Criteria for Prioritizing and Selecting Core International Crimes Cases

Morten Bergsmo (editor)

Third Edition

2024
Torkel Opsahl Academic EPublisher
Brussels

Editor of this volume:
Morten Bergsmo is the Director of the Centre for International Law Research and Policy (CILRAP).

Front cover: *'Criterion' derives from the Greek 'kritērion' ('means of judging'). The front cover therefore shows the fresco of the virtue Iustitia by Andrea del Sarto (1486–1530), a part of his remarkable, grisaille Chiostro della Scalzo cycle (1526), across the street from the CILRAP Bottega in Florence. Photograph: CILRAP.*

Back cover: *Building a sound portfolio of war crimes cases normally requires,* inter alia, *prioritization, criteria and strategic effort. It is nevertheless a relatively commonsensical process compared with the construction of a basilica such as that of Santa Chiara in Assisi, which depends on mastery not only of statics and construction, but multiple criteria-taxonomies including for the type, quality, cut and finish of every stone surface. Photograph: CILRAP.*

ISBNs: 978-82-8348-238-6 (print) and 978-82-8348-239-3 (e-book).

Dedicated to the memory of Trym Ivar Bergsmo (1962–2024),
whose nature photography and life
capture what is best in Norway

Preface by the Volume Editor

There are substantial changes in this Third Edition. It has seven new chapters and Chapter 1 has been reworked. Some chapters in the Second Edition have been left out of the present edition. Many of the old chapters have been materially updated (the status of each chapter is clarified in the star note on their first page), and all of them have been reviewed and updated with TOAEP's 2024 copy-editing standards (including hyperlinks to all relevant legal sources, better indexation, and e-book navigation).

My thoughts on the subject-matter of the book are spelled out in introductory Chapter 1 and Chapter 5, a more detailed analysis of main documents on prioritization criteria in Bosnia and Herzegovina, the International Criminal Tribunal for the former Yugoslavia and the International Criminal Court, three central laboratories for case selection and prioritization (with María Paula Saffon). Selection and prioritization criteria can be made and applied by prosecutors. They can serve as a professional response to backlogs or surges of cases, reducing the risk of politicization of prosecutorial discretion. It is a prosecutorial tool – of and for prosecutors – particularly relevant to territorial and international criminal jurisdictions. Prioritization seeks to bring the best-suited cases to trial first. It does not entail de-selection.

I would like to thank the authors for their contributions; Antonio Angotti, Rohit Gupta and Subham Jain for their excellent copy-editing; and Xabier Agirre Aranburu for exchanges on this Third Edition. The publisher's commitment to bringing new editions turns its books into dynamic knowledge-bases, not only digital public goods.

I hope this anthology will help criminal justice professionals who seek to develop or refine selection or prioritization criteria, and who would like to learn from the insights and experience of others.

Morten Bergsmo
Director,
Centre for International Law Research and Policy

FOREWORD BY SIRI S. FRIGAARD

When assuming my role as founding director of the Norwegian National Authority for Prosecution of Organized and Other Serious Crimes in August 2005, it had a backlog of approximately 80 war crimes cases, involving suspects from many different countries. Looking back, one may ask whether it was just a random case selection or whether the cases were prioritized in accordance with a specific set of criteria.

This anthology offers general perspectives on and understanding of the question of 'how to prioritize cases for full investigation and trial'. This issue is essential for all units working on war crimes cases. It is important not only for the international tribunals or hybrid courts, but also for the national units that have jurisdiction over the crimes committed in their own country as well as for those dealing with these cases as a third country.

It is unrealistic to expect that all crimes committed during an armed conflict will be tried in a court of law or that every perpetrator will be held criminally responsible for the offences committed. Some cases will most likely never be tried, some due to lack of resources, some for other reasons. All cases characterized as core international crimes are important. But some should be processed before others, and some need more immediate attention than others.

A proper selection process is therefore important.

In order to avoid unrealistic public expectations and accusations of, for instance, application of political pressure, it is important that the selection process is transparent and made known to those concerned through outreach.

The issue of case selection and prioritization opens many questions. For example, in order to prioritize and select the cases to be prosecuted we may ask whether there is a need for written criteria. If so, what should those criteria consist of? Who should decide on the criteria? How flexible should the criteria be? Should the same criteria apply for international tribunals, hybrid courts and national courts in the conflict area as well as national courts in third countries?

While discussing these and other questions arising from the topic, we should be conscious of the reasons and importance of prosecuting the most serious crimes occurring in armed conflicts. Understanding the rationale behind the prosecution of core international crimes is crucial. One thing is clear: it is not the self-interest of the international prosecutor or expert that prevails. We should ask ourselves whether we are doing it in order to reach sustainable peace in a country that has suffered the conflict. Or are we trying to contribute to reconciliation or prosecuting for reasons of deterrence? Are we seeking to bring justice to the victims, or is it to ensure trust in the criminal justice system in the country? Or could it be another motivation or a combination of several?

This leads back to the topic raised by the anthology, namely, how to prioritize cases for full investigation and trial. Does the answer to this question differ depending on which conflict we are dealing with? And does it depend on the type of unit that is dealing with it, international or national?

I worked in East Timor, in charge of the investigation and prosecution of crimes against humanity committed prior to October 1999, before being tasked with such cases in Norway. In both situations I have been confronted with a twofold dilemma: How to pick the best-suited cases for early trial? On which basis?

This volume offers reflections by an impressive selection of experts who expound on a variety of issues relating to case selection and prioritization. It presents the practice of some jurisdictions that have already dealt with the issue of prioritization and selection criteria, as well as views of leading experts in this field. Earlier editions of the book helped me when I introduced criteria in the Norwegian National Authority for Prosecution of Organized and Other Serious Crimes and subsequently proposed to fellow war crimes prosecutors in the Nordic countries and colleagues in the Eurojust Genocide Network that they should do the same.

Siri S. Frigaard
Former Chief Public Prosecutor and Director,
Norwegian National Authority for Prosecution
of Organised and Other Serious Crime
Former Deputy General Prosecutor for Serious Crimes,
East Timor

FOREWORD BY JULIJA BOGOEVA

The authors of this volume cover a number of jurisdictions, at different levels and in diverse legal, cultural and socio-political settings. They discuss the approach taken and the practice of case selection and prioritization in international criminal courts and some national jurisdictions. They offer extensive information on whether and how criteria for selecting and giving priority to war crimes cases are formulated, by whom, what form they take, whether they are implemented and what outcomes have been produced, in the legal, budgetary and strategic dimensions. The authors discuss what the main dilemmas and constraints in this area have been.

It is important to address the question of transparency in this context: is it necessary and why, and what does it entail? Moreover, when there is a large inventory of cases and a backlog, do case selection and prioritization necessarily mean that some perpetrators will not be prosecuted, as a *de facto* amnesty? Or can effective case selection and prioritization contribute to keeping all cases within the criminal justice system which may, for that purpose, have to undergo certain adjustments?

What more important task does any criminal justice system have than to ensure accountability for genocide, crimes against humanity and war crimes? Should the fact that such crimes imply large numbers of victims and perpetrators – an enormous challenge to any criminal justice system – be cause for giving up and giving in by prosecuting a few and granting *de facto* amnesty to many? Or should that hard reality be a call for doing what it takes to enable the criminal justice system to fulfil its purpose? Is there justification for prosecuting ordinary murderers while perpetrators of mass murder, rape, torture and other most serious crimes live freely and without stigma among us? What then of law and order and the rule of law and the claim that we are 'civilized'? Do we still prefer, regardless of the cost, a dangerous illusion that 'we' and 'our values' are safe as long as the war criminals are somewhere else, in front of the doorstep of 'the other'?

Here is my question: would optimal case selection and prioritization better persuade policy-makers that prosecuting war criminals should always be a priority because it is a strategic investment in long-term stability and security?

Julija Bogoeva

Formerly Analyst, Leadership Research Team, ICTY-OTP

TABLE OF CONTENTS

PART I: THE RELEVANCY, CONTEXT AND NATURE OF SELECTION AND PRIORITIZATION CRITERIA

1

On the Theme of Selection and Prioritization Criteria

Morten Bergsmo[*]

1.1. Many Crimes and Case-Files – Some Common Sense

It is widely recognized by now that wars can generate many more core international crimes[1] than criminal justice systems can investigate and prosecute. The task may be overwhelming in well-functioning jurisdictions, not to mention where the judiciary has been destroyed or severely weakened.[2] When case-files are opened, significant backlogs of core international crimes cases may emerge. This poses several challenges, among them (i) how to ensure a reliable overview of pending cases so that the workload can be meaningfully assessed based on a reasonable categorization; (ii) how to prioritize cases in the backlog for early investigation and trial; (iii) what to do with the large number of less-serious cases which the criminal justice system may not have the capacity to deal with; and (iv) determining how long the international community should remain involved in what are essentially national processes troubled by backlogs of cases, such as in Bosnia and Herzegovina or Colombia.

* **Morten Bergsmo** is the Director of the Centre for International Law Research and Policy (CILRAP) (see https://www.cilrap.org/bergsmo for his biography and list of publications). Relevant to this book, he has served, *inter alia*, as Senior Legal Adviser and Chief of the Legal Advisory Section, Office of the Prosecutor ('OTP'), International Criminal Court ('ICC') (2002–05); Legal Adviser, OTP, International Criminal Tribunal for the former Yugoslavia ('ICTY') (1994–2002); and as an adviser to core international crimes investigation and prosecution in several countries. He has worked on the dynamics of case prioritization since 1995, first in the ICTY-OTP, then in the ICC-OTP preparatory team, and later in research, writing and capacity-development. He thanks Xabier Agirre Aranburu and Devasheesh Bais for exchanges relevant to this chapter and the Third Edition as a whole.

1 For the purposes of this book, the term 'core international crimes' is used to refer to genocide, crimes against humanity, war crimes and aggression. The book, and the project-seminar of 26 September 2008 where several of its chapters were first presented, deal specifically with these crimes (and not others) in order to focus the discussion on key challenges facing criminal justice for atrocities in territorial states.

2 See Section 5.1. below, in Chapter 5 by Morten Bergsmo and María Paula Saffon.

Of these challenges, this anthology only concerns question (ii) on how the best-suited cases may be investigated and prosecuted first. As part of the multi-year research programme of the Centre for International Law Research and Policy (CILRAP) on fundamentals and weak links in the practice of criminal justice for core international crimes,[3] questions (i) and (iii) have been tentatively addressed in two separate TOAEP books, the monograph *The Backlog of Core International Crimes Case Files in Bosnia and Herzegovina*[4] and the anthology *Abbreviated Criminal Procedures for Core International Crimes*,[5] respectively. CILRAP has not yet contributed specifically to question (iv).

In Chapters 23 and 24 below, the civil society leaders Richard J. Dicker and late Christopher K. Hall make the general and well-rehearsed argument for more resources to criminal justice for core international crimes. Even if their plea were to be heard yet again, territorial states directly affected by war may well suffer too many allegations and case-files for their criminal justice system to process all. Whether the jurisdiction identifies with the principle of legality or opportunity of prosecutions, "choices have to be made in processing cases. All prosecutors in national systems are, to different degrees, accustomed to that", observes Ambassador Rolf Einar Fife in his incisive Chapter 3 below: "Prosecutorial directions are, however, useful or necessary to promote priorities and an optimal use of resources. They may also promote effectiveness. They may

3 This programme includes the books Morten Bergsmo (ed.), *Abbreviated Criminal Procedures for Core International Crimes*, Torkel Opsahl Academic EPublisher ('TOAEP'), Brussels, 2017 (http://www.toaep.org/ps-pdf/9-bergsmo); Morten Bergsmo, Alf Butenschøn Skre and Elisabeth J. Wood (eds.), *Understanding and Proving International Sex Crimes*, TOAEP, Beijing, 2012 (https://www.toaep.org/ps-pdf/12-bergsmo-skre-wood); Morten Bergsmo (ed.), *Thematic Prosecution of International Sex Crimes*, Second Edition, TOAEP, Brussels, 2018 (https://www.toaep.org/ps-pdf/13-bergsmo-second); Morten Bergsmo, Cheah Wui Ling and Antonio Angotti (eds.), *Old Evidence and Core International Crimes*, Second Edition, TOAEP, Brussels, 2024 (https://www.toaep.org/ps-pdf/16-2024); Morten Bergsmo and Carsten Stahn (eds.), *Quality Control in Preliminary Examination: Volume 1* and *Volume 2*, TOAEP, Brussels, 2018 (Vol. 1: https://www.toaep.org/ps-pdf/32-bergsmo-stahn; Vol. 2: https://www.toaep.org/ps-pdf/33-bergsmo-stahn); Xabier Agirre Aranburu, Morten Bergsmo, Simon De Smet and Carsten Stahn (eds.), *Quality Control in Criminal Investigation*, TOAEP, Brussels, 2020 (https://www.toaep.org/ps-pdf/38-qcci); and Gavin E. Oxburgh, Trond Myklebust, Mark Fallon and Maria Hartwig (eds.), *Interviewing and Interrogation: A Review of Research and Practice Since World War II*, TOAEP, Brussels, 2023 (https://www.toaep.org/ps-pdf/42-interrogation).

4 Morten Bergsmo, Kjetil Helvig, Ilia Utmelidze and Gorana Žagovec, *The Backlog of Core International Crimes Cases in Bosnia and Herzegovina*, Second Edition, TOAEP, Oslo, 2010 (https://www.toaep.org/ps-pdf/3-bergsmo-helvig-utmelidze-zagovec-second). This book also has a detailed discussion on prioritization, see pp. 81–127, which has since been further developed and significantly expanded, appearing as Chapter 5 below.

5 Bergsmo (ed.), 2017, see *supra* note 3.

enhance fairness and legitimacy. If combined with appropriate communication to the general public, they may contribute to consensus and increased support".[6] Prioritization and criteria are, in other words, relevant in criminal jurisdictions generally, whether civil or common law inspired.

The manner in which cases are prioritized affects the quality and legitimacy of criminal justice for core international crimes. Allegations of selective justice are commonplace in this field, not only from the ranks of perpetrators and their associates. Any evidence that the selection of cases has been instrumentalized by political considerations, other external actors or personal factors is likely to undermine – if not neutralize – the painstaking work of the teams that prepared and prosecuted the case. Were the impression to take hold that a case has been selected because of intense expectations among victim-intermediaries, non-governmental organizations, vocal social-media actors, government representatives or leaders of religious communities – for whom victim, ethical and political concerns often blur – the standing of the prosecution service in question can be weakened, irremediably in a worst-case scenario. This book is concerned with how criminal justice agencies can use prioritization criteria as a *professional shield against external pressure or personal considerations*, thus fending off or keeping at arm's length the threat of political curtailment of prosecutorial discretion.

This is why CILRAP's Forum for International Criminal and Humanitarian Law (FICHL) brought the topic of prioritization criteria to the fore of the international criminal justice discourse back in 2008,[7] with the objective of starting a more thorough discussion on prioritization and the use of criteria for core international crimes cases. It is encouraging, in this light, to see the subsequent development of and discussions on criteria in several jurisdictions and contexts,

---

6 See Section 3.2. below.

7 This book draws on several papers presented at a 2008-seminar in Oslo, conceptualized and convened by CILRAP's department FICHL in co-operation with a number of partners, reflecting the significant level of interest in the topic: the High Judicial and Prosecutorial Council of Bosnia and Herzegovina, the Organization for Security and Co-operation in Europe's ('OSCE') Mission to Bosnia and Herzegovina, Procuración General de la Nación (Unidad de Asistencia para causas por violaciones a los Derechos Humanos durante el terrorismo de Estado), Amnesty International, Belgrade Centre for Human Rights, Center for Legal and Social Studies (CELS), Center for the Study of Law, Justice and Society (DeJuSticia), Chr. Michelsen Institute, Documenta, Human Rights Watch ('HRW'), Humanitarian Law Centre, Research and Documentation Center Sarajevo, the Norwegian Centre for Human Rights (University of Oslo), the Norwegian Helsinki Committee, and the Norwegian Red Cross. For more information on the seminar and the associated research project (administered under the auspices of the Peace Research Institute Oslo (PRIO) where the present writer was a Senior Researcher at the time), see https://www.fichl.org/activities/criteria-for-prioritizing-and-selecting-core-international-crimes-cases.

including in Bosnia and Herzegovina, Colombia, the Democratic Republic of the Congo, Norway, among the Nordic countries, in the Eurojust Genocide Network, and at the International Criminal Court, as also referred to in the Foreword above by Siri S. Frigaard and in greater detail in Chapter 2 below by Devasheesh Bais as well as in Chapters 15 and 17. CILRAP has continued to contribute to discourse and practice on criteria through, *inter alia*, publications,[8] a 2018 manual which is discussed in Section 1.6. below,[9] and capacity-development activities.

CILRAP's contributions on this issue are informed by the early work of the preparatory team that established the ICC Office of the Prosecutor in 2002–2003.[10] Having carefully analysed the experience with case selection at the ICTY, the team asked two expert groups (one on length of proceedings and the other on the draft OTP Regulations) as well as individual experts to address the question of prioritization. The preparatory team focused on the critical "decision-making process to start investigations" in the mandate of the group that drew up the 2003 OTP Regulations. In draft Regulation 6 ("Preliminary examination report; draft investigation plan"), paragraph 6.5. contains detailed guidance on the draft investigation plan which shall provide an "explanation why the alleged offences warrant a full investigation against the backdrop of other alleged offences where such a step might not be recommendable".[11] It is precisely

[8] See, for example, Devasheesh Bais, "Prioritisation of Suspected Conduct and Cases: From Idea to Practice", in Aranburu, Bergsmo, De Smet and Stahn (eds.), 2020, pp. 563–585, *supra* note 3 (updated and modified as Chapter 2 in the present volume); and Jared O. Bell, "The Bosnian War Crimes Justice Strategy a Decade Later", Policy Brief Series No. 92 (2018), TOAEP, Brussels, 2018 (https://www.legal-tools.org/doc/eff713/).

[9] In 2015 several CILRAP-CMN colleagues co-authored the report "Prioritising International Sex Crimes Cases in the Democratic Republic of the Congo", including an outline of recommended criteria (see CILRAP-CMN, "Case Mapping, Selection and Prioritisation of Conflict and Atrocity-Related Crimes", June 2018, authored by Emilie Hunter and Ilia Utmelidze, with research support by Andreja Jerončič and Marialejandra Moreno Mantilla, section 3 ("Mapping of open case files and the extent of victimisation") ('CILRAP-CMN, "Case Mapping, Selection and Prioritisation"') (https://www.legal-tools.org/doc/fd5f42/).

[10] See Section 2.3.2. below in Chapter 2 by Devasheesh Bais.

[11] Draft Regulations of the Office of the Prosecutor, 3 June 2003, Regulation 6.5. The expert group on the draft Regulations included Mr. Tor-Aksel Busch (then Director General of Public Prosecution, Norway), Mr. Peter Lewis (then Business Development Director, Crown Prosecution Service, United Kingdom, later ICC Registrar), and Mr. Michael Grotz (then Bundesanwalt beim Bundesgerichtshof, Germany). For a detailed discussion of the Draft Regulations (including a comparison with the Regulations *ad interim* for the Office of the Prosecutor and its 2009 Regulations, accurately reproducing the texts of the Draft Regulations and the Regulations *ad interim*), see Carlos Vasconcelos, "Draft Regulations of the Office of the Prosecutor", in Morten Bergsmo, Klaus Rackwitz and Song Tianying (eds.), *Historical Origins of International Criminal Law: Volume 5*, TOAEP, Brussels, 2017, pp. 801–949 (https://www.toaep.org/

the justification of prioritization prescribed here that stands to gain from the existence of criteria.

A second thematic expert group on length of proceedings – similarly asked by the preparatory team to address prioritization criteria – observed emphatically in its report that it is "highly desirable to specify the general criteria guiding the selection of cases at the outset of the Court's operation", as this "could prevent the public from harbouring unrealistic expectations and also avoid any appearance of political bias in particular cases. An early declaration of the prosecution policy could also help preventing a backlog of non-priority suspects".[12] The expert group was well-informed of the relevant experience of the *ad hoc* tribunals for the former Yugoslavia and Rwanda.

Among the individual practitioners and experts invited by the preparatory team late 2002 to submit their reflections on topics relevant to the ICC-OTP, including on the issue of case selection and prioritization, was the United States ('US') prosecutor John Clint Williamson, later US Ambassador-at-Large for War Crimes Issues (2006–2009). He cautions against using even-handedness blindly to defend against critique of bias against a group that has committed more crimes and faces more charges. Rather, "the nature and scale of the crime [should be] the determining factor", thus preserving the selection rationale "by a largely objective methodology": "In the long run, this approach – using objective criteria – is more even-handed, is easier to defend and is less vulnerable to attack for politicisation of the process".[13] In Section 1.6. below, I discuss further the serious risks associated with misconceived, 'positive even-handedness'.

While we are indebted to the innovative work of the ICC-OTP preparatory team, which continues to exert considerable influence, the challenges of case selection and prioritization are not a creation of the International Criminal Court.

ps-pdf/24-bergsmo-rackwitz-song). The late Vasconcelos was a leading candidate to become the first ICC Prosecutor.

12 Report on Measures Available to the International Criminal Court to Reduce the Length of Proceedings, Section 4.1. ("Investigative Strategy"), para. 18. The members of the expert group were late Judge Håkan Friman, Dr. Fabricio Guariglia, Professor Claus Kreß, Professor John Spencer and Dr. Vladimir Tochilovsky. For the original text of the report and a discussion of its mandate, preparation and main ideas, see Morten Bergsmo and Vladimir Tochilovsky, "Measures Available to the International Criminal Court to Reduce the Length of Proceedings", in Bergsmo, Rackwitz and Song (eds.), 2017, pp. 651–693, *supra* note 11.

13 See Clint Williamson, "On Charging Criteria and Other Policy Concerns", Section 24.3., in Bergsmo, Rackwitz and Song (eds.), 2017, pp. 409–411, *supra* note 11.

1.2. Not a Challenge Unique to Contemporary International Criminal Justice

Prosecutors in territorial states directly affected by war are confronted by tangible dilemmas as they balance interests of gravity, probable outcome, community impact and consistency. Their prioritization of cases will often attract controversy, as we have seen in Bosnia and Herzegovina and Colombia. But this was also known at the time of the International Military Tribunal at Nuremberg, whose Prosecutor Telford Taylor conceded mistakes in selection decisions, referring to organizational failures to properly utilize in-house "informational resources".[14] He "circulated a memorandum on defendant selection in which [he] suggested some criteria".[15] The dilemmas also confronted the Tokyo Tribunal, in particular in connection with the so-called 'comfort women' and the shielding of the Japanese Emperor and his family from criminal responsibility while civilian cabinet members were pursued.[16] It has been remarked that the Tokyo Tribunal's "core selectivity problem was that the tribunal lacked sufficiently clear standards to justify its decision to immunise, among others, Emperor Hirohito, Unit 731 and the Americans from being prosecuted".[17]

The prosecutorial dilemmas became visible again following the decision of the UN Security Council in May 1993 to establish the ICTY. This triggered a relative surge in the political will of states to respond to war crimes, crimes against humanity and genocide with criminal justice. Criminal responsibility for atrocities in conflict – rather than impunity – became the rallying cry of a new movement. Mechanisms for the prosecution of core international crimes were

[14] Telford Taylor, *The Anatomy of the Nuremberg Trials. A Personal Memoir*, Alfred A. Knopf, New York, 1992, p. 117. The selection of defendants is criticized more than once (see pp. 87–88, 91–92, 113 and 567). The author thanks Agirre Aranburu for the page references.

[15] *Ibid.*, p. 90.

[16] Several TOAEP books address this problem, see, for example, Liu Daqun and Zhang Binxin (eds.), *Historical War Crimes Trials in Asia*, TOAEP, Brussels, 2016, Foreword by Liu Daqun (Judge, International Residual Mechanism for Criminal Tribunals), p. iv., and Chapter 2 by Zhu Dan, "From Tokyo to Rome: A Chinese Perspective", pp. 31 and 36 (https://www.toaep.org/ps-pdf/27-liu-zhang); see also, Morten Bergsmo, Cheah Wui Ling and Yi Ping (eds.), *Historical Origins of International Criminal Law: Volume 2*, First Edition, TOAEP, Brussels, 2014, pp. 3–117 (http://www.toaep.org/ps-pdf/21-bergsmo-cheah-yi); Viviane E. Dittrich, Kerstin von Lingen, Philipp Osten and Jolana Makraiová (eds.), *The Tokyo Tribunal: Perspectives on Law, History and Memory*, TOAEP, Brussels, 2020 (http://www.toaep.org/nas-pdf/3-dittrich-lingen-osten-makraiova). For other sources, see Yuki Tanaka, Tim McCormack and Gerry Simpson, *Beyond Victor's Justice? The Tokyo War Crimes Trial Revisited*, Martinus Nijhoff Publishers, Leiden, 2011, Chapter 4 by Awaya Kentaro ("Selecting Defendants at the Tokyo Trial") and Chapter 5 ("The Decision Not to Prosecute the Emperor").

[17] Liu Daqun and Zhang Binxin (eds.), 2016, p. 44, see *supra* note 16.

subsequently established for, *inter alia*, Rwanda, Kosovo, East Timor, Sierra Leone, Cambodia, Iraq, Indonesia and Colombia, as well as for 17 'situations' before the ICC, including Darfur, Libya, the Philippines, Uganda, Venezuela and Ukraine.[18] In addition to (i) international or (ii) hybrid jurisdictions and (iii) national jurisdiction on grounds of territory, active (perpetrator) or passive (victim) nationality, some states have enabled (iv) universal jurisdiction for crimes committed by foreign citizens in foreign countries. Most of these jurisdictions have faced prioritization challenges one way or the other.

This has been on particular display at the ICTY and related domestic jurisdictions, in part because of the sheer scope of the aggregated prosecution effort. During its indictment period (1994–2004), the Tribunal charged 161 persons, of whom 126 for alleged crimes in Bosnia and Herzegovina. Several states have also exercised universal jurisdiction and prosecuted crimes that occurred in Bosnia and Herzegovina in the 1990s. More importantly, the national war crimes mechanism established in Bosnia and Herzegovina saw thousands of case-files involving allegations of core international crimes open in the various prosecutors' offices at the state and entity levels of the country.[19] As we learn from Chapters 5, 8 and 17 below, of the three levels of criminal justice for atrocities in Bosnia and Herzegovina – international, foreign state and territorial state – it is clear that the latter has faced the largest burden of cases, hence the partial focus on criteria in that national jurisdiction and in Colombia.

The problem of crime or case-file inundation is in no way unique to the field of core international crimes in war. A number of national criminal justice systems are overwhelmed by rising crime combined with resource limitations, finding themselves examining ways to increase capacity and enhance prioritization so that deterrence and social cohesion are not further undermined. Even rule-of-law standard bearers such as Sweden and the United Kingdom see their criminal justice stretched. This book may therefore be relevant to justice policymakers beyond international criminal law.

---

[18] See the full list of the situations in which the ICC opened an investigation on the ICC's web site, 17 of them as of October 2024.

[19] It was notoriously difficult to obtain reasonably precise data on the number and nature of open core international crimes case-files in the criminal justice system of Bosnia and Herzegovina. In order not to proceed blindfolded, a 'database of open case-files' ('DOCF') was developed in 2007 under the auspices of the OSCE Mission to Bosnia and Herzegovina for the country's Office of the Prosecutor. It enabled the Prosecutor to establish a professional inventory of all open war crimes case-files according to a detailed information structure. For more information, see Bergsmo, Helvig, Utmelidze and Žagovec, 2010, pp. 53–79, see *supra* note 4. The generic DOCF has since been incorporated into the I-Doc system.

1.3. Risks in Case Selection

The subject-matter of the present book concerns not only public institutions but also civil society. When cases that are not best-suited for early prosecution are selected or prioritized first, public resources and trust are drained. It is not a birth right of prosecution services to fill their portfolios with cases against low-level perpetrators. Pursuing war criminals at considerable cost to the public, without plan or strategy, and with no prospect of addressing all crimes committed in the conflict, can hardly be justified by reference to prosecutorial independence or discretion alone. If a process selects and prioritizes cases in a way which does not correspond to the expectations of its donors, they may well end up challenging or restricting the autonomy of the criminal justice mechanism.

Claudia Angermaier describes how the UN Security Council did exactly that *vis-à-vis* the ICTY, in her Chapter 8 below.[20] More has been invested in criminal justice for atrocities in Bosnia and Herzegovina and Rwanda at the international and national levels combined than anywhere else. Bosnia and Herzegovina became in many ways the chief laboratory of criminal justice for atrocities in the 1990s. The precedent of the UN Security Council overruling the ICTY-OTP on case selection should therefore not be taken lightly, but rather remind criminal justice officials elsewhere to use their discretion to select and prioritize cases with integrity and responsibility.

In my experience with international criminal justice since 1994, some prosecutors hold the pragmatic and very basic view that criminal justice for atrocities cannot achieve more than putting a few of their authors on trial. Such trials, they say, show the world that atrocious conduct is not acceptable, and that is as much as we can expect of criminal justice in this area. The point is to keep the trials going, not so much who is prosecuted and for what. Chapter 5 shows the risks when this approach is combined with the rule of first come, first served (Section 5.1. below). Fortunately, other practitioners have seen the process in a broader light, not dismissing reasonable expectations of justice among victims or in the international community of states. The balance between these two perspectives has, however, often been precarious.

In conflicts involving mass atrocity, investigators as well as prosecutors may easily see crimes deserving prosecution left and right, wherever they look. Prosecutors in *ad hoc* war crimes mechanisms have often expressed a perceived need to show results in the form of indictments and trials as soon as possible after their establishment, even if the selected suspect was only one of many low-level perpetrators. This is what happened with the first ICTY and ICTR indictees, Tadić and Akayesu, two lesser actors whose main selection merit was simply

[20] See Chapter 8 below, Section 8.5.

that they could be detained. Prosecutors perceive a pressure to commence proceedings, with their webs of deadlines, submissions, defence challenges and related work requirements. Taking the time to first develop a strategy, a general plan of work, and specific case-preparation plans is easily dismissed as dwelling on 'methodology' rather than getting on with the work. Not only an expression of common sense, the impatient 'let us start and be guided by the evidence in the direction it takes us' has regrettably also been a common apology for focusing on the conduct of low-level perpetrators.

Criteria for case selection or prioritization can be a tool that tempers tendencies of random case selection. It is a professional tool of criminal justice, for criminal justice – not a political measure used to interfere with prosecutorial discretion. Case selection or prioritization by rational, clear and public criteria would normally seem to be preferable to selection by political interference (whether that happens directly or by use of the budget).

As the chapters in Parts II and III below illustrate, the challenge of case selection and prioritization is shared by international, hybrid, territorial state and universal jurisdictions, but in different ways. The need for effective case-selection and -prioritization criteria is most acute in the criminal jurisdictions confronted with the highest number of potential cases and largest backlogs, which often are the territorial states. They are meant to be the first line of investigation and prosecution of these crimes. That is confirmed by the complementarity principle on which the ICC – the only permanent international criminal jurisdiction – is based. It provides, as most readers would know, that the ICC can only step in when there is a lack of ability or willingness to process a case genuinely in national jurisdictions. The national level is therefore going to retain primacy and gradually become more important in the criminal justice for atrocities discourse, as we have seen in recent years.

1.4. Binding, Judicially-Enforced Criteria?

Even when there is agreement in a given jurisdiction that it should have and use case-selection or -prioritization criteria, there may be different opinions as to (i) whether these criteria should be binding, and (ii) whether the judges should have a role in making the criteria effective. Some prosecutors obviously prefer that the criteria function merely as internal guidelines in the exercise of prosecutorial discretion, with no judicial supervision. The answer to both questions depends on what type of jurisdiction it is.

In countries where there is only a relatively small number of alleged war criminals from war zones in the immigrant population (as is the case in, for example, Canada or Norway), relevant criminal justice actors may not feel a need to make criteria binding. The likelihood of serious public criticism of the criminal justice system for failing to deal with a large number of pending cases is rather low.

The situation is materially different in a territorial state with a large backlog of cases such as Bosnia and Herzegovina, Colombia or the Democratic Republic of the Congo. Here, the criminal justice system may suffer severe, sustained criticism when the expectations of justice for war crimes are dashed by the recognition that the system in its current form is unable to process all cases, especially if a (statutory) institutional mechanism has been established for such cases. Initial public acceptance of low-level cases may be overtaken by a sense that the criminal justice system is not adequately addressing the crimes.

Similarly, giving the judiciary a role in making criteria effective ((ii) above) will evoke different views in international, hybrid, territorial state, and foreign state jurisdictions. Prosecutors may be wary of giving judges a role, fearing erosion of the autonomy of hard-earned prosecutorial discretion. Judges and justice administrators may be concerned that criteria take on a mere paper existence in the prosecution service, not leading to professional case prioritization. In the case of the ICTY, criteria were not applied consistently and effectively by a prosecution service with a high number of war crimes cases until judges had the ability to enforce them, as described in Chapters 5 and 8 below. Critical voices will point out that it was the UN Security Council, a supremely political body, that gave the judges the relevant power to enforce criteria. Procedurally speaking, judges can easily be given such a role in jurisdictions where the prosecution needs to turn to the judiciary for the confirmation of indictments. In Chapter 17 below, Aida Šušić discusses relevant judicial review in Bosnia and Herzegovina (Section 17.4.4.).

1.5. Structure and Contents of the Book

This Third Edition has 26 chapters, by 29 authors from all continents. The chapters are organized in four *parts*, focusing on context (Part I), international(ized) and national jurisdictions (Parts II and III), and on some main considerations and substantive concerns (Part IV). A future fourth edition will hopefully include discussions of additional domestic jurisdictions and perhaps some empirical analysis of how relevant actors view the efficacy of criteria.

The five chapters in Part I set the stage for the book, explaining the nature of the challenge before us, how a lack of prioritization criteria has been a problem over several decades and in different jurisdictions, laying out the context and main issues involved, sharing some of the main insights in the book and from practice to date, and offering a substantive analysis of main criteria documents on core international crimes.

Devasheesh Bais' Chapter 2 gives an excellent overview of the origins of the discourse on prioritization criteria, how the issue has evolved within the ICC and the *ad hoc* tribunals, and the status of criteria in domestic jurisdictions such as Bosnia and Herzegovina, Colombia, the Democratic Republic of the Congo and the Central African Republic. He shows how an analysis commissioned by the Sarajevo office of the OSCE – drawing on the work of the preparatory team of the ICC-OTP as described in Section 1.1. above – has led thinking in this area, including by developing a criterion of 'representativity' that has "not yet been fully captured by the discourse on prioritization" and which he discusses, see Section 1.6. below. The chapter by Bais is important in order to understand this anthology and the contribution it makes to the field of criminal justice for core international crimes as a whole. His chapter should be read in tandem with this opening chapter and, for those who seek a more in-depth analysis of the nature of criteria, Chapter 5.

In his Chapter 3, Rolf Einar Fife – member of the UN International Law Commission and one of the founding diplomats of the ICC – highlights the importance of selection criteria from the perspective of state duties under international law. The chapter explains the risk of "theoretical myths" – such as formalistic "even-handedness" or "political fairness" – that may distract from genuine fairness for actual victims. Fife calls for planning as a safeguard for quality, a theme that permeates the volume. His chapter provides a wider contextual justification for prioritization criteria.

In Chapter 4, Ilia Utmelidze – a Georgian lawyer who has worked on the enhancement of national criminal jurisdictions and civil society documentation in Africa, Asia, Latin America and Europe for more than 20 years – presents a conceptual framework for prioritization, selection and criteria. He states the case for criteria based on comparative practice. He has developed this framework more fully in the CILRAP-CMN manual on "Case Mapping, Selection and Prioritisation of Conflict and Atrocity-Related Crimes" (2018), which is referred to several times in this anthology, including in Section 1.6. below.[21]

Chapter 5 by María Paula Saffon and the present writer offers a detailed analysis of criteria in key national and international documents relevant to the discourse on selection and prioritization of core international crimes cases, addressing head-on the nature of relevant criteria, their components and clustering, strengths and weaknesses, and some of the jurisdictional entanglements affecting their operation. Cutting across jurisdictions, the chapter gives a comparative perspective on criteria as such. First published in the original English in this

21 CILRAP-CMN, "Case Mapping, Selection and Prioritisation", see *supra* note 9. See the Annex to this book.

Third Edition, the 95-page chapter has been widely circulated since 2010 and was published in a Spanish translation in 2011. Following an introduction that discusses the concepts of selection and prioritization, the role of criteria in prosecution strategies, arguments for and against criteria, the context of backlogs of case-files, and some related risks (Section 5.1. below), the chapter offers a 40-page analysis of some documents on criteria in Bosnia and Herzegovina ('BiH') (5.2.): (i) the "Orientation Criteria for Sensitive Rules of the Road Cases" adopted by the BiH Collegium of Prosecutors (5.2.1.), (ii) the criteria included in Annex A of the National War Crimes Strategy adopted by the Council of Ministers of BiH (5.2.2.), and the criteria prepared by the Special Department for War Crimes of the Prosecutor's Office of Bosnia and Herzegovina in the framework of its Prosecution Guidelines on Charging, both (iii) an original 2007 version and (iv) a later 2009 version (5.2.3.). Chapter 5 then proceeds to analyse the 1995 and 1998 documents of the ICTY-OTP on criteria, with a subsequent analysis of criteria in the so-called 'completion strategy' process of the ICTY (5.3.1.), following which 2006 and 2007 policy documents of the ICC-OTP are analysed (5.3.2.). Section 5.4. concludes that "there are two major pillars at the centre of the landscape of criteria for selection and prioritization of war crimes cases: (a) 'gravity' and (b) 'representativity', and two lesser pillars: (c) policy considerations and (d) practical considerations", and then discusses each pillar. Chapter 5 engages the substance of criteria comparatively and in some detail, and may therefore be a useful resource to those who are drafting criteria.

Part II offers five chapters on criteria in international(ized) criminal jurisdictions, first two on the ICC, then one each on the ICTY, ICTR and ECCC. Together these chapters, with Chapter 5, contain more than 180 pages of discussion on criteria in international criminal justice, beyond the analyses that are found in Chapter 2 and other chapters.

Rod Rastan's Chapter 6 gives a reliable overview of selection criteria adopted by the ICC Office of the Prosecutor since its establishment. He has served the Office as a Legal Adviser for a number of years. The ICC-OTP criteria are similar in substance to those in other jurisdictions, while adjusted to the phases and procedure under the ICC Statute. Rastan summarizes the main ICC-OTP documents that define selection criteria: the first Policy Paper issued by the Prosecutor (2003),[22] the Policy Paper on the Interests of Justice (2007),[23] the

[22] ICC-OTP, "Paper on Some Policy Issues Before the Office of the Prosecutor", 5 September 2003 (https://www.legal-tools.org/doc/f53870/).

[23] ICC-OTP, "Policy Paper on the Interests of Justice", September 2007 (https://www.legal-tools.org/doc/bb02e5/).

OTP Regulations (2009),[24] the Policy Paper on Preliminary Examinations (2013),[25] the Policy Paper on Sexual and Gender-Based Crimes (2014),[26] the Report on the Basic Size of the OTP (2015),[27] the Policy Paper on Case Selection and Prioritisation (2016),[28] the Policy on Children (2016),[29] and two strategic plans.

Chapter 7 by Paul Seils, formerly head of the ICC-OTP Situation Analysis Section (2004–2008), discusses criteria in the ICC-OTP in the period 2003–2009. The chapter is not updated beyond this period, but it is included in the book for its insightful discussion of the 2006 ICC-OTP draft policy paper on "Criteria for the Selection of Situations and Cases" which was circulated for discussion[30] but not adopted until 2016 by which time the OTP had both selected several situations and brought charges against many (see Rastan's Chapter 6). Whereas the 2006 draft dealt with both situations and cases, the OTP later divided the two into separate policy papers of 2013 and 2016, as Rastan explains in the preceding chapter.[31] Seils warns that there will always be valid differing views about selection decisions, but as "long as these criteria are applied genuinely and faithfully, the Office has nothing to fear from reasonable disagreement".[32] Importantly, he warns against the danger of instrumentalization of prosecutorial discretion.

---

24 ICC, "Regulations of the Office of the Prosecutor", 24 April 2009, ICC-BD/05-01-09 (https://www.legal-tools.org/doc/a97226/).

25 ICC-OTP, "Policy Paper on Preliminary Examinations", November 2013 (https://www.legal-tools.org/doc/acb906/).

26 ICC-OTP, "Policy Paper on Sexual and Gender-Based Crimes", 5 June 2014 (https://www.legal-tools.org/doc/7ede6c/).

27 ICC Assembly of States Parties, "Report of the Court on the Basic Size of the Office of the Prosecutor", 17 September 2015, ICC-ASP/14/21 (https://www.legal-tools.org/doc/b27d2a/).

28 ICC-OTP, "Policy Paper on Case Selection and Prioritisation", 15 September 2016 (https://www.legal-tools.org/doc/182205/).

29 ICC-OTP, "Policy on Children", 15 November 2016 (https://www.legal-tools.org/doc/c2652b/).

30 The ICC-OTP received many comments on the draft policy, see, for example, International Federation for Human Rights (FIDH), "Comments on the Office of the Prosecutor's draft policy paper on 'Criteria for selection of situations and cases'", a letter from the FIDH President to the ICC Prosecutor of 15 September 2006 (https://www.legal-tools.org/doc/cf8ayhk4/); HRW, "The Selection of Situations and Cases for Trial before the International Criminal Court A Human Rights Watch Policy Paper", October 2006, in which they comment in detail on the draft paper (https://www.legal-tools.org/doc/753e9b/).

31 See *supra* note 28.

32 See Chapter 7 below, Section 7.5.

Claudia Angermaier's Chapter 8 – "Case Selection and Prioritization Criteria in the Work of the International Criminal Tribunal for the Former Yugoslavia" – offers an incisive analysis of criteria at the ICTY, showing how disagreement emerged between ICTY President Antonio Cassese and Prosecutor Richard J. Goldstone over case prioritization already in 1995, an important event in the development of the discourse on criteria. She explains how this initially led to what may be a nominal adoption of criteria by the ICTY-OTP in 1995 (Section 8.3. below); then to enhanced internal analysis and a review of the OTP case portfolio in 1998 (8.4.); the development of a 'completion strategy' through a remarkable interaction between the ICTY and the UN Security Council during 2000–2004, even leading the Council to introduce a substantive criterion for the confirmation of indictments (8.5.); the subsequent amendment of the ICTY Rules of Procedure and Evidence introducing an added review procedure for indictments empowering the Bureau to "determine whether the indictment, *prima facie*, concentrates on one or more of the most senior leaders suspected of being most responsible for the crimes within the jurisdiction of the tribunal" (Rule 28(A)) (8.6.); and the subsequent reduction by the ICTY Prosecutor of her case load (8.7.). Angermaier also shares some reflections on essential qualities that should define selection criteria, including clarity, publicity, impartiality and effective enforcement (8.8.).

In Chapter 9, Alex Obote-Odora, a former senior legal adviser at the ICTR-OTP, eloquently explains the experience of that Office. We learn about criteria that are similar to other jurisdictions, perhaps with the addition of "geographic spread" which the ICTR Prosecutor adopted to represent the nation-wide distribution of the alleged crimes. Obote-Odora shows how the Prosecutor prioritized allegations of genocide, consistent with the underlying gravity of the crimes. He justifies the decision by the Prosecutor not to prosecute crimes allegedly committed by members of the Rwanda Patriotic Front on grounds of gravity and national willingness. This was a difficult choice as the OTP was torn between the need to secure state co-operation and the duty to act with impartiality and integrity, a dilemma known in several jurisdictions both before and after the ICTR. But, importantly, Obote-Odora – like Fife and Williamson – warns against the idea that even-handedness is a selection or prioritization criterion: "The responsibility of the Prosecutor was not to balance the number of persons selected for prosecution so that all sides to the Rwanda crisis in 1994 could have equal representation in the dock".[33]

The crimes committed by the Khmer Rouge in Cambodia also called for prioritization, as Anees Ahmed and Margaux Day explain in Chapter 10 based

[33] See Chapter 9 below, Section 9.4.; see discussion on this also in Section 1.6. of the present chapter.

on their experience from the Extraordinary Chambers in the Courts of Cambodia ('ECCC'). The 2004 Statute of the ECCC limits its jurisdiction to "senior leaders of Democratic Kampuchea" and "those who were most responsible for the crimes", in a way similar to the 2002 Statute of the Special Court for Sierra Leone which codifies as binding law what has been a matter of prosecutorial policy in other jurisdictions. The resulting legal practice and debate sheds some light on concepts of senior criminal responsibility.

Part III has 10 chapters on prioritization criteria in domestic jurisdictions, covering seven jurisdictions, including the State Court of Bosnia and Herzegovina which is also discussed in Chapters 2 and 5.

Olympia Bekou's Chapter 11 offers an important articulation of the reasons why prioritization and selection criteria – including the criterion of 'representativity' discussed in Section 1.6. and Chapter 2 below – are important, with a practical case study. She proposes a set of selection criteria with detailed indicators, beginning with the gravity of the crime, to be applied in situations (such as that of the Democratic Republic of the Congo) where the prosecutorial theme of sexual crimes has been particularly relevant. Their implementation should be accompanied by a mapping of all relevant allegations and cases, adoption of a national policy, and actual implementation by the police and judiciary.

In Chapter 12, Terry M. Beitner – who, as former Director and General Counsel of the Crimes Against Humanity and War Crimes Section of the Department of Justice of Canada, was responsible for selecting cases – shares his experience of that office between 2000 and the Second Edition of this book. He considers in particular the File Review Subcommittee responsible at the time for applying selection criteria. Its practice was based on 21 substantive and operational criteria under the headings "Nature of allegation" (including "seriousness of the crime"), "Nature of investigation", and "Other considerations" (including "high-profile case" and "national interest considerations"). Beitner joins other authors in recommending a balance between principled and practical considerations, as "[c]reativity and flexibility will be the key while staying true to the rule of law" – "hard decisions must be made to demonstrate that public funds are spent wisely".[34]

In Chapter 13, Mirna Goransky and María Luisa Piqué provide an honest reflection on the important practice of Argentina which has seen a backlog of core international crimes cases generated during the period of military rule (1976–1983). Based on their long experience as prosecutors, they share insights on how cases have actually been prioritized. They remark that cases "seem to go faster through the system for at least one of the following 'reasons'": the

[34] See Chapter 12 below, Section 12.5.

"activity of the relatives of the victims and their lawyers", a "legal or bureaucratic reason that sometimes allows or pushes for a faster process" or the "efforts of individual justice operators who decide to prioritize these cases (apart from any official instruction)".[35] They underline the importance of criteria and a strategy, the need of consultation with victims and society, and the leading role that victims should play in long-term processes, unimpeded by shorter-term political considerations.

The volume has two chapters on Colombia, another territorial state with a high number of core international crimes cases. In chronological order, María Paula Saffon's Chapter 14 first offers a discussion on case selection in the early years of the justice and peace mechanism set up following the 2002 negotiations between the Colombian government and more than 30 paramilitary groups resulting in demobilization and development of a legal framework to investigate and prosecute crimes by demobilized individuals. Saffon shows how, in the early years of the justice and peace mechanism the "absence of clear and adequate criteria for the prioritization of cases to prosecute" led to "selection as an impunity strategy".[36] Her refreshing arguments for "clear, adequately justified, and publicly discussed prioritization criteria" resonate in several jurisdictions beyond Colombia,[37] and led to change in her country as we see in the next chapter.

In Chapter 15, Alejandro Aponte Cardona discusses in detail the evolution of a Colombian policy on selection and prioritization criteria after 2010. The chapter focuses on Directive No. 001 of 2012 of the Attorney General's Office and the Legal Framework for Peace. He also offers valuable, relatively detailed discussions of how he sees the conceptual differences between case selection and prioritization as well as on the criterion of representativity which is addressed in Section 1.6. below. Paradoxically, Colombia has one of the most extensive records of crime and among the most advanced criminal and transitional discourses in the world. This has led Colombians to develop sophisticated legal and investigative tools, including specific regulation of prioritization issued by the Attorney General (following publication of the Spanish version of Chapter 5 by Bergsmo and Saffon in a 2011 Colombian anthology)[38] and a dedicated *Unidad Nacional de Análisis de Contextos* within the Attorney General's Office. Colombia has also seen multiple peace negotiations with violent armed groups

[35] See Chapter 13 below, Section 13.9.

[36] See Chapter 14 below, Sections 14.2.–14.3.

[37] *Ibid.*, Section 14.4.

[38] Morten Bergsmo and María Paula Saffon, "Perspectiva internacional: Enfrentando una fila de atrocidades pasadas: como seleccionar y priorizar casos de crimenes internacionales nucleares?", in Kai Ambos (eds.), *Seleccion y priorizacion como estrategia de persecucion en los cases de crimenes internacionales*, Bogota, 2011, pp. 23–112.

over the years, adding complexity to the discussion on selection and prioritization criteria (through challenges of demobilization and 'peace v. justice').[39]

Chapters 16–19 concern the former Yugoslavia, in particular Bosnia and Herzegovina, Croatia and Serbia. Chapter 16 by Zekerija Mujkanović discusses how national prosecutors have had to consider jointly the jurisdiction of the ICTY and their own national system in Bosnia and Herzegovina, where many case-files were opened. Dividing the very large caseload required an elaborate system of review and selection. Mujkanović discusses the ICTY's 'Rules of the Road' unit, established in 1996 after a Bosnian-Serb general 'took a wrong turn' outside Sarajevo and was detained, apparently triggering a crisis in the peace process and the need to arbitrate among the different parties and jurisdictions. Both the ICTY and the Bosnian judiciary adopted classification schemes for cases, based on certain criteria. According to Mujkanović, the rating of the cases by the ICTY was not always reliable, as national prosecutors would find more evidence, or more meaningful interpretations of the available evidence, once they received the files. This raises questions about the evidence and contextual knowledge available to foreign actors, and the importance of professional prosecutorial discretion, in this and other situations.

In a second and extensive Chapter 17 on Bosnia and Herzegovina, Aida Šušić explains in detail the measures adopted by the national system, including the 'Orientation Criteria' adopted in 2004, the National War Crimes Strategy of 2008 and its 2020 revision, and the amendments in the Criminal Procedure Code adopted in 2009 to grant judicial oversight of the selection process. Her discussion of these sources and how they compare with the criteria frameworks of the ICTY and ICC is important. She also analyses preconditions for success of national criteria, including periodic review of war crimes cases, public information about the existence and use of criteria in case selection and prioritization, the equal and transparent application of the criteria, and judicial review of their application. The chapter has general value across war crimes jurisdictions, not only in Bosnia and Herzegovina which faced a backlog of several thousand open case-files.

Vesna Terselić, a leading human-rights activist, reflects on the experience of Croatia in Chapter 18. The change of government after the elections in 2000 brought greater impulse for war crimes proceedings in Croatia, as well as much better co-operation with the ICTY. Terselić explains the new cases that were possible only after 2000. The opening of the Bosnian-Croat military archives in

[39] Morten Bergsmo and Pablo Kalmanovitz (eds.), *Law in Peace Negotiations*, Second Edition, TOAEP, Oslo, 2010 (https://www.toaep.org/ps-pdf/5-bergsmo-kalmanovitz-second).

Zagreb was among the positive co-operation steps in that period. This is a reminder of the importance of government co-operation for effective investigations and prosecutions. In the view of Terselić, the priority for Croatia at the time of writing was to overcome denial and shielding of national actors.

In Chapter 19, Nataša Kandić, another prominent human-rights leader from the former Yugoslavia, tells a parallel story for Serbia. The chapter summarizes the main cases developed by the Serbian Office of the War Crimes Prosecutor in the period 2003–2024. The list of cases suggests that the Serbian Office applied at least three criteria implicitly: prioritization of killings, presumably considered as the gravest crimes; focus on low-level alleged perpetrators, presumably easier to investigate with direct evidence and politically more acceptable; and an effort to diversify among parties and avoiding dealing only with Serbian crimes, which, according to the author, was the result of undue political pressure.

All our authors from the former Yugoslavia (Mujkanović, Šušić, Terselić, Kandić and Tokača) concur that the ICTY came around to encouraging proceedings in their national systems and that this has been important.

Indonesia, with a population of more than 280 million, is much larger and complex than other countries discussed in Part III of the present volume. Chapter 20 by the late Fadillah Agus, a leading expert on international humanitarian law, analyses the situation in Indonesia. He summarizes for us the 12 cases heard by the *ad hoc* East Timor Human Rights Court, and the Abepura case heard by the permanent Human Rights Court, by the time of the Second Edition. The proceedings follow in three main steps: preliminary enquiry by the National Commission of Human Rights (of which Agus has been a member); criminal investigation and eventual indictment by the Attorney General; and trial before the permanent or *ad hoc* human rights courts. Agus explains that the National Commission does not have formal selection guidelines, but its practice has been guided by criteria of crime gravity and impact, the interest of the communities, and the degree of state involvement. The Commission has used the ICC Case Matrix to assist in the selection process. Agus recommends the adoption of formal selection guidelines.

In this Third Edition, Part IV contributes six chapters on key interests and considerations relevant to the development and implementation of criteria and their efficacy. In Chapter 21, Xabier Agirre Aranburu presents analytical techniques to assess the fundamentally important criterion of crime gravity and the term 'greatest responsibility', drawing on his experience from years of service at the ICTY and ICC. Aggravating circumstances available to judges at sentencing can also be used to assess gravity at the case-selection stage. Contrary to some views, the author explains how the mode of responsibility may affect the gravity of the conduct. In his view, it may also be advisable to define the concept of 'most responsible', if it is meant to have any bearing for the selection of cases. The updated chapter includes several examples of crime-pattern analysis and organizational structures relevant to selection processes.

Chapter 22 is dedicated to the selection criterion 'gravity of the crime' in the specific context of the ICC, following the relevant Chapters 5, 6, 7 and 21 above. Megumi Ochi reviews law and practice of the ICC regarding this criterion, drawing on rules, case-law and academic research on the subject. Her findings convey a critique of thinking at the Court, pointing out contradictions and a diversity of arguments, such as the gravity threshold differing between the OTP and Chambers (functioning as a 'sieve' before Chambers and only as one of the elements that guide OTP case selection). She highlights four weaknesses with the traditional understanding of gravity at the ICC: it can undermine the Court's deterrent effect, widen the impunity gap, prevent the Court from considering interests of justice, and offend the feelings of victims. In conclusion, Ochi proposes to "release the Prosecutor from the gravity constraint".

Chapter 23 is by one of the most influential civil-society actors in international criminal justice, Richard J. Dicker, who has served the field through HRW since the mid-1990s. He questions the legitimacy of overly economic prosecutorial approaches, and emphasizes the need for impartiality without favour for governmental actors. He argues for proper public explanation of criteria and transparency about their application, linking his discussion to experiences with the Democratic Republic of the Congo and Uganda. He suggests that preparing criteria is essential. Following the chapter's publication in earlier editions of the present volume, Human Rights Watch developed some of his points in a report on the ICC published in 2011, including calls for additional investigations across situations as well as for additional state support and budget increases.[40]

Chapter 24 is by another civil society leader in international criminal justice, the late Christopher K. Hall, who served as Senior Legal Advisor in Amnesty International for years and was perhaps the most consequential civil-society participant in the ICC negotiation process.[41] He warned the first ICC Prosecutor not to do justice 'on the cheap'. His chapter develops that warning, arguing that minimalistic policies are likely to produce failed investigations and prosecutions. Permeating the chapter is his concern for practices that lead to extensive de-selection of cases, in particular where case-files have not yet been opened.

[40] See HRW, "Unfinished Business. Closing Gaps in the Selection of ICC Cases", September 2011 (https://www.legal-tools.org/doc/738f10/), authored by Elizabeth Evenson, with guidance by Richard J. Dicker and contributions from several HRW lawyers and researchers.

[41] Christopher K. Hall passed away in 2013, three years after the publication of the first edition of this volume. See Nigel Rodley "Christopher Keith Hall obituary", *The Guardian*, 5 June 2013.

While prioritization criteria as advocated by this book do not entail de-selection, Hall's focus on means to increase the efficiency of war crimes proceedings – from plea bargaining to effective court management, and the importance of securing political will and state co-operation – are important.

In his concise Chapter 25, Mirsad Tokača – founder and Director of the Research and Documentation Center in Sarajevo – highlights the importance of selection criteria in view of his experience in Bosnia and Herzegovina. He argues that gravity of crime should be the main criterion for a fair and objective selection process, including quantitative and qualitative elements. The CILRAP-CMN guidelines of 2018 – annexed to this book – further acknowledged and developed this point, comprising both gravity of the offence and seriousness of the alleged responsibility.[42] For Tokača, objective consideration of the gravity of crime is necessary in order to avoid "ethno-religious balancing" or fallacious equivalence of blame, as discussed in the next Section.[43]

Finally, the last chapter of the Third Edition (Chapter 26) is by Vladimir Tochilovsky, a veteran trial prosecutor who served the ICTY-OTP for many years. In his practice-informed view, a "trial-oriented investigation" should guide the process,[44] and the three main selection criteria should be the gravity of crime, the strength of the evidence, and "the possibility of arrest of the suspect".[45]

1.6. Gravity and Representativity – Not 'Positive Even-Handedness'

Having established the relevant legal framework, drafting, fine-tuning or critiquing selection or prioritization criteria should first and foremost consult common sense, which investigation and prosecution agencies are expected to possess in abundance. Chapters in this book share insights that will resonate among investigators, analysts and prosecutors around the world. It also provides extensive information on relevant sources on selection, prioritization and criteria. Chapter 5, for example, offers detailed analysis of a careful selection of the key documents on criteria, Chapter 6 on ICC-OTP documents, and Chapter 17 on Bosnia and Herzegovina.

The 2018 CILRAP-CMN guidelines – "Case Mapping, Selection and Prioritisation of Conflict and Atrocity-Related Crimes", annexed to this book – may be a useful, customized resource for practitioners around the world.[46] It

42 See *supra* note 9, pp. 10–14.

43 See Chapter 25 below, Section 25.2.

44 See Chapter 26 below.

45 *Ibid.*

46 CILRAP-CMN, "Case Mapping, Selection and Prioritisation", see *supra* note 9, and available in an updated version in the Annex to this book.

draws on 15 years of relevant activities, starting with the work of the ICC-OTP preparatory team (as mentioned in Section 1.1. above and by Devasheesh Bais in Chapter 2 below), then the 2008 seminar on prioritization, earlier editions of this book, CILRAP-CMN's experience from field-work around the world, and specific legal and empirical analysis. The guidelines suggest steps that may be helpful when developing criteria: auditing of current practices, mapping of the overall universe of victimization and open case-files, combining consistency and flexibility in the process, the need to adopt a formal policy, and outreach to explain the process and criteria to concerned communities.[47] They explain how mapping and policies can be developed[48] and offer some 'model criteria', primarily gravity of the alleged crime, representativity *vis-à-vis* the relevant crime universe, and "policy and practical considerations", similar to Section 5.3. below.[49] An overview table offers a holistic view of relevant criteria under three main themes (see illustration in the Annex at the end of this book).

It may also be worthwhile to consider the ICC's experience with prioritization criteria, although the Court differs jurisdictionally and is resourced so much more generously than domestic criminal jurisdictions for core international crimes that it entails risk to view the Court as a relevant standard-setter for national prosecution services. As discussed by Rastan in his Chapter 6 below, the ICC-OTP issued a 2016 Policy Paper on Case Selection and Prioritisation[50] which adopts criteria that are largely similar to those discussed in the present volume and proposed in the CILRAP-CMN guidelines. The ICC-OTP paper refers to "prioritisation" as a subsequent step to "selection", guided by criteria like those under the "policy and practical considerations" of the CILRAP-CMN guidelines.[51]

The two documents both consider gravity and representativity as fundamental criteria. On the former, the 2016 ICC-OTP policy paper observes that *gravity* is the "predominant case selection criteria adopted by the Office and is embedded also into considerations of both the degree of responsibility of alleged perpetrators and charging".[52] The perceived gravity of core international crimes is often considered the main justification for international criminal justice since

47 *Ibid.*, section 2 ("General principles of case selection and prioritisation").

48 *Ibid.*, sections 3 ("Mapping of open case files and the extent of victimisation") and 4 ("Adoption of a policy on selection and prioritisation").

49 *Ibid.*, section 5 ("Model criteria for selection and prioritisation").

50 ICC-OTP, "Policy Paper on Case Selection and Prioritisation", see *supra* note 28.

51 *Ibid.*, section 6 "Case prioritisation criteria", including nine criteria, of which five "strategic" and four "operational"; for the CILRAP-CMN guidelines, see the section on "Policy and practical considerations", including 14 criteria.

52 ICC-OTP, "Policy Paper on Case Selection and Prioritisation", para. 6, see *supra* note 28 [sic].

the time of the Nuremberg Tribunal. It follows that gravity is widely expected to characterize cases brought under core international crime classifications. This basic point was explained in the 2009 monograph *The Backlog of Core International Crimes Case Files in Bosnia and Herzegovina*;[53] then in the present anthology in all three editions, by multiple contributors from across jurisdictions, Chapters 21 and 22 below being dedicated in their entirety to the gravity criterion, with significant discussions also in Chapter 5 (see synthesis in Section 5.4. below); it was included in both the 2016 ICC-OTP policy paper and the CILRAP-CMN guidelines; and was further referred to by the ICC Independent Expert Review ('IER') in 2020, whose report mentions that several sources suggested that the Court should apply a "higher gravity threshold",[54] with which the experts – but not the OTP – concurred.[55]

Chapter 22 explains how the gravity of the crime criterion is embedded in the ICC Statute itself. The closely related *level of authority and responsibility of the suspect* is referred to by both the 2016 ICC-OTP policy paper and the CILRAP-CMN guidelines.[56] As Agirre Aranburu explains in Chapter 21 below, this criterion is to some extent observed in the practice of the ICC, with approximately 55 per cent of the charged persons by June 2021 having been in senior positions in relevant structures. But this is a consideration that should be applied with its nature keenly in mind. The point is obviously not to select suspects of high position with less regard for the actual circumstances. Rather than a string of pearls, such a case portfolio would chain the prosecution to a succession of failed or soon-to-be-forgotten cases.

A case against an actor with a high level of responsibility in an armed group or force that has been involved in crimes in multiple incidents in different areas has the potential to speak to the victimization of surviving civilians from many villages and towns, sometimes entire regions, addressing the harm which they

53 See Bergsmo, Helvig, Utmelidze and Žagovec, 2010, pp. 120–125, *supra* note 4.

54 Independent Expert Review of the International Criminal Court and the Rome Statute System. Final Report, 30 September 2020, para. 647 (https://www.legal-tools.org/doc/cv19d5/).

55 *Ibid.*, recommendation R227: "In order to address the disparity between the OTP resources and the high number of PEs [preliminary examinations] resulting in investigations, the Prosecutor should consider adopting a higher threshold for the gravity of the crimes alleged to have been perpetrated. Gravity should also be taken into account at Phase 1 of PEs". The OTP has not followed this recommendation, referring to the need to involve the judges and the complexity of the gravity threshold, see ICC, "Overall Response of the International Criminal Court to the 'Independent Expert Review of the International Criminal Court and the Rome Statute System – Final Report': Preliminary Analysis of the Recommendations and information on relevant activities undertaken by the Court", 14 April 2021, paras. 410–413 (https://www.legal-tools.org/doc/e553hu/).

56 "Policy Paper on Case Selection and Prioritisation", section 5(b) ("Degree of responsibility of alleged perpetrators"), see *supra* note 28.

have suffered. A case against a lower-ranking actor in a unit responsible for a single incident of killing, rape or torture, on the other hand, may only speak directly to the victimization of a small number of survivors and their families, however notorious the relevant cruelty. It is widely assumed that the higher the level of authority over an armed group or force, the greater your ability to prevent or stop core international crimes by it – and if such harm is caused, the greater your responsibility. The level of authority and responsibility of a suspect may, in other words, bear on the perception and impact of core international crimes cases.

This brings us to the criterion of *representativity* which we find both in the CILRAP-CMN guidelines and the 2016 ICC-OTP policy paper, first put forward in the above-mentioned book *The Backlog of Core International Crimes Case Files in Bosnia and Herzegovina* with the explanation that, by "the end of a process of war crimes prosecutions, the accumulated case portfolio should reflect – or be representative of – the overall *victimisation caused by the crimes* in the conflict or situation at hand".[57] The monograph continued:

> The most serious crimes and the crimes that the most senior leaders are suspected of being most responsible for should have been prosecuted at the end of the day. The areas and communities most affected by the crimes should have seen more of these crimes or crime base prosecuted than in less affected communities. The most affected victim groups should have more of the crimes that caused the victimisation prosecuted than other groups. Organizations or structures causing the most serious crimes should have more of its responsible members – or more of the crimes caused by them – prosecuted than other such organizations or structures.[58]

This criterion suggests that the end-portfolio of prioritized cases should be "representative of the overall criminality" as much as possible, taking into account, *inter alia*, the extent of victimization or harm caused by the conduct, the existence of patterns of criminal conduct, their temporal and spatial scope, and the contribution of the suspect to the realization of the patterns.[59] The 2016 ICC-OTP policy paper recognizes the criterion, stating that the OTP seeks to "represent as much as possible the true extent of the criminality which has occurred within a given situation": "the charges chosen will constitute, whenever possible,

[57] See Bergsmo, Helvig, Utmelidze and Žagovec, 2010, p. 125, *supra* note 4 (italics added).

[58] *Ibid.* See also the discussion on 'representativity' in Chapter 5 below.

[59] CILRAP-CMN, "Case Mapping, Selection and Prioritisation", p. 14, see *supra* note 9. See also Section 15.4.3. below by Alejandro Aponte Cardona.

a representative sample of the main types of victimisation and of the communities which have been affected by the crimes in that situation".[60]

It is the overall victimization, and the criminality which has caused it, that should be objectively and adequately reflected in the portfolio of charges, not the expectations of organized victim groups or representatives who, as mentioned above, are sometimes driven more by political objectives than concern for surviving victims and their families. The political or ideological motivation can be so strong that, in some situations, those who speak most loudly for victims in their group have tragically instrumentalized them in a political struggle. By firing at the enemy from behind the backs of their own women and children, they may in fact cause their death. In extreme situations, this can take the form of a *suigenocide*. Should war crimes justice blur that – or who is the *hostis humani generis* – it may suffer significant loss of support.

The 'representativity' criterion is not about what we may describe as 'positive even-handedness' between different groups of victims and perpetrators – that if charges have been brought against, for example, Bosnian Serbs and Bosnian Croats, then they must also be brought against Bosnian Muslims – which is not equal treatment of equal cases. Rather, the 'representativity' criterion is intended to fully respect Clint Williamson's warning against using distorted 'even-handedness' in response to the direct or indirect lobbying of a group that has committed many crimes or its supporters, a warning echoed by Rolf Einar Fife, Alex Obote-Odora and Mirsad Tokača in their chapters. As mentioned above, Williamson wrote to the ICC-OTP preparatory team already in 2003 that the "nature and scale of the crime [should be] the determining factor".[61] The 'representativity' criterion seeks to do exactly that, focusing on the criminal conduct and the victimization it has caused. Proper representation therefore requires thorough analysis of the crime patterns, their social context, and the motives and behaviour of the criminal actors. The decision-makers will have to listen to those who do the requisite analysis, to make sure that decisions are driven by evidence, safeguarding longer-lasting credibility and legitimacy. The 'representativity' criterion, in other words, is not about diplomatic or political skills to manage how different groups will see the court in question.

A policy or practice of 'positive even-handedness' can even become an obstacle to 'representativity'. A view that charges must at all cost be brought against every side in a conflict, risks affording the same priority to grave and less grave crimes. This can generate a sense that the prosecution imposes moral equivalence through the 'even-handed' charges. Turning 'representativity' on its

---

[60] See *supra* note 28, para. 45.

[61] See Section 1.1. above.

head in this manner can severely undermine public acceptance of the cases concerned, if not of the jurisdiction as a whole. This is reinforced by the tendency to view suspects "as representatives of certain perpetrator groups (the Serbs, the Croats, the Hutus, the Tutsis) and thus the selection entails the distribution of blame to their respective states or groups".[62] Regrettably, some foreign ministries and civil society actors who in a conflict strongly advocate for one group – or against another – can end up lobbying for such 'positive even-handedness', sometimes inadvertently.

The 2016 ICC-OTP selection and prioritization paper says that applying "the same processes, methods, criteria and thresholds for members of all groups [...] may in fact lead to different outcomes for different groups".[63] It commits the Office to "not seek to create the appearance of parity within a situation between rival parties by selecting cases that would not otherwise meet the criteria set out herein".[64] This is a commitment which the Office should not compromise or abandon.

The 'representativity' criterion was coined by the present writer in response to the kind of particularistic, incident-centred charging practice which we saw in the first few years of the ICTY-OTP. At that time, cases were brought for grave local incidents in, for example, Prijedor, Bosanski Samač and Srebrenica, inadequately reflecting the wider patterns of victimization which these serious incidents were a part of, and the role of Bosnian Serb and Serbian leaders in those patterns. Through internal analysis and consultation in the ICTY-OTP, the limitations of the particularistic approach were better appreciated by the Office, which commenced more systematic pattern- and leadership-inquiry, leading, with time, to a more finely-tuned portfolio of charges, an incremental process which is described by Angermaier in Chapter 8 below.

A further difficulty in achieving 'representativity' can be political interference or pre-determination. The latter may be inherent in the jurisdictional design; the former, overt through various forms of pressure and sanctions or indirect through conditional budgeting or co-operation. There are no easy solutions to either challenge. 'Victor's justice' has been discussed for several decades as a limitation of early international criminal justice at Nuremberg and Tokyo, and some major World War II trials have been criticized for one-sidedness. The ICTY Prosecutor excluded from her investigations the allegations of NATO

62 Kai Ambos, "Introductory Note to Office of the Prosecutor", in *International Legal Materials*, 2018, vol. 57, no. 6, p. 1131.

63 See *supra* note 28, para. 20.

64 *Ibid.*

crimes during to the bombing of Serbia.[65] More obviously, the massive bombing of Cambodia was excluded from the jurisdiction of the ECCC.[66] The second ICC Prosecutor has been criticized for showing similar biases in self-referred situations (the Democratic Republic of the Congo, Uganda, Central African Republic and Mali) in which she needed to secure national co-operation.[67] The UN Security Council promoted the investigation of ISIL crimes in Iraq while not addressing those who ordered the invasion of the country in 2003 on legal grounds that many international lawyers question. The ICTR's experience with non-prosecution of alleged Rwandan Patriotic Front crimes has been much discussed,[68] while Obote-Odora eloquently defends the later ICTR Prosecutor Hassan Jallow's record in this regard in Chapter 9 below.

For all the reasons explained in the present anthology, and well-known to practitioners across situations and jurisdictions, the selection or prioritization of core international crimes cases is frequently necessary. It should be undertaken pursuant to criteria that are as precise, fair and transparent as possible. The purpose of such criteria should not be reduced to outreach or *ex post facto* justification of decisions. Rather, they should genuinely guide decision-making on prioritization, based on sound factual analysis. When applied consistently, selection or prioritization criteria will safeguard genuine equality under the law, so that similar crimes get similar responses, victims are treated fairly, and the process can be trusted.

As mentioned above and discussed in detail by Rastan in Chapter 6 below, the ICC-OTP has ended up with four policy papers on selection and prioritization, counting more than 75 pages. Although much thought has gone into these documents, this is obviously not an example for other core international crime jurisdictions. Criteria documents should be clear and concise, as we have seen in some of the documents in Bosnia and Herzegovina analysed in Chapter 5

---

65 For a discussion on this issue see, *inter alia*, the symposium "The International Legal Fallout from Kosovo", in *European Journal of International Law*, 2001, vol. 12, no. 3.

66 See William Shawcross (son of the Nuremberg prosecutor, Hartley Shawcross), *Sideshow: Kissinger, Nixon and the Destruction of Cambodia*, Touchstone, New York, 1979; Christophe Hitchens, *The Trial of Henry Kissinger*, Verso, London, 2001, Chapter 3 ("A Sample of Cases: Kissinger's war crimes in Indochina").

67 For a commentary on this issue, see "HRW Submission to the IER of the ICC", 15 April 2020, section on "Selection and prioritization of cases", pp. 4–5. Former ICC Prosecutor Bensouda did not alter her approach to Afghanistan investigations when sanctions were imposed against her by a permanent member of the UN Security Council.

68 See Carla Del Ponte and Chuck Sudetic, *Madame Prosecutor: Confrontations with Humanity's Worst Criminals and the Culture of Impunity*, Other Press, New York, 2009, pp. 224–239, suggesting that the Rwandan government threatened to stop co-operation with the genocide cases; Thierry Cruvellier, *Le tribunal des vaincus. Un Nuremberg pour le Rwanda?*, Calman-lévy, Paris, 2006, pp. 231–244.

below. They should also leave the prosecution services with adequate discretion,[69] while not being of a nature that could be used as a justification for misconceived 'positive even-handedness'.

The warning of Karim A.A. Khan KC in 2021 that the ICC must not be seen as a "vanity project"[70] applies to war crimes jurisdictions around the world, not only the ICC. "To have impact", he argued, "you need to prioritize against the greatest need, taking into account the gravity of the crimes committed and the jurisdictional issues in play".[71] Kai Ambos reminds us that the "rational and transparent selection and prioritization of situations and cases turns out to be of utmost importance for the success and legitimacy of the Court"[72] – and other core international crimes prosecution services, we might add.

---

69 See Lovisa Bådagård and Mark Klamberg, "The Gatekeeper of the ICC: Prosecutorial Strategies for Selecting Situations and Cases at the International Criminal Court", in *Georgetown Journal of International Law*, 2017, vol. 48, no. 3, pp. 639–733.

70 Interview of Karim A.A. Khan KC by Shehzad Charania, "Delivering the ICC Vision Through Deeds not Words: An Interview with Karim Khan QC", in *Opinio Juris*, 21 May 2021.

71 *Ibid.*

72 See *supra* note 62, p. 1131.

2

Prioritization of Suspected Conduct and Cases: From Idea to Practice

Devasheesh Bais*

2.1. Introduction

Quality of criminal investigation in fact-rich core international crimes cases can be enhanced by selecting and prioritizing cases that are best suited for the allocation of the limited resources of the prosecution. Some of the systemic bottlenecks[1] hindering criminal investigations, as identified by the 'Quality Control in Criminal Investigation' project, can be pre-empted by case selection and prioritization strategies.

In this chapter, the evolution of the case prioritization strategies for core international crimes will be discussed and its future prospects and challenges highlighted. The chapter starts with an explanatory background to the case prioritization strategies (Section 2.2.), and then proceeds to discuss the early beginnings of the concept (Section 2.3.), its gradual embrace by national and international prosecution services (Section 2.4.), challenges in the implementation of case prioritization strategies in national jurisdictions (Section 2.5.), and concludes with reflections on its future (Section 2.6.). At the end of the chapter, there is a table chronologically listing the development of case prioritization strategies for core international crimes.

---

* **Devasheesh Bais** is a Fellow at the Centre for International Law Research and Policy ('CILRAP') and Deputy Co-ordinator of the International Criminal Court Legal Tools Project. He is an Advocate at the High Court of Madhya Pradesh, India. The author wishes to thank Morten Bergsmo for his comment on the draft of this chapter, which was first published in Xabier Agirre Aranburu, Morten Bergsmo, Simon De Smet and Carsten Stahn (eds.), *Quality Control in Criminal Investigation*, Torkel Opsahl Academic EPublisher ('TOAEP'), Brussels, 2020 (https://www.toaep.org/ps-pdf/38-qcci/).

[1]

> a) the long duration and high cost of many investigations of core international crimes; b) loss of overview of information and potential evidence; c) lack of clear focus in the building of the case; d) vague formulation of criminal responsibility even after the organisation has in its possession enough potential evidence […].

See the web page of the CILRAP research project 'Quality Control in Criminal Investigation', with links to multiple resources (https://www.cilrap.org/events/190222-23-delhi/).

While the chapter is about *prioritization*, it is often used in conjunction with *selection*, as prioritization usually follows once cases to be investigated have been selected. Thus, the chapter refers to case selection at various points. However, this is not to say that a prioritization exercise cannot exist without a selection process.

2.2. Background

An armed conflict, civil war, or other events where mass crimes are committed involve a large number of instances of crimes and a complex factual narrative. Consider the Syrian situation, which is now in its thirteenth year, having started in 2011; it involves multiple States, multiple non-State actors, with serious crimes committed, including intentionally directing attacks against a civilian population, also by means of chemical weapons, sexual slavery, persecution and torture.[2] Imagine the difficult task of any accountability mechanism that may be set up to address the criminal conduct involved in the Syrian situation.

Prosecuting and adjudicating all those numerous crimes in a fair manner and without undue delay would be an overwhelming task. This will be true even for a jurisdiction with a well-functioning criminal justice system. However, the reality is that the judicial capacity of the State where these crimes were committed may have been destroyed, or severely impaired by conflict.

Given this context, with instances of alleged crimes exceeding judicial capacity, a significant backlog of opened or potential case-files may emerge. Years would have passed before most of these cases reach the trial stage, if ever. This challenge raises two important questions:

1) How to select the cases that will actually be investigated and tried?
2) How to rank the selected cases in an order of priority according to which they will be investigated and tried?

That is, how does a prosecution service select the cases or conduct that are to be investigated, and then amongst the selected cases and conduct identify those that should be prioritized?

The reality is that a decision on prioritization of cases is inevitable for any prosecution service, be it national or international, as it is likely that there will always be more cases to prosecute than what the concerned prosecution service can handle simultaneously while deploying its finite resources.[3] Thus, it is likely

[2] See, for instance, Report of the Independent International Commission of Inquiry on the Syrian Arab Republic, UN Doc. A/HRC/37/72, 1 February 2018 (https://www.legal-tools.org/doc/b01552/).

[3] See Section 1.1. above in Chapter 1 by Morten Bergsmo.

that any prosecutor would have to take a decision on the order in which the cases are rolled out.

In the absence of formal criteria for prioritizing cases, a decision on prioritization would be done on an informal basis, which could not only lack transparency but also consistency.[4] A prosecution service is also more susceptible to being influenced by governments, powerful organizations and individuals, and media coverage if it is not bound by formal prioritization criteria.[5] A formalized set of criteria, designed according to the circumstances of the jurisdiction it serves, not only protect the prosecution service from political pressure or accusation of bias, but could also, with a right set of criteria, increase its effectiveness and efficiency.[6]

2.3. The Idea

The idea started in a nascent manner with the International Criminal Tribunal for the former Yugoslavia ('ICTY'), progressed with the preparatory work on the International Criminal Court's ('ICC') Office of the Prosecutor ('OTP'), however, the real progress happened in the domestic context aided by international justice professionals and non-governmental organizations.

2.3.1. International Criminal Tribunal for the Former Yugoslavia

The Statute of the ICTY gave a general mandate "to prosecute persons responsible for serious violations of international humanitarian law committed in the territory of the former Yugoslavia since 1991".[7] Case selection and prioritization criteria were not addressed. However, the ICTY's OTP formally adopted case selection and prioritization criteria in October 1995.[8]

These criteria were organized in five different thematic groups:

(a) the person to be targeted for prosecution:[9]

---

[4] CILRAP-CMN, *Guidelines: Case Mapping, Selection and Prioritisation of Conflict and Atrocity-Related Crimes*, Brussels, June 2018, p. 1 (https://www.legal-tools.org/doc/fd5f42/). See Section 1.1. above in Chapter 1 by Morten Bergsmo.

[5] *Ibid.*, p. 9. See Section 1.1. above in Chapter 1 by Morten Bergsmo.

[6] See Section 1.1. above in Chapter 1 by Morten Bergsmo. Also see Section 3.1. below in Chapter 3 by Rolf Einar Fife.

[7] See Statute of the International Criminal Tribunal for the Former Yugoslavia, adopted 25 May 1993, amended 17 May 2002, Article 1 ('ICTY Statute') (https://www.legal-tools.org/doc/b4f63b/).

[8] See Morten Bergsmo, Kjetil Helvig, Ilia Utmelidze and Gorana Žagovec (eds.), *The Backlog of Core International Crimes Case Files in Bosnia and Herzegovina*, Second Edition, TOAEP, Oslo, 2010, p. 99 (https://www.toaep.org/ps-pdf/3-bergsmo-helvig-utmelidze-zagovec-second/).

[9] *Ibid.*, p. 99.

- position in the hierarchy under investigation;
- political, military, paramilitary or civilian leader;
- leadership at a municipal, regional or national level;
- nationality;
- role or participation in policy or strategy decisions;
- personal culpability for specific atrocities;
- notoriousness or responsibility for particularly heinous acts;
- the extent of direct participation in the alleged incidents;
- authority and control exercised by the suspects;
- the suspect's alleged notice and knowledge of acts by subordinates;
- arrest potential;
- evidence or witness availability;
- media or government or non-governmental target; and
- potential role-over witness or likelihood of linkage evidence.

(b) the serious nature of the crime:[10]

- number of victims;
- nature of acts;
- area of destruction;
- duration and repetition of the offence;
- location of the crime;
- linkage to other cases;
- nationality of perpetrators or victims;
- arrest potential;
- evidence or witness availability;
- showcase or pattern crime; and
- media or government or non-governmental target.

(c) policy considerations:[11]

- advancement of international jurisprudence (reinforcement of existing norms, building precedent, clarifying and advancing the scope of existing protections);
- willingness and ability of national courts to prosecute the alleged perpetrator;
- potential symbolic or deterrent value of prosecution;
- public perception concerning the effective functioning of Tribunal;

[10] *Ibid.*, p. 100.

[11] *Ibid.*, pp. 101–02.

- public perception concerning immediate response to ongoing atrocities; and
- public perception concerning impartiality or balance.

(d) practical considerations:[12]

- available investigative resources;
- impact that the new investigation will have on an ongoing investigation and on making existing indictments trial-ready;
- the estimated time to complete the investigation;
- timing of the investigation (for example, the impact initiating a particular investigation will have on the ability to conduct future investigations in the country);
- possibility or likelihood of arrest of the alleged perpetrator;
- consideration of other work carried out in relation to the case (including a check against Rules of Road cases);
- completeness of evidence;
- availability of exculpatory information and evidence; and
- consideration of other prosecution's investigations in the same geographical area, particularly those of opposite ethnicity perpetrators and victims.

(e) other relevant considerations:[13]

- The particular statutory offence or parts thereof, that can be charged;
- the charging theories available;
- potential legal impediments to prosecution;
- potential defences;
- theory of liability and legal framework of each potential suspect;
- the extent to which the crime base fits in with current investigations and overall strategic direction;
- the extent to which a successful investigation or prosecution of the case would further the strategic aims;
- the extent to which the case can take the investigation to higher political, military, police and civil chains of command; and
- to what extent the case fits into a larger pattern-type of ongoing or future investigations and prosecutions.

The thematic groups and their constitutive lists of factors, arranged at random, seemingly without any hierarchy, were to be considered as a set of relevant

[12] *Ibid.*, pp. 102–04.

[13] *Ibid.*, pp. 104–05.

considerations informing the decision to start investigations and prosecutions.[14] However, implementing a focused case selection and prioritization policy on the basis of this diffused list is a difficult proposition.[15] It is not surprising that these criteria were not adhered to in practice by the ICTY, as apparent in indictments against many low-level perpetrators despite a stated policy to focus on the higher-level perpetrators.[16]

The failure of this prosecution-led case selection and prioritization effort has led Bergsmo *et al.* to observe that the development and implementation of case selection and prioritization criteria is difficult to achieve by a prosecution service.[17]

It would have been difficult to implement a focused policy based on this catalogue of criteria.[18]

2.3.2. Early Efforts at the International Criminal Court

The preparatory team[19] for the establishment of ICC-OTP, led by Morten Bergsmo as its co-ordinator, was the first to suggest the use of a case selection and prioritization approach within the context of the ICC. This approach was born out of the concern that exercise of discretion by the OTP could be seen as "biased or lacking in independence".[20] It was thought that formal criteria for selection and prioritization could shelter OTP's decision-making from such risks.[21]

An expert group convened by the preparatory team to present some reflections "on measures available to the Court to reduce the length of trials as well

---

[14] *Ibid.*, p. 99.

[15] Claudia Angermaier, "Case Selection and Prioritization Criteria in the Work of the International Criminal Tribunal for the Former Yugoslavia", in Morten Bergsmo (ed.), *Criteria for Prioritizing and Selecting Core International Crimes Case*, TOAEP, Oslo, 2nd edition, 2010, pp. 33–34 (https://www.legal-tools.org/doc/7496ad/).

[16] Bergsmo *et al.*, 2010, p. 109, see *supra* note 8.

[17] *Ibid.*, p. 111.

[18] Angermaier, 2010, pp. 33–34, see *supra* note 15.

[19] The preparatory team for the ICC Office of the Prosecutor was instituted by the Advance Team for the establishment of the International Criminal Court. The preparatory team's work spanned from August 2002 to November 2003. The preparatory team identified several topics on which it formed expert groups to prepare non-binding reports "for the benefit of the ICC Office of the Prosecutor, ICC judges, and for those building relevant investigation and prosecution capacity in national jurisdictions". See Morten Bergsmo, "Institutional History, Behaviour and Development", in Morten Bergsmo, Klaus Rackwitz and Song Tianying (eds.), *Historical Origins of International Criminal Law: Volume 5*, TOAEP, Brussels, 2017, pp. 1–3 (https://www.legal-tools.org/doc/1c93aa/).

[20] *Ibid.*, p. 12.

[21] *Ibid.*

as pre-trial and trial preparation stage" found it "highly desirable" to have such criteria in place from the start of the Court's operations.[22]

In its report, the expert group, in the section on investigation strategy, began its rationale for case selection and prioritization with the need to effectively allocate the limited resources of the OTP:

> Given the limited investigative and prosecutorial resources of the Office of the Prosecutor (OTP) and the broad scope of investigations under Article 54(1)(a), the Prosecutor may not be able to investigate each and every incident arising from a single situation or to prosecute every perpetrator. It is essential to review each potential new investigation by a set of rational standards that will allow the effective marshalling of OTP resources.[23]

In addition, it considered that "[a] clear pronunciation of the prosecution policy, given in the abstract, could prevent the public from harbouring unrealistic expectations and also avoid any appearance of political bias in particular cases".[24] Importantly, the expert group suggested that such a prosecution policy could prevent a "backlog of non-priority suspects".[25]

The report goes on to suggest that in order to limit the number of cases before the Court, the policy should set out priorities, such as focusing on suspects in leadership positions or those accused of crimes of a particular gravity.[26] Underscoring the fact that lower threshold crimes and low-level suspects should not be of concern to the Court, but instead to the domestic jurisdictions, it said, material from ICC investigations on these other suspects can be made available for domestic accountability mechanisms.[27]

Similarly, in terms of charging, the expert group considered that an excessive charging policy will lead to lengthy trials and extensive evidence and thus questioned whether the OTP should avoid charging offences of relatively minor importance.[28] However, it considered reasons which may support an excessive

---

22 Morten Bergsmo and Vladimir Tochilovsky, "Measures Available to the International Criminal Court to Reduce the Length of Proceedings", in Morten Bergsmo, Klaus Rackwitz and Song Tianying (eds.), *Historical Origins of International Criminal Law: Volume 5*, TOAEP, Brussels, 2017, pp. 651, 653 (the report, which was submitted to ICC judges, Registry and Prosecutor, is annexed to the chapter) (https://www.legal-tools.org/doc/779b47/).

23 *Ibid.*, pp. 668–69.

24 *Ibid.*, p. 653.

25 *Ibid.*

26 *Ibid.*, p. 669.

27 *Ibid.*

28 *Ibid.*, pp. 674–75.

charging policy, such as the wish to address "the totality of crimes committed and the degree of victimisation".[29]

The report of the expert group on the length of proceedings was circulated to the judges of the Court, its Registrar and Prosecutor in 2003, however, it does not seem to have had an immediate impact on the Court in terms of its case selection and prioritization suggestions.[30]

The draft Regulations for the ICC-OTP, prepared by an expert group appointed by the preparatory team, enumerated case selection and prioritization criteria in its section on a draft investigation plan.[31] A draft investigation plan, as per the draft Regulations, was to be prepared at the end of the preliminary examination phase to aid the OTP's decision to start an investigation pursuant to Article 53(1) or request authorization for commencing investigations under Article 15(3).[32] In case of a positive decision, an investigation plan is developed from the draft investigation plan.[33]

The draft investigation plan was to include, *inter alia*, "an explanation why the alleged offences warrant a full investigation against the backdrop of other alleged offences where such a step might not be recommendable".[34] This element of the draft investigation plan brings forth the basic step necessary in a prioritization exercise: drawing comparisons with other conduct and cases and prioritizing some over others. The other elements of the draft plan are also of relevance in guiding a prioritization exercise, such as the position of the suspect in the relevant chain of authority, likelihood of arrest, and time or resources needed to complete the investigation.[35]

While an abridged version of the draft Regulations was adopted as Regulations *ad interim* of the ICC-OTP, draft investigation plans were not part of it.[36] There was no immediate outcome of the early meticulous efforts made at the ICC for case selection and prioritization criteria. However, as will be discussed later in this chapter, the ICC-OTP adopted a policy paper on case selection and prioritization in 2016.

---

29 *Ibid.*, p. 675.

30 *Ibid.*, p. 652.

31 Carlos Vasconcelos, "Draft Regulations of the Office of the Prosecutor", in Morten Bergsmo, Klaus Rackwitz and Song Tianying (eds.), *Historical Origins of International Criminal Law: Volume 5*, TOAEP, Brussels, 2017, Annex 1 (https://www.legal-tools.org/doc/678668/).

32 *Ibid.*, p. 865.

33 *Ibid.*, p. 869.

34 *Ibid.*, p. 861.

35 *Ibid.*

36 Bergsmo, 2017, p. 19, see *supra* note 19.

2.3.3. Bosnia and Herzegovina: The Turning Point

One of the major turning points of the concept of case selection and prioritization happened not in an international context, but domestically. In 2004, the Bosnia and Herzegovina ('BiH') Collegium of Prosecutors adopted the "Orientation Criteria for Sensitive Rules of the Road cases" ('Orientation Criteria'), annexed to the *Book of Rules on Internal Organization and Operations of the Prosecutor's Office of BiH*.[37] The purpose of the Orientation Criteria was to select cases to be "heard before Section I for War Crimes of the Criminal and Appellate Divisions of the Court of Bosnia and Herzegovina".[38] Amongst the selected cases, the Orientation Criteria served as a means of prioritizing the order in which they are investigated.[39]

The factors in the Orientation Criteria related to the general criterion of gravity, with its focus on the nature of the crimes alleged and the circumstances of the perpetrator.[40] Cases where the mode of liability was command responsibility, or which involved crimes committed by law enforcement or incumbent public officials, were to take priority.[41] Other factors included practical considerations such as general readiness to proceed and issues of witness security.[42]

The co-ordinator of the preparatory team for the establishment of ICC-OTP, Morten Bergsmo, working in 2007 as a consultant for Organization for Security and Cooperation in Europe ('OSCE') in BiH, wrote a report on the backlog of open case-files in BiH.[43] The report included commentary on the case selection and prioritization criteria at the Prosecutor's Office of BiH, ICTY and the ICC. The OSCE report and its follow-up had a lasting impact in BiH and the overall development of case prioritization strategies.

The OSCE report was followed by an expert conference 'Criteria for Prioritizing and Selecting Core International Crimes Cases' in Oslo on 26 September 2008. This was the first time the issue of case selection and prioritization was put on the agenda in a conference anywhere. An anthology of conference

37 Bergsmo *et al.*, 2010, p. 81, see *supra* note 8.

38 OTP of BiH, Book of Rules on the Review of War Crimes Cases, 28 December 2004, Article 10(1).

39 Bergsmo *et al.*, 2010, p. 84, see *supra* note 8.

40 *Ibid.*, pp. 85–87.

41 *Ibid.*, p. 84.

42 *Ibid.*, p. 87.

43 Jared O. Bell, "The Bosnian War Crimes Justice Strategy a Decade Later", FICHL Policy Brief Series No. 92 (2018), TOAEP, Brussels, 2018, p. 1 (http://www.toaep.org/pbs-pdf/92-bell/).

papers from Oslo was published on 26 March 2009, forming one of the most valuable resources on the topic.[44]

The OSCE report was widely circulated in BiH and the Oslo conference also invited wide West Balkan representation.[45] By the end of that year, on 28 December 2008, the BiH Council of Ministers adopted the National War Crimes Strategy. Its Annex A, titled "Criteria for the review of war crimes cases", listed criteria for case selection and prioritization for the Prosecutor's Office of BiH. The National War Crimes Strategy was motivated and influenced by the OSCE report.[46]

One of the objectives of the Strategy document was to assist the prosecution of most responsible perpetrators of war crimes before the Court of BiH through a case selection and prioritization criteria.[47] The case selection and prioritization criteria, though in an annex, were a 'constituent part' of the National War Crimes Prosecution Strategy.[48]

The "Criteria for the review of war crimes cases" were formulated using the Orientation Criteria and the practice of ICTY and ICC as reference.[49] It classified the criteria in three categories of (a) Gravity of criminal offenses; (b) Capacity and role of the perpetrator; and (c) Other circumstances.

The gravity criteria considered, logically foremost, whether the qualifications of one of the core international crimes (that is, genocide, crimes against humanity and war crimes) have been fulfilled.[50] The factors guiding the gravity assessment considered whether the offence involved: widespread and systematic killings; persecution; forced disappearance; serious forms of rape, torture, unlawful detention, or inflictions of sufferings on a civilian population; large number of victims or severe consequences for the victims; and particularly insidious means and methods of perpetrating the offence.[51]

The capacity and role of the perpetrator criteria included factors such as the position of the perpetrator in the hierarchy of military, police or paramilitary establishment; whether the perpetrator holds a political office or a judicial office,

---

44 Morten Bergsmo (ed.), *Criteria for Prioritizing and Selecting Core International Crimes Cases*, International Peace Research Institute, Oslo, 2009. A second edition was published on 23 July 2010 (http://www.toaep.org/ps-pdf/4-bergsmo-second/), followed by the present third edition.

45 Bergsmo *et al.*, 2010, p. 116, see *supra* note 8.

46 Bell, 2018, p. 1, see *supra* note 43.

47 BiH Council of Ministers, National Strategy for Processing of War Crimes Cases, 28 December 2008, Section 1.2 d., reproduced in Bergsmo *et al.*, 2010, p. 168, see *supra* note 8.

48 *Ibid.*, "Annex A: Criteria for the review of war crimes cases".

49 *Ibid.*

50 *Ibid.*

51 *Ibid.*

such as that of a judge, prosecutor, public attorney, or attorney at law; whether the perpetrator was in charge of a camp or detention centre; and modalities of participation in the perpetration of the offence, like involvement in planning and ordering the crime, manner of perpetration and the degree of intent.[52]

The third residual criteria included factors such as: relation to other cases and potential perpetrators; interests of victims and witnesses such as whether the witnesses are protected or need protection, or are insider witnesses; and a third factor considering the impact of the offence or its prosecution on the local community, such as demographic changes, societal trauma and disturbance in public order.[53]

2.4. The Idea in the Mainstream

The OSCE report, the Oslo conference, and the efforts in BiH heralded the dawn of case prioritization criteria. The Oslo conference and its anthology constitute the knowledge-base pursuant to which further progress has been made on several fronts, both internationally and domestically. It brought together cross-cutting research on prioritization from domestic and international courts and established case prioritization as a topic in international criminal justice.

Among its most significant impact is the ICC-OTP's policy paper on case selection and prioritization. But it has also formed the intellectual basis of efforts made in domestic jurisdictions by CILRAP's Case Matrix Network ('CILRAP-CMN') department.

2.4.1. ICC-OTP's Policy Paper on Case Selection and Prioritisation

On 15 September 2016, the ICC-OTP released its *Policy Paper on Case Selection and Prioritisation.*[54] While it is an internal policy document of the OTP, it was subjected to wide public consultation and published to increase transparency regarding the criteria guiding OTP's decisions on case selection and prioritization.[55]

The OTP Policy Paper lists considerations that guide the OTP in selecting cases to be investigated and prosecuted within a situation and prioritizing the selected cases both within and across the situations.[56]

---

52 *Ibid.*

53 *Ibid.*

54 ICC-OTP, "Policy Paper on Case Selection and Prioritisation", 15 September 2016 ('OTP Policy Paper') (https://www.legal-tools.org/doc/182205/).

55 ICC-OTP, "Report on the Implementation of the OTP Strategic Plan (2016 – 2018): Final Analysis and Evaluation of the Results", 23 August 2019, p. 14 (https://www.legal-tools.org/doc/5siv5j/).

56 OTP Policy Paper, para. 1, see *supra* note 54.

As the concept of prioritization is not in the Rome Statute, the OTP used Article 54(1)(b) that allows it to take appropriate measures to ensure the effective investigation and prosecution of crimes to articulate prioritization criteria.[57]

In order to aid the prioritization exercise, the OTP Policy Paper establishes a master document, titled the Case Selection Document, which lists potential cases across all situations that meet the case selection criteria of the OTP Policy Paper.[58] The prioritization criteria are used to determine the order in which cases listed in the Case Selection Document are "rolled-out over time".[59] Cases that are not prioritized still remain part of the Case Selection Document and could still be investigated and prosecuted when the circumstances permit such action.[60]

The OTP Policy Paper divides prioritization criteria into two categories: strategic and operational criteria. There is no hierarchy between the two categories and the weight to be given to each constituent criterion will depend on the circumstances of each case.[61] This gives broad discretion to the OTP to prioritize cases.

The strategic criteria include:

a) The gravity of crimes alleged, involving both quantitative and qualitative aspects. The factors that guide the assessment of gravity include the scale, nature, manner of commission, and impact of the crimes;[62]
b) Degree of responsibility of alleged perpetrators, highlighting the need to prosecute those most responsible. The extent of responsibility of an accused will be determined by the nature of the unlawful behaviour; the degree of their participation and intent; the existence of discriminatory motive; and any abuse of power or official capacity.[63]
c) Representativity: The office will prioritize cases where charges represent the true extent of the criminality which has occurred within a given situation, to constitute, whenever possible, a representative sample of the main

---

57 *Ibid.*, para. 49.

58 *Ibid.*, paras. 10–11. The Independent Expert Review ('IER') found in 2020 that the Case Selection Document had not been produced until then leading it to recommend that the OTP complete the development of Case Selection Documents. See "Independent Expert Review of the International Criminal Court and the Rome Statute System: Final Report", 30 September 2020, pp. 220, 221 ('IER Report') (https://www.legal-tools.org/doc/cv19d5/).

59 OTP Policy Paper, para. 48, see *supra* note 54.

60 *Ibid.*

61 *Ibid.*, para. 52.

62 *Ibid.*, para. 37.

63 *Ibid.*, para. 43.

types of victimization and involving the main types of victim communities.[64]

Beyond representative crimes, it will also prioritize investigation of crimes against or affecting children, sexual and gender-based crimes, and attacks against cultural, religious, historical and other protected objects as well as against humanitarian and peace-keeping personnel.[65]

d) "whether a person, or members of the same group, have already been subject to investigation or prosecution either by the Office or by a State for another serious crime";[66]
e) "the impact of investigations and prosecutions on the victims of the crimes and affected communities";[67]
f) "the impact of investigations and prosecutions on ongoing criminality and/or their contribution to the prevention of crimes";[68] and
g) "the impact and the ability of the Office to pursue cases involving opposing parties to a conflict in parallel or on a sequential basis".[69]

The operational criteria explore whether there are reasonable prospects of securing conviction by reviewing the quantity and quality of the available evidence, international co-operation and judicial assistance to the OTP, ability to conduct required investigations in a timely manner, security situation in the place of investigation, protection of persons co-operating with the court, ability to secure the presence of the accused.[70]

In the OTP's annual reports on preliminary examination activities, one can get a glimpse of the implementation of the case prioritization criteria. For instance, in Ukraine, the OTP sought to "prioritise certain types of alleged conduct believed to be most representative of the patterns of alleged crimes".[71] While in Gaza, it sought to prioritize "incidents for which there is a range of sources and sufficient information available to enable an objective and thorough analysis".[72]

---

64 *Ibid.*, para. 45.
65 *Ibid.*, para. 46.
66 *Ibid.*, para. 50.
67 *Ibid.*
68 *Ibid.*
69 *Ibid.*
70 *Ibid.*, para. 41.
71 ICC-OTP, "Report on Preliminary Examination Activities 2018", 5 December 2018, p. 27 (https://www.legal-tools.org/doc/39c2c1/).
72 ICC-OTP, "Report on Preliminary Examination Activities 2019", 5 December 2019, p. 58 (https://www.legal-tools.org/doc/lq7j94/).

Interestingly, by assessing cases being de-prioritized relative to others in the same situation, we can see OTP's application of prioritization criteria in a unique light. On 27 September 2021, the OTP filed a request before the Pre-Trial Chamber II to authorize resumption of investigation in the Situation in the Islamic Republic of Afghanistan ('situation in Afghanistan').[73] At the same time, the OTP released a media statement clarifying that, if authorized, the focus of the resumed investigation would be on crimes allegedly committed by the Taliban and the Islamic State – Khorasan Province ('IS-K') while it would "deprioritise other aspects of this investigation".[74] While the statement did not specify the reasons for de-prioritizing other crimes, it mentioned gravity, scale and continuing nature of crimes allegedly committed by the Taliban and IS-K, including thematic priorities such as persecution of women and girls and crimes against children, as reasons for prioritizing that aspect of investigation.[75] The OTP Policy Paper, however, does state that the OTP may choose to de-prioritize a case if it cannot conduct the necessary investigations leading to a prosecution with a reasonable prospect of conviction.[76] The OTP has separately cited the standard of "reasonable prospect of conviction" from the OTP Policy Paper when withdrawing charges against Maxime Mokom.[77]

The OTP's announcement of de-prioritizing aspects of investigation in situation in Afghanistan, which included alleged crimes committed by forces and intelligence services of non-States Parties was met with dismay from civil society and victims, with the former suggesting that OTP may have succumbed to pressure from powerful States.[78] Upon victims' representations that the Pre-Trial

[73] ICC, *Situation in the Islamic Republic of Afghanistan*, Pre-Trial Chamber II, Request to authorise resumption of investigation under article 18(2) of the Statute, 27 September 2021, ICC-02/17-161 (https://www.legal-tools.org/doc/pzfuq9/).

[74] ICC-OTP, "Statement of the Prosecutor of the International Criminal Court, Karim A.A. Khan QC, following the application for an expedited order under article 18(2) seeking authorisation to resume investigations in the Situation in Afghanistan", 27 September 2021 (https://www.legal-tools.org/doc/0nvy519m/).

[75] *Ibid.*

[76] OTP Policy Paper, para. 53, see *supra* note 54.

[77] ICC, *Situation in the Central African Republic II, Prosecutor v. Maxime Jeoffroy Eli Mokom Gawaka*, Pre-Trial Chamber II, Notice of Withdrawal of the Charges against Maxime Jeoffroy Eli Mokom Gawaka, 16 October 2023, ICC-01/14-01/22-275, para. 5 (https://www.legal-tools.org/doc/vaseup/).

[78] Amnesty International, "Afghanistan: ICC Prosecutor's Statement on Afghanistan Jeopardises His Office's Legitimacy and Future", 5 October 2021 (https://www.legal-tools.org/doc/1ew1v0cl/); ICC, *Situation in the Islamic Republic of Afghanistan*, Pre-Trial Chamber II, Public Redacted Annex I to Final consolidated report on Article 18(2) Victim Representations, 25 April 2022, ICC-02/17-190, para. 28 (https://www.legal-tools.org/doc/cwd2tf/).

Chamber ('PTC') should be able to review (under Article 53(3)(b) of the Statute) the OTP's decision to de-prioritize, the PTC opined that such review is not available in this instance since the investigation in the situation in Afghanistan was authorized upon the Prosecution's request to initiate a *proprio motu* investigation pursuant to Article 15(3).[79] The PTC's determination here leaves open the question whether it can review an OTP's decision to de-prioritize in a situation referred by States Parties or the United Nations Security Council ('UNSC').

In the Strategic Plan for 2019–2021, during Prosecutor Fatou Bensouda's tenure, the OTP had set a strategic goal of increasing "the speed, efficiency and effectiveness of preliminary examinations, investigations and prosecutions" which it aimed to achieve by implementing, *inter alia*, a strategy of "further prioritising amongst investigations and prosecutions".[80] Recognizing the expectations of stakeholders to deliver more and better results while using the existing resources, the OTP planned to stringently apply case prioritization criteria to cases identified across all situations under investigation which it warned could delay non-prioritized cases.[81] The OTP considered it necessary to undertake these 'difficult decisions' on prioritization, in order to build viable cases while working with limited resources.[82]

In 2020, the IER Report considered the issues of case and situation selection and prioritization at length, recommending several steps by the OTP including, *inter alia*, increasing the gravity threshold during the preliminary examination phase to reduce the number of ongoing investigations, introducing a hierarchy amongst the criteria for case selection with the gravity of crimes being the foremost criteria, followed by quality of evidence and the degree of responsibility of suspects.[83] With respect to prioritization criteria, the IER, recommended the OTP to come up with policy for prioritization, de-prioritization and hibernation of situations.[84] The following year the OTP released the Policy on Situation Completion which addresses aspects of de-prioritization or suspension of a case or situation.[85]

---

[79] ICC, *Situation in the Islamic Republic of Afghanistan*, Pre-Trial Chamber II, Decision pursuant to article 18(2) of the Statute authorising the Prosecution to resume investigation, ICC-02/17-196, 31 October 2022 (https://www.legal-tools.org/doc/psibag/).

[80] ICC-OTP, "Strategic Plan 2019–2021", 17 July 2019, paras. 18–19 ('Strategic Plan 2019–2021') (https://www.legal-tools.org/doc/raba4c/).

[81] *Ibid.*, para. 22.

[82] *Ibid.*

[83] IER Report, pp. 213, 219, see *supra* note 58.

[84] *Ibid.*, p. 224.

[85] ICC-OTP, "Policy on Situation Completion", 15 June 2021, pp. 15–18 (https://www.legal-tools.org/doc/mdl417/).

In the Strategic Plan for 2023–2025, under Prosecutor Karim A.A. Khan KC, the OTP is sharply focused on systematic and objective prioritization of situations and cases to reduce the total number of situations, allowing concentrated allocation of resources stated to yield better courtroom results.[86] Under the plan, the OTP will prioritize cases on the basis of gravity and prospect of success (conviction), as well as prioritize sexual and gender-based crimes and crimes against children.[87] The OTP has identified five priority situations: Bangladesh, Libya, Sudan, Ukraine and Venezuela where it has set up field offices or is in the process of establishing field presence.[88]

2.4.2. Colombia

Colombia's Office of the Attorney General adopted a directive on case selection and prioritization criteria in 2012, and is one of the early adopters of this strategy.[89] The directive categorizes prioritization criteria in three groups: (i) Objective: The objective criterion of prioritization examines the criminal conduct in terms of severity and its representativeness. Thus, combining considerations of gravity and representativity in the same cluster;[90] (ii) Subjective: this criterion considers the qualities of the victim such as their gender, age, membership of an ethnic group or profession such as human rights defender, journalist or judicial officer. It also considers the degree of responsibility of the accused;[91] (iii) Other complementary considerations: such as practical feasibility of prosecution, whether the conduct in question is being investigated by an international court, and the region or location of the crime.[92]

2.4.3. The Democratic Republic of the Congo

In 2018, the Democratic Republic of the Congo ('DRC') adopted Practice Direction for the Selection and Prioritisation of Crimes Against Peace and Security of Mankind, in Particular Sexual Violence at the Investigation Stage ('Practice

86 ICC-OTP, "Strategic Plan 2023–2025", 13 June 2023, para. 24 (https://www.legal-tools.org/doc/mu9jlt/).

87 *Ibid.*, paras. 24, 59.

88 ICC-OTP, "Annual Report 2023", 6 December 2023, p. 41 (https://www.legal-tools.org/doc/dcv6zxml/).

89 Colombia Office of the Attorney General, Por medio de la cual se adoptan unos criterios de priorización de situaciones y casos, y se crea un nuevo sistema de investigación penal y de gestión de aquéllos en la Fiscalía General de la Nación, 4 October 2012, Directiva No. 0001 (https://www.legal-tools.org/doc/e93910/).

90 *Ibid.*, pp. 30–31.

91 *Ibid.*, pp. 28–30.

92 *Ibid.*, pp. 31–32.

Direction').[93] CILRAP's CMN department assisted the DRC with methodology and technical support for the development of the Practice Direction.[94] The case selection and prioritizing criteria in the Practice Direction were themselves heavily influenced by a CILRAP-CMN report published in 2015.[95]

As a prerequisite of the case selection and prioritization exercise, it calls for a centralized statistical database on the number of open cases, number of suspects in those cases, nature of the offence and the number of victims.[96]

The case selection and prioritization criteria are divided into two broad sections: formal criteria, and policy and practical considerations. Formal criteria include consideration of the factual context of the commission of the crime on the basis of indicators that assess gravity, such as the number of victims, area of destruction, duration and repetition of the offence, *modus operandi* of the criminal conduct, discriminatory motive, defencelessness of victims and impact of crimes.[97] The factual context is also enriched by the location of the crime and ethnicity, tribe or nationality of the alleged perpetrators or victims, factors that are relevant in a domestic context.[98]

The formal criteria in the Practice Direction also include assessment of the degree of responsibility of the accused and a victim-centric representativity approach that focuses on the scale and nature of the victimization rather than the political, ethnic or religious affiliation of the accused or victims.[99]

93 DRC Conseil Supérieur de la Magistrature, Circulaire n°02/PCC-PCSM/2018 relative à la sélection et à la priorisation des affaires de crimes contre la paix et la sécurité de l'humanité, en particulier celles liées aux violences sexuelles, au stade de l'instruction préjuridictionnelle (Memo No. 02/PCC-PCSM/2018 on the Case Selection and Prioritisation of Crimes Against Peace and Security of Mankind, in Particular Those Relating to Sexual Violence at the Preliminary Stage), 19 March 2018 ('DRC Practice Direction') (https://www.legal-tools.org/doc/bf85a3/).

94 CILRAP-CMN, "Examples of Country-Work Undertaken by the CMN" (available on its web site).

95 CILRAP-CMN, "Prioritising International Sex Crimes Cases in the Democratic Republic of the Congo: Supporting the national justice system in the investigation and prosecution of core international crimes with a sexual element", Brussels, November 2015 (https://www.legal-tools.org/doc/2ee277/).

96 DRC Practice Direction, Chapter III – Mapping: prerequisite of prioritisation, see *supra* note 93.

97 *Ibid.*, Chapter IV, Section 1, Criterion 1.

98 *Ibid.*

99 *Ibid.*, Chapter IV, Section 1, Criteria 2 and 3.

Practical considerations for prioritizing cases include strategic and practical indicators to make an "early assessment of the effectiveness and efficiency" of prosecuting a given case.[100]

2.4.4. The Central African Republic

In December 2018, the Special Criminal Court ('CPS') of the Central African Republic ('CAR'), that exercises jurisdiction over core international crimes, launched an investigation and prosecution strategy that provides selection and prioritization criteria.[101] Its prioritization criteria have been localized extensively and they include:

1) Feasibility of investigation in terms of security: recognizing the safety and security issues persisting in the CAR, this criterion requires the prosecutor to consider the security issues, including witness and victim protection, the safety of investigators, judicial actors and all other persons who may be at security risk due to the prosecutor's activities.[102]
2) Representativity: the CPS uses a broad criterion of representativity. The cases to be prioritized should be representative of the a) victims including from different religious, ethnic and geographic groups; b) alleged perpetrators from various armed groups or State apparatus taking into account their ethnic and religious affiliations; c) geography – the incidents selected must, wherever possible, represent the different regions affected by the crisis in the CAR; d) different time periods of conflict in the CAR lasting from 2003 until the time of writing.[103] As is clear here, the CPS's use of the term representativity hints towards diversity in prosecution.
3) Possibility of identification, location and arrest of the suspect.[104]
4) Availability, credibility and reliability of evidence.[105]
5) Strategic considerations such as availability of resources, the time required to complete investigation, and the potential of developing future case-files.[106]

[100] *Ibid.*, Chapter IV, Section 2.

[101] CAR Cour Pénale Spéciale, Stratégie d'enquêtes, de poursuites et d'instructions, 4 December 2018 (https://www.legal-tools.org/doc/61skr0/).

[102] *Ibid.*, para. 64.

[103] *Ibid.*, para. 65.

[104] *Ibid.*, para. 66.

[105] *Ibid.*, para. 67.

[106] *Ibid.*, para. 68.

6) Public interests, such as developing trust in the CPS, emblematic value of certain incidents and crimes, and impact of prosecution in creating a deterrence to criminality.[107]

2.4.5. Representativity as a Case Prioritization Criteria: A Missed Opportunity

The OSCE report, referenced earlier, was also published as the monograph *The Backlog of Core International Crimes Case Files in Bosnia and Herzegovina* by Morten Bergsmo *et al.*[108] This book enunciated a unique concept of representativity that has not yet been fully captured by the discourse on prioritization.

In the words of Bergsmo *et al.*, the idea of representativity is:

> [T]hat at the end of a process of war crimes prosecutions, the accumulated case portfolio should reflect – or be representative of – the overall victimisation caused by the crimes in the conflict or situation at hand. The most serious crimes and the crimes that the most senior leaders are suspected of being most responsible for should have been prosecuted at the end of the day. The areas and communities most affected by the crimes should have seen more of these crimes or crime base prosecuted than in less affected communities. The most affected victim groups should have more of the crimes that caused the victimisation prosecuted than other groups. Organizations or structures causing the most serious crimes should have more of its responsible members – or more of the crimes caused by them – prosecuted than other such organizations or structures.[109]

As per that text, this approach towards representativity is born out of the concerns for the interests of the victims and the ability of criminal justice to contribute to reconciliation and deterrence, while commanding trust of all its stakeholders.[110]

However, the use of the superlative 'most' (most affected areas, communities and victim groups, most serious crimes, and so on) in the formulation of Bergsmo *et al.* exudes a utilitarian approach. From this perspective, representativity does not have victims at its core – if that were the case it would not differentiate between the most affected victims and lesser affected victims. This idea is all about efficiency – bringing out the maximum benefits from the criminal justice institution. This idea of representativity embodies the rationale of prior-

[107] *Ibid.*, para. 69.

[108] Bergsmo *et al.*, 2010, see *supra* note 8.

[109] *Ibid.*, p. 125.

[110] *Ibid.*

itization like no other criteria, that is, to have an efficient criminal justice machinery. In a way, representativity is what law intends to do: to maintain order and to do so in a way where benefits far outweigh the costs. To do it in a way that has the maximum impact is really about hammering the nail that sticks out the most.

The idea is not to seek shelter behind the poster incident or accused, which could be guided by popular media, but to tackle head-on what represents quantitatively the most serious form of victimization.

Donors, the international community, victims, and the general populace would surely recognize the effectiveness of a criminal justice system when those who faced the greatest suffering, the incidents which caused the greatest suffering, and those who caused the greatest suffering are processed by it.

The ICC-OTP has missed the opportunity to embrace the concept of representativity fully in its Policy Paper published in 2016. When making reference to representativity, the Policy Paper talks about representing the true extent of criminality in a situation and selecting charges that constitute a representative sample of main types of victimization and affected communities. The ICC-OTP's approach appears to be ensuring diversity and not effectiveness. As the institution that sits at the pinnacle of efforts to end impunity for mass crimes, a case prioritization strategy that ensures effective delivery of justice through representativity could bring larger benefits to the international community.

2.5. Challenges

In the context of the ICC, with its ever-burgeoning case load, a faithful and transparent application of the prioritization criteria remains critically important. As Morten Bergsmo notes in Chapter 1, the case selection and prioritization criteria should be "as precise, fair and transparent as possible" and their purpose should not be simply reduced to "outreach or *ex post facto* justification of [prioritization] decisions".[111] Nevertheless, the Prosecutor enjoys discretion in matters of case selection and prioritization, subject only to limited judicial review.[112] As such, the Prosecutor may decide to prioritize (or de-prioritize) a case or a whole situation with its underlying cases on the basis of criteria that are not included in the *Policy Paper on Case Selection and Prioritisation*. For instance, the Prosecutor has made several statements emphasizing that the OTP will extend particular prioritization to situations referred to it by the UNSC and allocate

[111] See Section 1.6. above in Chapter 1 by Morten Bergsmo.

[112] Kai Ambos, "Introductory Note to Office of the Prosecutor", in *International Legal Materials*, December 2018, vol. 57, no. 6, p. 1133.

sufficient staffing and technical capacity to these situations.[113] It is natural that as the OTP's practice evolves, it may identify novel priorities that it will want reflected in its case load. However, the OTP should consider updating its Policy Paper with the new priorities, so they can be placed and compared alongside existing criteria and guide the Prosecutor's discretion in a balanced manner. In this regard, the OTP's announcement of comprehensive review and consolidation of related policies on gravity, prioritization and completion of investigations is a welcome step.[114]

In the implementation of prioritization criteria in domestic jurisdictions, one important factor to consider is the operation of the principle of complementarity *vis-à-vis* the prioritization criteria in the domestic jurisdiction. Should the implementation of prioritization criteria in a domestic jurisdiction fall foul of the ICC standard of unable and unwilling, there is a possibility of those cases reaching the ICC. While prioritizing a case does not entail non-prosecution of the non-prioritized cases, realistically there are bound to be delays in managing the non-prioritized caseload. Under the ICC Statute, unjustified or undue delays could be considered as the unwillingness or inability of the domestic judicial system to carry out investigation and prosecution, and could invite the attention of the ICC-OTP.[115] Similarly, a broadly-worded, practical-considerations criterion could give wide discretion to the prosecutor, and if that discretion is used to deprioritize certain cases with the intent of shielding the accused from prosecution, it is likely to be treated as unwillingness to genuinely investigate or prosecute.[116]

The key to designing the domestic prioritization criteria is that they not be inconsistent with the ICC prioritization criteria: the gravity of offences and degree of responsibility of the accused should remain relevant, but the main types of victimization and affected communities should also be considered for prioritization.

While the ICC-OTP's Policy Paper is treated as an internal document not giving rise to any rights and obligations, it remains to be seen how the ICC-OTP

[113] See, for example, ICC-OTP, "Twenty-Second Report of the Prosecutor of the International Criminal Court to the United Nations Security Council Pursuant to Resolution 1970 (2011)", 23 November 2021, p. 1 (https://www.legal-tools.org/doc/27bt2cdo/), and ICC-OTP, "Twenty-Third Report of the Prosecutor of the International Criminal Court to the United Nations Security Council Pursuant to Resolution 1970 (2011)", 21 April 2022, p. 2 (https://www.legal-tools.org/doc/68bkdlh3/).

[114] Strategic Plan 2023–2025, see *supra* note 86, para. 57.

[115] Rome Statute of the International Criminal Court, 17 July 1998, Article 17(2)(b) and 17(3) (https://www.legal-tools.org/doc/7b9af9/).

[116] *Ibid.*, Article 17(2)(a).

will treat non-compliance by a domestic prosecution service of the relevant domestic criteria of prioritization.[117] Could the ICC-OTP consider such non-compliance as proof that the case has not been prioritized with a view to shielding the accused from criminal responsibility? It certainly can, as the ICC is likely to take into account all information available to it in order to assess the State's unwillingness and inability to prosecute core international crimes.

Thus, an ideal prioritization criterion in a domestic jurisdiction will not only address the local needs, but also be mindful of the ICC Statute, its prioritization criteria, and the operation of the principle of complementarity.

As a corollary to the ICC-aware or -sensitive domestic prioritization criteria, the ICC itself needs to design its prioritization criteria so that there is no impunity gap. That is, its prioritization criteria need to be specifically designed to cover cases, in line with the Rome Statute, that are not adequately covered by the domestic prioritization criteria, so that the operation of prioritization criteria at the domestic level and by the ICC-OTP complement each other and there is no impunity gap for the perpetrators of the most serious crimes.

2.6. The Future

As is evident in the adoption of case prioritization strategies in domestic jurisdictions, the idea of case prioritization is gaining wider acceptance due to its ability to meaningfully navigate bloated mass crimes case portfolios of States with stretched criminal justice systems.

Case prioritizing could also be a useful strategy for countries that suffer from judicial pendency. For instance, the Indian judicial system suffers from a massive backlog of civil and criminal cases.[118] In a recent Delhi High Court judgment on mass violence directed against the Sikh community in the aftermath of the assassination of former Prime Minister Indira Gandhi, the Court lamented the fact that it had taken 34 years to bring the perpetrators to justice:

> In India, the riots in early November 1984 in which in Delhi alone 2,733 Sikhs and nearly 3,350 all over the country were brutally murdered (these are official figures) was neither the first instance

[117] OTP Policy Paper, para. 2, see *supra* note 54.

[118] Law Commission of India, *Arrears and Backlog: Creating Additional Judicial (Wo)manpower*, July 2014, Report No. 245, p. 1 (https://www.legal-tools.org/doc/jwxv5v/):

> [T]he judicial system is unable to deliver timely justice because of huge backlog of cases for which the current judge strength is completely inadequate. Further, in addition to the already backlogged cases, the system is not being able to keep pace with the new cases being instituted, and is not being able to dispose of a comparable number of cases. The already severe problem of backlogs is, therefore, getting exacerbated by the day, leading to a dilution of the Constitutional guarantee of access to timely justice and erosion of the rule of law.

> of a mass crime nor, tragically, the last. The mass killings in Punjab, Delhi and elsewhere during the country's partition remains a collective painful memory as is the killings of innocent Sikhs in November 1984. There has been a familiar pattern of mass killings in Mumbai in 1993, in Gujarat in 2002, in Kandhamal, Odisha in 2008, in Muzaffarnagar in U.P. in 2013 to name a few. Common to these mass crimes were the targeting of minorities and the attacks spearheaded by the dominant political actors being facilitated by the law enforcement agencies. The criminals responsible for the mass crimes have enjoyed political patronage and managed to evade prosecution and punishment. Bringing such criminals to justice poses a serious challenge to our legal system. As these appeals themselves demonstrate, decades pass by before they can be made answerable. This calls for strengthening the legal system.[119]

Countries like India that suffer from inexplicable judicial delays due to massive backlogs of cases can benefit from prioritizing mass crimes cases. The criteria for prioritizing mass crimes need to be suited to the particular needs of the domestic jurisdiction. There can hardly be boilerplate prioritization criteria for domestic jurisdictions. As the case selection and prioritizing strategy from the CAR shows, States should design case prioritizing strategies that are best suited to their needs and realities.

As per the ICC-OTP's Strategic Plan for 2023–2025, it plans to prioritize situations and cases in aid of its overall goal of reducing the total number of situations under investigation at a time when the world is seeing increased armed conflicts and atrocity crimes.[120] This is a difficult goal and will necessarily require the OTP to meticulously and transparently apply the case-prioritization criteria, so it can be shielded from external pressure in making these decisions while also managing the expectations of victims and stakeholders. Thus, we are likely to witness a more proactive approach on case prioritization at the ICC, the method and results of which could be quite instructive for national jurisdictions that suffer from large backlogs of cases and limited resources.

---

[119] Delhi High Court, *State through CBI v. Sajjan Kumar and others*, Judgment, 17 December 2018, Criminal Appeal No. 1099/2013 and Connected Matters, para. 367.6 (https://www.legal-tools.org/doc/b08482/).

[120] Strategic Plan 2023–2025, see *supra* note 86, para. 24.

Annex

Date	Development
October 1995	ICTY's Office of the Prosecutor formally adopts case selection and prioritization criteria.
August 2002 to November 2003	Expert groups appointed by the preparatory team for the ICC Office of the Prosecutor prepares report "on measures available to the Court to reduce the length of trials as well as pre-trial and trial preparation stage" and draft Regulations for the OTP.
28 December 2004	BiH Collegium of Prosecutors adopted the "Orientation Criteria for Sensitive Rules of the Road cases".
2007	OSCE report on the backlog of open case-files in BiH.
26 September 2008	CILRAP expert conference on 'Criteria for Prioritizing and Selecting Core International Crimes Cases' held in Oslo.
28 December 2008	The BiH Council of Ministers adopted the National War Crimes Strategy with Annex A, titled "Criteria for the review of war crimes cases".
26 March 2009	Anthology of conference papers from Oslo expert conference 'Criteria for Prioritizing and Selecting Core International Crimes Cases' published by TOAEP.
17 September 2009	The OSCE report published as the monograph *The Backlog of Core International Crimes Case Files in Bosnia and Herzegovina* by TOAEP.
4 October 2012	Colombia's Office of the Attorney General adopts the directive on case selection and prioritization criteria.
November 2015	CILRAP's CMN releases *Prioritising International Sex Crimes Cases in the Democratic Republic of the Congo: Supporting the national justice system in the investigation and prosecution of core international crimes with a sexual element.*
15 September 2016	The ICC-OTP releases the *Policy Paper on Case Selection and Prioritisation.*
19 March 2018	The DRC adopts "Practice Direction for the Selection and Prioritisation of Crimes Against Peace and Security of Mankind, in Particular Sexual Violence at the Investigation Stage".
4 December 2018	The Special Criminal Court of Central African Republic launches the investigation and prosecution strategy with case selection and prioritization criteria.

A timeline on the development of the case prioritization criteria for core international crimes.

3

Criteria for Prosecution of International Crimes: The Importance for States and the International Community of the Quality of the Criminal Justice Process for Atrocities, in Particular of the Exercise of Fundamental Discretion by Key Justice Actors

Rolf Einar Fife*

Speaking on behalf of the Norwegian Ministry of Foreign Affairs at the seminar where this paper was presented, I should like to sincerely thank PRIO's Forum for International Criminal and Humanitarian Law, in particular Morten Bergsmo, for this timely initiative to engage not only in thorough but also systematic reflection on criteria for prosecutions of international crimes. An impressive array of international and national practitioners, many with hands-on experience from complex conflict situations, was invited to the seminar to share their insights.

The questions before us are usefully limited to the criteria for prosecutions within a situation. We are therefore not discussing the choice of general situations or conflict areas in which to consider engaging prosecutions.

Already at the outset, a brief proviso may be called for, in order to prevent or overcome some misleading pre-conceptions. Intuitively, the issue of *prosecution of international crimes* is often associated with the *international prosecution of crimes*. International or cross-border co-operation to bring criminals to justice, say of individuals suspected of murder or serious fraud, may admittedly raise a number of difficult questions. But this is not the kind of issue we are considering here. Instead, we are focusing on a particular category of offences, namely international crimes. These are distinguished by a specific international dimension and concomitant legal obligations. They are crimes of concern to the international community as a whole. Having been recognized as such

* Ambassador **Rolf Einar Fife** is a Special Adviser to the Royal Norwegian Ministry of Foreign Affairs and a Member of the United Nations International Law Commission. At the time of writing, he was Director General, Legal Affairs Department, Royal Norwegian Ministry of Foreign Affairs. This chapter has not been substantively updated since the Second Edition. He has previously served as the Norwegian Ambassador to France and the European Union.

under international law, they give rise to specific international legal obligations, irrespective of the state of national laws. These crimes include genocide, crimes against humanity and war crimes. Ideally and primarily, these crimes should be dealt with domestically. Initiatives at the international levels should only be undertaken, if and when the national system concerned is unable or unwilling genuinely to do so.

The perspective of criminalization of international crimes builds on recognition of key differences in scope and scale from ordinary crimes. Such a new paradigm is not only called for by international law. It is also largely, and increasingly, required by our national laws.

International crimes will usually concern mass crimes or crimes of particular gravity, potentially implicating large numbers of individuals, groups or social structures. Methodically, the emphasis is on the identification of large scale 'patterns'. How do you identify and select patterns, as opposed to individual events?

3.1. The Contribution of Legal Informatics to Grapple With Objective Assessments of Complex Patterns

An intuitive starting point for grasping challenges facing prosecutions of international crimes can be illustrated by the contributions of legal informatics. This discipline has increasingly demonstrated its relevance in the investigation of complex economic crimes and has been broadened to assist in identifying international crimes. We should here pause to congratulate Morten Bergsmo for receiving – just a few days prior to the seminar on which this book is largely based[1] – the international 'Dieter Meurer Prize for Legal Informatics'.[2] The prize was intended to mark the creation and development of the Case Matrix. This is a tool designed to make work on accountability for international crimes committed more precise and effective.

Upon reflection, it should come as no surprise that a vast and complex body of law, as applied to vast and complex patterns of events, can be aided by legal informatics. Indeed, we speak of *complex patterns* rather than of single events or isolated acts. Using legal informatics can contribute to the quality of the criminal justice process for atrocities.

But does the law actually allow for criteria for prosecutions? What do we mean by 'criteria' in this context? And are criteria even useful? In the following,

---

1 The seminar took place on 26 September 2008.

2 The prize was granted in Saarbrücken on 18 September 2008. The event was organized by the German Association for Computing in the Judiciary and the German-language legal information service provider juris GmbH (Germany's 'LexisNexis', for our American friends, or 'Lovdata', for our Norwegian friends).

I should like to share with you some reflections concerning prosecutorial discretion. Such reflections can of course not be expressive of official views of the Norwegian Foreign Ministry and are purely personal. I follow here the invitation by the convenors to engage in matters that not only are delicate, but belong to the independent realm of prosecutorial or judicial activities, as opposed to those of political bodies or States. My basic proposition is that the quality of prosecutorial work is essential, also as seen from the perspective of States, and that it may be aided by an in-depth reflection on criteria.

3.2. Criteria – Conceptual Approaches

The notion of criteria is more commonly embraced by the so-called exact sciences than by jurisprudence in the field of prosecutorial discretion. Typically, references to stated criteria are required when making assessments or evaluations relating to experimental and quantifiable phenomena. Is the notion then really appropriate, or even applicable, to the activities of justice actors? These do not have much in common with the working methods of, say, natural, computer or even social sciences.

Paradoxically, the very root of the notion of 'criterion' stems linguistically from the ancient Greek word for judging (*krino*, *krinein*: to judge). *Kritērion* came to signify a rule to distinguish between what is true from what is false. The noun was later taken up by Latin, now embracing the broader meaning 'judgement'.

The history of criminal procedure evolved without delving into an analysis of criteria for exercising prosecutorial discretion. Instead, as expressed for example by legal theory in the French continental tradition, two abstract ideals emerged. These were encapsulated in a debate on the principle of legality of prosecutions vs. the principle of opportunity of prosecutions (*la légalité* vs. *l'opportunité*). The first affords in principle no discretion at all to the prosecutor, it mandates compulsory prosecutions. The other allows for choices and screening, but leaves this largely to the discretion of prosecutors. In most if not all national legal systems the reality has been situated somewhere in a magnetic field between those two ideals.

Let us briefly recognize important differences between the main legal systems of the world, including civil law and common law. Differences in legal cultures inspire our understanding, our pre-judgement when interpreting the very role of prosecutors and judges. However, momentous developments of international criminal justice have demonstrated that we can surmount or transcend such cleavages. Let us just note that there are national systems where the notion of individualized justice runs deep, as in the American tradition:

> [...] enforcement of law is much more than applying to definite detailed states of fact the preappointed definite detailed consequences. Law must govern life, and the very essence of life is change. No legislative omniscience can predict and appoint consequences for the infinite variety of detailed facts which human conduct continually presents.[3]

It has been stated that some of these choices are controlled by standards, but that one must recognize that other choices have to be deemed standardless. Nowhere is there a full enforcement policy. One compelling reason is that it would be too costly. Screening is therefore necessary.[4]

So, choices have to be made in processing cases. All prosecutors in national systems are, to different degrees, accustomed to that. Prosecutorial directions are, however, useful or necessary to promote priorities and an optimal use of resources. They may also promote effectiveness. They may enhance fairness and legitimacy. If combined with appropriate communication to the general public, they may contribute to consensus and increased support.

3.3. Criteria in the Context of International Crimes

If selection and prioritization are classical questions for all prosecutors at national levels for ordinary crimes, they are, in fact, no less pressing in practice with regard to international crimes, particularly after armed conflict in the territorial State. This has to do with the mere quantity and scale of the issues involved. It has also to do with corresponding challenges relating to expectations among groups of victims and populations involved. A selection is necessary. Legitimacy of priorities requires identifying and communicating objective factors that have inspired them.

A discussion of criteria is thus, in my view, not only necessary, it is useful. To dispel misunderstandings, I should add that criteria should not mean prescriptive straightjackets. Nor should they exclude re-appraisal and adjustment.

Nevertheless, indication of priorities and working methods is important also as seen from the perspective of States. States have a standing and an interest as *members of the international community*, members of political organs of the United Nations, parties to international legal instruments, including the Rome Statute of the International Criminal Court, but not least as *territorial states* in relation to crimes that have been committed.

---

[3] Roscoe Pound, *Criminal Justice in America*, Harvard University Press, Cambridge, 1945, p. 36.

[4] Stephen A. Salzburg, *American Criminal Procedure*, Third Edition, West Academic Press, Eagan, 1988. For Criteria for screening in American law, see, for example, the National Advisory Commission on Criminal Justice Standards and Goals' reports of 1973.

Allow me here to suggest some possible or theoretical myths, for possible further discussion:

- That even-handedness would require indicting members of all groups, irrespective of objective criteria directing quality of prosecutions, including gravity of crimes and quality of evidence.
- That even-handedness would require that the same quantitative criteria must strictly apply in all cases, for example, as to numbers of victims of crimes concerned.
- That the appearance of even-handedness may be ensured by starting prosecutions, while awaiting in-depth determinations of evidence.
- That proceedings instigated out of political fairness may be necessary to ensure even-handedness, even if they later lead to acquittals based on poor evidence.

Allow me to suggest key elements that should instead command the attention when considering criteria:

- The timely formulation of certain criteria may play an important role in communication, outreach and management of expectations among populations.
- The initial priorities and the quality of direction of investigations will have a huge impact on the resource base for later prosecutorial activities. Awareness of criteria may be helpful already at this stage.
- In a politically charged environment, it must be the quality of objective and professional prosecutorial assessments, based on the evidence and the gravity of the international crime concerned, that in the long term will promote legitimacy, consensus and increased support.
- Readiness to reconsider and adjust criteria is not necessarily a weakness, if carried out on the basis of professional and objective assessments.
- Acquittals based on poor evidence could have a negative impact as to outreach and the appearance of even-handedness among certain groups.
- Stigmatization of persons through instigation of process is even more pronounced with regard to alleged international crimes. This should also be carefully weighed when making assessments.
- Respect for the principle of equality does not mean mathematical equality.
- Legitimacy, or trust, in prosecutorial matters must draw on professional experience and standards – as applied to the specific situation of international crimes.

I have now thrown in some postulates or rather questions. President Eisenhower once said that plans are nothing, and that planning is everything. I would not necessarily go as far here. But I would suggest that the main thrust of his point is still valid. Investing intellectual energy in a timely manner may prevent spending useless or expensive resources at later stages. Or, as encapsulated by the five celebrated 'p's in army parlance: Prior preparation prevents poor performance.

None of my remarks denotes any criticism of existing work or institutions. They are only meant to inspire a discussion in a field where the economy of the law, the management of expectations, the interests of victims and the long-term effects of re-establishing the rule of law all combine particular challenges – while having an important bearing on sustainable peace and security.

4

Requisite Resources and Capacity to Process Backlogs of Core International Crimes Cases

Ilia Utmelidze[*]

4.1. Introduction

The existing principles of international law place an obligation on the state to take action against mass atrocities that still persist in victimizing thousands, if not millions, of individuals worldwide, and to hold accountable those responsible for these acts. Several challenges make this task extremely difficult and invite reflection on what can be done to aid these processes.

This chapter presents some of the problems that any criminal justice system, especially of countries in transition, would face trying to deal with the consequences of large-scale victimization and backlogs of core international crimes.[1] It is argued that criteria for selecting and prioritizing[2] – combined with other relevant tools and strategies – could be the most sensible way to address backlogs of core international crime case-files in order to make meaningful progress towards full accountability. The chapter also discusses possible commonalities and differences between the concept of case selection and prioritization criteria and existing practices of prosecution.

---

* **Ilia Utmelidze** is the Director of CILRAP's department the Case Matrix Network. He is a Senior Legal Adviser at the National Human Rights Institution, the Norwegian Centre for Human Rights, University of Oslo, and advises the Norwegian Helsinki Committee on methodologies and tools for documentation of mass atrocities. Formerly, he served as Legal Adviser in the Human Rights Department of the Organization of Security and Cooperation in Europe's Mission to Bosnia and Herzegovina, advising on institution-building in areas such as domestic war crimes prosecution mechanisms (including the development of a national strategy for war crimes prosecution).

1 Bosnia and Herzegovina represents a clear case study on how backlogs of core international crimes may affect national justice systems. See Morten Bergsmo, Kjetil Helvig, Ilia Utmelidze and Gorana Žagovec (eds.), *The Backlog of Core International Crimes Case Files in Bosnia and Herzegovina*, Second Edition, TOAEP, Oslo, 2010, (https://www.toaep.org/ps-pdf/3-bergsmo-helvig-utmelidze-zagovec-second).

2 For more detail about the development of the concept of criteria for selection and prioritization, as well as examples, see Devasheesh Bais, "Prioritization of Suspected Conduct and Cases: From Idea to Practice", Chapter 2 above.

4.2. Obligation to Prosecute

By their very nature and the severity and scale of victimization caused, core international crimes[3] are considered a threat to international peace and security, a shock to the conscience of humanity, bringing untold sorrow to mankind. The consequences of such atrocities are not only affecting individual countries concerned, but the world as a whole.

In the aftermath of World War II and the Cold War, understanding of this fundamental interest led to several positive socio-political processes across the globe. As a result, a set of a new international rules and regulations have crystallised. This international criminal law aims to make illegal certain categories of conduct both during wartime and in other situations of conflict, and to make persons who engage in such conduct criminally liable. Concurrently, these norms also give authority or even impose the obligation upon states to prosecute and punish such crimes.

The publications of the most highly regarded experts in the field offer rather convincing evidence that states have an obligation to process[4] core international crimes. First of all, there are several international conventions that provide for such an obligation. Of particular note are the four Geneva Conventions of 1949 and the Convention on the Prevention and Punishment of the Crime of Genocide 1948.[5]

---

3 For the purposes of this chapter, the term 'core international crimes' refers to genocide, crimes against humanity and war crimes.

4 The state obligation is considered to include: duty to prosecute or extradite; the non-applicability of statutory limitation to these types of crimes; non-application of any immunities up to and including heads of state; the non-applicability of the defence of 'obedience to superior orders' (except for mitigation of sentence); the universal application of these obligations whether in time of peace or war; their non-derogation under 'states of emergency'; and universal jurisdiction over perpetrators of such crimes. See M. Cherif Bassiouni, "International Crimes: *Jus Cogens* and *Obligatio Erga Omnes*", in *Law and Contemporary Problems*, 1996, vol. 59, no. 4.

5 As of July 2024, 196 states were parties to the Geneva Conventions, whereas 153 states were parties of Genocide Convention. Geneva Conventions I, II, III and IV, 12 August 1949 (Convention I: https://www.legal-tools.org/doc/baf8e7/; Convention II: https://www.legal-tools.org/doc/0d0216/; Convention III: https://www.legal-tools.org/doc/365095/; Convention IV: https://www.legal-tools.org/doc/d5e260/); Convention on the Prevention and Punishment of the Crime of Genocide, 9 December 1948 ('Genocide Convention') (https://www.legal-tools.org/doc/498c38/).

Respectively Articles 49, 50, 129 and 146 to the four Geneva Conventions of 1949[6] provide that the High Contracting Parties must enact criminal legislation for all individuals having committed crimes qualifying as "grave breaches"[7] under these Conventions. Furthermore, with respect to these individuals, "[e]ach High Contracting Party shall be under the obligation to search for (these) persons […] and shall bring such persons, regardless of their nationality, before its own courts".

Article IV of the Genocide Convention 1948 also prescribes a duty to punish persons responsible for committing genocide, "whether they are constitutionally responsible rulers, public officials or private individuals".

Moreover, there are solid arguments suggesting that the 1998 Rome Statute of the International Criminal Court has, among other things, substantively contributed to the shaping of new customary international law or the crystallization and refinement of previously existing norms. The Preamble of the Statute provides "that it is the duty of every State to exercise its criminal jurisdiction over those responsible for international crimes".[8] This principle within the Rome Statute can substantially contribute to the position that customary international law not only establishes permissive jurisdiction over perpetrators of crimes against humanity and other crimes, but an obligation to process these crimes.[9]

The key objective of the principle of universal jurisdiction – which has been "nowadays acknowledged in the case of international crimes"[10] – is to ensure that there is no safe haven for those who have committed core international crimes. The principle of universal jurisdiction with its clear purpose to close impunity gaps can also be seen as a reinforcement of the view that states, by adopting the principle, accept the obligation to process core international crimes as a general rule.

---

6 The Geneva Conventions applies to virtually the entire community of states due to the high number of contracting states.

7 Articles 50, 51, 130 and 147 of the four Geneva Conventions define "grave breaches" as "[…] wilful killing, torture or inhuman treatment, including biological experiments, wilfully causing great suffering or serious injury to body or health, and extensive destruction and appropriation of property, not justified by military necessity and carried out unlawfully and wantonly".

8 The sixth preambular paragraph of the Rome Statute of the International Criminal Court, 17 July 1998 ('ICC Statute') (https://www.legal-tools.org/doc/7b9af9/).

9 Many authors agree that customary international law provides for a duty to prosecute crimes against humanity. However, there is also a viewpoint suggesting that there is no consistent state practice which would support this doctrinal point.

10 ICTY, *Prosecutor v. Tadić*, Appeals Chamber, Decision on the Defence Motion for Interlocutory Appeal on Jurisdiction, 2 October 1995, IT-94-1-AR72, para. 62 (https://www.legal-tools.org/doc/80x1an/).

However, as the international recognition of the principle of state obligation to prosecute these crimes is growing and the willingness to end impunity is increasing, both at international and national levels, the question still remains *how to ensure full accountability for core international crimes.*

The basis for this question is the existing gaps between legal expectations and legal reality, the frustration of victims, political scepticism, and some degree of disappointment in the donor community behind both international and domestic processes to deal with core international crimes.

4.3. Structural Obstacles

A distinguishing feature of core international crimes is that they, generally, occur outside the context of normally functioning societies, when there is total or partial failure of the rule of law and respect for human rights. As a consequence, these situations usually victimize thousands or even millions of individuals who may be killed or disappear, brutally and systematically tortured and raped, forcefully displaced and even ethnically cleansed, religious buildings desecrated, and thousands of households devastated.

Examples of such situations demonstrate that achieving even some small measure of accountability for these atrocities is very challenging and time- and resource-consuming. First of all, substantive progress normally requires a certain political and social transformation, a transitional process that can facilitate a political commitment to accountability and to end of impunity.

Consistent and genuine political will often requires international support and persuasion. The same applies to re-building or the building-up of domestic institutional and legal mechanisms to address mass violations of human rights which may amount to core international crimes. The requisite *de facto* capacity and technical ability to process these crimes, understanding their complexity and the need for specialized approaches can represent a serious challenge for justice systems in transition.

Core international crimes have to be processed with a clear understanding of the relevant laws and an appreciation of trial management skills, as well as a strong commitment to due process and fair trial principles. Any justice system's disregard of rule of law and the human rights of victims as well as those of the perpetrators can undermine the legitimacy of the procedure and turn justice into a political process or even blatant revenge.

International law can provide other forms of accountability like international or internationalized tribunals that usually limit their focus on the most high-ranking or notorious perpetrators, which in itself can be considered an immense step towards reducing impunity. It can give further impetus to greater accountability processes. Through their national criminal jurisdictions, other states can contribute in a direct way to processes of accountability. However, the lion's share of responsibility and effort to bring justice will always rest on the domestic institutions of the territorial states where the actual atrocities were committed.

It is vital to develop independent, impartial and efficient judiciaries in these countries, with the ability to understand the complex goals involved and have a clear strategy to address the challenge of limited resources and competing demands. However, one should keep in mind that it would require long-term commitment and broad support from domestic and often international actors to strengthen and develop national capacity to deal with core international crimes.

4.4. Backlog of Cases as a Common Phenomenon and the Role of Case Selection and Prioritization Criteria

A functional justice system that meets at least the minimum requirements of independence, effectiveness and fairness does not by default remove the full challenge that the processing of core international crimes cases involves.

It is a common phenomenon in countries which find themselves in this situation that their justice systems accumulate a large universe of unresolved investigation and case-files, with many suspects and incidents that are often not properly recorded and documented. There are typically a high number of complex criminal incidents, as well as multiple organizational structures and suspects, that have been involved in planning and carrying out such acts. There may also be issues linked to the available human resources with the necessary skills and knowledge to manage the complex nature of international crimes investigations.

Such backlogs of cases can represent a fundamental challenge not only to newly reformed and established justice systems, but also to the jurisdiction of the most resourceful and developed countries.

Existing examples indicate that there is no quick fix of backlog situations. There is no single remedy that can resolve the problem of a large backlog of cases in an immediate and responsible manner. It is therefore unavoidable that some cases will be completed before the justice system in question is able to process other cases.

Since resolving cases in a certain order is necessary, it seems both sensible and legitimate to suggest the development of a more formalized and regulated system of case selection and prioritization criteria – rather than disregarding this fact.

Clearly-defined case selection and prioritization criteria, designed as a part of an overall plan of action for justice systems, for example prosecutorial strategy or policy,[11] to address the legacy of mass atrocities, can play a crucial role in ending impunity and contributing to better and more comprehensive accountability for core international crimes.

First of all, well-crafted case selection and prioritization criteria can be instrumental in the process of streamlining institutional, legal and financial resources to ensure that the justice system will achieve maximum results.

The absence of a clear vision of where resources need to be mobilized can lead to uncertainty and hesitation within the justice sector and result in delayed justice or *de facto* impunity for perpetrators. *A contrario*, countries that undergo complex transitions can use case selection and prioritization criteria as a catalyst to jumpstart meaningful accountability processes.

Core international crime processes widely recognize the legitimate interest of victims and the general public to know how justice is done. In this regard, formalized case selection and prioritization criteria can be used as a tool to explain to the public in a clear and transparent manner why some cases will have to be processed before others. If case selection and prioritization criteria are based on considerations such as gravity of crime, seniority or level of responsibility of perpetrators, proportional representation of overall victimization,[12] or more practical considerations, there is a real need to explain this to the general public.

Understanding factors that define the order of cases can potentially minimize false expectations and help to build public confidence in the justice institutions. Any system for selection and prioritization of cases must be fair and should be perceived as fair by victim groups as well as the general public. The existence of formal criteria can help justice systems to demonstrate impartiality and fairness in this regard, in an open and transparent manner. This will help the overall strengthening of justice institutions in transition and to make them less susceptible to undue influence on case selection from outside or within the system.

---

[11] An action plan or strategy may also cover issues such as the establishment of a comprehensive overview of the backlog of cases, the need for assessment and resource planning, and defining the institutional machinery within the justice system that can tackle the backlog. See Bergsmo, Helvig, Utmelidze and Žagovec (eds.), 2010, *supra* note 1.

[12] The concept of proportional representation of victimization was first developed as a part of the effort to develop a war crimes prosecution strategy, including case selection and prioritization, in Bosnia and Herzegovina. It provides that cases are selected or prioritized based on the actual scale and nature of victimization rather than political, ethnic or religious affiliation of perpetrators or victims. See *ibid.*, p. 125.

4.5. Case Selection and Prioritization Criteria and the Limits of Prosecutorial Discretion

Case selection and prioritization criteria have both clear differences and similarities with how justice systems operate in more conventional situations. The general principle that applies in situations of ordinary crime can be characterized as 'first come, first served'. In other words, the cases are normally dealt with as they have been reported to the respective authorities.[13] However, depending on the legal tradition, there are also differences in how cases are advanced through the procedural stages of the justice system.

In many national jurisdictions the prosecutors are obliged to fully investigate every single reported crime and bring it forward to the national judiciary based on the principle of 'first come, first served'. However, other jurisdictions recognize the prosecutor's broad discretion to initiate and conduct criminal prosecutions. With the presumption that criminal prosecutions are undertaken in good faith and in a non-discriminatory manner, a prosecutor has broad authority to decide whether to investigate, grant immunity, or permit a plea bargain, and to determine whether to bring charges, what charges to bring, when to bring charges, and where to bring charges.[14]

Analysing essential inconsistencies and similarities between the notion of case selection and prioritization and these two traditional concepts of prosecution requires reflection. There are some self-evident issues that can be already identified and discussed.

---

[13] There seems to be exceptions to these general rules, especially when observing so-called high-profile cases such as high-level political cases; corruption, organized crimes and terrorism cases; some cases linked to sexual violence; and cases associated with racism and xenophobia. See Morten Bergsmo, *Thematic Prosecution of International Sex Crimes*, Second Edition, TOAEP, Brussels, 2018 (https://www.toaep.org/ps-pdf/13-bergsmo-second).

[14] The limitations to the prosecutor's discretion in the United States ('US') are noteworthy. The judiciary has a responsibility to protect individuals from prosecutorial conduct that violates constitutional rights. Such conduct usually involves either *selective prosecution*, which denies equal protection of the law, or vindictive prosecution, which violates due process. See District Court of Arizona, *US v. Redondo-Lemos et al.*, Order, 29 March 1993 (https://www.legal-tools.org/doc/1hbrq3bg/) (the court has a duty to closely scrutinize evidence of invidious discrimination); Supreme Court, *Yick Wo v. Hopkins*, Judgment, 10 May 1886, 118 US at pp. 373–74 (https://www.legal-tools.org/doc/vc5e8s1b/) (arrest and prosecution of Chinese laundry owners violated equal protection when similarly situated non-Chinese laundry owners were not arrested or prosecuted); Court of Appeals for the Tenth Circuit, *US v. Andersen*, Judgment, 29 July 1991 (https://www.legal-tools.org/doc/88djci8y/) (claim of selective prosecution must be supported by evidence that the prosecutor based the decision to charge on factors such as a "defendant's race, sex, religion, or exercise of a statutory or constitutional right").

As mentioned above, situations of core international crimes are quite different from the everyday routine of a justice system. The breakdown of the justice machinery makes it rather difficult to find objective ways to identify the crimes that have been reported first and therefore process first. Crimes may not have been properly reported and recorded. In some extreme situations, victims have been denied access to justice.

Moreover, the specificity of core international crimes provides that the same patterns of victimization can be dealt with as compartmentalized criminal acts or viewed as an overall, large-scale criminal enterprise in its entirety. Breaking down one such overall situation into smaller cases and using the principle of 'first come, first served' can prove to be difficult or even impossible. Furthermore, applying the 'first come' principle or even 'first committed, first processed' in a mechanical manner can lead to paradoxical situations. The consequence can be that a person without any significant role in the overall victimization process can face the full criminal process first, for example for pillaging, stealing a car, whereas persons masterminding and carrying out genocide will have to wait for years before the respective justice systems have time and resources to address their criminal conduct.

The concept of case selection and prioritization may be more immediately recognizable in those legal systems that provide for broad prosecutorial discretion, however, it is *de facto* common practice across different jurisdictions and legal traditions.[15] In these jurisdictions it is common practice to make decisions on whether cases should go to full trial or be subjected to other procedural steps.[16] Case selection and prioritization criteria used in the context of core international crimes are nevertheless based on more multifaceted standards and may require more formalized standards and mechanisms of enforcement, including clearly defined case selection criteria, than what is normally the case in such jurisdictions.

Factors like judicial efficacy and economy as well as overall resource management entail an active role for not only the prosecution. The judiciary has an important role to play through the development of its jurisprudence or even more directly by engaging in developing selection or prioritization criteria. It also has an obligation to guarantee the fairness of the criminal process and respect for the principle of equal protection of the law. Importantly, to be effective, case selection and prioritization criteria may require that the judiciary reviews its proper application, for example in connection with the confirmation of charges.

---

[15] See Rolf Einar Fife, Chapter 3 above, Section 3.2.

[16] For example, the prosecution may decide to grant immunity or permit a plea bargain.

A more active judiciary may limit prosecutorial discretion. But prosecution services still play the key role in the entire process of case selection and prioritization.

Avoiding inter-institutional misunderstanding in this regard is another strong argument in favour of the establishment of more formalized criteria for case selection and prioritization as well as a mechanism for their enforcement.

4.6. Conclusion

Honouring the international commitment to ensuring meaningful accountability for core international crimes remains challenging. It requires broadly-based political and popular support – as well as long-term, thorough institutional- and capacity-building processes. The nature, severity and scale of these crimes also necessitate a search for innovative solutions which respond more adequately to existing challenges. Case selection and prioritization criteria – as part of an overall plan to streamline and accelerate justice processes – can be an indispensable tool to ensure thorough and comprehensive accountability for core international crimes.

5

On the Nature of Selection and Prioritization Criteria: An Analysis of Select Documents

Morten Bergsmo and María Paula Saffon*

5.1. Introduction: The Importance of Case Selection and Prioritization Criteria

In the last decades of the twentieth century, the States' legal duty to investigate and prosecute perpetrators of serious violations of human rights and international humanitarian law consolidated, especially with regards to core international crimes, that is, genocide, crimes against humanity and war crimes.[1] This

* **Morten Bergsmo** is the Director of the Centre for International Law Research and Policy ('CILRAP'). At the time of writing, he was Visiting Professor of Law, Georgetown University. Relevant to this book, he has previously served as Special Adviser to the Office of the Director of Public Prosecution of Norway (2007–08); Senior Legal Adviser and Chief of the Legal Advisory Section, International Criminal Court ('ICC'), Office of the Prosecutor ('OTP') (2002–05); and Legal Adviser, International Criminal Tribunal for the former Yugoslavia ('ICTY') (1994–2002). **María Paula Saffon** is Assistant Professor at the Torcuato Di Tella University School of Law and a Research Associate at the Colombian Center for the Study of Law, Justice and Society (DeJuSticia). She received her Ph.D. in Political Science from Columbia University in New York, and a Bachelor's degree (*magna cum laude*) in law and an LL.M. degree from Universidad de Los Andes.

This chapter is based on Bergsmo's Chapter 5 ("Case Selection and Prioritization Criteria") in Morten Bergsmo, Kjetil Helvig, Ilia Utmelidze and Gorana Žagovec, *The Backlog of Core International Crimes Cases in Bosnia and Herzegovina*, Second Edition, Torkel Opsahl Academic EPublisher ('TOAEP'), Oslo, 2010, pp. 81–127 (https://www.toaep.org/ps-pdf/3-bergsmo-helvig-utmelidze-zagovec-second), which he expanded in 2010, followed by a further significant expansion by Saffon in 2010–2011. The chapter was translated into Spanish and first published in 2011, see Morten Bergsmo and María Paula Saffon, "Perspectiva internacional: Enfrentando una fila de atrocidades pasadas: como seleccionar y priorizar casos de crimenes internacionales nucleares?", in Kai Ambos (eds.), *Seleccion y priorizacion como estrategia de persecucion en los cases de crimenes internacionales*, Bogota, 2011, pp. 23–112.

[1] We use the notion of 'core international crimes' to refer to genocide, crimes against humanity, war crimes and aggression, as we believe these are the crimes with respect to which the states' international legal duty to investigate, prosecute and punish has been most clearly established, given their gravity and their consecration in special treaties aimed at preventing and sanctioning them. Note that the term 'international' used in this notion refers to the proscription of core crimes by international law, but it does not restrict their investigation, prosecution and punishment to international jurisdictions, due to the applicability of international law in national jurisdictions and to the States' duty to establish mechanisms for guaranteeing the efficacy of the

consolidation was the result of a series of international treaties that condemned the commission of such crimes and established specific procedural mechanisms for effectively combating impunity,[2] of the development of soft law and judicial precedents on the matter,[3] and, above all, of the creation of special tribunals for

duty to investigate, prosecute and punish, as established in the provisions referred to in the following footnote.

2 See the Convention on the Prevention and Punishment of the Crime of Genocide, adopted by Resolution 260 (III) A of the United Nations ('UN') General Assembly in 1948 (https://www.legal-tools.org/doc/498c38/), which establishes that States are committed to preventing and sanctioning genocide (Article 1), to providing effective penalties for perpetrators of acts of genocide (Article 5), and to granting extradition of suspects of genocide (Article 7); the Convention on the Non-Applicability of Statutory Limitations to War Crimes and Crimes Against Humanity, adopted by Resolution 2391 (XXIII) of the UN General Assembly in 1968 (https://www.legal-tools.org/doc/4bd593/), which forbids the application of statutory limitations of any sort to those crimes (Article 1), and establishes that those limitations should be abolished (Article 4) and that States should make extradition possible with regards to those crimes (Article 3); and the Convention against Torture and Other Cruel, Inhuman or Degrading Treatment or Punishment, adopted by Resolution 39/46 of the UN General Assembly on 10 December 1984 (https://www.legal-tools.org/doc/326294/), which establishes the States' duty to punish these crimes with appropriate penalties (Article 4) and foresees mechanisms to guarantee its efficacy, such as universal jurisdiction (Article 5) and extradition (Article 8).

3 Soft law documents have played an important role in the consolidation of the States' duty to prosecute, by establishing a series of principles on the struggle against impunity and the rights of victims of mass atrocity to justice, truth, reparations and the guarantee of non-recurrence, many of which have been adopted by the UN General Assembly and used by tribunals for the interpretation of human rights treaties. Some important documents on the matter are: UN, Human Rights Commission, 49th period of sessions, Question of the impunity of perpetrators of human rights violations (civil and political): Revised final report prepared by Mr. L. Joinet pursuant to Sub-Commission decision 1996/119, UN Doc. E/CN.4/Sub.2/1997/20/Rev. 1, 2 October 1997 (https://www.legal-tools.org/doc/ykahvz/); Diane Orentlicher, UN, Human Rights Commission, sixtieth period of sessions, Independent Study on Best Practices, Including Recommendations, to Assist States in Strengthening Their Domestic Capacity to Combat All Aspects of Impunity, UN Doc. E/CN.4/2004/88, 27 February 2004 (https://www.legal-tools.org/doc/7c388d/); and Theo van Boven and M. Cherif Bassiouni, 2004, UN, Human Rights Commission, sixtieth period of sessions, Basic Principles and Guidelines on the Right to a Remedy and Reparation for Victims of Gross Violations of International Human Rights Law and Serious Violations of International Humanitarian Law, UN Doc. E/CN.4/2004/57, 10 November 2003 (https://www.legal-tools.org/doc/tjdwei/). On the other hand, judicial decisions of human rights courts have also promoted the idea that States must prosecute and punish serious human rights and humanitarian law violations. The case of the Inter-American Human Rights Court is particularly illustrative of this point, as the Court has expressly condemned laws that establish amnesties for perpetrators of such violations, on the basis that they infringe the American Convention on Human Rights, in particular victims' rights to justice and truth. On this point, see Inter-American Human Rights Court, *Barrios Altos v. Peru case*, Ruling of 14 March 2001, Series C No. 75 (https://www.legal-tools.org/doc/f1439e/).

judging crimes of the sort, particularly when committed in war situations.[4] These advancements in international law have begun to replace amnesties and legal pardons with international, hybrid or national criminal processes as the main mechanism for dealing with mass atrocities committed in armed conflicts or in authoritarian regimes.

The existence of a clear and even more enforceable duty to investigate and prosecute perpetrators of core international crimes constitutes a significant achievement in the search for accountability and in the prevention of future atrocities, on the understanding that proportional and effective criminal punishment might deter the commission of such crimes. It is a particularly remarkable achievement given that it has mainly sprung from the political will of States to substitute impunity with criminal accountability in post-conflict or post-authoritarian situations. However, this achievement has brought along new challenges for institutions in charge of accomplishing the non-negligible goal of responding to past atrocities through criminal justice, which seems particularly ambitious when facing a legacy of mass atrocity.

Armed conflicts and some oppressive regimes tend to generate a very high number of core international crimes, often committed by many perpetrators. Prosecuting and adjudicating all those crimes in an adequate and timely manner constitutes an overwhelming task even in contexts where there is a well-functioning criminal justice system, not to mention the majority of contexts where the judiciary has been destroyed or severely weakened by war or authoritarianism. In transitional contexts where jurisdictions or mechanisms are created or specifically enabled to deal with such cases, it is quite likely that allegations of core international crimes will propagate to the point of exceeding judicial capacity. Those jurisdictions will be burdened with a significant backlog of cases.

A backlog of core international crimes cases implies the existence of a queue of past atrocities waiting to have their day in court. But many of such atrocities may never see that day, or might only see it after years have elapsed.

---

4 The pioneers were the Nuremberg and Tokyo Tribunals which judged some of those most responsible for atrocities committed during World War II. After them, a long period of lethargy concerning international accountability for serious human rights and humanitarian law violations took place during the Cold War. Since the early 1990s, there has been a boom of internationalized criminal justice, especially concerning post-conflict situations. The boom started with the *ad hoc* tribunals for the former Yugoslavia and for Rwanda established by the UN Security Council. It has been later followed by the establishment of hybrid and national tribunals in many other contexts, such as Sierra Leone, East Timor, Cambodia, Iraq, Argentina and Colombia. And it reached a climax with the creation of the ICC as a permanent international court for judging those most responsible for genocide, crimes against humanity, war crimes and the crime of aggression (Rome Statute of the International Criminal Court, 17 July 1998, Article 5 ('ICC Statute') (https://www.legal-tools.org/doc/7b9af9/)).

This situation raises at least two fundamental questions that are both complex and sensitive:[5] First, how do we choose the cases that the jurisdiction in question will actually prosecute and judge? Secondly, how should we organize and rank the selected cases so as to determine the priority order in which they will be investigated and judged? The answer to these questions necessarily entails the existence and use of criteria for the selection and prioritization of core international crimes cases.

However, due to the burden of their responsibilities and limited resources, the frequently perceived need to show prompt results, and the political pressures at work in the contexts they operate, prosecutorial services may be reluctant to thoroughly reflect upon such criteria and to choose them in a strategic and publicly justified way. As a result, core international crimes cases can be, and in fact often are, as referred to in Chapter 1 above, selected and prioritized on the basis of unintentional, inadequate or unjustified criteria, which do not guarantee – and can even impede – that the most important and best-suited cases are investigated and go to trial first.

For instance, prosecutorial services might apply the rule of first come, first served, which normally applies to queues in general and to judicial cases in particular, but which might not be the most convenient in a transitional context, as it may well lead to the prioritization of cases that cannot make the most substantive contribution to transitional goals or that are simply not ready for prosecution. On the other hand, prosecutorial services might consciously choose cases on the basis of the easiness to obtain evidence for indicting the suspects, which can be effective in producing quick results, but detrimental to the objective of investigating and judging the most important cases, since it may result in merely picking 'low hanging fruit'.[6] Finally, prosecutorial services might choose and prioritize cases directly or indirectly influenced by the political pressure exercised by other institutions or by external stakeholders, hence disregarding not only the importance and suitability of cases, but also and especially the independence of the prosecutorial activity.

---

5 As will be discussed below, other important issues entailed by backlogs of core international crimes cases are related to the question of what to do with unselected cases. However, these issues differ qualitatively from the questions formulated here, as their response does not necessarily require the use of criteria, but rather determination of whether and under what conditions some core international crimes should be dealt with through mechanisms different from ordinary criminal justice, such as truth commissions, reparations or reconciliation processes.

6 For the use of this expression by the former Registrar for the Special Department for War Crimes and the Special Department for Organized Crime, Economic Crime and Corruption of Bosnia and Herzegovina, see below note 23.

In contrast, the adoption of clear, adequate and publicly-justified criteria for selecting and prioritizing core international crimes cases does not only substantively reduce the risk of such negative effects; it is also crucial for guaranteeing the principle of equality before the law (and with it, other important transitional goals), the coherence, effectiveness and independence of the prosecutorial strategy, and the overall legitimacy of the criminal process.

Establishing criteria for selecting and prioritizing core international crimes cases is intrinsically important as a matter of distributive justice, since it requires deciding the way in which a scarce benefit (prompt access to criminal justice) should be allocated among persons with similar allegations (being victims of a core international crime), and it, therefore, determines whether such decision will respect the equality principle. Moreover, it is a particularly delicate matter, in the sense that the treatment of those allegations by the judiciary is key to the fulfilment of several essential goals sought in a transition, such as precluding impunity, consolidating the rule of law, recovering trust, and guaranteeing the non-recurrence of atrocities.

Indeed, the use of inadequate criteria can reduce the possibility of accountability for those crimes considered most important by institutions and the society at large – be it in terms of their gravity, authorship, systematic or massive character, among other things. This can also impede elucidating the truth about those crimes, facilitating the reparation of their victims, and preventing them from happening again. Furthermore, the use of inadequate or unjustified criteria can translate into new forms of discrimination and rights violations, which can undermine the transitional objectives of transcending the past of human rights violations and establishing a new social order based on justice and equal citizenship, and can even promote the renewal of violence by regenerating feelings of unfairness and resentment against institutions.

On the other hand, criteria for the selection and prioritization of core international crimes cases are relevant for developing a coherent, efficient and independent prosecutorial strategy. In fact, criteria can operate as important guidelines for the action of individual prosecutors, by establishing the general orientation and priorities of the prosecutorial strategy, thus restraining random or arbitrary case selection and prioritization, as well as enhancing the quality of decisions. Besides, criteria can substantially contribute to a rational allocation of the limited resources at the disposal of prosecutorial services, by assuring that only the best-suited cases for early prosecution – both in terms of relevance for the overall aims of the prosecutorial strategy and of evidence availability – will be dealt with first.[7] Further, criteria can help maintain the independence of prosecutorial services, by limiting the impact of political pressure exercised by other institutions or by groups with stakes in the judicial process with the aim of influencing the course of investigations.

Lastly, selection and prioritization criteria are determinant for the legitimacy of prosecutorial services and, more generally, of the whole criminal process aimed at dealing with core international crimes. The manner in which criteria are chosen and their specific content have a significant effect on the way victims, other social sectors of the context where atrocities took place, and the international community perceive the criminal process and the institutions in charge of carrying it out. In effect, the absence of clear and publicly justified criteria might give the impression that case selection and prioritization are being done in an arbitrary, biased or politicized way, and, hence, generate distrustful and disapproving attitudes against the judicial process. In contrast, formally adopted criteria may help explain selection and prioritization decisions. This is useful both for the prosecution to defend itself from accusations of discrimination, and for victims and other groups with stakes in the process to monitor those decisions and eventually challenge them when they do not adjust to the adopted criteria.

Even though they help fulfil common general goals such as those previously mentioned, selection and prioritization criteria have different concrete purposes, and therefore function in distinct ways. *Selection* criteria serve to determine which cases will be investigated and judged by a specific jurisdiction. Thus, they inevitably imply the de-selection of certain cases.[8] Furthermore, selection criteria operate as a threshold below which cases will not be dealt with

---

7 See Morten Bergsmo, "The Theme of Selection and Prioritization Criteria and Why It Is Relevant", in Morten Bergsmo (ed.), *Criteria for Prioritizing and Selecting Core International Crimes Cases*, Second Edition, Torkel Opsahl Academic EPublisher, Oslo, 2010 (https://www.toaep.org/ps-pdf/4-bergsmo-second); Claudia Angermaier, "Case Selection and Prioritization Criteria in the Work of the International Criminal Tribunal for the Former Yugoslavia", Chapter 8 of this book.

8 However, this does not necessarily mean that such cases will not be prosecuted and tried. Deselected cases can be expressly referred to another criminal jurisdiction by the jurisdiction in charge of applying selection criteria – as illustrated by the practice of referrals to national jurisdictions done by the ICTY in application of Rule 11*bis* of its Rules of Procedure and Evidence (https://www.legal-tools.org/doc/30df50/), described in Chapter 8 below by Claudia Angermaier. Besides, when the tribunal in question has a subsidiary or residual competence, cases that are excluded from selection can be taken on by the jurisdiction with general competence to investigate and try them – as it happens with cases that do not comply with the admissibility requirements established in the ICC Statute, see *supra* note 4, and that can, therefore, be investigated and tried by national jurisdictions.

by the jurisdiction in question.[9] In effect, these criteria normally consist in a catalogue of important elements that should be considered when deciding whether to exercise jurisdiction. And they are normally applied as if they were a checklist, in the sense that, when a case complies with all or with a specific number of them, it qualifies to be investigated and judged.[10] However, selection criteria do not *per se* determine which of the selected cases will be dealt with first, since they generally do not establish a hierarchy among cases, but rather put them on an equal footing once they have overcome the selection threshold.

In contrast, *prioritization* criteria serve precisely to rank cases within a jurisdiction, so as to determine the order in which they will be investigated and tried. Thus, they do not require the de-selection of cases, given that they can be applied to already selected cases, or to cases that have not gone through a filter of selection criteria – as it is the case in many national criminal jurisdictions. Moreover, prioritization criteria do not operate as a threshold, since all ranked cases should eventually be investigated and prosecuted. This means that, even though these criteria are also generally formulated as a catalogue of important elements that should be considered for ranking cases and, in fact, in many jurisdictions selection and prioritization criteria coincide, the latter cannot be simply applied as a checklist.

Indeed, especially when there has been a previous selection, all cases above the threshold tend to satisfy the catalogue of criteria; hence, no *a priori* hierarchy could be established among them. Consequently, prioritization should consist in interpretations of the catalogues of criteria, which determine the relative importance of some criteria over the others, as well as the relative importance of some components of each criterion over the others, in such a way that cases that comply with all criteria could still be prioritized in terms of the different levels or degrees in which they satisfy those criteria.[11] Otherwise, the mere use of catalogues of criteria for prioritizing cases could end up being a means to justify entirely discretionary decisions that are not actually based on prioritization criteria.

The difficult task of selecting or prioritizing core international crimes cases is faced by territorial States, international, hybrid and foreign States criminal

9 The idea that selection criteria work as a threshold is supported by Margaret M. deGuzman, "Gravity and the Legitimacy of the International Criminal Court", in *Fordham International Law Journal*, 2008, vol. 32, no. 5, pp. 1400–1465.

10 See also *ibid.*

11 See also, *ibid.*, where the author proposes the application of relative gravity as the main criterion for prioritizing cases in the Prosecutor's Office of the ICC, and criticizes the latter for failing to establish a distinction between selection and prioritization criteria.

jurisdictions. However, when engaging in that task, the challenges of these jurisdictions have a different scope and nature. In fact, territorial States' criminal jurisdictions carry the heaviest burden in terms of the number of cases they must prosecute and judge, given that atrocities took place in the territory of the State in question, that most victims and perpetrators normally reside therein, and that their mandate for prosecuting and judging crimes is ordinarily general or quite wide. In this matter, territorial States are followed by *ad hoc* international and hybrid tribunals specifically set up for dealing with the most important crimes committed in a conflict or in an authoritarian regime, and thereafter by jurisdictions with a general but subsidiary competence for prosecuting and judging core international crimes, such as the ICC and foreign States applying the principle of universal jurisdiction.

One could say that the task of selecting cases is much more important and demanding for jurisdictions facing a smaller number of cases, while the task of prioritizing cases is more crucial and difficult for jurisdictions that have to deal with a great backlog of cases. This is so because, in the case of the first type of jurisdictions, selection operates as a big filter aimed at guaranteeing that they will only deal with the most significant cases, given the subsidiary nature of international, hybrid and universal criminal justice. As a result, the application of selection criteria has a vast practical and symbolic impact, as it excludes many crimes – in fact, in most cases, the majority of crimes committed in the situation of conflict or authoritarianism in question – from the competence of the concerned jurisdiction, which are thus left to the uncertain possibility of ever being prosecuted and judged by another jurisdiction, and can be easily labelled as less important cases for not having been selected. Moreover, the impact and results of these jurisdictions will probably be judged on the basis of the nature and importance of the cases they selected for prosecution and trial.

In contrast, as it was previously mentioned, in the case of criminal jurisdictions of territorial States, the dimension of the backlog of cases tends to be enormous, both as a result of the conditions of the context, and of the broad competence of such jurisdictions for judging crimes committed in the State in question. Although this competence can be modified or restricted in a transitional or post-conflict situation in order to deal with a massive amount of cases, given the development of the international duty to prosecute described earlier, such modifications or restrictions tend to consist less in the exclusion of cases resulting from general amnesties, and more in the creation of special jurisdictions for the most important crimes, and in the investigation and trial of the rest of cases by ordinary jurisdictions, or by alternative mechanisms.

Consequently, the backlog of cases faced by these jurisdictions is not substantively reduced by selection criteria, and hence, prioritization criteria acquire a crucial role. Indeed, it is very likely that many cases will only see their day in court a number of years after their commission, if ever – since the passage of time might lead to the death of the suspect before trial or to a significant erosion of evidence. And prioritization criteria are determinant in figuring out which will be those cases that will receive a tardy or uncertain judicial response. This can notably affect the overall impact of the criminal process in terms of its capacity to deal with the most important cases, as well as victims' and social perceptions of its contributions to the struggle against impunity, truth elucidation, and the satisfaction of victims' needs.

In spite of the importance of selection and prioritization criteria for dealing with backlogs of cases – by ensuring that cases that are investigated and brought to trial are the most important and suitable ones – it must be recognized that, by themselves, these criteria are incapable of solving the problem of case backlogs. In fact, in situations of mass atrocity, even if selection and prioritization criteria were formulated and applied in the most coherent, clear and justified manner, core international crimes cases would very possibly remain too many for the criminal jurisdiction in question to be able to deal timely with them all. Therefore, the rigorous formulation and adequate application of these criteria should necessarily be complemented by a thorough reflection about and consistent implementation of abbreviated criminal procedures[12] as well as alternative mechanisms through which cases that would not make it to justice could still be dealt with in a satisfactory way, such as truth commissions or reparations and reconciliation processes.

The limitation of selection and prioritization criteria to solve the problem of backlog of cases does not reduce their importance for adequately dealing with core international crimes cases. This chapter seeks to add to the literature on the topic,[13] by offering an analytical study and comparison of key documents on criteria from central jurisdictions. By comparing the formulation, classification and inter-relationship of criteria, we hope to advance our understanding of their nature, their main taxonomies, jurisdictional parameters, and what may be the four main criteria for core international crimes cases. Our focus is on the criteria themselves.

---

[12] For a book on abbreviated criminal procedures for core international crimes, see Morten Bergsmo (ed.), *Abbreviated Criminal Procedures for Core International Crimes*, TOAEP, Brussels, 2017 (https://www.toaep.org/ps-pdf/9-bergsmo).

[13] For a few works on the subject, see Bergsmo, Helvig, Utmelidze and Žagovec, 2010, *supra* note *; the chapters of the anthology Bergsmo (ed.), 2010, see *supra* note 7; deGuzman, 2008, see *supra* note 9; Bergsmo and Saffon, 2011, pp. 23–112, see *supra* note *; and Kai Ambos, "Introductory Note to Office of the Prosecutor", in *International Legal Materials*, 2018, vol. 57, no. 6, pp. 1131–1134.

To that end, Section 5.2. starts by studying in some detail four documents prepared in the national criminal jurisdiction of Bosnia and Herzegovina ('BiH') on selection and prioritization criteria. The case of BiH receives particular attention because it in many ways has been the chief laboratory of criminal justice for atrocities, constituting perhaps the first territorial jurisdiction where this issue has been explicitly confronted, offering advanced developments on the issue of criteria for these crimes at the national level.

Section 5.3. analyses criteria for selection and prioritization of core international crimes cases in key documents of the ICTY and the ICC. The study of these documents is relevant not only to understand how some of the main international criminal tribunals have been dealing with the issue of case selection and prioritization, but also to inquire whether they have developed approaches that may be useful for correcting or complementing the BiH criteria or offering a precedent for future developments on the issue by other international and national jurisdictions.

Finally, Section 5.4. tries to synthesize the findings concerning criteria used in the different documents under study, by grouping them in four main clusters that facilitate the understanding of the practice of formulating and applying case selection or prioritization criteria. There is also a reflection on the further international discourse in this area.

5.2. Bosnia and Herzegovina: Experience in Formulating Case Selection and Prioritization Criteria

As suggested in the previous section, BiH has been in many ways the chief laboratory of criminal justice for atrocities. The magnitude of the crimes committed in the armed conflicts between 1992 and 1995, along with the fact that they were committed at an advanced stage in the development of the international legal duty to punish core international crimes, put the prosecution and judgment of those crimes as a key priority in the international and national agendas. In 1993, the ICTY was specifically created for the prosecution of the crimes committed in the armed conflicts of the Balkans during the 1990s.[14] However, at a quite early stage, it was understood that the tribunal would only be capable of dealing with a limited number of cases. Consequently, soon the ICTY began to refer cases to the national jurisdictions that were able and willing to prosecute and judge those crimes under the rules of fair trial.[15]

[14] The Tribunal was created by Security Council Resolutions 808 (1993), UN Doc. S/RES/808 (1993), 22 February 1993 (https://www.legal-tools.org/doc/20fa99/) and 827 (1993), UN Doc. S/RES/827 (1993), 25 May 1993 (https://www.legal-tools.org/doc/dc079b/).

[15] For the most part, referrals were the result of the implementation of the 'Rules of the Road Project' and of the 'completion strategy' of the ICTY, as discussed in Chapters 8, 16 and 17

In BiH, those referrals and the public pressure to prosecute other atrocious crimes generated the necessity of developing an efficient and independent judicial system capable of processing the majority of core international crimes cases committed during the conflicts. Indeed, even though BiH courts began to undertake the task of processing war crimes immediately after the conflicts, the judiciary was very weak and risked succumbing to political and ethnic bias.[16] In 2003, significant legal and institutional reforms were developed, including the creation of the BiH State Court and the BiH Prosecutor's Office, with primary jurisdiction over war crimes cases.[17] These advancements increased the confidence in the BiH judicial system, which, in 2004, led to the decision of the ICTY Prosecutor's Office to defer to the BiH Prosecutor's Office the function of reviewing "Rules of the Road" cases – that is, cases sent by domestic jurisdictions to the ICTY for it to determine whether they could be processed by local jurisdictions on the basis of available evidence and their consistence with international legal standards.[18]

As a result, the BiH Prosecutor's Office was suddenly faced with a quite heavy load of cases to review and approve for prosecution by other entities, on the one hand, and to process itself, on the other. The cases that such jurisdiction should process were composed of cases referred by the ICTY (in most of which

below. Created by the Rome Agreement of 1996, reached between the countries of the former Yugoslavia and the ICTY, the Rules of the Road established a special mechanism, in order, *inter alia*, to prevent unfair or biased trials. By virtue of that mechanism, domestic jurisdictions sent case-files to the ICTY for their review and approval. Once cases were recognized as worthy of prosecution and consistent with international legal standards, they were referred back to local authorities for their processing. The review function was transferred to the State Court of Bosnia and Herzegovina in 2004. On its turn, the ICTY completion strategy was foreseen by the Security Council in 2002 to put a temporal limit to the operation of the tribunal, and therefore, to restrict its efforts to cases concerning "the most senior leaders suspected of being most responsible for crimes within the ICTY's jurisdiction", and refer other cases to local authorities. These can include cases in which an indictment has already been issued (Rule 11*bis* of ICTY's Rules of Evidence and Procedure, modified in 2004, see *supra* note 8), and cases that have been investigated but that had not led to an indictment by the end of 2004 (which was the cutoff date under the ICTY completion strategy). See Bergsmo, Helvig, Utmelidze and Žagovec, 2010, see *supra* note *; Zekerija Mujkanović, "The Orientation Criteria Document in Bosnia and Herzegovina", Chapter 16 of this book; Serge Brammertz, "The Interaction Between International and National Criminal Jurisdictions: Developments at the ICTY", in Morten Bergsmo (ed.), 2010, see *supra* note 7. As we will see in Section 5.3. below, the ICTY has developed criteria for selecting both Rules of the Road cases and cases to be referred to local authorities by virtue of the completion strategy.

16 Bergsmo, Helvig, Utmelidze and Žagovec, 2010, see *supra* note *.

17 *Ibid.*

18 *Ibid.*

an indictment had not yet been issued, so significant investigation and prosecution work was still needed),[19] of cases that had been directly filed before the BiH Prosecutor's Office since its creation, and of cases submitted to the latter office by other prosecutors' offices in BiH.[20] At the time of writing, preliminary analysis suggested that core international crimes cases that needed to be processed in BiH involved *in toto* between 10,000 and 13,000 suspects.[21]

In the face of such a scenario, the need of criteria for selecting and prioritizing core international crimes cases became a prime concern in BiH. In fact, even if the speed by which cases were processed would have been substantially increased through improvements in the system, prosecuting and judging all existing cases in a reasonable time (that is, before the natural death of many suspects and witnesses) did not seem like a feasible task.[22] Therefore, the formulation and effective implementation of selection and prioritization criteria was vital to guarantee that the most important and best-suited cases would go to trial first. As Mr. David Schwendiman, an official of the State Prosecutor's Office, put it:

> It is *unrealistic to expect* that every case will be tried or to expect that every person who should be held criminally responsible for what they did during the war will be held accountable by a court. Many things that cannot be controlled, such as time, the death of potential defendants, and the age and failing memory of witnesses,

19 For the different referral mechanisms, see *supra* note 15. According to Bergsmo, Helvig, Utmelidze and Žagovec, only a small number of the cases referred to the BiH jurisdiction by the ICTY at the time of writing were Rule 11*bis* cases, meaning that the majority of referred cases had not been indicted, but were either investigated by the ICTY (as was the case with cases referred by virtue of the completion strategy) or reviewed to determine if there was sufficient evidence to justify prosecution (as was the case with Rules of the Road cases). The latter cases constituted the greatest number of referred cases with which the BiH judiciary had to deal with. *Ibid.*

20 Some of the last groups of cases were submitted to the BiH Prosecutor's Office by other prosecutors' offices in BiH by virtue of Article 6(2) of the *Book of Rules on the Review of War Crimes Cases*, Office of the Prosecutor of Bosnia and Herzegovina, 28 December 2004. See Bergsmo, 2010, see *supra* note 7.

21 According to Bergsmo, Helvig, Utmelidze and Žagovec, see *supra* note *:

> President Meddžida Kreso of the Court of BiH wrote in July 2007 that data from an HJPC analysis "showed that all prosecutors' offices in BiH reported 12,484 persons as possible perpetrators of war crimes in the period between 1992 and 2006" [161] [sic.]. Others in the criminal justice system at the State level have suggested that, whereas it is rumoured that there are 16,000 war criminals in BiH, there are in fact a total of 10,534 'named persons' […].

22 According to Bergsmo, Helvig, Utmelidze and Žagovec, such task would not be feasible even if the speed with which cases were processed were doubled through administrative, procedure and evidentiary improvements. *Ibid.*

> for example, conspire to make that so. It is not, however, unreasonable to expect that a person will be made to answer in a court or in some other forum in Bosnia and Herzegovina for what he or she did as an individual, for acts that had and still have great impact on the community.[23] [...]
>
> Time will conspire against all of the cases actually seeing the inside of a courtroom; a phenomenon that will occur notwithstanding the best efforts of the Court and the Prosecutor's Office. The challenge the caseload poses for the Prosecutor's Office is a management challenge that can be met, in part, by articulating criteria meant to identify the cases which should [be] done first and adopting guidelines to help ensure that cases are charged properly with a view to using resources in the most efficient way, to preserve resources so that more cases can be done. The Prosecutor's Office must also have the political courage to tell those affected by decisions ranking cases for investigation and prosecution how and why that was done. Case selection must be consistent, but flexible, taking into account newly acquired or developed evidence or information that may move a matter up or down on the priority lists.[24]

With the aim of facing this challenge, several institutional efforts were made in BiH to formulate clear and adequate criteria for the selection and prioritization of core international crimes cases. A closer study of these efforts is relevant not only because BiH is perhaps the first territorial jurisdiction where the issue of case selection and prioritization has been explicitly confronted, but also because it has substantively advanced in the formulation and justification of criteria, in such a way that it constitutes a precedent of significant importance for other territorial jurisdictions, as well as an extremely important interlocutor for international criminal jurisdictions dealing with atrocity crimes.

In what follows, we will describe and analyse three main documents in which selection and prioritization criteria were put forward in BiH: (i) the "Orientation Criteria for Sensitive Rules of the Road cases" ('Orientation Criteria'), adopted by the BiH Collegium of Prosecutors; (ii) the criteria included in Annex

---

[23] Working paper prepared by the Registry for the use of the Prosecutor's Office of BiH, "Selecting war crimes cases for investigation and prosecution: avoiding the opportunity costs of picking low hanging fruit", by Mr. David Schwendiman. The document was forwarded to one of the authors of this chapter via e-mail message on 6 November 2007, and a revised version of it was later handed personally to the same author on 10 October 2009 in BiH. The document is referred to here with permission of its author via e-mail on 22 November 2007.

[24] Paper prepared by the Registry for the use of the Prosecutor's Office of BiH, "Managing domestic war crimes caseloads", by Mr. David Schwendiman, forwarded to the authors of this chapter via e-mail message on 6 November 2007, pp. 6–7 (referred to here with permission of the author of the paper via e-mail on 22 November 2007) (emphasis added).

A of the 2008 National War Crimes Strategy adopted by the Council of Ministers of BiH; and (iii) the criteria prepared by the Special Department for War Crimes of the Prosecutor's Office of BiH in the framework of its Prosecution Guidelines on Charging. In Chapter 17 below ("Criteria for Selection and Prioritization of Core International Crimes in the National War Crimes Strategy of Bosnia and Herzegovina"), Aida Šušić of the Office of the High Representative in Sarajevo provides a further discussion of such documents.

5.2.1. The Orientation Criteria

As a result of the deferral by the ICTY Prosecutor's Office of the Rules of the Road cases oversight competence, the Special Department for War Crimes of the BiH Prosecutor's Office received 877 cases considered to contain sufficient evidence in accordance with international legal standards (designated as 'A' cases by the ICTY), 2,389 that did not yet have sufficient evidence for concluding that potential suspects possibly committed the crimes in question (designated as 'B' cases by the ICTY), and 702 cases that did not contain enough information (designated as 'C' cases by the ICTY).[25] In view of budgetary considerations, the Special Department for War Crimes of the Prosecutor's Office decided to focus mainly on the first type of case files first.[26]

With the purpose of sorting out those files and distributing them among the different jurisdictions in the country, on 12 October 2004, the BiH "Collegium of Prosecutors" adopted the document entitled "Orientation Criteria for Sensitive Rules of the Road Cases", and incorporated it as an Annex to the *Book of Rules on the Review of War Crimes Cases*.[27] The document sought to classify 'A' marked case-files into two sub-categories: 'highly sensitive' and 'sensitive' violations. While the first type of cases should be processed by the State Prosecutor's Office, the second type could be remitted to the criminal jurisdictions of the Cantonal and District levels.[28] The main goal of the Orientation Criteria was to guide the distribution of cases between jurisdictions or jurisdictional levels

[25] While the ICTY exercised the review function, it classified the Rules of the Road cases in several categories on the basis of the existing evidence for each case: cases were designated with the letter 'A' when they were considered to contain sufficient evidence in accordance with international legal standards, with the letter 'B' if they did not contain sufficient evidence for concluding that potential suspects possibly committed the crimes in question, with the letter 'C' if cases did not contain sufficient information to determine if they were 'A' or 'B' cases, and with the letters 'D', 'E', 'F' or 'G', if they had to be classified for reasons different from those related to the quality of evidence. See Mujkanović, 2024, see *supra* note 15 (Chapter 16 of this book).

[26] *Ibid.*

[27] *Book of Rules on the Review of War Crimes Cases*, Article 10(3), see *supra* note 20.

[28] See Bergsmo, Helvig, Utmelidze and Žagovec, 2010, see *supra* note *.

(the State Court and the courts at the Cantonal-District levels); however, they have also been conceived as a tool for prioritizing cases within each jurisdiction.

According to the Book of Rules, the Orientation Criteria "shall form an integral part of the Rules" and "shall provide guidance for the Prosecutor's Office of Bosnia and Herzegovina in the determination of the prosecutorial competence over the case".[29] More concretely, the Book of the Rules states that the Orientation Criteria offer "a basis for the selection of cases to be heard before Section I for War Crimes of the Criminal and Appellate Divisions of the Court of Bosnia and Herzegovina",[30] and that Section I shall "deal with the most serious cases, taking full account of the Court's resources".[31] Furthermore, according to the Orientation Criteria document itself, "[i]n principle it is desirable that only the most serious cases be heard before the Court of BiH, as the Court will have neither the resources nor the time to try all war crimes cases".[32] Now, the same document states that the criteria "are not intended to be 'set in stone' or exhaustive",[33] since "it is not advisable to adopt strict criteria, more a working model that may separate the most sensitive cases".[34]

Even though the main role of the criteria is to serve as a guide to the overall assessment of what is the right forum for a case, the process of file assessment outlined in the Orientation Criteria document suggests an additional role for the criteria, and particularly for the criterion related to gravity which, as we will see, is one of the main criteria in the document: to offer a basis for determining which of the cases found suitable for the State Court should receive priority treatment. In fact, in the assessment process, the consideration of the criteria is required at three different stages.[35] First, the criteria as a whole should be used for determining whether the forum for a particular case should be the Court of BiH or

29 *Book of Rules on the Review of War Crimes Cases*, Article 10(3), see *supra* note 20.

30 *Ibid.*, Article 10(1).

31 *Ibid.*, Article 10(2).

32 Second paragraph of the "Orientation Criteria for Sensitive Rules of the Road Cases", Annex to the *Book of Rules on the Review of War Crimes Cases. Ibid.*, section 2, paragraph 3 of the Orientation Criteria reiterates that "the War Crimes trials at the Court of BiH will be constrained by capacity, resources and limitation of time, not to mention the priority which will have to be given to cases transferred by the [ICTY] under Rule 11bis of its Rules of Evidence and Procedure [sic.]".

33 *Ibid.*, section 2, first paragraph.

34 *Ibid.*, section 1, second paragraph.

35 The Orientation Criteria document outlines seven stages of the assessment process: (i) "Assessing whether *the forum* for any particular case should be the Court of BiH or the Cantonal/District Courts, using the criteria [...]"; (ii) "In respect of cases which appear to be suitable for trial at Cantonal/District level, before they are remitted, a 'second eye', that is, a different Prosecutor or one of the legal advisors should look at the file to ensure that it is suitable to

the Cantonal or District courts. Second, cases that appear to be suitable for trial at the Cantonal or District level should be reviewed by a second lawyer to ensure that their remittal is appropriate, and such review would seem to involve consideration of the Orientation Criteria as well. Third, concerning the cases that are considered suitable for trial at the Court of BiH, the criteria, and specifically the gravity criterion, should be considered a second time for determining which cases should be treated first. According to the Orientation Criteria document, cases against persons in leadership positions or concerning grave crimes should normally take priority.[36]

The Orientation Criteria document opens for further prioritization of cases within jurisdictions in its last paragraph:

> It may also be necessary to prioritise cases depending upon the stage of the investigation and whether individual cases are ready to proceed, and if not, to establish the likely timeframe to completion so as not to set unreasonable deadlines. Accordingly, cases that fall into a particular category may be further divided by priority on the basis of readiness to proceed. Until such time as the "highly sensitive" cases have been isolated and reviewed, it is impossible to state which cases should take priority. As a point of reference command responsibility and crimes committed by public officials still in office and law enforcement officials may take priority.[37]

---

be remitted" [sic.]; (iii) "Once it has been established that a case is suitable for trial at the Court of BiH, the next part of the exercise should be an *assessment of its gravity*, for example, the allegations made are against a person in a leadership position, the nature of the crimes alleged; if not a leader, nonetheless is the person still in the area in which the crimes were allegedly committed and/ or still committing crimes and thereby an obstacle to reconciliation in the area. Subject to (iv) and (v) below such cases should take priority"; (iv) "Consideration should then be given as to the appropriate charges based on the available evidence and *whether* the information would seem to suggest that, with some investigation, *more serious offences would come to light*. If so, then clearly it would lose some of its priority rating"; (v) "The next part of the exercise is to assess *what work is required* before a case is trial ready. This would include such considerations as the availability of witnesses, whether further statements need to be taken from the witnesses or new witnesses found, whether the witnesses are likely to need protective measures and if so to what extent, whether documents are available in translation, whether further documents are available etc" (footnote omitted); (vi) "The next step is to assess the *likelihood of a quick arrest, or surrender*, of the accused, once an indictment has been issued"; and (vii) "The final assessment to be made is the *likely length of trial*". "Orientation Criteria for Sensitive Rules of the Road cases", Annex to the *Book of Rules on the Review of War Crimes Cases*, *ibid.* (emphasis added).

[36] *Ibid.*, section 2, fourth paragraph.

[37] *Ibid.*, section 2, last paragraph.

This passage makes a two-fold statement on prioritization. On the one hand, prioritization of cases within jurisdictions may be necessary – and may be done – on the basis of the readiness to proceed with the cases. On the other hand, as a general guideline, priority may be given to cases involving: (i) the mode of liability of command responsibility; (ii) crimes committed by public officials still in office regardless of mode of liability; or (iii) by law enforcement officials regardless of mode of liability. The second point would seem to correspond to gravity as in seniority of the suspect. As such, it may not add anything new to the consideration of cases that have been found suitable for trial at the State Court, but it would seem to extend this gravity consideration to all cases. Moreover, the reference to these three gravity criteria seem to suggest that highly sensitive cases should be prioritized on the basis of leadership or official positions rather than seriousness of crimes.

Hence, the Orientation Criteria document suggests a two-tier role for the criteria: first, they guide the *selection* of cases for different courts; second, the gravity criteria and, particularly, criteria related to seniority of the perpetrator also guide the *prioritization* of cases within the different jurisdictions. Let us proceed to examine the classification and content of these selection and prioritization criteria.

The Orientation Criteria document organizes criteria into three main groups: (1) "Nature of Crime alleged ('Crime')"; (2) "Circumstances of alleged perpetrator ('Perpetrator')"; and (3) "Other Considerations ('Other')". Groups (1) and (2) correspond to the general criterion of gravity, which includes both seriousness of the crime and seniority of the perpetrator. Group (3) mostly makes reference to the general criteria of "readiness to proceed". These groups of criteria are applicable to the selection and prioritization of both "highly sensitive" and "sensitive" cases, as each group has two lists of criteria corresponding to each of these categories of cases.

Thus, group (1), which refers to the nature of crimes, contains two lists of offences, one for each of the "highly sensitive" and "sensitive" categories of cases, structured in what may be an order of seriousness.[38] The lists cover a

[38] The list for "Category I – highly sensitive" cases contain the following crimes: (i) "Genocide"; (ii) "Extermination"; (iii) "Multiple Murders"; (iv) "Rape & other serious assaults as part of a system e.g. in camps or after attacks"; (v) "Enslavement"; (vi) "Torture"; (vii) "Persecutions on a widespread and systematic scale"; and (viii) "Mass forced Detention in Camps" [sic.]. The list for the cases in "Category II – sensitive" contains the following crimes: (i) "Murder committed as part of, or subsequent to, an attack, or in a camp"; (ii) "Rape and other serious sexual offences"; (iii) "Serious Assaults committed as part of a system"; (iv) "Inhuman and degrading treatment committed as part of a system"; (v) "Mass Deportation or Forcible transfer"; (vi) "Destruction or Damage to Religions and/or Cultural institutions on a widespread or systematic scale"; (vii) "Destruction of Property on a widespread or systematic scale"; (viii)

broad range of offences against life, physical integrity, personal liberty, freedom of movement, protection of religious or cultural institutions, and destruction of property. But the document makes no reference to these interests protected by the offences; much less does it discuss those interests, or justify their selection. Moreover, the document does not say what the indicated hierarchy of offences or the distinction between the offences in the two lists is based on.

On its turn, group (2), which refers to the circumstances of perpetrators, has two lists of past or present positions or roles of the suspect, and mentions the fact that the suspect is of "notorious reputation".[39] The listed categories cover military, paramilitary, police, political and judicial chains of authority. Even if only selected segments of these chains are included, the language is sufficiently vague to allow for wide discretion when applying the relevant criteria to individual cases. The lists also cover very practical roles like camp commanders and other persons "connected with the administration of camps", and it includes selective thematic functions like "[m]ultiple rapists" and persons "with a present or past notorious reputation" – one refers to the important theme of sexual assault and gender crimes, the other to the reputation of the alleged suspect, presumably to a large extent in the victim group. The selection of these two practical roles bears heavily on expectations of criminal justice for core international crimes in the specific BiH context.

It is fair to say that the categories included in group (2) cover the spectrum of leadership or prominent suspects very well. But again, the document does not indicate a justification for the apparent hierarchy in positions and roles listed, or for the differences between the lists. There is no reference to modes of liability or forms of participation in alleged criminal conduct, but rather to clusters of positions and roles and to notoriety, all of which are factual categories and not notions of criminal law. Limited reference is made to the specific organizations and structures to which alleged suspects belonged, as well as to the formal hierarchies of positions in these organizations.

"Denial of fundamental human rights e.g. medical care on a widespread or systematic scale"; and (ix) "Crimes which, although not within the range of gravity encompassed by Category I, are nonetheless notorious" [sic.].

39 "Category I" lists: (i) "Present or past Military Commander (including paramilitary formation)"; (ii) "Present or past Political leader (including Presidents of Municipalities/Crisis Staffs)"; (iii) "Present or past members of the Judiciary"; (iv) "Present or past Police Chiefs (CSB/SJB)"; (v) "Camp Commanders"; (vi) "Persons with a present or past notorious reputation"; and (vii) "Multiple rapists" [sic.]. "Category II" lists: (i) "Present or past police officer"; (ii) "Present member of the military"; (iii) "Persons who presently or in the past hold/held political office"; and (iv) "Persons connected with the administration of camps".

Finally, group (3), which refers to "Other Considerations", contains two lists that include a total of eight criteria regarding practical considerations.[40] Some of these criteria are uncontroversial, such as whether there are insider witnesses. Other criteria in this group – such as those concerning "Difficult issues of law" and "Cases involving perpetrators in an area which is sympathetic to him or where the authorities have a vested interest in preventing public scrutiny of the crimes" – require further justification for their possible merit to become readily apparent. One of the criteria in group (3) would also seem to be covered by gravity, namely "Crimes which may attract a lengthy prison sentence". The general criterion of 'readiness to proceed' is not listed specifically as a criterion in group (3), but four of the eight criteria in the group fall within this interest (see "Cases with 'Insider' or 'Suspect' witnesses", "Allegations connected with events which have already been the subject of a previous trial at ICTY", and "Case is document heavy", as well as the controversial "Difficult issues of law"). According to the Orientation Criteria document, all of these criteria can be considered during prioritization of cases within jurisdictions.

Of the remaining four criteria in group (3), two concern witness security ("Realistic prospect of witness intimidation" and "Witness Protection issues") and two have been referred to above ("Difficult issues of law" and "Cases involving perpetrators in an area which is sympathetic to him or where the authorities have a vested interest in preventing public scrutiny of the crimes"). The Orientation Criteria document says that these four criteria can be considered when distributing the cases between the State Court and the Cantonal or District courts.

As can be seen, the Orientation Criteria document is a flexible and quite comprehensive instrument as regards the use of criteria for the distribution of war crimes cases between BiH jurisdictions and for the prioritization of such cases within each jurisdiction. The document covers a broad range of reasonable criteria, almost all of which can be grouped under the considerations of gravity and readiness to proceed. According to the letter of the document, these criteria could also be used after case-files had been distributed between the State Court and the Cantonal or District courts, that is, in the prioritization of cases within jurisdictions or, more accurately, prosecutor's offices. As such, the utility of the document would not have been overlooked or underestimated in the search for

[40] "Category I" lists: (i) "Cases with 'Insider' or 'Suspect' witnesses"; (ii) "Realistic prospect of witness intimidation"; (iii) "Cases involving perpetrators in an area which is sympathetic to him or where the authorities have a vested interest in preventing public scrutiny of the crimes". "Category II" lists: (i) "Witness Protection issues"; (ii) "Difficult issues of law"; (iii) "Crimes which may attract a lengthy prison sentence"; (iv) "Allegations connected with events which have already been the subject of a previous trial at ICTY"; and (v) "Case is document heavy".

appropriate tools to deal with the large backlog of core international crimes cases in BiH. Furthermore, its existence and scope should continue to inform broader discussions on selection and prioritization criteria, whatever the forum of the discourse, as it establishes a relevant precedent for other territorial jurisdictions as well as for international tribunals and even for courts exercising universal jurisdiction. The makers of the Orientation Criteria and the Book of Rules deserve recognition for the foresight of formalizing criteria in this way, for including such a broad range of criteria, and for opening for the application of criteria also after cases have been distributed between the State Court and the Cantonal or District courts.

In spite of this, the Orientation Criteria have some limitations and have faced important challenges. On the one hand, the fact that they can operate both as selection and prioritization criteria is an important step in recognizing the crucial importance of the latter function for dealing with a significant backlog of cases in BiH as well as in other territorial jurisdictions. However, that fact is also problematic in the sense that it does not allow for a clear differentiation of the way in which criteria should function in order to fulfil each of those tasks. Indeed, as mentioned in the introduction, lists of criteria are quite useful for selecting or distributing cases among jurisdictions, since they can easily operate as a threshold below which cases are referred to lower-rank jurisdictions. But their role is different concerning case prioritization. Since all cases to be prioritized have already been selected for complying with the criteria in question, lists of the latter do not shed much light on the way in which they should be ranked, unless they specifically establish a hierarchy among the groups of criteria in which they are classified, as well as among the specific criteria contained in each group. The BiH Orientation Criteria document does not explicitly do this, and thus it seems to leave jurisdictions in charge of prioritizing cases wide room for the discretionary interpretation of criteria.

Nevertheless, the document does suggest at least two important elements that could be used in order to clearly define the way in which criteria should be interpreted to prioritize cases, and it therefore, offers grounds for countering this potential shortcoming. First, as mentioned earlier, when the Orientation Criteria document opens the possibility of further prioritization of cases within jurisdictions, it seems to recognize seniority as a more important or higher-rank criteria for prioritization purposes, when it indicates that "as a point of reference command responsibility and crimes committed by public officials still in office and law enforcement officials may take priority".[41] If this is the correct interpretation of the text, then a hierarchy between seniority and seriousness of crimes

[41] *Ibid.*, section 2, last paragraph.

could be established for prioritizing grave cases, but the ranking of these cases and those chosen on the basis of their readiness to prosecute should still have to be determined. Second, the Orientation Criteria document also seems to define, in a much more explicit way, the way in which criteria within each group of criteria should be ranked. In fact, each group contains two lists of criteria that can be considered hierarchically related – the list of criteria for highly sensitive cases being more important than the list for sensitive cases. Furthermore, the group that refers to the nature of crimes (group (1)) lists offences in such a way as to suggest an *order of seriousness*.[42] Therefore, this ordering could be used as a ranking on the basis of which grave cases could be prioritized.

On the other hand, the Orientation Criteria face a challenge related to the original case classification on which they were formulated. Indeed, they are founded on the distinction made by the ICTY between "highly sensitive" (type A) and "sensitive" (type B) cases. Thus, the Orientation Criteria document foresees that the criteria it formulates should only be applied to these types of cases. Moreover, it is on the basis of these categories that each group of criteria is divided into two distinct lists of criteria, which are to be applied to the so classified cases in order to establish the competent jurisdiction and the priority they should be given. Now, the problem is that, as Zekerija Mujkanović – Public Prosecutor of the Brčko District of BiH and Member of the Prosecutorial Council of the country – has noted:

> We have learned over time that the original review process carried out by the ICTY was not very reliable. Many of the received files were 'old'. The information contained in the electronic copies that had been returned was often of poor quality, by all relevant standards, and as such could not be authenticated. In many cases it turned out that victims, witnesses or suspects had deceased or were inaccessible. Using an analytical approach, it was established that even the files which the ICTY gave the standard designation "B" contain information which, when cross-referenced against other information, lead to suspects and evidence which can be instrumental in criminal prosecutions in Bosnia and Herzegovina. […]
>
> Some deficiencies were noted in the review process as well. In order to be able to complete the assignment, the staff engaged in the review had to take the information from the files as reliable, while time and experience showed that it was actually not. Furthermore, due to financial constraints, the staff conducting the review in 2005 was forced to process a large number of cases in a very limited period of time. The files were not only incomplete,

[42] See *supra* note 38.

> but they also contained statements and other documents in languages which the staff could not understand. The review and decisions were made on the basis of hastily prepared summaries and translations.

Hence, it is possible that the original case classification on the basis of which the Orientation Criteria were to be applied was not entirely suitable for determining the distribution of cases among jurisdictions and the priority they should receive within them. Although this is not a problem intrinsic to the formulation of the criteria, it had the capacity to deeply affect their operability and their chances of successfully dealing with the BiH backlog of cases in an appropriate and timely manner. Therefore, the BiH judiciary faced the additional challenge of making sure that the originally reviewed cases do comply in practice with the criteria for selecting and prioritizing them. For the more general discussion about criteria, this situation offers an important lesson for jurisdictions in charge of selecting and prioritizing cases of always making sure that the initial classifications of those cases are in accordance with the goals they seek to accomplish through the establishment of criteria.

5.2.2. Criteria in Annex A of the National War Crimes Prosecution Strategy

Despite the existence of the Orientation Criteria, a second instrument was developed and adopted in BiH that includes case selection and prioritization criteria as a mechanism for dealing with the heavy backlog of core international crimes cases. This instrument is the "National War Crimes Strategy of Bosnia and Herzegovina", which was elaborated by a Working Group established by the Ministry of Justice in September 2007, and which was formally adopted by the BiH Council of Ministers in December 2008, revised by the Council in September 2020 (but this chapter concentrates on the 2008 original).[43] Although the document only refers to war crimes, it specifies since the beginning that it uses the term in such a way as to also include "criminal offenses committed during the war in BiH (1992–1995), prescribed under Chapter XVII of the Criminal

[43] *National War Crimes Prosecution Strategy of Bosnia and Herzegovina*, adopted by the BiH Council of Ministers in December 2008. An English translation of the document is printed as an annex in Bergsmo, Helvig, Utmelidze and Žagovec, 2010, see *supra* note *. The 2020 Revised War Crimes Strategy was adopted as the timeline under the 2008 Strategy could not be met (see BiH Council of Ministers, *Usvojena Revidirana državna strategija za rad na predmetima ratnih zločina*, September 2020 (https://www.legal-tools.org/doc/dp6sk7km/)). The criteria in Annex A of the Revised Strategy are based on the 2008 criteria. We refer readers to Chapter 17 for more information on the 2020 Revised Strategy, as that falls outside the scope of the documents selected for analysis in the present chapter.

Code of Bosnia and Herzegovina, Crimes against humanity and values protected by international law committed in relation to the war in BiH".[44]

The Strategy document contains an Annex A entitled "Criteria for the Review of War Crimes Cases", which was drafted by the State Court and the Prosecutor's Office, and agreed upon by other prosecutor's offices and courts of the country, in order to guarantee "the selection and assessment of complexity of cases to be done in a uniform and objective manner".[45] According to the Strategy, Annex A constitutes an "integral part"[46] of it, and is therefore as binding as the rest of the measures implemented in the document. Annex A builds significantly on the Orientation Criteria document;[47] however, it includes some quite relevant variations in terms of the objectives and scope of criteria, which seem to explain in part why the Working Group that drafted the Strategy and the Council of Ministers that adopted it found it necessary to introduce a new document on case selection and prioritization criteria apart from the Orientation Criteria.

Indeed, according to the Prosecution Strategy, the rationale for drafting the latter includes, among other things, a concern with the "[i]nconsistent practice of the review, takeover and transfer of war crimes cases between the Court and the Prosecutor's Office and other courts and prosecutor's offices, and the lack of agreed upon criteria for the assessment of sensitivity and complexity of cases [...]".[48] Moreover, the Strategy indicates as two of its main objectives: (i) to "[e]nsure a functional mechanism of the management of war crimes cases, that is, their distribution between the State-level judiciary and judiciaries of the 5 entities and of Brčko District that will facilitate efficient prosecution within the set timeframe"; and (ii) to "[p]rosecute as a priority the most responsible perpetrators before the Court of BiH, with the help of the agreed upon case selection and prioritization criteria [...]".[49] These two objectives are also recognized in Annex A, according to which the criteria contained therein offer guidelines for

---

44 *Ibid.*, p. 3. As can be seen, then, it actually refers to a broader notion than that of 'war crimes' in a technical sense.

45 According to the Strategy, the following institutions participated in the process and agreed upon the criteria: "the RS Prosecutor's Office, FBiH Prosecutor's Office, the RS Supreme Court, the Prosecutor's Office of Brčko District BiH, the FBiH Supreme Court, the Appellate Court of Brčko District BiH". The process was assisted by the ICTY. *Ibid.*, p. 15.

46 *Ibid.*

47 Annex A explicitly asserts: "When these criteria were drafted, in terms of contents, *the orientation criteria for sensitive 'Rules of the Road' cases dated 2004 were used*", "Annex A", in *National War Crimes Prosecution Strategy of Bosnia and Herzegovina*, p. 1, see *supra* note 43.

48 *Ibid.*, p. 4, section 1.1., letter *e*.

49 *Ibid.*, pp. 3–4, section 1.2., letters *c* and *d*.

determining the right forum of cases, as well as for deciding the order in which cases should be prosecuted before the State Court.[50]

In that way, the criteria contained in the Strategy seek to accomplish the dual function of serving as grounds for both case selection and case prioritization. Now, as we saw in Section 5.2.1. of this chapter, the Orientation Criteria have a similar purpose. In fact, their main goal is to serve as guidelines for case distribution or selection among jurisdictions, but they are also conceived (that is the case of the gravity criterion in particular) as offering the grounds for case prioritization within each jurisdiction. This suggests that the creators and implementers of the Strategy document perceived the Orientation Criteria to be insufficient – at least on their own – to accomplish the former objectives. This is all the more relevant given that the subscribers of Annex A were members of the highest judicial institutions in charge of dealing with war crimes at the national, cantonal and district levels, that is, precisely the institutions in charge of applying case selection and prioritization criteria.

Therefore, even though it does not say so explicitly, Annex A of the National Strategy seems to abrogate the Orientation Criteria, or at least to complement it in such a way that the criteria therein contained can no longer be interpreted and applied without looking at the new set of criteria incorporated in the Strategy. Now, the classification and content of these criteria did not vary substantially in comparison with the Orientation Criteria. In fact, Annex A divides criteria into the same three clusters of the latter document, entitled in Annex A as: "Gravity of criminal offences", "Capacity and role of perpetrators" , and "Other circumstances".[51] Further, the criteria contained in each cluster do not

[50] *Ibid.*, p. 1.

[51] The first cluster, "Gravity of Criminal Offenses", includes the following criteria:

> a) Legal qualification of criminal offense – genocide, crimes against humanity (proving that there was a widespread and systematic attack), and war crimes against civilian population and prisoners of war, providing that some other criteria have been fulfilled as well; b) Mass killings (killing of a large number of persons, systematic killing); c) Severe forms of rape (multiple and systematic rape, establishment of detention centres for the purpose of sexual slavery); d) Serious forms of torture (taking into account the intensity and the degree of mental and physical injuries, large scale consequences); e) Serious forms of unlawful detention or another severe deprivation of physical liberty (establishment of camps and detention centres, escorting to and detention in the camps and detention centres, taking into account the large scale of or particularly severe conditions during the detention); f) Persecution; g) Forced disappearance (taking into account the consequences, circumstances and the large scale of forceful disappearance); h) Serious forms of infliction of sufferings upon civilian population (starvation, shelling of civilian building structures, destruction of religious, cultural and historical monuments); i) Significant number of vic-

vary in any radical way, but rather seem to respond to an effort of formulating the already existing criteria in more concise and precise terms. Consequently, the main changes in the criteria contained in Annex A with regards to the Orientation Criteria have to do with the collapse of the distinction between highly sensitive and sensitive cases, the substantial reduction of the list of criteria contained in each cluster – by excluding some categories and including others in more general categories – and the formulation of the remaining categories in a more precise way.[52]

> tims (or severe consequences suffered by the victims –degree of physical and mental suffering); j) Particularly insidious methods and means used in the perpetration of criminal offense; k) Existence of particular circumstances.

On its part, the second cluster, "Capacity and Role of the Perpetrator", refers to the following categories:

> a) Duty within unit (commander in the military, police or paramilitary establishment); b) Managing position in camps and detention centres; c) Political function; d) Holder of a judicial office (judge, prosecutor, public attorney, attorney at law); e) More serious forms and degrees of participation in the perpetration of a criminal offense (taking part in the planning and ordering of a crime; manner of perpetration; intentional and particular commitment to the planning and ordering of a crime; the degree of intent should be taken into account).

Finally, the third cluster, "Other Circumstances", includes these criteria:

> a) Correlation between the case and other cases and possible perpetrators; b) Interests of victims and witnesses (witnesses who have been granted protection measures before the ICTY and the Court of BiH – protected witnesses; necessity to provide witness protection; witnesses included in the program of protection; repentant witnesses); c) Consequences of the crime for the local community (demographic changes, return, possible public and social reactions or anxiety among citizens and the consequences for the public order in relation to the perpetration or prosecution of the crime).

"Annex A", in *National War Crimes Prosecution Strategy of Bosnia and Herzegovina*, pp. 2–3, see *supra* note 43.

52 If compared with the Orientation Criteria, Annex A incorporates the following variations. Concerning the first cluster, "Gravity of Criminal Offenses", Annex A adds the following criteria: (i) "Crimes against humanity" (a wide but also precise category that refers to the generality and systematicity of different offences referred to in the Orientation Criteria as a requisite for considering them of gravity); (ii) "Serious forms of unlawful detention or another severe deprivation of physical liberty" (a more comprising formula than the scattered references made to camps in the Orientation Criteria, and which includes: "establishment of camps and detention centres, escorting to and detention in the camps and detention centres, taking into account the large scale of or particularly severe conditions during the detention"); (iii) "Forced disappearance" (which takes into account the "consequences, circumstances and the large scale" of the crime); (iv) "Serious forms of infliction of sufferings upon civilian population" (which covers some of the more specific criteria referred to by the Orientation Criteria, thus forming a more comprehensive category that includes: "starvation, shelling of civilian building structures, destruction of religious, cultural and historical monuments"); (v) "Significant number of victims (or severe consequences suffered by the victims – degree of physical and mental suffering)";

(vi) "Particularly insidious methods and means used in the perpetration of criminal offense"; and (vii) "Existence of particular circumstances" (instead of listing additional criminal offences, the three last criteria refer to specific characteristics that may render any offence of gravity).

Moreover, concerning the first cluster, Annex A excludes the following criteria that appeared in the list of highly sensitive cases of the Orientation Criteria: (i) "Extermination" (which could possibly be covered by either the genocide or the mass killings category); (ii) "Multiple Killings" (which can certainly be included in the mass killings category if it is against a large enough number of persons); (iii) "Enslavement" (which could possibly be included in the category of serious forms of torture, although at the expense of the specificity of the crime of slavery); and (iv) "Destruction or Damage to Religions and/or Cultural institutions on a widespread or systematic scale" (which appears to be included as one of the cases of the more generic category "Serious forms of infliction of sufferings upon civilian population").

Also, Annex A excludes the following criteria that appeared in the list of sensitive cases of the Orientation Criteria: (i) "Murder committed as part of, or subsequent to, an attack, or in a camp" (which could be included in the "Mass Killing category if it complies with its particular conditions"); (ii) "Serious Assaults committed as part of a system" (which is certainly included in the "Crimes against humanity" category); (iii) "Mass Deportation or Forcible transfer" (which can possibly be covered by one of the following new categories: "Significant number of victims", "Particularly insidious methods and means used in the perpetration of criminal offense", or "Existence of particular circumstances"); (iv) "Destruction of Property on a widespread or systematic scale" (which can also possibly be covered by the three categories included in the previous parenthesis); (v) "Denial of fundamental human rights e.g. medical care on a widespread or systematic scale" (which could also possibly fit in the three categories mentioned in the same parenthesis); and (vi) "Crimes which, although not within the range of gravity encompassed by Category I, are nonetheless notorious" (an imprecise category that was probably replaced by the three categories mentioned in the referred parenthesis).

Finally, Annex A refers to certain categories in the first cluster that formulate criteria in a more precise way. Thus, instead of the categories "Rape & other serious assaults as part of a system e.g. in camps or after attacks" and "Rape and other serious sexual offences", which respectively appeared in the lists of highly sensitive and sensitive cases of the Orientation Criteria, Annex A uses the more comprehensive and precise formulation "Severe forms of rape (multiple and systematic rape, establishment of detention centres for the purpose of sexual slavery)". Also, instead of the categories "Torture" and "Inhuman and degrading treatment committed as part of a system", which respectively appeared in the lists of highly sensitive and sensitive cases of the Orientation Criteria, Annex A uses the formula "Serious forms of torture (taking into account the intensity and the degree of mental and physical injuries, large scale consequences)", which reduces the scope of the crime but also softens the requirement of systematicity. Further, instead of the category "Persecutions on a widespread and systematic scale", Annex A refers to persecutions in a general way, thus recognizing the gravity of this crime regardless of its systematicity. Finally, instead of the category "Mass forced Detention in Camps", Annex A refers to the wider but also more precise category of "Serious forms of unlawful detention or another severe deprivation of physical liberty (establishment of camps and detention centres, escorting to and detention in the camps and detention centres, taking into account the large scale of or particularly severe conditions during the detention)".

Concerning the second cluster, "Capacity and Role of the Perpetrator", for the most part, Annex A formulates the criteria in a more general and yet more precise way, so that they cover almost all the specific categories mentioned by the Orientation Criteria but through the use of a more technical and comprehensive language. Thus, Annex A used the more comprehensive category "Duty within unit (commander in the military, police or paramilitary establishment)" in replacement of the following more specific categories: "Present or past Military Commander (including paramilitary formation)", "Present or past police officer", "Present or past Police Chiefs (CSB/SJB)", and "Present member of the military", the first two of which appeared in the list of highly sensitive cases, and the latter two of which appeared in the list of sensitive cases of the Orientation Criteria. Also, Annex A used the category "Political function", instead of the following two narrower categories: "Present or past Political leader (including Presidents of Municipalities/Crisis Staffs)" and "Persons who presently or in the past holds/held political office", which respectively appear in the lists of highly sensitive cases and sensitive cases of the Orientation Criteria. Furthermore, Annex A used the category "Holder of a judicial office (judge, prosecutor, public attorney, attorney at law)", instead of the category "Present or past members of the Judiciary", which appeared in the list of highly sensitive cases of the Orientation Criteria. What is more, Annex A used the wider but more precise category "Managing position in camps and detention centres", instead of the more specific categories "Camp Commanders" and "Persons connected with the administration of camps", which respectively appear in the lists of highly sensitive and sensitive cases of the Orientation Criteria. Apart from the use of these more general and precise categories, Annex A excluded from the second cluster the quite equivocal categories "Persons with a present or past notorious reputation" and "Multiple rapists", both of which appear in the list of highly sensitive cases of the Orientation Criteria. Finally, Annex A added to the second cluster the criterion "More serious forms and degrees of participation in the perpetration of a criminal offense (taking part in the planning and ordering of a crime; manner of perpetration; intentional and particular commitment to the planning and ordering of a crime; the degree of intent should be taken into account)", which seems to be a residual category intended to cover relevant degrees of participation in the commission of crimes that could be left out by the other criteria of the cluster.

As for the third and final cluster of criteria, "Other Circumstances", Annex A also attempted to use more comprehensive categories, which cover most of those mentioned in the Orientation Criteria, but through a much more precise formulation. Thus, Annex A uses the category "Correlation between the case and other cases and possible perpetrators", which seems to cover the much narrower category "Allegations connected with events which have already been the subject of a previous trial at ICTY" included in the list of sensitive cases of the Orientation criteria, but which also covers many other relevant situations. Further, Annex A uses the category "Interests of victims and witnesses (witnesses who have been granted protection measures before the ICTY and the Court of BiH – protected witnesses; necessity to provide witness protection; witnesses included in the program of protection; repentant witnesses)" that covers the less precise and comprehensive categories "Cases with 'Insider' or 'Suspect' witnesses", "Realistic prospect of witness intimidation" and "Witness Protection issues", the first two of which appeared in the list of highly sensitive and sensitive cases of the Orientation Criteria, and the latter of which appeared in the list of sensitive cases of the same document. Moreover, Annex A uses the category "Consequences of the crime for the local community (demographic changes, return, possible public and social reactions or anxiety among citizens and the consequences for the public order in relation to the perpetration or

The latter suggests that the decision to adopt the new set of criteria contained in Annex A can be explained much less in terms of the need to change their content and classification than in terms of the need to adapt the already existing criteria to fully serve the new and broader purposes of case selection and prioritization criteria foreseen for them in the National Strategy. Indeed, the Strategy document expands the purposes of selection and prioritization criteria in at least three different ways.

First, Annex A of the Strategy document attempts to expand the scope of selection criteria, by extending their application to all prosecutorial and judicial activities involving the distribution of cases among jurisdictions, and especially by specifying that judges – not only prosecutors – should take those criteria into consideration in their decisions. On the one hand, it establishes that both the State Prosecutor's Office and the State Court of BiH should apply such criteria in decisions concerning the *transfer* of cases from the State jurisdiction to the entity and district jurisdictions.[53] According to the Strategy document, transfer decisions involve those cases that were brought before the courts after March 2003 (when the new criminal legislation entered into force) and that "fall under the exclusive jurisdiction of the Court and the Prosecutor's Office of BiH".[54] Thus, these cases require a formal transfer of jurisdiction in order to be dealt with by lower level jurisdictions. Now, the law that regulated this mechanism at the time of the Strategy (Article 27 of the BiH Criminal Procedure Code ('CPC')) did not require the use of selection criteria in the making of transfer decisions,

prosecution of the crime)", which covers but is in no way limited to the category "Cases involving perpetrators in an area which is sympathetic to him or where the authorities have a vested interest in preventing public scrutiny of the crimes", which appears in the list of highly sensitive cases of the Orientation Criteria. In addition to these reformulations of criteria, Annex A excluded from the third cluster of criteria the following problematic categories, which appeared in the list of sensitive cases of the Orientation Criteria: "Difficult issues of law", "Crimes which may attract a lengthy prison sentence", and "Case is document heavy".

[53] Concerning the State Prosecutor's Office, Annex A states:

> These criteria set out the guidelines that the Prosecutor's Office of Bosnia and Herzegovina will follow in the review of war crimes cases, in order for the Court to issue a decision whether a particular case, taking into account its complexity, would be prosecuted before the Prosecutor's Office and the Court of Bosnia and Herzegovina, or before the courts and prosecutor's offices of entities and the Brčko District of Bosnia and Herzegovina pursuant to Article 27 and Article 449 of the Criminal Procedure Code of Bosnia and Herzegovina.

On the other hand, concerning the State Court of BiH, Annex A establishes: "By using the stated criteria, the Court of BiH will review the complexity of cases ex officio, or at the proposal by parties or defence attorneys, in order to issue the decision on *transferring* or taking over a case pursuant to the CPC BiH" (emphasis added). *Ibid.*

[54] *National War Crimes Prosecution Strategy of Bosnia and Herzegovina*, pp. 11–12, see *supra* note 43.

but merely referred to the existence of "strong reasons" for transferring the case, which affected the application of the transfer mechanism due to the various possible interpretations of this legal standard.[55] The Strategy document therefore foresaw that the law in question should be modified "in an urgent procedure" so as to establish a more efficient mechanism for transferring less complex cases to lower level jurisdictions, including the consideration of selection criteria in the Prosecutor's Office's filing of proposals to the BiH Court for transferring cases, as well as in this Court's decisions.[56] Article 27a of the CPC, adopted on 13 November 2009, was the legislative response to this challenge.[57]

On the other hand, Annex A indicates that criteria should be applied in all acts concerning the *takeover* by the State jurisdiction of cases that were filed before March 2003 and therefore under entity and district courts.[58] The Prosecutor's Office of BiH assessed the sensitivity of some of those cases and proposed State Court takeover of those considered "very sensitive". Since the applicable law on the matter (Article 449, paragraph 2 of the BiH CPC) did not require the prosecutor's offices and courts of the country to report on pending cases in their jurisdictions, there was a risk that many such cases were highly sensitive but that the State Court could not take them over *ex officio* due to lack of information. In fact, by October 2008, a total of 1,216 cases were pending before these jurisdictions, but the State Prosecutor's Office had only made 161 requests to take over.[59] For that reason, the Strategy document established that prosecutor's offices and courts should immediately submit to the State Court a report of the number and complexity of pending cases before them, in order for it to be able to decide on takeovers.[60]

Hence, Annex A differs from the Orientation criteria in that it introduces the consideration of selection criteria to the different spheres in which case distribution is involved, and particularly in that it extends the application of such criteria to judges and not only to prosecutors. Thus, according to Annex A:

---

[55] *Ibid.*, pp. 12–13.

[56] *Ibid.*

[57] See BiH, The Law on Amendments to the Criminal Procedure Code of Bosnia and Herzegovina, 13 November 2009, Official Gazette of Bosnia and Herzegovina, 93/09 (https://www.legal-tools.org/doc/q5x12kqt/).

[58] *National War Crimes Prosecution Strategy of Bosnia and Herzegovina*, p. 14, see *supra* note 43.

[59] *Ibid.*

[60] The Strategy ordered an urgent procedure to amend the applicable law for it to admit the use of criteria in takeover acts, which include both the State Court's decision to takeover, and proposals of doing so presented to the Court by the State Prosecutor's Office as well as by other prosecutor's offices and courts in the country. *Ibid.*

> By using the stated criteria, the Court of BiH will review the complexity of cases ex officio, or at the proposal by parties or defence attorneys, in order to issue the decision on transferring or taking over a case pursuant to the CPC BiH. When filing the motion with the Court for transferring or taking over a case, the Prosecutor's Office of BiH will use the same criteria. Also, all courts and prosecutor's offices, by using these criteria, will file motions with the Court of BiH for taking over cases pursuant to Article 449 of the CPC BiH.[61]

Second, the adoption of Annex A appears to have been considered necessary for emphasizing the importance of criteria for prioritizing cases within the Prosecutor's Office. Indeed, in contrast with the Orientation Criteria (which only refers to case prioritization in its last paragraph), the Strategy document gives a central role to case prioritization as a function of the criteria contained in Annex A. Thus, as mentioned above, the Strategy identifies priority prosecution of the most responsible perpetrators as one of its main objectives, and points at criteria as the main mechanism for achieving that purpose. Moreover, Annex A explicitly states that the "Prosecutor's Office of BiH will apply these criteria to determine the level of priority of cases based on which the order of prosecuting the cases before the Court of Bosnia and Herzegovina would be determined".[62]

In spite of the central role given to case prioritization as a function of criteria, neither the National Strategy in general nor Annex A in particular advance much in distinguishing the different ways in which criteria should be applied in order to fulfil their two roles of case selection and prioritization. In fact, Annex A's only reference to the interpretation or application of criteria is the following:

> If a case meets the criteria below in terms of the gravity of criminal offense and the capacity and role of the perpetrator, whether separately or in their interconnection, and taking into account other circumstances, the proceedings will be conducted before the BiH Court. Otherwise, the case will be tried before another court in BiH pursuant to legal provisions on jurisdiction, transfer and taking over of cases.

[61] "Annex A", in *National War Crimes Prosecution Strategy of Bosnia and Herzegovina*, pp. 1–2, see *supra* note 43. Indeed, Article 449(2) of the CPC of BiH was amended on 13 November 2009 to require that "the gravity of the criminal offence, characteristics of the perpetrator and other circumstances important for assessment of complexity of the case" be taken into account (see Law on Amendments to the Criminal Procedure Code of Bosnia and Herzegovina, *supra* note 58).

[62] "Annex A", in *National War Crimes Prosecution Strategy of Bosnia and Herzegovina*, p. 1, see *supra* note 43.

Hence, Annex A indicates that criteria should be interpreted as a threshold above which a case should be selected for prosecution before the State Court in application of the criteria. However, it does not say anything about the way in which such criteria should be interpreted in order to accomplish the role of prioritizing cases within that jurisdiction. In particular, just as the Orientation Criteria and the Prosecutorial Guidelines referred to before, Annex A does not suggest a possible hierarchy of criteria that would allow to determine which of those criteria are more relevant for establishing the priority of a case that complies with some of them but not with others, and the threshold interpretation of criteria is not very helpful for this purpose.

Another limitation of Annex A concerning the case prioritization function of criteria is that it only refers to this function with regards to the State Prosecutor's Office, thus ignoring the potential usefulness of criteria for prioritizing cases within the entity and district level jurisdictions. These jurisdictions have also been quite overwhelmed with cases, and they could have benefitted greatly from having a clearly defined prioritization method, the application of which could be unified by the establishment of consistent parameters in the practice of the State jurisdiction.

Third, the creators of the National Strategy appear to have considered it important to establish mechanisms for guaranteeing their effective and unified application, and particularly to give judges the role of supervising such application. In fact, the Strategy establishes that the "Court and the Prosecutor's Office of BiH shall hold regular meetings aimed at ensuring consistent application of the agreed upon criteria".[63] Furthermore, in contrast with the Orientation Criteria – which gave a central role to the Prosecutor's Office concerning the application of criteria – the Strategy points at the Court of BiH as the body responsible for ensuring the consistent application of Annex A's criteria.[64]

In conclusion, Annex A of the National War Crimes Strategy constitutes a significant advancement in the formulation of case selection and prioritization criteria in BiH. This is so not only or mainly because it formulates a more concise and precise list of criteria than that contained in the Orientation Criteria, but also and especially because it widens the scope and purposes of the criteria therein contained, particularly by requiring their use in all the spheres and by all authorities concerned with case selection, by insisting on the relevance of their use for case prioritization within the State jurisdiction, and by envisaging mechanisms for supervising their effective application.

63 *National War Crimes Prosecution Strategy of Bosnia and Herzegovina*, p. 14, see *supra* note 43.

64 *Ibid.*, p. 40.

Annex A has faced some limitations related to the way in which criteria are to be operationalized, particularly concerning their role as case prioritization tools. Furthermore, it has not been obvious that Annex A's advancements would be enough for selection and prioritization criteria to substantively contribute to the difficult task of evacuating the large backlog of core international crimes cases in BiH. Indeed, the backlog proved to be too large for the timeline in the National Strategy to be implemented, so, as mentioned, a Revised Strategy was adopted in 2020, as discussed in Chapter 17 below. Be that as it may, what appears clear is that the advancements of the 2008 Annex A represent a contribution to the discussion about selection and prioritization criteria not only in BiH, but also in other international and territorial jurisdictions.

5.2.3. Criteria in the Charging Guidelines of the Prosecutor's Office of Bosnia and Herzegovina

In spite of the importance and usefulness of the Orientation Criteria and of Annex A of the War Crimes Strategy, the State Prosecutor's Office of BiH appears to have considered it necessary to develop case selection and prioritization criteria above and beyond those contained in such documents. In his letter of resignation as Registrar, Mr. David Schwendiman wrote that he and his colleagues had "started what [he] hope[s] will be a meaningful effort to develop prosecution guidelines and case selection criteria".[65] He attached to the letter a document containing "recommended prosecution guidelines for charging, pleas, immunity, and investigations", and described them as "core guidelines that any well managed prosecution office must have".[66]

This document, formally entitled "Prosecution Guidelines", was presented as a work in progress, which had been continually developed since 2007 by the Special Department for War Crimes of the Prosecutor's Office of BiH as a basis for its prosecution strategies.[67] In its initial version, the document included a

---

[65] Letter entitled "Registrar for the Special Department for War Crimes and the Special Department for Organized Crime, Economic Crime and Corruption; Notice of my resignation and report" from Mr. David Schwendiman to Chief Prosecutor Marinko Jurčević, Prosecutor's Office of Bosnia and Herzegovina, 28 September 2007, p. 6 (referred to here with permission of the author of the letter via e-mail on 22 November 2007).

[66] *Ibid.*, p. 3.

[67] Special Department for War Crimes Prosecutor's Office of Bosnia and Herzegovina, "Prosecution Guidelines", by Mr. David Schwendiman. The initial version of the document was forwarded to one of the authors of this chapter via e-mail message on 6 November 2007. A later version of the document, of February 2009, was handed personally to the authors by Mr. David Schwendiman on 10 October 2009 in Sarajevo, BiH. The document is referred to here with permission of its author via e-mail on 22 November 2007.

first section on the guidelines for the charging decisions of the Prosecutor's Office, which, among other things,[68] made reference to the "Public Interest test in war crimes cases" as a stage in the prosecution process in which the determination is made of whether a case should be charged or not.[69] This test was composed of a set of factors to be considered by the Prosecutor's Office, which seemed intended to operate as selection and prioritization criteria for establishing which cases should be charged, and which of them should be so first.

According to the original version of the document, its content was "available to the public for comment and criticism".[70] As a result, the Prosecutor's Office received substantial input from international organizations and individuals on the document in general and on the criteria therein included in particular.[71] On the basis of that input, the Special Department for War Crimes of the Prosecutor's Office updated the Guidelines, one of its most significant changes being that it included an entirely new section entitled "Prioritization", explicitly devoted to the Prosecutor's task of ranking war crimes cases in order to determine which should be prosecuted first.[72] The section is essentially composed of a list of prioritization criteria that corresponds significantly to a modified version of the criteria originally contained in the Charging section, which were consequently removed from the latter section.[73]

The analysis of the Prosecution Guidelines is quite relevant for identifying the contributions they make to the discussion about selection and prioritization criteria beyond the documents discussed in the previous two sections. Indeed,

---

68 *Ibid.*, "Prosecution Guidelines", "1. Charging", initial version of November 2007. Apart from the public-interest test, the document also referred to principles and standards for charging, to guidelines for determining what to charge, to criteria for establishing grounded suspicion, and to standards for indictments and pleadings.

69 *Ibid.*, section 1.7., pp. 9–10.

70 *Ibid.*, p. 1.

71 The document entitled "Some Remarks on the Handling of the Backlog of Core International Crimes Case Files in Bosnia and Herzegovina", written by Morten Bergsmo, Kjetil Helvig, Ilia Utmelidze and Gorana Žagovec was one contribution to the updating of the Charging document in general and for the reformulation of its criteria. As a Consultant to the Organization for Security and Co-operation in Europe – Mission to Bosnia and Herzegovina, Bergsmo led the team that prepared the report, which was later published as Morten Bergsmo, Kjetil Helvig, Ilia Utmelidze and Gorana Žagovec, *The Backlog of Core International Crimes Cases in Bosnia and Herzegovina*, see *supra* note *.

72 Special Department for War Crimes Prosecutor's Office of Bosnia and Herzegovina. "Prosecution Guidelines. 5. Prioritization", version of February 2009, see *supra* note 67.

73 In the newer version of the Charging section, in the place where criteria were originally formulated, one instead reads: "1.6. Public Interest test in war crimes cases. See Special Department for War Crimes, Prosecution Guidelines, 5. Prioritization, DRAFT, 09 Feb 09", see "Prosecution Guidelines. 1. Charging", version of February 2009, p. 10, *ibid.*

the inclusion of criteria of the sort in the Guidelines would normally suggest that the Department for War Crimes of the Prosecutor's Office did not consider either the Orientation Criteria or the criteria contained in Annex A of the War Crimes Strategy as adequate or sufficient for fulfilling the tasks of that Office concerning case selection and prioritization.

This consideration may be grounded in a particular concern of the State Prosecutor's Office to remain independent and immune to possible influences of the way cases should be selected and prioritized. Mr. Schwendiman had strongly recommended to the Chief Prosecutor of the BiH Prosecutor's Office to "resist every effort by anyone, OSCE [Organization for Security and Co-operation in Europe – Mission to Bosnia and Herzegovina], HJPC [High Judicial and Prosecutorial Council of Bosnia and Herzegovina], the State Court or anyone else, to dictate what your case selection criteria ought to be".[74] According to him,

> [s]electing cases and deciding who, what and whether to investigate and prosecute is at the heart of the prosecutor's independence, for good or bad, and are core concepts in the best systems of criminal justice. The court shouldn't be allowed to interfere in these central tasks. Neither should any other institution, including the press, victim's [sic.] associations, or politicians. The independence of both the prosecution and the judiciary is not simply an aspiration, it is essential and must be protected.[75]

Mr. Schwendiman's was a genuine concern, and the idea of formulating specific criteria within the internal Guidelines of the Prosecutor's Office for responding to the practical realities of the investigation and prosecution work was entirely reasonable and normal. However, in order for this idea to have practical results and to gain public acceptance, the need for additional criteria apart from those included in the Orientation Criteria and in Annex A, as well as the relationship between such criteria and those put forward by the Prosecutor's Office should have been explained and, ideally, this explanation and the Office's actual criteria should have been submitted for public discussion before their adoption.[76]

---

[74] Schwendiman, 28 September 2007, p. 7, see *supra* note 65.

[75] *Ibid.*

[76] This is what, for example, the ICC Office of the Prosecutor did before adopting its initial policy paper: it widely circulated a draft for comment, just as it conducted two days of open hearings at the Peace Palace in The Hague on the draft *Regulations* of the Office referred to in Section 1.1. above. Both documents had high quality, helping the first ICC Prosecutor to start from a position of strength. Even though the Prosecutor's Office of BiH did open the original version of its Guidelines for comments, their discussion could have been widened. Moreover, the later version of the Guidelines did not seem to be open to comments and criticism, although it significantly changed the list of prioritization criteria.

According to Mr. Schwendiman, the Prosecutor's Office criteria are intended to be articulated for the

> demographic analysis of the conflict to give management a more meaningful and systematic way of selecting the cases that ought to be investigated and prosecuted. All war crimes cases are important, but for a variety of reasons, all of which we have discussed at one time or another, some ought to be done before others and some need more immediate attention than others. Some will likely never be done. What we have been working on is a way to identify which those are and avoid the opportunity costs that come from simply picking low hanging fruit.[77]

Thus, in Mr. Schwendiman's opinion, the set of criteria of the Charging document could reduce the demographic analysis of the conflict to "workable lists",[78] as a "means for making the demographic analysis operational".[79] By applying them, it would be possible to "nominate cases throughout Bosnia and Herzegovina that merit close and early attention".[80] This suggests, then, that from the point of view of the BiH Prosecutor's Office, specific criteria for case selection and prioritization were needed in order to articulate the investigative activities of that Office with its decisions concerning which cases to charge and which to do so first. In particular, such criteria should be sensitive to and supplement the so-called demographic analysis undertaken by that Office at that time to map the patterns of select violations in BiH between 1992 and 1995.

In order to accomplish these specific goals, the original and the later versions of the Prosecution Guidelines incorporated different clusters of criteria, which were foreseen to operate in somewhat distinct ways. As we mentioned earlier, in the first version of the document, criteria were included in the Charging section of the Guidelines as factors aimed at informing the decision of whether or not to charge a given case. According to the Guidelines, this decision should take place only with regards to cases that had already been considered to have "grounded suspicion" – that is, sufficient and admissible evidence suggesting that a conviction is likely to take place and to survive appeal.[81] Moreover, the decision should be taken by applying a "Public Interest test" through which

---

77 Schwendiman, 28 September 2007, p. 7, see *supra* note 65.

78 *Ibid.*

79 Schwendiman, 6 November 2007, p. 8, see *supra* note 23.

80 Schwendiman, 28 September 2007, p. 7, see *supra* note 65.

81 "Prosecution Guidelines", "1. Charging", initial version of November 2007, section 1.5., pp. 7–8, see *supra* note 67.

cases to be charged could be selected not only on the basis of available evidence, but also of their relevance from the point of view of the public interest.[82]

Hence, the criteria included in the Charging section of the Prosecution Guidelines had the purpose of making such a test operational, by indicating the elements that should be taken into account for determining if the prosecution of a case was of public interest. This seemed to mean that criteria were to function as a checklist of requirements for cases to be chosen for charging, and hence as a threshold more characteristic of selection criteria. However, at various stages, the Charging document alluded to criteria as mainly accomplishing a prioritization function consisting in the identification of cases that should be charged first, despite the fact that it does not establish a clear hierarchy among those criteria.

The original version of the Prosecution Guidelines provided three clusters of criteria in its section on Charging: (a) "Factors that relate to the proposed defendant"; (b) "Factors that relate to the circumstances and the impact of the crime when it was committed"; and (c) "Factors that relate to the impact of the case on victims and affected communities".[83]

As regards cluster (a), the document notes that "[p]riority will be given to charging the people who were in positions to order, allow, or create the conditions necessary for the conduct, or who were in a position to prevent it and consciously chose not to, and those in positions of authority or influence who participated directly in the events themselves".[84] This was a very broad formulation. It could well encompass most of the applicable modes of liability in core international crimes cases and, as such, it was not clear how helpful it could be for a case selection process.[85] However, the document provided further elaboration, which somewhat specified the scope of the criteria:

> People on all sides of the conflict who planned and ordered operations, or made it possible for them to occur, those who set events in motion that led to catastrophe, and those who were simply the cadre that did the dirty work, the foot soldiers of the catastrophe, should all be candidates for criminal prosecution. To the extent resources can be committed to making it happen, they should be held to answer in a court as long as they can be identified, as long as there is legally obtained evidence that can be used in a Court in Bosnia and Herzegovina that is strong enough to lead to a conviction, and as long as they can be guaranteed a fair chance to defend

[82] *Ibid.*, section 1.7., pp. 9–10.

[83] *Ibid.*, section 1.5., pp. 9–10.

[84] *Ibid.*, p. 9.

[85] See Bergsmo, Helvig, Utmelidze and Žagovec, 2010, see *supra* note *.

> themselves so that the outcomes are credible and are respected as credible in Bosnia and Herzegovina, in the region and in the world.
>
> Nonetheless, in order to conserve resources and ensure that the greatest number of those who should be held accountable through the imposition of criminal sanctions can be reached, priority must be given to prosecuting those who exerted the greatest influence and occupied or wielded the greatest authority in relation to the crimes the evidence suggests were committed.[86]

In that way, the first cluster seemed to refer to the seniority or level of responsibility of the suspect mainly as a prioritization criterion. Now, as we saw above, this criterion is already covered by the Orientation Criteria and by Annex A of the War Crimes Strategy as an express group of criteria, and it is intended to serve both selection and prioritization purposes. Therefore, although it is a perfectly reasonable criterion, the material merits of which need not be disputed, it is not entirely clear why the Prosecutor's Office considered it necessary to include it in the Charging document again.

On the other hand, Mr. Schwendiman seemed to qualify the importance of seniority as a prioritization criterion when he made the following observation:

> As a practical matter, it may sometimes be necessary for tactical or strategic reasons to pursue smaller or simpler cases against lower-level perpetrators before taking on cases against the highest level leaders. This may be the case where, for example, the trial of lower-level offenders is needed to clarify the precise extent of the crime base. It may also be necessary in order to put potential witnesses, particularly insider witnesses, in a position to testify once convicted or after entering a plea. These should always be exceptions made for justifiable tactical reasons necessary to pursue those with greater liability. It must be understood that the priority that is placed on higher-level offenders in no way vests a person with the right not to be investigated or tried until all his superiors have been prosecuted.[87]

Even though the argument is persuasive, the admission of this kind of exceptionalism is dangerous when dealing with large backlogs of cases and scant resources, as it may be widely used to ignore or reduce the importance of established criteria, and therefore to transform selection and prioritization into mainly discretionary activities leading to unsatisfying results. Surely Mr. Schwendiman was well aware of this fact, both because of his years of experience and his direct knowledge of the ICTY portfolio, which, as we will see below, was for a long

[86] "Prosecution Guidelines", "1. Charging", initial version of November 2007, section 1.5., pp. 9–10, see *supra* note 67.

[87] Schwendiman, 6 November 2007, p. 8, see *supra* note 23.

time characterized by a high number of resource-demanding cases against low-level perpetrators. Copying the ICTY in this respect was likely to lead to a failure of the BiH war crimes process.

Concerning cluster (b), the document states that "in deciding which matters to do in which order, weight should be given to those cases in which the crimes had the greatest impact in the regions or communities where they were committed".[88] This is a novel prioritization criterion, the exact nature of which is elusive at first glance. How does one measure the impact of war crimes on communities? Which criteria are used for such an exercise? Mr. Schwendiman mentions an example of impact analysis:

> In eastern Bosnia and Herzegovina, for example, conduct that resulted in the reduction of the Muslim population in Visegrad Municipality from 60% to nearly zero between April and July 1992, will, in connection with consideration of the level of responsibility of the people involved, be given great weight in determining which matters and which people should be identified for investigation and prosecution by the Special Department for War Crimes.[89]

The Charging document provided some further guidance on how to operationalize this cluster of criteria:

> This determination will be based to a great extent on a credible demographic analysis of the conflict, including assessments based in a reasoned and well informed fashion on the number of confirmed civilian dead, the number of internally displaced persons and the percentage impact on the region from which they were displaced, and on the number, size and nature of camps in a region or community. Questions of ethnicity are at issue, of course, because of the nature of the conflict and the elements of two of the most significant offenses likely to be charged; that is, genocide (Article 171 of the Criminal Code of Bosnia and Herzegovina (CC)) and crimes against humanity (Article 173 of the CC). The demographic analysis of the conflict is the most objective and impartial way available to the Prosecutor's Office for sorting out which cases ought to be done first.[90]

We can see, then, that this is where criteria meet with the demographic analysis which Mr. Schwendiman insisted on when highlighting the need for

[88] "Prosecution Guidelines", "1. Charging", early version of November 2007, section 1.5., p. 10, see *supra* note 67.

[89] Schwendiman, 6 November 2007, p. 10, see *supra* note 23.

[90] "Prosecution Guidelines", "1. Charging", early version of November 2007, section 1.5., p. 10, see *supra* note 67.

criteria-formulation by the State Prosecutor's Office. The inclusion of this cluster of criteria could therefore be a key element in understanding the Office's objective when it formulated its own criteria, as a tool perceived as necessary to connect its demographic analysis of the conflict with case selection and prioritization. The demographic analysis was meant to provide the map of where alleged crimes had the greatest impact on communities and regions. Impact of crimes on communities may be another way of describing the victimization caused by the alleged crimes, and not only displacement. The most serious crimes would normally cause the most serious community impact. Prioritizing cases which caused the most serious victimization would seem to meet broad public acceptance insofar as this is another way of formulating the fundamental gravity consideration, here with reference to the seriousness of the alleged conduct itself.

But cluster (b) did more than reformulating the gravity criterion. By saying that those alleged crimes that caused the greatest impact on communities should be prioritized, the criterion suggests that the communities most affected should, relatively speaking, see more prosecutions of crimes. This entails an implied proposition of representation: there should be a representative relationship between the crimes committed or victimization, on the one hand, and the crimes prioritized for prosecution or the scope of prosecutions, on the other. In other words, the prosecution of war crimes should reflect the degree of victimization caused by the crimes. If understood correctly, this feature of cluster (b) is very important and its possible implications will be discussed further in the concluding remarks of this chapter, as it is also addressed in Section 1.6. above.

Evidently, the application of this feature of cluster (b) is context-specific, in the sense that it requires a prior analysis of the type, specific characteristics, and most significant outcomes of the conflict in question in order to determine which crimes and forms of victimization should be given priority. The four assessments on the grounds of which the demographic analysis of the BiH State Prosecutor's Office based its mapping of community impact seems to corroborate the relevance of context specificity. Such assessments were the following: (i) confirmed civilian dead; (ii) number of internally displaced persons and the percentage impact on the region; (iii) the number, size and nature of camps; and (iv) questions of ethnicity. Perhaps with the exception of the first factor (which is an important assessment element in any context), the other three appear to be specific to the Bosnian conflicts. Indeed, assessments (ii) and (iii) give particular importance to two of many core international crimes committed in the conflict, probably due to the magnitude of victims and to their special impact in certain regions or on certain populations. Also, assessment (iii) is presumably based on the recognition that detention facilities saw an accumulation of different crimes during 1992–1995, not only unlawful detention. Finally, assessment (iv) explicitly refers to the ethnic nature of the Bosnian conflicts.

For the purpose of adequately justifying the use of this feature of cluster (b), the selection of its components (in particular the specific crimes within a broad catalogue of core international crimes committed in BiH) should be explained well in order to avoid criticisms of partiality or arbitrariness that could weaken the case selection and prioritization undertaken by the Prosecutor's Office. Moreover, in order to evaluate the applicability and usefulness of this new cluster of criteria in other national jurisdictions, it should be noted that the specific content of such criteria would necessarily vary depending on the characteristics and outcomes of each particular conflict, which would make it possible to determine and justify which crimes should receive special consideration in terms of representativity.

Finally, regarding cluster (c), the Charging document observed: "consideration will be given to cases involving incidents or offenders where the outcomes are likely to have the greatest impact on a community, a region, or the nation as a whole".[91] Here, the perspective is prospective. The criterion requires an assessment of what the likely impact of criminal justice for crimes or suspects will be on a community wide or narrow. This criterion brings a new quality to the case selection criteria and it appeals to common sense, but it raises concerns at the same time. How can one reliably make the kind of predictions required by the criterion? Are additional criteria necessary to ensure that the predictions are as objective or consistent as possible? Do these additional criteria involve a vision of justice that is more victim-oriented in such a way that it responds to victims' needs and expectations and is not only concerned with delivering criminal justice under a fair trial? What would the implications of such a view be? If this cluster of criteria were to be applied in BiH or to inspire other jurisdictions, it would be useful to adequately address these questions also in order to avoid partiality-related criticisms.

To summarize, the Charging document brought three criteria for prioritization of cases before the State Prosecutor's Office to the table: (i) gravity as in the level of responsibility of the suspects, which did not seem to add much substance to the Orientation Criteria and Annex A of the War Crimes Strategy; (ii) community impact of crimes based on assessments focusing on select crimes and some quantitative information linked to the crimes, which offered a novel and important representative approach; and (iii) community impact of prosecutions, which also offered novel elements that were not present in the Orientation Criteria and Annex A, but which implied some implementation challenges. All

91 *Ibid.*

three criteria were reasonable and seemed to have been carefully considered. Furthermore, the introduction of the two latter novel criteria suggested that the Prosecutor's Office considered it necessary to have particular criteria for the prioritization of cases within that office beyond those contained in the Orientation Criteria and in Annex A, and especially that such criteria should be linked with its demographic analysis of the conflict.

Those considerations appear to be confirmed by the *later* version of the Prosecution Guidelines, which, as mentioned, introduced a new section specifically devoted to case prioritization that includes modified formulations of the clusters of criteria previously contained in the charging section, as well as other additional criteria.[92] According to the Prioritization section of the Guidelines, its criteria are intended to "avoid any appearance that the prioritization of matters is arbitrary or discriminatory, something that may adversely affect confidence in the Prosecutor's Office and the criminal system as a whole".[93] With this explicit goal in mind, the Prioritization section seems to take a step forward *vis-à-vis* earlier BiH documents on criteria, as it recognizes that case prioritization requires that criteria be applied in a particular way which differs from that used for case selection, and which corresponds to the specificities of the prosecutorial task. Indeed, the Prioritization document asserts that, for the purpose of prioritizing cases,

> it is important to have a set of reasonable defensible criteria comprised primarily of factors to be considered, rather than tests to be applied, to assess information and evidence developed from analysis, from reviews of existing files, and from additional investigation to make a reasoned decision regarding whether a matter ought to be taken up sooner rather than later.

And it adds:

> The following criteria are to be used by the Prosecutor to decide priorities for investigation and prosecution. These criteria are only general guidelines for managing subjectivity in selecting which matters will be done in which order. They should be used as a progressive set of sieves through which facts are sifted. They are imperfect because the matters that have to be reviewed are so varied and unique. Nonetheless, the Prosecutor must consider them when making any decision to investigate or prosecute.[94]

In that way, the Prioritization document clearly moves away from the approach of formulating selection and prioritization criteria in one and the same

[92] *Ibid.*, "5. Prioritization", version of February 2009.

[93] *Ibid.*, p. 3.

[94] *Ibid.*, pp. 3–4.

list and not distinguishing between the different ways in which such criteria should be applied for accomplishing each one of those functions. Indeed, the document establishes that its criteria will only serve the purpose of case prioritization, and that such purpose should be accomplished by applying criteria in articulation with the prosecutorial activities of investigation, file reviewing, and evidence assessment. Further, the document specifies that the task of prioritizing cases requires that criteria operate in a particular way, which should not consist in a test – or a checklist or threshold – through which it is assessed whether cases satisfy all the criteria or elements of the test, but rather in a progressive filtering system through which cases are assessed on the basis of criteria applied at different times to gradually sift the cases under consideration.

The Prioritization section of the later version of the Prosecution Guidelines formulates four main clusters of criteria: (a) "gravity", (b) "public interest", (c) case "viability", and (d) prosecutorial "capacity".

The *first* cluster refers to gravity mainly conceived in terms of the "nature and seriousness of the acts that were committed in connection with situations and events that gave rise to criminal activity during the war".[95] However, it also contemplates the status and role of the perpetrator as one of the factors of gravity, by indicating that this makes "part of the 'gravity added' calculus intended to further inform the process of deciding when things will be done".[96] Therefore,

---

[95] *Ibid.*, p. 4. The Prioritization document identifies the following two criteria as the main components of the gravity of crimes' cluster: (i) "Mass murder", "measured both by the number of victims and [...] the impact of the event on the communities affected"; and (ii) "Programmatic violence against the person, including programmatic rape and sexual violence, torture, murder, forcible dislocation, transfer of persons, detention, and programmatic violence to and theft of property of cultural, religious or social significance", the programmatic character of which can be determined by the "number of actors involved, along with the means, methods, and resources used by the actors", the "scale and level of organization involved", and the "improbability of the random occurrence of the acts associated with the violence", as well as by "[a]dditional factors" such as "a plan or policy, stated or implied, underlying the violence, the nature of the violence, the nature of the violence, identifiable patterns of violence and the results of the violence". *Ibid.*, pp. 4–6.

[96] *Ibid.*, p. 7. The factor concerning the status and role of the perpetrator, which is referred to as the "'added' part of the 'gravity added' calculus'", distinguishes between the following categories of perpetrators: (i) "Organizers", which are those "who organized, planned and ordered operations", and "generally […] who were in a position to order, allow, or create the conditions necessary for the events or acts to occur, or who were in a position to prevent them and consciously chose not to, who had the duty to but failed to punish conduct that was contrary to international law committed in connection with the events as required once on notice, and those positions of authority or influence who participated directly in the events and committed acts themselves"; (ii) "Implementers", that is, those who set events in motion that led to culpable

the Prioritization document reintroduces the gravity of crimes as a cluster of criteria that had been excluded from the Charging document contained in the initial version of the Prosecution Strategy, but that was present in both the Orientation Criteria and Annex A. In contrast with the latter two documents, it does not include it as a cluster separate from that of the status and role of perpetrators. Instead, the document incorporates the latter criterion as a relevant yet subordinate factor of gravity, which is to be considered only in case the other gravity factors are not enough to conclude that a case should be prioritized. That is why the document refers to the status and role of perpetrators as an "added" criterion within the gravity cluster, which establishes "additional sieves" "intended to further sift how the actors should be ranked for attention".[97]

Consequently, the Prioritization document establishes a hierarchy between the criteria referring to the nature and seriousness of crimes and the criteria referring to the status and role of the perpetrator, which enables the Prosecutor's Office to rank cases in terms of their priority for prosecution, firstly, on the basis of the gravity of crimes and, only if this is not enough, on the basis of the status and role of perpetrators. Moreover, the document also establishes a clear hierarchy among the criteria that compose the gravity cluster,[98] on the one hand, and among the elements that compose the "added" gravity factor of the status and

---

acts, most often acting according to instructions, directions or according to plans communicated to them in one way or another by the organizers; and (iii) "Foot Soldiers", corresponding to those "who committed individual acts of cruelty". *Ibid.*, pp. 7–8.

97 *Ibid.*, p. 7.

98 Within the gravity of crimes cluster of criteria, the Prioritization document establishes that mass murder is the "most grave of the acts committed during the war", and constitutes the "presumptive starting point for deciding when matters will be investigated and prosecuted by the Special Department for War Crimes". Later, the document points out that programmatic violence is "another presumptive starting point for deciding what the Special Department for War Crimes will do with its resources and when". However, it subsequently states:

> Programmatic violence may also feature acts short of murder and mass murder [...], but the events should be analyzed as a whole and after murder should be sifted in the following general order: [...] [i] Violence inflicted on a group, defined by nationality, ethnicity, race or religion, that included imposing conditions of life calculated to bring about the group's physical destruction, in whole or in part, as well as imposing measures intended to prevent births within such a group, forcibly transferring children from one group to another, causing serious mental and physical harm to members of a group, all with the aim to destroy the group, in whole or in part; [ii] Enforced disappearance; [iii] Sexual violence, including rape; [iv] Detention (imprisonment, severe deprivation of physical liberty), torture, enslavement, inhumane treatment; [v] Forcible dislocation and transfer of populations.

Consequently, the document ranks crimes in terms of their gravity in the following order: mass murder, programmatic violence leading to mass murder or murder, and other forms or programmatic violence. It then establishes a hierarchy among the latter acts ([i] through [v] in the previous quote). *Ibid.*, pp. 4–7.

role of the perpetrator,[99] on the other hand, which allows ranking cases *within* each of those groups of factors as well. In so doing, the document represents advancement with respect to the previous three documents on criteria developed in BiH concerning the operationalization of prioritization criteria. In fact, it does not merely recognize the need of applying prioritization criteria in a particular way; it also establishes a concrete mechanism through which such criteria can be actually applied in that way. Such mechanism consists in the establishment of hierarchies between different sets of criteria as well as within groups of criteria, which facilitates the ranking of cases on the basis of their priority.

A further advancement made with the formulation of this first cluster in the Prioritization document consists in the fact that it is able to group gravity criteria in more comprehensive and, at the same time, more precise factors, which makes it possible for the classification of criteria to distance itself from the particularism of concrete crimes, and to be grounded on wider categories applicable to different types of cases.

The *second* cluster of criteria, referred to as "public interest", includes six subgroups of criteria: (i) "Geographic and temporal impact";[100] (ii) "Community impact";[101] (iii) "Impact on [the likelihood of] Return";[102] (iv) "Impact on [the possibility of] Location, Recovery and Reunification of Remains";[103] (v) "Impact on Governance"[104]; and (vi) "Impact on the advancement or development

[99] Indeed, the Prioritization document specifies that perpetrators considered to have acted as organizers "are presumptive candidates for high priority attention", that "*[i]mplementers are also presumptive candidates for attention, but to a lesser degree than organizers*" (italics in the original), and that foot soldiers "are the lowest in priority, unless their conduct was widespread, occurring over large geographic areas, over prolonged periods of time, or involved acts that were so wanton and cruel in nature that they had and perhaps continue to have an effect on communities generally". *Ibid.*, pp. 7–8.

[100] Which refers to "[e]vents and acts that affected a large geographic area […] an took place over days or hours" and which are therefore "likely to have resulted in greater overall damage during the war". *Ibid.*, p. 8.

[101] Which refers to "[e]vents and acts that had significant impact on the communities affected […]; acts of such sustained wanton cruelty as to affect the long term physical or mental health of large numbers of people involved in an event or situation". *Ibid.*, p. 9.

[102] The document refers to the probability that the results of "[i]nvestigations and prosecutions of events and acts" will "significantly promote or create a reasonable likelihood for return". *Ibid.*, p. 9.

[103] The document refers to the likelihood that the results of "[i]nvestigations and prosecutions of events and acts" will "lead to the location, recovery and reunification of remains and the identification and return of the missing". *Ibid.*, pp. 9–10.

[104] The document refers to the probability that "[i]nvestigations and prosecutions of events […] are likely to result in the removal or suspension of individuals who occupy current positions of authority or governance […] and as to whom evidence suggests they are criminally liable for their conduct during the war". *Ibid.*, p. 10.

of international humanitarian law".[105] Thus, this cluster of criteria classifies cases of public interest in terms of the different types of impact that they can have and that would seem to justify their prioritization, even if they do not comply with the gravity criteria.

By using this comprehensive cluster, the Prioritization document collapses into one single category clusters (a) and (b) of the criteria contained in the Charging section of the initial version of the Prosecution Strategy, which referred, respectively, to the regional and community impact of the crime at the time of its commission and to the impact that its investigation and prosecution could have on communities. Indeed, some of the criteria contained in the Prioritization document refer to the impact of events and acts when they were committed (notably criteria (i) and (ii)) and others to the possible impact of the investigation and prosecution of such events and acts (criteria (iii) through (vi)). In that way, this second cluster of criteria is not original as it builds on the criteria already contained in the Charging document. However, it does constitute an advancement with respect to the latter document in the sense that it formulates these criteria in a more comprehensive and yet more precise manner, which identifies the common element among the different criteria of the cluster (their potential impact on communities), but also distinguishes them in terms of the different types of impact they produce.

In recognizing the novel criteria introduced by the Charging document, the Prioritization document endorses the former document's apparent concern with the relationship between the demographic analysis of the Prosecutor's Office and prioritization criteria. However, while doing so, the document does not progress much in overcoming the challenges faced by the formulation of such new criteria that were mentioned above (the need to justify the use of criteria that point at the degree of victimization or representativity as a relevant prioritization feature, as well as the difficulties of predicting the impact of criminal justice and of using victim-oriented criteria).

On the other hand, the second cluster is not as clear as the first in establishing a hierarchy among the criteria it contains. In effect, it refers to priority with respect to each one of those criteria. However, the way in which it formulates such references suggests that a hierarchy of the sort exists and functions in an ascendant order, the first criteria being higher ranked. Thus, the document es-

[105] With respect to this criterion, the document states: "Investigations and prosecutions should be conducted with a view to developing a war crimes jurisprudence in Bosnia and Herzegovina that is consistent with settled principles of international humanitarian law, both conventional and customary. They should also be conducted with the advancement and development of international humanitarian law in mind". *Ibid.*, p. 10.

tablishes that events corresponding to criteria (i) and (ii) are "presumptive candidates for priority attention", that events corresponding to criteria (iii) through (v) "should be considered candidates for priority attention", and that criterion (vi), "[t]hough not a governing factor", implies that "investigations and prosecutions that offer opportunities for advancing and developing international humanitarian law ought to be considered candidates for priority attention".[106]

The *third* cluster of criteria included in the Prioritization document refers to "Viability", conceived as the need of "determining whether it is likely that an event will yield viable prosecutions in the end".[107] According to the document, the application of this cluster defines "whether further resources […] should be invested in investigating a matter that is a candidate for priority attention".[108] And it includes as relevant factors for that purpose: whether there exist potential accused and witnesses who are living and available; whether it is likely that, at the time of trial, there will be enough evidence "to support a criminal conviction that will withstand reasonable appeal"; and whether there exist "adequate legal theories to support successful prosecutions".[109] In that way, the criteria within this cluster seem to work as a threshold or test because only if all such criteria are fulfilled can a case be considered viable.

As can be seen, the inclusion of the conditions required for a case to be considered viable from the point of view of criminal prosecution as a cluster of prioritization criteria is novel in the discussion about criteria in BiH. Indeed, none of the previously examined documents have referred to viability as a selection or prioritization criterion, but they have highlighted the relevance of assuring case viability for the prosecutorial strategy. Moreover, this cluster of criteria seems to be hierarchically superior to the first and second clusters, even though its applicability is dependent on the prior passing of the filters imposed by such clusters. Indeed, according to the Prioritization document, "[u]nless a matter is likely to yield viable prosecutions it should be set aside in favor of other matters that will".[110] This implies that although gravity and public interest seem to be required conditions for a case to be a candidate for priority by the Prosecutor's Office, such case should only be considered a priority if it complies with the viability criteria. In other words, the satisfaction of the two former clus-

---

[106] *Ibid.*, pp. 8–10.

[107] *Ibid.*, pp. 10–11.

[108] *Ibid.*, p. 10.

[109] *Ibid.*, pp. 10–11.

[110] *Ibid.*, p. 11.

ters of criteria is a necessary but not a sufficient condition for priority and, inversely, the satisfaction of the viability cluster is a sufficient but not a necessary condition for priority.

Assuring that cases selected for priority prosecution are viable constitutes a key objective for any successful prosecutorial strategy, especially for adequately dealing with the problem of a large backlog of cases. Nevertheless, it does not seem entirely accurate or convenient to treat case viability as a prioritization criterion. On the one hand, viability is so vital for the prosecution strategy in general and for the goal of dealing with case backlog in particular, that restricting it to the concrete task of prioritizing cases does not seem entirely appropriate. On the other hand, establishing viability as a sufficient criterion for case prioritization without which a case that complies with the gravity and the public interest criteria should not be considered a priority, risks rendering these other criteria irrelevant as their application could always be overridden by arguments pointing at the insufficient satisfaction of viability factors. This is all the more problematic given that, with respect to many of these factors (notably sufficiency of evidence and existence of legal theory), the determination of whether they have been fulfilled is a matter of interpretation and can therefore be submitted to subjective and even arbitrary readings aimed at rendering the other prioritization criteria inapplicable. This does not mean that viability is unimportant; quite on the contrary, it is its fundamental importance which suggests that it should be a central part of the prosecutorial strategy instead of a mere prioritization criterion, and also that it should not be used for blocking the operation of other prioritization criteria.

The *fourth* and last cluster of criteria refers to "Capacity", understood as the existence of "available resources in the Special Department for War crimes" for prosecuting priority cases.[111] The cluster includes as factors to be assessed for determining whether this criterion is met: an "[a]dequate number of staff" with the "[a]dequate and appropriate knowledge, abilities and skills", an "adequate space and appropriate facilities", an "adequate and appropriate witness protection capacity", and an "[e]ffective witness support".[112] According to the document, in "deciding whether a matter should receive priority attention a careful assessment of available resources in the Special Department for War Crimes must be made".[113] Hence, even though the Prioritization document puts it in less explicit terms than in the case of viability, it seems like the capacity factor also constitutes a sufficient (but not necessary) condition for a case to receive priority

[111] *Ibid.*

[112] *Ibid.*, pp. 11–12.

[113] *Ibid.*, p. 11.

attention (in the sense that a case considered to be a priority from the point of view of the gravity and public interest criteria, and even of the viability criteria, could possibly not receive priority prosecution in the event that there were not enough resources for that purpose in the terms of the capacity criteria).

Almost all the considerations made with regards to the viability criteria apply here as well. Indeed, the existence of capacity to prosecute, defined in terms of sufficient and appropriate resources, constitutes a further fundamental matter for prosecutorial services, not only from the point of view of the strategy, but also, at a more basic level, for their actual operation and outcome production. As such, the need to guarantee the existence of sufficient and adequate capacity should not be restricted to a matter of case prioritization. Furthermore, the use of capacity as a prioritization criterion can be problematic, especially if it is given a higher hierarchical status than that of other existing criteria, because it can easily be manipulated as a mechanism to block the operation of other criteria, thus rendering prioritization decisions arbitrary.

In brief, the Prioritization section of the later version of the Prosecution Guidelines incorporates four clusters of case prioritization criteria: (a) *gravity*, mainly understood in terms of the nature and seriousness of crimes, but including a complementary factor related to the status and role of perpetrators; (b) *public interest*, conceived in terms both of the impact of crimes at the time of their occurrence and of the impact of prosecutions; (c) *case viability*, understood as the likelihood of priority cases yielding feasible prosecutions; and (d) *prosecutorial capacity*, conceived in terms of the sufficiency and appropriateness of resources for prosecuting priority cases. The first two clusters do not introduce novel criteria with respect to prior documents on criteria developed in BiH, but rather reorient the approach and formulate the categories in more comprehensive or precise terms. In that way, these criteria reinforce the Prosecutor Office's view that they are needed for accomplishing its particular tasks. Yet, there are some questions concerning the convenience and operationalization of these criteria, especially of those contained in the public interest cluster. In contrast, the last two clusters are novel in the discussion about selection and prioritization criteria despite the fact that they refer to central issues for prosecutorial services around the world. In fact, the main issue that these new clusters raise is precisely whether they should be incorporated into prioritization criteria or should instead continue to be treated as key elements of the wider prosecutorial strategy.

The Prosecution Guidelines illustrate that the discussion on selection and prioritization criteria in BiH developed in a quite thorough and sophisticated way, making progress towards the goal of establishing adequate and applicable criteria for selecting and prioritizing cases in an impartial and transparent way in that country, as well as making key contributions towards the discussion on criteria in other territorial and international jurisdictions. The discourse on criteria in some of the latter jurisdictions will now be analysed.

5.3. Some Contributions of International Criminal Justice to the Formulation of Selection and Prioritization Criteria

The topic of case selection and prioritization criteria is not only important for national jurisdictions. By nature, international criminal tribunals can only deal with a handful of cases, since they are either established for a limited period of time (as is the case with *ad hoc* jurisdictions for a specific situation) or have subsidiary jurisdiction over core international crimes (as is the case with the ICC). In that sense, these tribunals must necessarily select a few cases from a pool of many – atrocities committed on a massive and systematic scale in a situation of armed conflict or authoritarianism in the first case, throughout the world in the second – and then decide which to process first. They must do so with the awareness that their efficacy and legitimacy will be largely assessed on the basis of the results such cases produce.

As mentioned in Section 5.1. above, for international criminal jurisdictions, the issue of case selection may be more pressing and thornier than that of prioritization – while the opposite could be said for territorial jurisdictions. Indeed, given that their incapability and unsuitability for processing the majority of cases over which they have potential competence is one of their key features, selecting cases constitutes not only one of their most relevant roles, but also probably the one that determines most clearly the impact that they will have on the struggle against impunity. However, case prioritization is also quite relevant for international criminal tribunals, as the length of their proceedings combined with the public's expectation of results may make the evaluation of their performance depend largely on the first cases they decide.

Despite the considerable importance of selection and prioritization in the activity of these tribunals, criteria for regulating such tasks did not receive much attention in the discussions on the establishment of the first contemporary international criminal tribunals, namely, the ICTY in 1993 and the International Criminal Tribunal for Rwanda ('ICTR') in 1994. Instead, the need to formulate and employ such criteria has mainly evolved in the practice of those tribunals, generating fragmented yet interesting solutions to the problems of selecting the most important cases and of deciding which of them to prosecute first. In contrast, the establishment of the ICC came to acknowledge the decisive relevance of case selection and prioritization, contributing to placing the issue of criteria more prominently in discussions and legal formulations.

In what follows, the criteria for case selection and prioritization that have been formulated and adopted first at the ICTY (5.3.1.) and subsequently at the ICC (5.3.2.) will be discussed. These jurisdictions exemplify two different ways in which, as just mentioned, criteria have been understood in international criminal justice: in the course of the tribunal's practice in the case of the ICTY, and with awareness at the time of the establishment of the tribunal itself in the case of the ICC. These two courts are important for the particularly relevant contributions they can make to the discussion on case selection and prioritization criteria. The ICTY's practice led to the recognition of a need to develop and use criteria, and to the first international advancements of such development. Both the ICC Statute and practice have acknowledged the importance of criteria and made contributions in terms of their formulation and application.

5.3.1. Criteria in the International Criminal Tribunal for the Former Yugoslavia

The establishment of the ICTY by the UN Security Council in 1993 was the first experience of international criminal justice after the Cold War,[114] and it was followed by a boom of international and mixed tribunals in different parts of the world as mentioned in Section 1.2. above.[115] In spite of the fact that the ICTY was created as a temporary jurisdiction – which underlined the practical impossibility of prosecuting all perpetrators of atrocity in the ex-Yugoslavia wars – its Statute and Rules did not contain any reference to case selection or prioritization criteria. Instead, the initial version of the Statute foresaw quite a broad mandate for the Tribunal, consisting in the prosecution and trial of "persons responsible for serious violations of international humanitarian law committed in the territory of the former Yugoslavia between 1 January 1991 and a date to be determined by the Security Council upon the restoration of peace".[116]

---

[114] Before the Cold War, quite important advancements towards the consolidation of international criminal justice had taken place, and the establishment of the Nuremberg and Tokyo *ad hoc* tribunals for prosecuting and judging perpetrators of atrocities committed during the World War II were the most important of them. However, these advancements and the trend to establish international criminal tribunals were brought to a standstill during the Cold War. They were renewed in the late 1980s with the issuance of new treaties (like the Convention against Torture and other Cruel, Inhuman or Degrading Treatment or Punishment, see *supra* note 2) containing core international cases and mechanisms to give efficacy to the struggle against impunity (such as extradition and universal jurisdiction). In the 1990s, these advances and trends were significantly accelerated by the creation of *ad hoc* international or hybrid tribunals (the first of which was the ICTY, followed by the ICTR) and by the establishment of the ICC.

[115] Apart from the ICTR, these tribunals include the special courts for Sierra Leone, Lebanon, Cambodia and East Timor.

[116] UN Security Council Resolution 827 (1992), "Establishing an International Tribunal for the Prosecution of Persons Responsible for Serious Violations of International Humanitarian Law Committed in the Territory of the Former Yugoslavia", see *supra* note 14. Since its issuance, the Statue has been amended by Resolutions 1166 (1998), 13 May 1998 (https://www.legal-tools.org/doc/96205a/); 1329 (2000), 30 November 2000 (https://www.legal-tools.org/doc/b1b6cc/); 1411 (2002), 17 May 2002 (https://www.legal-tools.org/doc/7fa380/); 1431 (2002),

This mandate does not suggest the existence of case selection criteria. Indeed, it does not distinguish between cases neither in terms of the degree of rank or responsibility of perpetrators nor the level of gravity of the violations referred to. According to Claudia Angermaier, even though some (notably the first President of the ICTY, Antonio Cassese) have

> argued that such a limitation can be inferred from Article 1 of the ICTY Statute – which provided that "persons responsible for serious violations of inter-national humanitarian law" were subject to prosecution before the Tribunal – the drafting process arguably suggests that there was a deliberate choice not to limit the jurisdictional mandate to senior persons. In establishing the Tribunal, the Security Council did not follow the only prior example of an international tribunal, the Nuremberg Tribunal, which had a clear division of competencies – namely that only the trial of major war criminals was to be conducted before the Nuremberg Tribunal, and minor war criminals were to be prosecuted by other courts.[117]

As Angermaier points out, the fact that the ICTY Statute did not make any explicit reference to a limitation in the Tribunal's jurisdiction or competencies shows that, in contrast with the Nuremberg Tribunal, the ICTY was originally conceived as a court with a wide competency over all perpetrators and crimes. This can also be deduced from a comparison between the ICTY Statute with that of later tribunals such as the Special Court for Sierra Leone ('SCSL') and the Extraordinary Chambers in the Courts of Cambodia ('ECCC'), which respectively refer to "persons who bear the greatest responsibility" and "senior leaders […] who were most responsible for crimes".[118]

So, from the beginning of the ICTY's proceedings, there were no restrictions concerning cases that the Tribunal should choose for investigation, prosecution and trial, nor were there criteria for deciding which to prosecute first. As a result, in the Tribunal's starting phase, cases were mainly selected on

---

14 August 2002 (https://www.legal-tools.org/doc/2e567b/); 1481 (2003), 19 May 2003 (https://www.legal-tools.org/doc/8a17e4/); 1597 (2005), 20 April 2005 (https://www.legal-tools.org/doc/2ad5a0/); 1660 (2006), 28 February 2006 (https://www.legal-tools.org/doc/bb44da/); 1837 (2008), 29 September 2008 (https://www.legal-tools.org/doc/84c4b4/); 1877 (2009), 7 July 2009 (https://www.legal-tools.org/doc/4b06b3/); and 2306 (2016), of 6 September 2016 (https://www.legal-tools.org/doc/68b41c/).

[117] Claudia Angermaier, Chapter 8 of this book, Section 8.2., citing Larry Johnson, "Ten Years Later: Reflections on the Drafting", in *Journal of International Criminal Justice*, 2004, vol. 2, no. 2, pp. 368–369.

[118] Cited in *ibid.*

the basis of evidence availability and of the interest of individual ICTY prosecutors in particular cases.[119] What is more, the early indictments concerned relatively low-level perpetrators such as camp guards.[120]

This generated deep concern among ICTY judges who thought the ICTY Office of the Prosecutor ('ICTY-OTP') was utilizing a "bottom-up approach" according to which low-level perpetrators should be prosecuted first, while, in their view, the Tribunal should "immediately target the military and political leaders or other high ranking commanders".[121] Judges decided to express their disagreement with the Prosecutor's approach both in a meeting they held with him and in a public declaration in which they stated to be concerned with the compatibility of the practice of indictments with the international community's expectations concerning the work of the ICTY.[122]

The first ICTY Prosecutor, Richard J. Goldstone, opposed the judges' intervention in the Prosecutor's affairs – especially their requests for reports on the progress of investigations – and thought it to be an attempt against the Prosecutor's independence, compromising the judges' impartiality.[123] Nevertheless, soon after the judges' criticisms, in October 1995, the ICTY-OTP decided to formally adopt an internal document that contained a list of "Criteria for Investigations and Prosecutions". These criteria were conceived as a set of rational standards that should allow the OTP to more effectively use its resources and enable it to fulfil its mandate, by guiding its decisions on "whether or not to initiate an investigation and/or prosecution in any particular case".[124]

Undoubtedly, this list of criteria could be seen as a significant advancement in the issue of case selection and prioritization both because it implied explicit recognition of the urgent need for criteria, and because it included many relevant factors mostly for selecting cases. However, the adoption of the list does not seem to have been enough to guarantee a rational and strategically sound practice of case selection, as it did not establish clear guidelines for the application

---

[119] Bergsmo, Helvig, Utmelidze and Žagovec, 2010, see *supra* note *.

[120] Angermaier, Chapter 8 of this book.

[121] Antonio Cassese, "The ICTY: A Living and Vital Reality", in *Journal of International Criminal Justice*, 2004, vol. 2, no. 2, p. 586, cited in *ibid.*

[122] Angermaier, Chapter 8 of this book.

[123] Richard J. Goldstone, "A View From the Prosecution", in *Journal of International Criminal Justice*, 2004, vol. 2, no. 2, pp. 380–381, cited in *ibid.*

[124] ICTY-OTP, "Internal Memorandum", 17 October 1995. This document was made available for consultation to one of the authors. The ICTY-OTP's work on criteria for case selection and prioritization involved at one and the same time selection criteria and attempts to formalize the decision-making process on selection.

of criteria and the latter were not consistently applied by prosecutors (some of whom were not aware of the existence of the criteria at the time).

The ICTY-OTP criteria were divided into five groups: (a) "Persons", which refers to "the position of the perpetrator"; (b) the "Serious violations", which refers to the "nature of the violation"; (c) "Policy Considerations"; (d) "Practical Considerations"; and (e) "Other Relevant Considerations".[125] Each group has a comprehensive list of factors, amounting more to a catalogue of relevant considerations than to a selective, focused list of binding criteria. Neither the groups of criteria nor the factors each of them contains were ranked according to weight. They were meant to be considered as a whole when evaluating the merits of potential investigations and prosecutions. Consequently, they were conceived more as selection than prioritization criteria, and even so they did not establish a solid ground for case selection as they included a mixture of factors that do not allow a clear identification of the threshold for cases to be selected.

Concerning *group (a)*,[126] the list represents quite a mixture of factors relevant to the suspect (including his or her "Position, formal and actual authority, role and notoriety"), combined with practical considerations (such as "Arrest potential" and "Evidence/Witness availability"), the policy consideration of specific "targets" (such as members of the media, government or non-governmental organizations ('NGOs')), and tactical considerations of an evidentiary nature (namely "Potential roll-over witness and likelihood of linkage evidence"). The combination of these factors makes it difficult to equate the group with any particular interest, such as gravity in the sense of level of responsibility. As a matter of fact, it is not easy to see what all the factors in the group have in common.

In that sense, this list could perhaps be useful for verifying whether any of its factors is explicitly referred to in the criteria documents developed in BiH, such as the suspect's knowledge of acts committed by his or her subordinates and the targeting of specific sectors (which could be included as gravity criteria), or the existence of roll-over witnesses or of the probability of linkage evidence (which could be included in the criteria that refer to practical considerations). However, it seems like the clusters of criteria that refer to the role and level of responsibility of the suspect in the three BiH documents – the "Perpetrator" cluster in the Orientation Criteria, the cluster referring to the seriousness of the level of responsibility of the suspect in the Charging document of the BiH Prosecutor's Office, and the "added" criteria on the status and role of the perpetrator

[125] *Ibid.*, pp. 2–4.

[126] Group (a) ("Persons") has the following factors listed: "Position in hierarchy under investigation", "Political Official", "Military Official", "Para-Military Commander", "Nationality", "Role/Participation in Policy/Strategy Decisions", "Personal culpability for specific atrocities", "Arrest potential", and "Evidence/Witness availability". *Ibid.*

contained in the gravity cluster of the Prioritization section of the later version of the Prosecution Guidelines – are both more comprehensive and precise lists of criteria linked to the suspect than ICTY's group (a).

As for *group (b)*,[127] related to the serious nature of the violation, several factors deal with the gravity of the alleged conduct, such as the number of victims and the duration and repetition of the offence. However, it is unclear exactly what is meant by some factors like "Nature of act(s)", "Area of destruction" and "Showcase or pattern crime". The nature of acts may refer to the seriousness of the crimes in question. The area of destruction, along with the location of the crimes and the nationality of perpetrators and victims (also included as factors in the list) may be relevant for the consideration that there should be 'representativity' between criminal victimization and the scope of prosecutions. And the reference to patterns seems to suggest that priority should be given to crimes committed in a systematic way, in accordance with prior research of the conflict's victimization trends. Besides these factors, the list adds a new tactical consideration: "Linkage to other cases". Also, it simply reproduces three factors from group (a), that is, arrest potential, evidence or witness availability, and the targeting of media, government and NGOs.

The factors included in group (b) seem to refer to the seriousness of the violation more in terms of its impact than in terms of the type of offence it constitutes. In that sense, as criteria related to the nature of crimes, both the first cluster of the Orientation Criteria (which refers to the nature of the crimes and seems to set an order of seriousness for them) and the first cluster of Annex A of the War Crimes Strategy of BiH (labelled "Gravity of criminal offences") are more precise. Nonetheless, these clusters could be enriched by some factors included in ICTY's group (b) of criteria, which refer to factual categories that are quite relevant for pinning down the gravity of a crime, such as the number of victims and the duration and repetition of the acts.

On the other hand, the emphasis of group (b) on the impact of crimes and its reference to categories that evoke the notion of representativity coincide with the second clusters of both the initial and later version of BiH Prosecution Guidelines – which refer to "Factors that relate to the circumstances and the impact of the crime when it was committed" and to "public interest" criteria, respectively. This is worth highlighting because it shows that there is a deep concern with assuring that criminal processes reflect the degree and types of

127 Group (b) ("Serious Violation") includes the following factors: "Number of victims", "Nature of act(s)", "Area of destruction", "Duration or repetition of the offence", "Location of crime", "Linkage to other cases", "Nationality of perpetrators/victims", "Arrest potential", "Evidence/Witness availability", and "Showcase or pattern crime". *Ibid.*

victimization that took place in the situation under analysis, which is shared by the Prosecutor's offices of BiH and the ICTY.

Despite their limitations, the criteria of the BiH Prosecutor's Office discussed above appear to constitute more comprehensive and precise categories for dealing with this issue than those offered by the ICTY-OTP, as they comprise more forms of crime impact that seem relevant for establishing representativity, and yet they are formulated in terms that point to the idea of impact in a clearer and more direct way. For this reason, as well as for the fact that – as we mentioned before – criteria related to the impact of crimes should be selected and applied on the basis of a previous demographic analysis, it is doubtful that criteria documents in BiH can benefit much from considering ICTY's group (b) criteria.

Concerning *group (c)*,[128] which refers to "Policy Considerations", the list includes a series of factors related to the potential impact that prosecutions and trials can have on the struggle against impunity, such as the willingness and ability of national courts to prosecute the alleged perpetrator and the potential symbolic or deterrent value of prosecution, the public perception of the ICTY's performance (concerning its immediate response, its functioning and its impartiality and balance), and the development of international jurisprudence in terms of precedent establishment and norm reinforcement.

Since they were created on the basis of the ICTY policy and strategy, some of these factors may not be directly applicable in national contexts like that of BiH, such as those concerning the advancement of international jurisprudence. Nevertheless, they all suggest interesting considerations that could be interpreted to serve the policy objectives of territorial jurisdictions. Thus, for instance, at the territorial level, the factors related to jurisprudence could be aimed at developing national jurisprudence on core international crimes that is consistent with the international standards on the matter, just as the sixth factor of the second cluster of the BiH Prosecution Guidelines ("Impact on the advancement or development of international humanitarian law") does. Also, at the territorial level, the factors concerning public perception could be formulated in terms of the legitimacy requirements of national courts.

Policy considerations tend to be practical realities in prosecution services – they are simply made in response to practical needs in the actual work on cases. When such considerations are made, it might be worth to articulate them and

[128] Group (c) ("Policy considerations") involves these factors: "Advancement of International Legal Jurisprudence" ("Indictments" to: "reinforce important existing norms and precepts", "build precedent", "clarify and advance the scope of existing protections"), "Willingness and ability of National Courts to prosecute the alleged perpetrator", and "Potential symbolic or deterrent value of prosecution". *Ibid.*

make them public in the interest of transparency, to the extent operational requirements allow. Whether policy factors such as those listed in group (c) *should* be included in a list of criteria for the selection and prioritization of cases is another matter.

None of the reviewed BiH documents on case selection and prioritization criteria contain an express reference to policy considerations among the listed criteria. However, some of the criteria included therein could well be described as policy considerations, such as the "Consequences of the crime for the local community" factor contained in the "Other Circumstances" cluster of Annex A of the War Crimes Strategy, and the third cluster of the initial and later version of the Prosecution Guidelines labelled "community impact of the prosecution". Indeed, these criteria indicate that cases should be selected and prioritized on the basis of their potentialities for producing a large and adequate impact on communities, which undoubtedly amount to important policy considerations.

The question that emerges is whether it would add any value to label such factors as policy considerations or criteria. There are at least two arguments against doing so. First, it would be less transparent insofar as such labelling may not allow clear identification of the specific criteria on the basis of which cases are selected, but would rather cover many possible categories under the less precise notion of policy considerations. Secondly, the term 'policy' is itself ambiguous and can easily be used as a synonym of broad discretionary decision-making, which could undermine the whole purpose of the establishment of criteria. Consequently, policy considerations should be used by prosecutors of core international crimes at both the international and national levels in a cautious manner, seeking to explain which specific criteria underpin the categorization in each case.

On its turn, *group (d)*[129] refers to "Practical Considerations", and it contains factors related to the availability of resources, information and evidence, as well as to the investigations' duration, timing and impact on other investigations. Thus, group (d) makes reference to resource availability just as the BiH Orientation Criteria does generically, and as the later version of the BiH Prosecution Guidelines does specifically under its fourth cluster of criteria related to the capacity to prosecute. As we said when we analysed the latter document, the availability of resources constitutes a fundamentally important element of any

[129] Group (d) ("Practical considerations") contains these factors: "Available Investigative resources", "Impact that the new investigation will have on ongoing Investigations and on making existing Indictments trial ready", "The estimated time to complete the Investigation", "Timing of the Investigation (for example, the impact initiating a particular investigation will have on the ability to conduct future investigations in the country)", and "Likelihood of arrest of the alleged perpetrator". *Ibid.*

prosecutorial strategy; nonetheless, it is doubtful that it should be included as a case selection or prioritization criterion, since it seems to be a more general goal that is not limited to these tasks, and since it could easily be interpreted in an arbitrary way to hinder the applicability of other criteria.

On the other hand, group (d) refers to other practical considerations related to the availability of information and evidence. As we have seen, groups (a) and (b) of the ICTY-OTP criteria both contain factors that constitute practical considerations, some of which are reproduced in this group once again – that is, arrest potential and completeness of evidence (described as evidence or witness availability in groups (a) and (b)). In order to avoid confusion, repeated factors should be eliminated, and each factor should only appear in the cluster in which it best fits, which, in the case of the latter factors, is evidently cluster or group (d). Apart from evidence completeness, group (d) contains three additional evidentiary and informational considerations: first, the existence of other work carried out in relation to the case, meaning fact-finding, investigative or prosecutorial work, with a view to benefiting from such efforts; second, the availability of exculpatory information and evidence, which would have a negative effect on the decision to prosecute; and third, the existence of other OTP investigations in the same geographical area, which can be conceived as an evidentiary consideration broadly speaking.

These new factors are quite relevant for the prosecutorial strategy of a jurisdiction dealing with core international crimes, as they point to the need of taking into account the state of the case, and especially its readiness to be prosecuted and the likelihood of it generating an indictment and a conviction. These factors were also considered in two BiH documents: the Orientation Criteria's third cluster labelled "Other Considerations", which included four criteria related to the readiness to proceed ("'Insider' or 'Suspect' witnesses", "Allegations connected with events which have already been the subject of a previous trial at ICTY", "Case is document heavy" and "Difficult issues of law"), and the more recent version of the BiH Prosecution Guidelines, the third cluster of which refers to the viability of cases in terms of their potentiality of yielding viable prosecutions, and includes criteria like accused and witness availability, evidence sufficiency and adequacy of legal theories.

Comparison of these different factors would have been useful for both the ICTY and the BiH Prosecutor's Office, to see whether they should have complemented their lists of practical considerations related to information and evidence availability. However, here again the question emerges as to whether such considerations should be formulated as criteria (selection or prioritization) or if they should instead be conceived as key objectives of the prosecutorial strategy that are not restricted to the application of criteria and that should not hinder it.

Indeed, depending on the function one wants to give to case selection and prioritization criteria, it could be argued that the latter should only be considered after inculpatory and exculpatory assessments have already been made, which would imply that evidentiary considerations should not be part of the criteria but should be considered before their application. This would surely be the case for files that have already been investigated and need to be prioritized for their prosecution and trial. However, for the selection of cases to be actually investigated by a jurisdiction, evidentiary considerations could be thought of as relevant criteria.

Finally, group (d) lists three temporal factors, one of which – the estimated time to complete the investigation – falls squarely within the general category 'readiness to proceed'. The other two – impact on ongoing investigations and on making existing indictments trial ready, and contextual timing of the investigation – point beyond the specific case at hand, and apparently have not been considered by any of the reviewed BiH documents on criteria. In contrast with the other components of group (d), these factors concern the impact of prosecutions, and they could therefore be useful for complementing the BiH Prosecution Guidelines' public interest cluster, which refers to the impact of prosecutions in many aspects, but not so much on other investigations or on the prosecution strategy as a whole as these factors seem to. Again, though, the use of criteria related to the impact of investigations should be adequately justified in order to guarantee transparency and to avoid perceptions of arbitrariness.

The last group of criteria conceived by the ICTY-OTP, *group (e)*,[130] refers to "Other Relevant Considerations". It offers an interesting and quite novel list of factors, several of which are legal in nature. First, the list refers to the "particular statutory offence or parts thereof, that can be charged". It does not explain which quality of the offence is relevant as a criterion. We are left to speculate that it might be its seriousness, but it could also refer to the evidentiary burden of the elements of the crime. Secondly, the list includes the "charging theories available" in the case, as echoed by the fifth factor referring to each potential suspect in the case ("theory of liability and legal framework of each potential suspect"). This factor may reasonably be construed as theories of criminal responsibility, which encompass the applicable modes of liability. Again, it is unclear whether the factor aims at the seriousness of the modes of liability which may apply in the case, or whether its inclusion is based on the differences in the evidentiary burden of the legal requirements of the modes of liability. As with the previous factor, an institution or legal system would of course be at liberty to fill either of the two factors with the content considered most relevant.

[130] Group (e) ("Other relevant considerations") includes the following factors: "The particular statutory offence or parts thereof, that can be charged", "The charging theories available", "Potential legal impediments to prosecution", and "Potential defences". *Ibid.*

Neither the BiH Orientation Criteria nor Annex A of the War Crimes Strategy contains equivalent factors. In contrast, the third cluster of criteria contained in the later version of the BiH Prosecution Guidelines refers to "adequate legal theories to support successful prosecutions", which seems to comprise theories of liability, but which does not specify either how the adequateness of theories should be assessed. It is reasonable to suggest that each factor should be more precisely defined prior to assessing which value, if any, they could add to the interested institution or jurisdiction. Gravity is arguably already a general criterion under the reviewed BiH criteria documents, and assessing the evidentiary burden which flows from alternative legal classifications would seem to be fairly standard procedure at a certain stage in the preparation of cases, regardless of whether there are case-prioritization criteria or not. In our view, the only way in which the evidentiary burden of cases that derives from different legal theories of liability could be conceived as important selection and prioritization criteria is if this was aimed at identifying pattern-based cases, that is, cases that could demonstrate systematicity in the commission of a crime or that could illuminate the characteristics of the criminal organization and its *modus operandi* beyond the particular case.

In addition to the former criteria, group (e) contains two further legal factors. On the one hand, "potential legal impediments to prosecution" are listed. This factor has its equivalent in the "Difficult issues of law" factor contained in the third cluster ("Other considerations") of the BiH Orientation Criteria. Thus, the merits of this criterion may be controversial for similar reasons, namely, that references to challenges of legal clarity or interpretation are often perceived as mere substitutes for other reasons motivating decisions not to proceed with an investigation or prosecution. If indeed there are real legal challenges, then the case should not feature in the group of cases from which selection or prioritization must happen. On the other hand, the list also includes "potential defences". This factor does not appear in any of the BiH criteria documents, but there will be differing opinions as to its suitability as a case-selection criterion insofar as cases with well-supported claims of grounds of exclusion of criminal responsibility should not be in the pool of strong cases within which a prosecution service must prioritize.

On the other hand, group (e) lists four non-legal criteria concerning the case and its context. First, "the extent to which the crime base fits in with current investigations and overall strategic direction", which reflects the essential aspiration to maximize the effect of the fact-work of the prosecution taken as a whole, and to avoid duplication in such work. This is important in war crimes processes where there is often an accumulation of large, fact-rich cases, which consume considerable resources. Drawing on the same evidence on, for example, the context in which crimes occurred in several cases can mean time and cost savings. This factor is a pertinent reminder of the need for a proper investigation strategy – or at least several co-ordinated investigation plans – in investigation and prosecution services responsible for war crimes cases. The resource drain of every case is simply so large that it is difficult to see how one can responsibly manage such agencies without these basic tools. Furthermore, this criterion allows including the identification of patterns of crimes as a key objective of the prosecutorial strategies on the basis of which the 'fitness' of a case in the overall strategic direction could be assessed. This is quite important for assuring that prosecutions would have a large impact both in terms of truth-telling (as criminal structures and patterns of actions could be elucidated) and of the struggle against impunity (since if structures and patterns are elucidated, they can also be stigmatized, which might impede recurrence).

Secondly, "the extent to which a successful investigation/prosecution of the case would further the strategic aims" is also listed as a factor. It is not clear what is meant by "strategic aims". If such aims differ from the investigation strategy, it may not be an entirely uncontroversial concept. However, if such aims include as part of the investigation strategy the prosecution of cases with the view of identifying patterns of crimes, then this selection factor could operate as a mechanism for determining whether the investigation of a specific case can contribute to such identification. In any event, whereas the previous factor refers to the contribution of the factual crime base of a case to the broader strategy, this factor refers to the contribution of a confirmed indictment or conviction in a case to the broader strategic aims.

Thirdly, group (e) also lists the factor "the extent to which the case can take the investigation to higher political, military, police and civil chains of command". This may be superfluous as an independent criterion alongside the previous two criteria, insofar as it seems to restate more precisely a chief characteristic of their content. Strategic direction and aims in war crimes investigations should be preoccupied exactly with how to ensure that criminal responsibility is established as high in the chains of authority as the evidence takes the work. Now, if this factor is interpreted as part of the strategic aim to identify patterns of crimes, the insistence in the hierarchy could be understood as a means to discover the internal structure of criminal organizations and their *modus operandi*, and it could therefore become quite a relevant factor worthy of autonomous consideration.

Fourthly, the last factor listed in group (e) is "to what extent the case fits into a larger pattern-type of ongoing or future investigations and prosecutions". This reinforces the importance of investigation strategy and plans, so that the relationship between larger investigations is clearly discussed, including the contribution of individual cases to the highest leadership cases in the same lines of inquiry. Moreover, the inclusion of this criterion seems to confirm that, as we have suggested in the previous paragraphs, the non-legal factors of group (e) are oriented towards the selection of cases in terms of the contributions they can make to the identification of patterns of crimes. If this is so, then this last factor could perhaps be better understood as a cluster that would comprise the previous three factors, each of which points at different ways in which cases should be assessed in order to determine if they can contribute to the strategic aims of the investigation in general, and to the key aim of identifying patterns of crimes in particular.

All four non-legal factors are essential indicators of how rationally and cost-effectively an investigation or prosecution service tasked with core international crimes is managed. They should be of direct interest to stakeholders who finance and administer war crimes processes. Such processes are proving to be expensive and drawn out in most jurisdictions. The decision to proceed with a full investigation or prosecution normally turns the key for a significant resource commitment. These decisions should not be made before the case has been considered in light of the broader investigation strategy. There should be a draft investigation plan before a decision is made to proceed with a full investigation, and the plan should explain how the case is expected to fit the strategy.[131] Furthermore, this draft investigation plan could be greatly strengthened if the identification of patterns of crimes was included as one of its key objectives and if, consequently, cases were selected among other things on the grounds of their potential for advancing in such identification. This would imply a tremendously important contribution to the organization and rationality of investigations, which could be understood as macro-processes aimed not only at bringing justice to the individual case, but at prosecuting and judging cases as part of a general strategy aimed at elucidating the patterns of criminality and victimization of a specific conflict situation. This would undoubtedly have a positive impact on resource-saving as well, since it would justify the prosecution of a case on the basis of its potential contributions to the overall strategic objectives. Certainly, donor States will not fail to note the importance of these tools.

None of the reviewed BiH documents on selection and prioritization criteria address these four strategic factors explicitly. Of course, that does not mean

[131] For instance, the Draft Regulations of the ICC Office of the Prosecutor prepared in 2002–2003 contains a strict requirement for the development of investigation plans, see Draft Regulations, 3 June 2003, Book 3, Part 2, Regulation 6 (https://www.legal-tools.org/doc/siibwo/). See also Antonio Angotti, "Investigation Plans in the Draft Regulations of the ICC Office of the Prosecutor: An Italian Perspective", in Xabier Agirre Aranburu, Morten Bergsmo, Simon De Smet and Carsten Stahn (eds.), *Quality Control in Criminal Investigation*, TOAEP, Brussels, 2020, pp. 821–849 (http://www.toaep.org/ps-pdf/38-qcci).

that the considerations have not been made within the relevant institutions. They may be reflected elsewhere in the regulatory infrastructure of the institutions or in their internal custom. This begs the question whether considerations of investigation strategy need to be included in case selection and prioritization criteria documents as opposed to another instrument. It is for each jurisdiction or institution to decide what suits its regulatory framework and work-processes best. However, excluding such considerations from the legal infrastructure all together risks undermining the quality of management and exposing the jurisdiction or institution to serious external criticism if the objectives or reasonable expectations are not met by the work. There must be a strong institutional self-interest in having a criterion of formal investigation strategy in connection with selection and prioritization of war crimes cases. Choosing not to formalize a requirement to consider how an investigation or prosecution will fit in with the overall investigation and prosecution agenda may benefit from a public explanation.

As we have seen above, the four strategic factors in group (e) overlap and seem to have a common wider goal. It may well be advisable to consolidate them into one cluster of strategic criteria when importing the strategic interest into a set of selection and prioritization criteria.

In conclusion, despite the repetitions and frequent overlap, the 1995 ICTY-OTP list of criteria is rich in content and accommodates many important interests in the selection and prioritization of core international crimes. It is almost a catalogue of relevant criteria, albeit incomplete and not particularly well edited or structured. As such, it can serve as a checklist in efforts to develop institutionalized selection criteria. However, it is far from being able to offer a sufficient basis for case selection, since it does not establish whether all criteria have to be satisfied in order for a case to be chosen for investigation, whether the different groups of criteria have different levels of importance and should therefore be considered hierarchically when selecting cases, and whether the different criteria within each group should all be satisfied, or if instead some should be given more weight than others for the purposes of selection.

Probably for that reason among others, the 1995 ICTY-OTP list of criteria did not bring about an adequate and consistent practice of case selection. In 1998, the Office acknowledged that only a few of the persons who had so far been indicted by the ICTY were in leadership positions.[132] As a result, it attempted to turn to a much more explicit focus on "persons holding higher levels of responsibility", which led Louise Arbour, the Chief Prosecutor at the time, to withdraw

[132] See Angermaier, Chapter 8 of this book.

charges against 14 persons who had been accused.[133] Further, the Office found it necessary to adopt a new internal document aimed at reviewing the procedure for opening new investigations or changing the direction of existing ones, with a view to rationalizing the selection of cases.[134]

This new document, adopted in 1998 and amended in 2000, contained a list of factors that amounted less to criteria than to a set of open-ended issues to be addressed in order to justify the selection of a specific case for investigation.[135] The issues were divided into seven types of considerations: (i) "Background", (ii) "Strategic considerations", (iii) "Character of violations and charging theory", (iv) "Characteristics of the alleged perpetrator(s)", (v) "Status of information and evidence", (vi) "Investigation plan", and (vii) "Other information".[136] This classification does not seem so adequate for case selection criteria, as it responds more to the wider concern of taking into account all the relevant information needed for opening and planning an investigation. Moreover, most of the considerations included in each group can be found in the list of criteria contained in the 1995 document, while some of the criteria included in the latter document cannot be found in the newer document. For those reasons, the 1998 document appears to be a useful complement to the 1995 criteria document, which contains a few new and relevant criteria and suggests some useful reclassifications, but which should not be understood as revoking the earlier document.

The first type of considerations of the 1998 document corresponds to the background of cases, and has the purpose of placing investigations in context.[137] As such, they refer to issues that can characterize cases in terms of place and time, circumstances of commission, number of victims, ethnicity of victims and perpetrators, and role and hierarchy of the latter. Some of these considerations constitute relevant selection criteria (such as the perpetrator's position in the relevant hierarchy and role, the number of victims, and even their ethnicity), but they should probably be classified into different clusters of criteria rather than

---

[133] *Ibid.*

[134] ICTY-OTP, "Internal Circular", amended on 20 November 2000. This document was made available for consultation to one of the authors of this chapter.

[135] Indeed, the document establishes that decisions to open new investigations should be preceded by the submission of a written proposal by the Team Leader and the Trial Attorney to the Chief of Investigations, and it sets the factors that should be outlined in such proposal. *Ibid.*, p. 1.

[136] *Ibid.*, pp. 2–3.

[137] *Ibid.*, p. 2. The list of "Background" considerations is the following: "Geographical area of crimes committed by size, main urban areas", "Dates of crimes", "Alleged perpetrator/s by name (if known), ethnicity, position in relevant hierarchy and role", "Alleged victims by number and ethnicity", and "Brief description of the crimes and the context in which they were committed".

grouped in a single one, as they point to different relevant issues for selection purposes (such as seniority, impact of the crime and representativity of the crime, respectively). However, many of the considerations included in this first group cannot be understood as selection criteria, but merely as relevant features of the cases for the purposes of investigation, which is the case of issues like the date and geographical area of the crimes, the name and ethnicity of perpetrators, and the description of the context in which crimes were committed. All the considerations contained in this group were already included in the 1995 ICTY-OTP document (particularly in group (b) of that document), with the exception of the ethnicity of victims and perpetrators, even though the relevant document referred to their nationality.

The second type of considerations refers to strategic issues,[138] all of which were already included in group (e) ("Other Relevant Considerations") of the 1995 ICTY-OTP document. The interesting thing about this group of considerations is that it only includes criteria related to the features of the case that are relevant for a pattern-based investigation (that is, whether "the crime base fits in with current investigations and overall strategic direction", "what added dimensions a successful investigation/ prosecution would bring to those aims", "realistically how high the political, military, police and civilian chains of command the case could take the investigation", and whether the case "fits in to [sic.] a larger pattern-type of on-going or future investigations and prosecutions"), instead of combining them with other types of considerations like the 1995 document did. This suggests a focused way of refining a cluster of selection criteria devoted to strategic considerations, by narrowing it down to issues related to the way in which the selected case can contribute to the aim of identifying the patterns of criminality developed during the conflict in question.

The third type of considerations is concerned with the "Character of violations and charging theory",[139] and it also includes issues which are all covered by group (e) of the 1995 ICTY-OTP document. However, once again, the 1998 document's contribution to the discussion about selection criteria seems to be

[138] These are the "Strategic Considerations" listed in the document: "where the crime base fits in with current investigations and overall strategic direction", "what added dimensions a successful investigation/prosecution would bring to those aims", and "realistically how high the political, military, police and civilian chains of command the case could take the investigation and/or where it fits in to [sic.] a larger pattern-type of on-going or future investigations and prosecutions". *Ibid.*, p. 2.

[139] The considerations related to the "Character of violations and charging theory" are: "Theory of liability and legal framework for each potential suspect", "Probable categories of charges for each potential suspect", and "Elements of potential offences, including those related to paras. 1 and 3 of Article 7 of the Statute". Note that the latter refers to the form of criminal participation and the positions in the criminal hierarchy.

the suggestion that criteria related to possible charges and theories of liability should be considered as a separate cluster of criteria. But it is not entirely clear why these criteria should be separate from those related to the characteristics of perpetrators, as they all seem to be aimed at giving prevalence to cases that include the most responsible perpetrators (both in terms of leadership and of degree of liability).

The fourth type of considerations refers to the "Characteristics of the alleged perpetrator(s)",[140] which, once again, are all included in the 1995 ICTY-OTP criteria document, this time under group (a) ("Persons"). However, several criteria contained in the latter are excluded from this fourth group, particularly those that (as said above) did not have a direct relationship with the cluster (such as "Arrest potential", "Evidence/Witness availability", "Media/Government/NGO target", and "Potential role-over witness/likelihood of linkage evidence"), or that could generate a lot of controversy if used as case selection criteria (like the perpetrator's nationality). In that way, the 1998 document makes an important contribution to this cluster of criteria, by protecting it against alien or problematic considerations.

The fifth type of considerations is related to the "Status of information and evidence",[141] and mainly deals with the availability of evidence and information sources. As such, most of the considerations it contains are covered by group (d) ("Practical considerations") of the ICTY-OTP document, with the exception of the categories "Information sources; including breadth and description, and those to be exploited" and "Immediate evidence gaps in case". These categories could be said to be covered by other criteria referring to the availability of information and evidence; nevertheless, they could be useful for pinning down the specific ways in which such information and evidence should be considered relevant for the purpose of case selection. On the other hand, this fifth type of considerations restricts the scope of the practical considerations to which the 1995 document referred to, as it only incorporates issues related to information and evidence, and it therefore, excludes the temporal factors related to the investigations' duration and timing, some of which are included in the following type of considerations.

---

[140] The document lists the following as "Characteristics of the alleged perpetrator(s)": "The suspect's role(s) and extent of direct participation in the alleged incidents", "The suspect's position in the command hierarchy (military, police or political)", "The authority and control exercised by the suspects", and "The suspect's alleged notice and knowledge of acts by subordinates".

[141] These considerations refer to the "current availability of": "Witnesses/victims of crimes", "Evidence and general information", "Information sources; including breadth and description, and those to be exploited", "Immediate evidence gaps in case", "Alleged perpetrators for arrest", "Exculpatory information and evidence", "Any work already carried out in relation to the case (including a check against Rules of Road cases), and "Possibility or probability of arrest".

The sixth type of considerations refers to the "Investigation plan",[142] and hence includes factors estimated to be relevant for the purpose of planning an investigation, such as the allocation of resources, a plan for resource spending, timelines to investigate and indict, and the consideration of other investigations in the area in question. These factors are to some extent covered by group (d) of the 1995 ICTY-OTP document. The main purpose of a draft investigation plan in time-consuming and expensive core international crimes cases is to properly inform the decision whether to proceed with a full investigation. As such, it is one of the most important instruments in the process of building rational case portfolios.

The seventh and final type of considerations generically refers to "Other information", which could cover "any other areas of immediate interest and information which assists in the justification of the case becoming an official investigation". If conceived as a case selection criteria cluster, the inclusion of this type of considerations is quite problematic, as it opens the door for any information and feature of cases considered relevant by the prosecutor in question to be used as justification for selecting it, and thus for subjective considerations to replace the existence of well-established criteria, and for arbitrariness to take the place of reasoned case selection. This type of considerations should, therefore, not be considered to add a new category of selection criteria.

In brief, the 1998 ICTY-OTP document is a useful complement to the 1995 document, which does not add many relevant case selection criteria to the list contained in the latter, but which does suggest some interesting reclassifications of such criteria.

Quite apart from the content and formulation of the ICTY-OTP criteria in the 1995 and 1998 documents, their fate within the ICTY-OTP can teach other national and international jurisdictions important lessons. It is evident from the ICTY case portfolio that the institution did not succeed to select and prioritize cases in a strategic manner, at least in its first years. There continued to exist many indictments against low-level perpetrators, contrary to the stated policy to focus on those on higher levels, which suggests that the case-selection criteria were never effectively enforced. The high number of such cases cannot be justified on tactical grounds. The criteria were not consistently adhered to in the practice of the Office, if at all explicitly referred to in the actual case-selection processes, which were controlled by investigation teams and team prosecutors,

[142] The document lists the following as considerations related to the investigation plan: "Resources required and/or allocation of existing resources", "Step by step plan of the tasking of resources", "Timelines to investigate and indict", and "A consideration of other OTP investigations in same geographical area, particularly those of 'opposite ethnicity' perpetrators and victims".

even though sometimes cases were selected by the Chief Prosecutor for reasons of policy.[143]

It has been suggested that the ICTY-OTP efforts to introduce case selection criteria and a formalized decision-making process for selecting cases were spearheaded by a small number of Office members not of traditional criminal justice background, and that they met resistance from some investigators and prosecutors who wanted case selection to be, on the whole, fact- and opportunity-driven.

Be that as it may, the ICTY case selection illustrates the risk of starting to select cases without clear and adequate criteria, and then attempting to introduce criteria. This might result in a random selection of cases (many involving lower-level perpetrators), in the expansion of this practice so that it becomes the standard mode of operation, and in a subsequent reactive attempt to *ex post facto* rationalize and justify a broad, fragmented and costly case portfolio, after investigations have been conducted and indictments confirmed. At such a stage, it may be too late to ensure an optimal or reasonable case selection. Indeed, donors and other main stakeholders in war crimes processes will normally only be able to address the capacity of the case portfolio to reflect the victimization caused by the conflict at a late stage in the work of the prosecutor's office in question.

Given the worrisome situation of the ICTY's case portfolio, it came as no surprise that from 2001 onwards, the so-called 'completion strategy' of the ICTY-OTP increasingly limited all new cases to higher-level leaders, excluding cases against notorious offenders at lower levels. The completion strategy is on its face a plan devised by the ICTY, aimed at ensuring the successful and timely conclusion of the Tribunal's mission. This policy was explicitly endorsed by the President of the Security Council in 2002,[144] and later emphasized and formally endorsed by Security Council Resolutions 1503 of 2003 and 1534 of 2004, as discussed in Chapter 8 below.[145] It is no secret, however, that several States wanted the ICTY to develop and adopt a completion strategy.

---

[143] Such as showing that the Tribunal was able to bring persons to account early in its existence (Tadić); that it could respond to crime themes such as sexual crimes (Furundžija); that it pursued particularly serious crimes (Srebrenica); and that it followed a balanced approach with regard to different parties of the conflicts (Bosnian Muslim and Bosnian Croat cases, especially during the Goldstone period). Chief Prosecutor Arbour also played a key role in withdrawing 14 indictments in 1998 issued during the Goldstone period mainly because they did not satisfy the criteria of 'most responsible' or 'notorious offenders'.

[144] Statement by the President of the Security Council, UN Doc. S/PRST/2002/21, 23 July 2002 (https://www.legal-tools.org/doc/bqwzzq/).

[145] Security Council Resolution 1503 (2003), UN Doc. S/RES/1503 (2003), 28 August 2003 (https://www.legal-tools.org/doc/05a7de/); Security Council Resolution 1504 (2003), UN Doc. S/RES/1504 (2003), 4 September 2003 (https://www.legal-tools.org/doc/1818e1/); Security

In Resolution 1503 of 2003, the Security Council reaffirmed "in the strongest terms" that the ICTY should concentrate on the prosecution and trial of "the most senior leaders suspected of being most responsible for crimes".[146] This represented in effect a shift in the political delineation of the scope of prosecutorial discretion as regards the selection and prioritization of cases before the ICTY. Further, in Resolution 1534 of 2004, the Council called on the ICTY and ICTR prosecutors "to review the case load" and, "in reviewing and confirming any new indictments, to ensure that any such indictments concentrate on the most senior leaders suspected of being most responsible for crimes within the jurisdiction of the relevant Tribunal as set out in resolution 1503 (2003)".[147] Although the Council's interference appeared to be dictated by the political 'need' to end the Tribunal's work and lifetime, it is difficult to detach it from the problematic state of the Tribunal's portfolio and completion in 2003 and 2004. That is very significant.

Moreover, subsequent to Security Council Resolution 1534, in 2004, the judges amended the ICTY Rules of Procedure and Evidence, and included Rule 28(A), which provided them with the possibility to review the indictments issued by the OTP in order to verify whether they concentrate "on one or more of the most senior leaders suspected of being most responsible for crimes within the jurisdiction of the Tribunal".[148] In that way, the judges assigned to themselves the role of determining whether the Security Council-endorsed criterion of "most senior leaders suspected of being most responsible" was satisfied by draft indictments, prior to the indictment confirmation procedure. This is of great importance, as it shows the ICTY's recognition of the prosecution's failure to adequately formulate and apply case-selection criteria capable of ensuring the prosecution of the most responsible perpetrators, and the acknowledgment of the need to establish a judicial review of case selection in order to guarantee the fulfilment of such goal.

Council Resolution 1534 (2004), UN Doc. S/RES/1534(2004) , 26 March 2004 ('Resolution 1534 (2004)') (https://www.legal-tools.org/doc/4e06ee/).

146 Resolution 1503 (2003), seventh preambular para, see *supra* note 145.

147 Resolution 1534 (2004), paras. 4 and 5, see *supra* note 145.

148 Rule 28(A), amended on 6 April 2004, see *supra* note 8, states (emphasis added):

> On receipt of an indictment for review from the Prosecutor, the Registrar shall consult with the President. The President shall refer the matter to the Bureau, which shall determine whether the indictment, prima facie, *concentrates on one or more of the most senior leaders suspected of being most responsible for crimes within the jurisdiction of the Tribunal*. If the Bureau determines that the indictment meets this standard, the President shall designate one of the permanent Trial Chamber Judges for the review under Rule 47. If the Bureau determines that the indictment does not meet this standard, the President shall return the indictment to the Registrar to communicate this finding to the Prosecutor.

However important, the remedies enforced after the completion strategy were in themselves of limited assistance in solving the problem of inadequate case selection at the ICTY. Indeed, they only involved cases selected after the beginning of the completion strategy, and thus left untouched the large bulk of previously selected cases, many of which, as has been observed above, deal with lower-level perpetrators.

In sum, the ICTY experience with criteria for case selection and prioritization sends a strong signal that the development and implementation of such criteria are difficult to achieve by prosecution services, and that timing is of fundamental importance in the sense that criteria developed once prosecutorial activities have already started might not be properly enforced. The risk of judicial or political interference with war crimes case selection increases significantly if prosecutors fail to adequately select cases and a less than optimal case portfolio emerges. The cost of criminal justice for perpetrators of core international crimes is so high that rational case selection becomes a matter of general interest and concern.

The practice of the ICTY shows that enforcement of criteria is the main challenge. Criteria should help ensure that the selection and prioritization of cases reflect the policies of a prosecution service. If its decision to select a specific case for prosecution is questioned, the service can defend it on the basis of rational, formal criteria. In the *Čelebići* case before the ICTY, for example, one of the accused unsuccessfully argued that he had been subjected to a selective prosecution strategy in contravention of the principle of equality enshrined in Article 21(1) of the ICTY Statute. He defined a selective prosecution as one "in which the criteria for selecting persons for prosecution are based, not on considerations of apparent criminal responsibility alone, but on extraneous policy reasons, such as ethnicity, gender, or administrative convenience".[149] The Appeals Chamber held that, although the Prosecutor has a broad discretion with regard to the initiation of investigations and the preparation of indictments, such a power is not unlimited but may be subject to certain restraints contained in the Statute and Rules of Procedure and Evidence of the Tribunal.[150] It stated that the Prosecutor was only allowed to exercise her functions in accordance "with full respect of the law", including "recognised principles of human rights",[151] one

[149] ICTY, *Prosecutor v. Mučić et al.*, Appeals Chamber, Judgment, 20 February 2001, IT-96-21-A, para. 596 (https://www.legal-tools.org/doc/051554/).

[150] *Ibid.*, para. 602.

[151] *Ibid.*, para. 604:

> The discretion of the Prosecutor at all times is circumscribed in a more general way by the nature of her position as an official vested with specific duties imposed by the Statute of the Tribunal. The Prosecutor is committed to discharge those duties with full respect of

such principle being equality before the Tribunal. It is understandable that prosecution services wish to protect themselves against such and similar challenges by using formal case selection and prioritization criteria. Had the prosecutor developed and publicized such criteria, a different story might have occurred in this case.

5.3.2. Criteria in the International Criminal Court

The creation of the ICC is so far the most important step in the process of consolidation of international criminal justice, after the Nuremberg and Tokyo Tribunals. Indeed, the ICC is a permanent tribunal with an open-ended territorial jurisdiction, which enables it to investigate many different situations in which crimes are presumably being committed in the territory of or by the nationals of the States that have accepted its jurisdiction, as well as to eventually prosecute many of those crimes.[152] In that way, the ICC differs from previous experiences of international criminal tribunals, including the ICTY, which have been characterized by having a temporary and *ad hoc* jurisdiction restricted to the investigation of crimes committed in a specific situation for a limited period of time.

The much wider jurisdiction of the ICC does not mean that it can or should investigate all those situations or prosecute all the crimes therein committed. Quite on the contrary, since the elaboration of the Statute, the need to choose situations to investigate and cases to prosecute has been recognized as a key issue in the exercise of the Court's jurisdiction. Consequently, a set of basic selection criteria was incorporated into the ICC Statute itself, and its application by the Office of the Prosecutor ('ICC-OTP') was subjected to judicial review by a Pre-Trial Chamber of the Court.[153] These selection criteria have been thoroughly interpreted and developed by the ICC-OTP in a few policy papers, and especially in the working paper "Criteria for selection of situations and cases", which has identified the elements that are necessary to apply such criteria, and

---

the law. In this regard, the Secretary-General's Report stressed that the Tribunal, which encompasses all of its organs, including the Office of the Prosecutor, must abide by the recognised principles of human rights.

152 These are the two basic or preliminary conditions for the exercise of the ICC's jurisdiction. In effect, according to ICC Statute, Article 12, see *supra* note 4:

> [...] [T]he Court may exercise its jurisdiction if one or more of the following States are Parties to this Statute or have accepted the jurisdiction of the Court in accordance with paragraph 3:
>
> (a) The State on the territory of which the conduct in question occurred or, if the crime was committed on board a vessel or aircraft, the State of registration of that vessel or aircraft;
>
> (b) The State of which the person accused of the crime is a national.

153 See notably *ibid.*, Article 53, paragraphs 1 and 2 for the selection criteria, and 3 for the judicial review of their application.

has also formulated prioritization criteria for the situations and cases that are selected on that basis.[154] Ten years later, in 2016, the ICC-OTP adopted a policy paper on selection and prioritization which is discussed in detail in Chapter 6 below by Rod Rastan to which we refer the reader.[155]

Thus, in contrast with previous experiences of international criminal tribunals, and especially with the ICTY, the need to formulate criteria was recognized since the creation of the ICC and, as a result, fundamental criteria were given a statutory basis and their application was subjected to judicial control. This illustrated the existence of broad consensus on the part of States that negotiated the statute about the need to formally adopt and adequately apply criteria. At the same time, the incorporation of criteria in the ICC Statute gave the specific criteria therein incorporated a much stronger authority, and offered solid grounds for their refinement and for the formulation of prioritization criteria beyond them.

The main rule of the ICC Statute concerning selection criteria is Article 53, which states:

> 1. The Prosecutor shall, having evaluated the information made available to him or her, initiate an investigation unless he or she determines that there is no reasonable basis to proceed under this Statute. In deciding whether to initiate an investigation, the Prosecutor shall consider whether:
>   (a) The information available to the Prosecutor provides a reasonable basis to believe that a crime within the jurisdiction of the Court has been or is being committed;
>   (b) The case is or would be admissible under article 17; and
>   (c) Taking into account the gravity of the crime and the interests of victims, there are nonetheless substantial reasons to believe that an investigation would not serve the interests of justice.
>
>   If the Prosecutor determines that there is no reasonable basis to proceed and his or her determination is based solely on subparagraph (c) above, he or she shall inform the Pre-Trial Chamber.
> 2. If, upon investigation, the Prosecutor concludes that there is not a sufficient basis for a prosecution because:
>   (a) There is not a sufficient legal or factual basis to seek a warrant or summons under article 58;
>   (b) The case is inadmissible under article 17; or

[154] See ICC, "Policies and Strategies" (available on its web site), and particularly the document: ICC-OTP, "Criteria for Selection of Situations and Cases", Draft Discussion Paper, 1 June 2006 (https://www.legal-tools.org/doc/sk0ratuy/).

[155] ICC-OTP, "Policy Paper on Case Selection and Prioritisation", 15 September 2016 (https://www.legal-tools.org/doc/182205/).

(c) A prosecution is not in the interests of justice, taking into account all the circumstances, including the gravity of the crime, the interests of victims and the age or infirmity of the alleged perpetrator, and his or her role in the alleged crime;

the [sic.] Prosecutor shall inform the Pre-Trial Chamber and the State making a referral under article 14 or the Security Council in a case under article 13, paragraph (b), of his or her conclusion and the reasons for the conclusion.

3. (a) At the request of the State making a referral under article 14 or the Security Council under article 13, paragraph (b), the Pre-Trial Chamber may review a decision of the Prosecutor under paragraph 1 or 2 not to proceed and may request the Prosecutor to reconsider that decision.

   (b) In addition, the Pre-Trial Chamber may, on its own initiative, review a decision of the Prosecutor not to proceed if it is based solely on paragraph 1 (c) or 2 (c). In such a case, the decision of the Prosecutor shall be effective only if confirmed by the Pre-Trial Chamber.

4. The Prosecutor may, at any time, reconsider a decision whether to initiate an investigation or prosecution based on new facts or information.[156]

Hence, Article 53 of the ICC Statute offers reasonably clear and precise grounds for the ICC-OTP to decide whether to initiate an investigation of a situation and a prosecution of a case, and it submits these decisions to some control of the ICC's Pre-Trial Chamber.

As can be seen, Article 53 establishes a clear distinction between the decision to choose a situation for initiating an investigation and the decision to choose a case for opening a prosecution, and provides similar selection criteria for each decision. As the ICC-OTP has put it when interpreting Article 53, "[u]nder the Rome Statute, the Prosecutor is required to consider selection criteria at different stages, including selection of situations for investigation and selection of cases for prosecution".[157] According to the OTP, the "Statute does not define a 'situation' or a 'case'", but they can be defined in the following terms:

> […] a situation may be described as a general context, defined by objective parameters such as territorial and temporal scope, in which crimes are alleged to have been committed, brought to the attention of the Prosecutor by a referral from a State Party or the Security Council or through information from other sources. […]

[156] ICC Statute, Article 53, see *supra* note 4.

[157] ICC-OTP, "Criteria for Selection of Situations and Cases", p. 1, see *supra* note 154.

> [A] 'case' is a narrower concept, comprising particular alleged crimes and particular suspects allegedly involved in those crimes.[158]

Therefore, according to the OTP's 2006 paper on criteria, the case selection process is divided into two main stages: first, after analysing the different situations or general contexts where crimes have allegedly been committed that have been brought to the attention of the Court by different possible sources, the ICC-OTP decides which of those situations to select for the purpose of investigating them; second, after reportedly formulating a case hypothesis for each situation, developing an investigation on its basis, and evaluating the gathered evidence, the ICC-OTP determines whether the hypothesis is confirmed or rejected, and consequently decides whether to prosecute the case and seek an arrest warrant, or to close the inquiry.[159]

For each of these two decisions, the Statute provides selection criteria that are quite similar but have a different scope in each stage of the process. As the OTP has noted, in both cases, the Statute divides the decision to select a situation or a case into three different steps, which are sequential in the sense that if the conditions of the preceding one are not satisfied, then there is no need to consider the following one, and the situation or case in question is ruled out for investigation or prosecution purposes.[160] Evidently, each of these sequences makes part of the more general sequence by which the decision to prosecute a case can only be taken if a decision to open an investigation in the situation to which such case belongs has been taken and implemented.

The division of selection decisions into stages, which has not been done in the other experiences analysed here – nor, to the knowledge of the authors, in other jurisdictions dealing with core international crimes – is a novel contribution to the adequate formulation and application of case selection criteria. It primarily reflects the interest of States that the exercise of prosecutorial discretion to select be sound, through Pre-Trial Chamber review, if necessary. Indeed, it sets up a clear procedure through which such criteria can be easily applied by the OTP, which implies the establishment of an order of priority to assess the criteria under consideration, and which therefore identifies a quite definite and distinct role for each criterion.

The first step of the selection process consists in determining whether there is a basis to proceed either to initiate an investigation of a situation, or to open a prosecution of a case in the context of such situation. In the first case, the

[158] *Ibid.*

[159] See the useful flowchart of this process contained in *ibid.*, p. 10.

[160] This point is made in *ibid.*, pp. 3–6.

statute refers to "a reasonable basis to believe that a crime within the jurisdiction of the Court has been or is being committed" (Article 53(1)(a)). According to the ICC-OTP's interpretation of the Statute, "the 'reasonable basis' test requires a degree of certainty more than mere suspicion".[161] However, since such degree of certainty concerns the possible commission of crimes and not the participation or mode of liability of perpetrators, it can be satisfied by establishing that:

(a) the event in question occurred,
(b) the event constitutes criminal activity under Article 5 of the Rome Statute, and
(c) the crime falls within the temporal and the personal or territorial jurisdiction of the Court.[162]

The second (b) condition of the test is satisfied, if the criminal activity in the analysed situation can be considered to constitute either genocide, crimes against humanity, war crimes, or aggression, which are the crimes conceived by the ICC Statute to be under the subject-matter jurisdiction of the Court. In order to conclude such a thing, the definitions of those crimes contained in the Statute must be considered.[163] This consideration necessarily implies a preliminary assessment of gravity, since their definitions suggest particular elements of gravity inherent to them.[164] In its turn, the third (c) condition is satisfied if such crimes were committed after the entry into force of the Statute and in the territory of or

---

[161] *Ibid.*, p. 3.

[162] *Ibid.*

[163] ICC Statute, Articles 6–8, see *supra* note 4.

[164] This point is made by scholar deGuzman, 2008, p. 1407, see *supra* note 9, but only with respect to genocide and crimes against humanity. According to her:

> For genocide and crimes against humanity, the contextual aspects of the definitions seek to distinguish these crimes from 'ordinary' crimes at least in part through elements suggesting gravity. Thus for genocide the Statute requires intent to destroy a listed group in whole or in part, and the Elements of Crimes mandate that the conduct occurred 'in the context of a manifest pattern of similar conduct directed against that group or was conduct that could itself effect such destruction.' Likewise, crimes against humanity are defined as one or more enumerated inhumane acts 'committed as part of a widespread or systematic attack' against a civilian population. The requisite 'attack' is 'a course of conduct involving the multiple commission of [enumerated] acts […] pursuant to or in furtherance of a State or organizational policy to commit such attack […].' Additionally, some of the enumerated acts contain references to gravity. For example, forms of sexual violence other than those listed must be of 'comparable gravity' to the listed acts and 'other inhumane acts' must be 'of a similar character.' Thus, the elements of genocide and crimes against humanity seek to ensure that only serious conduct is captured through such requirements as group targeting, scale, and systematicity.
>
> The definition of war crimes, on the other hand, does not contain required elements ensuring their gravity.

by the nationals of the States that ratified it, which are factors that respectively pin down the temporal, territorial and personal jurisdiction of the Court (Article 12).[165]

When determining whether to prosecute a case, the ICC Statute identifies the first step as implying the determination of whether there exists "a sufficient legal or factual basis to seek a warrant or summons under article 58" (Article 53(2)(a)). This determination is of course made on the basis of the information and evidence gathered during the investigation, which can point at patterns of criminality and individual responsibilities.[166] According to the ICC-OTP, the "test" for determining the viability of a prosecution is "more demanding", since it aims at resulting in a warrant or summons, and it therefore requires establishing that there are reasonable grounds for believing that a specific person participated in the commission of the crimes under investigation. In that way, the test does not only consider such crimes, but also "a particular individual (suspect) and a particular mode of liability and mental element".[167]

Note that the first stage of the process of selection of situations and cases refers to factors that, although not explicitly stated in previously analysed documents about case selection and prioritization criteria, require consideration in any decision to select a case. They cover quite basic conditions for a tribunal's jurisdiction to be exercised, such as a firm belief that a crime has been committed, and that it is covered by the subject-matter, temporal and territorial or personal jurisdiction of the court, as well as for a prosecution to be initiated, such as the belief that a particular person participated in the crimes in question. As such, these conditions are not prioritization criteria proper, as prioritization only takes place when there are two or more cases that meet such fundamental, preliminary requirements.

Be that as it may, it seems useful that these preliminary factors, which can be the subject of interpretation and disagreement, are clearly specified by the instruments that establish the jurisdictions under consideration, or in their absence by these jurisdictions themselves, so that the potential controversies that they can provoke are minimized and regulated by such factors.

The second stage of the selection process foreseen by the ICC Statute refers to the satisfaction of the conditions of admissibility contained in Article 17.[168]

---

[165] See *supra* note 152.

[166] ICC-OTP, "Criteria for Selection of Situations and Cases", p. 3, see *supra* note 154.

[167] *Ibid*., p. 4.

[168] This is the full text of Article 17:

> 1. Having regard to paragraph 10 of the Preamble and article 1, the Court shall determine that a case is inadmissible where:

According to Article 53(1)(b), the decision to select a situation requires that the case under analysis "is or would be admissible under article 17", while the decision to prosecute a case requires that it is in fact admissible under such disposition (Article 53(2)(b)). Even though both rules refer to the admissibility of the case, according to the ICC-OTP, the assessment of the admissibility conditions as selection criteria vary in the decisions to investigate a situation and to prosecute a case in its level of generality. In fact, since "at the stage of initiating an investigation there is not yet a 'case' […], it is necessary to consider admissibility in a generalized manner, taking into account the likely set of cases that would arise from investigation of the situation".[169] In contrast, the "assessment of gravity at the case selection phase considers the gravity of the particular 'case' in question".[170]

Although Article 17 refers to several admissibility conditions, their consideration for the purpose of selecting investigations and cases seems to be limited to two of those conditions: the sufficient gravity of the crimes in question (Article 17(1)(d)) and the complementary nature of the ICC's jurisdiction with respect to national jurisdictions (Article 17(1)(a) and (c) and (2)). Indeed, Article

---

(a) The case is being investigated or prosecuted by a State which has jurisdiction over it, unless the State is unwilling or unable genuinely to carry out the investigation or prosecution;
(b) The case has been investigated by a State which has jurisdiction over it and the State has decided not to prosecute the person concerned, unless the decision resulted from the unwillingness or inability of the State genuinely to prosecute;
(c) The person concerned has already been tried for conduct which is the subject of the complaint, and a trial by the Court is not permitted under article 20, paragraph 3;
(d) The case is not of sufficient gravity to justify further action by the Court.

2. In order to determine unwillingness in a particular case, the Court shall consider, having regard to the principles of due process recognized by international law, whether one or more of the following exist, as applicable:
   (a) The proceedings were or are being undertaken or the national decision was made for the purpose of shielding the person concerned from criminal responsibility for crimes within the jurisdiction of the Court referred to in article 5;
   (b) There has been an unjustified delay in the proceedings which in the circumstances is inconsistent with an intent to bring the person concerned to justice;
   (c) The proceedings were not or are not being conducted independently or impartially, and they were or are being conducted in a manner which, in the circumstances, is inconsistent with an intent to bring the person concerned to justice.
3. In order to determine inability in a particular case, the Court shall consider whether, due to a total or substantial collapse or unavailability of its national judicial system, the State is unable to obtain the accused or the necessary evidence and testimony or otherwise unable to carry out its proceedings.

[169] ICC-OTP, "Criteria for Selection of Situations and Cases", p. 5, see *supra* note 154.

[170] *Ibid.*

1 of the ICC Statute recognizes these two conditions as the central restrictions of the jurisdiction of the ICC, when it states that the Court "shall have the power to exercise its jurisdiction over persons for the most serious crimes of international concern […] and shall be complementary to national criminal jurisdictions".[171] Moreover, when interpreting the reference made to Article 17 by Article 53 of the Statute, the ICC-OTP ascertains that the assessment of admissibility factors required by Article 53(1)(b) and (2)(b) implies the consideration of "gravity and complementarity". According to the ICC-OTP, these two factors should be considered as distinct criteria that must be jointly satisfied[172] in order for a situation or a case found to have a reasonable basis to proceed to be selected for investigation or prosecution in the second stage of the process.

Chapters 21 and 22 below discuss the gravity criterion before the ICC in detail. We will nevertheless include some tentative reflections here based on the Statute and the 2006 draft document. On the one hand, as a selection criterion, gravity is not reduced to the condition that the crimes under analysis fit the definition of the crimes that constitute the subject-matter jurisdiction of the ICC or satisfy the specific elements of gravity identified by some of those definitions. Indeed, as it was mentioned above, this condition of gravity is already necessary for the first step of the selection process to be overcome. Therefore, the fact that the Statute refers to gravity once again with respect to the second step of the selection process implies that it is concerned with a consideration of gravity beyond those initial conditions. This appears to be confirmed by Article 8(2) of the Statute, which defines "war crimes" without any reference to their level of gravity, but which also establishes that the ICC should exercise its jurisdiction over such crimes "in particular when committed as part of a plan or policy or as part of a large-scale commission of such crimes", thus suggesting that the presence of these factors of gravity of war crimes is not a condition for determining that there is reasonable basis to proceed, but that it serves as a criterion to select investigations and cases concerning such crimes at a more advanced assessment stage.

For those reasons, the ICC-OTP concludes: "even where subject-matter jurisdiction is satisfied, it must still be determined whether the case is of sufficient gravity 'to justify further action by the Court'".[173] In order to arrive to such a

[171] ICC Statute, Article 1, see *supra* note 4.

[172] According to the ICC-OTP, the "Statute does not stipulate any mandatory sequence in the consideration of gravity and complementarity, but the Prosecutor must be satisfied as to admissibility on both counts (gravity and complementarity) before proceeding further", ICC-OTP, "Criteria for Selection of Situations and Cases", pp. 3–4, see *supra* note 154.

[173] *Ibid.*

determination, in its draft document on case selection criteria, the ICC-OTP proposed four relevant factors for the assessment of gravity: the "scale", "nature", "manner of commission" and "impact" of the crimes in question.[174] Furthermore, the OTP identified the elements that should be taken into account for each of these factors to be considered as offering grounds for justifying the selection of situations or cases on the basis of gravity.

First, concerning the scale of crimes, the OTP-document recognizes the "number of victims" as the main element of consideration,[175] but it also points at the "geographic and chronological spread of the crime" as other elements that should be examined.[176] Second, from the consideration of the nature of crimes, the OTP derives the conclusion that the "gravest crimes" are those that result in "deliberate death", closely followed by rape.[177] Third, concerning the manner of commission of crimes, the OTP provides a list of factors that should be considered for assessing gravity: the systematicity, organized or planned nature of crimes; the use of particularly cruel methods; the targeting of especially vulnerable victims; the commission of crimes on the basis of discriminatory considerations; and the abuse of power.[178] Fourth, the OTP interprets the impact of crimes in terms of their larger consequences both for the community in which the crimes were committed, and for "regional peace and security" in general.[179]

According to the OTP-document, these factors should be considered "jointly" in order to assess the gravity of situations and cases under consideration, in such a way that "no fixed weight should be assigned to the criteria, but rather a judgment will have to be reached on the facts and circumstances of each situation".[180] Therefore, the determination of whether a case is "sufficiently grave" to merit its investigation and prosecution by the ICC will still depend on the discretion of the OTP. However, this discretion is ruled by quite clear and precise factors of gravity and of indicators that measure the presence of such

[174] *Ibid.*

[175] According to the OTP, this is justified since information about deadly crimes is often the most reliable. However, the OTP explains that, if available, information about any other type of crimes can also be taken into account. *Ibid.*, p. 5.

[176] *Ibid.*

[177] *Ibid.*

[178] *Ibid.*

[179] According to the OTP, this last factor includes: "longer term social, economic and environmental damage", and particularly actions like "attacks on persons involved in humanitarian assistance and peacekeeping mission, as well as crimes intended to obstruct justice (particularly those targeting ICC witnesses or staff) and crimes committed with intent to spread terror". *Ibid.*

[180] *Ibid.*

factors, which should guide as well as justify the selection decision of the Prosecutor, thus reducing the risk of it being the product of arbitrariness or subjectivity. Thus, the ICC Statute does not limit itself to pointing at the gravity of crimes as a criterion, or at listing the elements that must be considered when assessing it, but it specifies the way in which each of those elements should be measured and interpreted in order to reach a selection decision.

It is worth noting that, in contrast to most of the documents on criteria analysed in this chapter, neither the ICC Statute nor the OTP-document include the role and status of perpetrators as part of the gravity criterion in the *selection* process, which is, therefore, restricted to the seriousness of crimes. As we will see, criteria related to the perpetrator are only considered relevant by the OTP-document when deciding which situations or cases to choose for investigation and prosecution from all those that satisfy the selection criteria included in the Statute. As such, they appear to be treated as case prioritization criteria rather than as case selection criteria in the sense that the ICC Statute gives to the latter.

On the other hand, the second stage of the situation and case selection process foreseen by the ICC Statute refers to complementarity as the second criterion to be considered along with gravity. Applying the categories of Article 17 of the ICC Statute (particularly (1)(a) and (b), (2) and (3)), complementarity should exist whenever the ICC's jurisdiction is exercised over a case that (i) is not being investigated or prosecuted by the state that has main jurisdiction over it; (ii) is being investigated or prosecuted by that state, but the latter is unwilling or genuinely unable to carry out such tasks; or (iii) has been investigated and has involved the issuing of a decision not to prosecute the person(s) involved, but such decision was the result of the unwillingness or inability of the State to genuinely prosecute.

As the OTP-document points out, the analysis of the complementarity criterion should be done in two steps: a first step aimed at answering "the empirical question of whether there have been or are national proceedings in relation to the cases that would likely be the focus for the ICC", and a second step aimed at solving "the normative question of whether the ostensible proceedings are vitiated by an unwillingness or inability to genuinely carry out the proceedings".[181] However, the second step should only be taken if the empirical question that corresponds to the first step is answered positively, since otherwise the complementarity criterion would be satisfied with the mere ascertainment that there have not been any investigations or prosecutions related to the crimes in which the ICC is interested in the State with the main jurisdiction over them. In that way, the assessment of the complementarity criterion does not necessarily imply

[181] *Ibid.*, p. 6.

the difficult consideration of the unwillingness or ability of territorial States to act, which should only take place when the latter have developed investigations or prosecutions concerning the crimes in question.

If proceedings of the sort are in place, the genuine inability or unwillingness of the State under consideration to carry them out should be assessed by referring to the factors recognized in Article 17. According to the latter, the inability of a State to investigate or prosecute a crime can be assessed by considering "whether, due to a total or substantial collapse or unavailability of its national judicial system, the State is unable to obtain the accused or the necessary evidence and testimony or otherwise unable to carry out its proceedings" (Article 17(3)). On the other hand, the unwillingness of a State to investigate or prosecute a crime can be established if such proceedings comply with one of the following conditions: (i) they were undertaken "for the purpose of shielding the person concerned from criminal responsibility"; (ii) they have been unjustifiably delayed in a way that is "inconsistent with an intent to bring the person concerned to justice"; or (iii) they "were not or are not being conducted independently or impartially, and they were or are being conducted in a manner which, in the circumstances, is inconsistent with an intent to bring the person concerned to justice" (Article 17(2)).

Here again, even though the factors considered necessary to assess the complementarity criterion – and particularly those related to situations in which investigations or prosecutions are taking place in the territorial State with main jurisdiction – require the ICC-OTP to make a judgment on whether they are satisfied in each concrete case, the formulation of such factors and the indication of the specific elements that should be taken into account when analysing them significantly reduce the probability of arbitrary or entirely subjective decisions, and impose the duty to justify those decisions.

Although the complementarity criterion can be described as a selection criterion, it is more accurate to refer to it as a fundamental admissibility principle, necessitated by the complementary nature of the ICC's jurisdiction.[182]

---

[182] Case selection is a crucial task for international tribunals, as it determines to a great extent the way in which their efficacy will be perceived by the international and national communities, and therefore the degree of legitimacy that they will obtain. These perceptions do not appear to depend only on the type of cases that such tribunals select, but also on the way in which, by selecting them, they can contribute to guarantee accountability and to counter impunity in the territorial States in question. And the consideration of the necessity of the international tribunal's intervention – conceived in terms of the absence of investigations and prosecutions concerning the crimes in question, or of the lack of capacity or will of the States to carry such proceedings out – seems to be quite relevant for that purpose.

The use of the complementarity criterion does not guarantee, on its own, that an international criminal jurisdiction will actually investigate and prosecute those cases in which its intervention is needed the most. For instance, many of the criticisms against the early activities of the ICC seem to point at the fact that the Court has applied that criterion to select cases where no investigations or prosecutions are taking place, thus ignoring the many and in some occasions much more complex and impunity-leading situations where such proceedings are taking place but with the only purpose of shielding perpetrators of the ICC intervention. Therefore, the incorporation of the complementarity criterion should always be accompanied by an adequate application and a rigorous justification of the selection of cases on its basis.

The third stage of the fundamental selection process foreseen by the ICC Statute incorporates a novel criterion for selecting situations to investigate and cases to prosecute: the 'interests of justice'. According to Article 53, this criterion implies inquiring whether the investigation or prosecution in question would not be in the interests of justice. Concerning decisions to select both situations to investigate and cases to prosecute, it requires doing such inquiry taking into consideration "the gravity of the crime and the interests of victims" ((1)(c) and (2)(c)). And concerning decisions to select cases to prosecute only, it also requires considering "all other circumstances, including […] the age or infirmity of the alleged perpetrator, and his or her role in the alleged crime" ((2)(c)).

As can be seen, concerning both types of decisions, the 'interests of justice' criterion operates in a negative way, in the sense that, if it is satisfied, then the situation or case in question will not be selected. As the OTP stated it in a 2007 paper specifically devoted to this criterion:

However, this consideration has not been used as a precise selection criterion in previous international criminal justice experiences, and especially not in the ICTY. Quite on the contrary, the latter tribunal initially exercised a non-subsidiary jurisdiction over the crimes committed in the Balkan Wars, which therefore led it to never selecting cases on the basis of which investigations and prosecutions were needed the most due to the absence of national proceedings of the sort, or the inability or unwillingness of national States for carrying them out. Rather, the competence of the ICTY appeared to be based on the general assumption that national jurisdictions were unable and unwilling to carry out such proceedings. Even though this was true in many cases, especially in the aftermath of the wars, it was not necessarily true for all jurisdictions or for all cases equally considered. But the lack of a criterion aimed at identifying where the exercise of the ICTY jurisdiction was most needed to complement national efforts hindered the identification of possible relevant differences. The consideration of these differences would have probably been relevant for the massive referral of cases to the national jurisdictions that ended up occurring, and that put the main responsibility of investigating and prosecuting core international crimes cases in the hands of national tribunals, thus suddenly assuming that they were all equally capable and willing to undertake such tasks.

> The interests of justice test is a potential countervailing consideration that might produce a reason not to proceed […]. [T]he Prosecutor is not required to establish that an investigation or prosecution is in the interests of justice. Rather, he shall proceed with investigation unless there are specific circumstances which provide substantial reasons to believe it is not in the interests of justice to do so at that time.[183]

Given the sequential nature of the selection process, this criterion is only to be considered if a situation or case has fulfilled both the first and second stages of the process and if, consequently, it is deemed to have a reasonable basis to proceed, to be concerned with crimes of sufficient gravity, and to justify the intervention of the ICC on the basis of complementarity. At that stage of the process, there seem to be quite powerful reasons for initiating an investigation of a situation or for opening a prosecution. For that reason, the 2007 OTP-document considers that a decision not to investigate a situation or prosecute a case on the basis of this criterion should only take place under "exceptional circumstances".[184] Moreover, there exists "a presumption in favour of investigation or prosecution wherever the criteria established in Article 53(1)(a) and (b) or Article 53(2)(a) and (b) have been met".[185]

In that way, as a general rule, the 'interests of justice' criterion should not operate to hinder a decision to initiate an investigation or to open a prosecution from being taken. It should only do so when exceptional conditions clearly show that such a decision would go against the important goals recognized in Article 53(1)(c) and (2)(c). The 2007 OTP-document offers a few examples where this could be the case. According to the OTP, if "a suspect's rights had been seriously violated in a manner that could bring the administration of justice into disrepute",[186] or if the suspect were "terminally ill" or had "been the subject of abuse amounting to serious human rights violations",[187] it would go against the interests of justice to prosecute him, even taking into consideration the gravity of the crime committed and the interests of victims in seeing justice done.

On the other hand, the ICC-OTP has indicated that the 'interests of justice' criterion should be distinguished from 'interests of peace', and it has made it clear that a decision not to investigate or prosecute should not be made on the

183 ICC-OTP, "Policy Paper on the Interests of Justice", September 2007, pp. 2–3 (https://www.legal-tools.org/doc/bb02e5/).

184 *Ibid.*, p. 1.

185 *Ibid.*

186 *Ibid.*, p. 4.

187 *Ibid.*, p. 7.

basis of the contributions it could make to a peace process. This is so both because the notion of 'interests of justice' has as goals "the prevention of serious crimes and guaranteeing lasting respect for international justice", and because interests of peace fall "within the mandate of institutions other than the Office of the Prosecutor".[188]

Thus, it seems like the pragmatic criterion related to the 'interests of justice' introduced by the ICC Statute will be rarely applied by the OTP and, when applied, it will operate as a criterion for *unselecting* rather than for selecting situations and cases. It is also quite evident that, due to its nature, the interpretation of this criterion will always require higher doses of discretion, since the factor to which it refers is imprecise and offers wide and fertile grounds for justifying decisions not to investigate or prosecute. Therefore, this criterion could easily open the door for arbitrary or subjective interpretations aimed more at restricting justice and the goals of crime prevention and respect for international justice than at preserving the interests of justice. These risks seem to be somewhat countered by the possibility of judicial review of decisions not to proceed on the basis of 'interests of justice' opened by Article 53(3)(b). Nonetheless, it is still doubtful that this criterion should be reproduced in documents on selection and prioritization criteria pertaining to other international or national jurisdictions.

Apart from the criteria that correspond to the situation and case selection process previously studied in this chapter, the ICC Statute seems to point at additional selection criteria related to practical considerations. In particular, such criteria have to do with the considerations that the ICC-OTP should make in order to comply with the obligations contained in Article 54(1)(b), which refer to the "respect [of] the interests and personal circumstances of victims and witnesses, including age, gender as defined in article 7, paragraph 3, and health, and take into account the nature of the crime, in particular where it involves sexual violence, gender violence or violence against children". Furthermore, according to the 2007 OTP document, such considerations also have to do with the need to examine the "availability of evidence and questions of security of victims, witnesses and staff, with a view to planning a potential investigation".[189] In the view of the OTP, these elements should be taken into account in "addition to considering the factors listed under Article 53",[190] and should therefore probably be considered as another cluster of situation and case selection criteria.

[188] *Ibid.*, pp. 8–9.

[189] *Ibid.*

[190] *Ibid.*

To summarize, the ICC Statute and its interpretation by the OTP point at four different clusters of criteria for selecting situations to investigate and cases to prosecute, which are to be assessed in a sequential manner: (a) criteria related to the jurisdiction of the ICC, aimed at establishing that there exists a reasonable basis to proceed (either to investigate or prosecute); (b) criteria related to the admissibility of cases, which refer to the gravity of crimes and to the subsidiary nature of the ICC's intervention; (c) the negative criterion consisting in the 'interests of justice' by which a decision not to investigate a situation or to prosecute a case could be exceptionally justified; and (d) criteria related to practical considerations that the OTP must take into account when selecting a case. Clusters (a) and (b) establish relatively novel criteria and precise factors through which such criteria can be assessed and measured. They concern fundamental jurisdictional and admissibility requirements. Cluster (c) is more problematic as it leaves open the possibility of arbitrary interpretations that could actually go against the interests of justice. And cluster (d) does not add much to the previously analysed clusters of criteria concerned with practical considerations of the prosecution.

Even though these are all the criteria that the ICC Statute refers to, the contributions to the discourse on selection and prioritization criteria by the ICC will continue through its practice. Indeed, the ICC-OTP's interpretations of the ICC Statute, and particularly its 2006 document, have strongly suggested that, apart from these selection criteria, the ICC can and should apply prioritization criteria in order to choose among the situations and cases that satisfy all the selection criteria only a few to be investigated and prosecuted:

> Case selection extends beyond admissibility: Any case, to be considered for prosecution before the Court, must meet the evidentiary and jurisdictional requirements as well as the admissibility requirements of the Statute (gravity and complementarity). Beyond that, however, it is the policy of the OTP to bring only a few cases from each situation. Not every case meeting the admissibility threshold of the Statute will be the subject of prosecution; it is necessary to select the cases most warranting prosecution. Among those cases meeting the admissibility thresholds, the OTP will consider factors such as the policy of focusing on persons most responsible for the most serious crimes as well as maximizing the contribution to prevention of crime.[191]

Hence, the document recognizes that the application of the selection criteria incorporated by the Statute will not be enough to select the cases that will actually end up being prosecuted by the ICC. Consequently, the OTP interprets

[191] ICC-OTP, "Criteria for Selection of Situations and Cases", p. 11, see *supra* note 154.

those criteria as a "threshold" or filter, the overcoming of which will determine which cases *could* be analysed by the ICC, but not necessarily which *will* actually be analysed or in which order of priority. Furthermore, it points at the need to formulate other criteria for accomplishing these two latter purposes, such as those related to the responsibility of perpetrators and to the potential contributions of cases to crime prevention.

The possibility of formulating this additional type of criteria and of conceiving them as prioritization criteria seems to be implicitly recognized by Article 53(4) of the ICC Statute, according to which the "Prosecutor may, at any time, reconsider a decision whether to initiate an investigation or prosecution based on new facts or information". Indeed, the admission of this possibility could be interpreted as implying that situations and cases that satisfy the threshold imposed by the selection criteria contained in the ICC Statute, but that nevertheless were not selected by a specific decision to investigate or prosecute, are not de-selected in the sense that they are excluded from the competency of the ICC, but rather are pushed behind in the list of priorities of the Court and can eventually be investigated and prosecuted. In that sense, all situations and cases that surpass the selection threshold are potential candidates for investigation and prosecution, and could thus be ranked by prioritization criteria.

Following a similar logic, in its 2006 document, the OTP proposed a list of criteria that are not included in the ICC Statute, and that are misleadingly labelled "selection criteria", when they are, in fact, prioritization criteria.[192] This list of criteria indicate factors that should be considered in decisions to select, among situations and cases that surpass the selection threshold, those that should be investigated and prosecuted with priority. Those factors are classified in terms of the decisions that may be needed for prioritizing regions, incidents, groups, persons, charges and crimes. This classification is interesting and novel for the discussion about prioritization criteria, as it is based on the different levels of analysis or detail from which a situation of rights violation can be considered, going from the wider or macro level of territories, to the more micro level of specific crimes committed by specific persons at specific times.

Thus, concerning *regions*, the ICC-OTP asserts that in territories that have been selected as relevant situations for investigation, the prioritization of a specific region may be needed for focusing the investigation and making it manageable. Further, the OTP proposes that such prioritization be "based primarily on gravity of the crimes and potential preventative impact of investigation, as

[192] *Ibid.*, pp. 11–12.

well as security considerations".[193] Hence, for the purpose of region prioritization, the OTP points at gravity and practical-considerations criteria that have been recognized by several of the criteria documents analysed in this chapter. But it also points at a semi-novel criterion related to the "potential preventive impact of the investigation", which has been recognized by other criteria documents in the sense of considering the impact of the investigation as a selection or prioritization factor, but that adds specificity to this criterion by focusing on prevention as the main relevant feature of the impact of investigations.

With regards to *incidents*, the 2006 document acknowledges that not all grave situations taking place in a selected region can be investigated by the ICC, and therefore establishes that the OTP will inevitably have to select "a comparatively small number of incidents as a basis for prosecution". For doing so, the OTP proposes to select such incidents so as "to provide a sample that is reflective of the gravest incidents and the main types of victimization" in so far as possible, given the need to guarantee the security and protection of witnesses, victims and staff as well as the access to evidence, particularly in situations of ongoing conflict.[194] Therefore, the OTP proposes and defends the use of a representativity criterion for the selection of incidents to investigate and prosecute – as discussed in Section 1.6. above – by arguing that the provision of a sample of the gravest incidents and main forms of victimization may counter the impossibility of the ICC to "establish a complete historical record".[195] As we showed in prior sections, this type of criterion has also been recognized by the BiH criminal justice system and by the ICTY. It is quite telling that the 2006 document – and later the 2016 policy paper on selection and prioritization, as discussed in Section 1.6. above and Chapter 6 below to which we are pleased to refer the reader – contemplates its use because it illustrates that representativity is an important piece in the prioritization puzzle and for prosecution strategy in war crimes jurisdictions.

With respect to *groups*, the 2006 document indicates that, in contexts of massive crime commission, the latter are often committed by several organizations or groups, such as armed groups. It consequently suggests that the responsibility for the gravest crimes and the potential preventive impact of their investigation should be the main factors to consider when deciding to prioritize the investigation and prosecution of one group over another.[196] The first factor is quite standard in lists of case selection and prioritization criteria, while the second has already been referred to in relation to the prioritization of regions. What

---

[193] *Ibid.*, p. 11.

[194] *Ibid.*

[195] *Ibid.*

[196] *Ibid.*

is interesting here is not so much the factors proposed as the aim that they intend to serve, which is to prioritize between different groups responsible for large-scale crimes, an aim that has not been acknowledged by other criteria documents reviewed by this chapter.

As regards *persons*, the OTP proposes the quite common and widely accepted notion of those "most responsible for most serious crimes" as the basis for prioritizing the prosecution of persons who have committed crimes in a context analysed by the ICC. Further, the OTP pins this notion down by referring to the also quite common criteria of "commanders and other superiors if their effective subordinates are involved in the crimes", of "those playing a major causal role in the crimes", and of "notorious perpetrators who distinguish themselves by their direct responsibility for particularly serious crimes".[197] Finally, it clarifies that mid- and low-ranking officials might be investigated and prosecuted if that is deemed "necessary for the whole case".[198] The OTP justifies the use of these criteria by establishing, as pretty much all prosecutors' offices concerned with core international crimes do, that "the policy of the OTP is to focus on those bearing the greatest responsibility".[199]

Therefore, the criteria proposed by the 2006 document on the responsibility and status of perpetrators are not innovative neither in content nor in scope. What is novel is that the OTP excluded criteria related to the role and status of the perpetrator from the considerations about the selection of situations and cases, and only incorporated them in the discussion about their prioritization. This can be explained at least in part by the fact that the ICC Statute did not point to the degree of responsibility as a relevant selection factor, and instead restricted the gravity consideration (present in both the jurisdiction and admissibility tests) to crimes, with no reference to perpetrators. However, in practice the operation of these criteria exclusively as prioritization and not as selection factors may not bring about different outcomes than those produced by jurisdictions exclusively or mainly focused on selecting cases concerning the most responsible perpetrators.

Concerning charges, the 2006 document asserts that it is its policy to select, among the crimes under its consideration, those that will be charged, and to formulate focused charges. Therefore, it proposes the "availability of evidence" as the main criterion that should guide the prioritization of the crimes to be charged.[200] However, it also recognizes as relevant criteria for this purpose the

---

[197] *Ibid.*

[198] *Ibid.*, p. 12.

[199] *Ibid.*

[200] *Ibid.*

"most serious crimes, representation of major crime patterns, impact, and the need for focused and expeditious trials".[201] Further, it establishes that it will "take particular account of crimes involving sexual violence and violence against children".[202] As can be seen, with the aim of prioritizing crimes to charge, the OTP refers to a variety of criteria that do not have much to do with one another, but that should rather belong to different clusters of criteria, as they do in other documents analysed in this chapter.

The choice of the practical consideration of evidence availability as the main criterion for prioritizing charges is understandable but could be criticized for leaving aside other considerations, such as the relative gravity of crimes and the impact of investigations, in favour of assuring that easier and more expeditious trials are conducted first. The suspicion that this could be the case is reaffirmed by the fact that the OTP refers specifically to the need for expeditious trials as another (less important) factor to take into consideration when prioritizing cases to charge. On the other hand, it is worth noting that the OTP seems to defend the notion of representativity once again when it refers to the representation of major crime patterns.

Perhaps the most interesting issue in this list of criteria is the introduction of what seem to be 'thematic prosecutions', that is, the priority prosecution of certain types of crimes (here, sexual violence and violence against children).[203] This does not seem to be based on their gravity (even though the OTP considers rape to be one of the gravest crimes, the reference to it is not linked to gravity here), but rather on their 'theme' or 'topic', perhaps because they have traditionally been under-represented in criminal justice. As such, thematic prosecutions seem to be used here as a quite novel prioritization criterion, which is absent or at least not explicitly recognized in other studied jurisdictions, and which therefore requires a strong and clear justification in terms of its need and convenience.

Finally, the 2006 OTP-document refers to the impact of the investigation, and particularly to its possible contributions to the prevention of crimes, as an additional criterion to be considered when prioritizing "sufficiently grave cases".[204] As an illustration of the importance of this criterion, it is noted that,

> the Office may for example pay particular attention to groups or individuals responsible for ongoing serious crimes, since arrest

[201] *Ibid.*

[202] *Ibid.*

[203] For more on 'thematic prosecution', see the first book on the topic: Morten Bergsmo (ed.), *Thematic Prosecution of International Sex Crimes*, Second Edition, TOAEP, Brussels, 2018 (http://www.toaep.org/ps-pdf/13-bergsmo-second).

[204] ICC-OTP, "Criteria for Selection of Situations and Cases", p. 12, see *supra* note 154.

> and prosecution of such persons can put an end to crimes. Consideration of impact may also lead to charges on matters such as the use of child soldiers, since this is a prevalent crime that is not widely prosecuted [...].[205]

As we mentioned above, the impact of the investigation is a relevant criterion, and its specification in terms of the possible contributions of the investigation to the prevention of crimes constitutes an important step forward in the definition of the content and scope of the impact criterion. Furthermore, this specification has the merit of focusing on the main goal that international criminal justice should pursue (crime prevention), and of indicating particular ways in which the application of this criterion by the ICC could contribute to the achievement of that goal. However, it is not entirely clear why this criterion is referred to independently from the other classification categories. On the one hand, it does not entirely correspond to the logic that underlies the classification (from more general to more detailed phenomena); and, on the other hand, it contains a criterion that was already referred to by several of those other categories. In that sense, it would be useful to explain how this criterion relates to the other prioritization criteria.

To conclude Section 5.3.2., apart from the selection criteria incorporated in the ICC Statute, the OTP documents that we have reviewed formulate prioritization criteria aimed at choosing situations to investigate and cases to prosecute from among those situations and cases that satisfy the threshold imposed by such selection criteria in the Statute. The contributions made by the formulation of these criteria do not consist so much in the novelty of their content as in the way in which they are classified, which does not correspond to the commonplace in criteria documents of topical clusters of criteria, but which rather refers to the different levels of analysis in which prioritization is considered relevant. Thus, going from the macro to the micro level, criteria are conceived for the prioritization of regions within territories, of incidents within regions, of groups that commit those incidents, of persons belonging to those groups, and of the charges that can be imputed to those persons. In that way, the criteria to which these different classifying categories refer to do not need to be hierarchically ranked in order to be applied as prioritization criteria, as they can easily serve the function of prioritization at each level of analysis.

5.4. Concluding Remarks

This chapter is grounded in the belief that the formulation and appropriate application of criteria for selecting or prioritizing core international crimes cases are important to deal with backlogs of cases in an adequate and justifiable way

[205] *Ibid.*

both at the national and international levels. We recognize that "the concrete application of any (selection or prioritization) criterion is always situation- and case-specific, i.e., the ultimate selection or prioritization decision cannot be precisely determined by abstract criteria".[206] Even though criteria cannot by themselves solve the problem of case backlogs, they can, when properly applied, ensure that the best-suited cases go to full investigation and prosecution first. That is essential when the capacity of a criminal justice system cannot process all cases in the backlog. It reduces and rationalizes the administration of the backlog and, in so doing, can enhance the efficacy and legitimacy of prosecutorial services.

In order to further the discourse on selection and prioritization criteria, this chapter describes in detail and critically analyses several key documents of national and international jurisdictions dealing with core international crimes in which criteria for selecting or prioritizing cases have been explicitly used.

The chapter first dealt with Bosnia and Herzegovina, which constitutes the seminal experience in criteria discussion, formulation and implementation at the national level – later followed by Colombia, as explained in Chapters 14 and 15 below – and which has without a doubt made one of the most important advancements in the consolidation of clusters of relevant criteria for selecting or prioritizing cases. Our chapter analysed three documents on the subject, produced by the most relevant representatives of the country's legal system, which have proved that the formulation of criteria constitutes a difficult and thorny process. Chapters 8, 16 and 17 below also discuss the experience of Bosnia and Herzegovina, whereas Chapters 11–20 consider other national jurisdictions (the Democratic Republic of the Congo, Canada, Argentina, Croatia, Serbia and Indonesia, in that order).

Later, our chapter scrutinized central documents of the ICTY and ICC, as two important examples of international criminal tribunals that have made significant contributions to the discourse on criteria formulation and implementation, both through their sound judgments and their mistakes. In particular, the ICTY exemplifies the risks of developing criteria in the course of the tribunal's practice, while the ICC shows the potentialities of foreseeing criteria early and thus being able to fine-tune them in practice. Chapters 9 and 10 below consider the ICTR and the ECCC, two additional international(ized) jurisdictions.

After having reviewed select criteria-documents proposed and employed by these jurisdictions, it can be suggested that there are two major pillars at the centre of the landscape of criteria for selection or prioritization of war crimes

[206] See Kai Ambos, "Introductory Note to Office of the Prosecutor", p. 1133, *supra* note 13.

cases: (a) 'gravity' and (b) 'representativity', and two lesser pillars: (c) policy considerations and (d) practical considerations.

The *gravity* pillar tends to encompass two types of criteria: the gravity or seriousness of the alleged crime, and the seriousness of the responsibility of the suspect. The two can be combined or presented separately, and they can be used as selection or prioritization criteria. Concerning the first type of criteria, a number of factors may serve as a basis for determining the gravity of crimes, including: (i) the number of victims, (ii) the area of destruction, (iii) the duration and repetition of the offence, (iv) the nature of the crimes, (v) the *modus operandi* of the criminal conduct (particular cruelty or flagrant disregard for the law), (vi) a discriminative motive, (vii) the defencelessness of victims (combatants/non-combatants, children, women), and (viii) the level of control of the alleged perpetrator. The seriousness of crimes has been recognized by all the documents analysed in this chapter, but they vary in terms of the factors they consider to indicate the gravity of crimes.

As regards the seriousness of the responsibility of the suspect, it depends, *inter alia*, on the *de jure* and *de facto* authority or role of the suspect, as well as on the form of participation or mode of liability. This criterion has been interpreted somewhat differently in the reviewed documents. Thus, with respect to the ICTY and the ICTR, the UN Security Council has formulated this criterion as "the most senior leaders suspected of being most responsible for crimes". In its turn, treating it as a prioritization criterion, the ICC Office of the Prosecutor has stated it as "those bearing the greatest degree of responsibility".[207] Arguably, the higher the rank of the suspect and the more directly this person is responsible for the crimes in question, the higher his or her level of responsibility is likely to be perceived. The commonly used category of 'notorious offender' should

[207] Other jurisdictions dealing with core international crimes cases have also recognized this criterion, and have formulated it in somewhat different ways. Thus, the Statute of the SCSL limits the jurisdiction of the Court to "persons who bear the greatest responsibility", reiterating Security Council Resolution 1315 of 2000. See Statute of the SCSL, 14 August 2000, Articles 1(1) and 15(1) (https://www.legal-tools.org/doc/aa0e20/) and Security Council Resolution 1315 (2000), UN Doc. S/RES/1315 (2000), 14 August 2000, para. 3 (https://www.legal-tools.org/doc/95897f/). Also, the Agreement on the Establishment of the Extraordinary Chambers in Cambodia and Law on the Establishment of Extraordinary Chambers, 10 August 2001, Articles 1 and 2 (https://www.legal-tools.org/doc/40d072/) stipulate that the Chambers have jurisdiction over "senior leaders of Democratic Kampuchea and those who were most responsible" for crimes committed between 1975 and 1979. See Article 2 of the Draft Agreement between the United Nations and the Royal Government of Cambodia concerning the Prosecution under Cambodian Law of Crimes Committed during the period of Democratic Kampuchea annexed to UN General Assembly Resolution 57/228, UN Doc. A/RES/57/228, 22 May 2003 (https://www.legal-tools.org/doc/533d2a/).

probably not be viewed as a sub-category of those who bear the greatest responsibility; rather, it should be viewed as giving more weight to the criterion of gravity of crimes based on a policy decision to address specific types of crimes or to address the concerns of specific victims. The determination of who bears the greatest responsibility should be conducted on the basis of objective factors. It is in the interest of transparency to keep policy and practical considerations conceptually separate.

Admittedly, these different thresholds for the seriousness of the responsibility of the suspect may seem somewhat confusing. Each institution or jurisdiction working on the formulation of criteria should choose what best serves its needs. The formulation chosen should provide adequate guidance to those who will work with it, it should be sufficiently clear to the public, and it should lend itself well to serve the interest of equal treatment of all cases.

The second pillar of criteria can be referred to as *representativity*. It simply means that, at the end of a process of core international crimes prosecutions, the accumulated case portfolio should reflect – or be representative of – the overall victimization caused by the crimes in the conflict or situation at hand. The most serious crimes and the crimes that the most senior leaders are suspected of being most responsible for should have been prosecuted at the end of the day. The areas and communities most affected by the crimes should have seen more of these crimes prosecuted than less affected communities. The most affected victim groups should have more of the crimes that caused the victimization prosecuted than other groups. Organizations or structures causing the most serious crimes should have more of their responsible members – or more of the crimes caused by them – prosecuted than other such organizations or structures. The reasoning behind this criterion seems rather self-explanatory. It is underpinned by concerns for the interests of victims, as well as by the capacity of the prosecutions of core international crimes to contribute to reconciliation and deterrence, as well as to truth elucidation. The balancing that this approach entails would seem necessary to ensure trust in the criminal justice system. We refer readers to the discussion in Section 1.6. above on how representativity differs from misconceived 'positive even-handedness'.

The first lesser pillar of criteria consists in *policy considerations*. This type of consideration is almost always made in prosecution services, but they may not be so visible to the public. However, they should be articulated and made public to the extent possible. Transparency is normally in the interest of the prosecution services and their work. Policy criteria for case selection or prioritization of core international crimes cases should be formalized and enforced equally in all cases. They have been recognized as criteria by most of the jurisdictions analysed in this chapter.

Finally, *practical considerations* are the bread and butter of criminal justice. There are major considerations that affect the selection or prioritization of core international crimes cases. But it is not clear whether these considerations should be treated as criteria in themselves. In any case, if they are, they should also be formalized and made public. That serves the interest of the prosecution services themselves. Again, most of the jurisdictions studied in this chapter have recognized these considerations as criteria.

It is not enough to formally adopt adequate selection or prioritization criteria if the way in which they should be applied is not established. One of the main problems faced by the jurisdictions analysed in this chapter is that the formulation of criteria is often not accompanied by guidelines that determine whether those criteria operate as a threshold (and therefore as selection criteria) or as a case-ranking mechanism (and therefore as prioritization criteria), and, in the latter case, that they do not establish a hierarchy among the criteria in question that would make such ranking easier.

On the other hand, having formally adopted criteria and even a clear set of guidelines for their application does not guarantee that the latter will always be done in an adequate way. We have seen in Section 5.3. above that the judges both at the ICTY and the ICC can play a role in ensuring that case-selection criteria are respected. This comes as no surprise if we consider the difficulties in only selecting suitable cases for prosecution in the internationalized criminal jurisdictions. It is not only the ICTY that has faced difficulties in this respect. As a matter of fact, it is not easy to point to any internationalized prosecution service that has without doubt succeeded with its case selection and prioritization. This is a common challenge and problem.

The understanding of criteria most commonly used by jurisdictions dealing with core international crimes might be useful for any jurisdiction facing the challenge of a large backlog of those types of cases. The management of such a queue of case-files on past atrocities can improve in efficiency, impartiality, transparency and legitimacy if criteria for selecting and prioritizing cases are formally adopted and appropriately applied. And the consideration, formulation and application of such criteria can be easier if jurisdictions have a clear idea of the menu of options existing in practice, as well as of the potentialities and limitations of those options. This chapter and book have hopefully contributed in some way to this end.

PART II: CRITERIA IN INTERNATIONAL(IZED) JURISDICTIONS

6

Case Selection and Prioritization at the International Criminal Court

Rod Rastan*

In 2016, the Office of the Prosecutor ('OTP') of the International Criminal Court ('ICC') issued its long-awaited *Policy Paper on Case Selection and Prioritisation.*[1] Many of the considerations contained in the policy paper are not new and had been a subject of earlier policy and strategic statement. For example, in 2003, in its first policy document, the OTP set out as a key consideration that it would, in principle, focus on those bearing the greatest responsibility:

> The global character of the ICC, its statutory provisions and logistical constraints support a preliminary recommendation that, as a general rule, the Office of the Prosecutor should focus its investigative and prosecutorial efforts and resources on those who bear the greatest responsibility, such as the leaders of the State or organisation allegedly responsible for those crimes.
>
> […] [the Office] will initiate prosecutions of the leaders who bear most responsibility for the crimes.
>
> [...] In some cases the focus of an investigation by the Office of the Prosecutor may go wider than high-ranking officers if, for example, investigation of certain types of crimes or those officers lower down the chain of command is necessary for the whole case.[2]

---

* **Rod Rastan** holds a Ph.D. from London School of Economics and an LL.M. from University of Nottingham. He serves as Legal Advisor in the Office of the Prosecutor ('OTP') of the International Criminal Court ('ICC'). The views expressed herein are solely the author's and do not necessarily reflect those of the ICC-OTP.

1 OTP, Policy Paper on Case Selection and Prioritisation, 15 September 2016 ('Policy Paper') (https://www.legal-tools.org/doc/182205/).

2 OTP, Paper on Some Policy Issues before the Office of the Prosecutor, September 2003, pp. 3, 7 ('OTP 2003 Paper on Policy Issues') (https://www.legal-tools.org/doc/f53870/). A similar focus had been recommended by a 2003 expert paper on complementarity, commissioned by the preparatory team of the ICC-OTP, see Morten Bergsmo and Song Tianying, "The Principle of Complementarity in Practice", in Morten Bergsmo, Klaus Rackwitz and Song Tianying (eds.), *Historical Origins of International Criminal Law: Volume 5*, Torkel Opsahl Academic EPublisher ('TOAEP'), Brussels, 2017 (https://www.toaep.org/ps-pdf/24-bergsmo-rackwitz-

This statement reflected certain conceptual consideration as to institutional design, in the Rome Statute's preambular emphasis on the most serious crimes of international concern and the Court's complementary relationship to national criminal jurisdictions, which would retain the primary responsibility to investigate and prosecute such crimes. The policy statement also mirrored the then evolving practice of the International Criminal Tribunal for the former Yugoslavia ('ICTY') and the International Criminal Tribunal for Rwanda ('ICTR'), not least as the initial 'primacy' gave way to completion strategies.[3] And it corresponded to the organizational reality of the Court's more limited capacity and budget, set against its vast potential personal and territorial reach: with each situation confronting the new Court capable of being as complex and grave as those that precipitated the establishment of prior *ad hoc* Tribunals.[4] The 2003 policy stated that this would require investigations focused on crime-pattern analysis and chains of command, and the collection of types of evidence establishing the criminal responsibility of those who designed the plans, gave the orders or otherwise supervised or failed to prevent the commission of crimes.[5]

Several other themes are treated in the 2003 policy paper that relate to case 'prioritization', even if they were not named as such at the time:

1. the prevailing situation in the country or region concerned, including the nature and stage of the conflict and any intervention by the international community;
2. 'practical realities', such as the availability of general security conditions on the ground as well as issues of witness protection, the availability of necessary assistance from national authorities or the international community, including on the arrest of suspects;[6]
3. the extent to which the OTP could prompt domestic action for crimes committed "within States or by State agencies which have normally functioning institutions", stating as "a general rule, the policy of the Office of the Prosecutor will be to undertake investigations only where there is a clear case of failure to act by the State or States concerned";

song), recommending a "prosecutorial policy focusing on persons most responsible" (p. 769, para. [60]).

3 See Chapter 8 below.

4 OTP 2003 Paper on Policy Issues, p. 6, see *supra* note 2.

5 *Ibid.*, p. 7.

6 The paper goes on to note: "the Prosecutor will need the support of national or international forces in order to investigate in situ. If these forces are not available, the Prosecutor will need to investigate from outside and rely on international co-operation for the arrest and surrender of the alleged perpetrators".

4. the need for co-operation and consultation on issues of forum determination where several States may have concurrent jurisdiction and the OTP is already investigating within a given situation;
5. the scope for thematic investigations, such as financial links with crimes, undertaken in tandem with national authorities, to prove the commission of crimes before the ICC as well as for the purpose of furthering domestic prosecutions;
6. the scope for deterrence;
7. the Court's limited budget and the need to be cost-effective; and
8. the need for consultation and co-ordination between national authorities, the international community and the Court to prevent the emergence of an 'impunity gap' as a result of the OTP's focus on those most responsible.[7]

A review of the OTP's past incarnations of a dedicated policy paper on case selection is treated separately by Paul Seils in this volume.[8] Unlike the 2006 draft policy paper discussed by him in Chapter 7 below and by Morten Bergsmo and María Paula Saffon in Chapter 5 above – which dealt jointly with 'Situation and Case Selection' – the OTP ultimately decided to separate out the two processes. In 2013, it issued a stand-alone *Policy Paper on Preliminary Examination*[9] which focuses on the stage leading up to the opening of investigations and in 2016 it issued its policy on case selection and prioritization during the course of such investigations.

The 2016 case selection and prioritization policy refers to two other strategic documents, the *Strategic Plan* and the *Basic Size Report*, which frame the context of policy and therefore deserve some introductory treatment below. A subsequent policy paper on 'Situation Completion', issued in 2021 and foreshadowed in the case selection policy paper, brings up the tail end of prioritization considerations by signalling when the OTP might consider it has brought forward all cases it intends to investigate and prosecute within a given situation.[10]

---

7 *Ibid.*, pp. 2–3.

8 See also Paul Seils, "The Selection and Prioritization of Cases by the Office of the Prosecutor of the International Criminal Court", in Morten Bergsmo (ed.), *Criteria for Prioritizing and Selecting Core International Crimes Cases*, Second Edition, TOAEP, Oslo, 2010, pp. 69–78 (https://www.legal-tools.org/doc/dd9ac0/).

9 OTP, Policy Paper on Preliminary Examination, November 2013 ('2013 Policy Paper on Preliminary Examination') (https://www.legal-tools.org/doc/acb906/).

10 OTP, Policy on Situation Completion, 15 June 2021 ('2021 Policy on Situation Completion') (https://www.legal-tools.org/doc/mdl417/).

6.1. OTP Strategic Plan

During the term of its first Prosecutor, Luis Moreno Ocampo, the OTP had developed an operational strategy based on 'focused investigations and prosecutions', corresponding to a limited number of charges and incidents while being reflective of the broader range of criminality within a given situation, and reliance on a limited number of witnesses to reduce the number of persons put at risk on account of their interaction with the Court. The aim of this strategy was to engage in high-impact investigations leading to efficient presentation of evidence or expeditious proceedings, in the light of the reality of limited resources stretched across multiple situations and cases. As set out in 2003, the strategy aimed at selecting for investigation and prosecution those bearing the greatest responsibility for the most serious crimes.

The 2012–2015 Strategic Plan, adopted under Prosecutor Fatou Bensouda, signalled a change in policy, emphasizing the need to collect more diverse forms of evidence, and replaced the notion of focused investigations with the principle of in-depth, open-ended investigations, namely, pursuing multiple case hypotheses throughout the investigation to strengthen decision-making with regard to the cases selected for prosecution.[11] The Strategic Plan more prominently adopted a strategy to build upwards where the responsibility of those most responsible could not be sufficiently established at the outset, and stressed the need to be trial-ready as early as possible. Although foreshadowed in 2003, it stated more explicitly that the approach might need to be adjusted in some situations due to the limited scope for investigative activities or a lack of co-operation. In such situations,

> A strategy of gradually building upwards might then be needed in which the Office first investigates and prosecutes a limited number of mid- and high-level perpetrators in order to ultimately have a reasonable prospect of conviction for those most responsible. The Office will also consider prosecuting lower level perpetrators where their conduct has been particularly grave and has acquired extensive notoriety.[12]

---

[11] See OTP, Strategic Plan: 2012–2015, October 2013, p. 6 ('OTP Strategic Plan: 2012–2015') (https://www.legal-tools.org/doc/954beb/). See also *id.*, para. 23: "The notion of focused investigations is therefore replaced by the principle of in-depth, open-ended investigations while maintaining focus to avoid over-expanding the investigations at the expense of efficiency".

[12] *Ibid.* See also *ibid.*, para. 22:

> In the light of limitations in investigative possibilities and/or a lack of cooperation and the required evidentiary standards, the Office is re-thinking its approach to proving the criminal responsibility of the most responsible. In such circumstances a strategy of gradually building upwards is needed. The Office would therefore first investigate and prosecute a

The classification of suspects into persons most responsible, mid- to high-level perpetrators, and notorious perpetrators also reflects the practice before other international courts and tribunals, as referred to elsewhere in this volume, including Chapters 8, 9 and 10 below.[13] Finally, in the light of the evidentiary

limited number of mid- and high-level perpetrators in order to ultimately have a reasonable chance to convict the most responsible. The Office will also consider prosecuting lower level perpetrators where their conduct has been particularly grave and has acquired extensive notoriety. Such a strategy will in the end be more cost-effective than having unsuccessful or no prosecutions against the highest placed perpetrators.

This approach had already been implemented in Darfur, where the OTP had first brought charges against one of the most notorious Janjaweed militia leaders and the then State Minister of Interior for Darfur, and only later built upwards towards the Head of State and the then federal-level Minister of Interior.

13 In the case of other *ad hoc* international courts and tribunals, this was guided as much by prosecutorial policy as by institutional design. Thus, the proceedings before the International Military Tribunal at Nuremberg focused on "major criminals whose offences have no particular geographical location and who will be punished by the joint decision of the Governments of the Allies," while others "responsible for or have taken a consenting part in the above atrocities, massacres and executions will be sent back to the countries in which their abominable deeds were done in order that they may be judged and punished according to the laws of these liberated countries and of free governments which will be erected therein"; Charter of the International Military Tribunal, 8 August 1945 (https://www.legal-tools.org/doc/64ffdd/); Agreement for the Prosecution and Punishment of the Major War Criminal of the European Axis, 8 August 1945 (https://www.legal-tools.org/doc/844f64/); Declaration Concerning Atrocities Made at the Moscow Conference, 30 October 1943 (https://www.legal-tools.org/doc/3c6e23/); Charter of the International Military Tribunal for the Far East, 19 January 1946, Article 1 (https://www.legal-tools.org/doc/44f398/). See also, United Nations Security Council Resolution 1534 (2004), UN Doc. S/RES/1534, 26 March 2004 (https://www.legal-tools.org/doc/4e06ee/), adopted as part of completion strategies of the ICTY and ICTR, calling on both tribunals to concentrate pending indictments on "the most senior leaders suspected of being most responsible for crimes within the jurisdiction of the relevant Tribunal" and to proceed with "the transfer of cases involving intermediate and lower rank accused to competent national jurisdictions" (see Chapter 8 below for a more detailed discussion). See also Statute for the Special Court of Sierra Leone, 14 August 2000, Article 1 (https://www.legal-tools.org/doc/aa0e20/) (stating that the "Special Court shall […] have the power to prosecute persons who bear the greatest responsibility for serious violations of international humanitarian law and Sierra Leonean law committed in the territory of Sierra Leone since 30 November 1996, including those leaders who, in committing such crimes, have threatened the establishment of and implementation of the peace process in Sierra Leone."); Law on the Establishment of the Extraordinary Chambers, with inclusion of amendments as promulgated on 27 October 2004, 10 August 2001, Article 1 (https://www.legal-tools.org/doc/9b12f0/) (stating that the "purpose of this law is to bring to trial senior leaders of Democratic Kampuchea and those who were most responsible for the crimes and serious violations of Cambodian penal law, international humanitarian law and custom, and international conventions recognized by Cambodia, that were committed during the period from 17 April 1975 to 6 January 1979.").

standards demanded already at the confirmation stage, the Strategic Plan emphasized the need to be trial-ready as early as possible.[14]

The subsequent 2016–2018 Strategic Plan built on the same elements with regard to prosecutorial policy, and also referred to a number of factors that have impacted on case prioritization.[15] In particular, it referred to the unforeseen events that had set back or delayed other cases that were under investigation or slated for investigation. This included the increase in investigation for Article 70 offences against the administration of justice arising from allegations of witness interference in the Central African Republic ('CAR') and Kenya situations, the transfers to the Court of wanted suspects who were long at large, including Bosco Ntaganda (Democratic Republic of the Congo ('DRC')), Charles Blé Goudé (Côte d'Ivoire), and Dominic Ongwen (Uganda), as well as the opening of new investigations in response to the outbreak of contemporary violence between Séléka and anti-balaka forces in CAR, leading to a new situation CAR II.[16] The Strategic Plan stated that the consequence of these developments was that the OTP had to deprioritize other "urgently needed activities" – these being identified as making previously investigated hibernated cases "trial-ready", starting its investigations against the other (pro-Ouattara) side of the conflict in Côte d'Ivoire, as well as pursuing additional cases in Libya, Darfur, Mali and the DRC.[17]

The 2016–2018 Strategic Plan made reference to prioritization not just across different cases, but also in relation to charges *within* cases, with particular emphasis given to investigating and prosecuting sexual and gender-based crimes and crimes against children, based on then extant and anticipated policy papers.[18] Also anticipated in the Strategic Plan was a policy document on its "exit strategy" (later called "situation completion") for closing investigations within a given situation.[19]

---

14 OTP Strategic Plan: 2012–2015, para. 4, see *supra* note 11.

15 OTP, Strategic Plan: 2016–2018, November 2015, paras. 35–40 ('OTP Strategic Plan: 2016–2018') (https://www.legal-tools.org/doc/2dbc2d/). See also OTP, Strategic Plan 2019–2021, July 2019, para. 24 (OTP Strategic Plan: 2019–2021) (https://www.legal-tools.org/doc/7ncqt3/).

16 OTP Strategic Plan: 2016–2018, para. 18, see *supra* note 15.

17 *Ibid.*

18 Referring to the OTP, Policy Paper on Sexual and Gender-Based Crimes, June 2014 (https://www.legal-tools.org/doc/7ede6c/), and anticipating the OTP, Policy on Children, November 2016 (https://www.legal-tools.org/doc/c2652b/). See also, OTP Strategic Plan: 2012–2015, pp. 16–17, see *supra* note 11.

19 OTP Strategic Plan: 2016–2018, para. 38, see *supra* note 15. The development of a policy on completion of situations is recalled as a priority in OTP Strategic Plan: 2019–2021, para. 23, see *supra* note 15.

Finally, echoing themes first mentioned in 2003, the 2016–2018 Strategic Plan stated, as a goal, the development with partners of "a coordinated investigative and prosecutorial strategy to close the impunity gap".[20] While the notion of the 'impunity gap' as used by the OTP traditionally focused on the need for greater burden sharing with national authorities on core international crimes, this section also focused on other types of criminality that intersect with such crimes (such as organized or transnational crimes, financial crimes and terrorism) and which often impede the closing of the impunity gap because they "fuel the continuation of a conflict and can lead to the commission of ICC crimes".[21] Framing this goal in terms of both prevention and suppression, the OTP expressed its interest in exploring collaboration and co-ordination on information, evidence and investigative standards both to strengthen its own investigations and to contribute to the efforts of others. The main thrust of the section was that a co-ordinated investigative and prosecutorial strategy to close the impunity gap for ICC crimes is not realizable without examining also inter-connected areas of criminal activity – and that while the OTP "has no mandate to deal with other instances of criminality closely associated with atrocity crimes", more could be done to exploit areas of overlap.[22]

6.2. Basic Size Report

The other OTP strategic document referenced in the case selection and prioritization policy, and set as a backdrop, is the OTP's 2015 Basic Size Report. This report focused on the essential question of what resources the OTP needs to sustain its activities and to determine its capacity model - and which, as a result, drives the workload of the Court as a whole. Submitted to the Assembly of States Parties ('ASP') as part of the budgetary process, it attempted to 're-set' the OTP's operating model by detailing for States Parties each of the processes and steps involved in bring cases to full cycle. According to the report, the 'Basic Size' proposed by the OTP would enable it "to adequately respond – with a rea-

[20] OTP Strategic Plan: 2016–2018, para. 100, see *supra* note 15.

[21] *Ibid.*, paras. 100–102.

[22] Suggested areas for exploration include exchanging best practices on specific investigative and prosecutorial challenges connected with ICC crimes; co-ordination on technological tools used by first responders to preserve evidence; a common open-source crime database between law enforcement agencies or alternatively the sharing of resultant analytical products; a platform for the exchange of confidential and operational information between law enforcement agencies investigating similar or related cases; and capacity building and technical assistance by third parties in post-conflict countries; *ibid.*, para. 104. See similarly, OTP Strategic Plan: 2019–2021, paras. 48–56, *supra* note 15, which states it "will maintain this strategic goal", formulated as "Strategic goal 6: to further strengthen the ability of the Office and its partners to close the impunity gap".

sonable degree of prioritisation – to demands for its intervention without undermining quality and efficiency".[23] Recognizing that a 'full' demand-driven approach would not be realistic, the OTP's report advocated "a demand-based approach, where prioritisation of activities will still be required, resulting in a pace below the level of full demand".[24] The projected aim of the Basic Size model was to enable the OTP to conduct up to six to seven parallel investigations a year, from the current four, with each investigation estimated to take an average of three years to complete, in order to service an average annual workload of five cases in pre-trial, five cases in trial, and two cases on appeal.[25] This includes the opening of cases within both existing and, as a result of preliminary examination activities, new situations.

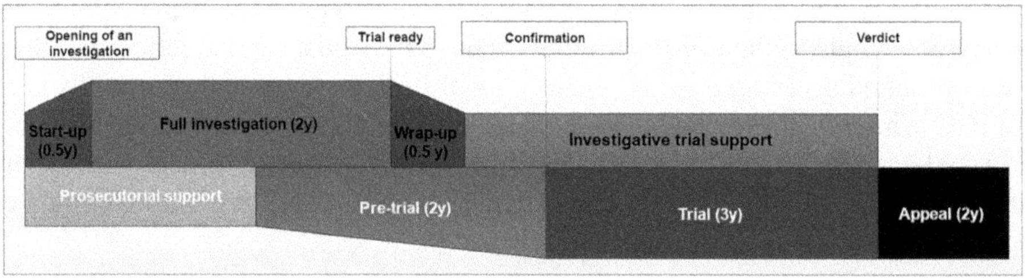

Figure 1. Diagram of average timelines, OTP Basic Size Report.[26]

Irrespective of whether the described basic size would have been attainable, if it had been approved and the required resources granted by the ASP, the report provides useful insights on the operational reality and capacity-constraints of the OTP, deconstructing the working processes involved in building and submitting a case for prosecution and thereby setting in context the number of the considerations set out in its policy and strategy documents. Although the budget

---

[23] ICC, Report of the Court on the Basic Size of the Office of the Prosecutor, 17 September 2015, ICC-ASP/14/21, para. 5 ('Basic Size Report') (https://www.legal-tools.org/doc/b27d2a/).

[24] *Ibid.*:

> The Office will not be in a position to immediately respond to all demands for its intervention. This would lead to a financially unpredictable and untenable situation. While recognising that a demand-driven approach is the only approach consistent with the purpose of the ICC as outlined in the Rome Statute: '*to put an end to impunity for the gravest crimes of international concern*', the OTP assesses that presenting a 'full' demand-driven approach would not be realistic, in particular, as this would require the Office to respond to all demands made to it simultaneously in a manner that would vastly outstrip existing budgetary assumptions (i.e. significant increases resulting in multiple cases in multiple situations). Instead, the Office has chosen a demand-based approach, where prioritisation of activities will still be required, resulting in a pace below the level of full demand.

[25] *Ibid.*, paras.7–9.

[26] *Ibid.*, para. 27.

does not dictate *which cases* are selected by the OTP within a given situation, it clearly has a direct impact on *how many cases* can be investigated and prosecuted at any given time. This might, in turn, affects the pace at which the Court is able to respond to atrocity crimes and the breadth and scope of its cases concerning different groups, both within a situation and across different situations, thereby impacting also perceived credibility and performance.

6.3. Policy Paper on Case Selection and Prioritisation

The Policy Paper on Case Selection and Prioritisation itself was circulated in draft for comments on 29 February 2016[27] and finalized on 15 September 2016. Given the progression of OTP activities from preliminary examination to investigation, there is a close correlation between the *Policy Paper on Preliminary Examination* and the 2016 policy paper in terms of the applicable legal principles, which derive largely from the independence of the mandate of the OTP, the impartiality flowing from the application of the law consistently and without any adverse distinction, and from the Office's duty of objectivity.[28] Similarly, the legal criteria established in the Statute for the opening of investigations mirror closely those required for bringing forward a case for prosecution.[29] Given this close correlation, discussion in the sections that follow will focus on the defining elements that distinguish case selection and prioritization from preliminary examinations.

The policy paper emphasizes that both the selection and prioritization criteria will be continuously evaluated during the course of investigations. This is axiomatic since any initial case hypothesis will need to be tested, revised and possibly abandoned in the light of the information and evidence collected. Similarly, prioritization criteria that depend on strategic or operational factors may need to be reassessed due to changes in the operating environment. A case that is initially selected and prioritized might later be abandoned, for example, because the evidence collected disproves the initial case hypothesis, exonerates the persons or groups under investigation, or otherwise fatally undermines the

27 OTP, Draft Paper on Case Selection and Prioritisation, 29 February 2016 (https://www.legal-tools.org/doc/aa1cfc/).

28 Rome Statute of the International Criminal Court, 17 July 1998, Articles 21(3), 42(1), 54(1) ('Rome Statute') (http://www.legaltools.org/doc/7b9af9/).

29 Compare, for example, the factors set out in Article 53(1)(a)–(c), which also find application at the Article 15 stage *via* Rule 48, with the case-specific requirements of Articles 17, 19 and 58(1). Although there is no mandatory requirement to assess the interests of justice at the stage of bringing cases for prosecution, the 2016 policy paper affirms, at paragraphs 24 and 33, that the OTP will nonetheless consider this factor as a matter of policy and best practice at the case selection and prioritization stage.

credibility or reliability of other evidence collected such that it is no longer supports a prosecution with a reasonable prospect of conviction. It may also be that the crimes alleged to have occurred in the incident(s) under investigation prove to be less grave than initially suspected (due to their scale, nature, manner of commission or impact) or the suspected degree of participation of the persons or groups under investigation may be diminished to such an extent that the case no longer meets the prescribed selection or prioritization criteria. Alternatively, an investigated case that had been de-prioritized might become viable because new evidence emerges, there is a unique opportunity to gather crucial testimonial or physical evidence, co-operation doors open, or there is a tangible arrest opportunity. Inevitably, how the different selection and prioritization criteria will interact in practice will perforce depend on the facts and circumstances of each case and, therefore, resist easy predictability.

6.3.1. Selection Criteria

Gravity serves as the predominant case selection criterion in the policy paper, consistent with the OTP's initial 2003 policy statement and subsequent strategy documents to focus, in principle, on the most serious crimes, or the gravest criminal conduct, within a given situation. The criteria for selection thus all revolve around notions of gravity, whether in terms of the crimes allegedly committed, the degree of responsibility of alleged perpetrators or charging policy. Chapters 21 and 22 below deal specifically with gravity.

6.3.1.1. Gravity of Crimes

The first selection criterion is based on the gravity of the crimes. There is some scope for confusion and overlap here between the notions of 'gravity of the crimes' and 'gravity of the case' as used in the Statute. The latter is arguably broader and encompasses all aspects of 'a case', in line with its usage under Article 17(1)(d) of the Rome Statute to determine admissibility (gravity). Other provisions of the Statute, particularly those related to sentencing, distinguish between the gravity of 'the crime' itself and the 'individual circumstances' of the convicted person.[30] In similar vein, the 2016 policy paper distinguishes as separate case selection criteria factors relevant to the crime itself from those relevant to the particular role and participation of the alleged perpetrator.

There remains, nonetheless, some scope for overlap between the different selection criteria since considerations such as 'manner of commission' which

[30] See, for example, Article 77(1)(b), in the context of determining a life sentence, where the Court is required to examine "[…] the extreme gravity of the crime and the individual circumstances of the convicted person". Rule 145(1)(b) similarly requires the Court to "[b]alance all the relevant factors, including any mitigating and aggravating factors and consider the circumstances both *of the convicted person* and *of the crime*" (emphasis added).

appears under 'gravity of the crime', includes "any motives involving discrimination held by the direct perpetrators" - which appears to coincide with "any motive involving discrimination" under the 'degree of responsibility' criterion. Such overlap may be unavoidable when relying on 'gravity' as the overarching thread of three selection criteria. It also does not pose a problem as such, as long as it is kept in view during its application and does not lead to some form of superficial double-counting.

There is also inevitable overlap in the way the factors constituting gravity are to be assessed – both as a legal criterion for the admissibility of a 'case' under Article 17(1)(d) (Section 4 of the policy paper) and as a discretionary assessment for the 'gravity of the crimes' for case selection (Section 5 of the policy paper). Thus, as with the Regulations of the OTP, the 2013 *Preliminary Examination Policy Paper* and the case law of the Court on Article 17(1)(d), this discretionary assessment contains both quantitative and qualitative considerations relating to the scale, nature, manner of commission, and impact of the crimes.[31] This should perhaps come as no surprise since the factors adopted by the OTP and Chambers for the assessment of Article 17(1)(d) have, in turn, drawn heavily from those listed under Rule 145 of the ICC Rules of Procedure and Evidence for purpose of determining the 'gravity of the crime' and the 'individual circumstances' of the convicted person.

The most obvious instance of overlap, however, is in the double iteration of the gravity assessment under Sections 4 (legal criteria) and 5 (case selection criteria) of the policy paper. The main stated difference is in the relative stringency applied at each stage – in that while a given gravity threshold might satisfy the legal test under Article 17(1)(d), a comparatively higher gravity threshold is needed for case selection. Considering the typically large-scale, widespread and systematic nature of conduct within a given situation, attributable to multiple persons at different levels of responsibility, many potential cases might meet the legal threshold under Article 17(1)(d), but not all can be investigated and prosecuted. Thus, selection among multiple possible cases becomes necessary - meaning that the OTP will need to select, as a function of its discretion, between the many cases that might all be legally admissible. As the factors that

[31] See, for example, ICC, *Prosecutor v. Bahar Idriss Abu Garda*, Decision on the confirmation of charges, 8 February 2010, ICC-02/05-02/09-243-Red, para. 31 (https://www.legal-tools.org/doc/cb3614/); *Situation in the Republic of Côte d'Ivoire*, Corrigendum to 'Decision Pursuant to Article 15 of the Rome Statute on the Authorisation of an Investigation into the Situation in the Republic of Côte d'Ivoire', 3 October 2011, ICC-02/11-14-Corr, paras. 203–204 (https://www.legal-tools.org/doc/e0c0eb/). See also, Regulations of the Office of the Prosecutor, 23 April 2009, Regulation 29(2) ('Regulations of OTP') (https://www.legal-tools.org/doc/a97226/).

are indicative of gravity remain the same, it is only the threshold that can be raised to a higher level.[32]

The table below summarizes the factors spelled out in the policy paper. As noted above, these are largely reflective of those set out in the 2013 *Policy Paper on Preliminary Examination*, and apply both to the assessment of gravity as a legal criterion and as a discretionary factor.[33]

Scale	number of direct and indirect victims
	extent of the damage caused by the crimes, in particular, the bodily or psychological harm caused to the victims and their families
	geographical or temporal spread (high intensity of the crimes over a brief period or low intensity of crimes over an extended period)
Nature	killings
	rapes, other sexual or gender-based crimes
	crimes committed against or affecting children
	persecution
	imposition of conditions of life on a group calculated to bring about its destruction
Manner of commission	means employed to execute the crime
	extent to which the crimes were systematic or resulted from a plan or organized policy or otherwise resulted from the abuse of power or official capacity
	existence of elements of particular cruelty, including the vulnerability of the victims
	any motives involving discrimination held by the direct perpetrators of the crimes
	the use of rape and other sexual or gender-based violence
	crimes committed by means of, or resulting in, the destruction of the environment or of protected objects
Impact	increased vulnerability of victims
	terror subsequently instilled
	social, economic and environmental damage inflicted on the affected communities, with particular consideration of Rome Statute crimes committed by means of, or that result in, *inter alia*, the destruction of the environment, the illegal exploitation of natural resources or the illegal dispossession of land

Table 1: Criteria for assessing gravity, *Policy Paper on Case Selection and Prioritisation*

32 Policy Paper, para. 36, see *supra* note 1.

33 See Policy Paper, paras. 32 and 36, see *supra* note 1.

The last set of factors relating to the assessment of impact generated widespread media reporting and some confusion at the time of the policy paper's issuance, with some suggestion offered that the OTP had decided to expand the Court's subject-matter jurisdiction to prosecute entirely new crimes. As should be obvious, the focus above is on the impact of *existing* Rome Statute crimes, not on a new category of crimes outside of the ICC's competence. The statement also builds upon notions already contained in the 2013 *Policy Paper on Preliminary Examination.*[34] What appears as new is the additional emphasis that the OTP will give "particular consideration" to the "Rome Statute crimes committed by means of, or that result in, *inter alia*, the destruction of the environment, the illegal exploitation of natural resources or the illegal dispossession of land". These are best understood as the secondary effects of Rome Statute crimes.

Practically speaking, this might mean that where, hypothetically, there are a number of incidents where the civilian population is attacked and in some such incidents the attack is committed by such means as, for example, poisoning wells or contaminating the land, thereby depriving the civilian population of the basis and their means of livelihood, such factors might elevate the impact of that particular attack. Or a particular attack might form part of competition between rival armed groups or forces to control territory in order to illegally extract the natural resources of the area. Another example might relate to the crime of deportation or transfer of the population as a crime against humanity committed by means of the destruction of the environment or the dispossession of land, to prevent return. Under the policy, the OTP might decide to focus on such incidents out of many others because of the resultant heightened impact.[35]

The close correlation of Rome Statute crimes to these three considerations (destruction of the environment, illegal exploitation of natural resources and illegal dispossession of land), which often fuel violence whether in conflict zones or peace-time, and can have such long-term repercussions for affected societies, lend themselves to an appreciative assessment of aggravated impact in these circumstances. They enable reflection of the broader context in which Rome Statute crimes are committed, including their economic and social drivers and the full range of actors involved. At the same time, it should be recalled that these considerations remain one of several impact factors, located within a broader cluster of factors relating to the nature, scale and manner of commission.

---

[34] 2013 Policy Paper on Preliminary Examination, para. 65, see *supra* note 9, describing factors for assessing impact as including "social, economic and environmental damage inflicted on the affected communities".

[35] This would mean that such secondary effects could be considered, as a matter of policy, as part of case selection to help identify the gravity of cases, even they would meet *per se* the high threshold required by Article 8(2)(b)(iv) for the charging of disproportionate attacks.

Hence, the totality of considerations will need to inform each case-selection decision.

6.3.1.2. Degree of Responsibility of Alleged Perpetrators

The second case-selection criterion relates to the OTP's long stated goal to focus on those who appear to be the most responsible.[36] Broadly consistent with earlier iterations of OTP policy, the 2016 policy paper has an in-principle focus with certain degrees of flexibility:

- most responsible;
- other mid- and high-level perpetrators to build upwards;
- low-level notorious perpetrators.

In this regard, the case selection policy paper recalls notes that the phrase 'most responsible' does not necessarily equate with the *de jure* hierarchical status, but will need to be assessed on a case-by-case basis.[37]

Drawing on Rule 145 of the ICC Rules of Procedure and Evidence, the policy paper states that as investigations progress the extent of responsibility of any identified alleged perpetrator(s) will be assessed on the basis of, *inter alia*:

- nature of the unlawful behaviour;
- degree of their participation and intent;
- existence of any motive involving discrimination; and
- any abuse of power or official capacity.

Clearly, elements relating to the specific role of individuals will only become apparent as the investigation unfolds and cannot be determined in advance in the initial case hypothesis. Hence, also recalled is the need to avoid the risk of a suspect-driven inquiry, instead of an objective and open-ended investigations focusing on the crime base to gradually identify the organization(s) and structure(s) involved and individuals allegedly responsible for the commission of the crimes.[38]

The internal organization of groups will also be context specific. Some organizations may be hierarchical, structured along *de jure* or *de facto* pyramidal lines. Others may be based on more flexible horizontal networks or flexible systems where members integrate to operationalize the commission of the crime without a charismatic or bureaucratic leadership structure. As the Appeals

[36] See Regulations of OTP, Regulation 34(1), see *supra* note 31; OTP 2003 Paper on Policy Issues, p. 3, see *supra* note 2; OTP Strategic Plan: 2016–2018, para. 34, last bullet point, see *supra* note 15.

[37] Policy Paper, para. 43, see *supra* note 1. See, for example, the notion of a person "effectively acting" as a military commander in Article 28(a).

[38] *Ibid.*, para. 42.

Chamber has observed, the role of persons or groups may vary considerably depending on the circumstances of the case and, therefore, should not be exclusively assessed or predetermined on excessively formalistic grounds.[39] Merely formal assumptions in this regard could "ignore the highly variable constitutions and operations of different organizations".[40] Xabier Agirre, in Chapter 21 below, illustrates some of the different models of internal organization and hierarchy, distinguishing between charismatic, bureaucratic and network types.[41] Some cases before the ICC, such as those concerning members of the Lord's Resistance Army ('LRA') have elements of charismatic and bureaucratic formations, based on Joseph Kony's charismatic style of leadership linking him directly with the mass of his subordinates as well as the tactical groupings in the LRA which are common to more conventional military units.[42] The case theories concerning the use of armed groups and armed forces in other cases in the DRC, CAR, Darfur, Georgia or Ukraine, concerning the role of civilian or military leaders or commanders within each organization, operate along a classical bureaucratic model of organized power apparatus, based on a hierarchy of echelons subordinated to a central authority. The Kenya cases displayed the interaction of a number of different actors in network formations, comprising a coalition of political, media, financial, tribal or police or military components which allegedly co-ordinated horizontally, as well as elements of formal bureaucratic hierarchies within such networks. There may thus be mixed types or complex variations of authority within different levels of organization in each case.

Since the OTP will typically select cases for prosecution which involve persons at the highest echelons of responsibility, direct or indirect linkage evidence as well as overall organizational theory will often be critical. The challenge of the OTP in these cases is to test counter hypotheses based, for example, on the malleability of formal hierarchies, elements of internal dysfunction, contextual factors affecting their cohesion, and the alleged inherent difficulty for the leaders to know or foresee the action of their subordinates.[43] The OTP will

39 ICC, *Situation in the Democratic Republic of the Congo*, Judgment on the Prosecutor's appeal against the decision of the Pre-Trial Chamber I entitled "Decision on the Prosecutor's Application for Warrants of Arrest, Article 58", under seal 13 July 2006, reclassified public 23 September 2008, ICC-01/04-169, paras. 69–79 (https://www.legal-tools.org/doc/8c20eb/).

40 *Ibid.*, para. 77.

41 Xabier Agirre Aranburu, "Gravity of Crimes and Responsibility of the Suspect", in Bergsmo (ed.), 2010, p. 229, see *supra* note 8 (https://www.legal-tools.org/doc/b32b70/).

42 *Ibid.*

43 Xabier Agirre Aranburu, "Prosecuting the Most Responsible for International Crimes: Dilemmas of Definition and Prosecutorial Discretion", in J. Gonzalez (ed.), *Protección Internacional de Derechos Humanos y Estado de Derecho*, Grupo Editorial Ibáñez, Bogota, 2009, pp. 381–404.

thus need to focus on gathering evidence sufficient to establish the hierarchy concerned and to attribute responsibility to the overall leaders who appear to bear the greatest responsibility for the crimes concerned.

Finally, the policy paper refers to the need to explore and present the most appropriate range of modes of liability to legally qualify the criminal conduct alleged, with particular emphasis on the deterrent and expressive effect of each mode of liability, referring in this context, in particular, to Article 28, relating to the responsibility of commanders and other superiors.

6.3.1.3. Charges

The final case-selection criterion relates to the charges that legally qualify the conduct. This criterion serves both to guide what type of criminal conduct the OTP wishes to focus on and to ensure that the conduct brought forward for prosecution is appropriately represented in the charging scheme. Citing Regulation 34(2) of the Regulations of the OTP, the policy paper states that the charges chosen "will constitute, whenever possible, a representative sample of the main types of victimisation and of the communities which have been affected by the crimes in that situation". At the same time, the policy paper states that the OTP "will aim to represent as much as possible the true extent of the criminality which has occurred within a given situation, in an effort to ensure, jointly with the relevant national jurisdictions, that the most serious crimes committed in each situation do not go unpunished". This remains consistent with those set out in earlier strategic documents of the OTP,[44] but adds the notion of burden-sharing. Thus, the goal of ensuring that "the most serious crimes committed in each situation do not go unpunished" is to be achieved "jointly with the relevant national jurisdictions". Again, this statement reflects the reality that, with its limited means stretched over multiple situations, the OTP will not be able to ensure a clear distinction between cases heard at the ICC and those at the national level on a clearly graduated basis of gravity. Instead, the OTP will be one among several actors, perhaps filling in gaps where others cannot or will not act, or serving as the lone jurisdiction but working to galvanize others to ensure accountability for other grave cases.

Finally, its terms of strategic choices guide the formulation of case hypotheses and their evolution. Specific reference in this context is made to crimes against or affecting children as well as rape and other sexual and gender-based

[44] See, for example, OTP, Report on Prosecutorial Strategy, 14 September 2006, p. 7 (https://www.legal-tools.org/doc/6e3bf4/).

crimes, which corresponds to the OTP's separate policy papers,[45] and to attacks against cultural, religious, historical and other protected objects as well as against humanitarian and peace-keeping personnel. The policy paper does not say that these crimes will be prioritized over other crimes, but that these crimes the OTP intends to "pay particular attention to", as a matter of policy, to promote their repression and prevention in the light of their traditional under-prosecution.[46]

6.3.2. Prioritization Criteria

As indicated by its title, a key feature of the 2016 policy paper compared to the 2006 draft is the explicit articulation of prioritization criteria that were left implicit in earlier policy documents and which also draw on insights gained from national and international comparative practice, such as those set out in earlier editions of this volume.

Prioritization flows from the practical reality that the ICC cannot do all things at once, since the demand for its intervention will always be greater than its capacity. Prioritization is also informed by conceptual considerations over the role and function of the ICC, which is neither intended to act as a surrogate for national jurisdictions, who retain the primary responsibility to investigate and prosecute, nor to function as the unique forum to hear such cases, given the notion of a Court that complements national criminal jurisdictions and thus shares with them the burden of closing the impunity gap.[47]

The policy paper defines prioritization as "the process by which cases that meet the selection criteria are rolled-out over time", stating that the OTP "aims to investigate and prosecute all cases that are selected pursuant to the case selection criteria set out above", and that all selected cases, including those not prioritized, remain part of the Case Selection Document (see below). The policy thus limits the scope of application of these criteria to prioritization, and not selection, meaning they cannot migrate from one context to another. Thus, for example, that practical and operational factors govern the likely success of evidence collection, or whether cases can be done in sequence or in parallel, will not govern whether a case is selected, but will form part of the calculation as to when it might be propitious to roll-out a particular case. Nonetheless, recognition is given to the fact that a case that is permanently de-prioritized might become effectively de-selected; thus, the paper states: a "case that is temporarily

[45] OTP, Policy Paper on Sexual and Gender-Based Crimes, June 2014 (https://www.legal-tools.org/doc/7ede6c/); OTP, Policy on Children, November 2016 (https://www.legal-tools.org/doc/c2652b/).

[46] Policy Paper, para. 46, see *supra* note 1.

[47] See Rome Statute, Preamble, para. 10 and Article 1, see *supra* note 28.

not prioritised is not thereby deselected: it remains part of the Case Selection Document and the Office will endeavour to investigate and prosecute such cases as circumstances permit, based on the criteria below".

The reality of the OTP's limited capacity to investigate and prosecute any particular number of cases any time means that prioritization will serve a key function.[48] At the same time, any decision to prioritize one case will come at the expense of another potential case, rendering decision-making on prioritization highly arduous and challenging.

The following prioritization criteria are set out in the policy, divided into 'strategic' and 'operational' clusters.

6.3.2.1. Strategic Prioritization Criteria

The five strategic prioritization criteria identified in the policy are:

a. a comparative assessment across the selected cases, based on the same factors that guide the case selection;
b. whether a person, or members of the same group, has or have already been subject to investigation or prosecution, either by the Office or by a State for another serious crime;
c. the impact of investigations and prosecutions on the victims of the crimes and affected communities;
d. the impact of investigations and prosecutions on ongoing criminality or their contribution to the prevention of crimes; and
e. the impact and the ability of the Office to pursue cases involving opposing parties to a conflict in parallel or on a sequential basis.

The first listed strategic prioritization criterion (a) requires a comparative gravity assessment – meaning a comparison between the different selected cases in terms of: (i) gravity of the alleged crimes, (ii) degree of participation of the alleged perpetrator(s), and (iii) charges under consideration. At the same time, a measure of situational perspective is warranted because the situations under investigation by the OTP vary so much. Thus, relying only on this one factor alone might result in the OTP prioritizing cases from one situation only or against one party to an armed conflict (for example, allegations of genocide committed in Darfur by the Government of Sudan or its agents), to the detriment of all other investigations. Thus, the first criterion must be weighed against other prioritization criteria, such as impact on victims and affected communities, on ongoing criminality or their prevention, or on the investigation or prosecution of cases involving opposing parties to a conflict in parallel or on a sequential basis. In relation to prioritization of cases against opposing parties, this assumes that

[48] See also Basic Size Report, paras. 4–9, see *supra* note 23.

cases against both or all opposing sides have previously met the selection criteria. This is clear from the fact that prioritization follows cases selection and focuses on prioritizing among such cases. It is also clear from the earlier statement on general principles in the policy paper that "impartiality does not mean 'equivalence of blame' within a situation" and that "the Office will not seek to create the appearance of parity within a situation between rival parties by selecting cases that would not otherwise meet the criteria set out herein".[49]

Strategic prioritization criterion (b) also deserves additional comment. The Court has been criticized by some commentators for pursuing cases against individuals where the national authorities appeared to be proceeding against the same person for a different crime (either for a core international crime or for another serious crime under national law) - or if not against the same person, then another comparably situated member of the same group. On closer examination of the cases heard before the Court in admissibility proceedings, it has not always been clear that this concern has actually materialized, since in the purported steps taken by the relevant national authorities (concerning 'other conduct' or 'other persons') appear not to have concretized in practice or were raised speculatively.[50] Nonetheless, irrespective of whether such action might

---

49 Policy Paper, para. 20, see *supra* note 1.

50 See, for example, rejected admissibility challenges by the Government of Kenya arguing that the Court should render its then cases against six individuals inadmissible due to Kenya's intention to launch a comprehensive national prosecution plan that might ultimately focus on "persons at the same level in the hierarchy being investigated by at the ICC"; ICC, *Prosecutor v. William Samoei Ruto, Henry Kiprono Kosgey and Joshua Arap Sang*, Application on Behalf of the Government of the Republic of Kenya Pursuant to Article 19 of the ICC Statute, 31 March 2011, ICC-01/09-01/11-19, para. 32 (https://www.legal-tools.org/doc/b9f9ef/); *Prosecutor v. Francis Kirimi Muthaura, Uhuru Muigai Kenyatta and Mohammed Hussein Ali*, Application on Behalf of the Government of the Republic of Kenya Pursuant to Article 19 of the ICC Statute, 31 March 2011, ICC-01/09-02/11-26, para. 32 (https://www.legal-tools.org/doc/426311/).

The issue has also been raised by scholars in the context of the *Lubanga* case, in which Lubanga was arrested and in pre-trial detention "*legally based* on charges of genocide [...] and crimes against humanity" (emphasis added) (*Prosecutor v. Lubanga*, Decision on the Prosecutor's Application for a Warrant of Arrest, 24 February 2006, ICC-01/04-01/06-8-Corr, para. 33 (https://www.legal-tools.org/doc/c60aaa/)), although the DRC authorities were not actually pursuing an investigation and there at least appears to have been a risk of his release upon a 12-month judicial review of his detention, precipitating thereby the timing of his surrender: see *id.*, at fn. 32; citing the Transcript of the Hearing of 2 February 2006, p. 6, lines 12–16 and p. 7, lines 19–22, available at *Prosecutor v. Lubanga*, Redacted Version of the Transcripts of the Hearing Held on 2 February 2006 and Certain Materials Presented During That Hearing, 22 March 2006, ICC-01/04-01/06-48 (https://www.legal-tools.org/doc/2a89be/). In the same transcript, the Prosecution observes, at p. 39, "[...] based on the fact that the file in respect of Thomas Lubanga Dyilo is empty – it is literally empty –

render a case inadmissible as a matter of law, it raises important questions for the proper exercise of prosecutorial discretion.

The legal test of complementarity, under Article 17 of the Rome Statute, cannot answer the question of whether the OTP should select one case over another when the national authorities appear to be pursuing a similar or broadly analogous case. This is because the admissibility test, as confirmed by the Appeals Chamber, is a relatively strict examination of whether there is a conflict of jurisdictions between the ICC and a national criminal jurisdiction over the same case: defined as a domestic case concerning the same person for substantially the same conduct as that being heard before the ICC.[51] Thus, as a legal criterion, a case before the ICC will not be rendered inadmissible due to the fact that a person, or a member of the same group, has already been subject to investigation or prosecution domestically for other conduct also proscribed under the Rome Statute or for another serious crime under national law.

Case selection and prioritization, because it is based on the exercise of prosecutorial discretion as to which cases the OTP should appropriately pursue, however, can factor in such considerations as a matter of policy. To this end, strategic prioritization criterion (b) examines whether a case that meets the selection criteria might nonetheless not be prioritized due to the fact that the same individual, or individuals from the same group, possibly at a similar level of responsibility, are being or have already been investigated and prosecuted at the national level for another serious crime, thereby warranting the possible prioritization of another case. Strategic prioritization criterion (b) also would apply to individuals or groups that have previously been the focus of OTP investigations, requiring consideration as to the most appropriate prioritization choices and allocation of limited resources among other possible selected cases. Thus, for example, there have repeated been calls for the OTP to seek additional arrest warrants against Joseph Kony and other members of the LRA for crimes committed

any judge who has to decide on the extension of detention of Mr Thomas Lubanga will have a very difficult time to extend the detention knowing that there is no investigation being done".

51 ICC, *Prosecutor v. William Samoei Ruto, Henry Kiprono Kosgey and Joshua Arap Sang*, Judgment on the appeal of the Republic of Kenya against the decision of Pre-Trial Chamber II of 30 May 2011 entitled "Decision on the Application by the Government of Kenya Challenging the Admissibility of the Case Pursuant to Article 19(2)(b) of the Statute", 30 August 2011, ICC-01/09-01/11-307, paras. 39-40 (https://www.legal-tools.org/doc/ac5d46/); *Prosecutor v. Francis Kirimi Muthaura, Uhuru Muigai Kenyatta and Mohammed Hussein Ali*, Judgment on the appeal of the Republic of Kenya against the decision of Pre-Trial Chamber II of 30 May 2011 entitled "Decision on the Application by the Government of Kenya Challenging the Admissibility of the Case Pursuant to Article 19(2)(b) of the Statute", 30 August 2011, ICC-01/09-02/11-274, paras. 38–39 (https://www.legal-tools.org/doc/c21f06/). See Rod Rastan, "What is 'Substantially the Same Conduct'? Unpacking the ICC's 'First Limb' Complementarity Jurisprudence", in *Journal of International Criminal Justice*, 2017, vol. 15, no, 1, pp. 1–29.

in the DRC, CAR and Sudan which are of a comparable (if not more serious) gravity than those allegedly committed in Uganda. Applying this criterion might mean that even if such conduct met case-selection criteria, it might not be prioritized as a new case for investigation due to the fact that the OTP already has a pending arrest warrant for similarly grave conduct against Joseph Kony, together with completed proceedings in *Ongwen*, thereby militating in favour of prioritizing other cases for investigation and prosecution.

By contrast, strategic prioritization criterion (b), which relates to the bringing of new cases, does not affect efforts to strengthen existing cases. It does not, for example, negate the seizing of investigative opportunities as they arise and evidence becomes available or the adding of additional charges within the context of the same overall case. Doing otherwise might contradict the case-selection criteria related to charges, whereby the OTP commits to "represent as much as possible the true extent of the criminality which has occurred within a given situation, in an effort to ensure, jointly with the relevant national jurisdictions, that the most serious crimes committed in each situation do not go unpunished". Thus, when the OTP added new charges in the *Ntaganda* case or in the *Ongwen* case, these were not outside of the scope of the initial investigation, but supplemental thereto. For example, in the *Ntaganda* case, the companion case to that against Lubanga, even though the crime base was significantly expanded to include, *inter alia*, a number of massacres that occurred in Ituri during 2002–2003,[52] investigation of such attacks were initially investigated for the joint case against *Lubanga and Ntaganda*, but were not advanced enough at the time to be included in the charges against Lubanga.[53] In the *Ongwen* case, by contrast, the charges added upon his arrest flowed from the way the initial case had been presented. In the arrest warrant against Kony and four other LRA commanders, Joseph Kony was alleged to be responsible for a representative sample of alleged crimes occurring principally in LRA attacks against different IDP camps in northern Uganda, with each of the other suspects allegedly involved as a co-perpetrator in one or more of such incidents. In this context, the warrant for Dominic Ongwen focused on his role in the attack on Lukodi IDP Camp.[54] When Ongwen was subsequently arrested and the proceedings against him were

[52] See ICC, *Prosecutor v. Bosco Ntaganda*, Decision on the Prosecutor's Application under Article 58, 13 July 2012, ICC-01/04-02/06-36-Red (https://www.legal-tools.org/doc/18c310/).

[53] ICC, *Prosecutor v. Lubanga*, Prosecutor's Information on Further Investigation, 28 June 2006, ICC-01/04-01/06-170, paras. 3–10 (https://www.legal-tools.org/doc/e668a0/) (referring to investigations into, *inter alia*, "allegations related to the intentional direction of attacks against the civilian population, murders committed during and after these attacks, the pillaging of towns and places […]").

[54] ICC, *Situation in Uganda*, Warrant of Arrest for Dominic Ongwen, 8 July 2005, ICC-02/04-01/05-10, para. 14 *et seq.* (https://www.legal-tools.org/doc/d2011f/).

severed from the case against the other suspects, supplementary evidence was gathered and charges were added concerning Ongwen's role and participation also in three of the other IDP Camps that had been previous investigated, namely, Pajule, Odek and Abok, and which formed part of the broader crime base involving other LRA suspects.[55]

6.3.2.2. Operational Prioritization Criteria

There are four operational prioritization criteria:

a. the quantity and quality of the incriminating and exonerating evidence already in the possession of the Office, as well as the availability of additional evidence and any risks to its degradation;
b. international co-operation and judicial assistance to support the Office's activities;
c. the Office's capacity to effectively conduct the necessary investigations within a reasonable period of time, including the security situation in the area where the Office is planning to operate or where persons co-operating with the Office reside, and the Court's ability to protect persons from risks that might arise from their interaction with the Office; and
d. the potential to secure the appearance of suspects before the Court, either by arrest and surrender or pursuant to a summons.

At first sight, these criteria might suggest that the OTP will try to avoid 'difficult' cases. In this regard, the policy paper makes the obvious point that challenges to evidence collection, co-operation, security and protection or managing arrest opportunities arise in every investigation, necessitating the routine adoption of mitigating measures to manage their effects. It is also clear that different cases will throw up a varied mix of operational challenges.

Most of the listed operational prioritization factors will be driven by opportunity. Thus, for example, there may be a risk that potential evidence contained in a mass grave site may degrade over time due to soil composition or seasonal variability. In a volatile security context, an area under the control of hostile groups might suddenly become accessible, opening up a window for access and deployment. Conversely, an area that was secure may become inhospitable to operational deployment and test the Court's witness protection capabilities. Other opportunities may arise due to sudden capture or surrender of other members of an armed group or force, providing a prospect for securing insider testimony and additional leads.

[55] See ICC, *Prosecutor v. Dominic Ongwen*, Public redacted version of "Notice of intended charges against Dominic Ongwen", 18 September 2015, ICC-02/04-01/15-305-Conf, ICC-02/04-01/15-305-Red3, 27 May 2016 (https://www.legal-tools.org/doc/a05da4/).

6.3.3. Case Selection Document

The other novel feature of the 2016 policy paper is the introduction of the notion of a 'Case Selection Document' to aggregate across all situations all possible cases that could be selected and prioritized for investigation and prosecution. The policy states that initially this will be based on the potential cases identified at the preliminary examination stage[56] and, as investigations proceed, the provisional case hypotheses that supersede them.[57] As investigations progress, these hypotheses will be tested and may be confirmed, abandoned or adjusted on the basis of additional information and evidence collected. The Case Selection Document is presented thus as "a dynamic document that will be reviewed and updated accordingly" and "will require regular updating on the basis of the information and evidence obtained in the course of investigations, any ongoing criminality, as well as the evolution of operational conditions that could impact the Office's ability to conduct successful investigations and prosecutions".[58] It is meant to serve as a tool to manage the overall workload of the OTP.

---

[56] The concept of a 'potential case' has developed in the context of the Article 15 procedure to explain how the Pre-Trial Chamber ('PTC') will assess admissibility under Article 53(1)(b) (*via* Rule 48) where no 'case' has yet been investigated. Such potential cases have been broadly defined as comprising (i) the groups of persons involved that are likely to be the focus of an investigation for the purpose of shaping the future case(s); and (ii) the crimes within the jurisdiction of the Court allegedly committed during the incidents that are likely to be the focus of an investigation for the purpose of shaping the future case(s); ICC, *Situation in the Republic of Kenya*, Pre-Trial Chamber II, Decision Pursuant to Article 15 of the Rome Statute on the Authorization of an Investigation into the Situation in the Republic of Kenya, 31 March 2010, ICC-01/09-19-Corr, paras. 50 and 59 (https://www.legal-tools.org/doc/338a6f/); ICC, *Situation in the Republic of Côte d'Ivoire*, Pre-Trial Chamber III, Decision Pursuant to Article 15 of the Rome Statute on the Authorization of an Investigation into the Situation in the Republic of Côte d'Ivoire, 3 October 2011, ICC-02/11-14-Corr, paras. 191 and 204 (https://www.legal-tools.org/doc/7a6c19/); ICC, *Situation in Georgia*, Pre-Trial Chamber I, Decision on the Prosecutor's request for authorization of an investigation, 27 January 2016, ICC-01/15-12, paras. 37 and 51 (https://www.legal-tools.org/doc/a3d07e/). Chambers have emphasized such identification "is preliminary, and as such, this may change as a result of the investigation" (ICC-01/15-12, para. 37; see also ICC-01/09-19-Corr, para. 50); while the assessment of gravity "involves a generic assessment (general in nature and compatible with the fact that an investigation is yet to be opened)" (ICC-01/15-12, para. 51).

[57] Policy Paper, para. 10, see *supra* note 1:

> Initially, the Case Selection Document will be based on the conclusions from the preliminary examination stage, including the potential cases identified therein. As investigations within each situation proceed, and bearing in mind the Office's strategy to conduct in-depth and open-ended investigations, the Office will gradually develop one or more provisional case hypotheses that meet the criteria set out in this policy.

[58] In this context, the policy paper cites to the 2016 OTP Strategic Plan, see Policy Paper, para. 10, see *supra* note 1:

The policy paper also states that the Case Selection Document will help the OTP determine when it should end its involvement in a situation.[59] This might mean that while the OTP and the Court would continue to complete existing cases – for example, by seizing investigative opportunities to shore up additional evidence, to track the movement of suspects, to tackle Article 70 offences, monitor ongoing protection issues, and ultimately to carry out relevant proceedings when suspects are apprehended – no additional cases concerning Article 5 crimes would be brought forward in that situation for investigation and prosecution.

6.3.4. Co-operation on Other Cases

By the nature of selection and prioritization, the OTP will never be able to exhaust or capture all relevant criminal conduct. As other chapters in Part II of this volume recall, even the *ad hoc* Tribunals with dedicated focus and larger resources available for a single situation over extended time periods have faced the necessity for selection. Thus, the policy paper also addresses the familiar question of co-operation with national jurisdictions to combat the impunity gap that may be left as a result of a case selection and prioritization at the ICC.[60] In the 2016 policy paper, the OTP recalls its pledge to encourage genuine national proceedings by relevant States with jurisdiction and to co-operate with States investigating and prosecuting individuals "who have committed or have facilitated the commission of Rome Statute crimes". This facilitation aspect might include the criminal liability of corporate agents for their complicity in such

> [T]he open-ended aspect of the investigations means that the Office first identifies alleged crimes (or incidents) to be investigated within a wide range of incidents. Following this meticulous process, alleged perpetrators are identified based on the evidence collected. This approach implies the need to consider multiple alternative case hypotheses and to consistently and objectively test case theories against the evidence – incriminating and exonerating – and to support decision-making in relation to investigations and prosecutions.

59 *Ibid.*, para. 12.

60 OTP 2003 Paper on Policy Issues, p. 3, see *supra* note 2:

> The strategy of focusing on those who bear the greatest responsibility for the crimes may leave an "impunity gap" unless national authorities, the international community and the Court work together to ensure that all appropriate means for bringing other perpetrators to justice are used. [...]. Urgent and high-level discussion is needed on methods to deal with the problem generally [...]. The organisation of the structure and work processes of the Office of the Prosecutor is based on the assumption that the Office should endeavour to maximise its impact while operating a system of low costs.

crimes, whether under national criminal law or relevant civil or administrative codes.[61] Additionally, the policy paper commits to

> cooperate and provide assistance to States, upon request, with respect to conduct which constitutes a serious crime under national law, such as the illegal exploitation of natural resources, arms trafficking, human trafficking, terrorism, financial crimes, land grabbing or the destruction of the environment.

Such assistance is foreseen in Article 93(10) of the Rome Statute, which provides that the "Court may, upon request, cooperate with and provide assistance to a State Party conducting an investigation into or trial in respect of conduct which constitutes a crime within the jurisdiction of the Court *or which constitutes a serious crime under the national law of the requesting State*" (italics added). The policy paper also particularizes the types of serious crimes under national law that it may often have information or evidence on.

This passage of the policy recognizes that, in many circumstances, Rome Statute crimes will be committed along-side and in the context of other types of criminality which may often be inter-linked with and causally connected to the persons and conduct under investigation by the OTP, as discussed earlier.[62] For example, the OTP may often seek to identify and trace financial information to help prove the structure of an organization, the role played by and the relationships between various actors, or the movement of means by which Rome Statute crimes are committed (instrumentalities of crime) or the benefits accruing therefrom (proceeds of crime). In the context of Article 70 offences, such information may go to direct proof of corruptly influencing witnesses or of soliciting the giving of false testimony.[63] While such financial information may be directly relevant to establishing the criminal responsibility of the person concerned under the Rome Statute, the OTP will clearly not rely on such evidence to charge fraud, embezzlement of public funds, or money laundering, but national prosecutors might. As such, the OTP commits to co-operate on information or evidence obtained in the course of its investigations.

61 See Rod Rastan, "Complementarity – Contest or Collaboration?", in Morten Bergsmo (ed.), *Complementarity and the Exercise of Universal Jurisdiction for Core International Crimes*, TOAEP, Oslo, 2010, pp. 126–131 (https://www.legal-tools.org/doc/4zl34o/), discussing proceedings in third States based on the accomplice liability of their nationals.

62 See *supra* Section 6.1.

63 See, for example, ICC, *Prosecutor v. Jean-Pierre Bemba Gombo, Aimé Kilolo Musamba, Jean-Jacques Mangenda Kabongo, Fidèle Babala Wandu and Narcisse Arido*, Trial Chamber VII, Judgment pursuant to Article 74 of the Statute, 19 October 2016, ICC-01/05-01/13-1989-Red, paras. 689–703 (https://www.legal-tools.org/doc/fe0ce4/).

The OTP also re-expresses in this section of the 2016 policy, within the broader context of transitional justice mechanisms of which the Court and national criminal justice systems form a part: "it fully endorses the role that can be played by truth seeking mechanisms, reparations programs, institutional reform and traditional justice mechanisms as part of a broader comprehensive strategy", recalling an earlier statement made in its 2007 *Policy Paper on the Interests of Justice*.[64]

As described below, many of the themes articulated in this section are given renewed emphasis and further impetus in the 2024 issued *Policy on Complementarity and Cooperation*.[65]

6.4. Situation Completion

In June 2021, the OTP issued its long-awaited policy paper on 'Situation Completion'.[66] The policy set out to explain how the Office will complete its work in a given situation. Noting the links with earlier policies, the new paper described itself as completing a trilogy of policy papers describing the life cycle of the Office's operations in a situation, and must be read with the *Policy Paper on Preliminary Examinations* (which describes the opening of an ICC investigation in a situation) and the *Policy Paper on Case Selection and Prioritisation* (which describes the selection of cases for investigation in a situation, and their prioritization in light of the multiple situations under investigation in the Office at the same time)".[67]

The key aspects of the Situation Completion policy paper lie in defining when the 'Investigation Phase' of a situation can be considered concluded, in the sense that the Prosecutor does not intend to seek any further warrants or summonses under Article 58 of the Rome Statute within that situation.[68] This does not mean that the OTP's work in a given situation is over, but that no new warrants should be expected to be sought for core crimes. Excluded from this is Article 70 crimes, since the Office must always be in a position to respond to alleged offences against the administration of justice.[69]

---

64 See OTP, Policy Paper on the Interests of Justice, 2007, p. 8.

65 OTP, Policy on Complementarity and Cooperation, 25 April 2024 ('2024 Policy on Complementarity and Cooperation') (https://www.legal-tools.org/doc/2hzyqht1/).

66 2021 Policy on Situation Completion, see *supra* note 10.

67 *Ibid.*, para. 1.

68 *Ibid.*, paras. 5–6, 21–23.

69 *Ibid.*, para. 5 (stating "the Office will make no further requests to the Pre-Trial Chamber to start proceedings for article 5 crimes in that situation"), contrasted with paras. 66–68, 79 (describing ongoing activity in relation to alleged Article 70 offences).

Concluding the investigation phase only explains the total number of cases the OTP intends to pursue in a given situation (also referred to as the OTP 'Prosecutorial Programme').[70] Those cases that have been brought to the Article 58 stage must still be brought to prosecution, a process that in some cases may take years to complete, either because of the length and complexity of proceedings, or because suspects remain at large. Thus, conclusion of the 'Prosecution Phase', according to the policy, only occurs when all legal proceedings relating to those cases as well as other residual activities have been completed.[71] As with the earlier case selection and prioritization policy, the Situation Completion policy calls for early formulation of an overall situation strategy, that is continually revised and updated.[72] The policy paper also emphasizes that it guides OTP practice only and does not address how the statutory activities of other organs of the Court may be completed within a given situation.

The Situation Completion policy paper was first put into effect during the term of Prosecutor Karim A.A. Khan KC. In December 2022, the Prosecutor announced the conclusion of the investigative phase in the situations in CAR I, CAR II[73] and Georgia,[74] meaning that no new case would be brought in those situations absent a significant change in circumstances, while the cases that had been brought would be carried through to the prosecution stage. In 2023, the situations in Kenya[75] and Uganda[76] were also announced as having entered the completion of investigations phase.

In announcing such decisions, the Prosecutor emphasized that they were "an essential part of articulating and implementing an effective prosecutorial strategy" and formed part of the discretion afforded to the Office under the Rome Statute to effectively manage the discharge of its mandate. The Prosecutor also referred to the need to enable a stable operating capacity for a Court with universal vocation, but limited capacity: "[t]he need for situational planning and

70 *Ibid.*, para. 5.

71 *Ibid.*, paras. 8–9, 21–23.

72 *Ibid.*, paras. 20–30.

73 OTP, "The Prosecutor of the International Criminal Court, Karim A.A. Khan KC, announces conclusion of the investigation phase in the Situation in the Central African Republic", 16 December 2022.

74 OTP, "The Prosecutor of the International Criminal Court, Karim A.A. Khan KC, announces conclusion of the investigation phase in the Situation in Georgia", 16 December 2022.

75 OTP, "Statement of ICC Deputy Prosecutor, Nazhat Shameem Khan, announcing her decision to conclude the investigation phase of the Situation in the Republic of Kenya", 27 November 2023.

76 OTP, "Statement of the Prosecutor of the International Criminal Court, Karim A.A. Khan KC, announcing his decision to conclude the investigation phase in the Situation in Uganda", 1 December 2023.

the adoption of accompanying completion strategies also reflects a growing, legitimate expectation that the Court will find ways and means to meaningfully sustain its work across multiple Situations within finite means".

This theme also appears in the OTP's 2023–2025 Strategic Plan, which stresses:

> To succeed, the Office will first have to define a realistic scope of operations and bring manageable cases. The Office will prioritize situations and cases systematically and objectively with the overall goal of reducing the total number of situations, thereby ensuring increased focus and resources on earmarked situations and cases. In so doing, and in line with its established policy framework, the Office will prioritize cases according to factors such as their relative gravity and prospect of success. It will progress each situation to complete its investigations appropriately, with the aim of reducing, overall, the number of open investigations.[77]

The role of completion strategies was also taken up by the Independent Expert Review commissioned by the ASP. In particular, the Experts urged for completion strategies to be considered a crucial part of the OTP's strategic planning and anticipated as early as possible during the life cycle of an investigation.[78]

The Experts further recommended that completion be tied to positive complementarity efforts and include modalities for establishing co-ordination between the OTP and other jurisdictions for the sharing of relevant information and evidence to assist local investigations and prosecutions.[79] In similar vein, the Prosecutor Khan's completion statement in relation to Georgia refer to "working collaboratively with competent national criminal jurisdictions to help reduce remaining impunity gaps" to support "new cases that might, through working in collaboration, be brought before domestic courts" as well as through technical and operational level exchanges.[80] The link between completion strategies and complementarity efforts is expressly made in the 2023–2025 Strategic

[77] OTP, Strategic Plan 2023–2025, 13 June 2023, para. 24 ('OTP Strategic Plan: 2023–2025') (https://www.legal-tools.org/doc/mu9jlt/).

[78] Independent Expert Review of the International Criminal Court and the Rome Statute System, Final Report, 30 September 2020, para. 691, recommendation R.249 ('IER Report') (https://www.legal-tools.org/doc/cv19d5/).

[79] *Ibid.*, para. 693, recommendations R.247, R.265.

[80] OTP, 2022, see *supra* note 74.

Plan and in the subsequently issued *Policy on Complementarity and Cooperation*.[81]

6.5. Policy Renewal

It is clear that any policy document will require testing through implementation, refining - brought on by learning and judicial practice - and, ultimately, revision. This applies no less to case selection and prioritization. Thus, while at the time of the Third Edition there exists a comprehensive policy framework to guide the exercise of prosecutorial discretion at all stages of the Office's work, this same framework stands in need of vigilance and renewal.

In this context, the OTP's 2023–2025 Strategic Plan set out, as one of its goals "a renewed policy framework for the Office", including "a comprehensive review and consolidation of its policy framework on gravity/prioritization/completion of investigations".[82] This follows more recent policy updates and revisions by the OTP on existing policies on gender-based crimes[83] on children,[84] and a separate policy on gender persecution,[85] and commitment that it would work on the development of new policies on slavery crimes, environmental crimes and cyber-crimes.[86] The issuance of the 2024 *Policy on Complementarity and Cooperation* has also significantly enhanced the Office's policy framework in relation to the OTP's role, alongside other national and international accountability actors, in closing the impunity gap.[87] Thus, the policies discussed in this chapter may well undergo further development and learning during the immediate years ahead.

Any development of OTP policies will need to reflect the evolving jurisprudence of the Court, which may sometimes cause it to revisit baseline assumptions on which foundational policy positions have been taken. For example, the March 2020 judgement of the Appeals Chamber, on the authorization decision with respect to the Afghanistan situation, articulated appellate opinion on one

---

[81] *Ibid.*, para. 40; 2024 Policy on Complementarity and Cooperation, see *supra* note 65, paras. 37, 95, 134, 142 and 174.

[82] OTP Strategic Plan: 2023–2025, para. 57, Strategic Goal 5, see *supra* note 77.

[83] OTP, Policy on Gender-based Crimes, 4 December 2023.

[84] OTP, Policy on Children, 7 December 2023.

[85] OTP, Policy on Gender Persecution, 7 December 2022.

[86] OTP Strategic Plan: 2023–2025, para. 57, see *supra* note 77; OTP, Delivering Better Together, Annual Report of the Office of the Prosecutor – 2023, 6 December 2023, p. 118 ('2023 OTP Annual Report') (https://www.legal-tools.org/doc/dcv6zxml/).

[87] 2024 Policy on Complementarity and Cooperation, see *supra* note 65, observing, in its preface, that the policy outlines "how through the mutually reinforcing principles of cooperation and complementarity we can strengthen and expand the common ground between all actors and reduce the accountability gap that persists with respect to international crimes".

crucial issue that had guided the OTP's policy approach towards situation and case selection. In its judgment, the Appeals Chamber observed that the Article 15 (*proprio motu*) and Article 53 (referral) routes were strictly distinguishable not only by the difference in applicable judicial review functions, but also by the asymmetric duties that followed for the Prosecutor under each route. In particular, the Appeals Chamber stressed that whereas the Prosecutor is obliged to proceed to open an investigation upon a reasonable basis determination following a referral, the Prosecutor enjoys far greater latitude under the Article 15 procedure. The Appeals Chamber observed that this was denoted by the use of the term "shall" in Article 53(1), and "may" in Article 15(1), signifying an intention by the drafters to ensure that the Prosecutor retained discretion in determining whether to seize a Chamber *proprio motu*.[88] By contrast, the OTP had previously interpreted the use of the word "shall" in Article 15(3) as signifying the existence of a common duty irrespective of the triggering route.[89] As a consequence, in its annual report of 2023, the Office reported that it was considering "how to adapt its operational practices in light of the Appeals Chamber's recent holding that the Prosecutor enjoys discretion in deciding whether to proceed under article 15 of the Statute", and that the "Office's recent experience [had] confirmed that the Prosecutor's discretion in deciding whether to proceed under article 15 forms an essential part of an effective prosecutorial strategy for the Court".[90] The injection of prosecutorial discretion at the 'situation' level at the Article 15 stage might, thus, warrant the articulation of applicable factors that will guide the exercise of such discretion under a renewed policy framework.

6.6. Conclusion

As other contributors to this volume have shown, the exercise of prosecutorial discretion in the selection of individual cases for prosecution is neither new nor unique to the ICC. The reality of selection is inherent in any accountability re-

---

88 ICC, *Situation in the Islamic Republic of Afghanistan*, Judgment on the appeal against the decision on the authorisation of an investigation into the situation in the Islamic Republic of Afghanistan, 5 March 2020, ICC-02/17-138, paras. 30–31 (https://www.legal-tools.org/doc/x7kl12/).

89 2013 Policy Paper on Preliminary Examination, paras. 12, 35 and 76, see *supra* note 9. See also, ICC, *Situation in the Islamic Republic of Afghanistan*, Separate opinion of Judge Luz del Carmen Ibáñez Carranza to the Judgment on the appeal against the decision of Pre-Trial Chamber II on the authorisation of an investigation into the situation in the Islamic Republic of Afghanistan, 5 March 2020, ICC-02/17-138-Anx-Corr, paras. 2 and 7 (https://www.legal-tools.org/doc/bfdi78/).

90 2023 OTP Annual Report, p. 20, see *supra* note 86.

sponse to situations of mass atrocity where there will typically be a large universe of crimes committed by numerous perpetrators against countless victims.[91] Faced with a situation of mass atrocity, the factual crime base may involve widespread acts of murder, rape, torture, destruction of property and forced displacement. The gamut of criminal liability may run from foot soldiers who physically perpetrated the crime, to the superior who directed the operation, to the military commander or political and business elite who masterminded and controlled their overall commission. Liability may also attach to support networks materially assisting perpetrators or contributing to the commission of crimes and fugitive flight. Victims may number in the tens or hundreds of thousands or, in the case of displacement, millions. Since comprehensive capture is impossible, selection becomes necessary. Nonetheless, the results of selection will always be unsatisfactory because not every crime will be prosecuted.

In this sense, the need for selection in the prosecution of atrocity crimes represents the most pressing and ethically challenging imperative in the task of bringing law to bear on situations of massive violence. International courts and tribunals must decide when and where they will direct the focus of their activities and be prepared to explain how they arrived at those choices. Although differences of opinions will persist over the selection of individual prosecution targets, to garner legitimacy, the process and methodology must be applied in a manner that is reasonable, based on established legal and policy criteria, and subject to overarching principles that demonstrate fairness. Selection must not lead to selectivity, resulting in arbitrariness or bias.[92] At the same time, the effort to articulate *ex ante* standards may itself invite criticism of tokenism and be

---

[91] This section borrows from Rod Rastan, "Comment on Victor's Justice and the Viability of *Ex Ante* Standards", in *John Marshall Law Review*, 2010, vol. 43, no. 3, pp. 569–602.

[92] See, for example, Allison Marston Danner, "Enhancing the Legitimacy and Accountability of Prosecutorial Discretion at the International Criminal Court", in *American Journal of International Law*, 2003, vol. 97, no. 3, p. 510; Fabricio Guariglia, "The Selection of Cases by the Office of the Prosecutor of the International Criminal Court", in Carsten Stahn and Göran Sluiter (eds.), *The Emerging Practice Of The International Criminal Court*, Brill Nijhoff, 2009, pp. 209–217; Richard J. Goldstone, "More Candour about Criteria: The Exercise of Discretion by the Prosecutor of the International Criminal Court", in *Journal of International Criminal Justice*, 2010, vol. 8, no. 2, pp. 383–406; Brian D. Lepard, "How Should the ICC Prosecutor Exercise His or Her Discretion? The Role of Fundamental Ethical Principles", in *John Marshall Law Review*, 2010, vol. 43, no. 3, pp. 564–565; Rastan, 2010, pp. 569–602, see *supra* note 91; Margaret M. deGuzman, *Shocking the Conscience of Humanity: Gravity and the Legitimacy of International Criminal Law*, Oxford University Press, 2020, pp. 26, 99; Mark Kersten, "Taking the opportunity: prosecutorial opportunism and the International Criminal Court", in Margaret M. deGuzman and Valerie Oosterveld (eds.), *The Elgar Companion to the International Criminal Court*, Edward Elgar Publishing, 2020, pp. 181–203. See also generally Asad Kiyani, "Re-narrating selectivity", in deGuzman and Oosterveld, *ibid.*, pp. 307–333, on the different ways selectivity operates in international criminal law.

perceived as disingenuous, designed to perpetuate a fiction of objectivity and legally obfuscate arbitrary decision-making.[93]

The choice of individual cases will always stoke controversy, inviting criticism of either engaging in uneven and biased prosecutions or, conversely, of painting with too broad a brush by suggesting an equivalence of blame between rival parties, thereby blurring relative levels of culpability. Due to the traditional prevalence of a culture of impunity, the uniqueness of trials in situations of mass atrocities also endows them with profound sociological import. Individual prosecutions resonate beyond the factual parameters of the specific case. They frame historical events in normative parameters. For societies brutalized by the accumulated patterns of violence, trials can serve vital expressive functions by identifying and individualizing guilt and reaffirming ingrained instincts toward justice. This representational function may be undermined if some, but not all, parties to a conflict are prosecuted, even if, according to sound legal and policy criteria, some groups warrant investigation and prosecution but not others. Thus, while consensus might more easily galvanize against blanket selectivity, case-by-case assessments will inevitably generate differences over the appropriate application of selection criteria.

Finally, as this volume bears out, the question of selection relates also to the wealth of practice emerging at the national level and the overall effectiveness of a criminal justice regime that relies on combined activity of international and national jurisdictions. Part of the challenge, therefore, is to operationalize the ever-present need for complementary mechanisms involving other international and state-level institutions to enable more complex and multifaceted responses to crimes.[94]

---

[93] See, for example, William A. Schabas, "Victor's Justice: Selecting 'Situations' at the International Criminal Court", in *John Marshall Law Review*, 2010, vol. 43, no. 3, p. 549; Sarah Nouwen and Wouter Werner, "Doing Justice to the Political: The International Criminal Court in Uganda and Sudan", in *European Journal of International Law*, 2011, vol. 22, no. 4, p. 951; Alana Tiemessen, "The International Criminal Court and the politics of prosecutions", in *International Journal of Human Rights*, 2014, vol. 18, nos. 4–5, p. 446; Asad Kiyani, "Third World Approaches to International Criminal Law", *AJIL Unbound*, 2015, vol. 109, pp. 255–259; Cale Davis, "Political Considerations in Prosecutorial Discretion at the International Criminal Court", *International Criminal Law Review* 2015, vol. 15, no. 1, p. 178; Phil Clark, *Distant Justice: The Impact of the International Criminal Court on African Politics*, Cambridge University Press, 2018, pp.172–174.

[94] Bergsmo (ed.), 2010, see *supra* note 61 (https://www.toaep.org/ps-pdf/7-bergsmo).

7

The Selection and Prioritization of Cases by the ICC Office of the Prosecutor (2003–2009)

Paul Seils*

This chapter will address three areas. First, it will identify the principal sources that indicate the criteria for the selection and prioritization of cases with respect to the public documents issued by the Office of the Prosecutor ('OTP' or 'Office') of the International Criminal Court ('ICC') by the time of the Second Edition of this book; in the process of identifying these sources, it will explore the process that has led to these criteria; and third, it will reflect on some of the particular challenges facing the ICC-OTP in the matters of selection and prioritization.

For the sake of clarity, it should be made clear that this chapter does not address the issue of the selection of *situations* for investigation by the Office. While the issue of situation selection is unquestionably complex, it is not the matter of the current study.

7.1. Public Statements of Policy by the ICC Office of the Prosecutor

There are three public documents that set out the criteria the Office has employed at the time of writing. These are the Policy Paper of September 2003,[1] a

---

* **Paul Seils** is Director of the Peace Practice and Innovation unit at the European Institute of Peace (EIP). At the time of writing, he was Head of the Situation Analysis Section of the Office of the Prosecutor of the ICC (August 2004-October 2008). Given the addition of Chapter 6 above by Rod Rastan, this chapter has not been substantively updated since the Second Edition. Seils has previously been Chief of the Information and Analysis Unit of the International Commission Against Impunity in Guatemala (CICIG), Vice President at the International Centre for Transitional Justice in New York (2001–2004), and Legal Director of Centre for Legal Action on Human Rights in Guatemala (1997–2001). He began work as a criminal defence lawyer in Scotland in 1991. He has directed investigations into mass crimes committed in internal conflict and advised several governments and other agencies on policy options in relation to accountability for such crimes in the context of political transitions. He has worked in a number of different situations including Guatemala, Peru, Colombia, East Timor, Afghanistan and the Democratic Republic of the Congo ('DRC'), and published several articles on related issues.

[1] ICC-OTP, "Policy Paper on Some Policy Issues Before the Office of the Prosecutor", 5 September 2003 (https://www.legal-tools.org/doc/f53870/).

draft policy paper on selection and prioritization of cases that was widely circulated to both states parties and civil society organizations in June 2006,[2] and the Office's first three-year report presented on 12 September 2006.[3] A number of internal documents have been developed throughout the time the Office has been in existence, but this chapter reflects those that were in the public domain at the time of the Second Edition of this anthology.

The policy paper of September 2003 sets out some of the key provisions that have informed selection policy from the earliest days of the Court. The draft selection paper of June 2006 offers a more detailed analysis of the relevant criteria as well as presenting some new matters for consideration; the three-year report provides some commentary on why certain selections were made in certain situations, particularly in relation to the DRC and Uganda, but does not add much to the principles enunciated in the earlier documents.

7.1.1. Key Provisions of the Policy Paper of September 2003

a. The Office will, in principle, seek to prosecute those bearing the greatest degree of responsibility.
b. The Office will take account of "the practical realities" of a situation when choosing and prioritizing cases, including the issue of witness security and access to witnesses.
c. The Office will carry out focused investigations with a view to ensuring expeditious court proceedings.

7.1.2. Draft Paper of June 2006

The draft paper on Criteria for Selection of Situations and Cases circulated in June 2006 did not change any of the preceding general principles, but made explicit that the pursuit of those bearing the greatest responsibility was necessarily dependent on the evidence that emerged in the course of an investigation. The idea of pursuing those bearing the greatest responsibility became the subject of a very significant decision in the case of Bosco Ntaganda. The Pre-Trial Chamber had rejected the Prosecutor's application for a warrant of arrest against Ntaganda on the basis that Ntaganda was not in a position of sufficient importance to render him among the most responsible and that, therefore, the case

[2] ICC-OTP, "Criteria for Selection of Situations and Cases", draft discussion paper, June 2003 (https://www.legal-tools.org/doc/sk0ratuy/).

[3] ICC-OTP, "Report on the activities performed during the first three years (June 2003–June 2006", 12 September 2006 (https://www.legal-tools.org/doc/c7a850/).

failed to meet the sufficient gravity test set out in Article 17(1)(d) of the Rome Statute.[4]

The Appeals Chamber ruled that the Pre-Trial Chamber had erred in law in several respects on this decision, but for present purposes the important consideration is that the Appeals Chamber found that the position of the person named in an arrest warrant application is not a relevant criterion in determining the gravity of a crime.[5] It agreed with the Office of the Prosecutor that, among other things, such a position would limit the potential deterrent effect of the ICC in that all but the very senior commanders of groups or organizations could expect to be prosecuted, therefore perhaps tempting others beneath them to believe they would enjoy impunity.

This part of the decision of the Appeal Chamber allows three reflections to be made. In the first place, the Chamber implicitly accepted that it was a legitimate policy decision on the part of the Prosecutor to pursue those bearing the greatest degree of responsibility but explicitly stated that it is not a legal requirement. Secondly, what the Prosecutor had thought obvious in fact had to be rendered explicit – namely that the concept of the greatest degree of responsibility depended on the evidence.

The reasoning of the Pre-Trial Chamber was deficient in two key respects which are important for the understanding of the concept. The Chamber seemed to understand the idea of those bearing the greatest responsibility in both a rigid, formulaic fashion, running a serious risk of entering the treacherous waters of strict liability, but also in an excessively narrow sense, guaranteeing impunity to all but the very top level.

This brings us to the third reflection: the concept of those bearing the greatest degree of responsibility is not only evidence-dependent, but can embrace a relatively large number of people depending on the crimes in question. This is seen, for example, in the case of Ali Kushayb, the first case brought in relation to the Darfur situation. If one were to have applied the logic of the Pre-Trial Chamber, it is extremely doubtful that one would ever have reached a local commander of the Janjaweed, but a proper understanding of the concept – relying on evidence concerning the specific crimes, not the position of the person in

[4] See ICC, *Situation in the DRC*, Pre-Trial Chamber I, Decision on the Prosecutor's Application for Warrants of Arrest, Article 58, 10 February 2006, ICC-01/04-01/07, especially paras. 42–62 (https://www.legal-tools.org/doc/d68b07/).

[5] ICC, *Situation in the DRC*, Appeals Chamber, Judgment on the Prosecutor's appeal against the decision of Pre-Trial Chamber I entitled "Decision on the Prosecutor's Application for Warrants of Arrest, Article 58", 13 July 2006, ICC-01/04-169, paras. 73–79 (https://www.legal-tools.org/doc/8c20eb/).

general – renders the selection of Kushayb eminently justified as being one of the most responsible *for those particular crimes*.

Therefore, while the June 2006 paper only briefly qualifies the concept of those bearing the greatest responsibility, it may be important to understand the context in which that explicit clarification was made.

7.2. The Gravity Criteria Developed

The June 2006 paper was significant in that it went into much greater detail on the Office's understanding of gravity as a selection criterion. The paper identifies four elements to be considered:

a. The scale of the crime in question, including the numbers of victims and possible consideration of temporal and geographic intensity.
b. The nature of the crime itself.
c. The manner of the crime (taking into account especially aggravating factors such as particular cruelty, targeting of especially vulnerable victims, the abuse of authority).
d. The impact of the crime.[6]

The paper explicitly states that the Office will not attempt to attribute specific weights to each of the elements to produce an arithmetic scorecard upon which to base selection: rather, it will consider all the facts, as it were, in the round. It is in this sense that one can say that the matter of selection cannot be regarded as a science, but nor is it so unattached to principle to be nothing more than artistic intuition: if anything, it might be considered a craft, based on guiding principles but sufficiently flexible to address the infinite variety of factual scenarios that will present themselves.

Nonetheless, it is also obvious that some factors set out by the Office raise a number of points worthy of discussion. The first issue of scale is relatively uncontroversial, as is the potentially useful reference to aggravating factors to assist in the selection of cases, but the other two bases provide fertile grounds for debate.

The idea that the nature of the crime provides a distinguishing factor to be considered in selection was based on the argument that while there is no explicit hierarchy of crimes in the Rome Statute, it is generally accepted that most national systems of law enforcement will prioritize certain kinds of crimes, in particular those dealing with loss of life or serious violation of physical integrity. On this basis the Office highlighted the crimes of killing and rape as among those of the utmost gravity.

[6] "Criteria for Selection of Situations and Cases", para. 29, see *supra* note 2.

Two problems emerged. In the first place, the Office elected to prosecute Thomas Lubanga in relation to the recruitment and use of child soldiers and brought no charges in relation to killings or rapes. In the second place, empirical research in the areas where the Office was investigating has indicated that the values reflected in the particular crimes highlighted in the draft paper may be insufficiently broad to capture what local populations consider as very serious crimes.

The latter of the problems can be addressed more simply. Research carried out by a number of non-governmental organizations ('NGOs') has indicated that local populations in areas where serious crimes have been committed may consider, for example, crimes involving looting or destruction of property as very grave indeed. On reflection, this ought not to be surprising: in the absence of any safety net in the form of welfare or humanitarian assistance, the loss of shelter and food can spell massive suffering for large groups of people. This not to say that the issues of killing and rape are not seen as very serious, but rather that it is not self-evident to those populations how a useful division of gravity between these and other crimes is likely to be drawn. In fact, as a matter of practice, the Office has acknowledged this reality in a number of warrant applications where such crimes are indeed charged.

The decision to charge Thomas Lubanga in relation to the recruitment and use of child soldiers provoked considerable dismay and criticism among national and international NGOs. While being prepared to acknowledge the seriousness of the crime itself, they felt that allegations of killings and sexual violence ought to have been reflected in the charging.

The Office's position in this regard was threefold: firstly, it highlighted the seriousness of the crime itself (although this was generally not publicly contested); secondly, it pointed out that the criteria applied to the selection of matters for investigation may have included other matters beside child recruitment and indeed indicated in its application for an arrest warrant that it wanted to leave open the possibility of bringing further charges. Thirdly, it argued on the basis of what is sometimes called in these contexts the principle of opportunity.

At the time in question, Lubanga had been detained for almost a year in Kinshasa by the DRC authorities in relation to matters not being investigated by the OTP. His detention was to be the subject of judicial review on the expiry of a 12-month period. The Office considered that in the particular circumstances that prevailed, there was a reasonable chance that a judge might order the release of Lubanga at that time. The Office did not claim it was anything more than a possibility, but it quite reasonably was not inclined to take unnecessary risks at that point: the arrest of suspects is quite easily the greatest challenge facing the

ICC – the efficacy of the Court depends significantly on suspects being brought to trial.

At that point, the Office was not in a position to bring charges in relation to matters other than the recruitment of child soldiers. It therefore elected to seek an arrest warrant on this limited ground in order to avoid the risk of Lubanga being released and rendering the prospect of his future arrest much more difficult.

This decision has been questioned by some as a departure from the criterion of gravity as the determining concept for case selection. It should be relatively obvious that the principle of opportunity in this context is exceptional. In all other warrant applications up to the time of writing, the Office had brought a wider array of charges. Faced with the choice of gambling on Lubanga's continued detention or ensuring his trial for the serious crime of recruiting child soldiers, the Office opted for the latter. Criticism on this basis seems pusillanimous if not wrong-headed. While not explicitly articulated in the paper of September 2003, the idea of a principle of opportunity seems to fit very comfortably within the considerations of the practical realities the Office indicated it would always take into account.

It is true that in due course, the Office indicated that it would not in fact bring further charges. There remains significant criticism among some parties for this decision that, among other things, they feel has never been properly explained. Whatever the reason for the failure to find sufficient evidence to prosecute Lubanga for other matters, it does not negate the legitimacy of the principle of opportunity on an exceptional basis as long as the crime itself meets the necessary threshold of gravity prescribed in Article 17(1)(d).

In retrospect, it may appear that the highlighting of killings and rapes as being of the utmost gravity is a less useful factor in assisting the office in selecting case hypotheses and finally cases for prosecution than originally thought. At the very least, the Office's own practice has normally embraced a broader range of crimes in its warrant applications and there appears to be an increasing tendency for the Office to avoid the suggestion of an inherent hierarchy of gravity in relation to the crimes themselves.

7.3. The Relevance of Impact

The fourth element identified in the paper of June 2006 was that of impact. The way in which it was presented there was explicitly on the basis that the prosecution of certain crimes may have a preventative impact on other (such) crimes being committed. On the other hand, public statements by the Prosecutor have indicated that the concept has another possible aspect: in speaking of attacks on peacekeepers, he has suggested that because such attacks may have the hugely negative impact of rendering local populations less secure, such attacks have an impact beyond the fact of the violence done to the victims themselves. This is an important consideration and is a reasonable attempt to indicate that a case focusing on peacekeepers does not suggest in any way that peacekeepers' lives are inherently more valuable than those of local people, but that rather it is the damage that such attacks are likely to do to the local people which might justify the selection of such a case. This approach seems to embody a qualitative aspect of aggravation rather than a preventative ambition. As such it seems to fit sensibly within the concept of gravity generally. However, the invocation of the concept of preventative impact in general, as a possible factor assisting in selection, appears confusing. The overall purpose of the Court as mentioned in the Preamble to the Statute is to end impunity and thus prevent such crimes being committed in the future. Since the primary objective of the Court is to help prevent the commission of all the crimes set out in the Statute, the value of preventative impact as a distinguishing factor justifying selection seems questionable.

One should not always presume that certain kinds of attacks will have specific kinds of impact. The impact of an attack on peacekeepers may not have the negative consequences presumed if there is any reason to believe that such peacekeepers, for example, had lost the confidence of the local population as result of an apparent lack of neutrality. Justifying the selection of a case partly on the basis of impact ought to require objective factual analysis that there was indeed such an impact.

7.4. Challenges for the ICC Office of the Prosecutor

7.4.1. Expectations

This is a challenge that faces all justice institutions, especially in the aftermath of mass atrocities. Effective and legitimate lobbying by groups with particular interests can somctimes nonetheless have the effect of raising expectations that for a variety of equally legitimate reasons are very unlikely to be met. The Office of the Prosecutor had done more than any other international justice institution at the stage of its life coinciding with the Second Edition to present relatively detailed documents explaining its policies and the criteria it will apply. This does not always help those whose expectations are not met, but it is an important recognition of the need for such institutions to take seriously the legitimate public interest in such matters and to make a serious attempt to do what it reasonably can to address matters of interest.

7.4.2. Representative Selection and Instrumentalization

A common criticism has been the unwitting victim of political instrumentalization which has in turn led to some suggesting the Office is not being seen to act impartially. The Office has consistently indicated that all of the cases it has sought to investigate are premised on a prior determination of gravity on the basis of the information available to be analysed.

It is clear that there is a perception issue where one is dealing with self-referrals from States, but the analysis of the substance perhaps needs to be more dispassionate. If it is correct that the cases that were selected for investigation in the DRC, Uganda and the CAR were all among the gravest for which credible and reliable information existed at the point of beginning the detailed investigation, these same cases would have been the ones selected even if they had begun by virtue of a *proprio motu* investigation rather than a referral. In the draft paper of June 2006 the Office made clear that it did not see the idea of the equivalence of blame as a legitimate criterion of selection. In practice the Office has in some cases brought proceedings against a variety of actors. For example, in the DRC, cases have been brought against leaders of the rival factions of the Union of Congolese Patriots and the Nationalist and Integrationist Front. These cases have not been brought to show that all are *in some way responsible*, but because on an objective analysis of the facts it was considered that FNI crimes were of sufficient gravity to merit prosecution.

It may well be the case that some perception difficulties could have been avoided if the two cases had been brought simultaneously. As a matter of prioritization this is a legitimate point. In the draft paper of June 2006, the Prosecutor indicated that he would follow a practice of sequential investigation. The precise reasoning for that position was not made explicit. It is noticeable that in subsequent *ad hoc* statements and briefings the idea of sequential investigations was not repeated.

The perception of instrumentalization will accompany much of the Prosecutor's work. A legitimate challenge to the prosecutorial choices on prioritization and selection has to demonstrate that there exists a reasonable basis to believe that other crimes of a similar or greater gravity have been committed. Much of the criticism in the Ugandan case relates to a failure to prosecute allegations of Uganda Peoples' Defence Forces crimes. A large part of that argument depends on whether one considers that allegations relating to forced displacement actually constitute crimes within the meaning of the Statute.

7.5. Conclusion

The ICC Office of the Prosecutor has been rightly praised for its more transparent processes from its earliest days compared to other similar institutions. Because the process of selection and prioritization is a craft rather than a science there will always be differing views about precisely what judgments should be made in particular circumstances. The nature of the process is likely to leave some, if not many, dissatisfied. These are issues about which reasonable people will very often disagree. In the final analysis, however, the Prosecutor must exercise his judgment and his discretion. The Office has gone quite far in indicating the criteria used in exercising its discretion. As long as these criteria are applied genuinely and faithfully, the Office has nothing to fear from reasonable disagreement.

8

Case Selection and Prioritization Criteria in the Work of the International Criminal Tribunal for the Former Yugoslavia

Claudia Angermaier*

8.1. Introduction

The selection of cases at the International Criminal Tribunal for the former Yugoslavia ('ICTY' or 'Tribunal') was an issue from the beginning of the Tribunal's work, as explained by Bergsmo in Chapter 1 above. Although there were initiatives in the Office of the Prosecutor ('OTP') to establish a framework and criteria for the selection of cases, it appears that a focused case selection policy was not consistently pursued in the early years of its work. It was only through strong political pressure from the United Nations Security Council and through changes in the procedural system of the ICTY, allowing for a wider judicial review of the Prosecutor's decisions, that the ICTY Prosecutor filtered its cases more thoroughly. This chapter explores some stages of this development and offers some general reflections in the last section.

8.2. Substantive and Procedural Framework

The ICTY Statute and Rules of Procedure and Evidence ('RPE') do not contain a list of case selection criteria. In comparison to the more recent international and internationalized tribunals, the ICTY was accorded a broad mandate, namely the prosecution of "persons responsible for serious violations of international humanitarian law committed in the territory of the former Yugoslavia

* **Claudia Angermaier** holds a doctorate in law from the University of Vienna, in addition to a Bachelor of Arts from the University of the Witwatersrand in South Africa. Formerly, she was Assistant Legal Advisor of the Legal Advisory Section, Office of the Prosecutor, International Criminal Court ('ICC') (2004–05); Research Assistant, Criminal Law Department, University of Vienna (2002–04); Country Manager for the FRY, International Centre for Migration Policy Development (2002). She researched selection criteria in international criminal justice when she worked for the ICC. This chapter, which brings together two contributions by the author in the Second Edition, has otherwise not been substantively updated since.

between 1 January 1991 and a date to be determined by the Security Council upon the restoration of peace".[1]

The Statute of the Special Court for Sierra Leone ('SCSL') specifically limited the jurisdiction of the Court, as well as the investigative and prosecutorial power of the Prosecutor, to "persons who bear the greatest responsibility".[2]

The Agreement on the Establishment of the Extraordinary Chambers in Cambodia stipulated that the Chambers have jurisdiction over "senior leaders of Democratic Kampuchea and those who were most responsible" for crimes committed between 1975 and 1979.[3]

While Antonio Cassese has argued that such a limitation can be inferred from Article 1 of the ICTY Statute – which provided that "persons responsible for serious violations of international humanitarian law" were subject to prosecution before the Tribunal[4] – the drafting process arguably suggests that there was a deliberate choice not to limit the jurisdictional mandate to senior persons. In establishing the Tribunal, the Security Council did not follow the only prior example of an international tribunal, the Nuremberg Tribunal, which had a clear division of competencies – namely that only the trial of major war criminals was to be conducted before the Nuremberg Tribunal, and minor war criminals were to be prosecuted by other courts.[5]

Article 16 of the ICTY Statute allocated the responsibility for investigations and prosecutions before the Tribunal solely to the Prosecutor. He or she was guaranteed independence in the exercise of prosecutorial functions both from the other organs of the Tribunal as well as external sources.[6] Once the Pros-

1 Security Council Resolution 827 (1993), UN Doc. S/RES/827 (1993), adopted 25 May 1993 (https://www.legal-tools.org/doc/dc079b/).

2 Statute of the SCSL, 14 August 2000, Article 1 (https://www.legal-tools.org/doc/aa0e20/)

3 "The present Agreement further recognizes that the Extraordinary Chambers have personal jurisdiction over senior leaders of Democratic Kampuchea and those who were most responsible for the crimes referred to in Article 1 of the Agreement.", see Article 2 of the Draft Agreement between the United Nations and the Royal Government of Cambodia concerning the Prosecution under Cambodian Law of Crimes Committed during the period of Democratic Kampuchea annexed to United Nations General Assembly Resolution 57/228, UN Doc. A/RES/57/228, 22 May 2003 (https://www.legal-tools.org/doc/533d2a/).

4 Antonio Cassese, "The ICTY: A Living and Vital Reality", in *Journal of International Criminal Justice*, 2004, vol. 2, no. 2, pp. 585, 587; ICTY Statute, Article 1 (https://www.legal-tools.org/doc/b4f63b/).

5 Larry Johnson, "Ten Years Later: Reflections on the Drafting", in *Journal of International Criminal Justice*, 2004, vol. 2, no. 2, pp. 368, 369.

6 ICTY Statute, Article 16(2), see *supra* note 4.

ecutor determined that a *prima facie* case existed, he or she submitted an indictment to a judge of the trial chamber.[7] In submitting the indictment, the Prosecutor selected a case for prosecution before the ICTY. Under Article 19, the judge of the trial chamber only had the possibility to review a decision of the Prosecutor on the basis of whether the evidentiary threshold of a "*prima facie* case" had been met. This did not allow judges to review the application of extra-evidentiary criteria for the selection of cases.

Antonio Cassese, who at the time was ICTY President, noted that already in the early stages of the Tribunal's work, the judges expressed their disagreement with the Prosecutor's prosecutorial policy. On 20 January 1995, a few months after Richard J. Goldstone took office as the first Prosecutor of the ICTY, the judges held an *in camera* meeting with the Prosecutor on the initial bottom-up approach of his Office – which entailed targeting low-level suspects and only at a later stage moving up the ladder of command to indict persons in senior positions.[8] The judges expressed their disagreement, arguing that it was the role of the Tribunal to "immediately target the military and political leaders or other high ranking commanders, based on the notion of command responsibility as laid down in the statute (Article 7(3))".[9] On 30 January 1995, the judges adopted a declaration in which they expressed their concern that the indictment practice be consonant with the expectations of the Security Council and the international community as expressed in Council Resolutions 808 and 827.[10] According to Cassese, this rather vague statement was meant to convey the judges' view that the purpose of the ICTY rested in the prosecution of "those persons who bore major responsibility".[11]

Goldstone held the view that the judges' insistence on receiving regular reports on the policy and progress of investigations constituted an encroachment on the independence of the Prosecutor, and that it was born out of frustration that there were yet no trials to be conducted.[12] He further argued that the exercise

---

7 *Ibid.*, Article 18(4).

8 See Cassese, 2004, p. 586, see *supra* note 4.

9 *Ibid.*, p. 586.

10 The declaration was made public the next day and is reprinted in ICTY, "The Judges of the Tribunal for the former Yugoslavia Express Their Concern Regarding the Substance of Their Programme of Judicial Work For 1995", 1 February 1995, Press Release CC/PIO/003-E (https://www.legal-tools.org/doc/d6scdqqb/).

11 Cassese, 2004, p. 586 at note 4, see *supra* note 4.

12 Richard J. Goldstone, "A view from the Prosecution", in *Journal of International Criminal Justice*, 2004, vol. 2, no. 2, pp. 380, 381.

of such judicial oversight on the investigative activities and policy of the Prosecutor could have resulted in a compromise of the judges' impartiality.[13] Cassese, on the other hand, maintained that the decision of the judges to 'meddle' with the case-selection policy of the Prosecutor was necessary because there did not at the time exist a procedural mechanism which would have ensured that the Prosecutor acted in conformity with the general goals laid down in the ICTY Statute.[14] He stressed that it was not a decision of individual judges but rather that the judges acted unanimously as a collective body.[15] He argued that because there was no interference with specific cases, but only a review of the general case-selection policy of the Prosecutor, the judges did not violate judicial ethics or propriety.[16]

The early indictments of the Office of the Prosecutor arguably demonstrate that the selection of cases was governed mainly by the availability of evidence and the interest of individual ICTY prosecutors in particular cases.[17] Moreover, the first indictments included such low-level perpetrators as camp guards in the list of accused persons, and therefore reflected the Prosecutor's stance that seniority was not a decisive criterion for the selection of cases.[18]

8.3. The 1995 Criteria

In October 1995, however, the ICTY Office of the Prosecutor formally adopted a set of case-selection criteria, in which the level of responsibility of the accused was defined as a criterion for the selection of cases. The stated purpose of these criteria was to enable an effective allocation of resources and the fulfilment of the Tribunal's mandate.[19]

The criteria were divided into five groups: "(a) person"; "(b) serious violation"; "(c) policy considerations"; "(d) practical considerations"; and "(e) other relevant considerations".[20]

---

[13] *Ibid.*, p. 381.

[14] Cassese, 2004, p. 587, see *supra* note 4.

[15] *Ibid.*, p. 588.

[16] *Ibid.*, pp. 587 ff.

[17] Morten Bergsmo, Kjetil Helvig, Ilia Utmelidze and Gorana Žagovec, *The Backlog of Core International Crimes Cases in Bosnia and Herzegovina*, Second Edition, Torkel Opsahl Academic EPublisher, Oslo, 2010, pp. 98–99 (http://www.toaep.org/ps-pdf/3-bergsmo-helvig-utmelidze-zagovec-second).

[18] See ICTY, "The International Tribunal for the former Yugoslavia Charges 21 Serbs With Atrocities Committed Inside and Outside the Omarska Death Camp", Press Release CC/PIO/004-E, 13 February 1995.

[19] Bergsmo, Helvig, Utmelidze and Žagovec, 2010, p. 99, see *supra* note 17.

[20] The content of these groups of criteria has been taken from *ibid.*, pp. 98 ff. They also provide an in-depth analysis of each of these sets of criteria.

The first list, "(a) person" contained the following factors:

- position in hierarchy under investigation;
- political, military, paramilitary or civilian leader;
- leadership at municipal, regional or national level;
- nationality;
- role, participation in policy, strategy decisions;
- personal culpability for specific atrocities;
- notoriousness and responsibility for particularly heinous acts;
- extent of direct participation in the alleged incidents;
- authority and control exercised by the suspects;
- the suspect's alleged notice and knowledge of acts by subordinates;
- arrest potential;
- evidence and witness availability;
- media, government or non-governmental organization ('NGO') target; and
- potential roll-over witness, likelihood of linkage evidence.

The group of criteria entitled "(b) serious violation" listed the following:

- number of victims;
- nature of acts;
- area of destruction;
- duration and repetition of the offence;
- location of the crime;
- linkage to other cases;
- nationality of perpetrators and victims;
- arrest potential;
- evidence and witness availability;
- showcase or pattern crime; and
- media, government or NGO target.

Under the section "(c) policy considerations" these criteria were listed:

- advancement of international jurisprudence (reinforcement of existing norms, building precedent, clarifying and advancing the scope of existing protections);
- willingness and ability of national courts to prosecute the alleged perpetrator;
- potential symbolic or deterrent value of prosecution;
- public perception concerning the effective functioning of Tribunal;
- public perception concerning immediate response to ongoing atrocities;
- public perception concerning impartiality or balance.

The section "(d) practical considerations" read as follows:

- available investigative resources;
- impact that the new investigation will have on ongoing investigations and on making existing indictments trial ready;
- the estimated time to complete the investigation;
- timing of the investigation (for example, the impact initiating a particular investigation will have on the ability to conduct future investigations in the country);
- possibility or likelihood of arrest of the alleged perpetrator;
- consideration of other work carried out in relation to the case (including a check against Rules of Road cases);
- completeness of evidence;
- availability of exculpatory information and evidence; and
- consideration of other Office of the Prosecutor investigations in the same geographical area, particularly those of 'opposite-ethnicity' perpetrators and victims.

And, lastly, the group "(e) other relevant considerations" included the following criteria:

- the particular statutory offence or parts thereof, that can be charged;
- the charging theories available;
- potential legal impediments to prosecution;
- potential defences;
- theory of liability and legal framework of each potential suspect;
- the extent to which the crime base fits in with current investigations and overall strategic direction;
- the extent to which a successful investigation or prosecution of the case would further the strategic aims;
- the extent to which the case can take the investigation to higher political, military, police and civil chains of command; and
- to what extent the case fits into a larger pattern-type of ongoing or future investigations and prosecutions.

Bergsmo, Helvig, Utmelidze and Žagovec maintain that these criteria merely provided a catalogue of considerations to be considered as a whole when deciding whether to pursue an investigation and prosecution. The considerations were not ranked according to their importance.[21] Arguably, a focused case-selection policy on the basis of this catalogue could hardly have been implemented.

[21] *Ibid.*, p. 99.

8.4. The 1998 Review of Cases

In 1998 an internal memorandum was prepared by Morten Bergsmo for Chief Prosecutor Louise Arbour which demonstrated that only few of the ICTY indictees were persons with leadership responsibility. This 1998 memorandum did not contain criteria but rather a guideline on some issues to be addressed for justifying the selection of a specific case for investigation.[22]

Nevertheless, the memorandum appears to have resulted in a re-evaluation of the Office of the Prosecutor's then-existing case portfolio. In May 1998, the Chief Prosecutor withdrew charges against 14 accused. In a press statement on 8 May 1998, she outlined the overall investigative and prosecutorial strategies of the ICTY Office of the Prosecutor:

> […] I have re-evaluated all outstanding indictments *vis-à-vis* the overall investigative and prosecutorial strategies of my Office. Consistent with those strategies, which involve maintaining an investigative focus on persons holding higher levels of responsibility, or on those who have been personally responsible for the exceptionally brutal or otherwise extremely serious offences, I decided that it was appropriate to withdraw the charges against a number of accused in what have become known as the Omarska and Keraterm indictments, which were confirmed in February 1995 and July 1995 respectively.
>
> This decision was taken in an attempt to balance the available resources within the tribunal and in recognition of the need to prosecute cases fairly and expeditiously. I wish to emphasize that this decision is not based on any lack of evidence in respect of these accused. I do not consider it feasible at this time to hold multiple separate trials for related offences committed by perpetrators who could appropriately be tried in another judicial forum, such as a State Court […].[23]

This statement by Arbour demonstrated a clear shift towards a more accused-centred approach, and reflected the course that the ICTY Prosecutor would be forced to pursue far more vigorously under the Security Council's so-called 'completion strategy'.

As a result of the withdrawal of charges, the accused Landžo in the Čelebići case sought to ensure a judicial review of the Prosecutor's decision. He alleged a violation of the principle of equality enshrined in Article 21(1) of the ICTY Statute because the Prosecutor had not, in accordance with her newly adopted

[22] *Ibid.*, p. 60.

[23] ICTY, "Statement by the Prosecutor Following the Withdrawal of the Charges Against 14 Accused", 8 May 1998, Press Release CC/PIU/314-E (https://www.legal-tools.org/doc/ro4u8xhj/).

prosecutorial strategy, withdrawn charges against Landžo – in spite of him being a 'low-level accused' – in order to give appearance of "even-handedness" (the accused was a Muslim, while those against whom charges had been withdrawn were Serbian).[24] Although the Appeals Chamber ultimately dismissed the appeal, it set out some guidelines regarding the case-selection policy of the Prosecutor. First, it stipulated that, despite the Prosecutor's broad discretion regarding the initiation of investigations and the preparation of indictments, this power was not unlimited but subject to certain limitations contained in the Statute and RPE of the Tribunal.[25] Accordingly, the Prosecutor was only allowed to exercise her functions in accordance "with full respect of the law", including "recognised principles of human rights",[26] one such principle being equality before the Tribunal. The Appeals Chamber then stated that it was for the accused to prove that this principle had been violated, by showing that the prosecution was based on an "unlawful or improper (including discriminatory) motive", and that "other similarly situated persons were not prosecuted". The Appeals Chamber rejected the grounds for appeal, holding that the prosecutorial policy was not only limited to persons holding higher levels of responsibility, but also included notorious offenders. In the Chamber's view, because the accused could be considered a notorious offender, the prosecutorial policy was not applied in a discriminate manner.

8.5. The Completion Strategy

With the adoption of the so-called 'completion strategy', the level of responsibility of the accused was defined as the decisive criterion for the selection of cases at the ICTY. The completion strategy was a result of the waning enthusiasm of donor-states for the Tribunal's work. The Tribunal was originally conceived as a temporary measure, however, in 1999 there was far from an end in sight for the Tribunal's activities.[27] In June 2000, ICTY President Claude Jorda presented a report to the Security Council in which he proposed a strategy for

---

[24] ICTY, *Prosecutor v. Zdravko Mučić et al.*, Appeals Chamber, Judgement, No. IT-96-21-A, 20 February 2001, para. 612 (https://www.legal-tools.org/doc/051554/).

[25] *Ibid.*, para. 602.

[26] *Ibid.*, para. 604:

> The discretion of the Prosecutor at all times is circumscribed in a more general way by the nature of her position as an official vested with specific duties imposed by the Statute of the tribunal. The Prosecutor is committed to discharge those duties with full respect of the law. In this regard, the Secretary-General's Report stressed that the tribunal, which encompasses all of its organs, including the Office of the Prosecutor, must abide by the recognised principles of human rights.

[27] Dominic Raab, "Evaluating the ICTY and its Completion Strategy", in *Journal of International Criminal Justice*, 2004, vol. 2, no. 2, pp. 82, 84.

completing first-instance trials by 2007.[28] This involved creating a pool of *ad litem* judges to be able to dispose of the heavy trial load. As a further measure, the report discussed the possibility of the ICTY focusing on high-level perpetrators, leaving those in the lower echelons to be tried by national courts in the West-Balkans. The report stated that the judges were not in favour of this option at that point in time, due to the political climate in the relevant states and the issues of safety for witnesses and victims.[29]

The Security Council approved the proposal for the creation of a pool of *ad litem* judges. Its Resolution 1329 (2000) also took "particular note" of the ICTY's position that "civilian, military and paramilitary leaders should be tried before them in preference to minor actors", and the possibility "to suspend an indictment to allow for a national court to deal with a particular case".[30] This resolution gave rise to the ICTY's so-called 'completion strategy'.

In a report submitted to the UN Secretary-General on 10 June 2002, the President of the ICTY laid out a comprehensive plan for the referral of cases involving intermediate and lower-level accused to national courts in the former Yugoslavia. This was presented as a measure to ensure the completion of first instance trials by 2008.[31] The report stressed the strong need for judicial reform in these countries, but in principle the report, in contrast to the earlier position in 2000, advocated for the referral of cases to these courts.[32] The report further proposed an amendment of Rule 11*bis* of the ICTY RPE, which already provided for the referral of cases under certain limited conditions. Besides broadening the possibility to refer cases to states other than the state in which the person was arrested and other procedural issues,[33] it was argued that it was in the interests of transparency *vis-à-vis* the international community as well as the states of the former Yugoslavia, to provide criteria for the referral of cases. It

---

[28] Security Council, "President of International Tribunal for former Yugoslavia Briefs Security Council, Asks for Change in Court's Statute", 20 June 2000, Press Release SC/6879 (https://www.legal-tools.org/doc/oys4kzt1/).

[29] See "Report on the Operation of the International Criminal Tribunal for the former Yugoslavia", 12 May 2000, in UN Doc. A/55/382-S/2000/865, 14 September 2000 (https://www.legal-tools.org/doc/f2nvb3/).

[30] See Security Council Resolution 1329 (2000), UN Doc. S/RES/1329 (2000), 5 December 2000, preambular paras. 7 and 8 (https://www.legal-tools.org/doc/6c89e1/).

[31] See Letter dated 17 June 2002 from the Secretary-General addressed to the President of the Security Council, UN Doc. S/2002/678, 19 June 2003 (https://www.legal-tools.org/doc/47c61zhc/), to which the "Report on the Judicial Status of the International Criminal Tribunal for the former Yugoslavia and the Prospects for Referring Certain Cases to National Courts" ('Report on the Judicial Status') is attached.

[32] Report on the Judicial Status, paras. 2 ff., *ibid.*

[33] *Ibid.*, paras. 38–41.

was suggested that the criteria should be formulated in broad terms, namely "the position of the accused" and "the gravity of the crimes with which he is charged", leaving the precise interpretation of these criteria to the Tribunal.[34] According to the report, the ICTY Prosecutor objected to the possibility of the Trial Chamber also deciding *ex officio*, and not only on an application of the Prosecutor, whether to refer a case to a national court, reasoning that such a procedural mechanism infringed on the statutory powers of the Prosecutor.[35]

By Presidential Statement of 23 July 2002,[36] the Security Council recognized that "the ICTY should concentrate its work on the prosecution and trial of the civilian, military and paramilitary leaders suspected of being responsible for serious violations of international humanitarian law committed in the territory of the former Yugoslavia since 1991, rather than on minor actors", and it endorsed the "broad strategy for the transfer of cases involving intermediary and lower-level accused to competent national jurisdictions".

Rule 11*bis* was amended accordingly on 12 December 2002. The President of the Tribunal could appoint a trial chamber after the confirmation of the indictment to determine whether the case should be referred to the authorities of a state.[37] Rule 11*bis*(B) stipulated that the trial chamber could take the decision on referral *proprio motu* or at the request of the Prosecutor. The criteria for the referral of cases were "the gravity of the crimes charged" and the "level of responsibility" of the accused.[38]

Although the procedural mechanism for implementing the proposed completion strategy was put in place, no decisions on the referral of cases were taken. On 28 August 2003, the Security Council adopted Resolution 1503 in which it recalled and reaffirmed the ICTY completion strategy.[39] It now called upon the ICTY to "take all possible measures" to implement the completion strategy which it defined in the following terms: first, the completion of all investigations by the end of 2004; secondly, the completion of all first-instance trial activities

[34] *Ibid.*, para. 42

[35] *Ibid.*, para. 43.

[36] Presidential Statement, UN Doc. S/2002/PRST/21, 23 July 2002, in "Security Council Endorses Proposed Strategy for Transfer to National Courts of Certain Cases Involving Humanitarian Crimes in Former Yugoslavia", 23 July 2002, Press Release SC/7461 (https://www.legal-tools.org/doc/vdtlbayw/).

[37] ICTY RPE, 11 February 1994, Rule 11*bis*(A) (https://www.legal-tools.org/doc/30df50/).

[38] *Ibid.*, Rule 11*bis*(C)

[39] Security Council Resolution 1503 (2003), UN Doc. S/Res/1503 (2003), 28 August 2003, preambular para. 7 (https://www.legal-tools.org/doc/b3d7d9/).

by 2008; and lastly the completion of all work in 2010.[40] Furthermore, the Security Council explicitly recalled "in strongest terms" some of the measures proposed by the ICTY to meet these deadlines, namely focusing prosecution and trial before the ICTY on "the most senior leaders suspected of being most responsible for crimes within the ICTY's jurisdiction"; transferring cases not meeting this requisite to the competent national courts; and thirdly, improving the domestic courts' capacity to deal with the these cases.[41] It then requested the Prosecutor and President of the ICTY to provide in their annual reports an explanation of the plans for implementing the completion strategy.[42] The Security Council hereby demonstrated its intention to exercise oversight on the prosecutorial and judicial activities of the ICTY. Most importantly, however, the Council formally imposed the completion strategy as a goal on the organs of the ICTY, as opposed to merely endorsing the Tribunal's self-imposed deadlines.[43]

With Resolution 1534, adopted only seven months later, on 26 March 2004, the Security Council took an even stronger stance towards the implementation of the completion strategy. Expressing its concern that the ICTY indicated that it might be impossible to fulfil the deadlines contained in Security Council Resolution 1503, it emphasized the importance of abiding by these deadlines and urged the Tribunal "to plan and act accordingly".[44] In this context, it called upon the ICTY Prosecutor to review the caseload with a view to deciding which cases to refer to national jurisdictions.[45] Furthermore, it called upon the Tribunal to ensure that all new indictments only concentrate on the most senior leaders.[46] One commentator argued that this was a response to the Prosecutor's stated intention to issue new indictments.[47] Lastly, the Security Council required that the President and Prosecutor of the Tribunal begin providing specific reports on the implementation of the completion strategy every six months.[48] It also explicitly declared its intention to review the progress made by the Tribunal and "to ensure that the timeframe set out in the Completion Strategies [...] can be met".[49]

---

40 *Ibid.*, operative para. 7

41 *Ibid.*, preambular para. 7

42 *Ibid.*, operative para. 6.

43 See also Raab, 2004, p. 85, see *supra* note 27.

44 Security Council Resolution 1534 (2004), UN Doc. S/RES/1534 (2004), 26 March 2004, preambular para. 8 and operative para. 3 (https://www.legal-tools.org/doc/ffe092/).

45 *Ibid.*, operative para. 4.

46 *Ibid.*, operative para. 5.

47 Raab, 2004, p. 87, see *supra* note 27.

48 Security Council Resolution 1534 (2004), operative para. 6, see *supra* note 44.

49 *Ibid.*, operative para. 7.

8.6. Rules 11*bis* and 28(A)

With Resolution 1534 the Security Council exercised its yet strongest oversight of the ICTY's performance. Most importantly, it introduced a substantive criterion for the confirmation of indictments, thereby forcing the Prosecutor only to select for prosecution the cases that targeted persons of the most senior level. On 6 April 2004, only a month after this resolution was adopted, the ICTY judges implemented the Security Council's request for additional judicial oversight of the Prosecutor's indictment practice. They amended Rule 28(A) of the ICTY RPE to include an added review procedure for indictments: upon receipt of an indictment, the President

> shall refer the matter to the Bureau which shall determine whether the indictment, *prima facie*, concentrates on one or more of the most senior leaders suspected of being most responsible for the crimes within the jurisdiction of the tribunal.[50]

This procedure constituted an additional measure of review to Rule 11*bis*. While the latter applied only after the confirmation of the indictment, the review under Rule 28(A) foresaw a review before the indictment was submitted to the competent judge for confirmation on the basis of the evidence submitted. It is also interesting to note that Rule 28(A) reflected the Security Council's language in speaking of most senior leaders being most responsible. Rule 11*bis* merely referred to the "level of responsibility of the accused".

The case law of the Referral Bench has shown that the criterion of "level of responsibility" in Rule 11*bis* was interpreted by reference to the rank of the accused coupled with his or her *de facto* and *de jure* extent of authority;[51] his or

---

[50] ICTY RPE, Rule 28(a), see *supra* note 37.

[51] See, for instance, *Prosecutor v. Rahim Ademi and Mirko Norac*, Referral Bench, Decision for Referral to the Authorities of the Republic of Croatia pursuant to Rule 11bis, 14 September 2005, Case No. IT-04-78-PT, paras. 29–30 (https://www.legal-tools.org/doc/4eee13/); *Prosecutor v. Dragomir Milošević*, Referral Bench, Decision on Referral of Case pursuant to Rule 11bis, 8 July 2005, Case No. IT-98-29/1-PT, para. 22 (https://www.legal-tools.org/doc/404de4/):

> The Referral Bench does not consider, however, that the phrase "most senior leaders" used by the Security Council is restricted to individuals who are "architects" of an "overall policy" which forms the basis of alleged crimes. Were it true that only cases against military commanders, who were at the highest policy-making levels of an army – in the case of the VRS the Republika Srpska highest political and supreme military levels – could not be referred under Rule 11 *bis*, this would diminish the true level of responsibility of many commanders in the field and those at staff level. […] The Referral Bench therefore considers that individuals are also covered, who, by virtue of their position and function in the relevant hierarchy, both *de jure* and *de facto*, are alleged to have exercised such a degree of authority that it is appropriate to describe them as among the "most senior", rather than "intermediate".

her role in the commission of the crimes including an assessment of the mode of liability by which he or she could be linked to the crime; and possibly any political role that the person additionally played.[52] It is also interesting that while the Security Council resolutions on the completion strategy stipulated the seniority of the accused as a case selection criterion, they did not refer to the gravity of the crimes charged. However, Rule 11*bis*(C) stipulated that the gravity of the crimes also constituted a criterion for deciding whether to refer cases to national courts. In order to determine the gravity of the crimes, the ICTY Referral Bench focused on the scale of the crimes by reference to such factors as the number of victims, the duration of the crimes, as well as the geographic scope.[53] In one case, the type of crimes also constituted a factor for determining gravity of the crimes.[54] At a later stage, additional criteria besides the level of responsibility of the accused and the gravity of the crimes were included in the 11*bis* regime: the judges were also to be satisfied that the accused would receive a fair trial and that the death penalty would not be imposed or carried out.[55]

8.7. Reduction of the Case Load

As a result of all these measures, the ICTY Prosecutor in 2004 substantially reduced her case load. First, the number of persons under investigation was reduced. Before then, in her annual report of 20 August 2003, the Prosecutor had categorized her investigations according to two priority lists. Priority list A referred to those investigations involving "the most serious crimes and the highest-level perpetrators" which would have been completed, in accordance with the completion strategy, by the end of 2004. Priority list B referred to investigations involving lower-level accused, which would have only been completed if sufficient resources remained before the end of 2004. She had identified 17 investigations involving 35 suspects as falling under list A.[56] After the Security Council issued Resolutions 1503 and 1534, the Prosecutor reduced the number

52 See *Prosecutor v. Gojko Janković*, Referral Bench, Decision on Referral of Case under Rule 11bis (With Confidential Annex), 22 July 2005, Case No. IT-96-23/2-PT, para. 19 (https://www.legal-tools.org/doc/95034b/).

53 See, for instance, *Prosecutor v. Željko Mejakić et al.*, Referral Bench, Decision on Prosecutor's Motion for Referral of Case pursuant to Rule 11*bis*., 20 July 2005, Case No. IT-02-65-PT, para. 21 (https://www.legal-tools.org/doc/7i67139y/); *Prosecutor v. Gojko Janković*, 22 July 2005, para. 19, *ibid.*

54 See *Mejakić et al.*, 20 July 2005, para. 21, *ibid.*

55 ICTY RPE, Rule 11*bis*(B), see *supra* note 37.

56 10th Annual Report of the International Tribunal for the Prosecution of Persons Responsible for Serious Violations of International Humanitarian Law Committed in the Territory of the former Yugoslavia since 1991, UN Doc. A/58/297-S/2003/829, 20 August 2003, para. 229 (https://www.legal-tools.org/doc/7c5dd7/).

of investigations and persons contained in list A. In her report to the Security Council on 24 May 2004, the Prosecutor listed only seven remaining investigations involving 13 suspects. She pointed out that her investigations had produced new results which indicated that some of the accused on her priority list B should rather be included in the priority list A. She then stated: "However, I do not expect to reevaluate additional accused from priority B to priority A".[57] Given the immense pressure to complete investigations by 2004, it appears the Prosecutor took a decision not to prosecute any additional persons, even if they fell into the category of being one of the most senior leaders.

In September 2004, the Prosecutor submitted her first motions for referral of cases under Rule 11*bis*. By the time of the Second Edition of this book, the Prosecutor filed 14 referral motions involving 22 accused. Two referral motions were denied by the Referral Bench. The Appeals Chamber reversed one decision of the Referral Bench in which it had granted a motion to refer. In two cases involving two accused the accused entered into guilty pleas. One case involving three accused was withdrawn by the Prosecutor. Thus, in total eight motions for referral, involving 13 accused, were granted.

8.8. Some Thoughts on Essential Qualities of Prioritization Criteria

Beyond the context of the ICTY, if we seek to define the essential characteristics of generally-applicable case prioritization criteria, it is important to consider the purpose served by these criteria. Case prioritization criteria may have a benefit at the internal level, meaning for the work of the prosecution office, as well as at the external level, for instance *vis-à-vis* the public.

8.8.1. The Purpose of Case Prioritization Criteria

At the internal level, criteria serve as guidelines for the decisions of individual prosecutors. They ensure that such decisions follow the overall prosecutorial strategy of the prosecutor's office. More importantly, however, they ensure that decisions are in consistency with the fundamental principle of equality before the law. Overall, they therefore enhance the quality of prosecutorial decision-making. Finally, they may allow for a rational allocation of limited resources.

At the external level, they provide a basis for justifying the prioritization of certain cases *vis-à-vis* victims, other interest groups, and the public at large.

---

[57] Assessment of Carla Del Ponte, Prosecutor of the International Criminal Tribunal for the Former Yugoslavia, provided to the Security Council pursuant to paragraph 6 of Security Council Resolution 1534 (2004), Enclosure II of Letter dated 21 May 2004 from the President of the International Tribunal for the Prosecution of Persons Responsible for Serious Violations of International Humanitarian Law Committed in the Territory of the Former Yugoslavia since 1991, addressed to the President of the Security Council, UN Doc. S/2004/420, 24 May 2004, paras. 14–15 (https://www.legal-tools.org/doc/532478/).

They may prevent the perception that decisions are taken arbitrarily. This is also of great importance for the individual accused. Criteria thus serve as a basis for holding the prosecutor accountable for his or her decision to prioritize a certain case for prosecution. However, they may also serve as a protection tool against various external actors who seek to influence the prosecutor's decision regarding the prioritization of cases. The requests of such actors to prioritize a specific case for prosecution can be evaluated against the defined and publicly available prosecutorial case-prioritization criteria. If requests are not in conformity with these criteria, they can be rejected as impermissible interferences with the work of the prosecution office. This has been described as second-order accountability.[58] Overall, the prosecutor's independence in his or her decision-making may therefore be strengthened. Moreover, such transparent and rational decision-making enhances the legitimacy of the prosecution office.[59]

8.8.2. Essential Qualities of Case Prioritization Criteria

Clarity and precision are essential qualities that case prioritization criteria should have for them to function effectively at the internal level. It is only when the content of criteria can easily be understood that they can be readily applied by individual prosecutors. These qualities are therefore important for ensuring that criteria function as clear guidelines for the work of prosecutors. Furthermore, the criteria should not be inherently biased or formulated in biased terms; otherwise, the application of such criteria may lead to a violation of the principles of fairness and equality.

There should be a balance between too vague or narrow a description of the criteria. If the criteria are formulated in very broad terms, there may be too much leeway in their application. This entails the risk of treating similarly situated cases very differently. On the other hand, too narrow a definition may render the criteria inapplicable because they lack the required flexibility to be applied to different cases.[60]

It does not, however, suffice to merely adopt criteria and hope for an equal and consistent application. Rather, there needs to be some form of review mechanism. This could be an internal review within the prosecution office, but may also be affected by an external review, for instance by the judiciary. Through an effective enforcement system, the consistency and equality of application can

[58] Allison Marston Danner, "Enhancing the Legitimacy and Accountability of Prosecutorial Discretion at the International Criminal Court", in *American Journal of International Law*, vol. 97, no. 3, 2003, pp. 510, 512.

[59] See *ibid.*, pp. 535 ff. for a discussion of the concept of legitimacy as both actual and perceived legitimacy.

[60] See also *ibid.*, pp. 549 ff.

be ensured. Furthermore, a fundamental prerequisite for objective prioritization of cases is a proper, comprehensive investigation of all facts – otherwise, it is likely that a skewed result will be achieved.

The issue of equal application is not only relevant at the internal level, but is essential to ensure the legitimacy of the prosecutor's actions *vis-à-vis* the public and in particular the victims. In relation to the prosecution of core international crimes, the charge that decisions are politically driven is quickly made. Without a set of publicly available criteria, it is more difficult to respond to such an attack. In order to provide accountability but also protection against political pressure, the criteria should be formulated in clear, non-political and confidence-generating terms.

The United Nations Guidelines on the Role of the Public Prosecutors of 1990[61] stipulate:

> In countries where prosecutors are vested with discretionary functions, the law or published rules or regulations shall provide guidelines to enhance fairness and consistency of approach in taking decisions in the prosecution process, including institution or waiver of prosecution.[62]

Similarly, the Recommendations of the Council of Europe on the Role of Public Prosecution in the Criminal Justice System (2000)[63] state:

> With a view to promoting fair, consistent and efficient activity of public prosecutors, states should seek to:
>
> […]
>
> – define general principles and criteria to be used by way of references against which decisions in individual cases should be taken, in order to guard against arbitrary decision-making.

[61] Guidelines on the Role of Prosecutors, Eighth United Nations Congress on the Prevention of Crime and the Treatment of Offenders, Havana, 27 August to 7 September 1990, UN Doc. A/CONF.144/28/Rev.I, p. 189 ('Guidelines on the Role of Prosecutors') (https://www.legal-tools.org/doc/658aba/), reprinted in Egbert Myjer, Barry Hancock and Nicolas Cowdery (eds.), *Human Rights Manual for Prosecutors*, International Association of Prosecutors, Wolf Legal Publishers, Nijmegen, 2003, p. 141.

[62] Guidelines on the Role of Prosecutors, para. 17, *ibid.*

[63] Recommendation Rec(2000) 19 of the Committee of Ministers to Member States on the Role of the Public Prosecution on the Criminal Justice System, adopted by the Committee of Ministers on 6 October 2000 at the 724th meeting of the Ministers' Deputies ('Recommendation Rec(2000) 19'), reprinted in Myjer, Hancock and Cowdery (eds.), 2003, p. 147, see *supra* note 61.

> b. The above-mentioned methods of organisation, guidelines, principles and criteria should be decided by parliament or by government or, if national law enshrines the independence of the public prosecutor, by representatives of the public prosecution.
>
> c. The public must be informed of the above-mentioned organisation, guidelines, principles and criteria; they shall be communicated to any person on request.[64]

The adoption of a set of criteria is, however, not sufficient. Only if the decision-making of prosecutors is actually governed by such criteria, can they enhance the public's confidence in the prosecutor's work.

[64] Recommendation Rec(2000) 19, para. 36.a, *ibid.*

9

Case Selection and Prioritization Criteria at the International Criminal Tribunal for Rwanda

Alex Obote-Odora*

9.1. Introduction

General principles of criminal law recognize the prosecutor's authority to decide whether or not to prosecute a given case.[1] The concept of case selection – or the exercise of prosecutorial discretion – is one on which defendants and the Office of the Prosecutor ('OTP') differed in cases before the International Criminal Tribunal for Rwanda ('ICTR'). The accused at the ICTR filed several motions before trial chambers, alleging that the ICTR Prosecutor was conducting selective prosecutions. All such motions filed by accused alleging selective prosecutions were dismissed, including one in which the accused sought an order from the Trial Chamber to authorize him to interview former ICTR Prosecutor Carla del Ponte.[2] The accused wished the former ICTR Prosecutor to provide the reasons why the RPF soldiers had not been prosecuted when the motion was filed. In the motion, the accused submitted that:

> Ambassador Carla del Ponte has firsthand information on the reasons why prosecution of RPF leaders, similarly situated to Mr. Nzirorera [the Accused], were not prosecuted. Therefore, the meeting sought with her is relevant to establish whether there may have

* **Alex Obote-Odora**, a legal consultant and author, was, at the time of the Second Edition, Chief of the Appeals and Legal Advisory Divisions, Office of the Prosecutor, International Criminal Tribunal for Rwanda, and an advocate of the Uganda judicature. [This chapter has not been substantively updated since the Second Edition.] He holds an LL.D. in international criminal law from Stockholm University, an LL.M. in international humanitarian law from Stockholm University, an LL.B. (Hons) from Makerere University, and a Post Graduate Diploma in Legal Practice from Law Development Centre, Uganda. The views expressed in this chapter are those of the author and do not necessarily reflect those of the Prosecutor, the Office of the Prosecutor, the International Criminal Tribunal for Rwanda or the United Nations.

1 I readily admit that this principle has been applied differently in different jurisdictions since prosecutors have different degrees of discretion, although all have some discretion.

2 See ICTR, *Prosecutor v. Édouard Karemera, Mathieu Ngirumpatse and Joseph Nzirorera*, Joseph Nzirorera's Motion for Request for Cooperation to Government of Switzerland, 12 September 2008, ICTR-98-44-T ('*Nzirorera* Motion') (https://www.legal-tools.org/doc/1cnq9fqq/).

> been a discriminatory motive in the decision not to prosecute the RPF.[3]

The accused's motion, denied on 21 November 2008,[4] erroneously cited the ICTY Appeals Chamber in *Prosecutor v. Delalić et al.* in support of the submission.[5] On the exercise of prosecutorial discretion, the *Delalić et al.* Appeals Chamber had opined:

> The discretion of the Prosecutor at all times is circumscribed in a more general way by the nature of her position as an official vested with specific duties imposed by the Statute of the Tribunal. The Prosecutor is committed to discharge those duties with full respect for the law. In this regard, the Secretary-General's Report stressed that the Tribunal, which encompasses all of its organs, including the Office of the Prosecutor, must abide by recognized principles of human rights.[6]

The accused at the ICTR appear to have equated the Prosecutor's exercise of prosecutorial discretion with selective prosecution, and generally argued as if selective prosecution is the same as or similar to the discredited defence of *tu quoque*. The Prosecutor's exercise of prosecutorial discretion, in the decision not to prosecute a person who committed crimes similar or identical to the crimes with which the accused is charged, is not a defence. Nor is the Prosecutor's decision not to prosecute a third person for a similar crime with which the accused is being charged a reason for the Prosecutor to discontinue the prosecution of the accused.

I need not labour the point that the exercise of prosecutorial discretion is legal, reasonable and recognized in all legal systems. On the other hand, selective prosecution is a discriminatory practice, improper and is not the norm in any judicial system known to me.

In this chapter, I will present the prosecution's understanding of the Prosecutor's exercise of prosecutorial discretion and submit that the Prosecutor, under the ICTR Statute, had the legal authority to exercise such discretion in the execution of his mandate as authorized by the United Nations Security Council. The exercise of this discretion was not arbitrary but grounded on sound legal

---

3 *Ibid.*, para. 13.

4 ICTR, *Prosecutor v. Édouard Karemera, Mathieu Ngirumpatse and Joseph Nzirorera*, Decision on Joseph Nzirorera's Motion for Binding Order to the Unites States of America and Motion for Request for Cooperation to Government of Switzerland, 21 November 2008, ICTR-98-44-T (https://www.legal-tools.org/doc/9cdd17/).

5 *Nzirorera* Motion, see *supra* note 2, para. 14, citing ICTY, *Prosecutor v. Delalić et al.*, Appeals Chamber, Judgement, 20 February 2001, IT-96-21-A ('*Delalić* Appeals Judgment') (https://www.legal-tools.org/doc/051554/).

6 *Ibid.*, *Delalić* Appeals Judgment, para. 604.

principles which encompass, *inter alia*, the principles of fair trial.[7] I will as well discuss the criteria that the ICTR Prosecutor used in the exercise of his prosecutorial discretion when deciding whether or not to prosecute, or – once prosecution was commenced – whether to discontinue criminal proceedings against any accused.

A brief background to the ICTR is necessary, if only to put the issues in context. The ICTR was established by United Nations Security Council Resolution 955 (1994).[8] The objective of the ICTR was the prosecution of persons responsible for serious violations of international humanitarian law ('IHL') committed in Rwanda and neighbouring States in 1994. The ICTR had three organs: the Chamber, the Registry and the Prosecutor. The Prosecutor was the head of the Office of the Prosecutor and his mandate was to conduct investigations and to prosecute persons responsible for serious violations of IHL in Rwanda and Rwandan citizens who committed such serious violations in neighbouring States between 1 January 1994 and 31 December 1994.[9] The Prosecutor was an independent and separate organ of the Tribunal and did not seek or receive instructions from any government or other source.[10]

In the exercise of his prosecutorial discretion, the Prosecutor had the responsibility to select cases that were to be investigated with a view to conducting prosecution in Arusha at the ICTR or to seek an order from a trial chamber and transfer the cases to national jurisdictions for prosecution as soon as practicable. The Prosecutor also had the power to transmit cases to Rwanda, without an order from a trial chamber, when investigations had not yet been completed or when investigations were completed but indictments had not been drafted and submitted by the Prosecutor to a trial chamber for confirmation.

Justice Hassan Bubacar Jallow, the ICTR Prosecutor from 2003 to 2016, developed criteria for case selection for prosecution, which were adopted and used by the ICTY-OTP.[11] The policy adopted by the ICTR Prosecutor outlined the process that the OTP used in selecting cases for trial in Arusha and cases

---

7 On fair trial, see United Nations Covenant on Civil and Political Rights, 23 March 1976, Article 14 (https://www.legal-tools.org/doc/2838f3/) and the commentary on Article 14 in Manfred Nowak, *U.N. Covenant on Civil and Political Rights: CCPR Commentary*, Second Edition, N.P. Engel Publisher, 2005, pp. 302–357.

8 Resolution 955 (1994), UN Doc. S/RES/955 (1994), 8 November 1994 (https://www.legal-tools.org/doc/f5ef47/).

9 ICTR, Statute of the International Criminal Tribunal for Rwanda, 8 November 1994, Article 1 ('ICTR Statute') (https://www.legal-tools.org/doc/8732d6/).

10 *Ibid.*, Article 15(2).

11 Hassan Bubacar Jallow, "Prosecutorial Discretion and International Criminal Justice", in *Journal of International Criminal Justice*, 2005, vol. 3, no. 1, pp. 145–161.

earmarked for transfer to national jurisdictions. It is significant that, while there are common criteria that may apply to every situation as well as in other jurisdictions for case selection, the context of the crime is a significant factor when deciding which of the many perpetrators are to be investigated with a view to prosecution. The case of Rwanda therefore provided a unique challenge. The case selection and prioritization criteria which were specific to the Rwandan situation may not necessarily apply to, or be easily replicated in, other situations.

There are many theories about the causes of the 1994 Rwandan crisis. However, the event that triggered the crisis on which many experts, scholars and legal practitioners agree is the shooting down of the plane carrying the President of Rwanda and his Burundi counterpart, by yet unknown persons, as it approached Kigali International Airport in the evening of 6 April 1994. As news began to spread that President Habyarimana was killed, allegedly by members of the minority Tutsi ethnic group, roadblocks were immediately erected throughout Kigali. At these roadblocks, the Tutsis were identified by the mandatory identity cards which every Rwandan had to carry at all times. The identity card classified Rwandans into the three ethnic groups: namely Hutu, Tutsi and Twa. The targeted ethnic group for elimination was the Tutsi.

From 6 April 1994 and over the subsequent three months, more than eight hundred thousand Tutsis and Hutus considered moderate and opposed to the Interim Rwandan Government were killed by the Hutu majority group. There were, however, some Hutus who sheltered and protected Tutsis at great risks for themselves and their families. Not every Hutu therefore, participated in the madness that saw women, children, the old and the disabled indiscriminately killed through government-inspired violence.

Simultaneously with the ongoing mass violence against the Tutsi ethnic group, there was a violent non-international armed conflict between the Tutsi-dominated rebel group, the Rwandan Patriotic Front ('RPF'), and its military wing, the Rwandan Patriotic Army ('RPA'), against the Rwandan Armed Forces ('FAR') under the control and direction of its political and military leaders, comprising the Hutu extremists who formed the Interim Government and senior military leadership after the death of President Habyarimana and the murder of the moderate Hutu Prime Minister Agathe Uwilingiyimana.

During the fateful three-month period in 1994 – from 7 April until mid-July – three distinct categories of crimes were committed in Rwanda. The crimes were genocide, crimes against humanity and war crimes. Of all the three crimes, genocide was the most profound and extensive. The deaths of an estimated eight hundred thousand people or more were a direct result of the genocide. As regards war crimes, it is not known how many people were killed in conjunction with the non-international armed conflict in Rwanda. However, the number of deaths that would result from war crimes is far lower, when compared to the genocide killings.

In the exercise of his prosecutorial discretion, the ICTR Prosecutor had to determine which perpetrators of the three categories of crimes he had to focus on. And, after making that determination, the Prosecutor had to determine the criteria to be used to identify each perpetrator. To place the Prosecutor's challenge in context, it is necessary to recall that in 1994, the population of Rwanda was about eight million. With at least 800,000 persons killed, that is, about 10 per cent of the population, by machetes, beatings and at roadblocks (what may be referred to as 'group killings'), it is reasonable to estimate that between three and five people, working in groups and providing support to each other, were involved in the killing of one person.[12] That translates into between 30 and 50 per cent of the population that was involved in the killing of Tutsis, or those who stood by, watched the killings and did nothing to protect the victims. Some of these persons who stood by and did nothing may, under criminal law principles, be classified as accomplices and therefore bear individual criminal responsibility for the substantive crimes committed by direct perpetrators, as persons who aided and abetted the crimes. The Prosecutor was faced with, potentially a criminal population in which there was good cause for him to institute criminal investigations against several thousand suspects with reasonable prospects for prosecution and conviction.

The ICTR Statute required the Prosecutor to prosecute those responsible for serious violations of IHL. The Prosecutor was therefore not expected, and the ICTR did not demand of the Prosecutor, to prosecute every person who violated international humanitarian law in Rwanda in 1994 or every Rwandan citizen who violated the law in neighbouring States. It was therefore not surprising that many low-level perpetrators at roadblocks or public places, including churches, schools and hospitals where many Tutsis were killed, were neither investigated nor prosecuted by the ICTR. These were the perpetrators who the Government of Rwanda later prosecuted through the ordinary courts and the *Gacaca* process.

[12] It is also correct that in some instances, particularly in churches and schools, places where many Tutsis sought shelter and safety, members of the FAR threw grenades in the midst of civilians, killings many of them. In other instances, members of the FAR shot at civilians indiscriminately. However, the preferred method of killing the Tutsi ethnic group was by use of machetes, and primarily by members of the Interahamwe.

The second limitation imposed on the Prosecutor were Security Council Resolutions 1503 (2003) and 1534 (2004).[13] These resolutions required the Prosecutor to complete all trial activities by 2008 and all appeals by 2010. A new Rule 11*bis* of the ICTR Rules of Procedure and Evidence (the "Rules") was adopted by the Judges of the ICTR.[14] Rule 11*bis* of the Rules must therefore be read together with Resolutions 1503 (2003) and 1534 (2004).

The new Rule 11*bis* allowed the Prosecutor to identify accused persons who were in custody or at large, and seek orders from a trial chamber to transfer them to national jurisdictions for prosecutions.[15] Rule 11*bis* was meant to address some of the constraints imposed by the ICTR Completion Strategy as stipulated in Resolutions 1503 (2003) and 1534 (2004). In exercising his authority to decide which cases were to be transferred to a national jurisdiction and which cases were to be retained for prosecution at the ICTR, the Prosecutor developed criteria to inform his decision.

---

[13] Resolution 1503 (2003), UN Doc. S/RES/1503 (2003), 28 August 2003 (https://www.legal-tools.org/doc/b3d7d9/); Resolution 1534 (2004), UN Doc. S/RES/1534 (2004), 26 March 2004 (https://www.legal-tools.org/doc/ffe092/).

[14] ICTR, Rules of Procedure and Evidence, 29 June 1995, Rule 11 *bis*(A) ('ICTR Rules of Procedure and Evidence') (https://www.legal-tools.org/doc/c6a7c6/) reads as follows:

> If an indictment has been confirmed, whether or not the accused is in the custody of the Tribunal, the President may designate a Trial Chamber which shall determine whether the case should be referred to the authorities of a State:
>
> (i) in whose territory the crime was committed; or
> (ii) in which the accused was arrested; or
> (iii) having jurisdiction and being willing and adequately prepared to accept such a case,
>
> so that those authorities should forthwith refer the case to the appropriate court for trial within that State.

[15] At the time of the Second Edition, the Prosecutor successfully sought the transfer of two accused to a national jurisdiction. They were transferred to France: Laurent Bucyibaruta (Case No. ICTR-05-85) and Father Wenceslas Munyeshyaka (Case No. ICTR-05-87). The Prosecutor had also filed five motions seeking the transfer of five accused to Rwanda. Four of these requests for transfer were subsequently rejected by the trial chambers: Yussuf Munyakazi, Case No. ICTR-97-36-A (Appeals Judgment, 28 September 2011 (https://www.legal-tools.org/doc/48cbd6/)); Idelphonse Hategekimana, Case No. ICTR-00-55 (Appeals Judgment, 8 May 2012 (https://www.legal-tools.org/doc/885b2c/)); Gaspard Kanyarukiga, Case No. ICTR-02-78 (Appeals Judgment, 8 May 2012 (https://www.legal-tools.org/doc/e6e1c9/)); and Jean Baptiste Gatete, Case No. ICTR-00-61 (Appeals Judgment, 9 October 2012 (https://www.legal-tools.org/doc/1d0b08/)). After the publication of the Second Edition, the Fulgence Kayishema case, No. ICTR-01-67, was transferred to the Rwandan authorities, see Decision on Prosecutor's Request for Referral to the Republic of Rwanda, 22 February 2012 (https://www.legal-tools.org/doc/c0aeb9/).

9.2. Case Selection Criteria: General Principles

There are general criminal law principles that inform prosecutors in every jurisdiction in the selection of cases for prosecution before national courts and tribunals. Some of these case selection criteria may be relevant before international criminal tribunals and courts, depending on the nature and scope of the crimes that are being investigated.

In making decisions on whether or not to prosecute a person in a national court, the prosecutor must take into account the interests of the victims, the accused[16] and the community at large. The initial consideration in the exercise of this discretion is whether the evidence is sufficient to justify prosecution. A proper evaluation of the available evidence, including an objective evaluation of the credibility and reliability of witnesses, is an important consideration. A prosecution should not be instituted unless the evidence, as collected by the investigators and evaluated by prosecuting counsel, is admissible, substantial, reliable and is sufficient to prove that there is a *prima facie* case to draft an indictment.

However, the fact that the collected and evaluated evidence proves that there is a *prima facie* case for the purpose of drafting an indictment is not sufficient to proceed to trial. Once a *prima facie* case is established, the prosecutor must consider the prospect of a conviction. The trial should not proceed if the prosecutor has formed an opinion that there is no reasonable prospect of a conviction. At this stage, the prosecutor may discontinue the proceedings by withdrawing the indictment and conduct further investigations, or amend the indictment and retain the counts which have reasonable prospects for sustaining a conviction.[17]

In deciding whether there is a reasonable prospect for conviction, the prosecutor shall assess and evaluate how strong the case is likely to be presented in court. There are a number of issues that the prosecutor must consider. First, the prosecutor must consider the availability of witnesses and the importance of each witness to the prosecutor's theory of the case. However good a witness is, if the witness is unable or unwilling to testify for the prosecution, the absence

[16] The term 'accused' in this chapter is used to include suspects, arrested accused in third countries awaiting transfer to the seat of the Tribunal, those indicted but at large, and accused persons in the custody of the Tribunal at the United Nations Detention Facility.

[17] The ICTR Prosecutor had, at the time of the Second Edition, withdrawn two indictments. In *Prosecutor v. Bernard Ntuyahaga*, Case No. ICTR-98-40, the Prosecutor withdrew the indictment but the accused was subsequently prosecuted in Belgium. The accused was a major in the FAR and was responsible for the death of Belgian soldiers, a crime he was prosecuted for by Belgium and convicted. He served his sentence in Belgium. In *Prosecutor v. Leonidas Rusatira* (Case No. ICTR-02-80) the Prosecutor withdrew the indictment for lack of evidence. The accused was a colonel in the FAR.

of that witness will weaken the prosecution's case. If two or more prosecution witnesses are either unwilling or unable to testify, the prosecutor will have to re-evaluate his strategy and the entire theory of the prosecution's case. The prosecutor may have to consider the nature of the witness-protection regime that is available to him, and whether he is able to persuade the key witnesses who are unwilling or unable to testify for security, personal or other reasons to be placed in a witness-protection programme. The outcome of the prosecutor's negotiations with the witnesses who fall under this category impacts on the prosecutor's eventual decision on whether to proceed with a trial or to discontinue the case.

Second, the prosecutor must consider the competence and credibility of each witness he intends to call and the likely impression of each of the witnesses before the court. A witness who is competent may not necessarily be credible. A competent witness who happens to be an accomplice, a serial killer or a drug addict may suffer some limitations even if he was an eyewitness and present at the scene of crimes. If the prosecutor finds himself in a situation where he has to use this particular witness, the prosecutor must consider whether there are other witnesses who can corroborate the testimony of this witness. If there are none, even if the witness is telling the truth, the prosecutor may have to consider dropping the witness, the counts in the indictment the witness was intended to support, or to drop both the witness and the count.

A competent witness may also be a co-perpetrator and, like 'insider witnesses', he may confess to crimes that he jointly planned, instigated, ordered, committed or otherwise aided and abetted in the planning, preparation or execution with the accused persons. The prosecutor shall evaluate the admissibility of the confession, its reliability and probative value, and whether the court can put any weight on it. A witness who is a co-perpetrator or an accomplice, as a general rule, needs to be prosecuted. Such a prosecution may function to enhance the credibility and reliability of the witness before the court.

In evaluating the evidence, the prosecutor shall take into account how the evidence was obtained and whether there are any possibilities that the court may exclude it for any reasons. If so, the prosecutor must consider if the exclusion of such evidence can substantially affect the decision of whether or not to institute or proceed with the prosecution. If, for example, the prosecution's case depends on the admissions or confessions of the accused, the prosecutor must still consider whether there are any grounds to believe that the accused is not withholding other relevant information, or embellishing the contributions of others while downplaying his own role in the commission of the crimes. The prosecutor therefore has to consider whether the accused, or a witness who is an accomplice, has motive for telling less than the whole truth. The fact that a witness has told lies in some parts of his testimony is not evidence that his entire testimony must be rejected on account of lies. The court may reject part of the testimony that has been proved to be lies while accepting other parts of the testimony that remained untainted or corroborated by other evidence. The prosecutor must, therefore, evaluate very carefully witness statements that are, *prima facie*, unreliable or lies.

In assessing the competence and credibility of a witness, the prosecutor must consider matters which the defence might put to the witness with the sole objective of attacking his credibility. The prosecutor must have a general idea of how the witness would respond to attacks on his credibility by the defence, evaluate what impression the witness is likely to make, and, further, how the witness can withstand cross-examination. In this context, the prosecutor must consider whether the witness suffers from any disability which is likely to affect his testimony and credibility. If the witness states that he was an eyewitness, it is necessary for the prosecutor to determine the respective distance between the witness and the accused; the time of day or night, visibility, and other relevant factors at the time the crime was committed. It is necessary for the prosecutor to consider, for example, whether the witness has good eyesight, that is, whether he wears glasses, or if he is colour blind. Thus, as far as is practically possible, the prosecutor should know whether the witness suffers from any physical or mental condition which is likely to affect his credibility.

The prosecutor must also consider whether there are conflicts of interests between the witness and the accused, discrepancies between statements of the same witness, if he has made more than one statement to investigators, or whether there are contradictions between eyewitnesses or different witnesses testifying about the same crimes an accused is alleged to have committed in a particular place, date and time. Clarifying areas of conflict or contradictions early in the investigations allows the prosecutor to know whether the accused may, for example, raise defence of alibi by claiming that he was elsewhere other than the place where the crimes were committed.

Having evaluated the competence and credibility of the witness, including the admissibility of his evidence, the prosecutor shall also consider any lines of defence which are open to, or have been indicated by, the accused, and any other factors which, in the view of the prosecutor, could affect the likelihood of a conviction. Assessing possible defences that the accused may raise is a difficult evaluation to make. However, a dispassionate assessment of the facts of the prosecution's indictment and supporting materials, an objective evaluation of the credibility of the witnesses, admissibility of their testimonies, and considering the lines of defence of the accused, is the recommended process to avoid the risk of prosecuting an 'innocent' person.

9.3. Case Selection Criteria: ICTR-Specific

The ICTR was an *ad hoc* tribunal with a limited lifespan. It was not expected to prosecute, and did not prosecute, every person who committed crimes in Rwanda that fell within its temporal jurisdiction. Yet, as pointed out in the introduction, more than eight hundred thousand persons were killed during the Rwandan crisis in 1994. It is estimated that persons responsible for serious violations of IHL may be as high as one million, if persons who stood by and watched others being killed are excluded from the estimate. The ICTR Prosecutor, or any prosecutor for that matter, would not be in a position to prosecute all perpetrators. The extensive nature of the crimes and the limitations of an *ad hoc* tribunal imposed on the Prosecutor a strategy of selecting only the most serious cases and adopting a policy of transferring the remaining cases for prosecution to national jurisdictions.

In 2004, the ICTR Prosecutor reviewed its case-load in the context of the Completion Strategy, as stipulated in Security Council Resolution 1503 (2003),[18] and developed criteria for selecting cases for prosecution at the ICTR and cases that were identified for transfer to national jurisdictions for immediate prosecution.[19] The policy adopted by the ICTR Prosecutor was to focus on prosecuting persons responsible for the most 'serious' violations of international law. However, while the ICTR Statute made references to "serious" violations of IHL,[20] it was silent on how the 'seriousness' of the crimes should be defined. It was therefore left to the Prosecutor to exercise his discretion in the determination of what constituted 'serious'. Many scholars, legal practitioners, and politicians will probably agree that the crime of genocide is 'serious', and has even been described as the 'crime of all crimes', and no one, I submit, can fault the ICTR Prosecutor for focusing principally on the prosecution of persons who committed genocide in Rwanda in 1994.

In determining what is 'serious', the Prosecutor considered a number of factors, but focusing on the nature of the crime and the role played by each perpetrator in the commission of the crime, the focus was on the prosecution of the crime of genocide. The Prosecutor consciously decided to include all the various groups represented in the atrocities, to ensure that different types of involvement were covered. Many of the individuals selected were as well the most guilty, as judged by their level of participation and their standing in society.

The Prosecutor's starting point was that the genocide in Rwanda was a result of a well-planned conspiracy by members of the government in power, the

[18] See *supra* note 13.

[19] Jallow, 2005, pp. 145–161, see *supra* note 11.

[20] ICTR Statute, Article 1, see *supra* note 9.

ruling party, the National Revolutionary Movement for Development ('MRND') and the senior military leadership. Individual members of the government participated in the commission of the crimes. Having made this determination, the primary targets for prosecution were, therefore, the members of the Interim Government including leaders of political parties,[21] ministers,[22] prefects,[23]

---

[21] Senior political leaders prosecuted by the ICTR include Joseph Nzirorera, Case No. ICTR-98-48 (Secretary General of MRND); Edouard Karemera, Case No. ICTR-97-24 (President of MRND). Nzirorera and Karemera were tried together with Matthieu Ngirumpatse, as joinder Case No. ICTR-98-44 (*Prosecutor v. Karemera, Ngirumpatse and Nzirorera*, Appeals Judgment, 29 September 2014 (https://www.legal-tools.org/doc/372a64/)), though Mr. Nzirorera passed away on 1 July 2010 and proceedings against him terminated in Decision Relating to Registrar's Submission Notifying the Demise of Accused Joseph Nzirorera, 12 August 2010 (https://www.legal-tools.org/doc/9cc2a7/).

[22] The Prime Minister and ministers of the Interim Government selected for prosecution include: Jean Kambanda, Case No. ICTR-97-23 (Prime Minister, he pleaded guilty; Trial Judgment, 4 September 1998 (https://www.legal-tools.org/doc/49a299/)); Jean de Dieu Kamuhanda, Case No. ICTR-99-54 (convicted; Appeals Judgment, 19 September 2005 (https://www.legal-tools.org/doc/bd4762/)); Emmanuel Ndindabahizi, Case No. ICTR-01-71 (convicted; Appeals Judgment, 16 January 2007 (https://www.legal-tools.org/doc/0f3219/)); Eliezer Niyitegeka, Case No. ICTR-96-14 (convicted; Appeals Judgment, 9 July 2004 (https://www.legal-tools.org/doc/35cd4f/)); Andre Rwamakuba, Case No. ICTR-98-44C (acquitted; Trial Judgment, 20 September 2006 (https://www.legal-tools.org/doc/b6ffa6/)); Jérôme-Clément Bicamumpaka, Case No. ICTR-99-49 (acquitted; Trial Judgment, 30 September 2011 (https://www.legal-tools.org/doc/7077fa/)); Pauline Nyiramasuhuko, Case No. ICTR-97-21 (convicted; *Prosecutor v. Nyiramasuhuko et al.*, Appeals Judgment, 14 December 2015, IT-98-42-A (volume 1: https://www.legal-tools.org/doc/b3584e/; volume 2: https://www.legal-tools.org/doc/93cee1/)); André Ntagerura, Case No. ICTR-99-46-A (acquitted; *Prosecutor v. Ntagerura, Bagambiki and Imanishimwe*, Appeals Judgment, 7 July 2006 (https://www.legal-tools.org/doc/5f76c1/)); Augustin Bizimana, Case No. ICTR-98-44 (Defence Minister, proceedings against him were terminated by the International Residual Mechanism for Criminal Tribunals on 4 November 2020 (https://www.legal-tools.org/doc/wcf819sb/)); Callixte Nzabonimana, Case No. ICTR-98-44 (convicted; Appeals Judgment, 29 September 2014 (https://www.legal-tools.org/doc/a1abb4/)); and Callixte Kalimanzira, Case No. ICTR-05-88 (convicted; Appeals Judgment, 20 October 2010 (https://www.legal-tools.org/doc/fad693/)).

[23] Prefects selected for prosecution include: Clement Kayishema, Case No. ICTR-95-01 (convicted; *Prosecutor v. Kayishema and Ruzindana*, Appeals Judgment, 1 June 2001 (https://www.legal-tools.org/doc/9ea5f4/)); Emmanuel Bagambiki, Case No. ICTR-97-36 (acquitted; *Prosecutor v. Ntagerura, Bagambiki and Imanishimwe*, Appeals Judgment, 7 July 2006, ICTR-99-46-A (https://www.legal-tools.org/doc/5f76c1/)); Lieutenant Colonel Tharcisse Renzaho, Case No. ICTR-97-31 (convicted; Appeals Judgment, 1 April 2011 (https://www.legal-tools.org/doc/0abb32/)); and Laurent Semanza, Case No. ICTR-97-20 (convicted; Appeals Judgment, 20 May 2005 (https://www.legal-tools.org/doc/a686fd/)).

bourgmestres[24] and other administrative personnel.[25] In this category, the Prosecutor included leaders of the various political parties who served in or supported the Interim Government. The leadership of the MRND youth wing and its members, commonly known as the 'Interahamwe', was also a target for prosecution.[26]

Members of the FAR, working jointly with the Interim Government and other political leaders in the commission of genocide and other crimes, were as well selected for prosecution. While the FAR was engaged in a non-international armed conflict with the RPF-RPA, linked to that armed conflict, the FAR and its allies, the Civil Defence forces and the Interahamwe, were killing Tutsi civilians deemed to be supporters of the RPF-RPA. The Prosecutor therefore selected senior members of the FAR, Civil Defence forces and the leaders of the Interahamwe for prosecution.[27]

The media in Rwanda played a significant and destructive role in 1994, particularly in promoting ethnic hatred and inciting people to acts of violence, murder and destruction of property. The radio (Radio Télévision Libre des Mille

---

[24] The *bourgemestres* selected for prosecution include: Jean Paul Akayesu, Case No. ICTR-96-4-T (convicted; Appeals Judgment, 1 June 2001 (https://www.legal-tools.org/doc/c62d06/)); Ignace Bagilishema, Case No. ICTR-95-1A (acquitted; Appeals Judgment, 3 July 2002 (https://www.legal-tools.org/doc/7cc2d0/)); and Sylvestre Gacumbitsi, Case No. ICTR-01-64 (convicted; Appeals Judgment, 7 July 2006 (https://www.legal-tools.org/doc/aa51a3/)).

[25] Other junior officials include 'sous-prefects' and 'conseillers'. Some of them are: Mikael Muhimana, Case No. ICTR-95-1B (convicted; Appeals Judgment, 21 May 2007 (https://www.legal-tools.org/doc/8b044b/)); Dominique Ntawukuriryayo, Case No. ICTR-05-82 (convicted; Appeals Judgment, 14 December 2011 (https://www.legal-tools.org/doc/42d81d/)); Vincent Rutaganira, Case No. ICTR 95-1C (pleaded guilty; Trial Judgment, 14 March 2005 (https://www.legal-tools.org/doc/cd2a8f/)).

[26] The Interahamwe leaders selected for prosecution include: Georges Rutaganda, Case No. ICTR-96-3 (convicted; Appeals Judgment, 26 May 2003 (https://www.legal-tools.org/doc/40bf4a/)); Obed Ruzindana, Case No. ICTR-95-1 (convicted; *Prosecutor v. Kayishema and Ruzindana*, see *supra* note 23); and Juvenal Kajelijeli, Case No. ICTR-98-44A (convicted; Appeals Judgment, 23 May 2005 (https://www.legal-tools.org/doc/2b7d1c/)).

[27] Military officers including leaders of the Interahamwe who were selected and prosecuted include: Colonel Théoneste Bagosora, Lieutenant Colonel Anatole Nsengiyumva, General Gratien Kabiligi and Major Aloys Ntabakuze, Case No. ICTR-98-41 (*Prosecutor v. Bagosora, Kabiligi, Nsengiyumva and Ntabakuze*, Trial Judgment, 18 December 2008 (https://www.legal-tools.org/doc/6d9b0a/); *Prosecutor v. Bagosora and Nsengiyumva*, Appeals Judgment, 14 December 2011 (https://www.legal-tools.org/doc/52d501/)); General Augustin Bizimungu, General Augustin Ndindiliyimana, Lieutenant Colonel François-Xavier Nzuwonemeye and Major Innocent Sagahutu, Case No. ICTR-00-56 (Trial Judgment, 17 May 2011 (https://www.legal-tools.org/doc/c71b24/); *Prosecutor v. Ndindiliyimana, Nzuwonemeye and Sagahutu*, Appeals Judgment, 11 February 2014 (https://www.legal-tools.org/doc/4c5065/); *Prosecutor v. Bizimungu*, Appeals Judgment, 30 June 2014, ICTR-00-56-B-A (https://www.legal-tools.org/doc/2a4ad3/)); and George Rutaganda (Interahamwe leader, see *supra* note 26).

Collines, 'RTLM') and the press (the *Kangura* newspaper) incited the public and announced on the radio places where Tutsis were hiding, or places where there were large concentrations of Tutsis for the FAR, Civil Defence forces and the Interahamwe to speedily travel there and kill Tutsis. The radio and the press provided running commentary on the various places where there were road-blocks, where Tutsis were being identified by FAR, Civil Defence forces and the Interahamwe and killed. The Prosecutor, therefore, selected the owners, directors and senior employees of the RTLM radio and *Kangura* newspaper for prosecution.[28]

The church, through the clergy, actively participated in serious violations of IHL in Rwanda. Many Tutsi civilians were killed in churches and schools under the control and management of the church. The Prosecutor therefore decided, based on their individual participation, to select members of the clergy for prosecution.[29]

The Prosecutor also considered some specific categories of crimes for prosecution, such as rape and other sexual violence. Early in the conduct of investigation by the OTP, evidence of widespread and systematic rape and other sexual violence began to emerge. Where evidence of rape and other sexual violence was discovered, the OTP investigators diligently pursued all leads.[30] Rape and other sexual violence were used as means in the commission of genocide, crimes against humanity and war crimes. In pursuit of this policy by the Prosecutor, any person, regardless of his or her status, found to have instigated or aided and abetted in the commission of the crime of rape or other sexual violence, was selected for prosecution.[31]

---

[28] Radio and newspaper owners including journalists selected and prosecuted include: Ferdinand Nahimana, Jean Bosco Barayagwiza and Hassan Ngeze, Case No. ICTR-99-52 (convicted; Appeals Judgment, 28 November 2007 (https://www.legal-tools.org/doc/4ad5eb/)); and Georges Ruggiu, Case No. ICTR-97-I (pleaded guilty; Trial Judgment, 1 June 2000 (https://www.legal-tools.org/doc/486d43/).

[29] The church leaders who were selected and prosecuted include: Bishop Samuel Musabyimana, Case No. ICTR-01-62 (died before trial, proceedings were terminated on 20 February 2003 (https://www.legal-tools.org/doc/045fcd/)); Pastor Elizaphan Ntakirutimana, Case No. ICTR-96-10 (died after release upon completion of sentence; *Prosecutor v. Elizaphan Ntakirutimana and Gérard Ntakirutimana*, Appeals Judgment, 13 December 2004 (https://www.legal-tools.org/doc/af07be/)); Father Emmanuel Rukundo, Case No. ICTR-01-70 (convicted; Appeals Judgment, 20 October 2010 (https://www.legal-tools.org/doc/d5b969/)); Father Athanase Seromba, Case No. ICTR-01-66 (convicted; Appeals Judgment, 12 March 2008 (https://www.legal-tools.org/doc/b4df9d/)).

[30] Extensive acts of rape and sexual violence committed by Muhimana are one such example. See *Prosecutor v. Mikaeli Muhimana*, *supra* note 25.

[31] The only female charged with rape and sexual violence is the former Minister for Women and Gender Affairs in the Interim Government, Ms. Pauline Nyiramsuhuko, see *supra* note 22.

To avoid creating any perception of possible bias, favouritism or discrimination which may have suggested that only individuals from certain locations in Rwanda committed serious violations of IHL, the Prosecutor decided to adopt the criteria for geographic spread with regards to targets and incidents.[32] Therefore, recognizing that the crimes committed in Rwanda were widespread and left no part of the country unaffected, the Prosecutor took a conscious decision to identify perpetrators across the geographic spread of Rwanda, ensuring that the perpetrators selected for prosecution represented all regions. The Prosecutor further decided to select crime scenes that covered the entire territory of the nation to ensure that crimes committed throughout Rwanda were investigated and prosecuted.

The pitfall of this policy, in the context of limited prosecution, meant that some targets in one location in Rwanda may have had to be excluded from the list of persons selected for prosecution, to accommodate other perpetrators from other administrative areas of Rwanda in order to meet the criteria of geographical representation.

9.4. Prioritization Criteria: Prosecution of Genocide

In 1994, the Government of Rwanda requested the Security Council to establish an international tribunal for the *sole* purpose of prosecuting persons responsible for *genocide* and other serious violations of IHL committed in the territory of Rwanda, and Rwandan citizens responsible for genocide and other such violations committed in the territory of neighbouring States, between 1 January 1994 and 31 December 1994.[33] The Security Council endorsed the request in Resolution 955 (1994)[34] establishing the ICTR and annexed the ICTR Statute to the resolution.

The Government of Rwanda was aware, at the time it made the request, that massive killings had taken place in the country. The Government was also mindful that other violations of IHL had to be investigated and prosecuted. Thus, Rwanda's request should not be seen as rejecting possible prosecution of persons responsible for crimes against humanity and war crimes. Rather, it must be viewed as prioritizing the prosecution of genocide.

Independent organizations and individuals who have conducted research in Rwanda generally agree that war crimes committed in the country pale when compared to the crimes of genocide and crimes against humanity committed during the 1994 Rwandan crisis. Africa Rights, one of the first human rights

32 Jallow, 2005, see *supra* note 11.

33 See Security Council Draft Resolution, UN Doc. S/1994/115, 3 February 1994 (https://www.legal-tools.org/doc/d1bmqw/).

34 See *supra* note 8.

organizations to issue reports on the mass killings in Rwanda, documented the killing of Tutsis throughout Rwanda.[35] Africa Rights named the perpetrators and their accomplices,[36] the elimination of political opposition, dissent and the adoption of a policy of massacre of the Tutsis by the Interim Government.[37] Africa Rights further described the policy of rape and abduction of women and girls, including violence against children, adopted by the Interim Government, the FAR, Civil Defence forces and the Interahamwe.[38] The widespread and systematic killing of Tutsi civilians in churches, hospitals and other public places were as well documented by Africa Rights.[39]

Human Rights Watch, another reputable human rights organization, published a detailed and informative report in March of 1999,[40] addressing the context of the Rwandan genocide,[41] the organization of genocide at the national level by the Interim Government,[42] and the organization of genocide at the local (grassroot) level.[43] The Human Rights Watch report went beyond Rwanda and described the role of the international community, first by denying and much later, acknowledging the genocide in Rwanda.[44]

Human Rights Watch stated that the RPF-RPA committed war crimes but also stressed that the RPF repeatedly declared its commitment to establishing accountability, including for soldiers who committed abuses against civilians.[45] Human Rights Watch further stated that: "In September 1994, authorities said they had arrested soldiers who killed civilians and executed two of them".[46] According to Human Rights Watch, when its "researcher presented evidence of the Mukingi massacre to Kagame in September 1994, the vice-president expressed his appreciation for being given the details of an affair that, he said, he had known about only in general terms. He stated that Major Sam Bigabiro had been

35 Africa Rights, *Rwanda: Death, Despair and Defiance*, revised edition, Africa Rights, August 1995.

36 *Ibid.*, pp. 100–176.

37 *Ibid.*, pp. 177–747.

38 *Ibid.*, pp. 748–853.

39 *Ibid.*, pp. 862–1060.

40 Alison Des Forges, *Leave None to Tell The Story*, Human Rights Watch, New York, Washington, London, Brussels, March 1999.

41 *Ibid.*, pp. 31–178.

42 *Ibid.*, pp. 180–301.

43 *Ibid.*, pp. 303–591.

44 *Ibid.*, pp. 595–690.

45 *Ibid.*, p. 733.

46 *Ibid.*

arrested for killing civilians and might have been in command at Mukingi".[47] Both Major Bigabiro and his subordinate, Colonel Denis Gato, were found guilty and sentenced to prison, Bigabiro for life and Gato for forty-five months.[48] Human Rights Watch further reported that:

> twenty-one RPF soldiers had been charged with killing civilians in November 1994. Hundreds of others have since been arrested, but it is not known how many of this group are charged with serious human rights violations. Of the twenty-one in 1994, six were tried by June 1998 and all found guilty.[49]

Human Rights Watch therefore acknowledged that, when members of the RPF committed war crimes, and the leadership of the RPF-RPA was made aware of the alleged crimes, investigations were conducted. Where sufficient evidence existed, the perpetrators were prosecuted. In its 25 July 2008 report Human Rights Watch noted that, as of April 2008, the ICTR Prosecutor "had not committed himself to prosecuting any RPA soldiers at the ICTR although he had not foreclosed the possibility of trying RPA soldiers at the ICTR".[50]

General Romeo Dallaire, the Commander of the United Nations Assistance Mission for Rwanda, is one of the few eyewitnesses to the genocide in Rwanda to have published an account of the genocide.[51] The other is his deputy, Brigadier Henry Kwami Anyidoho.[52] General Dallaire described how the 'Shadow Force' under the control of, among others, Colonel Bagosora organized assassinations and ambushes that eventually led to genocide after the killing of President Habyarimana.[53] Linda Melvern, writing after the genocide, provided detailed accounts in two of her books on Rwanda, both leading to the conclusion of mass killings of Tutsi civilians.[54]

The priority of the ICTR was the prosecution of genocide and crimes against humanity. The Prosecutor's decision was consistent with not only the

---

47 *Ibid.*

48 *Ibid.*

49 *Ibid.*

50 *Law and Reality: Progress in Judicial Reform in Rwanda*, Human Rights Watch, 25 July 2008, p. 87.

51 Romeo Dallaire, *Shake Hands With The Devil: The Failure of Humanity in Rwanda*, Random House, Canada, 2003.

52 Henry Kwami Anyidoho, *Guns Over Kigali: The Rwandese Civil War – 1994*, Fountain Publishers, Kampala, 1997.

53 See Dallaire, 2003, pp. 135–420, see *supra* note 51.

54 Linda Melvern, *A People Betrayed: The Role of the West in Rwanda's Genocide, Zed Books*, Cape Town, 2000; Linda Melvern, *Conspiracy to Murder: The Rwanda Genocide*, Verso, London-New York, 2004.

reports published by Africa Rights, Human Rights Watch and non-Rwandan eyewitnesses to the genocide, as for example, General Dallaire and Brigadier Anyidoho, but was also supported by the case law of the ICTR. Prime Minister Kambanda pleaded guilty to genocide and provided additional evidence on the planning and execution of genocide. The ICTR took judicial notice of the crime of genocide as committed in Rwanda in 1994.[55]

After genocide, the Prosecutor also focused on the selection of perpetrators who committed crimes against humanity. The Prosecutor's decision to select and indict many perpetrators was justified, as evidence of widespread and systematic killings were proved beyond reasonable doubt before the Trial and Appeals Chambers. In addition, the ICTR took judicial notice that there were, throughout Rwanda in 1994, widespread or systematic attacks against a civilian population based on Tutsi ethnic identification.[56]

Compared to genocide and crimes against humanity, the Prosecutor selected fewer perpetrators to prosecute for war crimes. This prompted accused at the ICTR to argue, without supporting evidence, that the Prosecutor had decided not to prosecute members of the RPF. Nothing could be further from the truth. The Prosecutor, in the exercise of his prosecutorial discretion, did not adopt a policy not to prosecute either the RPF or any person that the Prosecutor had sufficient evidence to prosecute. On the contrary, the Prosecutor had a policy of investigating all crimes as stipulated in the ICTR Statute, namely, genocide, crimes against humanity and war crimes; and selected perpetrators for prosecution whenever there was sufficient evidence. The Prosecutor did not prosecute Twas, Tutsis or Hutus, but individuals who committed serious crimes. It is of no consequence that a perpetrator selected by the Prosecutor for investigation and, whenever sufficient evidence was available, prosecution, happened to be Twa, Tutsi or Hutu. Significantly, since the Prosecutor did not prosecute individuals based on their ethnic backgrounds, there is no basis for making comparisons as to how many Twas, Tutsis or Hutus have been prosecuted by the ICTR. The proper test is whether there was sufficient evidence to prosecute any person who was alleged to have committed serious violations of international humanitarian law.

As researched and reported by Human Rights Watch, when information had been provided to the Government of Rwanda that RPF soldiers committed crimes, the perpetrators were investigated, and when evidence was available,

---

55 ICTR, *Prosecutor v. Edouard Karemera, Mathieu Ngirumpatse and Joseph Nzirorera*, Appeals Chamber, Decision on Prosecutor's Interlocutory Appeal of Decision on Judicial Notice, 16 June 2006, ICTR-98-44-AR73(C) (https://www.legal-tools.org/doc/67d818/).

56 *Ibid.* The Appeals Chamber took judicial notice of the existence of widespread and systematic attack, pp. 26–32. The Appeals Chamber also took judicial notice of genocide, pp. 33–38.

the accused were prosecuted. Similarly, the ICTR transmitted a case file involving the killing of some members of the clergy by RPF soldiers. The Prosecutor kept monitoring the trial, reserving the right to re-call it, had the monitors advised him that the conduct of the trial did not guarantee minimum international standards.

At the time of the Second Edition, the Prosecutor transmitted, as well, 35 case files to the Prosecutor-General of Rwanda to conduct further investigations and take appropriate action, if supported by sufficient evidence. While Human Rights Watch welcomed the Rwandan government's initiative to prosecute the persons whose files were transmitted to it by the ICTR, it noted that this did not absolve the ICTR of fulfilling its own mandate of trying RPA soldiers accused of crimes against humanity and war crimes.[57]

It is my submission that Human Rights Watch erred when it noted that transferring case files to Rwanda for prosecution did not absolve the Prosecutor of fulfilling its own mandate in the above-mentioned terms. I respectfully submit that the Prosecutor had no mandate to try RPA soldiers just because they happened to be RPA soldiers. Similarly, the Prosecutor had no mandate to prosecute any person because of who they were, or to which ethnic group they belonged. The Prosecutor, however, had the mandate to investigate and prosecute serious violations of international humanitarian law. If RPA soldiers or any other person fell within that category, the Prosecutor investigated and, where sufficient evidence was available, prosecuted them. The responsibility of the Prosecutor was not to balance the number of persons selected for prosecution so that all sides to the Rwanda crisis in 1994 could have equal representation in the dock. The Prosecutor was guided by the seriousness of the crimes, the availability of the evidence, and the Completion Strategy as stipulated in Security Council Resolutions 1503 (2003) and 1534 (2004).[58]

Human Rights Watch also erred when it submitted that the ICTR Prosecutor "had not committed himself to prosecuting any RPA soldiers at the ICTR although he had not foreclosed the possibility of trying RPA at the ICTR". Human Rights Watch appeared to place undue weight on the venue selected for trial. The imperative of a trial is not premised on the venue. A trial can be conducted anywhere as long as the court is independent, an accused can have a free and fair trial that provides all guarantees that meet minimum international standards. The Rules of Procedure and Evidence of the ICTR provided for the ICTR to hold hearings anywhere in the world, including Rwanda if the Chamber

[57] Human Rights Watch, "Law and Reality: Progress in Judicial Reform in Rwanda", 25 July 2008, pp. 89–90.

[58] See *supra* note 13.

deemed it necessary.[59] The concern of Human Rights Watch should have focused, in my submission, on whether the Rwandan judicial system could provide to an accused a free and fair trial, and not on where an accused was tried.

By transferring cases related to war crimes to Rwanda, there is no evidence to suggest that the Prosecutor abused his prosecutorial discretion. On the contrary, consistent with Resolutions 1503 (2003) and 1534 (2004),[60] and the letter and spirit of Rule 11*bis*,[61] the Prosecutor adopted a policy that facilitated a responsible closure of the ICTR. It must be noted, however, that the Prosecutor selected and prosecuted war crimes cases before the ICTR.[62] The priority for the selection and prosecution of perpetrators, however, remained the crimes of genocide and crimes against humanity.

9.5. Conclusion

On many occasions, the accused charged at the ICTR argued that a policy of selective prosecution was adopted towards them by the Prosecutor. This is, however, not supported by any evidence and it is an argument that can be entirely

---

59 See ICTR Rules of Procedure and Evidence, Rule 4, see *supra* note 14. Sittings Away from the Seat of the Tribunal: "A Chamber or a Judge may exercise their functions away from the Seat of the Tribunal, if so authorized by the President in the interests of justice". Judge Pillay authorized, as President of the ICTR, in the interests of justice, that a hearing take place on 28 February 2003 to take the testimony of Professor Guichaoua and that such hearing take place at the seat of the ICTY in The Hague (see *Georges Rutaganda v. Prosecutor*, The President's Authorisation for the Appeals Chamber to Sit Away From the Seat of the Tribunal, 20 February 2003, ICTR-96-3-A (https://www.legal-tools.org/doc/3fe572/)). In *Prosecutor v. Ferdinand Nahimana, Hassan Ngeze and Jean Bosco Barayagwiza*, Decision on the Prosecutor's Application to add Witness X to Its List of Witnesses and for Protective Measures, 14 September 2001, ICTR-99-52-I, para. 33 (https://www.legal-tools.org/doc/d380c9/), the Chamber stated:

> On the basis of the available material the Chamber accepts Witness X is in a particularly vulnerable position and that special security measures are required in connection with his testimony. It is undisputed by the parties that the Tribunal's Rules allow for the change of venue. Reference is made to Resolution 955 (1994) para. 6, according to which the Tribunal may meet away from its seat when it considers it necessary for efficient exercise of its functions. Rule 4 provides that a Chamber or a Judge may exercise their functions away from the seat of the Tribunal, if so authorized by the President in the interests of justice. Moreover, Rule 71(D) provides that a deposition may be given by means of a video conference.

60 See *supra* note 13.

61 See *supra* note 14.

62 See, for example, *Prosecutor v. Georges Rutaganda*, see *supra* note 26; *Prosecutor v. Laurent Semanza*, see *supra* note 23; *Prosecutor v. Bagosora, Kabiligi, Nsengiyumva and Ntabakuze* ('Military I Case'), see *supra* note 27; and *Prosecutor v. Bizimungu, Ndindiliyimana, Nzuwonemeye and Sagahutu* ('Military II Case'), see *supra* note 27.

sourced to the accused and their own particular situations, and one that has neither basis in the law nor in the practice of the Tribunal, and is distinct from the exercise of prosecutorial discretion which is permitted in law.

Case selection and prioritization criteria depend on the context of the crimes committed, the nature of the crimes, and what each prosecutor considers to be a priority within the discretionary legal framework. While there are general principles which provide useful guidelines, the prosecutor's ultimate decision on whether to select a particular perpetrator for investigation and, where sufficient evidence exists, prosecution depends on a number of factors as described in the chapter.

The ICTR having been established with a limited mandate and a definite period, its Chief Prosecutors realized that they would not be able to prosecute all the indictees, unless they were first apprehended and brought into custody of the Tribunal. To that extent, it was not a surprise when, on 9 December 2015, ICTR President Vagn Joensen made the Tribunal's last report to the UN Security Council, noting that, after 21 years, there were still pending issues the ICTR had not dealt with. One of them was the arrest, detention and prosecution of indicted fugitives selected by the ICTR-OTP for prosecution, but not arrested. The tracking, arrest and prosecution of all fugitives had not been successfully carried out.

As a whole, the ICTR's referral programme provided the international community with a model for how an international court can co-operate with national authorities to rebuild justice sectors in conflicts and post-conflict environments.

The ICTR formally closed on 31 December 2015. However, the President reported that activities would end during the first half of 2016, and that remaining cases, whatever stage they were at, would be passed to a new International Residual Mechanism for the ICTR and ICTY '(IRMCT') established for that purpose. On 15 May 2024, the IRMCT Prosecutor announced that the OTP Fugitive Tracking Team had accounted for all the ICTR fugitives. His fugitive break-down was as follows: the OTP confirmed the death of six fugitives, Augustine Bizimana, Protias Mpiranya, Pheneas Munyangarama, Aloys Ndimbati, Ryandikayo and Charles Sikibwabo; two fugitives were arrested, Felicien Kabuga (in Paris, France, in May 2020) and Fulgence Kayishema (in Paarl, South Africa, in May 2023).[63]

The arrest of fugitive Felicien Kabuga, the alleged mastermind of the genocide, was an important event for the ICTR. However, in August 2023, the IRMCT Appeals Chamber concluded that Kabuga's state of health no longer

63 IRMCT-OTP, "IRMCT Prosecutor Announces All ICTR Fugitives Successfully Accounted For", Press Release, 15 May 2024.

permitted his continued prosecution, even if the prosecutors and trial judges wanted to proceed with the trial. Thus, the ICTR was never able to prosecute Felicien Kabuga.

In conclusion, the policy adopted by the ICTR Prosecutor may not be the best suited for international courts and tribunals. The ICTR has recognized that one-size does not fit all situations, and that the ICTR did not necessarily set a precedent for other courts in the selection and prosecution of cases. However, the ICTR precedent does provide some useful principles and guidelines that other prosecutors dealing with mass atrocity may find useful at both domestic and international prosecution services.

10

Prosecution Criteria at the Khmer Rouge Tribunal

Anees Ahmed and Margaux Day*

10.1. Introduction

The Khmer Rouge Tribunal ('KRT'), formally known as Extraordinary Chambers in the Courts of Cambodia ('ECCC'), was established by a law passed by the Cambodian Parliament and promulgated on 10 August 2001 ('Statute').[1] Pursuant to an Agreement ('Agreement')[2] between the United Nations and the Government of Cambodia, extensive amendments were made to the Statute to implement the terms of that Agreement.[3]

Articles 1 and 2 of the Agreement confer personal jurisdiction to the KRT over the following two categories of persons:

i. *senior leaders* of Democratic Kampuchea ('DK') ('senior leaders' category'), and

* **Anees Ahmed**, a barrister, served as the Chief of Legal Affairs at the United Nations Mission in Liberia, as Chief of Judicial and Legal Affairs of the International Criminal Tribunal for Rwanda, and as the Senior Assistant Prosecutor of the United Nations Assistance to the Khmer Rouge Trials ('UNAKRT'). He was previously a prosecuting attorney at the International Criminal Tribunal for the former Yugoslavia. He is a graduate of the London School of Economics where he was a Chevening Scholar. **Margaux Day** is the Executive Director of Accountability Counsel. She previously worked for the International Law & Policy Group. She is a graduate of the Case Western Reserve University School of Law, and held a legal internship in the Office of the Co-Prosecutors of the Khmer Rouge Tribunal. This chapter has not been substantively updated since the Second Edition. The views expressed in this chapter are those of the authors and do not necessarily reflect the views of the United Nations or the KRT.

1 Law on the Establishment of Extraordinary Chambers in the Courts of Cambodia for the Prosecution of Crimes Committed During the Period of Democratic Kampuchea, promulgated on 10 August 2001, NS/RKM/0801/12 ('Statute') (https://www.legal-tools.org/doc/40d072/).

2 Agreement between the United Nations and the Royal Government of Cambodia Concerning the Prosecution Under Cambodian Law of Crimes Committed During the Period of Democratic Kampuchea, 6 June 2003 ('Agreement') (https://www.legal-tools.org/doc/3a33d3/). The Agreement was ratified by the Royal Government of Cambodia on 19 October 2004.

3 The Statute as promulgated, with amendments, on 27 October 2004 (NSRKM/1004/006) (https://www.legal-tools.org/doc/e66d31/). Also see, Agreement Article 2(2), see *supra* note 2.

ii. *those who were most responsible* for "the crimes and serious violations of Cambodian laws related to crimes, international humanitarian law and custom and international conventions recognized by Cambodia that were committed during the period from 17 April 1975 to 6 January 1979" ('most responsible persons category').

This enumeration of categories of persons subject to the jurisdiction of the KRT is identical to and mirrored in Article 2 of the Statute under the heading "Competence". For a person to be prosecuted before the KRT, he must fall under one of the two referred categories. To make such a determination it is essential to interpret the meaning of the terms (i) "senior leaders of Democratic Kampuchea"; and (ii) those who were most responsible for the crimes".

10.2. Interpretation

The 1969 Vienna Convention on the Law of Treaties ('Vienna Convention') applies to the Agreement.[4] Thus, principles of interpretation contained in that Convention shall be applicable to the Agreement. Further, since the Agreement "shall apply as law" in Cambodia, any interpretation of its articles regarding personal jurisdiction shall also apply to the identical provisions of the Statute.[5] Any other interpretation will result in the manifestly unreasonable consequence of two laws, with identical provisions, meaning differently.

Article 31 of the Vienna Convention states that instruments should be interpreted in good faith in accordance with the ordinary meaning to be given to their provisions in their context and in the light of the instrument's object and purpose. The context of a provision includes both the full text of the instrument as well as any other agreements that were made in connection with that instrument.[6] The legislative history of a provision may also serve as a "supplementary means of interpretation".[7]

10.3. Who Would Fall Under the Senior Leaders Category?

In terms of Article 31 of the Vienna Convention, the starting point for interpreting the term "senior leaders of Democratic Kampuchea" should be its ordinary meaning. Wherever necessary, the ordinary meaning can be supplemented by the negotiating history of the term.

---

4 *Ibid.*, Article 2(2).

5 Statute, Article 47, see *supra* note 1.

6 Vienna Convention on the Law of Treaties, 23 May 1969, Article 31(2) (https://www.legal-tools.org/doc/6bfcd4/).

7 *Ibid.*, Article 32.

The word 'senior' has several dictionary meanings, but the most relevant in the context of the current analysis is a "person with higher standing or rank".[8] A 'leader' is defined as "a person who leads" or "a person who has commanding authority or influence".[9] Consequently, the expression "leaders of Democratic Kampuchea" would refer to those individuals who had authority or influence in DK, while the addition of the word 'senior' would suggest a hierarchy amongst those who had authority or influence. Within that hierarchy, only those individuals who had "higher rank or standing" than other leaders would, thus, be considered 'senior leaders'. The expression "senior leaders of Democratic Kampuchea", however, does not require that the senior leaders would be only those who had the *highest*, as against *higher* rank.

The legislative history of the two instruments (the Statute and the Agreement) indicates that the term 'senior leaders' was meant to "target" a "small number" of people from the leadership of DK.[10] The selection of such individuals, however, was left to the Co-Prosecutors.[11] Indeed, when the idea for the establishment of a tribunal to try "leaders of Democratic Kampuchea"[12] was first mooted by the Group of Experts, the Group's Report was categorical that it did not believe that the term 'leaders' should be equated with all persons at the senior levels of the government of DK or even of the Communist Party of Kampuchea ('CPK'). It recommended that the proposed tribunal must "focus upon senior leaders with responsibility over the abuses as well as those at the lower level who were directly implicated in the most serious atrocities". This, the Group felt,

8 See Merriam-Webster Online Dictionary. The most common alternate meaning is "a person older than another". However, it seems unlikely that the jurisdiction of the ECCC was meant to be tied to the age of the accused, so this meaning will be discounted.

9 *Ibid.* An alternate definition of leader is "a person who directs a military force or unit". However, this meaning is too limited, as it is unlikely that the term leader was meant to limit the ECCC to jurisdiction over military personnel.

10 See comments of Mr. Sok An, the Deputy Prime Minister and the Minister of the Cabinet Council during the Debates on the Statute in the First Session of the Third Term of the Cambodian National Assembly, 4–5 October 2004. Translation by the Documentation Centre of Cambodia ('DC-Cam'), Phnom Penh. In the debate, it was indicated that the number of people expected to be prosecuted under the category of senior leaders would be "no more than ten people" ('National Assembly Debates 2004').

11 *Ibid.* Mr. Sok An also stated that, in deference to the prerogative of the Co-Prosecutors, it was not appropriate for the National Assembly to indicate as to who, within the DK hierarchy, would qualify for prosecution by the ECCC.

12 As against the expression "senior leaders of Democratic Kampuchea" that was finally incorporated in the two instruments.

would fully take into account the twin goals of individual accountability and national reconciliation.[13]

The term 'senior leaders' has also been interpreted by the International Criminal Tribunal for the former Yugoslavia ('ICTY') in the context of its mandate that similarly limits the scope of prosecution to a limited category of higher-level perpetrators. While interpreting the term "most senior leaders", the ICTY held that the term covered individuals who, "by virtue of their position and function in the relevant hierarchy, both *de jure* and *de facto*, [were] alleged to have exercised such a degree of authority that it [was] appropriate to describe them as among the 'most senior' rather than 'intermediate'".[14] The Tribunal's Appeals Chamber, in another decision, approved this criterion and clarified that this assessment of level of responsibility could not be restricted only to military responsibility but that it equally extended to political responsibility also.[15]

10.4. Who Would Fall Under the Most Responsible Category?

The next term that must be interpreted is "those who were most responsible" for the crimes that were committed between April 1975 and January 1979. 'Most' has two primary meanings, but the relevant one is "greatest in quantity, extent or degree".[16] 'Responsible' has multiple meanings as well, but the most relevant are "liable to be called to account as the primary cause, motive or agent", and "being the cause or explanation".[17] Taken together, these suggest that "those who were most responsible" are those individuals who bear the greatest quantity, extent or degree of responsibility for causing the crimes that occurred during the temporal jurisdiction of the court. It is important to note that responsibility has nothing to do with an individual's rank or title and depends on how their actions

---

13 Report of the Group of Experts for Cambodia Established Pursuant to General Assembly Resolution 52/135, 18 February 1999, para. 110 ('Group of Experts Report') (https://www.legal-tools.org/doc/3da509/).

14 ICTY, *Prosecutor v. Dragomir Milošević*, Decision on Referral of Case Pursuant to Rule 11*bis*, Case No. IT-98-29/1-PT, 8 July 2005, para. 22 ('Dragomir Milošević Decision') (https://www.legal-tools.org/doc/404de4/). The ICTY was evaluating the seniority of the Accused in the context of an application of the Prosecution to transfer this case to a national jurisdiction pursuant to the United Nations Security Council Resolution 1503 (2003), UN Doc. S /RES/1503 (2003), 28 August 2003 (https://www.legal-tools.org/doc/b3d7d9/), which called upon that Tribunal to complete its proceedings at the first instance by 2008: "by concentrating on the prosecution and trial of the *most senior leaders* suspected of being most responsible for crimes within the ICTY's jurisdiction and transferring cases involving those who may not bear this level of responsibility to competent national jurisdictions […]" (emphasis added).

15 ICTY, *The Prosecutor v. Gojko Janković*, Appeals Chamber, Decision on Rule 11*bis* Referral, 15 November 2005, IT-96-23/2-AR11bis.2, para. 29 (https://www.legal-tools.org/doc/db8af3).

16 See Merriam-Webster Online Dictionary. The primary alternate meaning is "the majority of".

17 *Ibid.*

contributed to the crimes that occurred. Thus, even relatively low-ranking individuals could bear the most responsibility for particular crimes.

The legislative history of the expression indicates that it was meant to target those who were not *senior leaders*, but those who committed crimes "as serious as those" by the *senior leaders*. No particular number of persons was contemplated as prospective candidates for prosecution, but it was felt that "there would not be too many, as in the case of the Sierra Leone Tribunal".[18] The Group of Experts contemplated that this term specifically covered "certain leaders at the zonal level, as well as officials of torture and interrogation centres such as *Tuol Sleng* [in central Phnom Penh]".[19]

Other international criminal tribunals have also interpreted the expression "persons most responsible". For example, in interpreting Article 17(d) of the Rome Statute that lays down that cases that were not of "sufficient gravity" should not justify action by the International Criminal Court ('ICC'), a Pre-Trial Chamber of the ICC held that this Article was intended to ensure that the Court initiated cases only against the *most senior leaders* suspected of being most responsible for the crimes within its jurisdiction.[20] It enumerated the following elements for the satisfaction of that threshold:

> the roles such person play, through acts or omissions, when the state entities, organization or armed groups to which they belong commit *systematic and large-scale crimes* within the jurisdiction of the Court […]. [Further,] the role played by such state entitles, organizations or armed groups in the overall commission of crimes within the jurisdiction of the Court [is also relevant].[21]

The ICTY has stressed factors such as the extent and the geographical and temporal spread of the committed crime, number of civilians affected, extent of property damaged, number of military personnel involved *et cetera* to assess whether such a criminal conduct could qualify to be tried before that Tribunal.[22] It has also considered as relevant the circumstances and context in which the

---

[18] See, again, the speech of Mr. Sok An in the National Assembly Debates 2004. He clearly indicated that there "is no specific amount of people to be indicted from the second group. Those committing atrocious crimes will possibly be indicted".

[19] Group of Experts Report, para. 110, see *supra* note 13.

[20] ICC, *Prosecutor v. Thomas Lubanga Dyilo*, Pre-Trial Chamber I, Decision Concerning the Pre-Trial Chamber I's Decision of 10 February 2006 and the Incorporation of documents into the Record of the Case Against Mr. Thomas Lubanga Dyilo, ICC-01/04-01/06-8, 24 February 2006, para. 50 (https://www.legal-tools.org/doc/c60aaa/).

[21] *Ibid.*, para. 52 (emphasis added).

[22] Dragomir Milošević Decision, para. 24, see *supra* note 14.

crimes were committed especially "in the context of the other cases tried by the tribunal".[23]

In interpreting its statute that mandated prosecution of "persons who bear the greatest responsibility" for the crimes enumerated therein, the Special Court for Sierra Leone ('SCSL') concluded that the expression includes, "at a minimum, political and military leaders and implies an even broader range of individuals".[24] For example, it suggested that children between the ages of 15 and 18 could constitute "persons who bear the greatest responsibility" for the crimes that occurred in Sierra Leone.[25] The Special Court recognized that "persons who bear the greatest responsibility" was a more limited jurisdictional standard than simply "persons most responsible".[26]

10.5. Practice at the Khmer Rouge Tribunal

The KRT began its judicial activities in June 2007 with the adoption of its Internal Rules.[27] Immediately afterwards, on 18 July 2007, the prosecution requested the Investigating Judges to investigate five suspects for various crimes committed during the period of three years, eight months and twenty days that the Khmer Rouge was in power in Cambodia. These crimes, according to the prosecution, were committed as part of a joint criminal enterprise ('JCE') constituting a systematic and unlawful denial of basic rights of the Cambodian population and the targeted persecution of specific groups. While requesting the prosecution of the first five suspects, the prosecution identified twenty-five distinct factual situations of murder, torture, forcible transfer, unlawful detention, forced labour and religious, political and ethnic persecution as evidence of the crimes committed in the execution of the alleged JCE.

The prosecution has declared that it is conducting additional investigations to identify further crimes and suspects.[28] The media and the civil society speculated about the total number of defendants that the KRT would finally prosecute. The number, however, became a function of the time and resources available to

---

23 ICTY, *Prosecutor v. Ademi and Norac*, Decision for referral to the authorities of the Republic of Croatia pursuant to Rule 11*bis*, 14 September 2005, IT-04-78-PT, para. 28 (https://www.legal-tools.org/doc/b1d79e/).

24 SCSL, *Prosecutor v. Brima et al.*, Decision on Defence Motions for Judgment of Acquittal Pursuant to Rule 98, 31 March 2006, SCSL-04-16-T, para. 34 (https://www.legal-tools.org/doc/ca0979/).

25 *Ibid.*, para. 37.

26 *Ibid.*, para. 32 ("The 'most responsible' formulation suggested by the Secretary-General of the United Nations was rejected by the Security Council, which insisted upon the 'greatest responsibility' formulation.").

27 ECCC, Internal Rules, 12 June 2007 (https://www.legal-tools.org/doc/a95fce/).

28 *The Court Report*, monthly e-newsletter of the ECCC, 15 November 2008, p. 3.

the Tribunal. Further, although the Prosecution has not published the criteria of selection of suspects or the crimes, in its filings it has identified the role of the suspects and how they fit into one or both of the categories of persons that can be prosecuted before the Tribunal. The first five suspects represented the surviving senior leadership of the Khmer Rouge at the national level. While Nuon Chea, Ieng Sary, Khieu Samphan and Ieng Thirith were senior members of the government of DK and the CPK, Duch was the chairman of the most notorious and central security centre of that regime where more than 14,000 people were tortured and then done to death as suspected enemies of the regime. In identifying these suspects in its initial list, the Prosecution stated that it was satisfied that these suspects were senior leaders of DK "and/or" those most responsible for the crimes committed within the jurisdiction of the KRT.[29]

Once the Prosecution extends its investigations to those beyond the senior leadership, it may identify criteria of choosing only a few suspects from amongst potentially numerous likely candidates for prosecution. These criteria would serve both legal and societal purposes: (i) they would make prosecutorial decision-making predictable, certain and systematic; and (ii) they would inform the Cambodian people and the international community that the prosecutorial discretion was exercised fairly and reasonably.

Some of the principles that may inform these criteria are decipherable from the basic documents of the KRT. For example:

i. The KRT prosecution is independent in the performance of its functions and mandate. It does not accept or seek instructions from any government or any other source.[30]
ii. The principal objective of the founding of the KRT was the pursuit of justice and national reconciliation, stability, peace and security in Cambodia.[31] One of the ways by which this objective can be achieved is to provide a true historical account of the crimes committed during the Khmer Rouge regime.
iii. Within the constraints of the KRT's finite financial resources and the limited temporal mandate within which it must conclude its operations, the prosecution cannot prosecute all those persons who may have committed crimes within this Court's mandate and fall under the above-noted two categories. For the same reasons, the prosecution cannot conduct investigations into all the criminal acts that may fall under the KRT's jurisdiction.

[29] Statement of the Co-Prosecutors of the Extraordinary Chambers in the Courts of Cambodia, 18 July 2007.

[30] Statute, Article 19, see *supra* note 1.

[31] Agreement, Preamble, see *supra* note 2.

Given the limited resources of the KRT and the fact that it can only prosecute a limited number of suspects, the prosecution would have benefitted from criteria for the selection of its crimes and suspects. On the basis of the experiences gained in other international criminal tribunals, it could have considered the following.

10.5.1. Criteria for Selection of Crimes

In selecting the crimes, the prosecution would have considered the diverse categories of crimes within the KRT's mandate. In formulating criteria, it could have focused on the severity, scope and systematic nature of the crimes committed, in particular selecting conduct most illustrative of the crimes committed during the period of DK. It should have identified the crimes with the greatest number of victims and broadest geographical impact, and consider the proportional magnitude of crimes inflicted upon specific sectors of the population.

10.5.2. Criteria for Selection of Senior Leaders

Under this category, the prosecution could have formulated the criterion of only prosecuting those persons who were in highest political, governmental or military positions of decision-making at the national or the regional levels during DK.[32]

10.5.3. Criteria for Selection of Persons Most Responsible

Under this category, the prosecution's formulations should have focused on persons who bear the greatest quantity, extent or degree of responsibility for causing the crimes within the jurisdiction of the KRT, including those persons who, apart from being most responsible for chargeable crimes, were also in positions of political, administrative or military leadership, such that they could effectively control the perpetrators of acts that were most illustrative of the crimes committed during the period of DK.[33]

10.6. Conclusion

Criteria tend to become visible as criminal jurisdictions move from investigative to prosecution stages of proceedings, with decisions identifying the criteria employed for selection of crimes and suspects. Articulation of selection criteria contribute to the wider field of prioritization of war crimes cases, and may assist harmonization of criteria between prosecution services.

[32] Direct individual criminal responsibility also necessarily includes 'committing' by way of participation in a JCE as a co-perpetrator.

[33] *Ibid.*

PART III:
CRITERIA IN DOMESTIC JURISDICTIONS

11

Applying Selection and Prioritization Criteria to Sex Crimes Cases in the Democratic Republic of the Congo

Olympia Bekou*

Contemporary armed conflicts are characterized by an overwhelming number of sexual and gender-based crimes, whose commission is often widespread and carried out in the context of a systematic campaign to brutalize and destroy targeted groups.[1] As evidenced by the multiple initiatives and organizations working on these issues, sexual and gender-based violence in the context of armed conflict has gained visibility and political momentum in recent years. Many States showed their will and determination to end conflict-related sexual violence by participating in the Global Summit to End Sexual Violence in Conflict, held in London in June 2014. This forum and subsequent work resulted in the "International Protocol on the Documentation and Investigation of Sexual Violence in Conflict", which sought to "serve as a tool to support efforts by national and international justice and human rights practitioners to effectively and protectively document Conflict and Atrocity-Related Sexual Violence (CARS)".[2]

The successive and concurrent civil wars in the Democratic Republic of the Congo ('DRC') have given rise to widespread sexual and gender-based violence both during the fighting as well as the transitional period, with the violence

---

* **Olympia Bekou** is Professor and Head of School at the University of Nottingham and also serves as Deputy Director of CILRAP's Case Matrix Network ('CMN'). This chapter is based on a report entitled: "Prioritising International Sex Crimes Cases in the DRC" (https://www.legal-tools.org/doc/2ee277/), which was drafted with the invaluable research assistance of Aikaterini Katsimardou-Miariti. The report draws on criteria initially developed by Ilia Utmelidze and forms part of CILRAP-CMN's "Enhancing the Rome Statute System of Justice: Supporting National Ownership of Criminal Justice Procedures Through Technology-driven Services" project.

1 United Nations Security Council Resolution 2106, UN Doc. S/RES/2106, 24 June 2013 (2013) (https://www.legal-tools.org/doc/2cfa22/).

2 United Kingdom Foreign and Commonwealth Office, "International Protocol on the Documentation and Investigation of Sexual Violence in Conflict: Best Practice on the Documentation of Sexual Violence as a Crime or Violation of International Law", Second Edition, London, March 2017, p. 11 (https://www.legal-tools.org/doc/55baa7/).

sadly continuing to the present day.[3] Cases involving sex crimes have flooded the DRC criminal justice system, making it unable to process them in a timely fashion. Infrastructural obstacles – exacerbated by armed conflict – including budgetary constraints, inadequate facilities, and a shortage of the necessary legal actors, coupled with poor conditions of service, greatly limit the capacity of the Congolese legal system to address the high criminality that has taken place in the context of or in relation to armed conflict.[4] These challenges inevitably result in delays, a backlog of cases, and the prevalence of a sense of impunity.

Many violations committed in the course of conflict in the DRC may constitute war crimes or crimes against humanity under the regime of the Rome Statute of the International Criminal Court ('ICC Statute').[5] The present chapter proposes that the rationale behind the selection and prioritization of core international crimes could be applied equally to the commission of sex crimes in the DRC insofar as sex crimes committed during the conflict are serious crimes of concern to the international community as a whole, occurring in a context of mass violence. In addition, it is proposed that prioritizing the investigation and prosecution of sex crimes is necessary in order to focus limited resources to build complex and time-consuming cases.

The present chapter discusses the application of a set of selection and prioritization criteria – customized for the use in the DRC – to support the investigation and prosecution of core international crimes with a sexual or gender-based element. It is argued that such criteria can enhance and optimize the capacity of the national criminal justice system, when adopted and habitually utilized by prosecutors and other actors, as evidenced in the DRC case.

11.1. Selection and Prioritization

The nature and scale of core international crimes give rise to numerous allegations against a great number of individuals. It would be unrealistic – or indeed impossible – to expect the investigation and prosecution of so many complex

---

3 Office of the High Commissioner for Human Rights ('OHCHR'), "Report of the Mapping Exercise documenting the most serious violations of human rights and international humanitarian law committed within the territory of the Democratic Republic of the Congo between March 1993 and June 2003", August 2010, para. 531 (https://www.legal-tools.org/doc/ae3026/); Office of the Special Representative United Nations Human Rights Council ('UNHCR'), "UNHCR Warns of Mounting Violence Against Women and Girls in Eastern DRC", Briefing Notes, 14 July 2023; Conflict-related sexual violence: Report of the Secretary-General, 4 April 2024, UN Doc. S/2024/292, paras. 31–34 (https://www.legal-tools.org/doc/cp8baklm/).

4 OHCHR, paras. 50–57, see *supra* note 3; Human Rights Watch, "A Human Rights Agenda for the Democratic Republic of Congo", 6 March 2024, Section 3.

5 ICC Statute, 17 July 1998 ('ICC Statute') (https://www.legal-tools.org/doc/7b9af9/).

cases to be carried out all at once; nor is it possible to bring to justice all the perpetrators of grave violations of international law.[6]

Prioritization is understood as the mapping and selecting of cases, according to formal criteria, so that the most suitable go to trial first. Prioritization has been proposed as a way to address the challenges faced by the jurisdictions that deal with mass atrocities, both on the international and national levels. In principle, prioritizing specific cases does not lead to the de-selection of others.[7] Case prioritization seeks to ensure a more efficient administration of justice, through objective criteria that maximize the impact of criminal prosecution. Case selection may be an inevitable result of the various operational challenges faced by a specific jurisdiction. However, formally adopted criteria based on an objective consideration of the commission of core international crimes is essential to ensuring that the prioritization of cases is not discriminatory or unfair; otherwise, a situation of *de facto* impunity for perpetrators of such crimes could ensue. Furthermore, such criteria should be formulated after an assessment of the factual events and the practical needs of a situation involving mass atrocities. Moreover, the criteria should be publicly presented and explained as "legitimacy of priorities requires identifying and communicating objective factors that have inspired them".[8]

A number of different criteria may be used in the prioritization process. The majority of these contribute to a fair and objective assessment of the gravity and impact of the crimes committed, while others introduce policy considerations that must be taken into account in order to create a comprehensive prosecutorial strategy. Delays and other infrastructural limitations justify the need to create a prioritization system, thereby allowing a better management of the caseload. However, the nature of core international crimes renders them sufficiently

6 David Schwendiman, "Selecting war crimes cases for investigation and prosecution: avoiding the opportunity costs of picking low hanging fruit", as cited by Morten Bergsmo *et al.*, *The Backlog of Core International Crimes Case Files in Bosnia and Herzegovina*, Torkel Opsahl Academic EPublisher ('TOAEP'), Oslo, 2009, p. 80 (https://www.toaep.org/ps-pdf/3-bergsmo-helvig-utmelidze-zagovec-second).

7 Morten Bergsmo, "The Theme of Selection and Prioritization Criteria and Why It Is Relevant", in Morten Bergsmo (ed.), *Criteria for Prioritizing and Selecting Core International Crimes Cases*, Second Edition, TOAEP, Oslo, 2010, p. 9 (https://www.toaep.org/ps-pdf/4-bergsmo-second).

8 Rolf Einar Fife, Chapter 3 above, "Criteria for Prosecution of International Crimes: The Importance for States and the International Community of the Quality of the Criminal Justice Process for Atrocities, in Particular of the Exercise of Fundamental Discretion by Key Justice Actors", in *ibid.* (https://www.legal-tools.org/doc/f5abed/).

different to and significantly graver than ordinary crimes so as to justify focusing the (often limited) resources available and efforts on their successful prosecution.

Prioritizing core international crimes is therefore justified because of their *gravity*. According to the Preamble of the ICC Statute, core international crimes shock the conscience of humanity and constitute a threat to international peace and security.[9] Gravity is determined based on a careful assessment of both quantitative and qualitative criteria, which, according to ICC Pre-Trial Chamber II, involve:

1. the scale of the alleged crimes (including an assessment of geographical and temporal intensity);
2. the nature of the unlawful behaviour or of the crimes allegedly committed;
3. the means employed to execute the crimes (that is, the manner of their commission); and
4. the impact of the crimes and the harm caused to the victims and their families.[10]

In 2016, the ICC Office of the Prosecutor issued a Policy Paper in which the criteria adopted for the selection and prioritization of cases were explained.[11] In short, it is their exceptional gravity that requires an immediate and efficient response to these crimes. Given the difficulties faced in post-conflict and transitional contexts, it is argued that such a response would be augmented by adopting a prosecutorial approach that focuses on the investigation and prosecution of core international crimes. Formally recognizing and adopting criteria for the prioritization of criminal cases requires method and a good understanding of all the relevant factors and indicators that may affect the quality of the investigations and prosecutions. The following section will consider general principles for establishing prioritization criteria and will proceed to identify the most important criteria, along with their constituent factors and indicators.

9 ICC Statute, Preamble, paras. 4 and 9, see *supra* note 5.

10 ICC, *Situation in the Republic of Kenya*, Pre-Trial Chamber II, Decision Pursuant to Article 15 of the Rome Statute on the Authorization of an Investigation into the Situation in the Republic of Kenya, 31 March 2010, ICC-01/09-19, para. 62 (https://www.legal-tools.org/doc/338a6f/). The criteria were referred to by Pre-Trial Chamber I in ICC, *Situation in the Republic of Côte d'Ivoire*, Pre-Trial Chamber I, Prosecution's Response to the Defence application pursuant to Articles 19(4) and 17(1)(d) of the Rome Statute, 20 October 2014, ICC-2/11-2/11, paras. 16–17 (https://www.legal-tools.org/doc/254d54/pdf)

11 ICC, OTP, "Policy Paper on Case Selection and Prioritisation", September 2016 (https://www.legal-tools.org/doc/182205/).

11.1.1. General Principles for Establishing Prioritization Criteria

A selective approach to the investigation and prosecution of criminal cases is followed by most national and international investigative and prosecutorial authorities.[12] Consequently, the chapter will briefly examine the process of selection and prioritization in general before discussing criteria for application in the DRC. When faced with a large backlog of cases, a number of approaches are available to prosecutorial services with regard to selection and prioritization. For example, cases may be selected as they enter the docket, that is, on a 'first come, first served' basis; alternatively, cases may be chosen based on the availability of evidence; in some instances, cases may be selected as a result of political pressure.[13]

Admittedly, the approach used to select and prioritize cases may "substantially affect the way in which the justice process is received by victims and others affected by the atrocities".[14] For example, applying a set of criteria may lead to a disproportionate number of prosecutions of certain types of crimes, while ignoring other types of criminal behaviour.[15] Moreover, any decision to select and prioritize criminal cases that is not based upon objective criteria calls into question the credibility and impartiality of the criminal justice process as a whole.

However, formally established criteria can help to prevent biased and unfair prosecutions, as well as the use of the criminal justice system as a political tool to yield power and perpetuate discriminatory tactics.[16] Formalized criteria are also able to guide a transparent and credible process of selection that would encourage prosecutors to take the most suitable cases to trial first,[17] based on objective criteria that take into account the gravity of the crime, its victims and their suffering. Publicly and officially articulated criteria can contribute towards a more coherent prosecutorial strategy that can be applied to all core interna-

[12] Fabricio Guariglia, "'Those Most Responsible' versus International Sex Crimes: Competing Prosecution Themes?", in Morten Bergsmo (ed.), *Thematic Prosecution of International Sex Crimes*, Second Edition, TOAEP, Beijing, 2018, p. 45 (https://www.legal-tools.org/doc/nqhbnx/).

[13] Morten Bergsmo, "The Theme of Selection and Prioritization Criteria and Why It Is Relevant", in Bergsmo (ed.), 2010, p. 9, see *supra* note 7.

[14] *Ibid.*

[15] Christopher K. Hall, "The Danger of Selective Justice: All Cases Involving Crimes Under International Law Should Be Investigated and the Suspects When There Is Sufficient Evidence, Prosecuted", in Morten Bergsmo (ed.), 2010, p. 176, see *supra* note 7.

[16] Morten Bergsmo and Cheah Wui Ling, "Towards Rational Thematic Prosecution and the Challenge of International Sex Crimes", in Bergsmo (ed.), 2018, p. 4, see *supra* note 12.

[17] Bergsmo, 2010, p. 9, see *supra* note 13.

tional crimes which, at the same time, can be adapted to a specific type of criminality, such as sex crimes. Indeed, fixed prioritization criteria that take into consideration both the crimes committed as well as the surrounding circumstances can serve as guidelines to "reduce the scope for arbitrariness".[18] Consequently, it can be concluded that not only do formalized prioritization criteria pose no threat to the fairness of the administration of justice, but they also offer an added guarantee for transparent and independent judicial proceedings addressing the most heinous of crimes.

As a general principle, case selection must be *consistent but flexible*, taking into account newly acquired or developed evidence – or any other new information – that may render a case more or less of a priority.[19] However, "exceptions made for justifiable tactical reasons necessary to pursue those with greater liability" are also justifiable and accepted.[20] Indeed, the decision to prosecute a specific case is a balancing exercise, requiring an assessment of the interests of the victims, the accused and the community as a whole.[21] Such a delicate balance can only be achieved through the establishment of fixed criteria possessing the following characteristics: allowing for an objective evaluation of the facts relevant to the commission of a core international crime on the one hand, while at the same time remaining flexible enough to accommodate the peculiarities and unique characteristics of each situation.

11.1.2. Prioritization Criteria for Core International Crimes

The need for objective criteria that help to 'frame' prosecutorial discretion and to ensure the fairness and objectivity of the criminal justice process in situations of mass atrocity is clear. The present chapter has identified two principal criteria to be considered in the selection and prioritization of national cases involving core international crimes. In turn, each criterion can be broken down into its constituent elements. The proposed criteria are: (i) the gravity of the offence, and (ii) the objective 'representativity' of the overall scope of the prosecutions.

Before proceeding to the analysis of each criterion, it is worth noting their varied nature. Not only do they aim to facilitate the fact-finding process, by taking into consideration both the number of victims and the location of the commission of crimes, but also necessarily involve a value judgement, by considering the role of the suspect in the crimes committed as well as in the general

[18] Daniel D. Ntanda Nsereko, "Prosecutorial Discretion Before National Courts and International Tribunals", in *Journal of International Criminal Justice*, 2005, vol. 3, no. 1, p. 143.

[19] Morten Bergsmo *et al.*, 2009, p. 81, see *supra* note 6.

[20] *Ibid.*, p. 94.

[21] Alex Obote-Odore, "Case Selection and Prioritization Criteria at the International Criminal Tribunal for Rwanda", in Bergsmo (ed.), 2010, p. 52, see *supra* note 7.

context of the conflict.[22] Furthermore, the criteria include wider practical and policy considerations surrounding the prosecution of core international crimes.

11.1.2.1. Gravity

Gravity is an important criterion in deciding which case should move forward and go to trial. The determination of gravity requires an assessment of (i) the seriousness of the offence in question and (ii) an examination of the level of responsibility of the alleged perpetrator.

11.1.2.1.1. Seriousness of the Offence

The seriousness of the alleged offence can, in turn, be deconstructed into a number of factual indicators allowing for an examination of the behaviour that may form the basis of criminal prosecution. The indicators listed below help investigators to properly establish the facts and context surrounding the criminal acts in question and to assess the gravity of the crimes in a fair and objective manner. They include quantitative aspects that measure the scale and extent of the criminal behaviour under examination, as well as qualitative factors that may later be reflected in findings of aggravating or mitigating circumstances. The proposed indicators to be taken into consideration when determining the seriousness of the offence are as follows:

- Number of victims;
- nature of acts;
- area of destruction;
- duration and repetition of the offence;
- location of the crime;
- nationality of perpetrators and victims;
- the *modus operandi* of the criminal conduct;
- discriminative motive;
- defencelessness of victims; and
- consequences of crimes.

11.1.2.1.2. Responsibility of the Alleged Perpetrator

The level of responsibility of the alleged perpetrator can also be broken down into a series of factual indicators enabling an examination of the position the suspect had in the leadership hierarchy and their involvement in the commission of crimes, as well the degree of personal culpability for crimes committed by leaders or their subordinates. The aim of this element of the gravity criterion is to hold to account the "people who were in positions to order, allow, or create

[22] See Luc Côté, "Reflections on the Exercise of Prosecutorial Discretion in International Criminal Law", in *Journal of International Criminal Justice*, 2005, vol. 3, no. 1, p. 169.

the conditions necessary for the conduct, or who were in a position to prevent it and consciously chose not to, and those in positions of authority or influence who participated directly in the events themselves".[23] It is assumed that the higher the position of the alleged perpetrator and their level of involvement in the commission of a (core international) crime, the greater their criminal responsibility, thereby rendering prosecution imperative.

Moreover, the following indicators also take into account the seriousness of the crime so as to include low-level perpetrators who have committed particularly egregious offences. In this regard, the following indicators related to the responsibility of the alleged perpetrator can be identified:

- Position in hierarchy under investigation;
- status as political, military, paramilitary, religious or civilian leader;
- leadership at municipal, regional or national level;
- nationality or tribe;
- role and participation in policy and strategy decisions;
- personal culpability for specific atrocities;
- notoriousness or responsibility for particularly heinous acts;
- extent of direct participation in the alleged incidents;
- authority and control exercised by the suspects;
- the suspect's alleged notice and knowledge of acts by subordinates.

11.1.2.2. The Objective 'Representativity' of the Overall Scope of the Prosecutions

Representative prosecutions seek to maximize the impact of prosecutorial work and minimize perceptions of unfairness and lack of justice that inevitably stem from the process of case selection and prioritization. This means that, at the end of a process of prosecutions of core international crimes, in a conflict, post-conflict or mass violence situation, the "accumulated portfolio should reflect – or be representative of – the *overall victimisation* caused by the crimes in the conflict or situation at hand".[24] A representative prosecution consequently requires a comprehensive knowledge and understanding of the criminality of a particular situation. It presupposes a mapping of the offences committed, which will include accurate and reliable data on the criminal offences, the alleged perpetrators and the victims. Representative prosecutions also seek to address any issues that may arise as a result of the selection and prioritization of cases – thereby

[23] Bergsmo *et al.*, 2009, p. 92, see *supra* note 6.

[24] *Ibid.*, p. 125 (emphasis added). See Chapter 2 above by Devasheesh Bais for the origins of the notion of 'representativity'.

reconciling the interests of victims and society as a whole with the reality of the finite resources enjoyed by certain criminal justice systems.

Contemporary criminal justice has been built upon the idea that victims of mass atrocities deserve to see justice done for their suffering. The concept of the 'interests of the victims' is complemented by considerations of their physical and psychological well-being, dignity and privacy.[25] Moreover, prosecutions aim to serve the interests of society as a whole, either by offering closure and contributing to the reconciliation process or by acting as a deterrent for potential perpetrators.[26] Analysing the philosophical foundations of the various justifications of the prosecution of core international crimes does not fall within the scope of this chapter. However, these considerations are relevant to the public role of the criminal justice system as both a guarantor of law and order and protector of the security and safety of the people.

In post-conflict and transitional situations, the State apparatus faces significant difficulties in carrying out its everyday functions. Justice systems are not exempt from these post-conflict realities: often operating in light of high levels of criminality and an impaired infrastructure. Representativity is therefore a key element for the conduct of effective and fair prosecutions. According to this criterion, cases involving offences committed in the areas and communities most affected by violence should be given priority or form a larger part of the prosecutorial work. In the same light, organizations or institutions most responsible for the commission of criminal offences should face justice to a greater extent than, or ahead of, organizations and institutions of lesser influence.[27] Representative prosecutions seek to address the impunity afforded to alleged perpetrators by the dysfunction of the criminal justice system[28] and to create a new public perception of the system that aims to re-establish the trust of the people.

11.2. Prioritization of Sex Crimes Cases in the Democratic Republic of the Congo

Before discussing the application of the foregoing selection and prioritization criteria in the DRC, it is important to recognize the context in which sexual violence occurs. Between 1998 and 2013, more than 5 million people lost their lives in the context of armed conflict in the DRC. Furthermore, the long-lasting

[25] ICC, OTP, "Policy Paper on the Interests of Justice", September 2007 (https://www.legal-tools.org/doc/bb02e5/).

[26] For a discussion of the various justifications of prosecutions of core international crimes, see Margaret M. deGuzman, "An Expressive Rationale for the Thematic Prosecution of Sex Crimes", in Bergsmo (ed.), 2018, pp. 13–44, see *supra* note 12.

[27] Bergsmo *et al.*, 2009, p. 125, see *supra* note 6.

[28] Maria Eriksson Baaz and Maria Stern, "Making sense of violence: Voices of soldiers in the Congo (DRC)", in *Journal of Modern African Studies*, 2008, vol. 46, no. 1, pp. 57–86 and 79.

conflict has led to a total collapse of the State's apparatus along with basic infrastructure, including roads and health facilities. As a result, reliable information has remained scarce. Both national State actors and civil society have attempted to map the situation in the country and to identify the diverse needs; various international organizations and independent experts have also contributed to this end.[29] Notwithstanding, it can be clearly stated that sexual and gender-based violence has been extremely prominent in the DRC since the outbreak of hostilities in 1998.

The armed conflict has also severely damaged the DRC court system, limiting its ability to function effectively. In 2022, there were only around 3,500 active magistrates nationwide. In 2023, 2,500 new magistrates were recruited and trained in the investigation and prosecution of international crimes, aiming to address the staffing shortages within the justice system.[30] They are responsible for investigating and prosecuting the crimes committed not only by the Congolese army and the national police force but also those committed by the thousands of armed group members. Moreover, these few judicial staff often face adverse circumstances, such as infrastructural issues, irregular payment of salaries and lack of the necessary training.[31]

All national prosecutorial systems are selective in one way or another. Decisions are made every day that consciously – or otherwise – give priority to one criminal case over another. The decision to focus on specific types of criminality is linked to the concept of prosecutorial discretion. Prosecutorial discretion involves the exercise of the prosecutor's independent professional judgement and "enables the decision maker to choose between two or more permissible courses of action and to adapt his decision to existing circumstances".[32] The decision to prioritize the investigation and prosecution of specific cases in the docket may be influenced by a number of factors such as limited resources, the availability

[29] See, for example, DRC, Ministère du Genre, de la Famille et de l'Enfant, "Ampleur des violences sexuelles en RDC et actions de lutte contre le phénomène de 2011 à 2012", June 2013 ('National Study on Sexual Violence'); Human Rights Watch, "Seeking Justice: The Prosecution of Sexual Violence in the Congo War", March 2007; Harvard Humanitarian Initiative and Oxfam America, "Now, the world is without me: An investigation of sexual violence in the Eastern Democratic Republic of Congo", April 2010; International Legal Assistance Consortium and International Bar Association, "Rebuilding courts and trust: An assessment of the needs of the justice system in the Democratic Republic of the Congo", August 2009.

[30] TRIAL International, "DRC: 2,500 New Magistrates Trained in the Investigation and Prosecution of International Crimes", 18 October 2023.

[31] OHCHR, "Progress and Obstacles in the Fight against Impunity for Sexual Violence in the Democratic Republic of the Congo", April 2014, p. 19 (https://www.legal-tools.org/doc/r1zo4v/).

[32] Nsereko, 2005, pp. 124–144, see *supra* note 18.

of legal actors in the criminal justice system, and the presence and quality of available evidence.

In post-conflict or transitional situations, State mechanisms, designed to protect the wider population and to ensure law and order, are severely impaired, if not completely destroyed. Moreover, the capacity of national criminal justice systems is challenged by high levels of criminality and the inability to react thereto in a timely and effective manner. In light of the many challenges faced by the DRC criminal justice system, the present chapter suggests the most relevant factors to be taken into consideration. The proposed criteria seek to hold accountable those most responsible for mass atrocities in the DRC and to address evidence and operational related issues. Moreover, they aim to provide judges with detailed and well-supported information regarding the commission of crimes, thereby allowing them to have a full overview of the facts of a given case and to identify and apply the relevant legislation.

It has been suggested that "[t]he issue of thematic prosecution of international sex crimes, and other core international crimes […] must be addressed by each jurisdiction on its own terms".[33] Every post-conflict and transitional situation presents unique characteristics, needs and gaps to be filled. As such, uniformly applying the same indicators would be unwise and ineffective. However, it is argued that the indicators listed above may be used as the starting point from which a prosecutorial strategy can be developed and adapted to the needs of any situation. Indeed, the indicators analysed in the preceding section may offer useful guidance in mapping the types of criminality and victimization that have taken place – and which may remain present – across the DRC. The following indicators can thus be identified as the most relevant to the DRC situation.

11.2.1. Nature of the Criminal Acts

Rape remains the predominant form of sexual and gender-based violence in the DRC.[34] It is indicative that in 2023 the vast majority of documented cases of conflict-related sexual violence were rape and gang rape.[35] Incidents of rape were followed by incidents of sexual slavery and other forms of sexual violence.[36] It is therefore proposed that the nature of the criminal acts ought to be

---

[33] Bergsmo and Cheah, 2012, p. 4, see *supra* note 16.

[34] National Study on Sexual Violence, 2013, see *supra* note 29; Denis Mukengere Mukwege and Cathy Nangini, "Rape with Extreme Violence: The New Pathology in South Kivu, Democratic Republic of Congo", in *PLoS Medicine*, 2009, vol. 6, no. 12, p. 1.; Conflict-related sexual violence: Report of the Secretary-General, 29 March 2022, UN Doc. S/2022/273, para. 28 (https://www.legal-tools.org/doc/a9vsjie9/).

[35] Conflict-related Sexual Violence: Report of the Secretary-General, 4 April 2024, para. 32, see *supra* note 3.

[36] National Study on Sexual Violence, 2013, p. 11, see *supra* note 29.

taken into consideration by national investigative and prosecutorial authorities in the DRC, with a particular emphasis on incidents of rape.

11.2.2. *Modus Operandi* of the Criminal Conduct

A comprehensive prosecutorial strategy requires that potential aggravating circumstances are taken into account when deciding which cases to prioritize for investigation and prosecution. In this regard, the nature of the act and the manner of its commission are the most important factors. The amount of violence involved, the number of perpetrators and the age of victim(s) therefore also ought to be taken into account by DRC investigators and prosecutors.

11.2.3. Location of the Crimes

In a country as vast as the DRC, it is very important to identify the locations where sexual and gender-based violence is most prominent. Eastern DRC has been the focal point of the contemporary armed conflict. The provinces of North and South Kivu in particular have been identified by studies as 'hot spots' of sexual violence.[37] Province Orientale is another region identified as a region with a high prevalence of sexual violence.[38] This is primarily due to the vulnerable geographical location of these regions, near the borders of the DRC with Uganda, Rwanda and Burundi. Their position means that the many armed groups active in the area originate not only from the DRC but also from neighbouring States. In this light, to spread prosecutions geographically so as to cover as much of the affected territories as possible would dismiss any claims of bias, discrimination or favouritism and would take into account broader parts of the population affected by sexual and gender-based violence.

11.2.4. 'Those Most Responsible': Command and Superior Responsibility

The possibility to pursue those 'most responsible' for the sex crimes committed in the DRC is perhaps the definitive criterion for the prioritization of crimes in this particular context. As the Secretary-General of the United Nations observes, "[m]ilitary personnel are responsive to training, unequivocal orders, disciplinary

---

[37] *Ibid.*; Conflict-related Sexual Violence: Report of the Secretary-General, 4 April 2024, para. 32, see *supra* note 3.

[38] Report of the Security Council mission to the Democratic Republic of the Congo (13 to 16 May 2010), 30 June 2010, UN Doc. S/2010/288, para. 8 (https://www.legal-tools.org/doc/w9f6vv/); Mpaka Kiansiku, "Rapport des Infractions de Violences Sexuelles: Statistiques des Infractions de Violences Sexuelles Rapportées en Province Orientale entre Septembre 2013 et Avril 2014", October 2014 (on file with the author); Conflict-related sexual violence: Report of the Secretary-General, 23 March 2015, UN Doc. S/2015/203, para. 23 (https://www.legal-tools.org/doc/kqkljq5s/).

measures and the example set by their hierarchy".[39] In the DRC, sexual violence has not been discouraged and punished; indeed, it has been used strategically.[40] Acts of sexual and gender-based violence have not only been used to garner political attention, but have also been employed as an instrument of control or as a way to terrorize the population in order to facilitate looting.[41] All the parties involved in hostilities across the DRC are responsible for committing sex crimes. To this end, civilians have been targeted either as a terrorization and domination technique or as a reprisal, on the basis of the real or perceived ethnicity of the population or their presumed political affiliation.[42]

Further difficulties are created by the complicated and delicate situation regarding the military. The disarmament, demobilization and reintegration procedures have created an army that is largely constituted by ex-members of armed militia groups.[43] As a consequence, multiple and parallel chains of command are observed, with the units remaining "responsive to the former and current belligerents, and not to the integrated command structures".[44] These contextual issues underline the need to bring an end to impunity for those high in the chain of authority, particularly in the military. Consequently, as a general principle, priority must be given by national investigative and prosecutorial authorities to cases involving (i) the mode of liability of command responsibility, (ii) crimes committed by public officials still in office, regardless of mode of liability, or (iii) by law enforcement officials, regardless of mode of liability.[45]

11.3. Concluding Remarks

Having identified a number of criteria for the selection and prioritization of cases that aim to assist the work of national criminal justice actors in the DRC, the chapter concludes by proposing a series of tailored steps to enable the prac-

---

[39] Conflict-related sexual violence: Report of the Secretary-General, 13 January 2012, UN Doc. A/66/657 and S/2012/33, para. 5 (https://www.legal-tools.org/doc/fcnn12/).

[40] LOGICA, "Sexual and Gender-based Violence in the Kivu Provinces of the Democratic Republic of Congo: Insights from Former Combatants", September 2013, pp. 60–61.

[41] *Ibid.*

[42] Conflict-related sexual violence: Report of the Secretary-General, 29 March 2022, para. 28, see *supra* note 34.

[43] Maria Eriksson Baaz and Maria Stern, "The Complexity of Violence: A critical analysis of sexual violence in the Democratic Republic of the Congo", Nordic Africa Institute, 2010, p. 19.

[44] Maria Eriksson Baaz and Maria Stern, "Why Do Soldiers Rape? Masculinity, Violence and Sexuality in the Armed Forces in the Congo (DRC)", in *International Studies Quarterly*, 2009, vol. 53, no. 2, pp. 495–518.

[45] Bergsmo *et al.*, 2009, p. 85, see *supra* note 6.

tical application of these criteria. In 2018, the Conseil Supérieur de la Magistrature adopted the prioritisation criteria outlined above as a practice direction, making them applicable to every single case dealing with sexual violence in conflict across the DRC, which is a significant step forward.[46] The implementation of the criteria enshrined in the practice direction, would be further enhanced if the specific steps during the pre-trial stage of the criminal justice process in the DRC were to be adopted as follows:

Step 1: Mapping Exercise. Both the Ministry of Justice and the Public Prosecutor (Ministère Public) ought to have a complete understanding of sexual and gender-based violence across the DRC. A mapping of the open case files, which will create records of the total number of crimes committed, as well as the total number of suspects, allows prosecution services to better understand where the need to address impunity is greater and more imperative.

Step 2: Design and Implementation of a National Policy. Having collected the data through the mapping exercise, the justice system should assess existing gaps and needs and create a comprehensive national policy to be used by the prosecution and courts.

By using the foregoing criteria, the policy created ought to assign clear tasks to all within the criminal justice system. The policy should, moreover, adopt an overall strategy for investigation and prosecution of core international crimes with a sexual element, taking into account the gravity of the crimes committed along with the overall recorded criminality and victimization.

It is noted that the adopted policy should be interpreted in line with fair trial standards at the national and international levels. Furthermore, it must respect the independence of the judiciary and seek the creation of an efficient and smooth system of case management, through the prioritization of cases. For the creation of such a policy, the need for extensive consultations at the national, regional and local levels ought to be emphasized alongside the need for co-operation between all national and international stakeholders in building national capacity and knowledge. This will enable the widest and most effective application possible.

Step 3: Practical Application in the Pre-Trial Stage. This step can be broken down into three sub-steps, as follows:

[46] Circulaire No 02 PCC-PCSM 2018 Relative à la sélection et la priorisation des affaires de crimes contre la paix et la sécurité de l'humanité, en particuliers celles liées aux violences sexuelles, au stade de l'instruction pré juridictionnelle, 19 March 2018 (https://www.legal-tools.org/doc/bf85a3/).

(a) Creation of a comprehensive case file: The officers within the Police Judiciaire are those who receive any complaints or reports of criminal offences.[47] They are required by law to create a case file (Procès-verbal) that will include information on:

1. The nature and circumstances of the commission of the offence;
2. the time and place of commission;
3. any evidence or indicators as to the identity of the perpetrator; and
4. any testimony that may be available by persons who were present during the crime or who have any other relevant information.[48]

This stage of the criminal justice process is the most crucial. These four elements provide the necessary information that will allow the Prosecutor to properly determine the gravity of the crimes allegedly committed. Collecting this information immediately after the commission of the alleged crime creates a solid base for the investigation and prosecution of the case.

(b) Respecting the legal timeframe: Article 7*bis* CCP provides that any investigation by the Police Judiciaire must be conducted immediately and with no intermissions, in order for the case to be transmitted to the relevant Public Prosecutor within a 24-hour timeframe.[49]

(c) Application of the prioritization criteria: At this stage of the investigative process, the Public Prosecutor must carefully examine the case file prepared by officers of the Police Judiciaire, proceed with the investigation and collect enough information and evidence in order to decide whether the case should be prioritized. Utilizing the information in the case file and the results of their own investigation, the Public Prosecutor must decide at this stage which cases should be prioritized, using the suggested indicators in the national policy, focusing on the gravity of the crimes committed and the representativity of the overall prosecutorial scope in regard to the criminality and the ensuing victimization in the DRC.

To conclude, it is not realistic to expect the investigation and prosecution of all core international crimes, particularly in situations of mass violence. Selection and prioritization criteria have therefore been proposed as a method to bring the most appropriate cases to trial first, based on formal criteria. The selection and prioritization of cases seek not only to respond to the challenges

[47] Décret du 6 août 1959 portant le Code de procédure pénale, 6 August 1959, Article 2 ('CCP') (https://www.legal-tools.org/doc/734d4e/).

[48] *Ibid.*

[49] *Ibid.*, Article 7*bis*.

faced in dealing with mass crimes, but also aim for a more efficient administration of justice. The adoption of such a selection and prioritization strategy for sex crime cases – coupled with its subsequent application by national criminal justice actors – can contribute towards the fight against impunity for sexual violence in the DRC and elsewhere.

12

Canada's Approach to File Review in the Context of War Crimes Cases

Terry M. Beitner*

12.1. Introduction

In its concept note to the 2008 seminar, CILRAP's department Forum for International Criminal and Humanitarian Law ('FICHL' or 'Forum') stated that the

> main concern of the seminar is how criminal justice systems can make use of prioritization criteria with regard to case files that have already been opened.[1]

The purpose of this chapter will therefore be to explore Canada's use of selection criteria in the file review process at the time of the Second Edition of this book. The ultimate objective of file review is the selection and application

---

* **Terry Beitner** is Professor of international criminal law at the University of Ottawa's Faculty of Law. At the time of writing, he was Director and General Counsel of the Crimes Against Humanity and War Crimes Section of the Department of Justice Canada, but the chapter does not necessarily reflect the views of the Department. The chapter was originally published in the Second Edition of this book in 2009, and it has not been substantively updated since. It described Canada's Crimes Against Humanity and War Crimes Program's historical practice regarding the use of selection criteria during the triage of allegations concerning the presence of alleged war criminals in Canada. The chapter also outlined the development of these selection criteria over time, up to the date of the Second Edition. The Program's practices have evolved since that edition and continue to undergo further refinement; therefore, the detailed procedural description below is outdated.

Beitner was responsible for selecting cases from among the Canadian inventory of war crimes matters under investigation by the Royal Canadian Mounted Police that may ultimately be put before the Attorney General of Canada with a recommendation that the Public Prosecution Service of Canada commence a criminal prosecution under Canada's Crimes Against Humanity and War Crimes Act. Since 2003, he delivered annual lectures at the Faculty of Law of the University of Ottawa and other universities on selected issues with respect to the application of the various remedies available to the Government of Canada under its Crimes Against Humanity and War Crimes Program to deal with the presence in Canada of individuals who may have been involved in the commission of war crimes or crimes against humanity. The War Crimes Section is involved in the application of all remedies employed by the Government of Canada when dealing with war crimes matters.

1 FICHL, "Criteria for prioritizing and selecting core international crimes cases", Seminar concept paper, 28 September 2008, p. 2, fn. 6 (see https://www.fichl.org/activities/criteria-for-prioritizing-and-selecting-core-international-crimes-cases).

of the appropriate legal remedy, under Canadian law, where an alleged war criminal is present in Canada. Before commencing an analysis on this specific process, it is important to first provide a contextual background of Canada's approach to the issue of war crimes.[2]

12.2. Canada's War Crimes Program

The Government of Canada established the War Crimes Program (hereinafter referred to as the 'Program') in 1998. The goal of the Program is to enforce Canada's *no safe haven* policy, a policy asserting that "Canada is not a safe haven for anyone involved in crimes against humanity, war crimes, or genocide".[3] The Program provides for a co-ordinated governmental response to specific allegations that individuals either already present in or attempting to gain entry into Canada were involved in war crimes. Canada's approach includes a robust effort at its ports of entry and processing overseas to screen out people ineligible to enter the country resulting from involvement in such crimes.[4] Although these efforts are fundamental aspects of the Program, this chapter will focus on the selection of remedies to be applied to individuals already located on Canadian soil.

The Program's objective is to respond to every credible allegation of the presence in Canada of an individual who may have committed war crimes. The Program's approach to the issue is consistent with the *no safe haven* policy. It also ensures respect for our obligations at international law. These international obligations include those arising from the various treaties adhered to over the years as well as those flowing from customary international law. The Program represents Canada's contribution to the international struggle against impunity for war crimes.

The Program brings together four key government departments and agencies: the Department of Citizenship and Immigration ('CIC'), the Department of Justice ('DOJ'), the Canadian Border Services Agency ('CBSA'), and Public Safety Canada represented by the Royal Canadian Mounted Police ('RCMP'). Other government departments also play critical functions in the enforcement

2 For the purposes of this chapter, a reference to 'war crimes' includes crimes against humanity and genocide.

3 See Canada's Program on Crimes Against Humanity and War Crimes, "Ninth Annual Report", English version, Canadian Border Services Agency, Ottawa, 2005–2006 ('Ninth Annual Report').

4 Canada, Immigration and Refugee Protection Act, 22 June 2009, Section 35 (https://www.legal-tools.org/doc/2cd12d/) provides that where there are "reasonable grounds to believe" that someone committed a war crime, then that person is "inadmissible" to enter or remain in Canada.

of the *no safe haven* policy, including the Public Prosecution Service of Canada and Foreign Affairs and International Trade Canada to name but two.

The Program ensures that separate government bodies do not operate at cross-purposes. It also avoids duplication of effort through the co-ordination of activities respecting individual cases. All of this is carried out with care so as not to fetter the independence of specific government authorities when charged with executing a particular mandate. For example, when the RCMP conducts an investigation into allegations, they remain in full control of their operations to the exclusion of other government players. With that said, this independence does not prevent the RCMP from seeking advice from analysts or counsel from the Crimes Against Humanity and War Crimes Section of the Department of Justice. In fact, one of the strengths of the Program is the co-ordination of efforts of all of the Program partners as well as the sharing of information between the departments. These activities are of course carried out in accordance with Canada's legal regime governing access to information and privacy.

The Program's infrastructure provides for co-ordination and periodic oversight by senior government officials from the operational tier up to the Assistant Deputy Minister ('ADM') level for all four departments. The ADMs meet annually and on an *ad hoc* basis when needed to review the activities of the Program and to receive reports from the Program Coordination and Operations Committee ('PCOC'). PCOC is the principal governing body of the operations of the Program. PCOC meets monthly and consists of the senior managers of all four partners. PCOC develops policy, co-ordinates operations and through a subcommittee assesses cases. The work of the File Review Subcommittee ('FRS') is the focus of the remainder of this chapter. This committee is responsible for applying the selection criteria.

12.3. The File Review Subcommittee

The File Review Subcommittee ('FRS') includes members of all four departments (CIC, CBSA, DOJ and RCMP) and reviews allegations of participation in war crimes made against individuals currently residing in Canada. The FRS recommends further review, investigation and analysis or legal action by a specific organization. The legal remedies include: deportation; revocation of citizenship and deportation; transfer to an international tribunal (upon request); extradition (upon request); and criminal investigation and prosecution pursuant to Canada's Crimes Against Humanity and War Crimes Act.[5]

[5] Canada, Crimes Against Humanity and War Crimes Act, C. 2000, c. 24, 31 December 2000 ('Crimes Against Humanity and War Crimes Act') (https://www.legal-tools.org/doc/0d3078/).

The most cumbersome and costly remedy is criminal investigation and prosecution in Canada. The majority of cases have been, and will no doubt continue to be, dealt with by employing remedies other than criminal investigation and prosecution. The practical realities surrounding the cost and complexity of carrying out international criminal investigations required to meet the rigorous legal burden on the prosecuting authority in Canada dictate that this remedy is to be used sparingly. What is meant by 'sparingly' in this context is a discussion I leave for another day.

It is worth noting that statistics published before the 2008 FICHL seminar indicate that there were 57 cases in the RCMP-DOJ criminal investigation inventory.[6]

In light of the foregoing, we now return to the Forum's current issue under study: "how criminal justice systems can make use of prioritization criteria with regard to case files that have already been opened".[7] Translated into Canadian terms, the question would be: what criteria were employed to place the aforementioned 57 cases into an active criminal investigation inventory?

12.4. File Review Subcommittee Selection Criteria

The criteria employed by the FRS at the time of the Second Edition was made public in the 2005–2006 Program annual report which stated the following:

> In order for an allegation to be added to the RCMP/DOJ inventory, the allegation must disclose personal involvement or command responsibility, the evidence pertaining to the allegation must be corroborated, and the necessary evidence must be able to be obtained in a reasonably uncomplicated and rapid fashion.[8]

In certain circumstances a file may be added to the RCMP-DOJ inventory where these conditions are not met. These include the following:

- The allegation pertains to a Canadian citizen living in Canada or to a person present in Canada who cannot be removed for practical or legal reasons.
- Policy reasons – such as the national or public interest, or overarching reasons related to the interests of the war crimes program, international impunity or the search for justice – exist.

The 'inventory' is a pool of matters from which the RCMP selects specific files to investigate. Files are typically placed into groups with complementary crime-base elements. The crime-base can consist of a common element that may

[6] Ninth Annual Report, see *supra* note 3.

[7] FICHL, 28 September 2008, see *supra* note 1.

[8] Ninth Annual Report, see *supra* note 3, p. 8.

bring a number of investigations together enabling the RCMP to deal with several cases at one time. For example, a specific event or series of events that took place at a particular geographic location can serve as the crime-base to allow for the concurrent investigation of several files.[9]

The criteria outlined above are the result of having previously employed different methods to select cases to be placed in the investigative pool. Previously, we engaged a two-stage process whereby the emphasis was placed on our obligations under international law (extradite or prosecute or *aut dedere aut judicare*) and the seriousness of the crime. If either element was satisfied at an early stage of the analysis, then the file was added to the inventory.[10] Subsequently, the files were assigned a specific priority that would, in theory, determine the order in which the allegations would be examined.

The criteria that were previously employed to assign a priority consisted of the consideration of the following elements:

a. Nature of allegation:
  - credibility of allegation;
  - seriousness of allegation;
  - seriousness of crime (genocide, war crimes or crimes against humanity);
  - military or civilian position;
  - strength of evidence.

b. Nature of investigation:
  - progress of investigation;

---

[9] Additionally, we must recall that Canada follows the British common law practice where the police are an independent investigative body that does not take direction from any other arm of the government. What is unique to the Program is the close co-operation between the police and the other departments involved in these investigations. Over time, Canadian police forces have formed 'integrated' units to investigate complex crimes. Therefore, the close co-operation between the RCMP and the other partners in the Program fits well in this modern trend. Other examples of Canadian integrated units include the Integrated Market Enforcement Teams (IMET) dealing with stock market fraud, the Integrated Proceeds of Crime units (IPOC) dealing with money laundering, possession of proceeds of crime, and the Integrated Border Enforcement Teams (IBET) dealing with border enforcement issues including drug interdiction and people smuggling. All of these units have a combination of various experts including police officers, lawyers, accountants and analysts working together to investigate these serious complex crimes.

[10] In practical terms, we translated the *aut dedere aut judicare* obligation, outside of an extradition situation where we are the receiving state of the request for extradition, to the obligation to submit the file to national authorities for investigation and, where appropriate under national law, prosecution. In Canada the decision to prosecute is governed by the following policy: the evidence must demonstrate that there is a *reasonable prospect of conviction and the prosecution must be in the public interest.*

- ability to secure co-operation with other country or international tribunal;
- likelihood of effective co-operation with other countries;
- presence of victims or witnesses in Canada;
- presence of victims or witnesses in other countries with easy access;
- likelihood of being part of group investigation in Canada;
- likelihood of parallel investigation in other country or by international tribunal;
- ability to conduct documentary research to test credibility of allegation;
- likelihood of continuing offence or danger to the public related to crimes against humanity and war crimes allegations.

c. Other considerations:
- no likelihood of removal (credible allegation of risk of torture upon return);
- no likelihood of removal (Canadian citizen);
- no reasonable prospect of fair and real prosecution in other country;
- high-profile case (publicity, representations, or interest from other countries);
- no indictment by international tribunal or no extradition request likely;
- likelihood of continuing offence or danger to the public not related to crimes against humanity and war crimes allegations;
- national interest considerations.

For a myriad of reasons this procedure was untenable because it led to an inordinate number of files to investigate.

Another factor that contributed to the development of the current practice outlined above is that we had to consider the singular situation where Canada has jurisdiction over the offence and the offender, but where it would be unreasonable to expend resources to such an investigation at the expense of other ongoing matters. Canada's legislation provides for broad jurisdiction over offences and individuals where, in some circumstances, the offender need not be present in Canada in order for our courts to assert jurisdiction. For example, Section 8(a)(iii) of the Crimes Against Humanity and War Crimes Act provides Canadian courts with jurisdiction if the victim of the alleged offence was a Canadian citizen.[11]

---

[11] Section 8 of the Crimes Against Humanity and War Crimes Act, see *supra* note 5, reads as follows:

When developing our criteria, we had to ask ourselves the following questions: Is it appropriate to expend limited resources if the alleged perpetrator is not in Canada while we have a considerable number of other viable cases related to people currently located in Canada? What if there is no reasonable prospect that the individual can be brought to Canada to undergo a trial?[12] On this issue we decided that it would be consistent with our *no safe haven* policy to give priority generally to those files relating to individuals in Canada. Finally, what if the evidence is not available to Canadian authorities for investigation, assessment or trial?

The articulation of the criteria stated above flows from an analysis of these and other considerations. Perhaps one of the most important, if not *the* most important element in the decision-making matrix, is cost. The investigation and prosecution of these matters are multi-million dollar undertakings. As in all major criminal investigations, a reasonable amount of money must be set aside for this work. Furthermore, there are justifiable limits to the amount of money to be attributed to such undertakings.

12.5. Conclusion

Like it or not, hard decisions must be made to demonstrate that public funds are spent wisely. Prosecutorial and police investigative discretion are recognized as important principles in the common law law-enforcement paradigm. Public interest considerations weighed by national law-enforcement bodies combined with international public policy considerations all contribute to the complexity of establishing and applying criteria. I believe that regardless of the approach adopted and of the decisions made as to whether or not criteria should be developed and employed, national authorities will have to remain flexible in their approach. They must not hem themselves into a mechanical application of a specific standard. I believe that, for some countries, large inventories will have

---

A person who is alleged to have committed an offence under section 6 or 7 may be prosecuted for that offence if

(a) at the time the offence is alleged to have been committed,
  - (i) the person was a Canadian citizen or was employed by Canada in a civilian or military capacity,
  - (ii) the person was a citizen of a state that was engaged in an armed conflict against Canada, or was employed in a civilian or military capacity by such a state,
  - (iii) the victim of the alleged offence was a Canadian citizen, or
  - (iv) the victim of the alleged offence was a citizen of a state that was allied with Canada in an armed conflict; or

(b) after the time the offence is alleged to have been committed, the person is present in Canada.

12 Canadian law does not provide for *ex parte* criminal trials as the accused has the right to be present at his trial.

to be managed and difficult decisions made. Creativity and flexibility will be the key while staying true to the rule of law.

13

(The Lack of) Criteria for the Selection of Crimes Against Humanity Cases: The Case of Argentina

Mirna Goransky and María Luisa Piqué*

13.1. Introduction

The thesis of this chapter is that when there is a decision to prosecute and judge crimes against humanity, there are always some criteria for the selection and prioritization of the cases. Sometimes these criteria are legal, rational, regulated, and follow elaborated strategies. Other times, they obey no rational rules.

In order to demonstrate this thesis, we will briefly explain the trials that took place in Argentina more than 30 years ago and those that were being carried out at the time of the Second Edition of this book. Two preliminary comments are needed: firstly, all the cases concern crimes against humanity; secondly, we cannot present a model of prioritization of cases or selection criteria, simply because such a model does not exist in Argentina for very important cases; rather, what we can offer is a model for the lack of criteria, so we will briefly present the combination of criteria and 'non-criteria' that has ruled the criminal prosecution of crimes against humanity during the last three decades.

---

* **Mirna Goransky** is Fiscal General Adjunta, Procuración General de la Nación Argentina. She formerly served as Prosecutor of the Special Unit to Investigate Human Rights Crimes during the 1976–83 Dictatorship, in charge of the trials against those accused of crimes against humanity in the Navy School of Mechanics and Operation Condor (2006–2012); Prosecutor of the Criminal Policy Unit (1996–1999); and Prosecutor of the first-ever decentralized prosecutor's office in the City of Buenos Aires (1999). She holds a Law Degree from the Law School of the University of Buenos Aires (1976–1982), where she was an Associate Professor teaching courses on criminal law and procedure and constitutional rights (1987–1997). She won the 2013 M.C. Bassiouni Justice Award. **María Luisa Piqué** is Fiscal, Procuración General de la Nación Argentina and a law professor at Universidad de Buenos Aires. She has a law degree from the University of Buenos Aires, and an LL.M. from Georgetown University Law Center. She has served as a member of the team that prosecuted several members of the Argentinean Armed and Security Forces involved in crimes against humanity committed during the 1976–1983 military dictatorship, in the Navy School of Mechanics and Operation Condor – the co-ordinated repressive effort of the Southern Cone military governments. This chapter has not been substantively updated since the Second Edition.

13.2. The Military Dictatorship (1976–1983)

During the military dictatorship that governed the country between 1976 and 1983, the Argentine armed forces implemented a plan for the systematic annihilation of political opponents, a category including not only armed activists promoting ideals antagonistic to those of the military, but also mere dissidents, their friends and their families. This plan included looting, the kidnapping, torture, murder and forced disappearance of a still undetermined number of people:

- more than 340 clandestine centres of detention throughout the country;
- between 20,000 and 30,000 'disappeared' persons;
- thousands of illegally executed people; and
- more than a thousand members of the armed and security forces involved in those crimes.

13.3. Transition to Democracy (1983–1985)

After the breakdown of the military regime and the re-establishment of democracy with the election of President Alfonsín in December 1983, the new administration began a process of controlled truth and justice. The beginning of this process was the creation of the National Commission on the Disappearance of Persons ('CONADEP') which worked as an official truth commission,[1] and by 1985, it had documented the disappearances of at least 8,900 people.

Alfonsín's government had a policy. As explained on numerous occasions by the President himself and his main advisers, they wanted to prosecute the highest authorities of the military repression and those who had gone too far, committing atrocious and abhorrent crimes.[2] To do so, they designed a blueprint for a trial, they passed the laws to implement it and, as a consequence, the trial took place.

13.4. The Trial Against the Juntas

By September 1984, thousands of crimes against humanity had been reported to CONADEP and in military courts, and the registered cases of disappeared persons at that moment increased to 8,900 people. It had to be decided which of

[1] The people appointed to the CONADEP were not professional politicians, but noteworthy personalities from Argentina's cultural, religious and journalistic elites, as well as activists from human rights organizations.

[2] The government's initial strategy was to engage the armed forces themselves in the prosecution of their own officials. However, in case that the Armed Forces Supreme Council failed to move forward with the proceedings, the government sought a reform of the Military Justice Code in order to enable the civil courts to take over these proceedings. When the Armed Forces Supreme Council upheld the orders given by the commanders of each army in order to eliminate 'terrorism', and ruled that they would not be punished because of them, on 26 September 1984, the Federal Court of Appeals of Buenos Aires took over and tried the juntas.

those crimes would be tried and against whom. That decision was finally taken both by the prosecutor and the court.

On the one hand, the prosecutor's office could use discretionary powers and decided to bring charges in almost 700 cases. The choice was made within the cases with the greatest ease of access to evidence. This represented less than 8 per cent of the totality of the documented cases.

The first hearing of the trial was on 22 April 1985. The verdict was rendered on 10 December of that same year. The members of the three military juntas that governed the country during 1976–1983 were in the dock of this historic trial.[3] And 869 persons – victims and relatives of the disappeared – declared as witness in the hearings.

The Court decided that each commander would be held accountable only for the crimes committed by his subordinates, not for every crime reported under his tenure as a junta member.

The trial concluded with two comprehensive and severe convictions, three lesser ones, and four acquittals. The judgment considered that the homicide of 73 people (near 10 per cent of the cases included in the debate and less of 1 per cent of the total of the people registered as disappeared) had been proven. Simultaneously, it left the door open to continue with the prosecution of those who followed in the military hierarchy. This decision was confirmed by the Supreme Court. Up until that point, publicly formulated criteria had been followed and, as a consequence, in less than two years a trial against the top hierarchy had been carried out and a seminal judgment rendered.

13.5. The End of the Human Rights Spring and the Impunity Years (1987–2003)

The casc selection made by the office of the prosecutor and the criteria adopted by the executive branch ruled the trial against the juntas, but were never 'legalized'. That is, there was no legislation that transformed these criteria into law –

---

[3] Jorge Rafael Videla (Commander of the Army, between 1976 and 1978), Emilio Eduardo Massera (Commander of the Navy, between 1976 and 1978) and Orlando Ramón Agosti (Commander of the Air Force, between 1976 and 1978) who belonged to the First Military Junta (1976–1980); Roberto Eduardo Viola (Commander of the Army, between 1978 and 1979), Armando Lambruschini (Commander of the Navy, between 1978 and 1981), Omar Domingo Rubens Graffigna (Commander of the Air Force, between 1978 and 1979) who belonged to the Second Military Junta (1980–1981); and Leopoldo Fortunato Galtieri (Commander of the Army, between 1979 and 1982), Jorge Isaac Anaya (Commander of the Navy, between 1981 and 1982), Basilio Lami Dozo (Commander of the Air Force, between 1979 and 1982) who belonged to the Third Military Junta (1981–1982). The judgment of the 'Junta Trial' is available in the Argentina Collection in the ICC Legal Tools Database (Part 1: https://www.legal-tools.org/doc/83efcc/).

mainly not to confront the demands of human rights organizations, the victims and their relatives and an important sector of the Argentine society, who claimed 'Justice for All'.

But, after the Juntas Trial, the courts responded to the demand of victims and human rights organizations and began to investigate and prosecute far beyond the expectations of the President. By 1987, there were hundreds of members of the armed and security forces who were being accused or were under investigation. After the Juntas Trial was over, an avalanche of complaints began, seeking prosecution of all perpetrators involved in the commission of gross human rights violations, and covering all instances of victimization.

One of the reasons why the strategy of President Alfonsín did not work was that, as more details became known about what had happened during the repression years, it also became apparent that (almost) all the members of the armed forces had been involved, one way or another, in the commission of atrocious crimes.

The armed forces began to exert strong pressure over the executive, trying to stop judicial investigations, and, as a result of that pressure, the well-known 'Full Stop' law was dictated.[4] This law established a purely temporary criterion governing prosecution: any prosecution could only continue against those who were summoned for questioning within 60 days after the law was passed, with the only exception of those suspects who had fled.

This law did not work as an impunity norm. Contrary to the expectations of the government – slow justice and only a handful of members of the military being prosecuted – the law provoked a wave of intense judicial activity aimed at summoning a substantial number of members of the armed and security forces. Two days before the expiration date, around 400 members of the armed and security forces were prosecuted.

That was an example of the different rationale and criteria governing the acts of various branches of the state: the executive, aiming at limiting the prosecutions and trials; and the judges, speeding up the inquiries into the conduct of the most questioned repressors (and not only for good reasons).

The consequence of this judicial activism was that those who were summoned began to refuse to appear before the judges. The senior officers in the military endorsed this attitude. The breaking point came when one of them not only refused to appear, but also incited a unit to rebel, beginning what was known as the 'Rebellion of Easter'.

Facing this surge of investigations and with military pressure to avoid the judicial citations, the government sanctioned the 'Due Obedience' law which

[4] Ley de Punto Final, 24 December 1986, No. 23.492 (https://www.legal-tools.org/doc/d464a5/).

established superior orders as a ground for full exclusion of criminal liability.[5] This law benefited practically all members of the military who had been reported and was a clear imposition of criteria by the executive on the judiciary.

The constitutionality of this law was challenged. However, the Supreme Court validated it in June 1987 with a divided bench.[6] The 'Due Obedience' law – and the Supreme Court's validation – blocked prosecutions and trials regarding crimes against humanity, and the defendants were released.

To make things worse, the first stage of prosecution of these crimes was ultimately demolished by the next President, Mr. Carlos S. Menem, who not only, in 1989, pardoned the few military who had been convicted in the historical trial, but also those senior officers who were not covered by the amnesty laws. By decree, he ordered that any proceedings against persons indicted for human rights violations who had not benefited from the earlier laws be discontinued. This legal shield from prosecution was maintained by the Supreme Court of Justice that guaranteed the laws and the pardons.

13.6. Between 1995 and 2003, a Slow Reopening Began

This paralysis pushed human rights organizations to look for possible loopholes in the legal system. Thus, they started a slow but constant effort to find all the legal opportunities that allowed them to retake the judgments to the perpetrators of these atrocious and aberrant crimes and to force state authorities to keep on investigating the whereabouts of the disappeared.

The process kept growing. Between the end of the 1990s and the first years of the new millennium, the spider web of impunity was broken. The fight for

---

5 Ley de Obediencia Debida, 8 June 1987, No. 23.521 (https://www.legal-tools.org/doc/a4be3b/).

6 The Court acknowledged the legislator's power to establish that certain facts could not be prosecuted and criminalized – not only the authority to create sanctions, but also to erase its effects. It also denied the existence of an acquired right to the simple maintenance of rules. Therefore, according to the Court's majority, the judiciary did not have the power to assess the ability of decisions by the legislator to reach its goals. At the most, the judges said, they could scrutinize the proportionality between the ends and the means, and whether the restriction of individual rights in a particular case was constitutional. Finally, the judges that upheld the law considered that this decision would not leave the crimes unpunished, but change the imputation towards other subjects. Justice Bacqué, on the other hand, in his dissenting opinion, denied the power of Congress to dictate amnesty laws when crimes against humanity were concerned, because of the primacy of international and *jus cogens* law. He also considered that the 'Due Obedience' law affected the division of powers, since only the judiciary can state, on a case-by-case basis, that somebody has acted in due obedience. Thus, the law replaced the independent factual determination of judges with an arbitrary decision of the legislator whose power is to establish rules for future acts. Consequently, Justice Bacqué considered the law unconstitutional. See Supreme Court, *Camps et al.*, Judgment, 22 June 1987 (https://www.legal-tools.org/doc/8ee6e3/).

justice found a new scenario. New proceedings against the repressors for the crimes committed in the years of the dictatorship began in different ways. The first step in this process was known as the 'search of the truth'.[7] Secondly, human rights activists and organizations fostered trials regarding those crimes that were not covered by the amnesty laws. Finally, this process was encouraged by international pressure and claims in favour of the prosecution of crimes against humanity committed within the last military government.

These proceedings contributed valuable data on the circumstances of the disappearance of victims of state terrorism and of the death and place of inhumation of many.[8]

During the late 1980s and the 1990s, Argentina came under strong pressure from abroad. Firstly, in late 1987, the Inter-American Commission on Human Rights ('IACHR') began to receive petitions against Argentina denouncing the legislature's adoption of impunity laws and their enforcement by the judiciary.[9]

Secondly, on 7 October 1998, the IACHR received a petition filed by the mother of a disappeared person, sponsored by several human rights organizations, against the Argentine state, alleging that the Argentine judicial authorities had denied her request to determine what had happened to her daughter, based

[7] The so-called 'Truth Trials' were a result not only of human rights activists and organizations, but also of the confessions made by some mid-level officers who felt scapegoated and left behind by the armed forces they had served. Those officers admitted the commission of atrocities during the illegal repression. These dramatic confessions brought about intense public pressure for the reopening of human rights trials. On the other hand, relatives of victims and human rights attorneys once again demanded information about the whereabouts of the disappeared persons from different courts. The courts acknowledged the petitioners' right of truth. Therefore, new proceedings began, justified by the principle that even though laws may be passed to prevent the prosecutions of those responsible for crimes, judicial investigations may continue in order to find out the truth. Judicial action was limited to investigation and documentation.

[8] Another advance in court investigations involved the discovery that many babies born to mothers in military detention were stolen and put into an illegal adoption ring to be given to couples under false identities. These cases were not covered by the 'Full Stop' and 'Due Obedience' laws. Thus, former officers were prosecuted in 1998 for crimes committed as a result of abducting children and altering their identities in order to enter them into an adoption ring – although they were still protected from prosecution for the murder of their parents.

[9] The IACHR indicated that the 'Full Stop' and 'Due Obedience' laws and presidential decrees on pardons were in conflict with Article XVIII (right to a fair trial) of the American Declaration of the Rights and Duties of Man, 2 May 1948 (https://www.legal-tools.org/doc/7f1088/), with Articles 1, 8 and 25 of the American Convention on Human Rights, 22 November 1969 (https://www.legal-tools.org/doc/1152cf/), and with the duty of Argentina to take the necessary steps to bring to light the events and identify the persons responsible for the human rights violations which occurred during the past military dictatorship (IACHR, *Consuelo et al. v. Argentina*, Decision, 2 October 1992, Case Nos. 10.147, 10.181, 10.240, 10.262, 10.309 and 10.311, Report No. 28/92 (https://www.legal-tools.org/doc/lhwy3gv2/)).

on the right to truth and the right to bereavement (case 12.059 IACHR). On 29 February 2000, the Argentine government signed a friendly settlement in which it accepted and guaranteed the right to the truth and declared that the right involved the exhaustion of all means to obtain information on the whereabouts of the disappeared persons.[10]

Meanwhile, trials took place in other countries, most of them within the region of Western Europe. Countries such as Italy, France, Spain, Sweden and Germany began demanding the extradition of various military personnel to be tried for the disappearances of their citizens during the period of military dictatorship, and also held trials *in absentia* against several officers and commanders (in Italy and France).

Finally, in 2001, in a ruling on the Barrios Altos case in Peru, the Inter-American Court of Human Rights declared that two amnesty laws introduced by the government of Peruvian President Alberto Fujimori in 1995 were incompatible with the American Convention on Human Rights and hence without legal effect.[11] This ruling was very influential, as the Inter-American Court's interpretations of the Convention are binding on the Argentine state.

13.7. Judicial Activism and the End of a Dark Phase for Justice

In a judgment handed down by a federal judge on 6 March 2001, the 'Full Stop' and 'Due Obedience' laws were declared unconstitutional and null and void in a case concerning forced disappearances and torture.[12] Therefore, the prosecution against some officers who had benefited from those laws was reopened. The ruling was confirmed by the National Chamber of Appeals for Criminal and Correctional Matters for Buenos Aires. Eventually, the Supreme Court on 14 June 2005, by a majority of seven to one, confirmed the previous judicial decisions affirming the invalidity and unconstitutionality of the 'Full Stop' and 'Due Obedience' laws as contrary to international norms of human rights – the so-called 'Simón ruling'.[13]

---

[10] In the settlement it was established that the fulfilment of the right to the truth was an obligation of means, not of results, which was valid as long as the results were not achieved, not subject to the statute of limitations.

[11] Inter-American Court of Human Rights, *Barrios Altos vs. Peru*, Judgment, 14 March 2001 (https://www.legal-tools.org/doc/f1439e/).

[12] Criminal and Correctional Federal Court No. 4, *Case of Julio Héctor Simón*, Judgement, 6 March 2001, Case No. 8686/2000 (https://www.legal-tools.org/doc/7d7b10/).

[13] Congress had tried – without success – to foster those trials. Firstly, in March 1998, it repealed the 'Full Stop' and 'Due Obedience' laws. But their repeal was interpreted as not having retrospective effect, and cases of human rights violations committed under the military governments therefore continued to be covered by them. Secondly, on 21 August 2003 Congress passed Law No. 25.779, Nulidad de las leyes de obediencia debida y punto final (https://www.legal-

What followed was the annulment of the impunity laws and the executive pardons. This means that, according to Argentine law, all the crimes committed in that period of time not only can, but must be prosecuted.

13.8. The New Trials (2003–2008)

The result of the endless struggle against impunity was the annulment of the laws, by the Supreme Court first and Congress later. This allowed for the reopening of all pending cases. As of September 2008, there were 1,120 persons involved in crimes against humanity in cases under investigation in Argentine courts:

- around 500 formally accused;
- 32 convicted;
- 2 acquitted;
- 436 in pre-trial detention; and
- 176 passed away.

Of the 1,120 persons, 446 were members of the upper ranks of the armed forces and 180 were from the upper ranks of the security forces. There were about 250 case files opened, but only around 150 were really moving forward. From 2003 up to the Second Edition of this book, there have been ten trials:

- In 2006:

- one trial against one low-ranking policeman (sentenced to 25 years in prison); and
- one trial against a high-ranking policeman (sentenced to life in prison).

- In 2007:

- one trial against a priest who was working with the police forces during the dictatorship (sentenced to life in prison); and
- one trial against seven high-ranking armed forces officials (sentenced to between 22 and 25 years in prison).

- In 2008, a much more active year:

tools.org/doc/94ffd6/), which established that the 'Full Stop' and 'Due Obedience' laws were null and void. This measure also led to some controversy: there was uncertainty as to the validity of this parliamentary decision. Nonetheless, after the annulment of the amnesty laws by Congress in 2003, several major cases against former military leaders were reopened despite uncertainty about their confirmation at the highest judicial level. With its decision in the Simón case, the Supreme Court removed that uncertainty and definitively cleared the path for judicial action (Supreme Court, *Case of Julio Héctor Simón*, Judgment, 14 June 2005, S. 1767. XXXVIII (https://www.legal-tools.org/doc/c624f4/)). For further analysis of these and other aspects of the ruling, see Christine A. E. Bakker, "A Full Stop to Amnesty in Argentina: The Simón Case", in *Journal of International Criminal Justice*, 2005, vol. 3, no. 5, pp. 1106–1120.

- six trials against 26 accused (24 convicted and two acquitted);
- 16 of the convictions were against high-ranking officials;
- one of these trials was against some of the most notorious repressors (but only based on four crimes); and
- two of them had more than 20 victims.

13.9. How Are Judges Selecting Cases That Come to Trial?

Faced by the legal obligation to prosecute, the questions are: Which are the actual investigations that are being carried out? How are cases selected and prioritized? Why have some cases come to trial?

Regrettably, in the majority of cases there are no criteria or regulated decisions for the selection of cases. Cases seem to go faster through the system for at least one of the following 'reasons' (in most of the ten cases judged at the time of the Second Edition, there was a combination of these reasons):

- the activity of the relatives of the victims and their lawyers pushed for the reopening of the case even before the impunity laws were revoked, so these cases were more advanced than others;
- a legal or bureaucratic reason that sometimes allows or pushes for a faster process (such as the fact that the defendant has been in pre-trial detention too long or a public defender missing the deadline to present an appeal); or
- the efforts of individual justice operators who decide to prioritize these cases (apart from any official instruction).

The whims of justice operators are the main reason why many other cases have not yet made it to trial. Compared with other inquisitorial criminal procedure systems, Argentina's is very attached to formalities. Judges, prosecutors and defence counsel have endless possibilities to delay a process. Prosecutors work in an isolated way, with no pro-activity to accelerate the main cases.

There are other problems that are not strictly related with the selection criteria but contribute to making this process even less efficient. There are very few courts judging these cases, only one in the capital city of Buenos Aires:

- during 2007, there was only one trial, which did not reach a verdict (because the defendant committed suicide/was killed in prison);
- in 2008, there were three trials but no major cases.

There is no centralized information system about these cases:[14]

- each court and prosecutor have to collect its own data;
- there is considerable duplication of work.

[14] We have used the ICC Case Matrix provided by the International Criminal Court and that has proved to be very helpful, but that is primarily a tool for individual cases.

13.10. The Mechanics School of the Navy (ESMA) Case

In our particular case, at the time of the Second Edition of this book we were appointed to prosecute crimes that took place in one of the most emblematic clandestine centres of detention of the city of Buenos Aires, the Mechanics School of the Navy ('ESMA'). The ESMA held thousands of political prisoners from 1976 to 1983:

- some of them remained in cruel detention;
- the overwhelming majority disappeared in the 'flights of death' (that means they were drugged and dumped into the River Plate from the air);
- a few survived this nightmare and many of them have been declaring about these atrocities for more than 30 years in endless judicial processes;
- the defendants in pre-trial imprisonment or house arrest are around 50 members of the navy and a few members of the security forces.

The judge in charge of the prosecution decided to split cases that should have been investigated together (there are cases that took place in the same clandestine centre of detention and they have an important number of victims and perpetrators in common). Secondly, he investigated the crimes committed in the ESMA separating them by year. This case was reopened in 2003, investigating facts which occurred in 1976, and five years later it was working on crimes that happened in 1977. Additionally, the judge separated different events occurring in the ESMA with reference to the 'complexity of the case'. For example, he decided to investigate in a separate process the murder and disappearance of a famous journalist, Rodolfo Walsh, or the kidnapping of a group of people in a church.

The problem is that all these cases share a great number of witnesses and victims as well as defendants. But each case advances at a different rhythm. No one can tell the reason why one case is brought to trial before another.

The result of all these decisions was that the first trial for crimes committed in the ESMA – against a low-ranking member of the security forces for his participation in numerous kidnappings, tortures, homicides, disappearances and thefts of babies – only involved charges for four cases of kidnapping and torture. Forty years after extremely serious crimes were committed by the navy, one single person was brought to trial. He was not even a member of the navy. And he was going to be judged only for a very small number of the crimes that he was involved in.[15]

[15] This case made it to trial because an acting defence counsel did not oppose the opening of the trial, probably due to an excessive workload.

The defendant was found dead four days before the verdict was to be read out. The autopsy found cyanide in his blood.

Many survivors and witnesses who will have to testify against other defendants in different trials, testified in this trial.

There are other examples. Out of all the hideous crimes that were committed in the ESMA, one case was about the seizure of an apartment and the robbery of a car and a bookcase. A woman was kidnapped, raped, tortured and kept under cruel conditions for months. And the first process in which she had to testify as a victim was about the robbery of her bookcase. The parents and their daughter disappeared, and the first trial was about the robbery of a car.

13.11. Concluding Remarks

The absence of legal regulation or criteria to select and prioritize cases makes decisions in some of Argentina's trials on when, how, why, by whom and who to prosecute depend mostly on (i) the dedication (or the lack thereof) of the justice operators in question; (ii) the greater or lesser attachment they have to empty formalities; and (iii) the initiative of the victims and their lawyers (in a sort of privatization of the decision of which cases are investigated first).

During the so-called 'spring of human rights', after the re-establishment of democracy, a major trial against the main accused behind the state terrorism apparatus was carried out in less than two years. The selection criteria defined by the executive were problematic, in that it was decided not to go beyond these high-ranking officials, but they made sense in terms of prioritization. Since 2003, there have been no prioritization criteria, and the result is small trials against a reduced number of defendants accused of a handful of crimes. Witnesses are forced to testify several times, with the associated emotional cost. Pre-trial detention is unduly prolonged and justice administration resources are wasted.

Argentina may be an example of what Bentham calls the 'madness of the erudition'. Justice administrators follow unreasonable procedural formalities, atomizing the trials, diluting the magnitude of the crimes.

However, there are important lessons to be learned from the Argentine experience on transitional justice – not only from the partial and incomplete attempts immediately after democracy was re-established, but also from those taking place several decades later, albeit in a slow and inefficient manner.

Firstly, political will is not enough to see these processes through. Without strategy and planning on how to pursue these trials – and without a serious decision-making process to establish the criteria for the selection of cases – even the best of intentions will end up buried in papers and files. Moreover, even if the proceedings moved forward, they cannot satisfy the victims' and society's legitimate expectations of learning the truth about human rights violations. Isolated from context, only particular and specific crimes are usually tried, while thousands of other crimes against humanity will most likely remain unpunished.

Secondly, the Argentine experience – in particular that of Mr. Alfonsín's government – suggests that case selection criteria cannot be imposed by the political power. On the contrary, the satisfaction of society's expectations of truth and justice is more likely to be reached through active consultation with, and participation by, victims' groups and the public in the determination of the criteria.

Finally, our experience also suggests that demands for justice and truth about past human rights violations from victims, human rights activists and society cannot be minimized. From 1983 onwards, several governments underestimated the moral legitimacy of victims to become leaders of a broader social movement that pursued justice as a social good. They did not understand that the victims, their lawyers and human rights organizations would continue their endless struggle until they saw justice done and that, eventually, society would back that demand.

14

Problematic Selection and Lack of Clear Prioritization: Early Justice and Peace Experience in Colombia

María Paula Saffon*

This chapter was written in 2008, when *Justicia y Paz* processes were only beginning and no signs of case prioritization existed in Colombia. Its publication in the first two editions of the book – together with the Spanish publication in 2011 of what appears as Chapter 5 in the present edition – amounted to an unequivocal argument for prioritization criteria. The situation in Colombia radically changed after 2012, when a Law was issued ordering case prioritization and investigations grounded on macro-criminality patterns (Law 1592 of 2012).[1] Chapter 15 discusses that Law and developments after 2012.

At the time of writing for the Second Edition of this book, the Colombian experience unfortunately offered an example of the dangers of ignoring the importance of the existence and the effective implementation of criteria for the selection and prioritization of atrocious crimes.[2] Indeed, the use of problematic selection criteria and the lack of clear prioritization criteria for the prosecution

* **María Paula Saffon** is Assistant Professor at the Torcuato Di Tella University School of Law and a Research Associate at the Colombian Center for the Study of Law, Justice and Society (DeJuSticia). She received her Ph.D. in Political Science from Columbia University in New York, and a Bachelor's degree (*Magna Cum Laude*) in law and an LL.M. degree from Universidad de Los Andes. She was a post-doctoral fellow in the Department of Political Science at Princeton University between 2015 and 2017. This chapter has not been substantively updated since the Second Edition.

1 Law 1592 of 2012, 3 December 2012 (https://www.legal-tools.org/doc/0ohmir07/).

2 Two terminology clarifications seem important. First, for the purposes of this chapter, I will rely on (without discussing) the distinction between selection and prioritization of cases offered by Morten Bergsmo in the introductory presentation of the Forum for International Criminal and Humanitarian Law's seminar on 26 September 2008 on the basis of which this publication was conceptualized. According to that distinction, selection may imply de-selection of crimes, whereas prioritization may not. Therefore, while the former may lead to the non-investigation or non-prosecution of crimes, the latter refers to the order in which cases are investigated or prosecuted. Second, I use the expression 'atrocious crimes' as a short form for 'serious violations of international human rights law' and 'violations of international humanitarian law', which are the notions used by the Colombian legislation.

of crimes committed during the armed conflict risk bringing about impunity under the appearance of the application of justice. However, this disquieting scenario is not irreversible: the risk of impunity may be mitigated, if appropriate action is taken towards the discussion and enforcement of clear, adequately justified, and publicly discussed criteria for the prioritization of atrocious crimes.

In this chapter, I attempt to make a first approach to these issues. In Section 14.1., I offer a very brief account of the Colombian armed conflict, in order to highlight the complexity of the criminal cases under discussion. In Section 14.2., I describe the legal framework that was implemented in the country by the time of the Second Edition to face the massive demobilization of paramilitary groups. In particular, I show that this framework operated as a very problematic mechanism of selection of the crimes to prosecute. In Section 14.3., I summarize the main outcomes of the first years of application of the framework in question, and argue that they are in part the product of the absence of clear and transparent criteria for the prioritization of cases. In Section 14.4., I insist on the importance of establishing appropriate criteria for the prioritization of cases under investigation, and identify some elements of the criminal processes under analysis that may offer the grounds for moving forward in that direction.

14.1. The Colombian Armed Conflict and the Complexities of Criminal Cases[3]

Several specific traits of the Colombian armed conflict make the investigation and prosecution of the crimes therein committed particularly complex. First, along with the Palestinian–Israel and the India–Pakistan conflicts, the Colombian has been one of the longest armed conflicts in the world.[4]

---

[3] This section of the chapter draws extensively from María Paula Saffon and Rodrigo Uprimny, "Uses and Abuses of Transitional Justice in Colombia", in Morten Bergsmo and Pablo Kalmanovitz (eds.), *Law in Peace Negotiations*, Second Edition, Torkel Opsahl Academic EPublisher ('TOAEP'), Oslo, 2010 (https://www.toaep.org/ps-pdf/5-bergsmo-kalmanovitz-second).

[4] See Colombian National Commission for Reparations and Reconciliation ('CNRR'), *Hoja de Ruta* [*Road Map*], 2006. The most cautious analysts point at 1964 as the contemporary origin of the Colombian conflict, since this was the year in which the Colombian Revolutionary Armed Forces ('FARC') – the strongest guerrilla group in the country at the time of writing – took up arms. See CNRR, *Fundamentos Filosóficos y Operativos. Definiciones estratégicas de la Comisión Nacional de Reparación y Reconciliación* [*Philosophical and Operational Foundations. Strategic Definitions of the National Commission for Reparations and Reconciliation*], 2006. However, many other analysts point at the period of violence between the liberal and conservative political parties in the 1940s as the origin of the conflict as we know it nowadays. See Gonzalo Sánchez and Ricardo Peñaranda, *Pasado y presente de la violencia en Colombia* [*Past and present of violence in Colombia*], CEREC, Bogota, 1991. The length and perpetuation of the conflict can be partially explained by the strong links between illegal armed groups and drug trafficking, as the latter constitutes an almost unlimited source of war financing. For the relationship between conflict and drug trafficking in Colombia, see Andrés López, 2006,

Second, the conflict includes various actors: subversive guerrilla groups,[5] the State[6] and right-wing paramilitary groups,[7] all of whom have committed atrocities against the civilian population on a significant scale.

"Narcotráfico, ilegalidad y conflicto en Colombia" ["Drug-traffic, illegality and conflict in Colombia"], in *ibid.*

5 At the time of writing, only two subversive guerrilla groups confronting the Colombian State's authority were still active: the Army of National Liberation (ELN), which was at the first stages of a peace negotiation with the government with still uncertain results, and, until the 2016 Peace Accord, the FARC, which had not shown any serious desire of holding peace negotiations with the government and continued the commission of atrocities against the civilian population. However, several other subversive guerrilla groups have confronted the State in previous times, such as the April 19 Movement ('M-19'), the Popular Liberation Army ('EPL'), the indigenous guerrilla group Quintín Lame, the Workers' Revolutionary Party ('PRT'), and the Current of Socialist Renewal ('CRS'). The latter groups received amnesties in the 1990s. At varying magnitudes, all these groups have committed atrocities against the civilian population, particularly homicides and kidnappings.

6 It is a notorious fact that the State, through its armed forces, participated in the armed conflict combating guerrilla groups and, subsequently, paramilitary groups. Paradoxically, however, the government in power at the time of writing denied the existence of an armed conflict in Colombia and instead referred to a terrorist threat, apparently with the objective of impeding the international political recognition of guerrilla groups as organized armed groups. See Rodrigo Uprimny, "¿Existe o no conflicto armado en Colombia?" ["Is there or is there not an armed conflict in Colombia?"], in Helena Gardeazábal Garzón (ed.); *Más Allá del Embrujo: Tercer año de gobierno de Álvaro Uribe Vélez*?" [*Beyond Enchantment: Third Year of Alvaro Uribe Vélez's Government*], Plataforma Colombiana Democracia, Derechos Humanos y Desarrollo, Bogota, 2005. It has also been judicially proven (both at the national and the international levels) that agents of the Colombian State have been responsible for international human rights and humanitarian law violations either by commission or omission. See, for instance, the five cases that have been decided by the Inter-American Court of Human Rights against Colombia, regarding atrocities committed by paramilitaries with the collaboration or omission of agents of the public force. Inter-American Court of Human Rights, *Case of the massacre of 19 merchants v. Colombia*, Judgment, 5 July 2004, series C No. 109 (https://www.legal-tools.org/doc/f93718/); *Case of the massacre of Mapiripán v. Colombia*, Judgment, 15 September 2005, series C No. 134 (https://www.legal-tools.org/doc/5830c0/); *Case of the massacre of Pueblo Bello*, Judgment, 31 January 2006, series C No. 140 (https://www.legal-tools.org/doc/cb12ef/); *Case of the massacres of Ituango v. Colombia*, Judgment, 1 July 2006, series C No. 148 (https://www.legal-tools.org/doc/1kg8g6/); *Case of the massacre of La Rochela v. Colombia*, Judgment, 11 May 2007, series C No. 163 (https://www.legal-tools.org/doc/0c7f35/).

7 In the 1980s, right-wing paramilitary groups appeared with the justification of the need to combat guerrilla groups in a stronger way. However, since the very beginning, paramilitaries committed heinous crimes against civilians, including massacres and forced disappearances. There have been more than 30 paramilitary groups in the country. See Office of the High Commissioner for Peace, "Peace Process with the Self-Defences" (available on its web site). Although paramilitary groups are not organized hierarchically and do not have a united or centralized mandate, in 1997 most of them joined to create the Colombian Confederation of United Self-Defences (AUC). The leaders of most of the groups included in that Confederation participated

Third, the conflict has produced approximately three million victims of internal forced displacement,[8] and more than 100,000 victims of other atrocious crimes, including massacres, forced disappearances, kidnappings, sexual violence, torture and arbitrary detentions, among others.[9] In general, these victims belonged to the least favourable sectors of society before the commission of atrocities, and most are under conditions of severe deprivation.[10]

Fourth, in the subsequent developments of the conflict until the time of the Second Edition, prior to the 2016 Peace Accord, there were no general peace agreements, but rather partial negotiations between the State and some armed groups.[11] Therefore, these negotiations have taken place in the middle of conflict, and have not brought about a real or complete transition from war to peace.

---

in the peace negotiations with the government in 2002, and their members demobilized the following years. However, quite a few of those groups refused demobilizing and took up arms again. Moreover, since the demobilizations, new paramilitary groups – commonly known as 'emergent bands' or 'black eagles' – have been created, composed both of demobilized and non-demobilized paramilitaries.

8 In 2009, official sources mentioned a little more than two million forcedly displaced persons in the country. See Acción Social, "Estadísticas de la población desplazada" ["Statistics of displaced population"], 2009. This, however, only took into account the number of persons who were officially registered in the government's 'Displaced Population Only Register' and, thus, excluded displaced people who were unable to register. That is why other sources, such as the United Nations High Commissioner for Refugees ('UNHCR'), mentioned around three million forcedly displaced people. See UNHCR, "Global Trends Refugees, Asylum-seekers, Returnees, Internally Displaced and Stateless Persons", June 2007.

9 For some preliminary calculations of the total number of victims in Colombia and the cost of their reparations, see Camillo González, "Prólogo" ["Prologue"], in Diego Otero Prada (ed.), *Las cifras del conflicto* [*The numbers of the conflict*], INDEPAZ, Bogotá, 2007; Mark Richards, *Quantification of the Financial Resources Required to Repair Victims of the Colombian Conflict in Accordance With the Justice and Peace Law*, CERAC, Bogotá, 2007.

10 This is so, perhaps with the exception of some victims of extortion kidnapping. In this, the Colombian situation is similar to that of Guatemala (where the majority of victims belonged to Mayan ethnic groups) and Peru (where the majority of victims were rural), and very different to that of Argentina and Chile (where victims were mostly from the middle classes).

11 There were general peace agreements and consequent amnesties during the period of violence between the liberal and conservative political parties between the 1940s and 1960s. See Colectivo de Abogados José Alvear Restrepo, *¿Terrorismo o Rebelión? Propuestas de regulación del conflicto armado* [*Terrorism or Rebellion? Proposals for the Regulation of the Armed Conflict*], Bogotá, 2001; Gonzalo Sánchez and Donny Meertens, *Bandits, Peasants, and Politics: The Case of "La Violencia" in Colombia*, University of Texas Press, Austin, 2001. However, in the subsequent developments of the conflict, there have only been partial peace negotiations with some factions of the conflict, notably with the M-19, EPL, Quintín Lame, PRT and CRS guerrilla groups during the 1990s, with paramilitary groups in 2002, and with the FARC leading to the 2016 Peace Accord. See Iván Cepeda, "Pacto de lealtades e impunidad" ["Loyalty Pacts and Impunity"], 23 December 2003; Colectivo de Abogados José Alvear Restrepo, *idem*. Many

Fifth, the 2002 negotiations between the Colombian government and most paramilitary groups ascribed to the Colombian Confederation of United Self-Defences, resulted in the demobilization of 35 paramilitary groups and over 30,000 individuals belonging to them.[12] These were the first negotiations that led to the development of a special legal framework intended to investigate and prosecute the crimes perpetrated by demobilized individuals.[13] However, for various reasons, the nature of paramilitary groups imposes difficult challenges for the investigation and prosecution of their crimes.

On the one hand, paramilitary groups are pro-systemic, not anti-systemic actors.[14] They never intend to overthrow the government or to defeat the army, but rather to support their struggle against guerrilla groups through illegal means. Moreover, for many years the State did not persecute them, and even benefited from their support.[15] On the other hand, paramilitary groups have created strong economic and political power structures. In fact, since their origins, they have held strong ties with economic elites and with drug lords, which have allowed them to amass substantive fortunes and to accumulate great extensions of land.[16]

---

have argued that negotiations with paramilitary groups should not be considered a peace agreement, due to the fact that these groups never confronted or even opposed the government. On this, see Cepeda, *idem*.

[12] According to the Office of the High Commissioner for Peace, at the time of the Second Edition, the number of demobilized paramilitaries was 31,671, see Office of the High Commissioner for Peace, *supra* note 7.

[13] Indeed, the peace agreements with guerrilla groups in the 1990s brought about individual pardons or the ceasing of criminal procedures for the members of these groups, but excluded from these benefits those individuals who had committed certain atrocious crimes and crimes without a political intention. However, no special criminal procedures were established for the purpose of prosecuting the excluded individuals, who were therefore submitted to the ordinary criminal laws. See Cepeda, 2003, and Colectivo de Abogados José Alvear Restrepo, 2001, *supra* note 11.

[14] For this distinction, see Leopoldo Múnera, "Proceso de paz con actores armados ilegales y parasistémicos (los paramilitares y las políticas de reconciliación en Colombia)" ["Peace Process With Illegal and Para-Systemic Armed Actors (Paramilitaries and Reconciliation Policies in Colombia)"], in *Revista Pensamiento Jurídico*, 2006, no. 17.

[15] For an analysis of the Colombian legal framework, on the basis of which many paramilitary groups were created, see the five cases that have been decided by the Inter-American Court of Human Rights against the Colombian State, regarding atrocities committed by paramilitaries with the collaboration or omission of agents of the public force, *supra* note 6.

[16] See Mauricio Romero, *Paramilitares y autodefensas, 1982–2003* [*Paramilitaries and Self-Defences, 1982–2003*], IEPRI-Planeta, Bogota, 2003; Gustavo Duncan, *Los señores de la guerra: de paramilitares, mafiosos y autodefensas en Colombia* [*The Warlords: Of Paramilitaries, Mafia and Self-Defences*], Planeta, Bogota, 2006; María Paula Saffon, "Poder paramilitar y debilidad institucional. El paramilitarismo en Colombia: un caso complejo de incumplimiento de normas" ["Paramilitary Power and Institutional Weakness. Paramilitarism in Colombia: A Complex Case of Disobedience to Law"], M.A. thesis, Los Andes University, Bogota, 2006.

Furthermore, paramilitary groups have established strong relations of collaboration and complicity with State agents, who have not only included members of the public force,[17] but also agents of intelligence, local politicians, and national Congressmen.[18] Finally, paramilitary groups have not organized hierarchically and do not have a united or centralized mandate, but rather function as semi-autonomous cells belonging to a nodal structure.[19]

The aforementioned characteristics of the Colombian situation make the task of criminally investigating and prosecuting the crimes therein committed particularly difficult. Indeed, it is an attempt to carry out, in the middle of an armed conflict, the investigation and prosecution of a myriad of crimes, many of them of a systematic nature, committed over a quite long period of time by individuals belonging to different groups with complex political, economic and military structures.

14.2. The Legal Framework of the Demobilization Process: Selection as an Impunity Strategy?

As was mentioned in the previous section, negotiations between the Colombian government and paramilitary groups in 2002 resulted in the formulation of a special legal framework aimed at dealing with atrocities committed by members of armed groups who decide to demobilize either individually or collectively.[20] This legal framework constituted an innovation in the Colombian context for at least two reasons. On the one hand, it moved away from the historic tendency

[17] On this, see also the five cases decided by the Inter-American Court of Human Rights about the State's responsibility in relation to paramilitary crimes, *supra* note 6.

[18] See Duncan, 2006, and Saffon, 2006, *supra* note 16. At the time of the Second Edition, criminal investigations for links with paramilitaries had been opened against 65 Congressmen, representing 23 per cent of the total number of members of the legislative. See "Cifras del escándalo de la parapolítica dejan al descubierto su dimension" ["Numbers of the Parapolitics Scandal Expose Its Dimension"], *El Tiempo*, 26 April 2008.

[19] On this, see Manuel A. Alonso Espinal, Jorge Giraldo Ramírez and Diego Jorge Sierra, "Medellín: El complejo camino de la competencia armada" ["Medellin: The Complex Way of Armed Competition"], in *Diálogo Mayor: Memoria colectiva, reparación, justicia y democracia: el conflicto colombiano y la paz a la luz de experiencias internacionales* [*Major Dialogue: Collective Memory, Reparations, Justice and Democracy: The Colombian Conflict and Peace in Light of International Experiences*], Universidad del Rosario, Bogota, 2005.

[20] This legal framework is composed by Law 782 of 2002, 23 December 2002 (https://www.legal-tools.org/doc/83b644/) and Law 975 of 2005, 25 July 2005 (https://www.legal-tools.org/doc/a4e2c0/), their governmental decrees, and the rulings in which the Constitutional Court has analysed the constitutionality of such laws. Although the laws were formulated as a response to the negotiations with paramilitary groups, they are also applicable to members of guerrilla groups who decide to demobilize. However, they exclude State agents, who have to be investigated and prosecuted through pre-existing criminal laws that regulate the prosecution of public servants (Law 975 of 2005, Article 2).

to confer amnesties or individual pardons to the actors of conflict[21] because it established that demobilized individuals could receive legal pardons unless they have committed atrocious crimes.[22] On the other hand, instead of leaving the investigation and prosecution of atrocious conduct to the ordinary functioning of the criminal justice system,[23] it created a special criminal procedure for the investigation, prosecution and judgment of atrocious crimes committed by demobilized individuals, as well as special prosecutorial and judicial units in charge of implementing it.

The main objective of the special criminal procedure, commonly known as the 'justice and peace procedure', is to grant a substantial reduction of the criminal sentence (a minimum of five and a maximum of eight years, regardless of the quantity and gravity of the crimes committed) to those demobilized individuals who cease their illegal activities, fully and trustworthily confess the crimes in which they participated, and give in assets for the reparation of their victims.[24]

According to the law, in order to verify the satisfaction of these conditions, and particularly the one referred to confessions, the Peace and Law Unit of the General Prosecutor's Office must carry out public hearings in which each demobilized individual delivers a confession.[25] Subsequent to each public hearing, the Unit must undertake an investigation aimed at determining the veracity of the confession, after the conclusion of which it formulates an indictment.[26] If the Unit establishes that the concerned individual lied or omitted confessing crimes she committed, the indictment only covers the confessed crimes, and the rest must be prosecuted and judged in the ordinary criminal process, thereby losing the benefits of the sentence reduction.[27]

After the indictment, the process would pass to the judgment stage, the competence of which falls on the justices of the Superior Tribunals of Justice

---

21 See *supra* note 11. As stated in note 13 above, this historic tradition started to break in the amnesty processes carried out in the 1990s in relation with some guerrilla groups, which imposed certain conditions to the concession of pardons and the ceasing of criminal procedures.

22 Literally, the law refers to "atrocious acts of ferocity or barbarianism, terrorism, kidnapping, genocide, non-combat homicide or homicide against victims in a state of defencelessness", Law 782 of 2002, Article 5, see *supra* note 20.

23 As did the legal framework that regulated the negotiation processes carried out in the 1990s, by contemplating the possibility of prosecution of demobilized individuals who had committed certain atrocious crimes, but not instituting special criminal laws for that purpose.

24 Law 975 of 2005, Article 11, see *supra* note 20.

25 *Ibid.*, Article 17. The Peace and Law Unit of the General Prosecutor's Office was created by Article 34.

26 *Ibid.*, Articles 17 and 18.

27 Constitutional Court, Judgment, 18 May 2005, No. C-370/06 (https://www.legal-tools.org/doc/ebdde4/).

and Peace, also specifically created by this framework.[28] This stage starts with a hearing of conciliation in which the demobilized individual and her victims try to reach an agreement regarding the reparations owed to the latter.[29] Subsequently, the competent justice issues the criminal sentence, which also contains either the reparations agreement – if it was reached – or an order to repair based on the justice's discretion.[30] The sentence may be appealed before the Criminal Chamber of the Supreme Court of Justice.[31]

Although this legal framework constituted an important advancement towards the accountability of perpetrators of atrocities, it was implemented in such a way to potentially lead to significant levels of impunity. This is so because the government issued a decree which offered a lax interpretation of the legal disposition according to which demobilized individuals who have committed atrocities cannot receive legal pardons. Such interpretation contemplated that only those demobilized individuals who had been convicted or who were being prosecuted for the commission of atrocious crimes in 2003 would be excluded from those legal pardons.[32] Even though this interpretation seemed reasonable at first sight, in a country in which the impunity rate was exceptionally high,[33] it risked exonerating many perpetrators of atrocities. Indeed, many of the demobilized paramilitaries who received legal pardons could have participated in the commission of atrocities, but might not have had processes opened against them at the moment in which legal pardons were conceded. To a great extent, this explains why more than 90 per cent (28,544) of the demobilized paramilitaries in 2008 ended up benefiting from such pardons.[34]

The government's interpretation can be understood as a measure of selection of atrocious crimes because it excluded certain individuals who might be responsible for the commission of such crimes from criminal investigation and prosecution. It is true that the pardoned individuals are not entirely armoured against prosecution; they could eventually be prosecuted if a criminal investigation proved their participation in an atrocious crime. However, it seems highly

[28] Law 975 of 2005, Article 68, see *supra* note 20.

[29] *Ibid.*, Article 23.

[30] *Ibid.*, Article 24.

[31] *Ibid.*, Article 26.

[32] Decree 128 of 2003, 22 January 2003, Article 21 (https://www.legal-tools.org/doc/47eb94/).

[33] For the different ways in which such rate has been calculated, see Elvira María Restrepo and Mariana Martínez Cuéllar, "Impunidad penal: mitos y realidades" [Criminal Impunity: Myths and Realities], in *Documentos Cede*, no. 24, June 2004.

[34] See the 2008 report elaborated by a group of human rights organizations on the Colombian State's compliance with human rights standards: "Informe para el Examen Periódico Universal de Colombia" [Report for the Periodic Universal Exam of Colombia], July 2008.

unlikely that this will happen, given that, at the time of the Second Edition, the Prosecutor's Office was already overloaded with the task of investigating the more than 3,000 demobilized paramilitaries who had entered the peace and law procedure, likely without the time and resources necessary to investigate the other more than 28,000 perpetrated atrocities.

For those reasons, this selection measure has been criticized as a veiled amnesty, which brought about impunity under the appearance of accountability.[35] Apart from this very disturbing feature, the measure was also problematic because it was never presented as a selection measure, and therefore it was never justified nor publicly discussed, in spite of the significance of its impact.

14.3. The Development of the Criminal Processes: Arbitrary Prioritization?

Despite the problematic selection measure referred to in the previous section, a substantial number of demobilized paramilitaries were considered eligible by the government to apply for the criminal benefits of the justice and peace procedure.

The workload that more than 3,000 suspects imposed on the Prosecutor's Office was not negligible, especially since the law required that each render a full confession in an individual hearing, and that the Prosecutor's Office develop an investigation to verify the confessed crimes and to determine whether the individual committed other non-confessed crimes.

To manage this workload, the Peace and Law Unit of the General Prosecutor's Office had, at the time of the Second Edition, three sub-units and 22 prosecutors. Each prosecutor was in charge of one or two of the 35 demobilized paramilitary groups, which means that she had to undertake the public hearings, investigation and prosecution of all the members of the group(s) who entered the justice and peace procedure.[36]

Two years after the beginning of the justice and peace procedures, 1,431 confession hearings were initiated, 1,142 were concluded and 289 were on course.[37] However, the vast majority of the concluded hearings (941 by December 2007) was not the result of an efficient management of the cases, but is rather

---

[35] *Ibid.* See also Gustavo Gallón, "La CNRR: ¿Dr. Jekyll o Mr. Hyde?" [The CNRR: Dr. Jekyll or Mr. Hyde?], in Guillermo Hoyos Vàsquez (ed.), *Las víctimas frente a la búsqueda de la verdad y la reparación en Colombia* [*Victims in Search for Truth and Reparations in Colombia*], Pontificia Universidad Javeriana, Bogota, 2007.

[36] This information was supplied by Mr. Luis González, the Chief of the Justice and Peace Unit, in a written response to an information petition that I presented, on 28 July 2008.

[37] General Prosecutor's Office, "Informe de gestión despacho del Fiscal General de la Nación" [Management Report of the Office of the Nation's General Prosecutor], 2008.

explained by the fact that the demobilized individuals did not ratify their decision to have recourse to the law.[38]

Not a single sentence had been issued at the time of the Second Edition. The most advanced process, against alias 'El Loro' ('The Parrot'), was at the stage of the reparations hearing. However, it was not in any way an exemplary case: at an advanced stage of the process, it had to be annulled due to procedural irregularities. Moreover, in spite of being a case against a paramilitary commander who had an important degree of responsibility, he was only indicted for three crimes.[39]

At least in part, this discouraging situation was the result of the absence of clear and adequate criteria for the prioritization of cases to prosecute. Indeed, the fact that many processes were initiated but very few advanced efficiently or produced substantive results shows that such criteria were not an important part of the Prosecutor's Office strategy.

This is also confirmed by the fact that it was not possible to identify any clear prioritization criteria in the practice of the Prosecutor's Office as examined by this chapter. Thus, according to the chief of the Justice and Peace Unit of the Prosecutor's Office in 2008, the Unit received 2,695 cases simultaneously in 2006,[40] which means that it could not have applied a 'first-come, first-served' criterion. Moreover, the chief of the Unit also recognized that confession hearings of commanders and other demobilized individuals have been carried out simultaneously,[41] which means that a seniority criterion was not used either. On the other hand, it is possible to conclude that the gravity of crimes has not been a criterion for the prioritization of cases, given that, as mentioned above, prosecutors developed the cases with a focus on the individuals who pertained to a demobilized group, and therefore were investigating and prosecuting all sorts of crimes committed by those individuals at the same time.[42] Finally, it can also be concluded that cases were not prioritized on the grounds of their readiness for being prosecuted either; otherwise, the most advanced case at the time of writing would not have been against 'El Loro', which apparently lacked the necessary evidence to indict the paramilitary leader for more than three crimes.[43]

---

[38] See "Report for the Periodic Universal Exam of Colombia", July 2008, *supra* note 34.

[39] Colombian Commission of Jurists, *Colombia: El Espejismo de la justicia y la paz* [*The Mirage of Justice and Peace*], Chapter 5, Colombian Commission of Jurists, Bogota, 2007.

[40] Information supplied by Mr. Luis González, see *supra* note 36.

[41] *Ibid.*

[42] *Ibid.*

[43] Colombian Commission of Jurists, 2007, see *supra* note 39.

Therefore, the outcomes of the justice and peace procedures in the examined time-period seem to be the product of the lack of clear criteria for the prioritization of cases, perhaps added to the political pressure to produce results, regardless of their quality and effective impact. These results may be counterproductive, as they may highlight the inefficiency of the procedures, worsen the backlog of cases, and be interpreted as the product of arbitrary and non-transparent criteria, all of which may discredit the work of the Prosecutor's Office.

14.4. The Importance of Clear, Adequately Justified, and Publicly Discussed Prioritization Criteria

The use of problematic criteria for the selection of crimes and the lack of clear criteria for the prioritization of crimes have generated notorious risks in Colombia. Nevertheless, this does not create an irreversible situation, at least with regards to the issue of prioritization. In effect, the justice and peace procedures were undertaken only a few years prior to the examined period, and still had a lengthy and thorny way ahead. In such situations, it is important to take action towards the selection and enforcement of clear, adequately justified, and publicly discussed criteria for the prioritization of atrocious crimes.

Despite the need to initiate this discussion in Colombia, at the time of the Second Edition no one seemed willing to take the first step. The Prosecutor's Office seemed more interested in producing any type of results than in defining a consistent strategy for producing the best and most efficient results possible. Moreover, a reason could be fear of the strong criticisms that would probably confront the Office if it were to raise the issue of criteria only after several years, as this could be interpreted as an admission of not having used clear or adequate criteria up to that point. On the other hand, human rights and victims' organizations seemed reluctant to support the use of prioritization criteria, probably out of fear that they would have ended up being used as selection criteria, by indefinitely delaying the resolution of certain cases.

Although the former concern is relevant, it is worth noting that the enforcement of clear prioritization criteria has the potential to diminish, instead of accruing the risk of indefinite delays of cases. In fact, if prioritization criteria are adopted, their selection would necessarily have to be made in a public and transparent way, and would thus allow the participation of all interested parties. Furthermore, such selection would require a solid justification, which, in case it is inadequate or insufficient, could be openly criticized and challenged. Finally, the existence of enforceable criteria would allow interested parties to exercise permanent control of their implementation and to challenge the non-application or the inadequate application of the chosen criteria. This would surely reduce the discretion of prosecutors and enhance their accountability.

At the time of the Second Edition, each prosecutor of the Justice and Peace Unit was in charge of investigating and prosecuting the crimes committed by the members of one (or in some cases two) specific paramilitary group(s). In order to accomplish this task, they undertook the strategy of investigating and widely documenting the ways in which each paramilitary group, as a whole, acted in its regions of influence, before initiating the criminal procedures. As a result, they accumulated important information about the context of operation of such groups, their internal structures, their logics of operation, and the patterns of crimes they committed, among other. The information was accumulated with the aims of contributing to the elucidation of the truth and adequately planning the subsequent criminal investigations.

Such information could also be used to identify the most adequate criteria for the prioritization of cases. It may, for example, clarify the command structures of each group, allowing for prioritization of cases based on the criterion of seniority. Or it may provide relevant information about the crime patterns of each group, allowing for the prioritization of paradigmatic cases based on different types of crimes.

During the first years of justice and peace practice, it seemed clear that the subject of prioritization criteria should be discussed in greater detail by the Colombian community. This chapter was written to prompt such discussion.

15

Selection and Prioritization in Colombia With Emphasis on the Attorney General's Office and the Legal Framework for Peace

Alejandro Aponte Cardona*

15.1. Introduction

In July 2014, the Attorney General's Office and a major journal in Colombia organized a forum on forms of attribution of international crimes in Bogotá, and the first Prosecutor of the International Criminal Court, Luis Moreno Ocampo, and former President of the Inter-American Court of Human Rights, Diego Garcia Sayan, were invited. Taking into account the ongoing transitional process in the country, the two guests agreed that the Colombian case was so challenging that there were no legislative, jurisprudential or political guidelines that could be applied consistently and almost automatically to the situation. They also emphasized that, precisely because of this circumstance, it was a case that in several respects did not have an international precedent. If that is so, the result of the Colombian experience may have world-wide effects.

This chapter reviews some aspects of Colombia's transitional process, while informing its readers of structural changes in the Attorney General's Office and, with it, at the centre of Colombia's criminal justice system on the way to investigate and charge offences that constitute international crimes. This is essentially the Attorney General's prioritization strategy of 2012. The author of the present chapter participated directly in its conception as an advisor to the Attorney General's Office. It was an ambitious strategy, accompanied by structural administrative reform of the prosecuting body. It can be seen as an investigation strategy for crimes of organized structures.

---

* **Alejandro Aponte Cardona** is Professor and Head of the Department of Criminal Law and Transitional Justice at Universidad de La Sabana. He holds a Ph.D. in criminal law and legal theory from University of Saarland. At the time of writing, he was a university professor and advisor and consultant to national and international agencies. The author thanks, especially, Emilie Hunter, for her interest in the Colombian case and dedication to reflect on it from the point of view of comparative law; he also thanks his research assistants Daniel Castellanos (who maintains an ongoing reflection on these issues) and Ligia Maria Vargas (for the care and dedication in presenting the text in its English version).

The chapter is basically descriptive, though it contains analysis of specific events and contextualizes relevant questions, such as the relationship between selection and prioritization, the harmonization of a general policy of national prosecution of international crimes, the criminal-political decisions related to the application of constitutional and legislative frameworks of transitional justice, as well as the harmonization, always mandatory and necessary, of any criminal strategy and the rights of victims. It is a text that, while outlining structural changes in how to investigate international crimes, presents a reflection on challenges presented by an ongoing situation.

15.2. Background of the Prioritization Strategy of the Attorney General's Office

15.2.1. The Special Process for Justice and Peace

In June 2005, Law 975 (2005) – the "Justice and Peace Law" – was issued, as described in the chapter by María Paula Saffon.[1] Law 1592 of 2012 amended it. It is linked to the demobilization of paramilitary members which took place at that time, although the text of the law refers to members of "illegal organized armed groups" in general. For this reason, there were also a significant number of men and women who were combatants in the guerrillas, especially the Revolutionary Armed Forces of Colombia ('FARC-EP'), who fell within the group of people covered by the Law. In its original Article 2, the Law stated:

> The present law establishes the regulation regard to the investigation, prosecution, punishment and legal benefits to all persons linked to groups that operate outside the law, as authors or participants in crimes committed during and because of their membership to those groups, who have decided to demobilize and contribute decisively to national reconciliation.

On the other hand, the new articles introduced by Law 1592 of December 2012, while maintaining the same meaning, added a reference to the prioritization strategy to be driven by the Attorney General's Office, which has a direct relation to the evolution that is described in this chapter. The new Article 2 states:

> The present law establishes the regulation regard to the investigation, prosecution, punishment and legal benefits to all persons linked to groups that operate outside the law, as authors or participants in crimes committed during and because of their membership to those groups, who have decided to demobilize and contribute decisively to national reconciliation, according to the prioritization

[1] Law 975 of 2005, 25 July 2005 ('Justice and Peace Law') (https://www.legal-tools.org/doc/ca98de/).

criteria applicable to the investigation and prosecution of those conducts.[2]

From the beginning, it has been discussed whether the law was conceived in a transitional dynamic as it was not necessarily clear whether the demobilization of paramilitaries was conceived as part of a peace process, or rather mainly as a process of demobilization and weapons-delivery in exchange for favourable punitive treatment. However, from the outset and institutionally, it was conceived as a process in a 'transitional code', though it was not a transitional process in a conventional or orthodox sense, because it was another effort to incorporate illegal armed actors into the civil society and the law, in an ongoing armed conflict scenario.[3]

In any case, it has been a fundamental chapter in the institutional history of the national prosecution of international crimes. This history is the context of the prioritization strategy and the debate on selection, introduced by the so-called 'Legal Framework for Peace'.[4]

---

2 Law 1592 of 2012, 3 December 2012, Article 1 (https://www.legal-tools.org/doc/0ohmir07/), amending Article 2 of Law 975 of 2005.

3 As an example, in the decision that evaluated the constitutionality of the Justice and Peace Law, the Court, in the discussion about reparation, asked itself: "In the first place, it is necessary to decide if, in transitional justice processes, as the one that the sue law regulates, it is a constitutional requirement that the responsible for the crimes attend with their patrimony the compensations for the victims", see Constitutional Court, Sentence C-370/06, 18 May 2006, para. 6 (https://www.legal-tools.org/doc/ebdde4/). In the same way, this statement has been reiterated by the Criminal Chamber of the Court and by the Tribunal of Justice and Peace. Furthermore, as an example and concerning the requirements for access to alternative punishment, the Criminal Chamber in Supreme Court of Justice, Judgment, 9 March 2009, no. 31048 (https://www.legal-tools.org/doc/b3b4rbgs/), stated:

> If someone that demobilized from an illegal armed group is being investigated or prosecuted by ordinary justice for a killing crime committed during his membership to that group, and it occurred before the 25 July of 2005, it is not enough to participate in the process against him in the frame of the transitional justice process regulated in the Law 975 of 2005, and confess that crime so he can be beneficiated automatically with the alternative punishment.

4 At the time of writing, there was a significant number of members of paramilitary groups who, after several years of being deprived of freedom and having served the maximum alternative sentence, were beginning to regain their freedom, having fulfilled certain conditions. This was a particularly critical aspect in the process as the Attorney General and the criminal justice system was advancing towards the consolidation of important and emblematic judgments (expecting several within a few years).

15.2.2. A Fundamental Fact: The Massive Nature of the Crimes Committed and the Factual Impossibility of the Criminal System to Account for All

From the beginning of the implementation of the Justice and Peace Law, a central circumstance became notorious: the massive factual nature of what took place, the extraordinary complexity of the power structures that were investigated, and the inability of the system to account in criminal investigation for every fact and last person responsible.

The present author – in his capacity as director of the justice area of an international observatory that was monitoring the implementation of the law – during a voluntary statement-hearing that took place at the request of the Justice and Peace Unit of the Attorney General's Office, found a singular fact narrated by a prosecutor investigating an entire block of paramilitary activity. By 2007, the prosecutor told the author not only about the drama she lived personally, but also one suffered by virtually every prosecutor:

> I have about 100 cases investigated, each with multiple events and dozens of victims. I was able to go very well with about 20 cases and I have very precarious and fragmented information for the other cases. What should I do? Do I go ahead with the cases already investigated and cleared or should I wait to complete all cases and linger with them many years? On one hand, victims of advanced cases, are calling me forward to conclude the allegations and, on the other hand, the many victims of cases missing, are pushing me too. What should I do?

This crossroads – quite widespread throughout the criminal justice system – led to the need to move the process forward. A concerted output within the judiciary was the formulation of *partial charges*. It was an emergency mechanism, endorsed by the Criminal Chamber of the Supreme Court, which allowed moving forward with partial and not total charges, according to the facts that were being investigated and illustrated, without setting aside other facts.[5]

It was a purely procedural way out, but it is important to note that there were major tensions, which around the year 2012 originated the prioritization strategy driven by the Attorney General's Office: it was the enormous weight posed on any criminal system, not only in Colombia, but in every nation given

[5] A review of the process through which the 'partial charges' were implemented can be found in the comprehensive document by the present author on the process of justice and peace, entitled *El proceso especial de justicia y paz. Alcances y límites de un proceso penal concebido en clave transicional*, Monográfico 2, Observatorio Internacional DDR-Ley de Justicia y Paz, Centro Internacional de Toledo para la Paz, Bogotá-Madrid, 2011, pp. 148 ff.

the task of investigating and punishing every last fact and the ultimate responsibility. These tensions, and the drama lived by prosecutors, created the need to take action in order to advance the investigation and prosecution of cases, and the need to change the mindset in the research, so that no individual fact was investigated in isolation, but rather within the true macro criminal structures: more precisely, the need to investigate major criminal structures based on prioritization criteria.

But the legal community was not ready in 2008–2009 to conduct this discussion. Opinions were polarized in such a way that the partial charges were conceived by some as a source of impunity and, in any case, a sign that the criminal justice system was still being pushed to produce results in a counterproductive environment, because the higher the pressure was, the slower the system was moving. It should be emphasized, however, that during this time fundamental, pioneering decisions of the criminal system were made.

One example is the iconic Manpuján judgment of the Justice and Peace Chamber of the Superior Tribunal of the Judicial District.[6] The ruling was appealed and deserved a response from the Supreme Court of Justice's Criminal Chamber.[7] In this judgment the main issues raised in the justice and peace process can be found, and beyond them, the main problems of the investigation and punishment of massive crimes committed by criminal organizations. These are the challenges in the investigation and punishment of acts constituting international crimes, such as those posed by the forms of attribution of those crimes, the extreme difficulty of repairing their many victims, possible forms of liability of officers currently working in the same areas where the crimes were committed.

15.2.3. The Prioritization Strategy of the Attorney General's Office: Change in the Culture of the Investigation of Criminal Organizations

It was only in 2012 that the Attorney General, Eduardo Montealegre, began to think concretely about the need to adopt criteria for prioritizing cases, in order to really advance in the investigations and produce results. Before then, in 2010, a large forum about prioritization and selection took place in Colombia. It was clear then that international courts, in some form or other, adopted such criteria

[6] Superior Tribunal of the Judicial District of Bogotá, Justice and Peace Chamber, Judgment, 29 June 2010, no. 2006-80077 (https://www.legal-tools.org/doc/lpijhq80/).

[7] Supreme Court of Justice, Criminal Chamber, Judgment, 27 April 2011, no. 34547 (https://www.legal-tools.org/doc/cmpg358b/).

to give momentum to their investigations. At the same time, the early works on the subject were being published.[8]

From April 2012, the Attorney General and his closest team, with which the author of this chapter worked as an external consultant, began working on boosting the prioritization strategy in connection with a radical change in the way of investigating international crimes. There was a need to identify the real contexts in which the facts occurred, in such a way that the criminal justice system would not be exhausted by investigating isolated facts and individuals, but rather concentrate the investigation on, *inter alia*, the conduct of the main suspects and the relations between perpetrators and civilians, military officials and private individuals. This could reveal the counter-state actors who rely on legal actors of all kinds to commit crimes.

The prioritization strategy began with public working meetings or hearings in which all state institutions were involved. In addition, there was a meeting with the main organizations of victims in the form of a process of open, public reflection which had the support of all agencies of international co-operation linked to these issues and of several experts, national and international.[9]

15.2.4. Year 2012: Adequate Legal and Political Context for Institutional Adaptation to Prioritize

The concept of prioritization was an ambitious enterprise – looking for a change of paradigm in the investigation of criminal structures – that ran parallel to two unique events that also took place in 2012: (a) the adoption of Legislative Act 1 (2012),[10] a constitutional reform conceived as a complex network of transitional justice mechanisms to be developed and implemented in an open process of peace with the FARC-EP guerrillas; and (b) a process of legislative reform of the Law of Justice and Peace that sought to resolve structural failures in the process, also based on prioritization. As an example, Law 1592 (2012) added to Law 975 (2005) a new Article 16A, which reads as follows:

> Criteria of prioritization of cases. In order to guarantee the rights of victims, the Attorney General's Office will determine the prioritization criteria for the exercise of criminal justice, that shall be binding and shall be made public. The prioritization criteria will

[8] As an example, the work co-ordinated by Kai Ambos (ed.), *Selección y Priorización como estrategia de persecución en los tribunales internacionales. Un estudio comparado*, GIZ-Profis, Bogotá, 2011, with long chapter by Morten Bergsmo and María Paula Saffon, a Spanish translation of Chapter 5 above in the present anthology.

[9] The meetings on prioritization that took place from May to July 2012 are outlined in a publication by the Attorney General's Office: *La priorización: memorias de los talleres para la construcción de los criterios del nuevo sistema de investigación penal*, Bogotá, 2012.

[10] Legislative Act 1 of 2012, 31 July 2012 (https://www.legal-tools.org/doc/dee32b/).

> be aimed at clarifying pattern of macro-criminality in the actions of organized illegal armed groups and reveal the context of those actions, the causes and the reasons for it, concentrating investigative efforts on the most responsible. For these purposes, the Attorney General shall adopt by resolution the "Comprehensive Plan for Prioritized Investigation".[11]

Meanwhile, and as was ordered by this law, a Legal Framework for Peace (in transitional Article 66 amending the Constitution) gave the Attorney General the task of developing criteria for prioritization.[12] The third paragraph of the constitutional provision reads: "The Attorney General's Office will determine prioritization criteria for the exercise of criminal action".[13]

15.2.5. Some Forms of Selection Prior to the Legal Framework for Peace

It should now be clear that the Attorney General's strategy outlined above is a *prioritization* strategy, and has no relation with the selection of cases. The latter notion appears only in the design of the Framework for Peace. This does not mean that the application process for those who are subject to the Justice and Peace special process (developed by the executive power) does not constitute a kind of selection process. It is not a selection mechanism as the one conceived by the Framework for Peace – that is, a jurisdictional threshold to establish which cases should enter the criminal justice system and which not – but it is selection to the extent that it is a decision about who enters the Justice and Peace process and who not. The choice, in general, always involves a more political decision.[14]

It is also an eminently political action, a policy-making process, because when the government decides whether a paramilitary leader linked, for example, to drug trafficking enters the process or not, it is a choice grounded in a political decision. Even the decision taken by former Colombian President Uribe in May 2008, criticized at the time, to extradite paramilitary leaders who were confess-

[11] Law 1592 of 2012, Article 13, see *supra* note 2.

[12] See *supra* note 10.

[13] As will be shown later, the Framework for Peace dwelled in particular with the concept of selection. The only reference to prioritization is the one just reviewed, which is understandable to the extent that it was a strategy launched by the Attorney General and was already at an early stage of operation when the Framework for Peace came into force.

[14] The author has addressed this issue in diverse forms, and he used the notion of 'technical discretion', and not merely 'political discretion', to implement selection processes. In any case, in the Framework for Peace, the selection of cases should not respond to purely political and pragmatic decisions, but must be influenced by a sequence of criteria that reflects the reality of the facts and violence committed by the actors.

ing particularly sensitive facts in the Justice and Peace process with the argument that they were committing crimes, was also a kind of selection, related to political decisions.

15.3. Prioritization Strategy in Directive No. 001 of 2012 of the Attorney General's Office

Since the mechanism of selection of cases that could be implemented through statutory laws authorized by the legal Framework for Peace must be in accord with the prioritization system, it is necessary to analyse some specific aspects of the investigation strategy of the Attorney General's Office embodied in Directive No. 001 of 2012.[15] For this, a brief summary of the operating basis of prioritization will be presented in the following sub-sections, to illustrate properly the process and evolution of the conception of the strategy.

15.3.1. Central Notions Contained in Directive No. 001 of 2012

15.3.1.1. Defining Criteria

Dealing exclusively with the prioritization policy, the Directive defines 'standard' as a logical parameter put in place to focus the investigative action of the prosecutors to certain situations and cases. Similar to prioritization in its operational aspect, selection would also be designed based on criteria that constitute logical parameters, containing the minimum material elements that a case must meet to satisfy the special requirements of jurisdiction or competence.

15.3.1.2. Classification Criteria

According to the Directive, there are three kinds of basic criteria in prioritization: objective, subjective and additional criteria: (1) objective criteria examine the elements of gravity and crime-representation, each of which is detailed by factors, in turn divided into sub-factors; (2) subjective criteria address the special qualities of the perpetrators and the victims (degree of responsibility and vulnerability, respectively). The elements of these criteria are also defined by factors and sub-factors; and (3) the complementary approach incorporates considerations of availability of proof, teaching value of a case, its review by an international body, among others. They are additional elements to establish the need to give priority to a case.

This classification of prioritization criteria in the Directive into three broad categories (divided into elements, which in turn are divided and subdivided) is one of several possible designs of a policy of selection and prioritization of sit-

[15] Attorney General's Office, Directive No. 0001, 4 October 2012 (https://www.legal-tools.org/doc/e93910/).

uations and cases. It is important to pay attention to the deductive, logical structure (from general to specific) of the policy (criterion-element factor and sub-factor) which may be retained to design the mechanism of selection of cases even though, as indicated by the legislative act, it refers to selection criteria.

15.3.2. Operation of the Prioritization Criteria

Directive No. 001 of 2012 established a "Comité de priorización de situaciones y casos" ('Committee') as the body responsible for implementing the criteria for prioritizing and managing the new system of criminal investigation,[16] with a Technical Secretariat responsible for implementing and co-ordinating all functions, lend technical and administrative support, and follow the development of the decisions, among other functions.[17]

The prioritization system was developed on three levels through which situations and cases to potentially be prioritized were to be put for approval or recommendation. To decide on prioritization, the Committee were to apply a test known as 'test for prioritization', defined in the directive as the "judgment that allows a balancing of the various prioritization criteria in order to recommend or decide on a situation or event". The methodology for performing this test consisted of the following stages: (i) perform a previous analysis which involves associating the different criminal cases to find patterns and situations that can be prioritized; (ii) apply the prioritization criteria to the situation or event to potentially prioritize; and (iii), in a reasoned manner, adopt the recommendation or decision.[18]

In the first level of the prioritization system, situations or cases potentially to be prioritized may come from (i) the request of any member of the Committee or (ii) a citizen petition. Either way, requests for prioritization must have a solid argument. The prioritized cases in this first level were to be entrusted to the Unidad de Análisis y Contextos de la Fiscalía ('UNAC'), which in turn may also,

---

16 Decree Law 016 of 2014, 9 January 2014 ('Decree Law 016 of 2014') (https://www.legal-tools.org/doc/80wdi7uy/) defined and modified the organizational and functional structure of the Attorney General's Office (including by creating a Comités de priorización de situaciones y casos responsible for implementing the policies and strategies defined by the Attorney General, to adopt a prioritization plan, and propose and decide situations and priority cases).

17 In the Committee participate (i) the Deputy Attorney General, (ii) a delegate of the Deputy Attorney General, (iii) the National Prosecution Director, (iv) the National Technical Investigation Director, (v) the Chief of the Prosecution Unit Delegate to the Supreme Court, (vi) the Chief of the National Prosecution Unit for Contexts and Analysis, and (vii) the Head of the Technical Secretariat.

18 See Attorney General's Office, National Unit for Analysis and Contexts, *Informe de rendición de cuentas 2012–2013*, Bogotá, 2013, p. 10.

according to Decree Law 016 of 2014, identify and delineate situations and susceptible cases of prioritization and propose them to the Committee.

In the second and third levels, in addition to sources (i) and (ii) above, situations or cases can be nominated for prioritization by (iii) the action plans to be submitted to the Committee for approval by each of the National Units and Sectional Directions.[19] Similarly, and with good reason, in the action plans the arguments why a situation or event is presented should be strong.

Action plans are an instrument that allows transparent, rational and controlled application of the prioritization system. National Units and Sectional Directors can only apply the prioritization criteria once the Committee has approved its plan of action, whose first two points match with the test for prioritization, and a third point on the methods and administrative measures that should be employed to make prioritization effective is added. Thus, the action plan must contain a specific timetable for the implementation of the prioritization policy through the goals to be attained within the life of the plan (the term for the action plans is one year). In any case, as the prioritization strategy is in no way equivalent to the waiver of prosecution in respect of cases that are not prioritized, the action plan must contain an estimate of the strategies and plans to be implemented in relation to those cases. The monitoring and follow-up of the action plans are tasked to the Technical Secretariat of the Committee.

15.3.2.1. Investigation Methodology

On the first level, UNAC has designed and implemented a four-stage methodology of work, by which the reconstruction of the contexts goes hand-in-hand with the criminal investigation, and is constantly feeding the progress back.[20] Prosecutors, investigators and analysts are involved in a co-ordinated manner, allowing the investigative hypothesis to be nourished by the perspectives of different disciplines. This methodology starts after the prosecutor accepts the suggestions or Committee assignments. According to a report by UNAC in October 2013, the four stages of the work are: (i) delimitation and characterization of situations; (ii) identification of the most responsible; (iii) investigation for the prosecution of the most responsible; and (iv) judgment.[21]

---

[19] Decree Law 016 of 2014, see *supra* note 16, modified the name of the Unidades Nacionales de Fiscalía to Direcciones de Fiscalías Nacionales. It was not just a change of name, but a structural transformation, that falls outside of the scope of this document.

[20] On the second and third levels of postulation of situations and cases, the implementation of the new prioritizing system was done through action plans, the methodology of which has been explained above.

[21] See Attorney General's Office, 2013, p. 41, see *supra* note 18.

Although a detailed analysis of investigation methodologies goes beyond the scope of this chapter, it is necessary to make a brief reference given their importance for the upcoming discussion on the selection of cases. Accordingly, the first phase of work focuses on the definition, description and strategic analysis of the prioritized problems. Given the breadth of these problems, they are clustered in situations or cases as part of the development of global contexts; the delimitation of situations or cases can be done through inductive (from the particular to the general) or deductive analysis (from the general to the specific).[22] The inductive process begins with the concrete analysis of a case, from which common patterns are identified. Deductive analysis is performed on the basis of a thematic delimitation based on the association of cases.[23]

Secondly, once the situations or cases are defined and the construction of the context is initiated, the work goes beyond descriptive. In this sense, context analysis is addressed in a more detailed way and the descriptive work is overcome, to identify and focus on the most responsible within the organizations, alliances or criminal networks. The construction of investigative hypotheses and the development of methodological research programmes are directed in this way. The processes of creating contexts have complexities that require the use of various tools, procedures and techniques for the systematic and interdisciplinary study of crime.[24]

The third stage is the approach of the research hypothesis, based on the formulated context. This step should lead mainly to present charges against the most responsible, identified according to the level they occupy in the command structure of the criminal organization or for committing particularly egregious crimes. Such formulated contexts allow prosecutors and judicial police to strategically organize criminal investigations in order to concentrate on prosecuting those most responsible.

---

22 The Directive 001 of 2012, see *supra* note 15, defines 'context' as the frame of reference that contains the essential aspects of (i) geographical, political, economic, historical and social elements, in which the crimes have been performed by the illegal armed groups, including those in which public servants and particulars are involved. It should also include, (ii) a description of the strategy of the criminal organization, its regional dynamics, logistics essential aspects, communication networks and maintenances of the supports network, among others.

23 The thematic delimitation can be of different kinds, so, the problem may comprise, according to the report presented by UNAC, *supra* note 18: "1. Violence in a given region (Montes de Urabá or Maria); 2 A group of victims who share similar qualities (union members or members of the Unión Patriotica); 3 Tort behaviours of the same type (child recruitment and sexual violence in armed conflict) and; 4 Criminal organization (FARC-EP or some criminal gangs)".

24 While the analysts work on the elaboration of contexts and identify the structure of the criminal organizations, the prosecutors and the investigators of the judicial police begin the preliminary investigation on the situations identified in the first stage of the work. Additionally, the participation of victims is essential for the construction of contexts.

The fourth and last stage, the trial stage, is where the contexts developed to present the charges against those most responsible are tested. Jointly with evidence, contexts stand as a suitable tool to strengthen criminal charges. If it is considered appropriate for the case strategy, analysts can participate as expert witnesses in trials.

These different stages of work are in constant feedback as the products of the construction of context can contribute to the development of a methodological plan of criminal investigation. The results of the investigation stage and the work performed by the judicial police officers are called to confirm, extend and, in some cases, even challenge assumptions found in the developing context.

At the time of writing, UNAC had nine thematic working teams: (i) Investigation Group for the FARC-EP, (ii) Investigation Group for labour union violence, (iii) Investigation Group for violence against members of the Patriotic Union, (iv) Investigation Group for extrajudicial killings, (v) Investigation Group for Urabá, (vi) Investigation Group for government contracts in Bogotá, (vii) Investigation Group for assassinations, (viii) Investigation Group for Montes de Maria, and (ix) Investigation Group for violence committed against journalists.

15.3.2.2. The Strategy's Relevance to Challenges in Implementing the Legal Framework for Peace

The work done on prioritizing cases by the Attorney General's Office in general, and UNAC in particular, is a cornerstone when facing new challenges posed by the implementation of the Legal Framework for Peace, especially with regard to the selection of cases.

For example, the research strategy of UNAC on the first level of prioritization is a central reference point to determine how the selection process will be. Indeed, the strategy for identifying employed by UNAC provides general situations and contexts to subsequently investigate and prosecute those most responsible for committing certain crimes. While the prioritization strategy is a comprehensive strategy that includes a variety of topics, ranging from threats to labour unions to state contracts in Bogotá, there are specific developments within the prosecution of international crimes committed in armed conflict scenarios.

In this sense, taking into account the requirements and the context in which Legislative Act 1 of 2012 was issued, it may be helpful to consider for illustration purposes the work of UNAC in the Investigation Group for FARC-EP guerrillas: developing a context, focusing on the history and operation of the armed group, as a prerequisite and indispensable approach that contributes to the research hypotheses for further formulation of charges against those most responsible for crimes against humanity and war crimes.[25]

As noted above, the progress of this research group and, more generally, the methodological tools developed in identifying contexts and the most responsible criminal actors, if they are bound to the context of the armed conflict, represent significant input to defining how cases are selected, as provided by Legislative Act 1 of 2012. For example, tools like inductive and deductive analysis and contexts, developed by the Investigation Group of the FARC-EP, are a central tool for those who, depending on the statutory regulation, are responsible for deciding which cases will be selected.

As will be shown below, in its judgment of the constitutionality of paragraph 4 of transitory Article 66, modifying the Constitution, introduced by Legislative Act 1 of 2012,[26] the Constitutional Court failed to make specific reference to developments in the Attorney General's Office in implementing a prioritization strategy, which raises some questions regarding the possible link between the selection and prioritization of cases. These are issues that should be resolved taking into account the previous advances of the prosecuting body.

15.3.3. Restructuring the Attorney General's Office: Decree Law 016 of 2014

The outlined process of adaptation of the Attorney General's Office, based on the new research strategy and general prioritization system, has its counterpart in a complex process of administrative modernization. The institution was updated in accordance with new requirements to combat the organized apparatus of power and crime in its various forms. In that sense, the Colombian President, in exercise of the extraordinary powers conferred upon him by Act 1654 of 2013, issued Decree Law 016 of 2014 on 9 January 2014, which restructured the functional organization of the Attorney General's Office.[27] Below are the most important elements of the restructuration, focusing only on the matters of transitional justice and prioritization.

First, within the functions assigned to the Attorney General, established in Article 4 of the decree, there is the duty to formulate and direct the prioritization policy, based on objective and subjective criteria. Also, the Attorney General is required to give special relevance to the context of crime, by geographic area, with the aim of ensuring the right to justice.[28] Article 15 establishes the functions

[25] Attorney General's Office, 2013, p. 54, *supra* note 18.

[26] See *supra* note 10.

[27] Decree Law 016 of 2014, see *supra* note 16.

[28] *Ibid.*, Article 4, no. 7:

of the Deputy Attorney General, and Section 13 of this article gives this officer the duty to co-ordinate the prioritization committees, according to the guidelines given by the Attorney General. These committees are created by the same decree, in Article 46, in order to adopt the plan for prioritizing and implementing policies in this area.[29] According to later decisions of the Attorney General, there may be various committees at the national and branch levels.

Secondly, Article 2 of the decree establishes departmental agencies that depend on the office of the Deputy Attorney General's Office, within which is the National Directorate of Analysis and Context that advises the Attorney General on the prioritization strategy and performs the investigation to identify criminal contexts, among others. Furthermore, the Directorate of Joint Specialized National Prosecution is also attached. Within it, it is important to mention the National Directorate of the Special Prosecutor for Transitional Justice, whose functions include "execute prioritization plans approved by the National Committee for Prioritization of Situations and Cases according to their competences".[30] Finally, it is worth mentioning the creation of the Special Judicial Police Directorate of Human Rights and International Humanitarian Law, by paragraph 3 of Article 23, responsible for advancing investigation in this field.

15.3.4. Conceptual Differences Between Case Selection and Prioritization

While the binomial selection–prioritization shares a common genesis in international criminal law, it should be noted that the effects of each of these institutes

> Formulating, directing, setting policies and strategies for prioritizing the exercise of investigative activity by the Attorney General's Office, taking into account, *inter alia*, subjective, objective, especially complementary and social context of crime the geographic area that would provide a care order cases in order to ensure, on a basis of material equality, the realization of the fundamental right to justice. For the purpose he may organize committees that are required to decide the situations and priority cases.

29 *Ibid.*, Article 46:

> Prioritization committees must be created and they will be responsible for implementing the policies and strategies of prioritization defined by the Attorney General's Office, to adopt the plan and propose prioritization and decide when it is assigned this competition, situations and priority cases. The policies and strategies of prioritization in the criminal investigation will take into account, among others, subjective, objective, complementary and especially social context of crime in the geographic area, aimed at establishing a care order cases, in order to ensure in conditions of material equality, the realization of the fundamental right to justice. Similarly, the Attorney General's Office may take into account in the policies and strategies for prioritizing the suggestions, for reasons of public order, asked by the Superior Council of Criminal and Penitentiary Policy. The Attorney General shall organize committees on prioritization required at a national or sectional level, determine their number, integration and other functions.

30 *Ibid.*, Article 20, no. 5.

differ, making it inconvenient to assimilate the formulation of their identity, their contents and their various modes of operation.

To understand this, it should be noted that *selection* criteria are aimed at determining "which cases can be investigated and prosecuted by a specific jurisdiction".[31] For this reason, selection involves more discrimination or exclusion of certain cases that do not meet the necessary requirements to activate a previously-established special jurisdiction. So, in general, it can be argued that the selection of cases determines the competence or jurisdiction required to activate the functions of investigation, prosecution and punishment of the criminal justice system. Selection criteria are minimum parameters (a threshold for jurisdiction or competence) that must meet certain punishable acts and their perpetrators for their cases to be known and handled by a particular criminal justice apparatus.

Thus, selection criteria introduce a filter for understanding certain cases, and they should be applied as part of a checklist; that is, all the elements or criteria laid down must be present in a particular case for it to be selected, investigated and tried, through the special procedure provided for it. Under this assumption, and analysed from the context of national jurisdictions, non-selected cases either go to ordinary courts, as both generic and residual, or are processed through alternative mechanisms of transitional justice, such as truth commissions or reconciliation and reparation programmes designed by the state.

For example, if a peace agreement enables the implementation of programmes authorized under the Legal Framework for Peace, the net effect of non-selection could be a conditional waiver of prosecution. Instead, as a parallel, with the regulations in force at the time of writing, if there was not compliance with the eligibility requirements for the Justice and Peace process, the ordinary criminal courts would be called to process the case.

From the international point of view, the adoption of selection criteria is also explained by the existence of different kinds of jurisdictions that are sometimes concurrent: territorial jurisdiction of the state in which the crime was committed, personal jurisdiction by the active or passive subjects of the crime, international jurisdiction of international courts (with primacy or complementarity), hybrid jurisdictions, or universal jurisdiction of foreign states.[32]

---

[31] María Paula Saffon and Morten Bergsmo, "Enfrentando una fila de atrocidades pasadas: ¿cómo seleccionar y priorizar casos de crímenes internacionales nucleares?", in Kai Ambos (ed.), *Selección y priorización como estrategia de persecución en los casos de crímenes internacionales. Un estudio comparado*, *supra* note 8, p. 29.

[32] On the territorial jurisdiction of any state where widespread violence has been presented, it has been considered the difficulty of handling all cases through a single mechanism. Thus,

Internally, case selection has a more complex connotation because it involves balancing the duties of criminal prosecution by the state and the requirements for the ending of a given conflict, or the deposition and transition between different regimes, depending on the context. It is a decision with a high political and reconciliatory content that is determined in accordance with the material parameters.

Contrary to the selection strategy, *prioritization* criteria should be understood as the criteria which serve to classify cases within one jurisdiction and determine the order in which they will be investigated and those responsible punished. In this sense, prioritization criteria do not involve the choice of cases based on their respective knowledge, but involve a rational organization as to the order and the way in which they will be investigated. Relations between selection and prioritization acquire different levels of complexity according to the contexts in which they are applied. Such is the case, as will be seen below, with the relationship between these two models within the so-called Legal Framework for Peace.

15.4. Legal Framework for Peace: New Challenges for Selection and Prioritization Strategies

15.4.1. Introduction of the Case Selection Mechanism

The Legal Framework for Peace, created by Legislative Act 1 of 2012, provides a fundamental filter through the selection of cases that will be known by the criminal justice system: only those most responsible for conduct that constitute core international crimes will be brought to ordinary justice. Transitional Article 66, amending the Constitution, reads in the relevant part:

> Without prejudice to the general obligation of the State to investigate and punish serious violations of Human Rights and International Humanitarian Law, in the context of transitional justice, the Congress, at the initiative of the Government, may, by statutory law determine selection criteria that allow focusing efforts of the criminal investigation into the most responsible of all crimes that

---

in fact, the criminal courts of territorial states carry the heaviest burden in terms of the number of cases that must prosecute and judge, because the atrocities were carried out in the territory of the state concerned, most victims and perpetrators usually reside in it and that its mandate to pursue and prosecute crimes is usually general or broad. In this area, the territorial states are followed by *ad hoc* international tribunals and hybrid ones created specifically to deal with more important crimes in a conflict or authoritarian regime, and then by jurisdictions with general competence but subsidiary jurisdiction to prosecute and try core international crimes, such as the ICC and foreign states under the principle of universal jurisdiction.

Ibid.

> suit the connotation of crimes against humanity, genocide, or war crimes committed in a systematic manner [...].[33]

As is evident, the selection is both about people – who are the most responsible – and offenses; as also seen above, it is required that the offences are committed in a systematic manner. This last point can be understood in the general *telos* of the law, which is a way of raising the threshold requirement for selection, because had it not been limited to crimes, including war crimes, committed in a systematic manner, there would have been tens of thousands of possible cases for selection, because of the number of crimes that were committed – more, if the rule had referred to 'all crimes'. But this point resulted in a widely criticized, anti-technical interpretation, in the constitutionality judgment of this norm: Judgment C-579 of 2013, which will be outlined later in central fragments, but mentioned here in this critical context. The Constitutional Court sees the 'systematic' required by the standard as the material context – armed conflict – typical of war crimes. The Court seems to assimilate, as a context, the very systematic crimes against humanity to the notion of armed conflict, which is the material context required for war crimes:

> The Court wrongly equates the meaning of 'systematically committed' to the contextual material element that characterizes war crimes. War crimes are behaviours by definition linked to an armed conflict; do not require a pattern or course of conduct, thus systematic practice, as with crimes against humanity.[34]

However, the cases that are selected are to be investigated, prosecuted and punished by the criminal justice system and, in that sense, may be subject to legal benefits, alternative sanctions, not total but partial suspension of the execution of penalty, and special procedures for implementing and enforcing it.[35] While, for unselected cases which are understood to constitute the largest number of cases committed by the demobilized population, the mediation of a truth commission is authorized, as is the imposition of extrajudicial sanctions, as possible mechanisms of clarifying the truth and the attribution of individual criminal responsibility for participation in the armed conflict.

---

[33] Legislative Act 1 of 2012, see *supra* note 10.

[34] Kai Ambos and John Zuluaga, "Análisis del fallo sobre el marco jurídico para la paz", in *Ámbito jurídico,* 27 January 2014. This topic is also analysed in a paper about the judgement, in its diverse problematic aspects, titled *Justicia de transición y constitución*, Temis, 2014, published with the co-ordination of Kai Ambos (ed.) and with the participation of several authors. In this particular case, seek for the contribution of Gustavo E. Cote and Diego F. Tarapués, "El marco jurídico para la paz y el análisis estricto de sustitución de la constitución realizado en la sentencia C-579 de 2013", pp. 251 ff.

[35] Constitutional Court, Judgment C-579/13, 28 August 2013, para. 8.3.2.(vi) (https://www.legal-tools.org/doc/ede533/).

We must clarify that the Legal Framework for Peace states that, during a critical period which can be up to ten years, the Congress should enact statutory laws, most demanding and complex, in which the issues arising from the Framework are regulated: for example, the most responsible figure, the nature of crimes against humanity, and the political participation of ex-combatants.

Once this clarification has been made, it should then be added that the selection of cases makes a distinction between the members of the armed organization most responsible for the facts of the conflict: it highlights guerrilla members with a wide ideological formation, directing members, those in a political or driving organizational level, and other lower-level fighters whose criminal responsibility apparently rests, unless proven otherwise, on the basis of the imputation of the crime of rebellion. This differentiation in the universe of members who make up the armed structure is essential to the justification for the application of alternative and extrajudicial sanctions, for either category of combatants.

A fundamental fact should be clear: it has been discussed so far, and public discussion has emphasized, that members of the guerrillas are the subjects of the Legal Framework for Peace. However, the constitutional amendments also include civil servants and members of the army or police or civilians who have committed international crimes. The country needs transitional justice formulas that can be applied to all, from the explicit recognition of their responsibility in the commission of heinous crimes. Their attribution of responsibility and punishment should be commensurate with their status.

Those most responsible are, as the expression implies, members who bear the greatest responsibility for the atrocities committed by their illegal group in the course of the armed conflict. They are those leaders or managers with command over military units, that is, people who have enjoyed the power to issue orders and enforce them, for example, on issues relating to the formulation of a group policy or the conduct of a military operation, executed through chains of command and established with a protocol. These people have a high level of military and political formation, and are also responsible for the discipline of the troops and for the consolidation and the dissemination of the ideological discourse that identifies the organization. The leaders also function as speakers and co-ordinate the various military units that structure the armed group. The judgment commenting on this role, stated, for example, the following:

> In conclusion, from the above specified international criteria can be noted that the most responsible is a person who has an essential role in the criminal organization and in the commission of each offense, that is that he had addressed, controlled or funded the commission of crimes against humanity, genocide and war crimes committed in a systematic manner. Within this concept should be

> included then, not only leaders who ordered the crime, but also behaviours through which this has been funded as drug trafficking.[36]

The conditional waiver of prosecution applied to the rank-and-file guerrillas who have no decisive responsibility for the commission of serious and representative crimes that acquire the connotation of international crimes. The state's response would not be strictly punitive for this category of combatants. In many cases, a double condition must be recognized, that of victimizer and victim.

15.4.2. Consistent Implementation of the Mechanisms of Selection and Prioritization

In the case of the Legal Framework for Peace, a specific relationship between the selection and prioritization strategies can be expressed as follows. All selected cases are unlikely to be hundreds, but those absolutely essential must be investigated and those responsible must be effectively punished: these are the cases in which the effective combination of criteria occurs, such as the action of the most responsible, as well as the representativity of the most serious offenses in respect of the territories where the events took place, and taking into account the nature of the victims – women, indigenous people, members of Afro-Colombian communities, for example. In other words, these are cases that cannot be suspended in time because of both the expectations of the victims and the parties responsible. If such a case is selected, the crime must be investigated and punished.

In general, it can be said that the conceptual distinction between selection and prioritization described above comes from the fact that the effects of the selection of cases differ from those of their prioritization. Taking into account that Legislative Act 1 of 2012 orders to include, by way of 'selection criteria', the notions of most responsible (for the commission of all offenses considered crimes against humanity, systematic war crimes or genocide), along with gravity and representation, and that there is a working definition of prioritization, it is understandable how important it is to develop harmoniously, and with a broader development of the objectives of criminal policy, the relations between these two kinds of 'filter system'.

It is also important to understand that, regardless of the selection mechanisms developed within the Framework for Peace, the Attorney General's Office will continue to apply the prioritization criteria and, in general, its prioritization

[36] *Ibid.*, paras. 8.3.3. ff.

strategy. As mentioned, this strategy, that was being promoted at the time of writing, is set to produce results with a significant impact on the country.

15.4.2.1. Integrating Normative Unity of Article 4, Sub-Section 4 of Legislative Act 1 of 2012

With its Judgment C-579 of 28 August 2013, the Constitutional Court decided the constitutional claim presented (by a group of citizens belonging to the Colombian Commission of Jurists) against the terms 'most', 'committed systematically' and 'all' in the first article of Legislative Act 1 of 2012.[37] According to the plaintiffs, the expressions referred to above replaced a founding pillar of the Constitution of 1991, namely the duty to guarantee human rights and the correlative obligation to investigate, prosecute and, if applicable, punish serious violations of human rights and international humanitarian law.[38]

Broadly speaking, the issue addressed by the constitutional judge in this lawsuit was whether in the context of transitional justice (when the values of peace and justice are in tension) the expressions replaced the aforementioned essential pillar.

It should be noted that the Constitutional Court, in a fundamental initiative to spark community dialogue by creating spaces for discussion, conducted a public hearing on 25 July 2013, with representatives of all institutions and experts – within which the author of this chapter was invited to discuss the constitutionality of the constitutional reform. The discussion was important and helped the Court decide. Thus, as will be described below, the Court declared the Framework for Peace constitutional, both transitional Article 66, more relevant to this chapter, and transitional Article 67 related to the possible political participation of ex-combatants. This provided constitutional backing to efforts related to peace processes.

To address the lawsuit, the Constitutional Court's initial consideration was the integration of normative unity of Article 1, paragraph 1, of Legislative Act 1 of 2012. The Court held that the expressions should be studied together with all tools and judicial benefits provided in sub-section 4 of the article, since those expressions were part of a complex system of transitional justice whose operation and proper interpretation depended on its full study. So, its constitutionality

[37] Legislative Act 1 of 2012, see *supra* note 10.

[38] The petitioners argued that the expressions constitute a replacement of the constitutional pillar of human rights protection, because they imply that the state is only required to pursue some of those responsible (only the most responsible and not all involved) by the commission of certain violations of human rights and international humanitarian law (in this sense, the argument is directed against the expression 'systematically committed' in relation to war crimes), see Constitutional Court, 28 August 2013, para. 2.3., see *supra* note 35.

could be determined only by coherently studying all legal provisions included in that sub-section.[39]

Although the lawsuit did not specifically refer to unconstitutionality of selection and prioritization criteria as inherent transitional justice instruments, the Court did make reference to them and to the interpretation that should be given. While judgment C-579 of 2013 is extensive, rich in sources and reflections, this chapter is only concerned with studying its sections on the possibility of focusing investigative efforts through the use of selection criteria and prioritization, naturally in conjunction with the 'most responsible' concept and criteria such as the gravity and representativeness of the crimes.[40]

15.4.2.2. Alternatives to Focusing Investigative Efforts on the Most Responsible Actors and on the Most Grave and Representative Cases

In addressing the constitutional analysis regarding the possibility of focusing criminal investigation efforts, through prioritization criteria and upon the terms set by the Legal Framework for Peace, the Court stated that such a focus is justified in a context of transitional justice when the prosecution of all those responsible and all crimes committed in the armed conflict would be impossible and counterproductive to the demands and expectations of justice for victims.[41]

---

[39] *Ibid.*, para. 4.

[40] The structure of the relevant part of the judgment is as follows: (i) integrating unit regulations in fourth paragraph of Article 1 of the legislative act; (ii) limits to the power of reform and the replacement of the Constitution; (iii) transitional justice in the rule of law; (iv) the rights of victims; and (v) the substitution test of the plaintiffs. It is a judgment that includes central reflections on transitional justice, but most of these issues go beyond the scope of this chapter's document analysis.

[41] In the analytical structure raised in its Judgment C-579 of 2013, the Constitutional Court referred to the selection criteria and prioritization at different times. However, analysis of the constitutionality of such instruments focused on the study of minor premise (including instruments by legislation) in carrying out the strict test of substitution and the establishment of the conditions for the interpretation of the rule. On the possibility of focusing research efforts, the Court stated:

> The ability to focus the criminal investigation in a number of cases came from the inability to have a maximalist research strategy appropriate legal action against all the suspects, as stressed by the Presentation for First Debate in the House of Representatives: There is now an international consensus on the matter. As has warned the Office of the UN High Commissioner for Human Rights, when there are thousands of people who participated in the systematic commission of crimes, it is impossible to take legal action against all. It is essential to establish a clear set of criteria to explain the strategy of identifying suspects who are to be investigated and prosecuted.

Constitutional Court, 28 August 2013, para. 8.2.2., see *supra* note 35.

While the Court recognized that the adoption of strategies for prioritizing and selecting "can substantially affect the way in which judicial proceedings are received by the victims", it also claimed that a correct and transparent application of them serves to (i) clarify the patterns, systems and massive violations of human rights, (ii) macro-deconstruct the criminal organizations, and (iii) "significantly improve the satisfaction of the rights of victims to truth and ensure non-repetition".[42]

The Court considered that criteria for selection and prioritization are consistent with the Constitution and with the specific demands of transitional justice. The Court stated:

> Transitional Justice in itself does not changes the pillar of guaranteeing Human Rights, but instead is a special form of joint various mechanisms to safeguard the rights to truth, justice, reparation and non-repetition in situations of massive IHL or HR violations, requiring the use of special criteria, as this Court recognized in Case C-370 of 2006, C-771 of 2011, C-052 of 2012, C-253 and C-781 of 2012 and as pointed out by various documents of the United Nations as the "Body of principles for the protection and promotion of Human Rights, for the fight against impunity" and Resolutions 1503 of 2003 and 1534 of 2004 of the Security Council.[43]

15.4.2.3. On the Impulse to Gravity and Representativeness Criteria: Searching for Truth

According to the Constitutional Court, gravity and representativeness criteria are key to implement the shift in the conception of investigating crimes committed by macro-criminality structures. The Court, reflecting on how the categorization of these factors would take shape following the enactment of the necessary statutory laws, stated:

> The system raised by the Legislative Act is not about meeting the cases, but it involves the construction of macro-judgments determined by a number of common elements; factors related to the severity and representation such as location, time, the form of commission, victims or affected social groups, active subjects, the

[42] *Ibid.*, para. 8.2.2.

[43] Carrying out the strict judgment of substitution, the Court also holds:

> In this way, the approach of the Legislative Act No. 01 of 2012 is not aimed at enshrining impunity for some offenses, but to change the research strategy "case by case", which makes it difficult to guarantee the right to justice for victims of gross human rights violations by structuring macro processes in which there is a massive participation of all victims and not structured by chance, but pursuant to investigations based on contexts and structural analysis of organized crime.

Ibid., para. 8.3.2.

scale of commission or the evidence available. Under this situation, a process can be developed for a particular type of crime that is committed in a particular region of Colombia, during a given time by a group of people and against a particular section of the population, which is representing those with the same characteristics or a strategy that is representative of the commission of the offense in several regions.

This form of investigation permits the disclosure of macro criminal structures and facilitates the construction of individual and collective truths that go beyond individual cases and for determining the causes of violence, promoting the transitional justice process. In this sense, it seeks to identify patterns of violence, degree of victimization, a possible deterrent effect and obtaining reconciliation and truth.[44]

15.4.3. Real Impact of Implementation of the Criterion of Representativeness

Furthermore, there are considerations on choosing cases that illustrate and make visible forms of horror, very specific dynamics full of violence of cultural, symbolic and even mythical content that have influenced them and, at the same time, that give content to subsequent mechanisms of guarantees of non-repetition which must be developed based on the rights of the victims. Thus, the fragmentary and limited nature of criminal law acquires a renewed sense, also emphasized in this chapter: in a transitional logic, making visible multiple elements based on the representativeness of the cases offsets the limitations of criminal law by contributing to the reconstruction of truth, thereby mobilizing basic elements for the non-repetition of the conduct. Therefore, a key input from the representativeness criterion consists in finding or illustrating the truth of the operations of the criminal apparatus. From its limitations, criminal law develops specific advantages.[45]

The most serious and representative crimes may be established – that is, those who have acted as superiors are located and a representative case is built – when a criminal apparatus or a machine of war (understood not only as a whole, but as units operating with effective control of specific acts and crimes) is identified. For example, a representative case may be one where specific types of sexual assault (including forms different from violent sexual intercourse on a

[44] *Ibid.*, para. 8.2.6.

[45] For a reflection on the value of representivness as criterion, see Alejandro Aponte Cardona, "La priorización como estrategia de reducción de complejidad: un ensayo de interpretación", in *id.*, *Derecho Penal Internacional, textos escogidos, volumen II*, Universidad Javeriana, editorial Ibáñez, Colección estudios no. 5, Bogotá, 2014, pp. 429–439.

protected person as in the case of forced marriage or forms of sexual slavery) are committed on certain groups of victims – such as indigenous women or country youth – and conducted by commanders or superiors who implemented this policy for specific periods. Similarly, cases in which the most responsible have intervened, occurring in specific territories, and involving, for example, several acts of illegal recruitment of children would be another example of a genuinely representative case that should be selected.

The Constitutional Court mentioned the following conduct:

> Given their severity and representativeness the investigation and punishment of the following crimes should be prioritized: extrajudicial executions, torture, forced disappearances, sexual violence against women in armed conflict, forced displacement and illegal recruitment of children, if they are qualified as crimes against humanity, genocide and war crimes committed in a systematic manner.[46]

These are cases in which all criteria converge: most responsible, both relative gravity of offenses and respect of the victims, and representativeness for the victims and the patterns in which the crimes are committed. However, the criterion of representativeness also allows focusing on cultural, mythical forms of action against women, along with their conception and rooted structures, which may provide reconciliation and genuine non-recurrence policies.

The transformation in the investigative strategy in Colombia has been studied by various Latin American countries that may wish to learn from this experience. With regards to peace processes and the implementation of the mechanisms contained in the Framework for Peace, Colombia and its legal community should seek new paths to meet the challenges. This entails an educational process for victims and the entire community who should know that this process involves the whole country. It is not the responsibility of a few actors, but our common responsibility.

15.5. Perspectives

Today, as it is well known, there is a complex model of transitional justice. It is composed by three main institutions: the Truth and Reconciliation Commission (*Comisión de la Verdad y Reconciliación*), which ended its mandate and produced several volumes, all very complex, with dozens of testimonies and interviews from all territories. The second institution is the Search Unit for Missing Persons (*Unidad de Búsqueda de Personas dadas por Desaparecidas*), which has undertaken enormous efforts and continues to operate across the country. It

[46] Constitutional Court, 28 August 2013, para. 9.9.4., see *supra* note 35.

has found dozens of bodies of missing persons and delivered them to their families. The third component is the Special Jurisdiction for Peace (*Jurisdicción Especial para la Paz* ('JEP')) a complex jurisdiction tasked not only with administering justice in transitional terms but also with focusing on victims and seeking the truth. In fact, the author of this article has argued that the true function of punishment, applying a transitional justice logic, should not only be retribution, which in any case is not the primary function, but rather the construction of narratives aimed at creating true social scenarios of non-repetition.

In this sense, the JEP has not only produced, to date, very complex rulings, known as Determination of Facts and Conducts Orders (*Autos de Determinación de Hechos y Conductas*), among other decisions, but has also made significant progress in reconstructing truths that are now essential for any possibility of reconciliation. In some contexts, it is even said that the JEP also functions as a true centre of historical memory.

Regarding the matter at hand, the JEP has embraced, from the very beginning, the entire system of prioritization developed by the Attorney General's Office in 2012, which was also included in the reform of the Justice and Peace Law in 2013. Of course, based on the criteria and basic strategy, the JEP has given it its own content, emphasized certain criteria, and progressed based on them. It has created the general methodology of the so-called 'macro-cases', which, in turn, and depending on the type of conduct, have been subdivided into 'sub-cases', either thematic or especially regional.[47] Notably, the two basic prioritization criteria of the Jurisdiction are gravity and representativeness. In addition, of course, to criteria such as the highest-ranking official and the Jurisdiction's own creation, the notion of the "determining participant".[48]

In the initial prioritization strategy of the Attorney General's Office, the notion of representativeness was initially conceived as a complementary criterion. However, from the Attorney General's own work, it was recognized that this criterion was not complementary; it was and had to be a primary criterion, precisely because of the need to build emblematic, genuinely representative cases that could illustrate dozens of acts which, for various reasons, cannot be investigated and prosecuted. Today, the JEP has made the criterion of representativeness, alongside the criterion of gravity, the fundamental criterion.

---

[47] To delve deeper into this structure, refer to the JEP's web site, which is very comprehensive and pedagogically structured to help understand this complex model. Additionally, the web site *ObservaJep* is cited here. It is an academic, university-based observatory that aims to permanently monitor the work of the jurisdiction and publish reviews of the most relevant decisions. It can be found at the following page: https://recursos.observajep.com/.

[48] To delve deeper into the study of the criteria and decisions, see the page "Jurisdicción Especial para la Paz" on the JEP's web site.

It is also noteworthy, and one of the challenges for the process of accusation, that the transitional model brings with it an open system of sources: not only human rights law, international humanitarian law, international criminal law, and domestic criminal law can be used, but they are all regulated, both legislatively and constitutionally. Indeed, there are decisions that have been made based on domestic law and others based on international criminal law, all of which are valid from the perspective of sources. There is a dialogue between domestic law and international law. [49]

Precisely this more open use, this 'open texture' of the system of sources, has also allowed significant progress in refining doctrinal concepts, not only for imputing criminal acts but also, for example, in applying forms of liability. Thus, concepts rooted in the continental tradition, such as co-perpetration, have been filled with new content to be applied based on domestic criminal law, while also using international criminal law. Similarly, concepts like indirect perpetration through organized power structures and superior responsibility are now used by the JEP, in a dialogue between domestic criminal law and international criminal law.

There are critics of the JEP who, rightly, point out the slow pace of the processes, and this is partially true. The first final decisions are only expected soon, and the process is indeed very slow. Progress is needed. Additionally, alternative sentences, which are very interesting within a transitional justice framework, are not yet being applied. However, the system is moving forward, especially in recognition of responsibility hearings, where state agents in cases of extrajudicial killings of civilians out of combat, the so-called 'false positives' (*falsos positivos)*, and in cases of hostage-taking by the former FARC-EP guerrillas, have created real scenarios of reparation and dignification of the victims. Likewise, scenarios of non-repetition. It is expected, as mentioned, that the first substantive rulings by the JEP will take place soon.

Finally, and in perspective, it is added that the current government is implementing, with great difficulties but firm purpose, a policy called 'Total Peace' (*Paz Total*). It is a very risky proposal to carry out peace or demobilization processes with a wide variety of armed and illegal actors. Dialogues are underway, and progress has been made with some of them. It is not clear yet, but it is certain to be expected that, in the various normative models being advanced, whether with those recognized as having a political character or with those acting more

---

[49] To study various decisions made by the JEP, their impact, and to read diverse publications from the *Ibero-American Yearbook on International Humanitarian Law* published by the University of La Sabana with the support of the International Committee of the Red Cross office in Bogotá, see: https://www.unisabana.edu.co/programas/unidades-academicas/facultad-de-derecho-y-ciencias-politicas/anuariodih/.

in organized crime contexts, the processes will also move forward based on selection and prioritization strategies, with formulas such as 'maximum responsible' being applied, among others. It is now a global strategy internalized in the most diverse legal-political frameworks.

16

The Orientation Criteria Document in Bosnia and Herzegovina

Zekerija Mujkanović*

16.1. Introduction

The war raged on for four blood-stained summers and three long brutal winters throughout my country, Bosnia and Herzegovina, between 1992 and 1995. When the fighting stopped, at least 97,000 soldiers and civilians of all ethnicities had lost their lives in the violence[1] and over one million people were displaced. The lack of trust had severed the relations of old neighbours. Hostilities could not be covered up. State institutions – including the police, the prosecution and the courts – were unable to operate as was expected and no longer enjoyed the trust of the citizens they served.

Thus, it is of no surprise that, during the first post-war years, very little was achieved on any side towards resolving the legacy left by the war crimes. After the war (even during various periods of the war), the police, the prosecution, investigative judges and the courts selected cases themselves to investigate and to criminally prosecute their enemies. Rarely was there any re-examination regarding the accountability of anyone from the same ethnic group. Due to divisions in the State and the continued insecurity of free movement through the (sometimes) invisible internal borders of post-war Bosnia and Herzegovina, few of them were able to collect sufficient evidence for any given case. To make things worse, complete archive materials were secretly moved out of the country. Large segments of valuable evidence that could have been used in local case-processing were delivered to the International Criminal Tribunal for the Former

* **Zekerija Mujkanović** is Chief Prosecutor of Brčko District of Bosnia and Herzegovina. At the time of writing, he was Public Prosecutor of Brčko District of Bosnia and Herzegovina and a member of the High Judicial and Prosecutorial Council of Bosnia and Herzegovina. This chapter has not been substantively updated since the Second Edition. He graduated from the Law Faculty of the University of Sarajevo in 1984. His professional career in the justice sector started in 1994 as a judge in Municipal Court of Brčko. He was President of the Municipal Court of Brčko 1997–2001 and became Public Prosecutor of Brčko District in 2001.

1 Correspondence with Ewe Tabe, demographer, International Criminal Tribunal for the former Yugoslavia ('ICTY') Office of the Prosecutor, 10 September 2008.

Yugoslavia in The Hague ('ICTY'), while the victims had moved on to all parts of the world.

Significant efforts were made with the aim of reforming the judicial sector, beginning in 2002, and in part started to resolve some of these issues. As a result of the Exit Strategy which the United Nations ('UN') Security Council imposed on the ICTY in 2003,[2] even more was done to deal with the war crimes issues of Bosnia and Herzegovina.

This chapter was written against the background of these events.

16.2. 'War Crimes'

To begin with, it is important to clarify what is to be understood with the term 'war crimes'. Whenever I use the term 'war crimes' in this chapter, I mean genocide, crimes against humanity or violations of the customs of war, including conventional and common international criminal law.

I also view the term 'war crimes' through the prism of domestic law, that is, crimes as defined in the Criminal Code of Bosnia and Herzegovina which came into effect in 2003 as part of the above-mentioned reform of the judicial sector,[3] as well as the law that was in effect in Bosnia and Herzegovina prior to 2003.

There was some confusion regarding the application of domestic law in war crimes cases, that is, whether to apply the laws that were in effect at the time of the conflict in the 1990s[4] or the 2003 Criminal Code of Bosnia and Herzegovina. This is a significant issue, though I will not address it in this chapter.

I consider the roles of both conventional and customary international criminal law in the practice of Bosnia and Herzegovina in defining 'war crimes', both in the practical and conceptual sense.[5] I am also aware of the potential in-

2 See UN Security Council ('UNSC'), Resolution 1503 (2003), UN Doc. S/RES/1503 (2003), 28 August 2003 (https://www.legal-tools.org/doc/05a7de/); UNSC, Resolution 1534 (2004), UN Doc. S/RES/1534 (2004), 26 March 2004 (https://www.legal-tools.org/doc/ffe092/).

3 Criminal Code of Bosnia and Herzegovina, 1 March 2003, Articles 171–184 ('Criminal Code of Bosnia and Herzegovina') (https://www.legal-tools.org/doc/46b8dc/).

4 See, for example, Chapter 16, Criminal acts against humanity and international law, Criminal Code of the Socialist Federative Republic of Yugoslavia, 28 September 1976 (https://www.legal-tools.org/doc/jie2pin6/).

5 See Criminal Code of Bosnia and Herzegovina, Article 4a, see *supra* note 3; also see European Convention on Human Rights, 4 November 1950, Article 7 (https://www.legal-tools.org/doc/8267cb/), which is applied through the application of Article 2 of the Constitution of Bosnia and Herzegovina, 14 December 1995 (https://www.legal-tools.org/doc/6876c3/); see also International Covenant on Civil and Political Rights, 16 December 1966, Article 15

fluence on the development of customary international criminal law of the hundreds of cases which we will ultimately investigate and prosecute in Bosnia and Herzegovina.[6]

I am aware that international law requires Bosnia and Herzegovina to punish perpetrators of war crimes and genocide. This duty encompasses in my opinion a responsibility to, as thoroughly as possible, identify, investigate, prosecute and punish the most serious crimes and their perpetrators.[7] In this regard, this chapter addresses decision-making as to what needs to be done and by whom.

16.3. What Was Done Prior to the Second Edition

A book published in 2007 states that local courts throughout Bosnia and Herzegovina, in the ten years between 1995 and 2005, rendered 55 final verdicts in war crimes cases.[8] During that same period, the ICTY issued indictments against approximately 100 individuals for crimes committed during the conflict in the former Yugoslavia.

Apart from this, the Special Department for War Crimes of the Prosecutor's Office of Bosnia and Herzegovina, in little under three months, issued indictments against 99 individuals charged with war crimes, in 45 cases. We achieved major success in these cases in a relatively short period, and we have since gotten better and more efficient.

(https://www.legal-tools.org/doc/2838f3/). Furthermore, Bosnia and Herzegovina is the successor to the conventions, including the Geneva Convention (1949) and the Protocols.

6 For example, Criminal Code of Bosnia and Herzegovina, Article 171, see *supra* note 3 defines the crime of genocide, using terms almost identical to those used in Article 6 of the Rome Statute of the International Criminal Court, 17 July 1998 (https://www.legal-tools.org/doc/7b9af9/). We tried one exceptionally important domestic case for genocide dealing with the Kravica warehouse in Srebrenica 1995 in which convictions were rendered at the main hearing in August 2008. Article 172 of the Criminal Code of Bosnia and Herzegovina, see *supra* note 3, defines crimes against humanity using terms almost identical to those in Article 7 of the Statute of the International Criminal Court. We have held trials and verdicts have been passed, including final verdicts in cases qualified as crimes against humanity. These first and second instance verdicts have been published. They provide domestic interpretation of the law and the way it was applied in each case. They are a potential source for commentaries on international criminal law, as will be the ever-growing number of decisions from Bosnia and Herzegovina. The judgments are available on the ICC Legal Tools Database, in the comprehensive 'Court of Bosnia and Herzegovina Collection' under 'Other International(ised) Criminal Jurisdictions'.

7 See, for example, the Convention on the Prevention and Punishment of the Crime of Genocide, 9 December 1948 (https://www.legal-tools.org/doc/498c38/).

8 *War Crimes in Bosnia and Herzegovina: Legally Effective Criminal Sentences in Bosnia and Herzegovina, 1992-2005*, American Bar Association, Rule of Law Initiative, Sarajevo, 2007.

16.4. Historical Context

The topic I have been invited to address has to be positioned in a brief historical context. When the Dayton Peace Accord was signed in 1995, there were probably a couple of hundred *major war criminals* at large in Bosnia and Herzegovina. At the same time, there were even a greater number of *war criminals who had committed serious crimes* who were also at large. Of course, there were also many *common soldiers* who had committed separate brutal offences. There were those who had participated in these offences on all levels.

They all require attention. No one should go unpunished for their unlawful ways. However, in practical terms, it is not possible to reach all perpetrators on every level. Even with more resources it would be wrong, and still is, to create a feeling of expectation that investigations and criminal prosecution will be brought against all those who have committed war crimes and that they will be convicted and punished severely. This would, quite definitely, lead to disappointment, which would diminish confidence in the institutions that are responsible for processing war crimes cases, as well as the whole criminal justice system.

At the same time, everything cannot be done at once. And there is no point in processing one case at a time, as will be explained further. A more regulated method is needed so as to take on the task of applying both domestic and international criminal law to process the crimes that were committed during the war.

The Special Department for War Crimes of the Prosecutor's Office of Bosnia and Herzegovina, as well as the prosecutors of the cantonal and district prosecutor's offices, are tasked with investigating and prosecuting war crimes. I will describe this task and some things the Special Department has done to bring order to the processing of these cases. There are questions that require attention, such as whether the division of tasks between the Special Department and the cantonal and district prosecutor's offices makes sense and whether additional measures should be developed.

I will elaborate on some tools that we use to give the process meaning, though the decision basically on 'who will do what' is a political one, and one which requires a satisfactory answer. The National War Crimes Strategy, discussed in detail in Chapter 17 below, gives some answers to this and other questions, although we knew before its adoption that we should not wait for the development of a National Strategy to achieve better methods to organize our workload. I believe we have a doable way to complete the work, a method that will continue to be valuable regardless of which political decisions are made.

16.5. The Task

In 2004, when the Rules of the Road Unit of the ICTY closed down, electronically-scanned copies of materials from its files were returned to Bosnia and Herzegovina for review. The Rules of the Road files are cases which, according to the Rome Agreement that was reached in 1996[9] between the countries of the region and the ICTY, were sent to the ICTY for review and approval to be processed by the local authorities.[10]

There is a background to the Rules of the Road. But the files that existed at the time of the Rome Agreement were packed and sent, which also happened to the new files that were compiled between 1996 and the end of 2004, when the Unit was closed. The files that were returned to the Special Department for War Crimes in 2004 were, in principle, in the same state as when the ICTY received them in 1996. No additional investigation had been undertaken in the meantime.

The Rules of the Road Unit of the ICTY Prosecution had assigned a 'standard designation' to each file:

- **Standard Designation 'A'** was given to files which the ICTY review team considered to contain sufficient 'evidence', pursuant to international standards, to provide probable cause to conclude that the individuals named as potential suspects or accused had committed serious violations of international law;
- **Standard Designation 'B'** was given to files which the ICTY review team considered to *not* contain sufficient 'evidence' for the rendering of such conclusion;
- **Standard Designation 'C'** was given to cases which the ICTY review team considered to not contain sufficient information to be able to make a decision; and
- **Standard Designations 'D', 'E', 'F' and 'G'** were given to cases for a variety of other reasons which did not necessarily refer to the 'quality' of the information contained.

From October 2004, the Special Department for War Crimes started receiving e-copies of 877 files that received the Standard Designation 'A'. Electronic copies of materials from 2,389 files with Standard Designation 'B' were ultimately returned. Standard Designation 'C' was given to 702 files that were also returned to Bosnia and Herzegovina.

[9] Rome Agreement on Agreed Measures, 18 February 1996; see para. 5, Cooperation on War Crimes and Respect for Human Rights (https://www.legal-tools.org/doc/vlstvw26/).

[10] See Procedures and Guidelines for Parties for Delivering Cases to the International Criminal Court for the Former Yugoslavia in accordance with the agreed measures of 18 February 1996 ('Rules of the Road').

16.6. Deciding Who Will Do What

The Special Department for War Crimes was tasked to sort out the returned files. A decision was made to focus on those files with Standard Designation 'A'. The decision was primarily based on the available funds.

Similar to what had been done by the ICTY staff tasked with the case review, the review initiated by the Special Department in 2005 was based only on what had been received. Additional investigations were not carried out.

Once a strategic decision was made that both the cantonal and district prosecutor's offices and the Prosecutor's Office of Bosnia and Herzegovina would be engaged in the processing of returned cases, the Special Department adopted rules regulating the review of files designated 'A'.[11] The rules were used to divide files with standard designation 'A' into the categories 'VERY SENSITIVE' and 'SENSITIVE'.

VERY SENSITIVE category

a. CRIMINAL OFFENCE
   - i. Genocide[12]
   - ii. Extermination
   - iii. Multiple murders
   - iv. Rapes and other sexual acts being part of the system (for example, in concentration camps or during the attacks)
   - v. Enslavement
   - vi. Torture
   - vii. Persecution, widespread and systematic
   - viii. Mass, unlawful detention in concentration camps

b. PERPETRATOR
   - i. Current or former commanders (including paramilitary forces)
   - ii. Current or former political leaders (including municipal presidents and crisis headquarters)
   - iii. Current or former judicial office holders
   - iv. Current or former heads of police forces
   - v. Concentration camp commanders
   - vi. Notorious persons
   - vii. Multiple rapists

[11] The Prosecutor's Office of Bosnia and Herzegovina, KTA-RZ-47/04-1, Book of Rules on the review of war crime cases, 28 December 2004; Addendum, A-441/04, Guiding criteria for sensitive cases of the Road Map, 12 October 2004.

[12] This should be considered as an accusation in every Srebrenica-related case.

c. OTHER
   i. Cases in which witnesses are 'members of a smaller group of people' or 'accused'
   ii. Realistic chances for intimidation of witnesses
   iii. Cases including perpetrators in the territory which is benevolent to them or where the interest of the authorities is to prevent public investigation of crimes.

SENSITIVE category

a. CRIMINAL OFFENCE
   i. Murder committed as a part of or after the attack, or in the camp
   ii. Rapes and other serious sexual criminal offenses
   iii. Serious attacks committed as part of the system
   iv. Inhuman and degrading treatment committed as part of the system
   v. Mass deportations or forcible transferring of people
   vi. Destruction or damage made to religious or cultural institutions on a large scale and systematically
   vii. Destruction of property on a large scale and systematically
   viii. Deprivation of fundamental human rights such as medical treatment on a large scale and systematically
   ix. Crimes belonging to notorious crimes, although not classified under Category I

b. PERPETRATORS
   i. Current or former police officials
   ii. Current members of the army
   iii. Persons holding or who used to hold political function
   iv. Persons affiliated with the camp management

c. OTHER
   i. Witness protection issues
   ii. Difficult legal issues
   iii. Crimes for which a potential long-term prison sentence could be imposed
   iv. Allegations connected with events that were already tried before the ICTY
   v. Cases with extensive documentation

Out of 877 files, 202 were estimated 'VERY SENSITIVE' and were kept by the Special Department for War Crimes. The remaining files were deemed 'SENSITIVE' and were sent for further investigation to the cantonal and district prosecutor's offices in the places where these incidents took place as stated in the files.

The rules and criteria used to carry out this review used to be the best way to share the work among one small unit for processing war crimes in the Prosecutor's Office of Bosnia and Herzegovina and cantonal and district prosecutors.

We have learned over time that the original review process carried out by the ICTY was not very reliable. Many of the received files were 'old'. The information contained in the electronic copies that had been returned was often of poor quality, by all relevant standards, and as such could not be authenticated. In many cases it turned out that victims, witnesses or suspects had deceased or were inaccessible. Using an analytical approach, it was established that even the files to which the ICTY gave the Standard Designation 'B' contained information which, when cross-referenced against other information, led to suspects and evidence which could be instrumental in criminal prosecutions in Bosnia and Herzegovina.

We also learned that in 2005 the cantonal and district prosecutor's offices did not fully adopt the criteria set by the Special Department for War Crimes and the presuppositions they were based on. Even though the criteria were reasonable at the time, there were significant delays in their adoption.

Some deficiencies were noted in the review process as well. In order to be able to complete the assignment, the staff engaged in the review had to accept the information from the files as reliable, while time and experience showed that it was actually not. Furthermore, due to financial constraints, the staff conducting the review in 2005 were forced to process a large number of cases in a very limited period of time. The files were not only incomplete, but also contained statements and other documents in languages which the staff did not understand. The review and decisions were made on the basis of hastily prepared summaries and translations.

The review made in 2005 was the best that could be undertaken in the circumstances, but the presumptions deriving from the review could not be justified. That was particularly true if the number of disputed cases was taken into account. The review did not adequately address the issue of unnecessary documents contained in the files. A number of those refer to the same cases, events or situations, but it was almost impossible to detect or anticipate the overlapping without a thorough analysis. If you disregarded the unnecessary documents,[13] numerous consequences could be expected in terms of investigation and criminal prosecution.

[13] Including minutes of numerous, well-intentioned but useless hearings of the same witnesses and victims by prosecutors and investigators who operated independently of each other, at the state, cantonal and district levels.

I will not go deeper into the method by which the cases had been selected prior to 2007, nor will I dwell further on the messy discussion on whether war crimes should be prosecuted at the state or cantonal and district levels. Rather, what is important is what we did in the 18 months prior to this Second Edition to improve our work and better organize the process of identification and selection of cases requiring investigation and prosecution, irrespective of the level at which the cases were processed.

Precious experience acquired in conducting investigations and preparing cases for prosecution – starting with the cases bearing the 'A' designation, classified as 'VERY SENSITIVE' and retained in the Prosecutor's Office of Bosnia and Herzegovina, as well as the experience from the field – have shown that a case-by-case prosecution is neither efficient nor effective. Such an approach did not lead us in the desired direction and only deepened the ongoing mess about what should be done, how and by whom.

Whatever the term 'core international crimes' might imply, the mere focusing on the existing files in order to determine what needs to be done, what can and must be done and who will do it, simply did not work in Bosnia and Herzegovina. Neither did it promise to fulfil the expectations by the courts and prosecutor's offices. The databases were not very useful in that sense (except for identification of potential sources of evidence pertaining to committed war crimes), partly due to the condition in which the documents were returned from the ICTY. Databases themselves can never offer specific assessments or the functions required by prosecutors. They are not an adequate replacement for the smart and focused exercise of a discretionary right which each prosecutor should use in the public interest. Databases can be used for collecting and sorting information, but they cannot 'make decisions'.

In 2006, it became clear that we needed a new approach to the issue of war crimes prosecutions in Bosnia and Herzegovina. The response to this was an analytical approach, considering cases, events and situations instead of files. This approach sought to address the issue of prioritization of war crimes cases in the Prosecutor's Office of Bosnia and Herzegovina.

17

Criteria for Selection and Prioritization of Core International Crimes in the National War Crimes Strategy of Bosnia and Herzegovina

Aida Šušić*

17.1. Introduction

Armed conflicts in which many core international crimes are committed entail numerous suspects. When many case files involving such crimes have been opened, the criminal justice system may face big challenges in processing all or a large proportion of open cases, as discussed in Chapters 1, 3 and 4 above. Core international crimes are severe and massive offences, with consequences that shock and affect the whole world-community. International instruments impose on states an obligation to prosecute and punish those who commit such crimes.[1]

---

* **Aida Šušić** is Legal Advisor for Public and Constitutional Law at the Office of the High Representative ('OHR') of Bosnia and Herzegovina ('BiH'). Previously, she worked at the High Judicial and Prosecutorial Council of BiH and at the Improving Judicial Efficiency Project. She obtained her LL.M. in public international law at Oslo University and her Bachelor's degree at the University of Sarajevo. Views expressed in this chapter are the author's and they are not necessarily shared by the Office of the High Representative or the High Judicial and Prosecutorial Council.

[1] Geneva Convention for the Amelioration of the Condition of the Wounded and Sick in Armed Forces in the Field, 12 August 1949 (https://www.legal-tools.org/doc/baf8e7/); Geneva Convention for the Amelioration of the Conditions of Wounded, Sick and Shipwrecked Members of Armed Forces at Sea, 12 August 1949 (https://www.legal-tools.org/doc/0d0216/); Geneva Convention Relative to the Treatment of Prisoners of War, 12 August 1949 (https://www.legal-tools.org/doc/365095/); Geneva Convention Relative to the Protection of Civilian Persons in Time of War, 12 August 1949 (https://www.legal-tools.org/doc/d5e260/), namely Articles 49, 50, 129 and 146, respectively; Convention on the Prevention and Punishment of the Crime of Genocide, Article IV (https://www.legal-tools.org/doc/498c38/); and the sixth preambular paragraph of the Rome Statute of the International Criminal Court ('ICC'), 17 July 1998 ('ICC Statute') (http://www.legaltools.org/doc/7b9af9/). See also Otto Triffterer (ed.), *Commentary on the Rome Statute of the International Criminal Court*, Second Edition, C.H. Beck, Hart, Nomos, Munich, 2008, p. 11. The obligation to prosecute crimes against humanity is still disputed by some. The obligations to prosecute crimes of genocide and war crimes are firmly rooted in conventional law, as specified above. On the contrary, there is no specialized con-

Notwithstanding the doctrine of universal jurisdiction and other legal grounds of jurisdiction, such as the active and passive nationality principles, the majority of cases involving core international crimes will probably be processed by the authorities of the state where those crimes were committed.[2] Ideally, in order to comply with the said obligation, the relevant authorities should search for and prosecute all those who have committed core international crimes. Moreover, international human rights instruments[3] promote certain values that all states consider important and call for their protection.[4]

Additionally, the concept of transitional justice, which emerged in the late 1980s and the early 1990s, expects that societies in their transition to democracy address past human rights abuses.[5] The transitional justice approach includes a

---

vention with respect to crimes against humanity. Thus, it has to be established that the obligation is a part of customary international law. It is highly questionable whether a multilateral treaty, such as the ICC Statute, is indeed a codification of a pre-existing customary obligation to prosecute crimes against humanity. Nonetheless, it is warranted to stress that the obligation to prosecute crimes against humanity is advocated for by many scholars. See for instance M. Cherif Bassiouni, "Accountability for Violations of International Humanitarian Law and Other Serious Violations of Human Rights", in M. Cherif Bassiouni (ed.), *Post-Conflict Justice*, Transnational Publishers, 2002, pp. 12, 13; Michael P. Scharf. and Nigel Rodley, "International Law Principles on Accountability", in *ibid.*, p. 94; Antonio Cassese, "Balancing the Prosecution of Crimes Against Humanity and Non-Retroactivity of Criminal Law, The Kolk and Kislyiy v. Estonia Case Before the ECHR", in *Journal of International Criminal Justice*, 2006, vol. 4, no. 2, pp. 410–418. In this regard, see also the ruling of the International Criminal Tribunal for the former Yugoslavia ('ICTY'), *Prosecutor v. Duško Tadić*, Appeals Chamber, Decision on the Defence Motion for Interlocutory Appeal on Jurisdiction, 2 October 1995, paras. 137–142 (https://www.legal-tools.org/doc/80x1an/). In addition, many argue that crimes against humanity have reached the status of *jus cogens* norms, thus entailing the obligation *erga omnes* to prosecute those who commit them. For instance, see generally M. Cherif Bassiouni, "International Crimes: Jus Cogens and Obligation *Erga Omnes*", in *Law and Contemporary Problems*, 1996, vol. 59, no. 4, pp. 63–74.

2 For discussion on legal grounds of jurisdiction see more Antonio Cassese, *International Law*, Second Edition, Oxford University Press, 2005, pp. 431, 452.

3 See Universal Declaration of Human Rights, 10 December 1948, Preamble (https://www.legal-tools.org/doc/de5d83/); European Convention for the Protection of Human Rights and Fundamental Freedoms, Article 1 ('ECHR') (https://www.legal-tools.org/doc/8267cb/).

4 In order to address human rights breaches as specified in the ECHR, the Human Rights Chamber was established in BiH under the Annex 6 to the Dayton Peace Agreement and its Protocols (https://www.legal-tools.org/doc/bycwxsm3/); see the Human Rights Chamber's web site.

5 Inter-American Court of Human Rights, *Case of Velasquez – Rodriguez v. Honduras*, Judgment, 29 July 1988, paras. 161–188 (https://www.legal-tools.org/doc/18607f/). In this case, the Court found that any state has four fundamental obligations in the field of human rights: taking measures to prevent violation of human rights, conducting serious investigation in case of breach, imposing suitable actions on those responsible and ensuring reparations for the victims. These findings are in part the basis for the transitional justice concept (see the International Center for Transitional Justice's web site).

range of mechanisms: criminal prosecutions, truth commissions, reparations, justice system reforms, reconciliation, *et cetera*.[6] Post-conflict justice is a way to deal with the past by promoting peace and reconciliation for the future. It also calls for the restoration and development of the justice system which may have been damaged by the conflict.[7] However, transitional societies affected by past atrocities may face extraordinary difficulties in trying to deal with the accumulated backlog of core international crimes cases and its consequences for victims and society.

From 1992 to 1995, a great number of gross violations of international humanitarian law were committed in BiH. The armed conflict, which lasted for almost four years, was conducted with such cruelty and scale that it caused enormous human losses, displacement, refugees, missing persons and destroyed property. Despite a clear determination of the international community and the BiH criminal justice system to deal with the atrocities committed during the war, the number of outstanding cases remained extremely high. Numerous suspects were still at-large. In December 2008, as an attempt to comprehensively and systematically tackle this issue, the Ministry of Justice of BiH adopted the National War Crimes Strategy[8] with the aim to process the most complex and highest-priority cases within a seven-year time limit, and all other war crimes cases within 15 years of its adoption. The case selection and prioritization criteria meant to facilitate this process formed an integral part of the Strategy.

This chapter discusses the following question: What are the prospects and obstacles of these criteria effectively addressing the backlog of the core international crimes cases in BiH? The experience of BiH will be presented as a case study that may serve as a useful model for other societies facing similar challenges.

Chapters 1 and 2 above analyse the evolution of the discourse on criteria. They emerged in the 1990s with the creation of the ICTY as a response to mass atrocities in ex-Yugoslavia, especially in BiH. As a consequence of the ICTY's completion strategy,[9] the epicentre of the issue moved from the international to

6 See the International Center for Transitional Justice's web site. See also Luis Bickford, "Transitional Justice", in *The Encyclopaedia of Genocide and Crimes Against Humanity*, Macmillan Library Reference, 2004, vol. 3, pp. 1045–1047.

7 Bassiouni, 2002, p. xv, see *supra* note 1.

8 Ministry of Justice of BiH, "National War Crimes Strategy", 29 December 2008 ('National War Crimes Strategy' or 'Strategy').

9 According to the Report of 19 November 2010, submitted by the President of the ICTY to the United Nations ('UN') Security Council ('UNSC') regarding the implementation of the completion strategy, the majority of trials were expected to be completed in 2012. In the case of *Prosecutor v. Radovan Karadžić* the judgment was expected to be rendered during 2014. The

the domestic level. It became clear that only a limited number of cases would be prosecuted by the ICTY[10] and that the majority of cases would be processed in BiH.[11] Domestic trials are necessary to combat impunity and ensure respect for the rule of law.[12]

The chapter is organized as follows. Section 17.2. provides some background information on specific post-conflict political, social and legal circumstances in BiH. Section 17.3. discusses the case selection and prioritization criteria in BiH as well as those created under the auspices of the ICTY and ICC. Section 17.4. sets forth relevant requirements for the criteria's success in the post-war transition of BiH. Finally, Section 17.5. provides some concluding remarks.

For the purposes of this chapter, the term 'core international crimes' should be considered synonymous with the term 'war crimes' *lato sensu*, and both will be used interchangeably to refer to crimes of genocide, crimes against humanity and war crimes *stricto sensu*, as defined by international legal documents such as the Statutes of the ICTY and ICC.[13]In BiH's context these expressions should include genocide, crimes against humanity and war crimes *stricto sensu* as defined by the Criminal Code of BiH,[14] the entity and district Criminal Codes, as well as the Criminal Code of the Socialist Federal Republic of Yugoslavia as applicable at the time of the alleged perpetration of the offences. 'Criminal justice system' is defined as collective institutions through which an accused of-

proceedings in the case of *Prosecutor v. Goran Hadzic* were anticipated to commence in January 2013. The preliminary assessment in the case of *Prosecutor v. Ratko Mladic* was that the trial would not commence before November 2012. See UNSC, Letter dated 15 November 2011 of the President of the ICTY addressed to the President of the Security Council, UN Doc. S/2011/716, 16 November 2011 (https://www.legal-tools.org/doc/qxcyj4/).

10 As of 20 May 2012, the ICTY indicted 161 persons. Out of this number, 90 cases including 126 accused had been completed, and 15 cases with 35 accused were still ongoing.

11 UNSC Resolution 1503 (2003), UN Doc. S/RES/1503 (2003), 28 August 2003 ('S/RES/1503 (2003)') (https://www.legal-tools.org/doc/05a7de/) noted that the establishment and functioning of the War Crimes Chamber of BiH Sate Court is "an essential prerequisite to achieving the objective of the ICTY Completion Strategy".

12 Human Rights Watch, "Narrowing the Impunity Gap: Trials Before Bosnia's War Crimes Chamber", February 2007, vol. 19, no. 1(D), p. 3.

13 See ICC Statute, Articles 6, 7 and 8, *supra* note 1; Statute of the International Criminal Tribunal for the former Yugoslavia, 25 May 1993, Articles 2, 3, 4 and 5 ('ICTY Statute') (https://www.legal-tools.org/doc/b4f63b/).

14 See Criminal Code of BiH, 24 January 2003, Articles 171–175 (https://www.legal-tools.org/doc/gnnveg00/).

fender passes until the accusation has been disposed of or punishment administered.[15] The 'best suited case' is a case that meets the agreed criteria, which normally seem to include a consideration of the gravity of the crime, the seniority of the suspect, the strength of the evidence and other relevant considerations. 'Selection of cases' refers to a process of reaching a decision on which forum or venue is the most appropriate to process a certain case. It signifies the distribution of cases between relevant courts. 'Prioritization of cases' means deciding to proceed with a certain case before other cases, that is, giving priority to a particular case. Case selection and prioritization criteria may be used as a tool in order to reach both types of decisions. 'Transitional justice' is a response to systematic or widespread violations of human rights. It seeks recognition for victims and to promote possibilities for peace, reconciliation and democracy.[16]

17.2. The Background

17.2.1. Post-Conflict Constitutional Realities

Understanding the complexity of the design of the state of BiH is crucial for the appreciation of its post-war transition. "It's a state by international design and of international design".[17]

The war in BiH lasted from 1992 to 1995. It was brought to an end by the conclusion of the General Framework Peace Agreement for Bosnia and Herzegovina ('the Dayton Peace Agreement'),[18] which was signed on 14 December 1995 in Dayton, Ohio in the United States. It was signed by Alija Izetbegović, Franjo Tuđman and Slobodan Milošević on behalf of their respective countries, namely BiH, the Republic of Croatia and Serbia. The fact that this agreement ended the war in BiH is undisputable, but its implementation remains an ever-struggling battle. Built on the foundations of ethnic cleansing, leaving the society deeply divided and "polarized on the most basic issues – the question on the legitimacy of the state, its common institutions and its borders"[19] had led to a long-lasting battle "to buil[d] a 'single multi-ethnic country' in any meaningful sense".[20]

---

15 Bryan A. Garner *et al.* (eds.), *Black's Law Dictionary*, Deluxe Eighth Edition, West Group, Saint Paul, 2004, p. 403.

16 See the International Center for Transitional Justice's web site.

17 Sumantra Bose, *Bosnia After Dayton, Nationalist Partition and International Intervention*, Hurst and Company, London, 2002, p. 60. It is well-known in BiH that the Dayton Peace Agreement was mainly the work of the lawyers from the United States.

18 See the Dayton Peace Agreement and its Protocols, *supra* note 4.

19 Bose, 2002, p. 3, see *supra* note 17.

20 *Ibid.*, p. 53.

Pursuant to the Dayton Peace Agreement, BiH is divided into two entities: Federation of BiH ('FBiH') and Republic of Srpska ('RS'). In 1999, the status of Brčko was finally settled by the Arbitration Tribunal for the Dispute over the Inter-Entity Boundary Line in Brčko Area. Brčko District is established as a separate administrative unit with local self-governance placed under the sovereignty of BiH.[21] The FBiH is administratively divided into ten federal units called cantons. Republic of Srpska consists of five administrative units referred to as districts. The Constitution of BiH[22] established a complex political structure with very limited powers for the central institutions.[23] The central government consists of a bicameral legislative body, the three-member Presidency (one from each constituent peoples: Bosniacs, Serbs and Croats), the Council of Ministers (consisting of nine ministries, including the Ministry of Justice), the Constitutional Court (composed of mixture of national and international judges) and the Central Bank.[24]

17.2.2. Aspects of the BiH Post-Conflict Transition

The war in BiH was undoubtedly among the most horrible armed conflicts in Europe since World War II. It is estimated that the war resulted in 97,207 dead persons; out of this number, 39,684 persons were civilians. In terms of ethnicity, 65.88 per cent were Bosniacs, 25.62 per cent Serbs, 8.01 per cent Croats and 0.49 per cent belonged to other groups.[25] Around 2.2 million people became

---

[21] Statute of Brčko District of BiH, 7 December 1999, Article 1(1) (https://www.legal-tools.org/doc/0ih60q/).

[22] Constitution of BiH, Annex 4 of the Dayton Peace Agreement, 14 December 1995 ('BiH Constitution') (https://www.legal-tools.org/doc/6876c3/).

[23] *Ibid.*, Article III(1).

[24] *Ibid.*, Articles IV, V, VI and VII.

[25] These figures are the result of the research conducted by the Research and Documentation Center, Sarajevo, under its project "Population Losses in BiH '91–'95". The presented numbers include only direct victims of war, that is, persons whose death was the result of direct military operations. The second part of the project aims to establish a record of the indirect victims of the war in BiH. It is useful to mention that this project is important not only for the fact that it presents a valuable database on number of victims in the BiH war, but also for the fact that it will as such help reduce the possibility to play with the numbers of war victims. For a long time, the number of victims was manipulated and has been a source of lots of controversy, for numerous political and other reasons. The estimations ranged from 25,000 to 200,000 war victims. See Balkan Investigative Reporting Network ('BARN'), "100 Days of Government", 21 November 2012 (available on the BARN's web site). Also see Report of the Secretary-General on the UN Mission in Bosnia and Herzegovina, UN Doc. S/2002/1314, 2 December 2002, p. 2 (https://www.legal-tools.org/doc/brr2ew/).

refugees. In addition, 1.3 million were internally displaced.[26] Some 10,000 persons have remained missing in BiH.[27]

It therefore does not come as a surprise that, in the aftermath of the armed conflict in BiH, the functioning of its judicial system suffered numerous difficulties. The war brought about a great loss of skilled members of the legal profession and the judiciary, alongside with the physical destruction and lack of proper equipment and facilities. As a consequence, the courts and prosecutors' offices throughout the country were filled by judges whose appointment was based on political and ethnic grounds. This has significantly hampered the ability of the courts to administer justice in a proper and efficient manner.[28] The complex constitutional structure of BiH, as explained above, has aggravated the situation. Strengthening the rule of law in BiH was therefore considered a priority in its post-conflict transition.[29] From 2002 and 2003 onwards, comprehensive legal and institutional reforms were carried out (see Section 17.2.3. below).

One of the important specificities of the BiH post-conflict transition is the position assumed by the international community. The international community exercised and still has a significant role in BiH's day-to-day life. Different international organizations were called to assist in the enforcement of the Dayton Peace Agreement.[30] Most importantly, the High Representative, was designated in order to supervise the implementation of the civilian aspects of the Dayton Peace Agreement on behalf of the international community.[31] The High Representative was given such broad powers that it was declared to be the final authority regarding the implementation of the civilian aspects of the Agreement. These powers[32] were further expanded by the Peace Implementation Council

[26] Press Release by the United Nations High Commissioner for Refugees ('UNHCR'), "Representation in Bosnia and Herzegovina", May 2006. See also UNHCR, "Update of UNHCR's Position on Categories of Persons from Bosnia and Herzegovina in Need of International Protection", August 2009, p. 1.

[27] See International Commission for Missing Persons, Press Release, 31 August 2009.

[28] Organization for Security and Co-operation in Europe ('OSCE'), Mission to BiH, *War Crimes Trials Before the Domestic Courts of Bosnia and Herzegovina, Progress and Obstacles*, Sarajevo, March 2005, p. 4.

[29] "Declaration of the Peace Implementation Council", Madrid, 16 December 1998, para. 12; "Final Report of the Independent Judicial Commission, January 2001–31 March 2004", November 2004, p. 3.

[30] Some of them are OSCE, UN Development Programme, European Union Police Mission and UNHCR.

[31] Annex 10 of the Dayton Peace Agreement, see *supra* note 4. UNSC has also supported the appointment of the High Representative; see UNSC, Resolution No. 1031, UN Doc. S/RES/1031 (1995), 15 December 1995 (https://www.legal-tools.org/doc/22278c/).

[32] Also known as 'Bonn powers'.

Conference held in Bonn in December 1997. They included the powers to remove from office public officials who violate legal commitments and the Dayton Peace Agreement, and to impose laws that the High Representative deems appropriate, if BiH's legislative bodies fail to do so.[33]

BiH remains a divided country, not only in terms of its administrative structures, but in social terms as well. The national interests of the three constituent peoples[34] – Bosniacs, Croats and Serbs – are used by the political parties to achieve different political objectives and politically-motivated decisions.[35] National polarization and division are still present and govern the main political, judicial[36] and other processes in BiH. This remains a stumbling block on its path towards achieving full participation in European integration.

17.2.3. BiH System for the Prosecution and Adjudication of Core International Crimes

The state of the BiH judiciary was an issue of concern in the years after the war.[37] The need for a comprehensive reform was apparent and it was advocated for by different parties.[38] Such reform was considered crucial for the enhancement of the rule of law and the independence and professionalism of judges and

---

33 Peace Implementation Council Bonn Conclusions, 10 December 1997, Article XI.2. The High Representative used the Bonn powers in many instances. On the role of High Representative in BiH, see also Bose, 2002, pp. 6 and 7, see *supra* note 17.

34 See the last preambular paragraph of the BiH Constitution, see *supra* note 22. In the case *Sejdić and Finci v. Bosnia and Herzegovina*, the European Court of Human Rights found discriminatory the provisions of the Dayton Peace Agreement which stipulated that only those belonging to one of the three constituent peoples of BiH were permitted to stand for elections of the House of Peoples or for the Presidency, thereby excluding members of the 14 other national minorities in the country. The European Court of Human Rights found that this amounted to a breach of Article 14 of the ECHR taken in conjunction with Article 3 of Protocol 1, as well as of Article 1 of Protocol 12. In order to implement the decision of the Court, vital changes to the Constitution of BiH are required. See European Court of Human Rights, *Case of Sejdić and Finci v. Bosnia and Herzegovina*, Grand Chamber, Judgment, Strasbourg, 22 December 2009 (https://www.legal-tools.org/doc/249bae/).

35 See, generally, European Stability Initiative, "Reshaping international priorities in Bosnia and Herzegovina, Part One: Bosnian Power", *Structures*, 14 October 1999.

36 UN Mission in BiH, Judicial System Assessment Programme, "Thematic Report IX, Political Influence: The Independence of the Judiciary in Bosnia and Herzegovina", November 2000, p. 13.

37 UN Mission in BiH, Judicial System Assessment Programme, "Thematic Report VII, Prosecuting Corruption: A Study of the Weaknesses of the Criminal Justice System in Bosnia and Herzegovina", November 2000.

38 UN Mission in BiH, Judicial System Assessment Programme, "Thematic Report X, Serving the Public: The Delivery of Justice in Bosnia and Herzegovina", November 2000; UN Mission in BiH, Judicial System Assessment Programme, "Thematic Report IX, Political Influence: The Independence of the Judiciary in Bosnia and Herzegovina", November 2000; International

prosecutors throughout the country.[39] The Independent Judicial Commission was created under the auspices of the Office of the High Representative in order to facilitate the judicial reform programme in BiH.[40] This task was taken over by the High Judicial and Prosecutorial Council in 2002.[41] Subsequently, broad reforms of the judicial and prosecutorial systems,[42] combined with substantive and procedural criminal legislation reforms,[43] both at the state and entity level, were carried out in 2002 and 2003, respectively.

The prosecution and adjudication of core international crimes is shared between the state and the entity, that is, the Brčko District prosecutorial and judicial institutions.[44]

At the state level, in 2000 the Court of BiH was established by the decision of the High Representative, but it became operational in May 2002 when the first judges were appointed. The Court of BiH (also known as the 'State Court') was created in order to ensure the effective exercise of the competencies of the state of BiH and the respect of human rights and the rule of law.[45] In January

---

Crisis Group, "Courting Disaster: The Misrule of Law in Bosnia and Herzegovina", 25 March 2002.

39 OHR, Criminal Institutions and Prosecutorial Reform Unit, *Restructuring of Bosnia and Herzegovina Prosecutorial System*, 2002, p. 3.

40 Press Release by the OHR, "Independent Judicial Commission Takes on Development of Judiciary in BiH", 30 November 2000.

41 "Final Report of the Independent Judicial Commission, January 2001–31 March 2004", November 2004, pp. 76–81.

42 The courts and prosecutor's offices were restructured and all judges and prosecutors were reappointed.

43 The new Criminal Code of BiH incorporated core international crimes, that is, genocide, crimes against humanity and war crimes, while the 1977 Criminal Code of the Socialist Federal Republic of Yugoslavia, which was in force during war in BiH, criminalized the acts prohibited under the Geneva Conventions. The new Criminal Procedure Code ('CPC of BiH') (https://www.legal-tools.org/doc/0a301a/) was a shift towards more adversarial model of criminal justice, while at the same time some typical inquisitorial components were abolished (the most significant one is the role of investigative judge). In this way, a mixed model of investigation and court proceedings was created, with several important new institutes: plea bargaining, a preliminary hearing and preliminary proceedings judges, new rules on presentation of evidence, cross-examination of witnesses, *et cetera*. See in general OSCE, Mission to BiH, *Trial Monitoring Report on the Implementation of the New Criminal Procedure Code in the Courts of Bosnia and Herzegovina*, Sarajevo, December 2004.

44 Lilian A. Barria, and Steven D. Roper, "Judicial Capacity Building in Bosnia and Herzegovina: Understanding Legal Reform Beyond the Completion Strategy of the ICTY", in *Human Rights Review*, 2008, vol. 9, no. 3, pp. 3–5; Swedish International Development Agency, *Justice Chain Analysis, Bosnia and Herzegovina*, Sarajevo, June 2007, Chapters 2 and 3.

45 High Representative's Decision on Law Establishing the State Court of BiH, 12 November 2000, Official Gazette of BiH No. 29/00 (https://www.legal-tools.org/doc/4e4ths55/); Law on

2005, the War Crimes Chamber[46] was established within the Criminal Division of the State Court in order to process the most serious war crimes cases committed during the conflict in BiH, including both the cases transferred by the ICTY as a result of its completion strategy and the cases initiated locally.

The Prosecutor's Office of BiH is the institution responsible for the investigation and prosecution of cases before the State Court. It was established by the decision of the High Representative in August 2002.[47] For the purpose of the prosecution of war crimes cases, the War Crimes Department within the Prosecutor's Office of BiH was created in January 2005.

In FBiH, there are 32 municipal courts with the jurisdiction over lower-level cases, that is, those cases for which the maximum sentence of 10 years of imprisonment may be prescribed[48] and 10 cantonal courts acting as courts of first instance for the adjudication of cases concerning crimes with a minimum 10 years of imprisonment sanctioned, as well as the second instance courts when municipal courts' decisions are contested.[49] The 10 cantonal courts have jurisdiction to try war crimes. In addition, at the Federation level there is also the Supreme Court of FBiH serving as an appeal court for decisions of cantonal courts.[50]

At the Federation level, there are 11 prosecutors' offices, namely the Prosecutor's Office of the FBiH[51] and 10 cantonal prosecutors' offices.[52]

The RS court structure is parallel to the FBiH court system: there are 19 basic courts competent to adjudicate lower-level criminal offences for which imprisonment up to 10 years may be pronounced, and five district courts serving as first instance courts for crimes punishable with minimum sentence of 10 years

Court of BiH, 3 July 2002, Official Gazette of BiH No. 16/02, Article 1 (https://www.legal-tools.org/doc/2xsja4wl/).

46 OSCE, Mission to BiH, 2005, p. 10, see *supra* note 28; see also UN, "Security Council briefed on establishment of War Crimes Chamber within State Court of Bosnia and Herzegovina", Press Release, 8 October 2003, No. SC/7888.

47 Law on the Prosecutor's Office of BiH, Official Gazette Nos. 24/02, 03/03, 37/03, 42/03, 09/04, 35/04, 61/04 and 61/09), in OHR, "Decision Enacting the Law on the Prosecutor's Office of Bosnia and Herzegovina", 6 August 2002 (https://www.legal-tools.org/doc/dqqjfrsy/).

48 Law on Courts of the FBiH, 4 July 2005, Official Gazette of FBiH No. 38/05 (https://www.legal-tools.org/doc/5xm0ehkr/).

49 *Ibid.*, Articles 17, 25 and 28.

50 *Ibid.*, Articles 18 and 29.

51 The work of this service is governed by the Law on the Federation Prosecutor's Office of the FBiH, in OHR, "Decisions Enacting the Law on the Federation Prosecutor's Office of the Federation of Bosnia and Herzegovina", 21 August 2002 (https://www.legal-tools.org/doc/gzo5hcn7/).

52 The work of cantonal prosecutor's offices is regulated by the individual cantonal laws.

of imprisonment and as second instance courts competent to decide upon appeals to basic courts' decisions.[53] War crimes cases are adjudicated before the district courts of RS. The Constitutional Court of RS is the appellate court sitting in judgment on appeals on district courts' decisions.[54]

In the RS entity, the work of prosecution services is governed by the Law on Prosecutor's Offices of RS. Besides the Republic Prosecutor's Office of RS, there are also five district prosecutor's offices.[55]

The prosecution of war crimes in Brčko District is under the jurisdiction of the Basic Court of Brčko District. The Appellate Court of Brčko District acts as the second instance court.[56] The Prosecutor's Office of Brčko District is the body in charge of prosecution of cases before the courts of this district.[57]

17.3. Criteria in the BiH Criminal Justice System

17.3.1. Backlog of Core International Crimes Cases in BiH

It is estimated that war in BiH resulted in almost 100,000 human lives lost,[58] an even greater number of injured and wounded people, enormous property destruction, and displaced persons and refugees. In addition, the whole system, including its political and judicial infrastructures, was almost destroyed. International as well as domestic efforts to hold accountable those suspected of committing war crimes started before the war ended. At the international level, the ICTY was established by the UNSC Resolution 827, adopted on 25 May 1993 as a response to mass atrocities committed in the territory of the former Yugoslavia, with primary jurisdiction over such crimes. During the war, at the national level, war crimes prosecutions were conducted by military and civilian courts, but were mostly directed against enemy perpetrators. Moreover, trials were conducted under political pressure. There were also concerns regarding

[53] Law on the Courts of the RS, 15 December 2011, Official Gazette of RS Nos. 111/04, 109/05, 37/06 and 119/08, Articles 16, 17, 22 and 25 (https://www.legal-tools.org/doc/cgkt3l1z/).

[54] *Ibid.*, Articles 18 and 28.

[55] Law on Prosecutor's Offices of RS, "Decision Enacting the Law on the Prosecutor's Offices of the Republika Srpska", 21 August 2002 (https://www.legal-tools.org/doc/k7u3r5ts/).

[56] Law on Courts of Brčko District, 26 June 2007, Official Gazette of Brčko District Nos. 19/07 and 20/07, Articles 17, 18, 19, 21 and 22 (https://www.legal-tools.org/doc/niw9kx8n/).

[57] Law on the Prosecutors Office of Brčko District, 26 June 2007, Official Gazette of Brčko District No. 19/07, Article 11 (https://www.legal-tools.org/doc/m67mv6u2/).

[58] Research conducted by the Research and Documentation Center in Sarajevo, under its project "Population Losses in BiH '91–'95", see *supra* note 25.

lack of evidence.[59] This continued for some time after the war ended.[60] The inability of the domestic system to deal with war crimes prosecutions in an unbiased and fair manner, alongside with the prevailing fear of arbitrary arrests, prompted further action by the international community.

On 18 February 1996, the Rome Agreement was signed between the ICTY and the countries of the region.[61] The Agreement provided for the review mechanism known as the Rules of the Road which allowed the ICTY to supervise the war crimes proceedings carried out by national institutions. In 2003, extensive institutional and legal reforms took place in BiH allowing its criminal justice system to approach war crimes prosecutions in a more responsible and organized manner.

As a consequence of the completion strategy of the ICTY, in 2003 the War Crimes Chamber within the Court of BiH was established.[62] Subsequently, the war crimes review process was transferred to the Prosecutor's Office of BiH. The Orientation Criteria Document[63] was adopted in order to assist the Prosecutor's Office in pursuing this task. As of 1 March 2003, the State Court was accorded primary jurisdiction over war crimes cases in BiH.[64] Accordingly, the cases pending before other courts in BiH before the said date fell under the competence of those courts.[65] Thus, it should be noted that, according to domestic laws, the jurisdiction for war crimes within BiH criminal justice system is divided between the State and entity level.

More than 10 years after the war ended, the large backlog of unsolved core international crimes cases in BiH still existed. With a view to solve this issue in a comprehensive and systematic fashion, the Ministry of Justice of BiH adopted the National War Crimes Strategy in December 2008.[66] One of its objectives was to prosecute the most complex and highest-priority cases within a seven-year time limit, and all other war crimes cases within 15 years of its adoption.

---

59 UN Development Programme, *Transitional Justices Guidebook for Bosnia and Herzegovina: Executive Summary*, Sarajevo, June 2009, Chapter I, Section 3. See also Iavor Rangelov and Marika Theros, *Maintaining the Process in Bosnia and Herzegovina, Coherence and Complementarity of EU Institutions and Civil Society in the Field of Transitional Justice*, Working Group on Development and Peace, November 2007, pp. 4 and ff.

60 OSCE, Mission to BiH, 2005, pp. 3 and 4, see *supra* note 28.

61 See further below, Section 17.3.8.1.

62 For more details, see the Court of BiH's web site.

63 See *infra* sub-Section 17.3.8.1.

64 CPC of BiH, Article 449, see *supra* note 43.

65 The possibilities of taking over of a case by the State Court from any lower-level court and the transfer of jurisdiction from the State Court to lower-level courts are provided for in the CPC of BiH.

66 See *supra* note 8.

The National War Crimes Strategy offered a complete overview of unsolved cases pending before the courts and prosecutor's offices throughout BiH. According to data available up until 1 October 2008 presented in the Strategy, the number of unsolved cases before all courts and prosecutors' offices in BiH was as high as 4,990 case files in total. This included 9,879 suspected or accused persons. Some 2,409 cases involving almost half of the alleged perpetrators[67] were pending before the prosecutors' offices of FBiH. The Prosecutor's Office of BiH was about to carry out a slightly smaller amount of this burden. The total number of cases pending before the state prosecutor's office was 1,581, including 3,819 alleged perpetrators. 927 cases involving 1,758 potential perpetrators were pending before the judicial institutions of the RS. The least number of cases was pending before the judicial institutions of Brčko District, that is, 76 cases in total, concerning 202 persons.

17.3.2. Limitations of the BiH Post-Conflict System to Process Core International Crimes Cases

In a situation in which many war crimes have been committed with numerous potential suspects, and accordingly many case files open, the BiH post-war system was inevitably faced with the dilemma: How to best deal with so many open case files in a responsible manner? Taking into account the existing state obligation to search for and prosecute those responsible for such heinous crimes, the question seems to acquire even greater importance.

In the course of the work of the two *ad hoc* tribunals for the former Yugoslavia and Rwanda, it became clear that these courts would only be able to prosecute and punish those who were the most responsible.[68] Other cases would have to be left to national authorities. The consequence of this approach was a shift of the workload from international bodies to the relevant national authorities.[69]

In the context of BiH, this meant that a much higher number of cases would be tried before national courts, in comparison to cases completed by the ICTY.

[67] More precisely 4099.

[68] These tribunals have concentrated on trying only the most serious cases. Less serious cases have been transferred to relevant national authorities for trial. In this regard see Rule 11 *bis* of the Rules of Procedure and Evidence of the two tribunals: ICTY, Rules of Procedure and Evidence, 11 February 1994, IT/32/Rev.50 ('ICTY RPE') (https://www.legal-tools.org/doc/30df50/); International Criminal Tribunal for Rwanda, Rules of Procedure and Evidence, 29 June 1995 (https://www.legal-tools.org/doc/c6a7c6/).

[69] In his book *International Criminal Law*, Antonio Cassese explains the main problems besetting the ICTY and ICTR proceedings. Cassese also puts forward the grounds for, as he calls it a "new trend" of national courts taking over the workload from the international tribunals. See Antonio Cassese, *International Criminal Law*, Second Edition, Oxford University Press, 2008, pp. 340 and 341.

Already at the time of the adoption of the National War Crimes Strategy there were 28 cases (55 accused) prosecuted before national courts in BiH, while the ICTY had concluded proceedings against 126 accused by June 2012. However, there are several impediments that may jeopardize the whole process of prosecuting core international crimes at the national level.[70]

Core international crimes occurred in a context in which the criminal justice system was not functioning at all, or at least not functioning normally, and had proven to be biased. A common feature of modern armed conflicts is that they usually entail the failure of democratic institutions and the rule of law, resulting in a dysfunctional, biased and unprofessional criminal justice system. This was the situation in BiH as well.[71] During the conflict, the BiH criminal justice system was destroyed and, as a consequence, unresolved case files accumulated at a great rate. Alongside the transition from war to peace, BiH was going through the transition from an authoritarian to a democratic regime. The Dayton Peace Agreement proclaimed that BiH shall be a democratic state operating under the rule of law, and obliged the state and its entities to ensure respect for human rights and fundamental freedoms.[72] Thus, the democratic and judicial institutions had to be built. In order to be able to fulfil the internationally-recognized obligation to try and punish the perpetrators of war crimes, the criminal justice system had to be re-built from the ground up. Many reforms, including institutional and judicial, had to be implemented.[73] And once the system started to deal with the war crimes cases, there was already a backlog of cases with different categories of crimes, different gravity, different victimization, seniority, *et cetera*. The system was inevitably faced with the problem –how to deal with so many cases?

Even though the domestic war crimes trials started before the war in BiH was brought to its end, and the ICTY was established, a large backlog of cases accumulated over the years. As stated above, domestic prosecutions were an object of criticism for many reasons; those were the trials of enemy perpetrators, there was a lack of evidence, political pressure was high, concerns were raised regarding the independency of the judges, *et cetera*.[74] At the same time, the

---

70 Katie Zoglin, "The Future of War Crimes Prosecutions in the Former Yugoslavia: Accountability or Junk Justice?", in *Human Rights Quarterly*, 2005, vol. 27, no. 1, pp. 46 and ff.

71 See, generally, "Declaration of the Peace Implementation Council", Madrid, 16 December 1998, para. 12; "Final Report of the Independent Judicial Commission, January 2001–31 March 2004", November 2004.

72 BiH Constitution, Articles I(2) and II(1), see *supra* note 22.

73 See OHR, "Judicial Reform Programme", 15 May 2000.

74 See for instance Human Rights Chamber of BiH, *Sretko Damjenović v. the Federation of BiH*, 5 September 1997, Decision No. CH/96/30 (https://www.legal-tools.org/doc/yyav6oit/).

ICTY was equipped to deal with a limited number of cases. The case-review process established under the Rules of the Road Agreement required all the case files to be sent to the ICTY for its review. Once it was decided that BiH was able to conduct trials responsibly, the cases were sent back to the BiH authorities which took over the war crimes proceedings. But at that time, there was already a gap between the time of the commission of the crimes and that of their prosecution. When the system had been established and the war crimes prosecutions started, the 'rule of law backlog' was formed and a large backlog of cases produced. Months or even years passed without the proper system functioning, entailing the lack of prosecution of open cases. This created the so-called 'backlog gap'. Therefore, a dilemma emerged: How to start the prosecutions? Where to start? How to organize the work? "Existing examples indicate that there is no quick fix of backlog situations. There is no single remedy that can resolve the problem of large backlog of cases in an immediate and responsible manner".[75] Finding A responsible and best-fitting manner to deal with the accumulated case load was a fundamental challenge to the BiH post-war society.

17.3.3. Ensuring That the Most Suitable Cases Go to Trial First

The scale and severity of the atrocities of the war placed a legal, political and moral responsibility on BiH to take action against their legacy, and thereby lay foundations for a sustainable peace and reconciliation for the future generations.

On 16 June 2008, BiH signed the Stabilisation and Association Agreement, clearing the first barrier towards full integration into the European Union within the following decade. Further, comprehensive reforms in the judicial sector and overall progress in establishing the rule of law are conditions *sine qua non* for achieving progress towards this goal. The European Union accession places paramount importance to fighting impunity, strengthening the rule of law, as well as to development of justice sector.[76] In this regard, substantial progress was made. However, the challenge of a large backlog of war crimes cases entails the need for strong strategic vision, political commitments and innovative solutions to the problem.

Several years of efforts in fighting impunity made by the international community and domestic actors resulted in the adoption of the National Strategy for War Crimes in December 2008, setting the ambitious objective to resolve the

[75] See Chapter 4 above by Ilia Utmelidze, "Requisite Resources and Capacity to Process Backlogs of Core International Crimes Cases", Section 4.4.

[76] Council Decision on the Principles, Priorities and Conditions Contained in the European Partnership with Bosnia and Herzegovina Repealing Decision 2006/55/EC, 2008/211/EC, 18 February 2008; OHR, Peace Implementation Council, "An Agenda For Reform Agreed Between the Government of Bosnia and Herzegovina and the International Community: A Message to The People of Bosnia and Herzegovina, The Rule of Law", 4 October 2002.

large backlog of all open war crimes case files within a 15 years' time-frame. According to this document, the backlog was to be resolved by the use of the selection and prioritization criteria that would ensure that the most serious cases would be processed within seven years, and all other cases within 15 years, of the adoption of the Strategy.[77] The importance of the implementation of these strategic goals is underlined by several considerations. In many instances, the international community and the ICTY itself stressed the importance of domestic war crimes prosecutions.[78] The war crimes prosecutions in BiH are the precondition for full transition into a democratic society and BiH's progress on its way to European integration. They are recognized as the first step in facing the past.[79] The role of war crimes prosecutions is recognized in the rule of law-rebuilding process in post-conflict BiH, which is essential to ensure the strengthening of domestic judicial capacity. The existence of an independent and efficient judiciary that enjoys the confidence of the citizens is a pre-condition for building a democratic and just society.

By processing those that are the most responsible as a priority, BiH can show its determination not to shield the masterminds of the crimes committed during the war, which is important for the perceptions of the domestic and international audiences. BiH's determination to hold accountable all those responsible will allow it to face its past maturely and turn to the future without unresolved issues of such importance that may jeopardize its development.

17.3.4. Ensuring That the Most Suitable Cases Go to Trial First or Before It Is Too Late

Ideally, any criminal justice system faced with past atrocity crimes should design a plan on the approach to address a large backlog of core international crimes cases. Notwithstanding the clear and strong determination of BiH criminal justice system to deal with the past atrocities, 13 years had passed when the Strategy was adopted. In such a long period of time some relevant material evidence may have disappeared. In addition, witnesses, who are the most used type of evidence in war crimes trials in BiH, may have passed away. Therefore, the BiH authorities decided to address the large caseload of war crimes cases by the adoption of case selection and prioritization criteria.

In August 2004, the Chief Prosecutor of the ICTY transferred the review process to the Prosecutor's Office of BiH.[80] In order to be able to conduct this

---

77 National War Crimes Strategy, p. 4, see *supra* note 8.

78 See ICTY, "Capacity Building" (available on its web site).

79 National War Crimes Strategy, p. 3, see *supra* note 8.

80 Prosecutor's Office of BiH, "Book of Rules on the Review of War Crimes Cases", 28 December 2008, Articles 2(4) and (5) ('Book of Rules').

process, the Collegium of BiH Prosecutors adopted the "Orientation Criteria for Sensitive Rules of the Road Cases" with the purpose "to assist the Prosecutor's Office of Bosnia and Herzegovina with the selection of cases to be heard before the Special War Crimes Chamber of the Court of Bosnia and Herzegovina".[81]

Later on, in December 2008 the National War Crimes Strategy adopted the case selection and prioritization criteria against which all war crimes cases would have to be measured, with a view to assign the cases to an appropriate forum, that is, to differentiate among cases to be tried before the State Court and other courts within BiH. The most complex cases were to be processed before the Court of BiH. Other cases deemed to be less complex were to be tried at the courts of the Federation, Republic of Srpska or Brčko District. Moreover, the criteria also played a role in making a strategic decision on the priority of certain cases among others.

17.3.5. Case Selection and Prioritization Criteria in BiH Came as a Logical Choice in Light of the ICTY Experience

It seems that the BiH criminal justice system took the desirability of criteria for case selection and prioritization for granted. The institutions concerned decided to follow the approaches taken by the international courts, namely the ICTY and ICC, and their practices and to adopt the criteria as a tool designed to address the large war crimes caseload. Thus, they skipped the question of the criteria's desirability and proceeded straight to the formulation and articulation of the content and its specifics. Other criminal justice systems have opted for other methods of dealing with the past, such as *Gacaca* trials in Rwanda or the Truth and Reconciliation Commission in South Africa.

However, given the specific post-war realities, constitutional and political specificities of BiH society, the case selection criteria seemed a normal and natural way to follow. Since the end of the war, BiH's development, as noted in the previous section, is marked and measured by the level and power of international influence in so many respects. The war crimes prosecution-process itself was seriously triggered when the international community decided to create the ICTY. After the ICTY completion strategy was introduced, Bosnian domestic war crimes prosecutions were the natural follow-up mechanism, with the international community having a considerable role.[82] In light of these circumstances,

[81] *Ibid.*, Addendum, A-441/04, "Orientation Criteria for Sensitive Rules of the Road Cases", 12 October 2004, Section 1, first paragraph.

[82] Law on Court of BiH, Article 24, see *supra* note 45, allows for the appointment of international judges. In the beginning of the war crimes prosecutions, the first instance panels at the State Court of BiH in war crimes cases were composed of two international and one national judge. After the initial phase, all international judges should be replaced with national ones. The Registry was in charge for providing the support and coordination of this process. See Office of

both the jurisprudence of the ICTY as well as its methods of selecting cases became a model for domestic prosecutions. In the years after the war, many laws were imposed by the High Representative, including some important provisions concerning war crimes cases.[83] Similarly, the National War Crimes Strategy project was supported by the international actors in BiH. Staff members of the OSCE and the Office of the High Representative participated in the Working Group meetings where the Strategy was negotiated. In my view, these specific circumstances surrounding BiH post-conflict development, taken together with the strong determination to deal with the war crimes cases within its criminal justice system, may be seen as an explanation of why the desirability of the criteria was not disputed as such by the local legal community. The concerned local actors tried to formulate the criteria that would suit best the BiH criminal justice system, and to find a solution to the question of how to include them in the legal framework with the intention to make them applicable in practice.

17.3.6. The Role of Criteria in the Selection and Prioritization of Core International Crimes in BiH

The main objective set by the Strategy was to prosecute:

- the most complex and top priority war crimes cases within the period of seven years from the time of adoption of the Strategy and
- all other war crimes cases within the period of 15 years of its adoption.

For this purpose, the case selection and prioritization criteria were developed and formed an integral part of the Strategy as its Annex A. They served as guidelines for the Prosecutor's Office of BiH and the Court of BiH in determining whether a particular case should be prosecuted at the state, entity, or Brčko District level. The intention of the drafters of the Strategy and the determination of the state of BiH was clearly stated: the most complex cases were to be tried before the Court of BiH. The complexity of the case was the criterion for the appropriate forum selection.

In this light, it is necessary to distinguish between two groups of cases dealt with by the Strategy. According to Article 449(1) of the Criminal Procedure Code of BiH ('CPC of BiH') that entered into force on 1 March 2003[84] all war

the High Representative, "Project Implementation Plan, Registry Progress Report", 20 September 2004, pp. 3 ff.

83 For instance, provision on the length of custody after pronouncement of verdict. These amendments to the Criminal Procedure Code were imposed by the High Representative. See Law on Amendment to the Criminal Procedure Code of Bosnia and Herzegovina, Article 1 (Amendment to Article 138), Official Gazette of BiH No. 16/09, 20 February 2009.

84 Official Gazette of BiH, No. 3/03, see *supra* note 64.

crimes cases that are initiated after the stated date fall under the exclusive jurisdiction of the State Court. In accordance with Article 27 of the CPC of BiH, which provides for the transfer of jurisdiction, these cases may be transferred to other courts in the entities or Brčko District by a decision of the State Court (at the request of the parties or *proprio motu*). These cases fall under the first group of cases differentiated by the Strategy – 'group I' cases.

The second, more numerous, group of cases consists of war crimes cases that were pending before courts other than the Court of BiH prior to entry into force of the CPC of BiH (1 March 2003) – 'group II' cases. Pursuant to Article 449, the entity and district courts which have territorial jurisdiction are under the obligation to finalize these cases, except when the Court of BiH decides to take over. The State Court has the possibility to take over a case from this category, by way of a procedural decision, either on its own initiative or upon request of the parties.

Until 1 October 2008, the Prosecutor's Office of BiH had 565 cases classified under 'group I'. At the same time 146 cases falling under 'group II' had been taken over by a decision of the State Court, pursuant to Article 449, and would be handled by the Prosecutor's Office of BiH.

Certain amendments to the existing criminal legislation were necessary in order to make prosecution of the most complex cases before the State Court applicable in practice. In that regard, Articles 27 and 449 of CPC of BiH were amended in November 2009, incorporating the main elements of the selection criteria (Annex A of the Strategy), as legal reasons for decisions on takeover or transfer of jurisdiction.[85]

Before these amendments, the transfer of jurisdiction as provided for in Article 27 of the CPC of BiH was possible only in the presence of "strong reasons" justifying it.[86] Having strong civil law origins, judges in BiH were generally keen to interpret the law strictly. Traditionally the legal standard of 'strong reasons' was read to mean, for instance, that the transfer of a case would be justified if conducting the trial before the State Court would involve enormous costs of the proceedings, or unnecessary loss of time. These interpretations thus include considerations on where the proceedings would be more easily and effectively conducted.[87]

85 See CPC of BiH as amended in November 2009, Official Gazette of BiH No. 93/09, Articles 27 and 449, see *supra* note 43.

86 *Ibid.*

87 See for instance Court of BiH, *Case No. X-KRN/06/222 Against Boro Milojica*, Decision on transfer of jurisdiction, 28 August 2006.

With the intention to make Article 27 a functioning mechanism for the transfer of jurisdiction, an additional article, namely Article 27a, was added to be applied only to war crimes cases. This amendment incorporated significant improvements. The transfer of jurisdiction could be justified by the reference to criteria, that is, "the gravity of criminal the offence", "the capacity of the perpetrator" and "other circumstances of importance" instead of ineffective and obsolete 'strong reasons' legal standard contained in Article 27.[88]

As indicated above, there were much more cases falling under the 'group II' cases differentiated by the Strategy, in comparison to 'group I' cases. The former are the cases under the jurisdiction of cantonal and district courts. Some of these cases were subjected to the review by the Prosecutor's Office of BiH, prior to the adoption of the Strategy, using the Orientation Criteria, and were found to be 'very sensitive' thus requiring a trial before the Court of BiH. Subsequently, 136 such cases were taken over by the State Court pursuant to Article 449(2) of the CPC of BiH. However, the majority[89] of 'group II' cases had never been subjected to such a review since the territorially competent courts were not under any obligation to inform the Court of BiH about this kind of cases, leaving the State Court without any insight into them. Thereby, the possibility of the Court of BiH to take over such a case *ex officio* was made practically impossible. Hence, it is very likely that at least some of 'group II' cases were of such complexity that they would have required the prosecution at the state level. For these reasons, the Strategy imposed obligations on the prosecutors' offices throughout BiH to inform the State Court on their caseload. Additionally, it formally introduced selection criteria – Annex A, the Orientation Criteria (previously covered by internal rules of the Prosecutor's Office of BiH) and called for amendments of Article 449 to include them.[90] Subsequently, Article 449 was amended in November 2009[91] and the references to the main features of the Annex A selection criteria such as "the gravity of criminal offence", the "capacity of the perpetrator" and "other circumstances of importance", were included therein, to guide the assessment of the complexity of cases for the purpose of taking over them. In

[88] CPC of BiH, Article 27a.

[89] According to the National War Crimes Strategy, see *supra* note 8, up until 1 October 2008 there were 1216 such cases in total.

[90] It should be noted that the selection criteria adopted by the Strategy (Annex A) are called "case complexity criteria" while the previously existing criteria used by the Prosecutor's Office of BiH were called "sensitivity criteria". The difference in terminology here is not of importance, given that both sets of criteria refer to the same substantive elements, and that the Strategy criteria practically substituted the orientation criteria, making them formally part of the National War Crimes Strategy and subsequently introducing them into relevant legal provisions of the CPC of BiH. It would seem that this was just a matter of choice in terminology.

[91] Official Gazette of BiH, No. 93/09, see *supra* note 85.

addition, the Strategy also clearly instructed the entity prosecutors' offices and the Prosecutor's Office of Brčko District to provide the Court of BiH with the data on the number of cases within their jurisdiction, and with enough details so as to allow the Court to take over cases *ex officio* if the complexity so required.

It bears to note what is clearly spelled out by the adopted amendments, namely, the intention of the Strategy drafters to strengthen the role of judges in the war crimes cases review process. With the subsequent amendments of November 2009, the judges formed an indispensable part of the case selection and prioritization agenda.

17.3.7. Criteria at the International Criminal Tribunal of the Former Yugoslavia and International Criminal Court

17.3.7.1. International Criminal Tribunal of the Former Yugoslavia

Cassese observed that the "United Nations Security Council set up *ad hoc* Tribunals pursuant to its power to decide on measures necessary to maintain or restore international peace and security".[92] This was the first time that the UNSC took such a measure acting on the strength of Chapter VII[93] of the UN Charter.[94] By its resolution 827 the UNSC established the ICTY on 25 May 1993. The UNSC decided to:

> establish an international tribunal for the sole purpose of prosecuting persons responsible for serious violations of international humanitarian law committed in the territory of former Yugoslavia between 1 January 1991 and a date to be determined by the Security Council upon the restoration of peace.[95]

The ICTY was given a very broad mandate. Article 1 of the ICTY Statute states that:

> The International Tribunal shall have the power to prosecute persons responsible for serious violations of international humanitarian law committed in the territory of the former Yugoslavia since 1991 in accordance with the provisions of the present Statute.[96]

In the initial phase of the Tribunal's work, case selection and prioritization were mainly governed by the availability of evidence and the particular interests

92 Cassese, 2008, p. 325, see *supra* note 69.

93 UN Charter, 24 October 1945, Articles 39 and 41 (https://www.legal-tools.org/doc/6b3cd5/).

94 In this regard see UNSC Resolution No. 955 (1994), S/RES/955 (1994), 8 November 1994 (https://www.legal-tools.org/doc/f5ef47/).

95 UNSC Resolution No. 827 (1993), S/RES/827 (1993), 25 May 1993, para. 2 (https://www.legal-tools.org/doc/dc079b/).

96 ICTY Statute, see *supra* note 13.

of individual prosecutors in a certain case.[97] It seems that, in the beginning of the Tribunal's functioning, the position and level of responsibility of the perpetrators was not a key factor for the case selection. This is apparent from the selection of its first case, *Prosecutor v. Duško Tadić*.[98] As Carla Del Ponte described in her article:

> Although the crimes committed by Duško Tadić were indeed horrific and despicable in themselves, it is still probably true that this convicted man is not among those most responsible for the crimes committed in the former Yugoslavia.[99]

This may easily be the consequence of the fact that the criteria were not contained in the ICTY Statute or in the RPE.[100] Neither document contained a list of case selection standards or guidance as how to organize such a selection.

In October 1995, the ICTY Office of the Prosecutor ('ICTY-OTP') reportedly adopted a document containing a set of criteria for the selection of cases. Its purpose was to enable an effective allocation of the Tribunal's resources and to facilitate the fulfilment of its mandate.[101] The criteria included in the 1995 document were divided into five groups: "(a) the person to be targeted for prosecution; (b) the serious nature of the crime; (c) policy considerations; (d) practical considerations; and (e) other relevant considerations".[102]

In 1998, a debate on criteria emerged at the ICTY. It was pointed out in an internal memorandum drafted by Morten Bergsmo, a Legal Officer in its Office of the Prosecutor at that time, that only a small number of alleged perpetrators who were indicted before the Tribunal were persons with leadership responsibility. The Chief Prosecutor's decision to withdraw the indictments against 14 low-level accused in the Omarska and Keraterm cases showed that the ICTY-OTP's charging policy changed. In a press release of 8 May 1998, the Chief Prosecutor explained her decision and confirmed that the overall strategy of her office was to concentrate on those who bear the highest level of responsibility

---

97 See Morten Bergsmo, Kjetil Helvig, Ilia Utmelidze and Gorana Žagovec, *The Backlog of Core International Crimes Case Files in Bosnia and Herzegovina*, Second Edition, Torkel Opsahl Academic EPublisher and Peace Research Institute Oslo, Oslo, 2010, p. 98 (https://www.toaep.org/ps-pdf/3-bergsmo-helvig-utmelidze-zagovec-second).

98 ICTY, *Prosecutor vs Duško Tadić*, IT-94-1.

99 Carla Del Ponte, "Prosecuting the Individuals Bearing the Highest Level of Responsibility", in *Journal of International Criminal Justice*, 2004, vol. 2, no. 2, p. 516.

100 ICTY RPE, see *supra* note 68.

101 Bergsmo *et al.*, 2010, p. 99, see *supra* note 97.

102 For the content of each group of criteria see *ibid.*, pp. 99–105.

or those who have been personally responsible for extremely brutal and serious offences.[103]

In 2000, the UNSC adopted Resolution 1329 (2000), approving the proposal of the ICTY President to create a pool of *ad litem* judges.[104] By this resolution the UNSC also took note "of the position expressed by the International Tribunals that civilian, military and paramilitary leaders should be tried before them in preference to minor actors".[105] This was the first of the UNSC resolutions on the so-called 'completion strategy' of the ICTY.[106] In this regard, two additional UNSC resolutions bear mentioning, namely 1503 and 1534, of 2003 and 2004 respectively,[107] whereby the UNSC reaffirmed that the ICTY should concentrate "on the prosecution and trial of the most senior leaders suspected of being most responsible"[108] for crimes within its jurisdiction. Subsequently, the judges of the ICTY amended Rule 28(A) of the RPE in 2004, thereby allowing for the review of the indictment in order to examine whether it concentrates on the criterion of level of responsibility as specified in the UNSC Resolution referred to above.[109]

In sum, the 1995 document contained a very broad list of relevant criteria to be considered when deciding whether to try a case before the ICTY. Although it had little impact on the early selection policy of the ICTY, as shown above, the value of this document may be seen in light of the ICTY being some kind of an experiment with international criminal justice in the early 1990s. Its value is recognized in the creation of the selection criteria in BiH, which are heavily influenced by the ICTY criteria.

As regards the 1998 Prosecutor's decision, contained in the press release issued in May that year, notwithstanding the fact that it did not contain the actual criteria but rather formed the guidelines for prosecutorial charging decisions, its

103 ICTY, "Statement by the Prosecutor following the withdrawal of the charges against 14 accused", Press Release, 8 May 1998, CC/PIU/314-E.

104 The letter of the President of the ICTY addressed to the UNSC contained the strategy for completion of all first instance trials until the end of 2007, UNSC, Press Release, 20 June 2000, No. SC/6879.

105 UNSC Resolution No. 1329 (2000), S/RES/1329 (2000), 5 December 2000, seventh preambular paragraph (https://www.legal-tools.org/doc/b1b6cc/).

106 Dominic Raab, "Evaluating the ICTY and Its Completion Strategy", in *Journal of International Criminal Justice*, 2005, vol. 3, no. 1, p. 85.

107 S/RES/1503 (2003), see *supra* note 11; UNSC Resolution No. 1534 (2004), S/RES/1534 (2004), 26 March 2004 (https://www.legal-tools.org/doc/4e06ee/).

108 See *ibid.*, S/RES/1503 (2003), seventh preambular paragraph.

109 ICTY RPE, Rule 28(A), see *supra* note 68.

importance may be best seen as a crystallization of the level of responsibility or seniority of the accused as a critical element in case selection.

17.3.7.2. International Criminal Court

As the first permanent international criminal jurisdiction, the importance and content of criteria in the work of the ICC must be analysed through the prism of that function and the purpose of its creation, namely to put an end to impunity for the perpetrators of such serious crimes that are of concern to the whole international community.[110] The ICC has jurisdiction over "the most serious crimes", as defined by the Statute,[111] that are of "sufficient gravity"[112] to substantiate its action. The ICC is global in nature, since its territorial jurisdiction is not limited to a certain conflict or area. The Court may investigate and prosecute crimes committed in different countries. This trait makes it distinct from other international courts, since their jurisdiction is limited to a certain conflict or situation, as is the case of the two *ad hoc* tribunals ICTY and ICTR.[113] Thus, case selection and prioritization criteria plays an important role in the work of the ICC.

The ICC Statute itself provides for the criteria that the Prosecutor has to take into account when deciding on the initiation or continuation of an investigation. In order to initiate an investigation, Article 53(1) prescribes that the Prosecutor must consider three elements: whether the information available provides a reasonable basis to believe that a crime falling under the ICC jurisdiction has been or is being committed;[114] whether the admissibility requirements specified in Article 17 of the Statute are satisfied;[115] and whether there exist "substantial reasons to believe that an investigation would not serve the interests of justice", taking into consideration "the gravity of the crime and interests of victims".[116] Similarly, Article 53(2) stipulates the factors to be considered in determining whether a certain investigation provided sufficient basis to proceed with prosecution: whether the "legal or factual basis" is sufficient to seek a warrant or summons pursuant to Article 58; the other two elements are the same as in Articles 53(1)(b) and (c) respectively, with the only exception that Article 53(2)(c),

110 ICC Statute, preambular paras. 4 and 5, see *supra* note 1.

111 *Ibid.*, Article 5 in relation preambular para. 9. Article 5 lists crimes that fall under the jurisdiction of the court: genocide, crimes against humanity, war crimes and aggression.

112 In this regard see *ibid.*, Article 17 (1)(d), that proclaims inadmissible cases of insufficient gravity.

113 ICTY Statute, Article 8, see *supra* note 13 and Statute of the International Criminal Tribunal for Rwanda, 8 November 1994, Article 8 (https://www.legal-tools.org/doc/8732d6/).

114 ICC Statute, Article 53(1)(a), see *supra* note 1.

115 *Ibid.*, Article 53(1)(b).

116 *Ibid.*, Article 53(1)(c).

unlike 53(1)(c), refers to "all the circumstances" to be taken into consideration.[117] There are some limitations to prosecutorial discretion in case selection and prioritization. The decision of the Prosecutor based on Articles 53(2)(c) and 53(1)(c)[118] is subject to review by the judges of the Pre-Trial Chamber.[119] The judicial review of prosecutorial selection decisions is important for the appearance that such decisions are not arbitrarily made.

In sum, not every situation brought before the ICC Prosecutor will be formally investigated. After having concluded that the situation involves crimes within the jurisdiction of the Court, the Prosecutor must determine whether the case is of sufficient gravity to proceed with prosecution. This includes considerations of complementarity, as described in Article 17 of the ICC Statute,[120] and gravity (its components are analysed below).

As discussed in detail in Chapter 6 above by Rod Rastan, there are several ICC-OTP public documents that are worth some analysis in the context of case selection criteria. Initially these documents included the "Paper on some policy issues before the Office of the Prosecutor" of September 2003,[121] the draft paper on "Criteria for Selection of Situations and Cases" of June 2006,[122] the ICC-OTP's "Report on the activities performed during the first three years (June 2003–June 2006)" dated 12 September 2006,[123] and the "Policy Paper on the

---

[117] *Ibid.*, Article 53(2)(c) suggests the circumstances to be taken into account when deciding whether to continue with an investigation: gravity of the crime, the interests of victims, the age or infirmity of the alleged perpetrator, and his or her role in the alleged crime.

[118] *Ibid.*, Articles 53(3) and 19(1)

[119] In this regard it is interesting to see the developments in the case *Prosecutor v. Bosco Ntaganda*, Case No. ICC-01/04. The gravity test was an issue before the Pre-Trial and Appellate Chamber of the ICC. See particularly the ICC, *Situation in the Democratic Republic of the Congo*, Appeals Chamber, Judgment on the Prosecutor's Appeal Against the Decision of Pre-Trial Chamber I entitled "Decision on the Prosecutor's Application for Warrants of Arrest, Article 58", 13 July 2006, ICC-01/04-169, para. 54 (https://www.legal-tools.org/doc/8c20eb/).

[120] The ICC is not meant to replace national courts, but instead to act only when and if a state is unwilling or unable to conduct the investigations or proceedings genuinely. For discussion on complementarity, see also Cassese, 2008, pp. 342 ff., *supra* note 69.

[121] ICC-OTP, "Paper on some policy issues before the Office of the Prosecutor", September 2003 (https://www.legal-tools.org/doc/f53870/).

[122] ICC-OTP, "Criteria for Selection of Situations and Cases", draft discussion paper, June 2006 (https://www.legal-tools.org/doc/sk0ratuy/). The content of this document is presented in Chapter 7 above by Paul Seils, "The Selection and Prioritization of Cases by the ICC Office of the Prosecutor (2003–2009)", Section 7.1.2.

[123] ICC-OTP, "Report on the activities performed during the first three years (June 2003–June 2006)", 12 September 2006 (https://www.legal-tools.org/doc/c7a850/).

Interests of Justice" of September 2007.[124] The policy paper of September 2003 suggests that the OTP's intention was to concentrate its activities on those bearing the greatest degree of responsibility.[125] Furthermore, the document recognizes the problem of "practical realities" the Prosecutor might face, such as witness protection issues, questions of security and availability of means of investigation.[126] The aim is to employ a strategy that would allow the Court to use its potential to the maximum, while at the same time recognizing the need to use its limited resources most efficiently. Accordingly, the importance of conducting expeditious and focused proceedings was acknowledged.

The draft paper on the "Criteria for selection of cases and situations" of June 2006 added some clarification to the gravity standard announced already in 2003 as the guiding prosecutorial standard in case selection. The assessment of the gravity of a case involves consideration of the following relevant factors: nature of the crime, its scale taking into account the number of victims and its intensity (temporal and geographical), the manner of commission of the crime in question, as well as its impact on the affected communities. This policy paper was adopted in 2016 and is discussed in detail by Rod Rastan in Chapter 6 above.

The ICC-OTP's first three-year report of 12 September 2006 did not add much to what was already proclaimed in the previous documents. It restated its strategy to concentrate activities on those who bear the greatest responsibility and reiterated the main elements that form part of the gravity threshold considerations requited to support further Court action.

The "Policy Paper on the Interests of Justice" lists three elements relevant for case selection determinations. Firstly, the gravity of the crime is described with reference to higher gravity considerations set forth in Article 17(1)(d) as a part of the admissibility test. It is reiterated that gravity is measured by the scale of the crimes, their nature, the manner of their commission and the impact on affected communities. The second criterion for case selection, that is, the interests of victims "includes the victims' interest in seeing justice done, but also other essential interests such as their protection".[127] "The particular circumstances of the Accused" is the last criterion suggested by the Paper. As indicated above, the ICC-OTP previously declared its strategy to focus on those who bear the highest responsibility. In this regard, the Policy Paper catalogues factors to

[124] ICC-OTP, "Policy Paper on the Interests of Justice", September 2007 (https://www.legal-tools.org/doc/bb02e5/)

[125] *Ibid.*, p. 7.

[126] *Ibid.*, p. 2.

[127] *Ibid.*, p. 5.

be taken into consideration when determining the most responsible accused in the following words:

> [T]he alleged status or hierarchical level of the accused or implication in particularly serious or notorious crimes. That is, the significance of the role of the accused in the overall commission of crimes and the degree of the accused's involvement (actual commission, ordering, indirect participation).[128]

17.3.8. Criteria in the BiH Criminal Justice System

17.3.8.1. The Orientation Criteria of the Collegium of Prosecutors

On 18 February 1996, the Rome Agreement was signed between the ICTY and the countries of the region, as also discussed by Zekerija Mujkanović in Chapter 16 above.[129] Based on Part 5 of the Rome Agreement, the 'Rules of the Road' procedure was developed. This mechanism enabled the ICTY to supervise the war crimes processes conducted by domestic authorities. In accordance with the Agreement, a Rules of the Road Unit was formed within the ICTY-OTP. The signatories agreed that the ICTY Prosecutor "would review domestic war crimes investigations in order to advise whether or not the evidence was sufficient by international standards to justify either the arrest or indictment of a suspect or continued detention".[130]

The Rules of the Road obliged judicial authorities in BiH to deliver all files referring to investigated war crimes cases to the Rules of the Road Unit for assessment.[131] Therefore, all case files that existed at the time were sent to the ICTY, as well as those of the cases that were opened in the period ranging from after the conclusion of the Rome Agreement to 2004, when the Unit ceased to exist.[132] The Rules of the Road Unit reviewed a significant number of cases. The assessment depended on the evidence in the case file being enough to substantiate prosecution.[133] All reviewed files were classified into seven categories on a descending scale, with different standard markings from 'A' – where evidence was sufficient to provide reasonable grounds for believing that the individual

---

[128] *Ibid.*, p. 7

[129] See Section 16.5. above.

[130] Book of Rules, Article 2(1), see *supra* note 80.

[131] See UN Development Programme, *Transitional Justices Guidebook for Bosnia and Herzegovina: Executive Summary*, Sarajevo, June 2009, Chapter I, Section 3.

[132] See Chapter 16 above by Zekerija Mujkanović, "The Orientation Criteria Document in Bosnia and Herzegovina", Section 16.5.

[133] Book of Rules, Article 2(2), see *supra* note 80.

subject of the report has committed a serious violation of international humanitarian law, to 'G' for when evidence was not sufficient.[134]

On 27 August 2004, the Prosecutor's Office of BiH took over the review of war crimes cases.[135] In order to be able to conduct this process, on 12 October 2004, the Collegium of BiH Prosecutors adopted the Book of Rules which set out the "conditions and arrangements"[136] for the war crimes review process. The "Orientation Criteria for Sensitive Rules of the Road Cases" were annexed to the Book of Rules document.

The purpose of these criteria is "to assist the Prosecutor's Office of Bosnia and Herzegovina with the selection of cases to be heard before the Special War Crimes Chamber of the Court of Bosnia and Herzegovina".[137] The document gives preference to trying the war crimes cases before the lower courts since the Court of BiH "will have neither resources nor the time to try all the war crimes cases".[138]

The Orientation Criteria document divides all cases into two categories: 'Category I – highly sensitive' and 'Category II – sensitive' cases. The first group of cases must be tried before the Court of BiH, whereas the second group may as well be tried before lower-level courts.[139]

The criteria are designed to function on two levels. Firstly, they are used to select cases to be tried on different jurisdictional levels, namely the State Court and district or cantonal courts. Moreover, they function as criteria for prioritizing cases once the appropriate forum has been determined, that is, prioritizing the cases within a specific court.

For both categories of cases, Category I and II, the criteria are divided into three groups: (i) "Nature of Crime alleged ('Crime')", (ii) "Circumstances of alleged perpetrator ('Perpetrator')" and (iii) "Other Considerations ('Other')". Under the first heading the offences for both categories of cases are listed. The list is rather broad and includes various protected values. It includes offences against persons as well as against property.[140] The criteria under the second group titled 'Perpetrator' are quite broad. They include not only past and present military and civilian leaders, but also paramilitary, police and judicial authorities.

---

[134] *Ibid.*

[135] *Ibid.*, Articles 2(4) and (5).

[136] *Ibid.*, Article 1.

[137] "Orientation Criteria for Sensitive Rules of the Road Cases", Section 1, first paragraph, see *supra* note 81.

[138] *Ibid.*, second paragraph.

[139] *Ibid.*, Section 2, second paragraph.

[140] *Ibid.*

There is also a reference to the notoriety of a potential suspect and multiple rapists. It should be noted that the lists do not refer to any mode of liability or any form of participation in a criminal offence, but solely to the hierarchical positions and roles of potential perpetrators.[141]

In the closing paragraph of the Orientation Criteria document, an important statement regarding the prioritization of cases is made: that there may be a necessity "to prioritize cases depending upon the stage of the investigation and whether individual cases are ready to proceed". The text continues by recognizing the criterion of "readiness to proceed" with a case as a criterion for case prioritization. The paragraph ends with a general guideline for prioritization of cases, which may be made based on the examination of the following aspects: command responsibility as mode of liability of a suspect, offences committed by a public official who is still in office, and crimes committed by law enforcement officials.

17.3.8.2. The National War Crimes Strategy

In December 2008, the Ministry of Justice of BiH adopted the National War Crimes Strategy. There are several reasons for which the Strategy was initially drafted. First of all, there was a great number of unsolved war crime cases. Secondly, establishing a centralized record of all war crime cases in the BiH judiciary was necessary as recommended by a detailed report prepared under the auspices of the Sarajevo office of the Organization for Security and Co-operation in Europe that was later published as a monograph.[142] This was a prerequisite for planning efficient subsequent prosecutions.

The third reason was lack of a harmonized judicial practice in war crimes cases throughout BiH courts.[143] The most significant aspect of this problem was the application of different substantive laws applicable to war crime cases. Namely, the State Court of BiH applied the new Criminal Code of BiH, enacted in 2003, when trying war crimes cases. On the other hand, the entity courts had different legal standings on this matter. They applied the substantive law that was in force at the time of the commission of war crimes, that is the Criminal Code of the Socialist Federal Republic of Yugoslavia. From the human rights point of view, the problem could lead to grave human rights concerns. As a consequence, the constitutional principles of legal certainty and equality before law

---

141 Bergsmo *et al.*, 2010, see *supra* note 97, pp. 86 and 87.

142 *Ibid.*, pp. 53-77. Morten Bergsmo was the OSCE Consultant who led this work.

143 See generally OSCE, Mission to BiH, *Moving Towards a Harmonized Application of the Law Applicable in War Crimes Cases Before Courts in Bosnia and Herzegovina*, Sarajevo, August 2008.

could be seriously infringed.[144] The Strategy called for some legal amendments to address this issue.

Deficiencies in the management of war crime cases are named as the fourth *rationale* for drafting the Strategy. The last two motivations underlying the making of this Strategy are the fact that the regional co-operation with regard to war crime cases had not been on a satisfactory level[145] and the support and protection of witnesses and victims in war crime proceedings within BiH's judicial system was insufficient.[146]

In relation to the Orientation Criteria, which was an internal document of the Prosecutor's Office, the Strategy offered a way to integrate their essence into legal provisions governing the distribution of cases amongst different jurisdictions in BiH. The criteria adopted in the Strategy, largely based on the Orientation Criteria, through legal amendments of the relevant provisions of the CPC of BiH, became the official mechanism to which judges could refer when transferring cases, thereby harmonizing the then-existing practice in case selection and prioritization.

17.3.8.2.1. The Specific Criteria Developed by the Strategy

The Strategy states that the most complex cases from both groups should be processed before the Court of BiH. Less complex cases are to be tried at the lower courts. This would be ensured by the transfer mechanism and the mechanism of take-over of cases (provided for in Articles 27 and 449 of the CPC of BiH) which both incorporate the complexity criteria as defined in the Strategy.[147] The features of the "gravity of the criminal offence" criterion, "the capacity and role of the perpetrator" criterion, and "other circumstances" criterion are listed in Annex A of the Strategy. All war crimes cases have to be measured against these criteria with a view to assign the cases to an appropriate forum, that is, to differentiate among cases to be tried before the State Court and other courts having jurisdiction. Moreover, the criteria also play a role in determining the priority of a certain case among others. These criteria are based on those stipulated in the Orientation Criteria document of the Collegium of BiH Prosecutors, as well as the relevant documents and the case law of the ICTY and ICC.

---

144 The Constitutional Court of BiH decided in favour of the application of the new Criminal Code. For more details see Constitutional Court of BiH, *Abduladhim Maktouf*, Decision on admissibility and merits, 30 March 2007, Case No. AP 1785/06 (https://www.legal-tools.org/doc/hopsfbfc/).

145 National War Crimes Strategy, p. 4, see *supra* note 8.

146 *Ibid.*

147 Amendments to the CPC of BiH of November 2009.

Pursuant to the Strategy, the roles of criteria are multiple. Firstly, they serve as a guiding instrument for the Prosecutor's Office of BiH when submitting a proposal to take over a case (in accordance with Article 449(2) of the CPC of BiH) or for the transfer of jurisdiction (in accordance with Article 27a of the CPC of BiH) by the Court of BiH. Secondly, in order to request the taking over of a case in accordance with Article 449(2) of CPC of BiH, all lower-level prosecutors' offices and courts should justify the motions by the use of criteria. Finally, by measuring war crimes cases against the stated criteria, the Court of BiH is in position to decide, *proprio motu* or on the proposal of the parties, whether a case should be prosecuted before the Court of BiH or alternatively at the entity or district level. This novel and important possibility of the Court itself to take part in the selection and distribution process was, in my view, influenced by the role accorded to judges at the ICTY and ICC. The Orientation Criteria document did not provide for such possibility. This changed with the adoption of the Strategy. Accordingly, Articles 449 and 27 of the CPC of BiH were amended by inclusion of the criteria therein which allowed for a more active role of the judges in the implementation of the criteria.[148] The judges of the Court of BiH thus became the ones who, by the application of criteria, decide on the complexity of a case, as opposed to the Orientation Criteria that were not binding for the Court as such since they were part of an internal prosecution document. According to data available to the author, in 2010 there have been 63 decisions[149] in which the Court applied the criteria from the Strategy, referring to the newly adopted Article 27a of the CPC of BiH.

In its decisions rendered in accordance with Article 27a, the State Court referred not only to the criteria stipulated in Article 27a, but also to their essence as detailed in Annex A of the Strategy. Cases with accused persons having no command responsibility, less grave consequences of the crime, and without any need of protective measures for witnesses, were transferred to lower courts for prosecution.[150] On the other hand, the transfer of cases involving accused persons who were commanders in the military, paramilitary or police establishments was rejected by the Court.[151] In addition, the presence of a need for protective measures for witnesses, even when only concerning one witness, was the

[148] Official Gazette of Bosnia and Herzegovina, No. 93/09, see *supra* note 85.

[149] E-mail correspondence with the Head of the Court Management Section in December 2010.

[150] See, for instance Court of BiH, Decision of the Court of BiH on transfer of jurisdiction, Case No. X-KRO-07/476, 8 June 2010; Case No. X-KRO-07/433, 1 September 2010; Case No. X-KRO-09/673, 22 November 2010.

[151] See Court of BiH, Decision of the Court of BiH on transfer of jurisdiction, Case No. X-KRO-07/428, 28 June 2010.

reason for rejecting the motion for transfer of jurisdiction.[152] It seems that the criteria have been more or less equally applied to all cases, which should positively influence the overall war crimes prosecution process. This most probably ensures that the most complex cases are tried as a priority and before the appropriate forum, in this case the Court of BiH. This aspect undoubtedly enhanced the chances of the BiH judiciary to accomplish the goal set forth by the Strategy.

17.3.8.2.2. Work on the Strategy After 18 October 2011

The Strategy set an obligation for the entity prosecutors' offices, the Prosecutor's Office of Brčko District and the Prosecutor's Office of BiH to submit to the Court of BiH a report on war crimes cases which contained sufficient information for the Court of BiH to form an insight into the number and complexity of these cases, so as to plan the capacity required for their trial and potential rendering of a decision on transfer of conduct of the proceedings in accordance with Article 27 of the CPC of BiH, or making a decision *ex officio* on taking over a war crimes case in accordance with Article 449 of the CPC of BiH.

After the adoption of the Strategy, and with a view to efficiently conduct the review of cases in accordance with the complexity criteria, the Court of BiH set up an internal mechanism for review of war crimes cases. In the beginning of 2011, the president of the Court of BiH formed a Panel of judges responsible to conduct the review based on the information delivered from the entity prosecutors' offices, the Prosecutor's Office of BiH and the Prosecutor's Office of Brčko District, as well as for deciding on any change of jurisdiction following a request by the prosecutor or on its own initiative.

Until 18 October 2011, approximately 80 per cent of prosecutors' offices submitted to the Court of BiH the reports containing enough information to assess the complexity of war crimes cases pending before them. However, since the majority of war crimes cases were pending before the Prosecutor's Office of BiH, the date when this Office delivered the necessary information can be seen as a turning point in the management of war crimes cases in BiH judiciary.

On 18 October 2011, the Prosecutor's Office of BiH fulfilled its obligation by delivering relevant data on all war crimes cases pending before his office. This allowed the Court of BiH to start an intensive work on the review of the submitted reports. In essence, the Court's Panel reviews the delivered reports, which contain enough information to measure the complexity of war crimes cases, and makes a preliminary assessment of complexity. This preliminary assessment is then delivered to the Prosecutor's Offices of BiH in the form of a

[152] See Court of BiH, Decision of the Court of BiH on transfer of jurisdiction, Case No. X-KR-10/948, 19 July 2010.

report. Based on this report, the Prosecutor's Office of BiH makes a substantiated request to transfer the conduct of proceedings as suggested by the Panel's preliminary assessment.

From the beginning of its work until 22 May 2012, the Court of BiH transferred the conduct of the proceedings in 237 cases in total. After the adoption of the Strategy until 22 May 2012, the Court made 232 transfers of the conduct of the proceedings. This means that only 5 cases were transferred to the entity courts before the Strategy's adoption.

The conduct of the proceedings was transferred to the lower courts in 77 cases, from the beginning of the Court's work until the report on war crimes cases was submitted by the Prosecutor's Office of BiH. From 18 October 2011 to 22 May 2012, the Court of BiH made 160 decisions on transferring the conduct of proceedings.

17.3.8.3. Revised War Crimes Strategy

Given that not all the goals outlined in the 2008 War Crimes Strategy were achieved within the set deadlines, and considering the number of processed war crimes cases in the prosecutors' offices in BiH, there was a need to amend and supplement the Strategy. For this purpose, the BiH Council of Ministers established a Working Group on 12 April 2017 to draft amendments and additions to the State Strategy concerning how to deal with war crimes cases. The Working Group was composed of experts from all levels of government in BiH, as well as representatives of the international community. After two and a half years of drafting, the Revised War Crimes Strategy was adopted in September 2020 by the BiH Council of Ministers.[153]

The goal of the Revised Strategy was to improve the prosecution of war crimes cases in courts and prosecutors' offices in Bosnia and Herzegovina through adequate mechanisms, especially the proper distribution of war crimes cases between the judiciary at the state level, the entities, and the Brčko District of BiH. Above all, it aimed to ensure more efficient prosecution of the most complex and high-priority war crimes cases within set deadlines.[154]

The Revised Strategy reiterated the goals and results as set out in the 2008 Strategy, and extended the time limit for completion of all war crimes trials that was set to the end of 2023.

---

[153] Revidirana Državna Strategija Za Rad Na Predmetima Ratnih Zločina, May 2018 ('Revised Strategy') (https://www.legal-tools.org/doc/dp6sk7km/).

[154] Ministry of Justice of BiH, "Usvojena Revidirana državna strategija za rad na predmetima ratnih zločina", Press Release, 24 September 2020.

In November 2023, the BiH Council of Ministers extended the deadline for processing the remaining complex war crime cases until the end of 2025, because it was clear that they were not going to be completed as previously envisaged. At the time, the Council of Ministers stated that the dynamics of resolving war crimes cases and the number of remaining cases not yet completed by the Bosnian judiciary indicated the impossibility of resolving them within the previously-set deadline of the end of 2023.[155]

The Revised Strategy adopted the modified criteria for assessing the complexity of cases (listed in Annex A to the Revised Strategy) and provided a harmonized interpretation in order to enable the transfer of a larger number of war crimes cases from the State-level judiciary to the entity-level or Brčko District of BiH. In the development of these criteria, the criteria established by the 2008 Strategy were used as a substantive basis, along with best practices established by domestic courts and prosecutors' offices, while also consulting ICTY and ICC practice.[156]

If a case meets the criteria set out in Annex A regarding the gravity of the criminal offense and the characteristics and role of the perpetrator, either individually or in their inter-relationship, the trial will be conducted before the Court of BiH. Otherwise, the case will be tried before another competent court in BiH, in accordance with the legal provisions on jurisdiction, referral or transfer of cases.[157]

17.3.8.3.1. Comparison of Some Criteria of Domestic and International Institutions

By comparing domestic and international approaches to criteria many similarities may be noted, as well as certain differences in their perception. This is understandable due to the varying circumstances that have led to their adoption. The particular conditions in which these judicial mechanisms operate cannot be underestimated. The ICTY and the ICC unavoidably have to cope with the demanding task of picking only those cases that are the most suitable for international prosecution.

Certain difficulties registered in this process have to be recognized, especially regarding the ICTY, since it was accorded a broad mandate and primacy over national jurisdictions concerning core international crimes. In the beginning of its work, the ICTY lacked a clear prosecutorial strategy. Only later, with the introduction of the completion strategy, it became clear that the Tribunal

155 Haris Rovčanin, "Deadline Missed: Bosnian War Cases Not Completed on Time Again", *Balkan Insight*, 28 December 2023.

156 See the Revised Strategy, p. 51, *supra* note 153.

157 *Ibid.*

should focus "on the prosecution and trial of the most senior leaders suspected of being most responsible".[158] In this context, it is warranted to repeat the Rules of the Road procedure as established by the Rome Agreement in 1996. Pursuant to this document, the relevant national authorities were restricted in their jurisdiction over core international crimes inasmuch as the ICTY was granted a supervisory function in relation to their prosecution. By the adoption of its completion strategy, the Tribunal's primacy took a different shape. From that point onwards, national jurisdictions were given the leading role in war crimes prosecutions in the former Yugoslavia. As anticipated, these circumstances had an impact on war crimes prosecutions within national jurisdictions. In the BiH judicial system, they are reflected in the adoption of the Orientation Criteria document in 2004, as well as in the National War Crimes Strategy in 2008, which are aimed to facilitate the national authority's efforts to fight impunity in a systematic and organized manner.

The situation is, in some respects, different when it comes to the ICC. Unlike the ICTY, which has primacy over national jurisdictions, the ICC has jurisdiction over "the most serious crimes" that are of "sufficient gravity",[159] which can be exercised only it if a state is unwilling or unable to genuinely proceed with a case. Thus, it is not surprising that the criterion of gravity of the case, encompassing both the gravity of the crime and the degree of the responsibility of the perpetrator, lies at the heart of the ICC's work.

As regards the gravity of the crime, it seems that both BiH national instruments on criteria address its content by linking it with the hierarchical status of the crime. The hierarchy is to be measured with reference to the interest protected by the particular criminal offence such as life, physical integrity, property, *et cetera*.

Circumstances pertaining to the perpetrator seem to be more comprehensively dealt with by the Orientation Criteria document than in international documents. The lack of reference to any mode of liability or any form of participation in a criminal offence, but solely to the hierarchical positions and roles of potential perpetrators in the Orientation Criteria document was remedied in the Strategy. The Strategy explicitly states that the "most serious forms and degrees of participation in the perpetration of a criminal offence"[160] make a case eligible for trial before the State Court. The mode of liability of the perpetrator, that is, direct perpetration, co-perpetration, participation in joint criminal enterprise, in-

[158] S/RES/1503 (2003), Preamble, see *supra* note 11.

[159] See *supra* notes 111 and 112.

[160] National War Crimes Strategy, Annex A, p. 42, see *supra* note 8.

citement, ordering, aiding and abetting, *et cetera*, is a relevant factor in the determination of the seriousness of the perpetrator's responsibility. The Strategy specifies that more serious forms and degrees of participation in the perpetration of a criminal offence, that is, taking part in planning and ordering of a crime, manner of perpetration, intentional and a particular commitment to planning and ordering of a crime, the degree of intent, justify prosecution before the State Court.[161] The Strategy states that commanders in the military, police or paramilitary establishments are to be tried before the Court of BiH. It seems that the actual distribution of cases before the State Court as opposed to other courts has been in accordance with these criteria. The cases including criminal offences that are not systematic and massive, in which the consequences of the crime are significantly less severe than those of the other crimes normally prosecuted before the State Court, and in which the accused persons had no command responsibility at the time of the perpetration of the crime, were transferred to lower courts for trial, provided that other relevant circumstances substantiated such decision.[162]

Furthermore, the criteria document of the ICTY seems to be more extensive in addressing what factors are to be considered as "Other relevant considerations". This document lists certain factors that are not present in other documents, neither in BiH or at the ICC, such as the available charging theories, potential defences, theory of liability and legal framework of each potential suspect, the extent to which the crime base fits in with the ongoing investigation and overall strategic direction, *et cetera*.

Close examination of different documents and practices on criteria reveals the following factors to be considered in the determination of the gravity of the crime: the nature of the crime; the scale of the crime, including the number of victims[163] and the temporal and geographical circumstances of the crime; the manner of commission, which may include special cruelty or heinous commission of the crime or a systematic and planned commission;[164] and defencelessness of the victims of the crime. The nature of the crime is closely connected with the interest protected by the criminal offence such as life, physical integrity or property.

161 *Ibid.*

162 See, for instance, the Decisions of the Court of BiH in cases Nos. X-KRO-07/476, X-KRO-07/433 and X-KRO-09/673, *supra* note 150.

163 See, for instance, ICTY, *Prosecutor v. Gojko Janković*, Decision on Referral of case Under Rule 11 *Bis*, 22 July 2005, IT-96-23/2-PT, para. 19 (https://www.legal-tools.org/doc/95034b/).

164 ICC Statute, Articles 7(1) and 8(1), see *supra* note 1.

Similarly, all scrutinized documents give due consideration to interests of the victims or witnesses. Issues like witness security, the need for their protection and similar, are commonly addressed by both national and international documents. The 'representativity' criterion is spelled out through the examined documents in different parts and groups of criteria they list. For example, the ICTY criteria document lists "nationality of perpetrators/victims" and "area of destruction" as relevant consideration to the gravity of the alleged conduct, but they rather seem to be adequate factors in determination of 'representativity' as a criterion demanding for a balance between the degree of criminal victimization and overall prosecution scale. The Strategy also spelled out this requirement by the reference to "consequences of the crimes to the local community" as a relevant consideration in the case selection and prioritization process. This may be very important given the specific social and political circumstances of BiH. As noted above, alongside the existing trend to politicize the number of victims of the war, local courts are often attacked as being biased and under political pressure for trying mainly Serb perpetrators rather than Croat and Bosniacs.[165] Thus, it may be important to clearly spell out this criterion to the public in BiH. The public should be explained that in the BiH conflict, violent acts occurred throughout the territory, but some parts or areas were more affected by the crimes than other. Similarly, some communities have suffered more harm. Accordingly, certain communities have more of its members among those who inflicted such suffering. Giving detailed clarifications to the public that the degree of victimization is to be reflected in the overall prosecution of war crimes in BiH may help reduce such unfounded criticism and enhance public trust in judiciary in general.

17.4. Requirements for the Criteria's Success in the BiH Post-Conflict Transition

17.4.1. Periodic Review of War Crimes Cases

The Court of BiH, as stated above, set up an internal mechanism for review of information submitted by all prosecutors' offices throughout BiH on war crimes cases pending before them, in order to ensure that the cases are distributed to the courts and prosecutors' offices respecting the complexity criteria specified in Annex A of the Strategy, and the overall goal of the Strategy of trying the

[165] See, for instance, the press release by the President of the State Court, "Court of BiH strongly denies all accusations of biased work"; see also the article "The Court of BiH ignores Serb victims", *Nezavisne novine*, No. 3758, 21 January 2009; OSCE, Mission to BiH, "Spot Report, Independence of the Judiciary: Undue Pressure on BiH Judicial Institutions", December 2009, pp. 3 and 4 ('"Spot Report", December 2009').

more complex cases at the state level and the less complex ones at the entity level.

Considering the large backlog of war crimes cases and the Strategy's time frame of 15 years to finalize them, which was not achieved, it was important to secure continuous monitoring mechanism which would ensure an adequate and most efficient distribution of the resources of the BiH judiciary, at all times. This includes the periodic monitoring of the dynamics of investigations and trials. Therefore, the Court of BiH should be able to consider a potential redistribution of cases, that is, transfer of cases to entities or taking over cases from entities, in accordance with human, financial and other capacities, and the dynamics of the work accomplished. For this purpose, the prosecutors' offices in BiH should have an obligation to deliver data on war crimes cases on a regular basis, once a year, for instance. The Court's determination should be done by reviewing data provided by prosecutors' offices, respecting the complexity criteria and the overall goal of the Strategy that more complex cases are to be tried at the State level and less complex at the entity-level courts.

The establishment of such a continued periodic review of war crimes cases would allow for a most efficient use of available resources at any moment. By doing so, BiH would be on the right track to fulfil its goal of putting an end to impunity for atrocities committed during the past war.

17.4.2. Public Access

The legitimate interests of victims and society in general to see and know the way that justice is being done is widely recognized in the prosecution of core international crimes as a part of criminal justice.

The BiH society that has suffered from mass atrocities in the past faces great expectations towards the criminal justice system from numerous victims, witnesses and other stakeholders. In BiH there are many associations of victims of war.[166] These organizations have very high expectations for the judicial system. In many instances so far, they have been dissatisfied with certain judicial decisions, namely the length of prison terms and the slow process of trying war criminals. In addition, the judiciary has been criticized as being under undue political pressure.[167]

Undoubtedly, victims and the public have the right to be informed of why certain cases are prosecuted before others. The case selection criteria may serve as a professional mechanism for the prosecution service to explain case selection and prioritization decisions to the victims and other external interested groups.

---

[166] See for instance the association 'Woman Victim of War', Sarajevo or the Association of Detainees of BiH.

[167] "Spot Report", December 2009, see *supra* note 165.

By the use of the criteria, the public is explained why it is justified to prosecute certain cases prior to others. The criteria show to the public that the cases are not selected randomly or arbitrarily, or with any kind of political, ethnic or similar connotations, but rather as a result of considerations where the criteria played a major role. This may significantly reduce unwanted pressure and critique coming from the outside, increase public confidence in the judicial system which, in turn, enhances the independence and legitimacy of the prosecution in general. As a result, the war crimes trial process as a whole would be perceived as fairer by the general civil society.

The National War Crimes Strategy, containing case selection and prioritization criteria, is available to the general public on the web site of the Ministry of Justice of BiH. However, the mere fact that the criteria are accessible on the Internet is not enough for public appreciation of the criteria in any meaningful sense. There is a danger that the criteria are still not reachable and understandable to the majority of the public in BiH. Given the complexity of war crimes proceedings and the sensitivity of the post-conflict situation in BiH, further steps towards full understanding of the criteria should be taken. In order to mitigate the dangers of unwanted pressure and criticism from outside, the Annex A criteria should be presented in a manner that is easily understandable to the general public, possibly through public debates and presentations. This would enhance their prospects in achieving accountability for the crimes committed.

17.4.3. Equal and Transparent Application

'Equal application' requires that all the cases within the existing case portfolio are measured against the set of previously formulated criteria. Each case needs to be evaluated against the set of criteria in order to ensure that the cases are not selected arbitrarily, but rather in pursuance of a prosecutorial strategy to end impunity in a responsible manner. Transparency may enhance the ability of the justice system to tackle accountability for core international crimes. It works in favour of the prosecution service and the criminal justice system itself. The transparent application of criteria may have a positive impact on the BiH society. In addition, decision-making processes driven by the criteria and made transparent to the general public may provide fertile ground for a reduction of external pressure of any kind.

Thus, in order to ensure an equal and transparent application of criteria in BiH, it was necessary to include them directly into the Criminal Procedure Code. By doing so, through amendments of Articles 449(2) and 27 of the CPC of BiH, the judiciary was obliged to apply such criteria when taking over a case or transferring jurisdiction to a court.

It could be concluded that by changing the CPC of BiH both requirements, equal and transparent application, are covered to some extent. The mere fact that the essence of the criteria became part of the law, accessible to all, is an important step towards a transparent understanding of the criteria for the distribution of cases. However, more is required for full transparency. In that regard, the project on "Support to the judiciary in BiH – Strengthening prosecutors in the criminal justice system" carried out by the High Judicial and Prosecutorial Council of BiH has been commendable. One of the objectives of this project was to improve the quality of public information on cases and enhance the public perception of the prosecution's work.[168] Such activities, aimed at professionalizing the work of prosecutors in relation to their ability to adequately inform the public on the cases they are tasked with, may help reduce public criticism and pressure resulting from the lack of knowledge of prosecutorial work by the public in general.

17.4.4. Judicial Review

At the ICTY and ICC, the judges were given a role in securing the proper application of criteria for selection of cases. Rule 28(A) of the RPE of the ICTY provides for the review of the indictment in order to examine whether the selection standards are met. Likewise, there are some limitations to discretionary prosecutorial decisions in the case selection process at the ICC. Prosecutorial decisions based on Articles 53(2)(c) and 53(1) (c) of the ICC Statute are subject to review by the judges of the Pre-Trial Chamber. Similarly, by making a decision on the transfer of jurisdiction or take-over of a case, the judges of the State Court of BiH are in a position to ensure that the criteria are properly applied.

Judicial review is a mechanism that ensures proper application of the criteria. It ensures that decisions on case selection are not made arbitrarily but rather as a result of a thorough examination based on a set of criteria. Judicial review also provides the possibility of an appeal, which would be impossible if decisions were made internally within the prosecution service. An effective judicial review may guarantee that the criteria would be equally and consistently applied in practice. In BiH, a society affected by past mass atrocities that is quite susceptible to various kinds of influence, the role of the judiciary in ensuring the correct application of criteria seems to be quite important. As stated above, around 60 decisions based on Article 27(a) of the CPC of BiH were pronounced in the first period following the amendments to the CPC of BiH which adopted containing the essence of the criteria. It is commendable to see that, in these decisions, the judges referred to the list of considerations pertaining to each criterion as specified in the Strategy, which were not listed in the CPC of BiH itself.

---

[168] High Judicial and Prosecutorial Council, "Project Document, Support to the judiciary in BiH – Strengthening prosecutors in the criminal justice system, Final Draft", 5 August 2010, p. 19.

The Orientation Criteria document did not provide for such a possibility for judges to ensure that the criteria are applied properly. By amending Articles 449 and 27 of the CPC of BiH and including the criteria therein, the prospect that the cases will be selected in line with the selection criteria are enhanced. The judges of the Court of BiH are the ones who, by the application of the criteria, guarantee that the cases will be selected and distributed depending on their complexity, as opposed to the Orientation Criteria that were not binding for the Court as such since they were part of an internal prosecution document.

17.5. Concluding Remarks

The war in Bosnia and Herzegovina, which lasted for almost four years in the early 1990s, resulted in massive human life losses, wounded and injured persons, refugees and displaced persons and destroyed property. Numerous war crimes were committed, involving many suspects. The mass character of the crimes committed, combined with the fact that the national judicial system was not functioning normally for years and the limited performance by the ICTY, caused a large number of case files to accumulate. There were nearly 2,000 opened war crimes cases, including almost 10,000 suspects.[169] In 2008, BiH decided to systematically and responsibly address this issue. A National War Crimes Strategy was adopted in order to prevent impunity and prosecute all, or at least most of, the perpetrators in the 15 years following the adoption of the Strategy. It incorporated case selection and prioritization criteria, the essence of which later became part of the CPC of BiH.

Against this background, the chapter began with the question: What are the prospects of and obstacles to the criteria effectively addressing the backlog of core international crimes cases in BiH?

The role of criteria is twofold. They ensure that the most complex cases are tried before the State Court, and that due priority is given to the most serious cases. Each case should be measured against the criteria so they fulfil their function. Criteria should be made public and applied equally and transparently with a certain degree of judicial review. There is, however, a risk that this is not entirely the case.

The core of the criteria was included in the CPC of BiH through amendments in November 2009. Detailed lists of considerations to be taken into account in order to decide whether each criterion is satisfied remained, however, only available in the National War Crimes Strategy. On the other hand, these amendments ensured, to some extent, that the criteria would be equally and transparently applied to each case by giving the judges of the State Court a role

[169] National War Crimes Strategy, p. 7, see *supra* note 8.

to decide on the complexity of cases with reference to the criteria. The amendments of Articles 449 and 27 of the CPC of BiH increased the prospects of the criteria's effectiveness. The practice of the Court of BiH has shown that the judges used not only the essence of the criteria, but they also referred to the Strategy's list of considerations pertaining to each criterion to justify their decisions taken in accordance with Articles 27a and 449 of the CPC of BiH.

However, as stated above, further steps have to be taken in order to fully use the criteria's potential to effectively address the backlog of core international crimes cases in BiH. Improving the prosecutors' capacity to inform the public about cases and enhancing the public perception of the prosecution's work may further improve the prospects of the criteria's usefulness in fighting impunity for war crimes, as well as reduce public criticism of and pressure on the prosecution service. The Strategy itself has been available to the general public via the web site of the Ministry of Justice of BiH, but this may not have been enough to reach the broader public. It is advisable to ensure broad public access to the criteria in order to mitigate unwanted pressure on and criticism of war crimes justice. This can enhance the effectiveness of the criteria in the prosecution service.

More important for the successful application of the criteria in practice is to ensure that available human, financial and other resources in the institutions competent to process war crimes are fully employed at all times, by establishing an obligation for those institutions to regularly inform the Court of BiH on the war crimes cases pending before them, thus enabling the Court to consider redistribution of cases if the situation so requires.

18

Criteria for Prioritizing and Selecting Core International Crimes Cases: The Situation in Croatia

Vesna Terselić*

In Croatia, criteria for prioritization were not formally adopted by the time of the Second Edition of this book. In the prosecution of war crimes in the 1990s, one set of criteria was used for war crimes against Croats and another for crimes committed against Serbs. Double standards, typical of many other countries in the immediate aftermath of war, became the norm. Although the difference in attitude towards crimes committed on different sides of the war has become less obvious and striking over time, it has lingered.

Landmark cases were thresholds in becoming less partial on the road to possible insignificant partiality. To mention just two: indicting and later sentencing General Norac and others for war crimes committed in 1991 around Gospić,[1] or indicting and later sentencing of perpetrators for torture in the military prison Lora,[2] which became possible after political changes linked to the elections held on 3 January 2000. Both cases have contributed to creating a better social climate for other war crimes trials. The gradual – in the beginning, grudging –

---

* **Vesna Terselić** is the founder and former Director of Documenta – Center for Dealing with the Past ('Documenta'). She has been Director of the Center for Peace Studies, Zagreb, co-ordinator of Antiwar Campaign Croatia, and a lecturer in peace and women's studies. She has broad practical experience as a trainer and facilitator in conflict situations, mostly in Bosnia and Herzegovina, Croatia, Kosovo and Kirgizstan. Her publications include handbooks on facilitation and mediation. She is a Right Livelihood Award Laureate (1998) and Nobel Prize Nominee (1997). This chapter has not been substantively updated since the Second Edition.

[1] Tihomir Orešković, Mirko Norac and Strepan Grandić have been sentenced for war crimes (liquidation of civilians at Lipova glavica) and given 15, 12 and 10 years of imprisonment. The first instance verdict of the Municipal Court in Rijeka of 24 March 2003 (https://www.legal-tools.org/doc/5ciiqw57/) was approved by the Supreme Court in 2004 (https://www.legal-tools.org/doc/dq41eneo/).

[2] Tomislav Duić, Tonči Vrkić, Miljenko Bajić, Josip Bikić, Davor Banić, Emilio Bungur, Ante Gudić and Anđelko Botić have been sentenced (for torture and liquidation of imprisoned civilians in the Lora military prison) and given 8, 7 and 6 years of imprisonment. The first instance verdict of the Municipal Court in Split of 2 March 2006 was approved by the Supreme Court on 6 February 2007 (https://www.legal-tools.org/doc/7wxwfjaf/).

change of heart of government institutions after 2000 can also be attributed to international pressure and the effort to prove that the judiciary in Croatia could prosecute suspected war crimes as efficiently as the International Criminal Tribunal for the former Yugoslavia ('ICTY').

The summary of the 2008 war crimes trials report stated:[3]

> The greatest problems occurring year after year are yet again the adverse political context, the insufficient personnel and technical conditions for the processing of war crimes, and a large number of verdicts reached in absentia. The defects observed in the criminal procedures in progress include repetition of procedures, mistrials, inconsistent court practice and the fact that many of the accused are still being tried in absentia. Inefficient trials marked by frequent and long interruptions and repetitions of procedures, along with an inconsistent policy on detention result in the apathy and disinclination among witnesses to take the stand, and even greater frustration of the victims and the injured persons. The worrying practice in the work of the State Attorney's Office has been the issuance of imprecise indictments against a large number of the accused persons, some of whom are not charged with a single specific crime. Consequently, investigations end up being conducted during the main hearing, and prosecutors repeatedly change the indictments (sometimes to the extent that none of the original incriminations remain included), which leads to dismissals of cases or acquittals. In more than a half of the war crime cases reported to the State Attorney's Office, the perpetrators have remained unknown. We urge that the role and capacity of special units for war crimes be strengthened, and pre-trial investigations and other investigating actions be intensified through increasing the capacity of the Ministry of the Interior both at the national level and the level of police departments.

Findings presented in a *Transitional Justice in Post-Yugoslav Countries* report still pointed to "the bias that has for years characterized the judiciary of the Republic of Croatia in trials for war crimes primarily concerns [...] the application of unequal criteria, depending on ethnic background of suspects and victims, when deciding which offences will be prosecuted as war crimes".[4]

Around the time of the Second Edition of this book, the State Attorney mapped all reported cases in Croatia. According to the data on the processing

---

3 Centre for Peace, Non-Violence and Human Rights in Osijek, Documenta and Civic Committee for Human Rights, *Monitoring of War Crimes Trials: A Report for the Period of January–June 2008*, 26 September 2008.

4 Humanitarian Law Center and Documenta (eds.), *Transitional Justice in Post-Yugoslav Countries: 2007 Report*, 2007, p. 8.

war crimes presented in the annual report of the State Attorney of Croatia,[5] until 1 April 2008, 3,827 criminal proceedings had been started and 1,776 indictments issued. For the first time, data was organized by particular situations (for example, war crimes in Vukovar, war crimes in Osijek, *et cetera*), and not by name of suspected or indicted person. The total number of war crimes presented in this way (committed on Serbian and Croatian sides of the war in Croatia) and registered by the State Attorney was 703, for which proceedings were started regarding 301 reported war crimes. For 402 crimes perpetrators were not known and proceedings were not started; 391 investigations were ongoing at that time; and 255 investigations were interrupted. Some 645 suspects were indicted without verdict, and 615 perpetrators were sentenced.

Since 2001, the highest judicial instances of the Republic of Croatia worked on improving the standards of war crimes prosecution by several measures:

- synchronizing the activities of the Croatian judiciary with the Statute of the International Criminal Court;
- analysing and revising the working practice of the State Attorney, by its insistence on ceasing a practice of conducting trials in absence and by opening investigations for crimes committed against ethnic non-Croats and of those accountable on the basis of command responsibility;
- the corrective role of the Supreme Court of the Republic of Croatia;
- setting the legal conditions and strengthening institutional prerequisites for witness protection and support; and
- strengthening the regional co-operation on war crime trials.

Prior to the Second Edition, between 23 and 35 first-instance trials for criminal acts against values protected by international humanitarian law were conducted annually in Croatia. Despite the pressure exerted by a part of the public – and facing serious political resistance as well as obstructions within the state institutions – the war crimes which were committed by members of Croatian military units have also been brought to courts. Croatian Army generals have been among those charged for crimes pursuant to command responsibility, for example, the case of war crimes in Medački džep, against Mirko Norac and Rahim Ademi, transferred to Croatia from the ICTY; the case of war crimes in Osijek against Branimir Glavaš *et al.*; the case of war crimes in Cerna against Tomislav Madi *et al.*; and the retrial in the case of war crimes in Paulin Dvor against Enes Viteškić.

5 Republic of Croatia, Office of the State Attorney, "Izvješće o radu državnih odvjetništava u 2007. Godini", Zagreb, June 2008.

In that period of time, the following problems arose and were reported by human rights organizations:[6]

- negative consequences of the practice of conducting trials against accused persons in absence during the early 1990s;
- numerous reinstitutions of first-instance proceedings due to verdicts based on insufficiently established facts;
- a significant number of committed crimes still had not been investigated or prosecuted; and
- insufficient support for witnesses and insufficient visibility and inclusion of victims in criminal proceedings.

The reported deficiencies pointed to the fact that the observed achievements of the judiciary in conducting war crimes trials coincided with the peak of the judiciary's capacity and what internal organization could allow. Therefore, the human rights organizations which monitored the war crime trials advocated for:

- strengthening of the capacity and roles of the war crimes investigation centres;
- intensification of investigations;
- analysis of the adjudication processes in the 1990s, especially verdicts brought in the absence of the accused and the cancellation of criminal proceedings through application of the General Amnesty Law;
- improvement of victims' support and position in the criminal proceedings; and
- further development of regional co-operation between the judicial systems in war crimes trials.

Personally, I am not convinced that criteria for prioritization should be proposed in a situation where crimes are neither fully documented nor investigated. A complete mapping of war crimes, although very much needed, was not done in Croatia. Unfortunately, a full overview of the human losses – disclosing the identity of each killed or missing citizen of Croatia – was not done either. The names of all victims on the different sides of the war in Croatia are not known.

In my opinion, a precondition for setting criteria would be the full establishment of the relevant facts, including documenting the human losses and subsequent mapping of the war crimes. Croatian institutions and society have had some way to travel before accepting that all suspected war crimes, on different

---

6 Katarina Kruhonja and Veselinka Kastratović (eds.), *Praćenje suđenja za ratne zločine, izvještaj za 2007*, Centre for Peace, Non-Violence and Human Rights in Osijek, Documenta, Civic Committee for Human Rights and Croatian Helsinki Committee, Osijek, 2007.

sides of the war, have to be investigated.[7] Judging by the judicial practice at the time of writing, achieving that goal seemed closer then than in the 1990s, but it still did not seem to be within easy reach, although human rights organizations insisted on achieving it.

---

7 Support for prosecution of war crimes in Croatian society, at least on general level, was not insignificant at the time of publication of the Second Edition. One of the findings of public opinion research on dealing with the past done by Documenta in 2006, showed that 61 per cent of the interviewed persons were of the opinion that all war crimes should be prosecuted.

19

The Strategy for Prosecuting War Crimes in the Early Years of the Serbian Office of the War Crimes Prosecutor

Nataša Kandić*

The Republic of Serbia Office of the War Crimes Prosecutor ('OWCP') was founded on 1 July 2003, when the Law on War Crimes was passed.[1] In 20 years of its work, it filed 106 indictments against 239 individuals. By the Third Edition of this book, after 20 years of trials, 96 individuals have been convicted in final proceedings, while eight have been convicted in first instance proceedings. This chapter presents the work of the OWCP in those early years, in the context of a strategy for prosecuting war crimes and, therefore, points to the reasons or criteria the prosecution has set in the selection of cases for investigation and indictment. I seek to analyse whether the Office had priorities and a strategy in the prosecution of war crimes in its first five years.

19.1. The *Ovčara* Case

The OWCP filed the first indictment on 4 December 2003, against eight members of the Serbian Territorial Defence Unit and the 'Leva Supoderica' volunteer unit for war crimes against prisoners of war committed on 20 November 1991 at the Ovčara farm in Croatia. For the same crime, the second indictment was filed on 24 May 2004,[2] against 11 individuals. On 26 May 2004, an indictment[3]

* **Nataša Kandić** is Co-ordinator of the RECOM Reconciliation Network and Founder of the Humanitarian Law Center ('HLC') – a Belgrade-based human rights non-governmental organization. Campaigning for truth and justice for victims, at the time of writing she was the Executive Director of the HLC, which she led in its mission to assist post-Yugoslav societies to re-establish the rule of law and to come to terms with the legacy of large-scale and systematic human rights violations. She is a recipient of over 20 international, regional and national human rights awards, and is a member of the Order of the Croatian Morning Star of Katarina Zrinska.

1 Law on Organisation and Competence of Government Authorities in War Crimes Proceedings, 1 July 2003 ('Law on War Crimes') (https://www.legal-tools.org/doc/b2993b/).

2 OWCP, *Prosecutor v. Milan Lančužanin et al.*, Indictment, 24 May 2004, No. KTRZ 4/03 (https://www.legal-tools.org/doc/t9734uig/).

3 OWCP, *Prosecutor v. Predrag Dragović*, Indictment, 26 May 2004, No. KTRZ 4/04 (https://www.legal-tools.org/doc/6rwpd9p4/).

was filed against one more individual. Two more individuals were indicted on 13 April 2005 and 8 April 2008. Proceedings were suspended against one individual who died in 2004, while two individuals received the status of witness-collaborator. Due to the illness of the accused Milan Bulić, the proceedings against him were separated and ended as a separate case. For these reasons, on 16 September 2005, the Prosecutor specified the indictment charging a total of 16 accused. There are serious indications that the prosecution selected the case of the murder of at least 200 Croat prisoners of war for two reasons: (i) the International Criminal Tribunal for the former Yugoslavia ('ICTY') Office of the Prosecutor had already indicted three officers of the former Yugoslav People's Army ('JNA') for the same crime, and the prosecution could obtain relevant documents and organize an efficient investigation in a short period of time; and (ii) by initiating criminal proceedings against 16 immediate perpetrators, the OWCP attempted, and partially succeeded, in alleviating the criticism of the Serbian public caused by the arrest of the former JNA officers with the explanation that the trials of immediate perpetrators would have shown that the accused officers were innocent.

Even though the court adduced numerous pieces of evidence proving, among other things, the accountability of several JNA officers for the crimes committed in Ovčara, the OWCP had not indicted a single officer at that time. The highest-ranking officer indicted was a territorial defence commander and his deputy. The Serbian Supreme Court rendered a decision on 18 October 2006 reversing the War Crimes Chamber's first instance verdict of 12 December 2005[4] and returned the case for retrial.[5] In the meantime, two more persons were indicted for the commission of the same crime – proceedings against these two individuals were joined with the main case. In retrial, the proceedings were conducted against 18 individuals in total. On 27 September 2007, the trial against the three officers conducted before the ICTY was completed by the first instance trial chamber: the primary accused was convicted to 20 years of imprisonment, the secondary accused to five years of imprisonment, and the third accused was acquitted of all charges. The first instance court delivered a decision in retrial on 12 March 2009 convicting 13 individuals and acquitting five. The Court of Appeal in Belgrade delivered a decision on 23 June 2010[6] by mostly confirming the first instance court decision, while increasing and reducing the sentence for

4 District Court in Belgrade, *Prosecutor v. Miroljub Vujović et al.*, War Crimes Chamber, Judgment, 12 December 2005, No. K.V. 1/2003 (https://www.legal-tools.org/doc/a5f8e9/).

5 District Court in Belgrade, *Prosecutor v. Miroljub Vujović et al.*, War Crimes Chamber, Judgment (retrial), 12 March 2009, No. K.B. 4/2006 (https://www.legal-tools.org/doc/b236a6/).

6 Court of Appeal in Belgrade, *Prosecutor v. Miroljub Vujović et al.*, Judgment, 14–18, 21 and 23 June 2010, No. Kž1, Po2-1/2010 (https://www.legal-tools.org/doc/4d2mcswx/).

two of the convicted. One of the convicted, Saša Radak, filed a constitutional appeal against the first instance judgment and the judgment of the Court of Appeal in Belgrade claiming violation, among others, of the right to a fair trial under Article 6, paragraph 1 of the European Convention on Human Rights. In 2013, the Constitutional Court of Serbia ruled that Saša Radak's right to a fair trial was violated because Judge Siniša Važić participated in both the first instance and appellate proceedings in his case, raising concerns about impartiality.[7] Judge Važić had made key decisions in the first instance trial and later presided over the appeal, which the court deemed a conflict of interest. The Constitutional Court's decision also applied to other defendants in the case.

In June 2014,[8] the Supreme Court of Cassation accepted requests from defence attorneys, annulling the Court of Appeal's conviction due to violations of the right to an impartial trial, and sent the case back for reconsideration, extending the ruling to other defendants who had not filed similar requests. On 1 December 2014, the Court of Appeal re-opened the appeals proceedings and decided to re-open the hearing process as well, and, in September 2017, the trial had to begin anew, owing to a change in the composition of the chamber. Defendant Đorđe Šošić died in the course of the trial, and the proceedings against him were terminated. On 24 November 2017,[9] the Court of Appeal delivered a judgment upholding the first instance judgment with respect to four convicts, reduced the sentence of three convicts, and increased the sentence for one convicted individual. Four individuals who had been sentenced to imprisonment by the court of first instance were all acquitted. This judgment represents a stark departure from the previous Court of Appeal's judgment of 2010, which was based on the very same set of evidence. By this second judgment, the Court acquitted four defendants, including those who had previously been sentenced to as much as 15 and 13 years (Vojnović and Perić respectively), and drastically reduced the sentences on two defendants, Đanković and Radak, from the original maximum sentence of 20 years in prison to a mere five years.

19.2. The *Zvornik* Case

In mid-2004, the ICTY Office of the Prosecutor transferred a partially investigated case of war crimes committed in Zvornik Municipality in eastern Bosnia and Herzegovina ('BiH') to the OWCP. This case required further investigation

---

7 Constitutional Court of Serbia, Decision, 12 December 2013, No. Už-4461/2010 (https://www.legal-tools.org/doc/0biiax9l/).

8 Supreme Court of Cassation, Judgment, 19 June 2014, No. Kzz RZ 2/2014 (https://www.legal-tools.org/doc/1edn3fwf/).

9 Court of Appeal in Belgrade, *Prosecutor v. Vujović et al.*, Judgment, 24 November 2017, No. Kž1, Po2-2/2014 (https://www.legal-tools.org/doc/dh2xq8mq/).

against seven individuals for war crimes against the civilian population. The indictment was filed on 12 August 2005 against eight individuals (one had deceased in the meantime).[10] After the indictment was filed, the HLC and the Association of Family Members of the Killed and Missing in Zvornik Municipality ('Association of Family Members') asked for a meeting with the OWCP. The meeting took place in December 2005, during which they protested that the indictment did not include the most serious crime after the genocide in Srebrenica: the banishment of the Muslim population from villages in Zvornik Municipality, the separation of men from women and children on 1 June 1992, the imprisonment of these men in the Technical High School in Zvornik, and finally the execution of approximately 700 prisoners. The Chief Prosecutor and the Acting Prosecutor promised that they would collect documents and decide on opening an investigation on the basis of this material. The HLC continued putting pressure on the OWCP, using every opportunity in the media to mention its demand that the investigation of the most serious crime after the genocide in Srebrenica, the execution of 700 prisoners, be initiated.

The trial of seven defendants in the case *Zvornik I* was completed on 12 June 2008 when the verdict of four accused was announced.[11] Three defendants were sentenced to prison, while one was acquitted. In its ruling of 8 April 2009,[12] the Supreme Court of Serbia reduced the sentences of two defendants and upheld the conviction of one, as well as the acquittal of another. The trial against the accused Grujić and Popović was separated by a trial chamber decision of 26 May 2008. The indictment against these two individuals – Branko Grujić, the former President of the Provisional Government, Crisis Headquarter, Mayor, and President of the War Headquarter in Zvornik, and Branko Popović, the former commander of the Zvornik Territorial Defence Unit – was announced on 22 October 2008. The indictment included the acts from the previous indictment as well as the acts of forcible separation and taking hostage of 600–700 Muslim civilians from villages in Zvornik Municipality, who were executed in various manners after their detention. The court of first instance delivered a judgment on 22 November 2010,[13] pronouncing both of them guilty and sentencing Grujić to 6 years and Popović to 15 years in prison. The Court of Appeal in Belgrade

[10] OWCP, *Prosecutor v. Dragutin Dragićević et al.*, Indictment, 12 August 2005, No. KTRZ 17/04 (https://www.legal-tools.org/doc/ae5a28/).

[11] District Court in Belgrade, *Prosecutor v. Branko Grujić et al.*, War Crimes Chamber, Judgment, 12 June 2008, No. K.V. 5/2005 (https://www.legal-tools.org/doc/9679f4/).

[12] Supreme Court of Serbia, *Prosecutor v. Dragan Slavković et al.*, Judgment, 8 April 2009, No. Kž1 r.z. 3/08 (https://www.legal-tools.org/doc/9a6712/).

[13] Higher Court in Belgrade, *Prosecutor v. Branko Grujić and Branko Popović*, War Crimes Department, Judgment, 22 November 2010, No. K-Po2-28/2010 (https://www.legal-tools.org/doc/874ecd/).

fully confirmed the first instance judgment on 3 October 2011;[14] it dismissed as unfounded appeals from the Prosecutor as well as the defendants. The request and constant pressure by the HLC and the Association of Family Members was fruitful and contributed to the initiation of a trial for one of the most serious war crimes committed in BiH.

19.3. The *Scorpions* Case

The OWCP filed an indictment against the commander and four members of the Scorpions unit on 7 October 2005[15] for war crimes against the civilian population on the basis of video footage of the execution of six Muslims, which the HLC obtained and handed over to the prosecution on the condition that the latter would not file any indictment before the owner of the tape had left Serbia.

After the witness (the owner of the video tape) received protection by the ICTY and left Serbia, the HLC demanded that the prosecution initiate proceedings against members of the Scorpions who were showed in the tape killing unarmed Muslims. On 1 June 2005, one of the ICTY prosecutors, Mr. Geoffrey Nice KC, presented a part of the video footage showing the execution of six Muslims in the *Milošević* case before the Tribunal. The HLC decided to play the entire footage and several TV stations broadcast the footage the same evening. That night the police arrested five members of the Scorpions. A trial chamber rendered a verdict on 10 April 2007, becoming final on 13 June 2008, except insofar as the defendant Aleksandar Medić was concerned.[16] In its judgment, the Supreme Court of Serbia, as the second instance court, quashed the judgment relating to the defendant Aleksandar Medić and ordered a retrial. In the judgment after retrial on 28 January 2009,[17] the first instance court convicted Aleksandar Medić again and imposed the same sentence of five years imprisonment. In November 2009, the Supreme Court of Serbia upheld that decision.

19.4. The *Tuzla Column* Case

The OWCP filed an indictment against the Bosnian Croat Ilija Jurišić on 9 November 2007 for using illegal means of fighting.[18] He was charged with having

[14] Court of Appeal in Belgrade, *Prosecutor v. Branko Grujić and Branko Popović*, Judgment, 3 October 2011, No. Kž1, Po2-6/11 (https://www.legal-tools.org/doc/s4z44qel/).

[15] OWCP, *Prosecutor v. Aleksandar Medić et al.*, Indictment, 7 October 2005, No. KTRZ 3/05 (https://www.legal-tools.org/doc/cb447f/).

[16] District Court in Belgrade, *Prosecutor v. Slobodan Medić et al.*, War Crimes Chamber, Judgment, 10 April 2007, No. K.B. 6/2005 (https://www.legal-tools.org/doc/d2c374/).

[17] District Court in Belgrade, *Prosecutor v. Aleksandar Medić*, War Crimes Chamber, Judgment, 28 January 2009, No. K.V. 8/08 (https://www.legal-tools.org/doc/2eccbc/).

[18] OWCP, *Prosecutor v. Ilija Jurišić*, Indictment, 9 November 2007, No. KTRZ 5/04 (https://www.legal-tools.org/doc/b1d9bb/).

ordered an attack on a JNA column despite the previously reached agreement between the representatives of the Tuzla military and civilian authorities, and is thus accused of having utilized means of combat prohibited by international law. At least 92 members of the JNA were killed on this occasion and at least 33 wounded.

Ilija Jurišić was arrested at the Belgrade airport on 11 May 2007. Until that moment, he had been in Serbia on numerous occasions. The BiH Ministry of Justice demanded his extradition and transfer of his criminal case, recalling Article 30 of the European Convention on the Transfer of Proceedings in Criminal Matters, acceded to by Serbia and BiH.[19] However, the Belgrade District Court War Crimes Chamber rejected this request and never forwarded any official document on its decision.

The OWCP filed (and announced in the media) the indictment against Ilija Jurišić before the investigation was closed. On that day (9 November 2007), the BiH Office of the Prosecutor, upon the request of the War Crimes Chamber, examined witnesses in the presence of an investigative judge from the War Crimes Chamber of the Belgrade District Court (Milan Dilparić) and the Deputy Prosecutor for War Crimes (Dragoljub Stanković).

The filing of an indictment before closing the investigation, and the persistent refusal of the Serbian judicial authorities to transfer the case to the BiH Office of the Prosecutor that conducted an investigation into the same event, bring us to the conclusion that the OWCP was influenced by political considerations and the need to show to the public that it does not prosecute Serbs only. The Serbian Radical Party and other extremely nationalistic parties and groups had attacked the prosecution on this basis on numerous occasions.

The initial verdict by the first instance court, which found Ilija Jurišić guilty, was delivered on 28 September 2009.[20] Because of the first instance court's failure to determine a number of key facts, the Court of Appeal had to open a main hearing to hear evidence that the first instance court had omitted to hear. On 11 October 2010,[21] the Court of Appeal ruled and sent the case back to the first

---

[19] European Convention on the Transfer of Proceedings in Criminal Matters, 15 May 1972, Article 30(1) (https://www.legal-tools.org/doc/0289ef/):

> Any Contracting State which, before the institution or in the course of proceedings for an offence which it considers to be neither of a political nature nor a purely military one, is aware of proceedings pending in another Contracting State against the same person in respect of the same offence shall consider whether it can either waive or suspend its own proceedings, or transfer them to the other State.

[20] District Court in Belgrade, *Prosecutor v. Ilija Jurišić*, War Crimes Chamber, Judgment, 28 September 2009, No. K.V. 5/2007 (https://www.legal-tools.org/doc/03f60c/).

[21] Court of Appeal in Belgrade, *Prosecutor v. Ilija Jurišić*, Ruling, 11 October 2010, No. Kž1, Po2-5/10 (https://www.legal-tools.org/doc/7d7b24/).

instance court for retrial, ordering that the case be heard by a chamber composed of judges other than those who had heard it in the initial trial. On 2 December 2013,[22] the War Crimes Department of the Higher Court delivered its judgment upon retrial, which was exactly the same as the first one and, for the second time, sentenced the defendant to 12 years in prison. On appeal, the Court of Appeal ruled to re-open the main hearing. Over the course of 2015, the Court heard two expert witnesses. On 25 December 2015,[23] the Court of Appeal in Belgrade acquitted Ilija Jurišić.

19.5. The *Lekaj* Case

Anton Lekaj, an Albanian from Kosovo and a former member of the Kosovo Liberation Army ('KLA'), was arrested in Montenegro and transferred to Serbia on the basis of a Serbian Ministry of Interior warrant. The OWCP filed an indictment against Lekaj on 7 July 2005 for crimes against Serb civilians.[24] The final verdict of Lekaj was rendered on 26 February 2007.[25] He was convicted to 13 years of imprisonment. The HLC demanded that the OWCP transfer the case to the United Nations Mission in Kosovo ('UNMIK'), but the OWCP claimed that it had the jurisdiction to prosecute individuals responsible for war crimes committed in Kosovo.

19.6. The *Morina* Case

Sinan Morina, an Albanian from Kosovo, was arrested in Montenegro and he was transferred to Serbia on the basis of a Serbian Ministry of Interior warrant. As in the case of Lekaj, the HLC advised the OWCP to transfer the case to UNMIK, but the Office firmly held its position that it had jurisdiction to prosecute war crimes committed in Kosovo.

The OWCP filed an indictment on 13 July 2005 for the attacks in July 1998 in Kosovo which resulted in deaths of a certain number of Serbs.[26] The Trial Chamber completed the trial on 20 December 2007 with an acquittal,[27] with the

---

[22] Higher Court in Belgrade, *Prosecutor v. Ilija Jurišić*, War Crimes Department, Judgment, 2 December 2013, No. K.Po2, b.r. 53/10 (https://www.legal-tools.org/doc/le81lfjl/).

[23] Court of Appeal in Belgrade, *Prosecutor v. Ilija Jurišić*, Judgment, 25 December 2015, No. Kž1, Po2-5/14 (https://www.legal-tools.org/doc/rmt0bz/).

[24] OWCP, *Prosecutor v. Anton Lekaj*, Indictment, 7 July 2005, No. KTRZ 7/04 (https://www.legal-tools.org/doc/9a1f9f/).

[25] Supreme Court of Serbia, *Prosecutor v. Anton Lekaj*, Judgment, 26 February 2007, No. K.Z. I P3 3/06 (https://www.legal-tools.org/doc/7oc57sm1/).

[26] OWCP, *Prosecutor v. Sinan Morina*, Indictment, 13 July 2005, No. KTRZ 1/07 (https://www.legal-tools.org/doc/58a7a3/).

[27] More information on the case is available in "War Crimes Prosecutor v. Sinan Morina", in *International Crimes Database*, Asser Institute, Ministry of Justice and Security of the Netherlands, International Centre for Counter-Terrorism (https://www.legal-tools.org/doc/21633c/).

explanation that the indictment was generic and that it was not proven that the defendant had committed what he was charged with. On 3 March 2009,[28] the Supreme Court of Serbia revoked the decision and ordered a retrial. The retrial has not yet been held because the accused is unavailable to the authorities of Serbia.

As in the *Lekaj* case, there are indications that the OWCP quickly filed an indictment in this case only to prove to the public and the associations of victims' family members that it was able to serve justice for Serbian victims.

19.7. The *Bytyqi* Case

The OWCP filed an indictment for the murder of three Bytyqi brothers, Kosovo Albanians and United States ('US') citizens, on 24 August 2006, under pressure from the US Department of Justice.[29] The trial was conducted against two members of the Ministry of Interior who aided the commission of this crime and not against the masterminds or immediate perpetrators. The District Court in Belgrade delivered a judgment on 22 September 2009,[30] acquitting the accused of charges for lack of evidence. On 1 November 2010,[31] the Court of Appeal quashed the judgment and sent the case back to the first instance court for retrial. After a retrial, the first instance court delivered a judgment on 9 May 2012[32] acquitting the defendants, holding that the Prosecutor had failed to prove the existence of an armed conflict at the time of the commission of the offence, a precondition for incrimination. The Court of Appeal in Belgrade later delivered a judgment on 18 January 2013[33] which upheld the judgment and acquitted Sreten Popović and Miloš Stojanović of charges of aiding and abetting the commission of a war crime against prisoners of war.

19.8. The *Orahovac* Case

Two members of the Serbian Ministry of Interior (a reserve police officer, Boban Petković from Velika Hoča, and a regular police officer, Đorđe Simić from

[28] District Court in Belgrade, *Prosecutor v. Sinan Morina*, War Crimes Chamber, Judgment, 20 December 2007, No. K.V. 2/07 (https://www.legal-tools.org/doc/npyrttnf/).

[29] OWCP, *Prosecutor v. Sreten Popović and Miloš Stojanović*, Indictment, 24 August 2006, No. KTRZ 5/06 (https://www.legal-tools.org/doc/b32728/).

[30] District Court in Belgrade, *Prosecutor v. Sreten Popović and Miloš Stojanović*, Ruling, 22 September 2009, No. K.V. 3/2006 (https://www.legal-tools.org/doc/90bc2d/).

[31] Court of Appeal in Belgrade, *Prosecutor v. Sreten Popović and Miloš Stojanović*, Ruling, 1 November 2010, No. Kž1, Po2-7/2010 (https://www.legal-tools.org/doc/5b60c9/).

[32] Higher Court in Belgrade, *Prosecutor v. Sreten Popović and Miloš Stojanović*, War Crimes Department, Judgment, 9 May 2012, No. K-Po2-br. 51/2010 (https://www.legal-tools.org/doc/ebba05/).

[33] Court of Appeal in Belgrade, *Prosecutor v. Sreten Popović and Miloš Stojanović*, Judgment, 18 January 2013, No. Kž1, Po2-5/12 (https://www.legal-tools.org/doc/e0213a/).

Orahovac) were indicted on 12 November 1999 for murder (Boban Petković) and complicity (Đorđe Simić). The Deputy Prosecutor of the District Prosecution of Požarevac, Dobrivoje Perić, filed the indictment. He was a prosecutor in the District Prosecution Office of Prizren prior to June 1999. The Trial Chamber, presided by Judge Jovica Mitrović, sentenced Boban Petković to four years and ten months of imprisonment for two murders, while Đorđe Simić was sentenced for complicity to one year of imprisonment.[34] The Supreme Court of Serbia reversed the verdict on 18 December 2001, ordering a retrial.[35]

The District Prosecutor in Požarevac (Dimitar Krstev) amended the indictment on 19 February 2003[36] by indicting Boban Petković for war crimes against the civilian population pursuant to Article 142(1) of the Criminal Code of the Socialist Federal Republic of Yugoslavia; and Đorđe Simić for complicity in such war crimes pursuant to Articles 142(1) and 24.[37]

On 21 August 2003, the Trial Chamber President, Judge Jovica Mitrović, rendered a verdict[38] finding Boban Petković guilty of war crimes committed against civilians, sentencing him to five years of imprisonment, and imposing a safety measure of compulsory psychiatric treatment in a medical institution. Đorđe Simić was acquitted.

On 25 May 2006, the Supreme Court of Serbia, deciding on appeals of the District Public Prosecutor in Požarevac and the defence counsel, reversed the verdict in its entirety and returned the case to the first instance court for retrial.[39] The second retrial commenced on 22 January 2008, before the District Court in Požarevac. However, due to a change in the judicial panel, the trial started anew on 20 September 2011 before the Higher Court in Požarevac. On 21 February 2013,[40] the Higher Court in Požarevac delivered a judgment convicting Boban Petković of the charges against him and acquitting Đorđe Simić of the charges.

[34] District Court of Požarevac, *Prosecutor v. Boban Petković and Đorđe Simić*, Judgment, 19 July 2000, No. K. 96/99 (https://www.legal-tools.org/doc/e19b45/).

[35] Supreme Court of Serbia, *Prosecutor v. Boban Petković and Đorđe Simić*, Decision, 18 December 2001, No. Kz. I 1955/00 (https://www.legal-tools.org/doc/2ddc77/).

[36] District Prosecutor of Požarevac, *Prosecutor v. Boban Petković and Đorđje Simić*, Amended Indictment, 19 February 2003, No. Kt. 118/99-108 (https://www.legal-tools.org/doc/12814a/).

[37] Criminal Code of the Socialist Federal Republic of Yugoslavia, Official Gazette No. 44, 1 July 1977, Articles 24 and 142(1) (https://www.legal-tools.org/doc/0tyfo7hz/).

[38] District Court of Požarevac, *Prosecutor v. Boban Petković and Đorđe Simić*, Judgment, 21 August 2003, No. K.P. 17/2002-(35) (https://www.legal-tools.org/doc/a81896/).

[39] Supreme Court of Serbia, *Prosecutor v. Boban Petković and Đorđe Simić*, Judgment, 25 May 2006, No. K.Z. I 1955/00 (https://www.legal-tools.org/doc/b59cd2/).

[40] Higher Court in Požarevac, *Prosecutor v. Boban Petković and Đorđe Simić*, Judgment, 21 February 2013, No. 2K 25/11 (https://www.legal-tools.org/doc/kvedhmf6/).

The Court of Appeal in Belgrade delivered a judgment on 18 December 2013[41] reducing the sentence from five to three years in prison for Boban Petković.

It is not possible to make a certain conclusion as to why the OWCP was not interested in taking over this case. This was the only case in which witnesses and victims from Kosovo were not participating.

19.9. The *Rambo* Case

The ICTY transferred this case to the OWCP according to Rule 11*bis* of the ICTY Rules of Procedure and Evidence.[42] Vladimir Kovačević, also known as 'Rambo', was indicted for war crimes against the civilian population pursuant to Articles 142(1) and (2) and Article 22 of the Criminal Code of the Socialist Federal Republic of Yugoslavia.[43] As a JNA officer under the command of the convicted Admiral Miodrag Jokić and convicted General Pavle Strugar, he allegedly ordered soldiers in his unit to attack the Old Town of Dubrovnik by indiscriminate shelling, in which two civilians (Pavo Urban and Tonči Skočko) were killed and three other civilians were wounded, six buildings were destroyed, and 46 more buildings were damaged.

In 2007, the Higher Court in Belgrade dismissed the indictment against Vladimir Kovačević, 'Rambo', with the explanation that the defendant was unable to follow the trial due to illness.

19.10. The *Slunj* Case

Based on the evidence collected by the Republic of Croatia Attorney General's Office and on the basis of the investigation that was conducted, the OWCP indicted the Serb Zdravko Pašić on 7 November 2007 for war crimes against the civilian population (murder of a Croatian doctor) in the town of Slunj in Croatia.[44] The District Court in Karlovac sentenced Zdravko Pašić *in absentia* in 2001 to 12 years of imprisonment. They also sentenced Milan Grubješić who, at the time of writing, was serving his sentence in Croatia. The District Court in Belgrade ruled that this did not constitute a violation of the principle of *ne bis*

---

41 Court of Appeal in Belgrade, *Prosecutor v. Boban Petković and Đorđe Simić*, Judgment, 18 December 2013, No. Kž1 6826/13 (https://www.legal-tools.org/doc/81fvz23i/).

42 ICTY, Rules of Procedure and Evidence, 11 February 1994 (https://www.legal-tools.org/doc/30df50/).

43 Criminal Code of the Socialist Federal Republic of Yugoslavia, Articles 22 and 142, see *supra* note 37.

44 OWCP, *Prosecutor v. Zdravko Pašić*, Indictment, 7 November 2007, No. KTRZ 11/07 (https://www.legal-tools.org/doc/ca6e49/). See also District Court in Belgrade, *Prosecutor v. Zdravko Pašić*, Judgment, 8 July 2008, No. K.V. 4/2007 (https://www.legal-tools.org/doc/2da2b7/).

in idem, as under domestic law, the rule holds relative rather than absolute significance. Given this legal framework, and considering that the defendant neither served a sentence nor was acquitted for the same offense abroad, nor was prosecution barred by time limitations in a foreign country, the Court determined that a trial before a domestic court was permissible. On 8 July 2008,[45] the District Court in Belgrade rendered a judgment convicting Zdravko Pašić and sentencing him to eight years in prison.

19.11. The *Velika Peratovica* Case

On the basis of the evidence of the Office of the Prosecutor of the Republic of Croatia and of the conducted investigation, the OWCP indicted the Serb Bora Trbojević for war crimes against Croat civilians (murder of five civilians) on 21 May 2008.[46] On 27 May 2009,[47] the District Court in Belgrade rendered a judgment, convicting Bora Trbojević and sentencing him to 10 years in prison.

19.12. The *Lovas* Case

The trial of a group of 17 Croatian Serbs for war crimes against Croatian civilians committed in October 1991 was conducted before the District Court in Vukovar *in absentia* for years. The primary accused, Ljuban Devetak, contacted the HLC in 2005 for help in order to, as he said, prove his innocence. He expressed his willingness to be prosecuted before the ICTY or before the courts in Serbia, while he found the courts in Croatia to be biased. The HLC conducted an interview with Devetak and forwarded it to the Vukovar District Court and the OWCP, thus introducing them to Devetak's position.

The OWCP started co-operation with the Office of the State Prosecutor in Vukovar, who in turn has turned over all the evidence it possessed. After investigation, the OWCP, on 28 November 2007, indicted 14 individuals, former JNA, Territorial Defence and 'Dušan Silni' ('Dušan the Mighty') members, for war crimes committed against Croatian civilians (murder of 69 civilians) in October and November 1991 in Lovas, Croatia.[48] This was the first indictment against officers and reserve members of the former JNA. The amended indictment of 28 December 2011 reduced the number of civilians stated to have lost their lives

---

[45] District Court in Belgrade, *Prosecutor v. Zdravko Pašić*, War Crimes Chamber, Judgment, 8 July 2008, No. K.V. 4/2007 (https://www.legal-tools.org/doc/2da2b7/).

[46] OWCP, *Prosecutor v. Boro Trbojević*, Indictment, 21 May 2008, No. KTRZ 4/07 (https://www.legal-tools.org/doc/fb9c27/).

[47] District Court in Belgrade, *Prosecutor v. Boro Trbojević*, War Crimes Chamber, Judgment, 27 May 2009, No. K.V. br. 5/08 (https://www.legal-tools.org/doc/ec01eb/).

[48] OWCP, *Prosecutor v. Dragan Bačić et al.*, Indictment, 28 November 2007, No. KTRZ 7/07 (https://www.legal-tools.org/doc/b1fa38/).

from 69 to 44. On 26 June 2012,[49] the Higher Court in Belgrade delivered a judgment finding all the accused guilty of a war crime against the civilian population as co-perpetrators, and sentenced them to terms of imprisonment ranging between 4 and 20 years. On 9 December 2013,[50] deciding in appellate proceedings, the Court of Appeal in Belgrade ruled to overturn the judgment of the Higher Court and remanded the case for retrial. The retrial began on 4 March 2014, before a new chairperson; by the completion of the retrial, there had been two more changes of the presiding judge. The proceedings were terminated in respect of the five accused who had died in the meantime, including Devetak. The proceedings were severed in respect of one of the accused for reasons of expediency. On 1 December 2015[51] and 5 January 2017,[52] the OWCP amended the indictment. As the amended indictment reduced the number of indictees to eight, the number of victims was reduced accordingly, with only 27 victims who had lost their lives encompassed. Also, the OWCP omitted from the indictment that the attack on the village of Lovas had been carried out on the orders of Dušan Lončar, commander of the 2nd JNA Proletarian Guards Mechanized Brigade, which during the attack also comprised the Tovarnik Territorial Defense and the 'Dušan Silni' volunteer detachment. On 20 June 2019,[53] the Higher Court in Belgrade rendered a judgment upon retrial declaring the defendants guilty of a war crime against the civilian population and sentencing them to terms of imprisonment ranging between four and eight years. On 20 November 2020,[54] the Court of Appeal in Belgrade ruled to reverse the retrial judgment of the Higher Court in Belgrade, absolved two defendants of criminal responsibility and commuted the prison sentences of the other six defendants. The imposed sentences ranged from six to three years of imprisonment.

19.13. The *Suva Reka* Case

On 25 April 2006, the OWCP indicted eight members of the Serbian Ministry of Interior, including the Assistant Commander of the Gendarmerie, who was

[49] Higher Court in Belgrade, *Prosecutor v. Dragan Bačić et al.*, War Crimes Department, Judgment, 26 June 2012, No. K-Po2-22/2010 (https://www.legal-tools.org/doc/2217b2/).

[50] Court of Appeal in Belgrade, *Prosecutor v. Dragan Bačić et al.*, Ruling, 9 December 2013, Kž1, Po2-3/13 (https://www.legal-tools.org/doc/c4d9c0/).

[51] OWCP, *Prosecutor v. Ljuban Devetak et al.*, Amended Indictment, 1 December 2015, No. KTRZ 7/07 (https://www.legal-tools.org/doc/ju89xvbo/).

[52] OWCP, *Prosecutor v. Ljuban Devetak et al.*, Amended Indictment, 5 January 2017, No. KTRZ 7/07 (https://www.legal-tools.org/doc/j3h0926e/).

[53] Higher Court in Belgrade, *Prosecutor v. Darko Perić et al.*, War Crimes Department, Judgment, 20 June 2019, No. K-Po2-1/2014 (https://www.legal-tools.org/doc/5e13pmck/).

[54] Court of Appeal in Belgrade, *Prosecutor v. Darko Perić et al.*, War Crimes Department, Judgment, 20 November 2020, No. Kž1, Po2-2/20 (https://www.legal-tools.org/doc/gbtwke5i/).

also a former commander of the Suva Reka Police Station, and the assistant of the aforementioned police commander, for the murder of 49 members of the Berisha.[55] This was the first indictment against a high-ranking member of the police (Gendarmerie Assistant Commander). It is interesting that the indictment covered only one event (the murder of 49 members of the Berisha family), even though other murders and serious criminal offences were also committed at the same time for which there are indications of involvement of high-ranking members of the military of the Federal Republic of Yugoslavia. The trial began on 2 October 2006 before the War Crimes Chamber of the District Court in Belgrade. The first instance decision was delivered on 23 April 2009.[56] Two defendants were sentenced to 20 years, one to 15, and one to 13 years in prison. Three defendants were acquitted, and following the Prosecutor's decision not to proceed with the prosecution, charges against one were withdrawn. One of the acquitted defendants was Radoslav Mitrović, the commander of the 37th Special Police Units Detachment during the armed conflict in Kosovo, who after the war became the deputy commander of the Gendarmerie. On 30 June 2010,[57] the Court of Appeal in Belgrade delivered a decision which confirmed the first instance judgment with regard to the sentencing of three defendants, and with regard to the acquittal of three defendants. Radojko Repanović's 20-year prison sentence was quashed and a retrial was ordered. On 15 December 2010,[58] the Court again sentenced the defendant Radojka Repanović to 20 years in prison. On 6 June 2011,[59] the Court of Appeal in Belgrade confirmed the judgment.

19.14. The *Podujevo* Case

This is the second indictment against members of the Scorpions unit for war crimes committed against Albanian civilians. According to the first indictment from 2002, one member of the Scorpions was convicted on the basis of 'insider' evidence and the children who survived, whose participation was facilitated by the HLC.

Three years after the final verdict of Saša Cvjetan (the primary accused), the OWCP indicted four more members of the Scorpions incriminated by the

[55] OWCP, *Prosecutor v. Radoslav Mitrović et al.*, Indictment, 25 April 2006, No. KTRZ 5/05 (https://www.legal-tools.org/doc/93fd6a/).

[56] District Court in Belgrade, *Prosecutor v. Radoslav Mitrović et al.*, War Crimes Chamber, Judgment, 23 April 2009, No. K.V. 2/2006 (https://www.legal-tools.org/doc/4ad437/).

[57] Court of Appeal in Belgrade, *Prosecutor v. Radoslav Mitrović et al.*, War Crimes Department, 30 June 2010, No. Kž1, Po2-4/2010 (https://www.legal-tools.org/doc/b8cbb4/).

[58] Higher Court in Belgrade, *Prosecutor v. Radojko Repanović*, War Crimes Department, Judgment, 15 December 2010, No. K-Po2-49/2010 (https://www.legal-tools.org/doc/6d9eb5/).

[59] Court of Appeal in Belgrade, *Prosecutor v. Radojko Repanović*, War Crimes Department, Judgment, 6 June 2011, No. Kž1, Po2-4/11 (https://www.legal-tools.org/doc/8txsgdk5/).

'insider' mentioned above.[60] On 14 April 2008, the Prosecutor issued an indictment against four members of the Scorpions for the criminal offense of war crimes against civilians. The District Court in Belgrade delivered the judgment on 18 June 2009,[61] finding the defendants guilty, and sentencing three of them to 20 years in prison and one to 15 years. On 24 and 25 May 2010,[62] the Court of Appeal in Belgrade upheld the first instance judgment for three of the defendants, while overturning the judgment for one defendant and ordering a retrial. Following a retrial and amended indictment, the Higher Court in Belgrade delivered its judgment on 22 September 2010,[63] finding the defendant guilty and sentencing him to 20 years in prison. On 11 February 2011,[64] the Court of Appeal in Belgrade upheld that decision.

19.15. The *Banski Kovačevac* Case

According to the Agreement on Co-operation in the Prosecution of Perpetrators of War Crimes concluded between the Croatian Attorney General's Office and the OWCP, and pursuant to the Law on co-operation between the two countries in legal assistance in civil and criminal matters,[65] the OWCP took over the case and indicted Pane Bulat and Rado Vranešević for war crimes against Croatian civilians (murder of six civilians) on 16 April 2008.[66] On 15 March 2010,[67] the War Crimes Chamber of the Higher Court in Belgrade convicted Pane Bulat and Rade Vranešević, sentencing them to 15 and 12 years respectively for war crimes against civilians. However, on 14 February 2011,[68] the Court of Appeals

60 OWCP, *Prosecutor v. Željko Đukić et al.*, Indictment, 14 April 2008, No. KTRZ 12/07 (https://www.legal-tools.org/doc/5ce9f6/).

61 District Court in Belgrade, *Prosecutor v. Željko Đukić et al.*, War Crimes Chamber, Judgment, 18 June 2009, No. K.V. 4/2018 (https://www.legal-tools.org/doc/281672/).

62 Court of Appeal in Belgrade, *Prosecutor v. Željko Đukić et al.*, Judgment, 24 and 25 May 2010, No. Kž1, Po2-3/2010 (https://www.legal-tools.org/doc/26bf7c/).

63 Higher Court in Belgrade, *Prosecutor v. Željko Đukić et al.*, War Crimes Department, Judgment, 22 September 2010, No. K-Po2-44/2010 (https://www.legal-tools.org/doc/6573ed/).

64 Court of Appeal in Belgrade, *Prosecutor v. Željko Đukić et al.*, War Crimes Department, Judgment, 11 February 2011, No. Kž1, Po2-2/2011 (https://www.legal-tools.org/doc/bd5098/).

65 Agreement Between the Federal Republic of Yugoslavia and the Republic of Croatia on Legal Aid in Civil and Criminal Matters, 15 September 1997, Official Gazette (International Treaties) No. 1/1998.

66 OWCP, *Prosecutor v. Pane Pulat and Rade Vranešević*, Indictment, 16 April 2008, No. KTRZ 13/07 (https://www.legal-tools.org/doc/6988de/).

67 Higher Court in Belgrade, *Prosecutor v. Pane Pulat and Rade Vranešević*, War Crimes Department, Judgment, 15 March 2010, No. K-Po2-25/2010 (https://www.legal-tools.org/doc/8a493e/).

68 Court of Appeal in Belgrade, *Prosecutor v. Pane Pulat and Rade Vranešević*, Judgment, 14 February 2011, No. Kž1, Po2-8/2010 (https://www.legal-tools.org/doc/1223b2/).

in Belgrade overturned the original sentences and imposed harsher penalties, increasing their prison terms to 20 years for Bulat and 13 years for Vranešević.

19.16. The *Pakšec* Case

On 9 June 2006, the Novi Sad District Public Prosecutor Veronika Vencel indicted Slavko Petrović, Petar Ćirić and Nikola Dukić for murder (Article 114 of the Criminal Code of the Republic of Serbia) and rape (Articles 178(1) and (2))[69] for killing four members of the Pakšec family in Croatia on 9 April 1992, and for forcing a woman of Serbian nationality to sexual intercourse. The trial was closed to the public.

The Trial Chamber, presided over by Judge Zoran Drecun, rendered its verdict on 19 October 2007 and found the indictee Slavko Petrović guilty of both charges and convicted him to 40 years of imprisonment. Nikola Dukić was sentenced to 30 years of imprisonment, taking into consideration that he pleaded guilty. Petar Ćirić was acquitted for the charges of rape and sentenced to 12 years of imprisonment. In its ruling on 2 December 2008, the Supreme Court of Serbia upheld the prison sentences for Petrović and Dukić, while reducing Ćirić's sentence from 12 to 10 years.

19.17. Investigation and Pre-Trial Proceedings

According to the European Commission 'Serbia 2023 Report', the OWCP has a backlog of over 1,700 pre-investigative cases.[70] According to information from the OWCP, 13 investigations were pending at the time of writing, three of which related to war crimes committed in Kosovo. Excluding 728 criminal complaints and 26 pre-trial proceedings for crimes committed by the KLA, 10 pre-trial proceedings referred to crimes committed in Kosovo against Albanian civilians. Data indicates that Kosovo crimes were at the centre of attention of the OWCP. However, no information indicates which – if any – criteria were used for the selection of cases and for the prioritization process.

19.18. Findings

The described cases unambiguously show that the OWCP did not act independently in the first five years, but rather filed indictments under political pressure, and pressure imposed by victims' families and nationalist political parties (*Tuzla column*, *Lekaj*, *Morina*, *Ovčara*). The indictment in the *Zvornik I* case was the result of the ICTY's referral. Several indictments follow close co-operation with the Croatian State Attorney General's Office, which contributed to

69 Criminal Code of the Republic of Serbia, 1 January 2006, Official Gazette Nos. 85/2005, 88/2005, 107/2005 (https://www.legal-tools.org/doc/9fdf3d/).

70 European Commission, Directorate-General for Neighbourhood and Enlargement Negotiations, "Serbia 2023 Report", 8 November 2023, SWD/2023/695 final, p. 30.

faster and more efficient prosecution of war crimes and the termination of *in absentia* trials in Croatia. At least three indictments were the result of investigations conducted pursuant to the HLC's activities (*Zvornik III, Lovas*) or on the basis of evidence collected by the HLC (*Scorpions*). The OWCP was most willing to prosecute crimes in the cases of *Lovas* and *Suva Reka* – the indicted individuals were high-ranking members of the police and military.

This is indicative that the OWCP did not have criteria for the selection of cases to be investigated or for filing indictments in its early years. The prosecution of war crimes in Serbia was an *ad hoc* process and it greatly depended on the political circumstances in the country.

20

Human Rights Courts in Indonesia: A Brief Outline

Fadillah Agus*

20.1. Background

Indonesia an archipelago state which consists of more than 17,000 islands, and is populated by more than 280 million people: there are more than 300 ethnic groups and 500 local dialects, and it is the largest South-East Asian country. Indonesia is one of the initiators of the Non-Aligned Movement where it plays an active role in this movement.

Indonesia was under Dutch colonization for more than 350 years. During World War II, it was occupied by Japan for about three and a half years. After a long struggle against the Dutch and Japanese, Indonesia succeeded to proclaim its independence on 17 August 1945.

It is no wonder, given this long history of colonization, that Indonesia's legal system is very much influenced by the Dutch legal system. The Civil Code, Penal Code and Military Penal Code at the time of writing come from the Netherlands. More recently, some Anglo-American legal systems have influenced Indonesian law, particularly in the fields of business and commercial law. In addition, as there are many ethnicities and cultures, the legal system of Indonesia is also influenced by the so-called 'Adat' law (local law born and developed within communities in particular areas and groups). Furthermore, as the largest Muslim country in the world, there is a strong influence of Islámic law, particularly with regards to family law.

* The late **Fadillah Agus** was one of Indonesia's leading experts on international humanitarian law. As the author has sadly passed away, his chapter has not been substantively updated since the Second Edition. At the time of writing, he was pursuing a Ph.D. at Padjajaran University, Bandung, on the topic of the application of international humanitarian law in internal armed conflicts, and was one of three partners in the FRR Law Office in Jakarta, a law firm which he used as his base for his prominent human rights work in Indonesia, including training for the Indonesian Armed Forces. He lectured at the Syiah Kuala University in Banda Aceh and in De La Salle University in Manado. From 1998 to 2004, he worked as Legal Adviser for the International Committee of the Red Cross in Jakarta. In 2005–2006, he was a member of the inquiry team under the National Commission of Human Rights investigating disappearances (abductions of activists) during the final days of Suharto's New Order regime that was toppled in 1998.

Since independence, the country has seen some insurgencies and separatism – ethnic as well as religious conflicts. The Aceh freedom movement was one of the famous insurgencies, settled by the Helsinki process. Another well-known conflict is that of East Timor which led to the establishment of the state of Timor Leste and war crimes trials. There are still active separatist movements within Indonesia, in Papua and the Moluccas. In addition, a religious conflict occurred in the Moluccas and Sulawesi, and an ethnic conflict (Madurese against Dayak) in Kalimantan. There was also a Communist insurgency in 1965 which led to hundreds of thousands killed, both on the side of the Communist Party and nationalist and Muslim groups.

Right after independence, Indonesia was led by the famous President Soekarno and his Vice-President Hatta. Following the failure of the Communist Movement in 1965, Soekarno stepped down from the Presidency and was replaced by Suharto. The smiling General Suharto led the country for more than 30 years: this period is known by the Indonesian people as the authoritarian regime of President Suharto. The country was under his strong control, and he used the military, the police and government agencies (particularly the intelligence) as tools of domestic control. There are many accusations of human rights violations committed during Suharto's regime.

20.2. Legal Framework

President Suharto was toppled by the reform movement in 1998. The following President, Yudhoyono, was elected through a direct and peaceful election. The reform process started in 1998 and was marked by a greater interest of the people in human rights issues. The People Consultative Body (the highest institution in the country, with jurisdiction to amend the Constitution) issued a decree on human rights. Then the country issued Laws 39 of 1999 and 26 of 2000 on human rights and the Human Rights Court.[1] The National Commission of Human Rights ('Komnas HAM') was also established right after Suharto's fall. Since then, there has been a significant human rights movement in the country.

As opposed to human rights courts elsewhere in the world, the Indonesian Human Rights Court – regulated by Law 26 of 2000 – is close to being a penal court with the power to impose penal sanctions. According to Law 26 of 2000, there are two types of human rights court: the permanent Human Rights Court,

1 Indonesia, Legislation No. 39 of 1999 Concerning Human Rights, 23 September 1999 ('Law 39 of 1999') (https://legal-tools.org/doc/abced1/). Legislation No. 26 of 2000 Concerning Human Rights Courts, 23 November 2000 ('Law 26 of 2000') (https://legal-tools.org/doc/8d6ceb/): the linked document is an unofficial translation; the original text is also available in the Legal Tools Database (https://www.legal-tools.org/doc/fbaf18/).

which has jurisdiction to process cases of gross violations of human rights committed after the passing of the Law; and the *Ad Hoc* Human Rights Court, which has jurisdiction to hear cases of gross violations of human rights committed before the issuance of the law, meaning that the latter is, in a way, using a retroactive principle.

Retroactivity is normally not acceptable in criminal justice, but there are some exceptions. According to Law 26 of 2000, an *Ad Hoc* Human Rights Court has to be established by Presidential Decree after the recommendation by Parliament to the President.

As mentioned above, the Human Rights Court under Law 26 of 2000 has jurisdiction over gross violations of human rights, that is, genocide and crimes against humanity. No elements of crime are described under said Law. There is also no special procedural law for the Court; it applies ordinary criminal procedural law. Komnas HAM is the fact-finding body of the Court. It takes the first step when there is an accusation of gross violations of human rights. The formal investigation and indictment are made by the Attorney General's Office, and the case is heard by five Judges (two career judges and three *ad hoc* judges).

20.3. Cases

At the time of writing, there have been three main clusters of cases processed before Indonesian human rights courts: the East Timor, Tanjung Priok and Abepura cases. The East Timor and Tanjung Priok cases were heard by the *Ad Hoc* Human Rights Court (because the alleged crimes occurred prior to the issuance of Law 26 of 2000), while the Abepura cases were heard by the permanent Human Rights Court as the charged offences occurred after the issuance of Law 26 of 2000.

There have been 12 cases with 20 defendants before the East Timor *Ad Hoc* Human Rights Court. Most of the accused were from the Indonesian National Military ('TNI'). The other defendants were from the Indonesian Police (Polri) and civilians. All the indictments involved crimes against humanity, while the modes of liability used in the indictments were individual criminal responsibility and command responsibility.

The *Ad Hoc* Human Rights Court of East Timor was established pursuant to Presidential Decree No. 53 of 2001,[2] which was strengthened by Presidential Decree No. 96 of 2001.[3] These regulations constitute the legal basis to investi-

[2] Indonesia, Presidential Decree No. 53 of 2001, 23 April 2001 (https://www.legal-tools.org/doc/svhfak/).

[3] Indonesia, Presidential Decree No. 96 of 2001, 1 August 2001 (https://www.legal-tools.org/doc/on6vnh91/).

gate human rights violations that occurred in East Timor. According to Presidential Decree No. 96 of 2001, the Court has jurisdiction over crimes committed in three areas (Dili, Liquica and Suai) between April and September 1999. All tribunals have operated out of the District Court of Central Jakarta.

At the time of writing, all defendants had been acquitted. Six defendants were sentenced by the court of first instance, but then acquitted by the Appeals and Supreme Courts. The more controversial case was the one against Major General Adam Damiri (Commander of the Regional Command of Bali and Nusa Tenggara), who was ordered to be released by the Attorney General.

Some commented that the Court had failed to bring justice, particularly to the victims. However, the good intention of the government of Indonesia to process the cases should be appreciated. This was the first time that Indonesia tried such cases – the Human Rights Court itself had to learn by doing. The lack of capacity in the Attorney General's Office was the main reason leading to its failure in proving its indictments.

The Tanjung Priok case[4] was started by the arrest of members of Musholla As Saadah, a small mosque in the Tanjung Priok area, in north Jakarta. They were accused of damaging the motorcycle of Sergeant Hermanu because, according to members of Musholla As Saadah, Sergeant Hermanu was entering the mosque without taking off his shoes (as was normal procedure for everyone). The police then transferred the four persons to the Military District Command of North Jakarta. A few days later, members of Musholla As Saadah, led by Amir Biki, came along to the North Jakarta Military District Command with the intention of asking for the release of their fellow members. On their way to the District Command, they were confronted by some ten military personnel led by Sergeant Mascung. The military personnel unexpectedly opened fire directly at the group, wounding 55 persons and killing 24. The leader of the group, Amir Biki, was killed. Without informing their families, the dead were buried by the military in several graveyards. Some of them did not have a gravestone. Those who were wounded were taken to the Gatot Subroto Military Hospital by military truck; others were treated at Koja Hospital and Suka Mulia Hospital before being transferred to Gatot Subroto Hospital. The wounded victims were transferred to several military posts in Jakarta shortly after the treatment and recovery. The military took them into custody and tortured them during their detention.

In 2000, Komnas HAM formed a commission for the inquiry of human rights violations in Tanjung Priok ('KP3T'). On 11 October 2000, KP3T released a report stating that there were at least four severe violations of human

---

4 The author is thankful to Ben Biran Ananda, who helped in carrying out part of the research on the Tanjung Priok case.

rights which occurred during the incident. Those violations are summary killing, unlawful arrest and detention, torture, and involuntary disappearance. The whole series of incidents was the responsibility of the perpetrators in the field and the commanders. Based on the report, there were at least 23 people who were responsible as field perpetrators and operational commander in the incidents. The suspects were divided into three categories: field perpetrators, operational commander in charge, and the commander, who did not take any action to prevent the violations.

Soon afterwards, Komnas HAM submitted its final report to the Attorney General's Office. The investigation by the Attorney General's Office was completed in July 2003. After 19 years, in September 2003, the Human Rights Court started its proceedings. The Court examined 15 defendants who were charged as field perpetrators and operational commander. The first Tanjung Priok trial was against defendant Sutrisno Mascung and ten military co-accused, including Pranowo, R.A. Butar-Butar and Sriyanto. In 2004, the first instance sentenced Butar-Butar to ten years of imprisonment. Mascung was sentenced to three years, and his military co-accused to two years. The prosecutor did not prove the guilt of Pranowo and Sriyanto. In the second instance in 2005, the judge acquitted Butar-Butar and Mascung. In 2005–2006, the Supreme Court ordered the release of all defendants.

The judges at the first instance had included compensation for the victims in their judgment. This had, in the end, no effect, as the Appeals Court and Supreme Court annulled the judgment.

The Abepura case was processed by the permanent Human Rights Court. The defendants were two members of the police; one was the commander of a special police task force (Mobile Brigade), and the other Head of the District Police at Papua. Following demonstrations and incidents between students and the police, the police went to homes and arrested some of the students, most of whom came from particular tribes and areas in Papua. Torture occurred during the operation and at the place of detention in the police station.

Crimes against humanity and command responsibility were at the core of the indictment brought by the Attorney General's Office. The two police officers were acquitted by the judges, as they were of the opinion that the Attorney General had not proven that crimes against humanity were committed by the defendants. The judgment says that the element of systematic or widespread attack directed against the civilian population was not proven, so the judges did not continue with the modes of liability and ordered the release of the defendants.

20.4. Case Selection and Prioritization

The three clusters of cases discussed above – East Timor, Tanjung Priok and Abepura – show that no defendant has been found guilty by the human rights courts. This should not lead to the pessimistic conclusion that it does not make sense to try to improve human rights courts in Indonesia. At the time of writing, there are some 20 cases that potentially qualify as gross violations of human rights which would fall within the jurisdiction of the human rights courts.

One needs to consider how the judicial system is working in human rights cases. When there is an allegation of gross violations of human rights, Komnas HAM makes an inquiry if there is sufficient evidence.[5] Based on Article 19 of Law 26 of 2000,[6] Komnas HAM can start its inquiry if, based on the nature and scope of the alleged incidents, it can be reasonably suspected that one or more gross violations of human rights were committed.

Based on the case practice to date, we can identify some criteria used by Komnas HAM to select and prioritize cases:

- the pattern, scope and geographical range of crimes (East Timor and Tanjung Priok cases);
- the victim's approach and impact on the community (Tanjung Priok cases);
- the attention of the community towards the case, leading to political pressure (East Timor and Abepura); and
- the degree of involvement of the state apparatus.

Shortly before the publication of the Second Edition of this book, Komnas HAM used the Case Matrix (an International Criminal Court tool) as one of its supporting tools to select a case.

Based on the inquiry made by Komnas HAM, the Attorney General's Office conducts the investigation in the case. Article 12 of Law 26 of 2000[7] stipulates that the Attorney General is the investigator and prosecutor for gross violations of human rights. According to Articles 106 and 140 of the Code of Criminal Procedure,[8] the investigation and indictment will be made by the Attorney General if there is sufficient evidence in the case. As mentioned above, there is no special procedural law that applies as a supplement to Law 26 of 2000. The ordinary criminal procedure law applies (Article 10 of Law 26 of 2000).[9]

One of the critical issues in cases involving gross violations of human rights is the criteria for selection and prioritization of cases. There are no written guidelines that have to be followed by Komnas HAM when it selects and prioritizes cases. Such guidelines would seem even more important for the Attorney

---

5 Law 39 of 1999, Article 91, see *supra* note 1.

6 See *supra* note 1.

7 *Ibid.*

8 Indonesia, Code of Criminal Procedure, Act No. 8 of 1981 (https://www.legal-tools.org/doc/a8a8ef/).

9 See *supra* note 1.

General's Office. The East Timor and Tanjung Priok cases are good examples of cases where there were significant differences of opinion between Komnas HAM and the Attorney General's Office on selecting the case to be processed by the Court. There was a substantial number of persons to be prosecuted. In the East Timor cases, the Attorney General's Office reduced the number of cases that were presented by Komnas HAM for prosecution.

Law 26 of 2000 and Law 39 of 1999 do not stipulate criteria for the selection and prioritization of cases. There is no regulation or guideline which has to be followed on this matter. In practice, the selection and prioritization of cases fall within the discretion of the Attorney General's Office. This can lead to intervention in the selection of cases based on political or security considerations. Usually, there is a misuse of the 'national interest' consideration to influence the selection and prioritization of the gross violations of human rights cases.

There is, therefore, a need to develop guidelines, or even regulations, concerning the selection and prioritization of human rights cases that should apply to the institutions involved in the proceedings. Furthermore, Law 26 of 2000 should be amended to include the category of war crimes and special procedural provisions for human rights cases, as well as the elements of the crimes, which should be provided for in the law.

PART IV: INTERESTS AND EFFICACY

21

Gravity of Crimes and Responsibility of the Suspect

Xabier Agirre Aranburu*

21.1. Introduction: Definition and Elements of a Case

The meaning of 'case' is not the same in different national and international systems, and even within the same system the usage of the term is not always consistent. For the purpose of the investigation and prosecution of core international crimes (war crimes, crimes against humanity, genocide and aggression), the most common understanding is that a case comprises the whole of facts and charges attributed to one or several accused jointly, as stated in an indictment or warrant of arrest. A case is formed by the following elements of fact and law:

a. the facts or criminal events;
b. the suspect or accused;
c. the charges, that is, the legal characterization of the facts;
d. the mode of responsibility; and

---

* **Xabier Agirre Aranburu** is Senior Coordinator at the Office of the Prosecutor ('OTP') of the International Criminal Court ('ICC') since 2022. He has been Senior Analyst and Head of the Investigative Analysis Section at the ICC-OTP (2004–2024), Associate Analyst and Strategic Analyst at the OTP of the International Criminal Tribunal for the former Yugoslavia ('ICTY') (1997–2003), Legal Officer with the United Nations ('UN') Office of the High Commissioner for Human Rights in Colombia (2001), Visting Professor at the American University Washington College of Law (2009) and Senior Investigator with the Truth and Reconciliation Commission in Honduras (2011). He is also author of several relevant publications, including "Methodology for Investigations", in Dinah Shelton (ed.), *Encyclopaedia on Genocide and Crimes Against Humanity* (MacMillan, New York, 2004), "Selection Criteria and the Use of Sampling Techniques in the Investigation of International Crimes", in Uwe Ewald and Ksenija Turković (eds.), *Large-Scale Victimisation as a Potential Source of Terrorist Activities* (IOS Press, Amsterdam, 2006), "Sexual violence beyond reasonable doubt: using pattern evidence and analysis for international cases", in *Leiden Journal of International Law*, 2010, vol. 23, pp. 609–627 and "Prosecuting the most responsible for international crimes: dilemmas of definition and prosecutorial discretion", in Joaquín González Ibáñez (ed.), *Derechos Humanos, Relaciones Internacionales y Globalización*, Second Edition (Gustavo Ibáñez Ediciones Jurídicas, Bogotá, 2009). The views expressed in this paper are the exclusive responsibility of the author and do not necessarily represent the views of the ICC-OTP nor the ICTY-OTP. The author was invited to the 2008 CILRAP conference to give independent advice on analysis, while his colleague Paul Seils represented the ICC-OTP. The author thanks Ali Amjad for data collection, inputting and coding, and Susie Kemp and Paul Seils for their review and comments.

e. the standard of evidence (depending on the phase of development of the case).

To select a case implies selecting the above elements, either at the same time or, what is most common, gradually. The process is based always on a blend of legal and factual judgment, a combination of inductive and deductive thinking (from the specific facts to the legal inferences, and *vice versa*) and a dialogue between the officers focused on the facts and those focused on the law. This process grows along two main scales of certainty and specificity. The graph on the next page shows the correlation of these two parameters and the corresponding phases of the legal process; the graph is illustrated with references to the Statute of the ICC, but the process and milestones are similar in most systems of criminal law.

Certainty. The question is 'how sure' the actor (prosecutor or judge) is about the alleged facts. The lowest level 'suspicion' requires a mere notice of the crime (*notitia criminis*) that is deemed sufficient to trigger some analysis or collection of evidence. The second level of 'reasonable basis' is reached when the prosecutor, who is by definition a reasonable person using logical methods, believes the allegations. The third and highest level indicates absolute certainty about the alleged facts by the judges.

Specificity. The scope of relevant facts may initially be very broad, comprising all crimes that have been reported and fall within the formal scope of jurisdiction. The next step to narrow down the scope is to identify the entities that were instrumental to the crime (institutions, armed groups, armies, political parties, networks, *et cetera*): this is not a legal requirement, but it is the most logical step in the analysis because core international crimes are usually the result of some form of collective action through established groups or institutions. The final and most specific stage refers to the identification of a particular accused, within the scope of the investigated crimes and organizations.

At the initial stage, what needs to be selected is a case *hypothesis* rather than a case as such. Just like in scientific methodology, the hypothesis is the provisional explanation of the facts that shall be subject to investigation and then consolidated into a thesis, which will be the case.

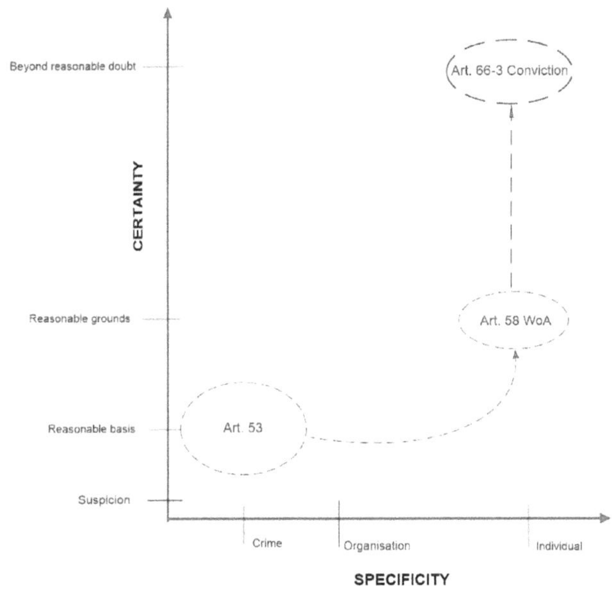

Graph 1: Scales of certainty and specificity.

The design of a solid case hypothesis (logically consistent, objective, clearly defined, factual and legally sound) is fundamental for successful selection and investigation. Using a standard format to design case hypotheses will help to advance more promptly and efficiently. The case hypothesis must flow as a syllogism, that is, a logic proposition whereby a chain of factual premises leads to the conclusion of responsibility of the accused in question. The main premises of fact that the hypothesis must cover are usually: (a) status of authority or role of the suspect; (b) structure of the organization instrumental to the crime and subordinated or associated to the suspect; (c) pattern and *modus operandi* of the criminal events; and (d) conclusion on mode of responsibility.

Rather than a vague idea or 'common knowledge', it is advisable to formulate the case hypothesis in written form, circulate it and subject it to the investigating team, first for review, and then as the framework that shall direct the investigation.

21.2. The Gravity of the Crimes

International criminal law ('ICL') was conceived and developed to deal with crimes of the highest gravity.[1] In the words of the ICC Statute,[2] these are the "most serious crimes of concern to the international community as a whole", and past "unimaginable atrocities that deeply shock the conscience of humanity" (Preamble). The ICC Statute further mentions a requirement of "sufficient gravity" for case selection and admissibility (Article 17(1)(d)). The gravity criterion is discussed in detail in Chapters 5 and 6 above and 22 below.[3]

The requirement of gravity is clear in the origin of each of the core crimes: each one includes qualifiers of gravity in its legal definition that operate as restrictors to limit their application to extraordinarily grave conduct. Concerning war crimes, 'grave breaches' are differentiated from 'other, presumably less grave violations', particularly for international armed conflicts (after the 1949 Geneva Conventions and their 1977 Additional Protocols).[4] The ICC Statute includes an advisory provision in Article 8(1) for the "particular" consideration of war crimes "when committed as part of a plan or policy or as part of a large-scale commission", mirroring similar qualifiers of gravity in the definition of crimes against humanity.

'Crimes against humanity' were created mainly as a reaction to the Holocaust, that is, the systematic, racist murder of millions of civilians, and it is clear that the references to 'widespread' or 'systematic' were designed to limit the scope to crimes that were extraordinarily grave because of the vast scale or methodical commission. The ICC Statute has further emphasized the element of systematicity by requiring that the 'attack' must result from a higher State or organizational policy (Article 7(2)). Concerning genocide, the most significant qualifier of gravity, and usually the most difficult element of the crime to prove in a court of criminal law, is the specific intent to destroy one of the protected groups.

While some qualifiers of gravity are built-in as elements of the legal definition of the crimes, a further analysis of gravity will be necessary beyond the

---

1 Note on terminology: 'seriousness' and 'severity' are frequently used as synonyms of gravity in the relevant law and commentaries.

2 Rome Statute of the International Criminal Court, 17 July 1998 ('ICC Statute') (https://www.legal-tools.org/doc/7b9af9/).

3 For some recent academic debate on the issue, see Margaret M. deGuzman, *Shocking the Conscience of Humanity: Gravity and the Legitimacy of International Criminal Law*, Oxford University Press, 2020, and Priya Urs, *Gravity at the International Criminal Court. Admissibility and Prosecutorial Discretion,* Oxford University Press, 2024.

4 Frits Kalshoven and Liesbeth Zegveld, *Constraints on the Waging of War*, International Committee of the Red Cross, Geneva, 2001, p. 80.

formal test of legality. For example, only a 'widespread' (or 'systematic') attack on a civilian population may constitute a crime against humanity, but some crimes against humanity may be more 'widespread' than others, or some acts within the 'widespread' pattern are graver than others and hence should merit selection or prioritization.

Therefore, the focus on crimes of the highest gravity is a fundamental principle of ICL that should not be undermined with its use for relatively minor offences or frivolous prosecutions.[5]

21.2.1. Substantive Gravity of the Offence

The first question that needs to be addressed is whether some offences are graver than others.[6] In most national and international systems, there is a hierarchy of gravity between the offences, so that, for example, offences against life and physical integrity may be considered graver than offences against property (it is graver to kill than to rob a person). The penalty attributed to different offences is the clearest indicator of their perceived gravity (whether those penalties are codified in a criminal code, or developed through judicial decisions).

Regarding core international crimes, there is not such a thing as a codified set of penalties. There is only some emerging case law and developing empirical research on sentencing, and the investigating authorities may be reluctant to take a position on whether some offences are graver than others because they may see this as constraining their discretion.

It is safe to regard offences resulting in deliberate death of protected persons as gravest (murder or extermination as a crime against humanity, wilful killing or attack on civilians as a war crime, killing as an act of genocide). This is the case in most national systems. Furthermore, the right to life is the first one consecrated in the Universal Declaration of Human Rights (Article 3) and every international crime initiates the enumeration of constituent offences with reference to those resulting in death.[7] As a matter of methodology, killings are often

---

5 For an extensive analysis of the issue in the ICC context, see the report *The Gravity Threshold of the ICC*, by the War Crimes Research Office of the Washington College of Law, American University, March 2008.

6 This is about the underlying offences of the crimes. Regarding the core international crimes as such (war crimes, crimes against humanity, genocide and aggression), the prevailing opinion in jurisprudence is that there is no hierarchy of gravity among them. Victims and public opinion do usually consider genocide the gravest, and alternative characterizations may be the cause of disappointment or a feeling of 'under-estimating' the gravity of the crime (see, for example, the reaction of Bosnian victims to the acquittal on genocide charges in the Krajišnik and other ICTY cases).

7 As in the ICC Statute, see *supra* note 2, "killing members of the group" as an act of genocide (Article 6(a)), "murder" as a crime against humanity (Article 7(a), followed by "extermination"

the best indicators for crime-pattern analysis because the information available is usually of better quality and lesser ambiguity; killings attract a lot of attention, bodies or forensic evidence may be available, and the elements of the crime are generally less ambiguous than other offences.

Rape is also considered a crime of the highest gravity in most national systems and in the emerging international jurisprudence. Hence, the selection of cases primarily focused on rape before, among others, the ICTY (Foča, Furundžija) and the ICC (Bemba).

Attacks against peace-keepers have been considered as particularly grave crimes by international tribunals for reasons akin to those of the national systems when dealing with violence against police or other public officers: attacking them affects their ability to protect and threatens the society as a whole. Hence, the charges for using peace-keepers as hostages and human shields by the ICTY (in the case of Karadžić and Mladić) and the case for an attack on a base on African Union peace-keepers by ICC (in the Darfur investigation).

In addition to the legal criteria, opinion surveys may help to adjust the assessment of gravity to the needs of the victimized population. For example, a recent survey conducted in eastern Democratic Republic of the Congo ('DRC') confirmed that killing was the highest priority for the local population (92 per cent demanded accountability), followed by rape (69 per cent), and looting (41 per cent).[8] As one of the participants in the seminar mentioned, this may trigger some dilemmas of "cultural relativism *versus* international law". In reality, the perception of the victims is unlikely to contradict substantially the criteria of international law when dealing with massive violence.

21.2.2. Quantitative Aspects

The number of victims is a basic parameter to define the gravity of the crime. The judges of the UN international tribunals have referred consistently to this key aspect of gravity (in the context of sentencing). Quantitative estimates of large numbers of victims in the context of war or mass violence require complex methodology and are often open to controversy in the trials as well as in the public opinion. The two main strategies are basically counting reported victims or estimating them based on samples and extrapolations. Both approaches have been accepted by judges and ideally the best result would come from combining and complementing them.

Article 7(b)), "wilful killing", "violence to life and person, in particular murder of all kinds, mutilation, cruel treatment and torture" as war crimes (Article 8(a)(i) and Article 8(c)(i)).

8 Patrick Vinck, Phuong Pham, Suliman Baldo and Rachel Shigekane, *Living With Fear: A Population-Based Survey on Attitudes about Peace, Justice, and Social Reconstruction in Eastern Democratic Republic of the Congo*, August 2008, pp. 40–41.

The graph below is an example of counting reported victims from the Peruvian Truth and Reconciliation Commission showing their chronological distribution for a period of 20 years.[9] The very sharp peaks around 1983–1985 give a clear indication of the periods of gravest crime.

Graph 2: Reported victims from the Peruvian Truth and Reconciliation Commission (1980–2000).

A limitation of this method is that it only covers the *reported* victims, and so it is likely to under-represent the real figures (assuming that all reports were truthful). Usually, this method is most helpful to identify the periods and areas of gravest crime (assuming that there are no significant biases on the chronology and geography of the sources), rather than to assess the overall figures of victimization. Other limitations of this kind of analysis may be related to the quality of the underlying data (definition of the operational concepts, accuracy, completeness, *et cetera*).

A similar model was used in 2004 by the OTP for the initial analysis that led to the selection of the first cases in the DRC investigation. Killings were used as the main indicator because of the inherent gravity of the crime, the relatively better quality of the information (more accuracy on the figures, locations, dates and attributions than other crimes), and because killings were considered a valid indicator of the broader pattern of multiple crimes (killings were usually committed in association with rape, destruction, expulsions, *et cetera*). The legal

[9] Peru, Comisión de la Verdad y la Reconciliación, *Informe Final* [Final Report], 28 August 2003, Chapter II ('El despliegue regional'), p. 107 (https://www.legal-tools.org/doc/nos1ri5j/).

definition of 'murder' or 'killing' was utilized (under Articles 7 and 8 of the ICC Statute), so that deaths of combatants in war actions were excluded. The sources of the information comprised mainly the UN, as well as some non-governmental organizations ('NGOs') and media, all of them subject to critical source evaluation (to control possible biases in the sources) and correction of duplications (what is known in different systems as 'false collaterals' or 'circular reporting', that is, the same incident being reported by different sources under different names or aggregate categories). In case of conflicting or ambiguous information, ranges of minimum and maximum figures were used for the number of victims of the incident. The figures were inputted by reported incident, and then aggregated by months to produce the table. The underlying dataset has been then updated until 2008 (for new incidents as well as for new data on old incidents) to monitor trends.

The first table in the appendix of this chapter shows the chronological distribution of reported killings for the whole of the DRC. The second table, based on the same data, shows the chronological distribution by regions within the DRC. The chronological line between the two tables shows key events in order to visualize correlations. The resulting pattern analysis indicates the regions and periods of gravest crime, and their correlation with the armed conflict.

The data on reported killings were also analysed by entities (armed groups or institutions), with the result of the illustration below. Of the 10 entities whose members had reportedly committed relevant killings, two featured with a significantly higher profile (nos. 1 and 2 in the table). These were actually the two main entities in the armed conflict in Ituri during 2002–2003 and they were selected for the first two cases to be investigated in the DRC, which ultimately led to the convictions in *Lubanga*, *Ntaganda* and *Katanga* for most serious offences.

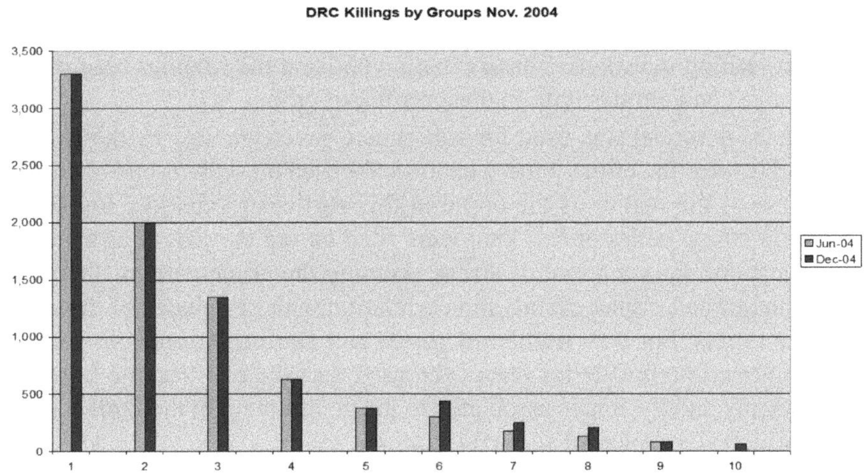

Graph 3: Reported killings in the DRC by groups (November 2004).

This analysis requires first to define the identity of each of the entities, the boundaries of their membership. Often a given armed group or institution is described with different names by different sources (victims or others). Sometimes the attribution is vague or based on generic characterization (for example, in Bosnia 'Chetniks' for all Serb forces or 'Ustasha' for all Croat forces, or, in the DRC, 'Rwandan rebels' for a series of groups, *et cetera*). Consolidation tables will need to be designed to control these terminological variations and translate, in the most objective way, the reported categories into a consolidated entity, within a given temporal and geographic context. This exercise is similar to acknowledging the *emic* and *etic* perspectives about a culture, as linguists and anthropologists would say, that is, the internal and external understandings of a culture, and then defining clear definitions and semantic boundaries for analytical consistency.

To produce the descriptive statistics and graphs is not that difficult, the examples above were produced with basic Excel and Visio applications. What is difficult is to design the right parameters (with the right criteria of substantive law and jurisdiction), to identify the right sources and evaluate them correctly (taking into account all kinds of potential biases), to collect the adequate mass of data, and to complete the inputting with sufficient accuracy and consistency (all of the above within usually short deadlines). For that matter, it is necessarily a deal of teamwork (including investigators, analysts and prosecutors), good database design (including clear written protocols, as well as possibly prototypes testing), and proper quality control.

Along with the in-house analysis of the crime data, the opinion of different researchers with extensive field experience was gathered through a series of open non-leading questions. These experts validated the findings regarding the periods, areas and entities with highest profile of crime.

The same model was used for subsequent investigations by the OTP. For northern Uganda, the crime-pattern analysis focused on killings and abductions, in response to the reality of the crime in this particular situation. For the first two Darfur cases, tables of this kind were filed before the judges as annexes to the applications for a warrant of arrest, showing the crime pattern (focused on killings and forced displacement) and correlation with key phases of the conflict and other events. For both northern Uganda and Darfur, the analysis showed a much higher crime profile for one of the parties of the conflict (the Lord's Resistance Army and the forces associated to the government of the Sudan, respectively), which were selected for investigation.

Crime mapping techniques may help to identify the 'hot spots' or areas with highest concentration of crime. The maps below are an example of analysis of this kind conducted by the OTP at an early stage of the Darfur investigation (2005, internal draft working version). A crime database similar to the one explained above (see the DRC example) was developed, and geographic coordinates were assigned to each reported incident resulting in a significant number of killings. Geographic and ethnographic information was collected and collated to build a layer showing administrative divisions and approximate presence of the tribes.[10]

[10] An updated and animated version of this map (to show chronological evolution, built on the Flash software) was submitted before the judges as an annex to the application for a warrant of arrest for the second Darfur case, and further used for public communication in 2008.

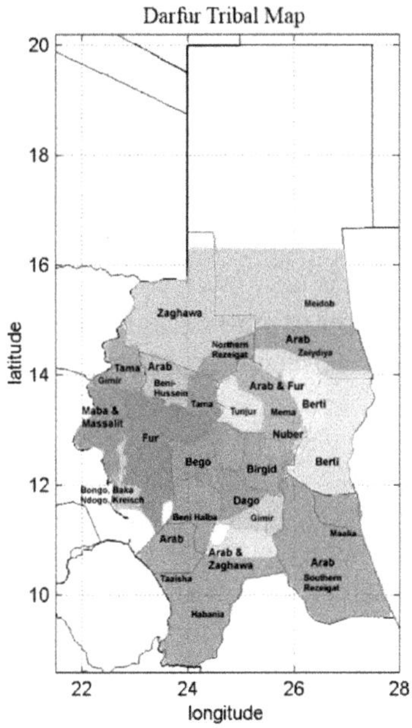

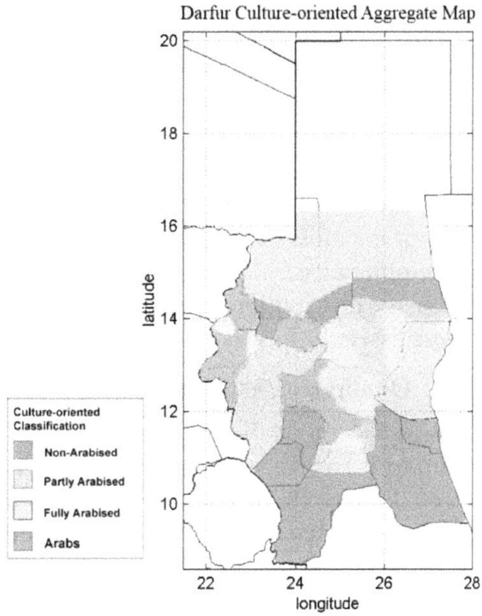

Image 1: Darfur tribal map. Image 2: Darfur culture-oriented aggregate map.

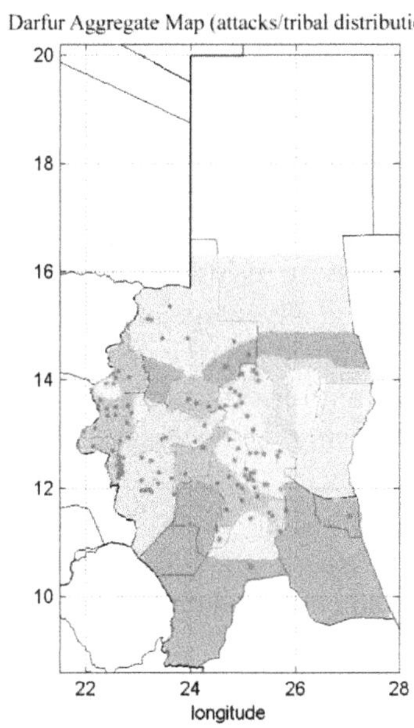

Image 3: Darfur aggregate map (attacks/tribal distribution).

As explained before, to produce the graphic output is not the most difficult part of the exercise (in this case, produced with the Matlab and ArcGIS software). What is most difficult is to have the correct database design, to gather the right data, and to input it correctly. Specific difficulties may arise from the poor geographic data (including lack of official toponyms, and issues of transliteration).

The plotting of the crime data on the layer of geographic information shows particularly grave concentrations of crime and correlations with certain tribal areas. For the most complete objective analysis, it is also advisable to take into account other elements, such as overall distribution of population and population density, distribution of military formations and objects, and roads and other strategic assets.

21.2.3. Qualitative Aspects

Judges consider a set of aggravating (and mitigating) circumstances for sentencing purposes, which usually refer to qualitative aspects of the conduct of the accused, the profile of the victims or the context of the crime. These circumstances are deemed to be assessed at the end of the trial, and they are specific to the individual suspect and the evidence presented before the judges. At a more general level, they may also provide guidance for an assessment of gravity at the investigation stage. These are the most common aggravating circumstances for core international crimes, as provided by treaty and case law:

a. *Reoccurrence or persistence*. Repeated or continuing commission of the crime, or prior conviction for a similar crime (Rule 145(2)(b)(i) of the ICC Rules of Procedure and Evidence).[11]
b. *Abuse of power*. For State officials or other actors with a position of power, to abuse the trust vested on them by the national or international community to commit a crime (Rule 145(2)(b)(ii)). This has been repeatedly highlighted by international judges that relate the level of the accused in a power hierarchy to the gravity of his or her responsibility.
c. *Victim vulnerability*. Taking advantage of the particular vulnerability of the victim because of their defenceless or weak condition (Rule 145(2)(b)(iii)). This is particularly relevant for offences against children.
d. *Particular cruelty*. Causing unnecessary pain on the victim (Rule 145(2)(b)(iv)).
e. *Discriminatory intent*. On racial, ethnic, national, religious, political, gender, socio-economic, linguistic, or other grounds considered offensive to the values of diversity, equality and underlying peaceful coexistence (Rule 145(2)(b)(v)).

---

[11] ICC Rules of Procedure and Evidence, 9 September 2002 (https://www.legal-tools.org/doc/l3a64k/)

f. *Impact*. When the action has a broader or long-term impact beyond the immediate victim or damage (including violence on peacekeepers, magnicide, long-term trauma, economic deprivation, or environmental damage).
g. *Iniquity*. Special efforts or machinations (long-term, sophisticated) in the planning or execution of the crime that indicate a particularly evil disposition.
h. *Specific notice*. When the accused fails to react upon specific and qualified notice of the crime and the resulting damage.

Some of these circumstances may be equivalent to elements of the legal definition of the crimes or modes of responsibility: still, as explained above, these aspects require factual analysis beyond the formal legal test to determine degrees of gravity among multiple crimes or within a broad pattern of crime.

21.2.4. Gravity and Mode of Responsibility

It is fair to assume that some modes of responsibility or mental elements are graver than others. It is clear that, all other circumstances being the same, it is graver to pursue deliberately an act of violence than to allow it to happen out of negligence (unless notorious tolerance before subordinates becomes deliberate instigation). The ICC Statute does suggest such a scale of gravity when limiting the responsibility to cases in which the perpetrator "means to engage in the conduct" and "means to cause that consequence or is aware that it will occur in the ordinary course of events" (Article 30, 'Mental Element'). The ICC Rules of Procedure and Evidence further refer to the "degree of intent" as a sentencing factor (Rule 145(1)(c)).

To be the principal perpetrator of the crime, the primary causal actor, should be considered as graver than being an accessory, and to order or instigate a pattern of crime should be considered as graver than executing a part of it. Among deliberate contributions to a crime some may be graver because they are fundamental to achieve the result, and others may be less decisive and so less grave. Hence, the reference to "degree of participation" as a sentencing factor in the ICC Rules of Procedure and Evidence (Rule 145(1)(c)).

While these are valid considerations of gravity, they are suspect-specific and it will be difficult to make a valid assessment at an early stage of case selection: it often takes a full investigation to determine the precise mental element and mode of responsibility of the perpetrator.

21.3. The Level of Responsibility of the Suspect

21.3.1. Origin and Definition

There is a long tradition in the prosecution of core international crimes of focusing on a limited number of senior leaders. The main trials of Istanbul in 1919 for the massacres of Armenians dealt with 19 leaders, including the top State authorities.[12] After World War I, the Commission on the Responsibility of the Authors of the War and on Enforcement of Penalties, established as part of the peace agreements, recommended trials for "persons of authority" and "civil or military authorities".[13] The Nuremberg International Military Tribunal ('IMT') trial was designed for the "Major War Criminals of the European Axis", defined in Article 1 of the London Agreement as "war criminals whose offenses have no particular geographical location whether they be accused individually or in their capacity as members of organizations or groups or in both capacities".[14] This provision was meant for higher leaders accountable for crimes across the territory of multiple states.[15] They were also referred to as "the leaders of the European Axis and their principal agents and accessories".[16] Similar provisions defined the personal jurisdiction for the International Military Tribunal for the Far East, at Tokyo ('IMTFE').

A certain international custom of selecting senior suspects has developed also from multiple and more recent national experiences. In 1975, the Greek judiciary put to trial the 20 top leaders of the military junta who then had sponsored systematic persecutions and torture during their dictatorial regime. In 1979, the government of Cambodia tried (*in absentia*) the two most senior leaders of the Khmer Rouge regime, which were regarded as "ringleaders" of their "clique" and planners and instigators of genocide.[17] In 1983, the government of Argentina focused on "a small group of people who had promoted and conducted state terrorism, as well as those who had executed the most cruel and perverse acts". The 'deliberative capacity', ranks and command within the military regime would the basis of selection for the senior suspects, which led to the trial of the nine top leaders of the Argentine military juntas in 1985.[18] In the

[12] Guenter Lewy, *The Armenian Massacres in Ottoman Turkey: A Disputed Genocide*, University of Utah Press, 2005, p. 76.

[13] Sheldon Glueck, *War Criminals: Their Prosecution and Punishment*, Alfred A. Knopf, New York, 1944, p. 21.

[14] Agreement for the Prosecution and Punishment of the Major War Criminal of the European Axis, 8 August 1945 (https://www.legal-tools.org/doc/844f64/).

[15] For the first definition of this concept, see Declaration Concerning Atrocities Made at the Moscow Conference, 30 October 1943 (https://www.legal-tools.org/doc/3c6e23/).

[16] United States, Executive Order on Providing for Representation of the United States in Preparing and Prosecuting Charges of Atrocities and War Crimes Against the Leaders of the European Axis Powers and Their Principal Agents and Accessories, 2 May 1945, No. 9547 (https://www.legal-tools.org/doc/3e7885/).

[17] See Howard Denike, John Quigley and Kenneth Robinson (eds.), *Genocide in Cambodia: Documents from the Trial of Pol Pot and Ieng Sary*, University of Pennsylvania Press, 2000.

[18] Carlos Santiago Nino, *Radical Evil on Trial*, Yale University Press, New Haven, 1996, p. 64. For an account of the trial by Luis Moreno Ocampo based on his direct experience, see Luis Moreno Ocampo, *Cuando el Poder Perdió el Juicio*, Buenos Aires, Planeta, 1996.

1980s, several German and French senior officers were selected for prosecution by the French judiciary because of crimes against humanity.[19] In 1992, the Berlin prosecutor indicted the former head of State of the German Democratic Republic for being a "key figure in everything that happened" with "unlimited influence" on the border control system that ran "like a clockwork" and resulted in the shooting and killing of a number of fugitives.[20] In 1994, the Ethiopian Federal High Court started the trial of the former head of State and other 54 senior officers for genocide and crimes against humanity. In 1996, the Genocide Law of the Republic of Rwanda included in the top category of perpetrators (category 1 of 3) the "planners, organisers, instigators, supervisors and leaders" and the "persons who acted in positions of authority" at different levels (along with "notorious murderers" and perpetrators of sexual violence).[21] In 1998, the Spanish judiciary indicted the former head of State and the armed forces of Chile for ordering killings, torture and other crimes.[22]

The Statute of the Special Court for Sierra Leone ('SCSL')[23] specifically limits the jurisdiction of the Court to "persons who bear the greatest responsibility" but with a broader meaning, including references to the national law and the peace process, in the following terms (Article 1(1)):

> The Special Court shall, except as provided in subparagraph (2) [(peacekeepers)], have the power to prosecute persons who bear the greatest responsibility for serious violations of international humanitarian law and Sierra Leonean law committed in the territory of Sierra Leone since 30 November 1996, including those leaders who, in committing such crimes, have threatened the establishment of and implementation of the peace process in Sierra Leone.

The defence in the case of Moinina Fofana before the SCSL challenged the indictment on the grounds that the accused was not among those "bearing the greatest responsibility". Fofana was indicted together with two other top leaders of the Civilian Defence Forces and, according to the indictment (as it was con-

19 See Sorj Chalandon and Pascale Nivelle, *Crimes contre l'Humanité: Barbie, Touvier, Bousquet, Papon*, Paris, Plon, 1998.

20 A. James McAdams, *Judging the Past in Unified Germany*, Cambridge University Press, 2001, p. 35. The case against former President Hönecker was preceded by two cases on lower-ranking officers.

21 Rwanda, Loi Portant Répression du Crime d'Idiologie du Génocide, 23 July 2007, No. 18/2008 ('Genocide Law') (https://www.legal-tools.org/doc/343c65/).

22 Auto de Prisión by investigating judge Baltasar Garzón of 18 October 1998.

23 Statute of the Special Court for Sierra Leone, 14 August 2000 (https://www.legal-tools.org/doc/aa0e20/).

firmed by the judges), he was second-in-command at the top of the military hierarchy. The defence argued that the concept of "persons who bear the greatest responsibility" is rather vague, but, in any event, the accused did not fall within any of the two possible interpretations, which were: (a) "The leader of the parties (or the states) that had the greatest responsibility for the (continuation of the) conflict and the threat to the establishment and implementation of the peace process in Sierra Leone"; and (b) "Those individuals who were responsible for the majority of crimes committed during the conflict in Sierra Leone".[24]

In his response, the prosecutor rejected the two interpretations proposed by the defence, but he did not propose any definition of his own, claiming instead that the issue remains within his legitimate discretion. On the specifics of the case, the prosecutor re-stated the status of command of the accused (which had not been contested by the defence) and his allegation that "the Accused committed the specific crimes with which he is charged".

The judges referred to the *travaux préparatoires* of the Statute to suggest a broad interpretation of the concept, and so they decided to support the discretion of the prosecutor and to dismiss the challenge from the defence. In the *travaux préparatoires*, quoted in the decision, some guidance is given to define the concept:

> While those "most responsible" obviously include the political or military leadership, others in command authority down the chain of command may also be regarded "most responsible" judging by the severity of the crime or its massive scale. "Most responsible", therefore, denotes both a leadership or authority position of the accused, and a sense of the gravity, seriousness or massive scale of the crime. It must be seen, however, not as a test criterion or a distinct jurisdictional threshold, but as a guidance to the Prosecutor in the adoption of a prosecution strategy and in making decisions to prosecute in individual cases.[25]
>
> [...] the draft Statute, as proposed by the Security Council, does not mean that the personal jurisdiction is limited to the political and military leaders only. Therefore, the determination of the meaning of the term "persons who bear the greatest responsibility"

[24] SCSL, *Prosecutor v. Moinina Fofana et al.*, Decision on the Preliminary Defence Motion on the Lack of Personal Jurisdiction Filed on Behalf of Accused Fofana, 3 March 2004, SCSL-04-14-PT (https://www.legal-tools.org/doc/7d58c6/).

[25] UN Security Council, Report of the Secretary-General on the establishment of a Special Court for Sierra Leone, UN Doc. S/2000/915, 4 October 2000, para. 30 (https://www.legal-tools.org/doc/4af5d2/).

> in any given case falls initially to the prosecutor and ultimately to the Special Court itself.[26]

The competence of the Extraordinary Chambers in the Courts of Cambodia ('ECCC') is also limited by its Statute to "senior leaders of Democratic Kampuchea and those who were most responsible". This language suggests, however, that the 'senior leaders' and the 'most responsible' might be different categories, that is, the leaders could be prosecuted just because of their status.

This trend, as well as the experience of the UN *ad hoc* tribunals, led the ICC Prosecutor to decide in 2003 that:

> as a general rule, the Office of the Prosecutor should focus its investigative and prosecutorial efforts and resources on those who bear the greatest responsibility, such as the leaders of the State or organisation allegedly responsible for those crimes.[27]

The ICC judges have expressed their support for this policy by the Prosecutor.

The elements for a definition suggested by the SCSL and other sources above remain still rather open, and they may be problematic in saying too much in some aspects and too little in others. It is excessive to cast suspicion on leaders just because of their formal status without qualifying clearly what circumstances justify a presumption of individual responsibility. It is not appropriate to exclude from the definition issues of causation (primary causation versus accessory responsibility) and degrees of participation. Bringing the gravity of the criminal acts as such into the definition of degrees of responsibility (as suggested at SCSL) may lead to confusion. The practice of using broad theories of liability (common purpose or joint criminal enterprise) does not help to differentiate the 'most responsible' from the rest. Unclear doctrine on causation in some legal systems is an additional difficulty.

In conclusion, a clearer definition should understand that the greatest responsibility for core international crimes corresponds to those persons who were the primary causal actors (as opposed to accessory actors) for the pattern or incident of crime as a whole by means of ordering, incitement or notorious tolerance. At the investigation stage, senior leaders should be presumed to be most responsible for the crime if: (a) there was a hierarchical structure in place, whether civilian, military, economic or other; (b) that structure was instrumental to the crime as a matter of policy; and (c) the leader had effective control or influence on the structure in the relevant period and area. Instigators of the crime

[26] UN Security Council, Letter dated 12 January 2001 from the Secretary-General addressed to the President of the Security Council, UN Doc. S/2001/40, 12 January 2001, para. 2 (https://www.legal-tools.org/doc/e4h6dt/).

[27] ICC-OTP, "Paper on some policy issues before the Office of the Prosecutor", September 2003, p. 7 (https://www.legal-tools.org/doc/f53870/).

should be presumed to be most responsible for the crime, regardless of their hierarchical status, if they effectively led a substantial segment of the leaders or direct executioners to commit the crime.

21.3.2. Practice

To what extent have the international tribunals focused on the most responsible? To address this question, first note the important differences in the number of accused. The ICTY has prosecuted a much higher number of individuals than any other international tribunal (161), followed by the International Criminal Tribunal for Rwanda ('ICTR') (88) and then all others in much smaller figures (see graph below, figures as of July 2008).

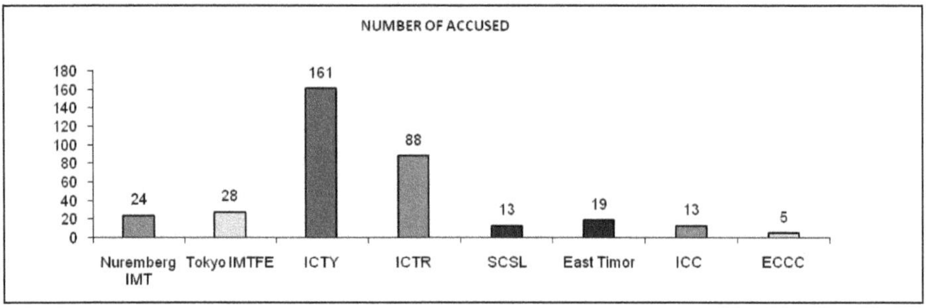

Graph 4: Number of accused by international(ized) jurisdiction.

The question can be addressed from two perspectives: first, to identify all known clusters of 'most responsible persons' and check whether their members were selected for prosecution or not; second, to review all persons that have been actually selected for prosecution and verify their level of responsibility. The data of the ICTY have been analysed using both methods.

Concerning the first approach, the table below shows the 15 main reported clusters of allegedly 'most responsible persons' (leadership groups) within the jurisdiction of the ICTY and an assessment of whether they were selected for prosecution or not (in a meaningful way, not necessarily every member of the group). The groups are identified by reference to a particular pattern and period of crime. Some groups may feature more than once because reportedly they were responsible for multiple patterns of crime, at different points of time (such as the leadership of the Federal Republic of Yugoslavia for Croatia (1991), Bosnia and Herzegovina (1992–1995) and Kosovo (1999)).

No.	Period	Leadership Group	Selected
1.	1991	Republic of Serbian Krajina	Yes
2.	1991	Federal Republic Yugoslavia (Belgrade)	Yes

3.	1991	Republic of Croatia	Yes
4.	1992-95	Republika Srpska	Yes
5.	1992-95	Federal Republic of Yugoslavia (Belgrade)	Yes
6.	1992-95	Republic of Bosnia and Herzegovina	Yes
7.	1993-94	Republic of Herceg-Bosna	Yes
8.	1993-94	Republic of Bosnia and Herzegovina	Yes
9.	1999	Federal Republic of Yugoslavia (Belgrade)	Yes
10.	1995	Republic of Croatia	Yes
11.	1995	Republic of Serbian Krajina	Yes
12.	1999	Kosovo Liberation Army (Albanians)	Yes
13.	1999	North Atlantic Treaty Organization (re: Kosovo)	No
14.	2001	Republic of Macedonia	Yes
15.	2001	National Liberation Army (Albanian Macedonian)	No

It is clear that the ICTY Prosecutors in the end selected for prosecution almost all the relevant leadership groups. Only two of the 15 clusters were not selected, two of them in the relatively lower range of crime gravity.[28]

Concerning the second approach, a scale has been defined to assess the profile of responsibility of each accused in five levels, from the top level of highest authorities, to level 5 for executioners without any authority or role beyond their immediate actions.[29] According to this scale, less than a third of the

[28] The Prosecutor's decision not to investigate North Atlantic Treaty Organization officers referred mainly to allegations of disproportionate or indiscriminate aerial bombardment that resulted in damage of dual-purpose (civilian–military) facilities and the death of several hundreds of civilians in Serbia in 1999. It was a controversial decision, much criticized by the victims, the Serbian authorities and opinion leaders, and a sector of academia and NGOs. The crimes allegedly committed by members of the National Liberation Army in Macedonia seem of relatively lesser gravity in the overall scale of crimes within the ICTY jurisdiction (this gap has raised questions about impartiality, since crimes of similar gravity committed by Macedonian forces were selected for prosecution, but this is a different issue).

[29] Definitions for each level: 1 = 'Top authority' – highest authorities at the top of the organized structure, namely, head of State, prime minister, top military commanders, president of a major political party, or leading instigator of the relevant patter of crime as a whole; 2 = 'Individuals immediately subordinated or accessory to the top level' – deputies with command authority to level 1 individuals, ministers, senior advisors, or instigators affecting a large part of the pattern; 3 = 'Regional leaders, corps commanders, commander or head of a branch or institution, police chief, military zone commander, brigade commander, instigator at the regional level'; 4 =

ICTY accused belong in the top two levels (11 per cent in level 1 and 16 per cent in level 2), while level 3 comprises 28 per cent and the two lowest levels make up 45 per cent (30 per cent in level 4 and 15 per cent in level 5).

The data of the ICTR show a similar share: less than a third of the accused belong in the top two levels (2 per cent in level 1 and 28 per cent in level 2), while level 3 comprises 27 per cent and the two lowest levels make up 40 per cent (42 per cent in level 4 and 1 per cent in level 5).

Significant differences appear when comparing two of the main municipalities investigated by the ICTY, Prijedor and Srebrenica: in the former, a number of low-level perpetrators were indicted, while, in the latter, indictments focused on senior officers (with the exception of Erdemović). There are also significant differences in the level of indictees in relation to certain types of offences; rape and sexual violence have originated relatively lower-level indictees and convictions (like the Furundžija and Foča case), while crimes related to artillery attacks on cities have originated higher-level indictees (like in the indictments for the shelling of Zagreb, Dubrovnik and Sarajevo).

In conclusion, the ICTY did select many persons that were apparently most responsible (including the most notorious top leaders), but also many more that were not. A review of years of practice at the ICTY-OTP suggests that those 'lesser responsible' were selected for a number of reasons (often contributing jointly to a single selection):

a. Arrest opportunities (beginning with Tadić, the very first case) in a context of limited co-operation and difficulties to obtain any arrest;
b. Notorious perpetrators in areas of very grave crime (like Jelisić in Brčko);
c. Expectations of national (mainly Bosnian) authorities, victims and NGOs;
d. Investigative value to build higher cases (such as Erdemović for Srebrenica) in a context of difficulty to obtain key insight evidence;
e. To address particularly grave types of offences (like Furundžija for rape);
f. Because the officers in charge of the case had obtained the evidence (including evidence files submitted by the UN and national agencies) and discretion was not restricted.

A stricter focus on the 'most responsible' could have released resources and sped up the most important cases. For example, Milošević was indicted only after six years of the establishment of the Tribunal, while the investigation on him and other Serbian leaders could have progressed faster allocating resources that had been invested in smaller cases. A more selective approach of this kind could have limited prosecutions to less than half the total number of 161 accused,

'Lowest authority' – any person superior to or instigating one or more immediate executioners; and 5 = 'No authority' – immediate executioners.

while the smaller cases could have been deferred to the emerging national systems in the different ex-Yugoslav republics.

The death of senior suspects is another aspect that has affected, to some extent, the ability of the ICTY to focus on higher levels. This is particularly the case with forces of the Republic of Croatia and its surrogate the so-called Republic of Herzeg-Bosna, several of whose senior suspects passed away before the prosecutor managed to indict them.[30]

The data of the SCSL and ECCC show a higher profile of their accused (with total numbers being much smaller). For the SCSL, 92 per cent of the accused belong in the top two levels, 8 per cent (which is just one accused) in level 3, and there is none in the lowest levels. For the five accused of the ECCC, four would belong in top two levels (which is 80 per cent) and 1 in the third level, with none in the lowest levels. This is consistent with their statutory competence.

The ICC also shows a high profile for the persons that the OTP selected for prosecution in the period 2005–2024 in 17 situations.[31] About 55 per cent of the accused belong in the top two levels. This is consistent with the policy adopted by the ICC Prosecutor in 2003, although the average level of the accused has become slightly lower since 2012, as the second and third ICC Prosecutors have been more open than the first one to indicting lower-level perpetrators; this is noticeable particularly in the second Central African Republic, Mali and Libya situations.

21.3.3. Analysis of Structures

To identify the most responsible is not always self-evident. Assumptions based on formal hierarchy are often valid as hypotheses, but they cannot be regarded as axiomatic. The true authority of leaders may vary depending on the type of political structure (the president of the republic has very different powers in Italy and France), territorial structure (a federal state and a centralized state may work very differently), the strength of the institutions (while international crimes often take place in the context of weak or collapsed institutions), or organizational changes over time.

[30] Among them, the President of the Republic of Croatia Franjo Tuđman, his Minister of Defence Gojko Šušak, and the President of the so-called Republic of Herceg-Bosna Mate Boban. Their suspect status is apparent by their mention in indictments, evidence and public arguments put forward by the prosecutor in public for a number of related Croat and Bosnian-Croat cases. The Nuremberg IMT had a similar problem with the death of Hitler, Himmler and Göbbels prior to any indictment.

[31] Data of publicly known persons for whom the OTP applied for warrants of arrest or summons to appear, as of 23 October 2024 (available at the ICC official web site). Defendants for Article 70 cases are not included (offences against the administration of justice).

Consider the following types of organizational structures, in which the same 10 individuals are organized in different ways:

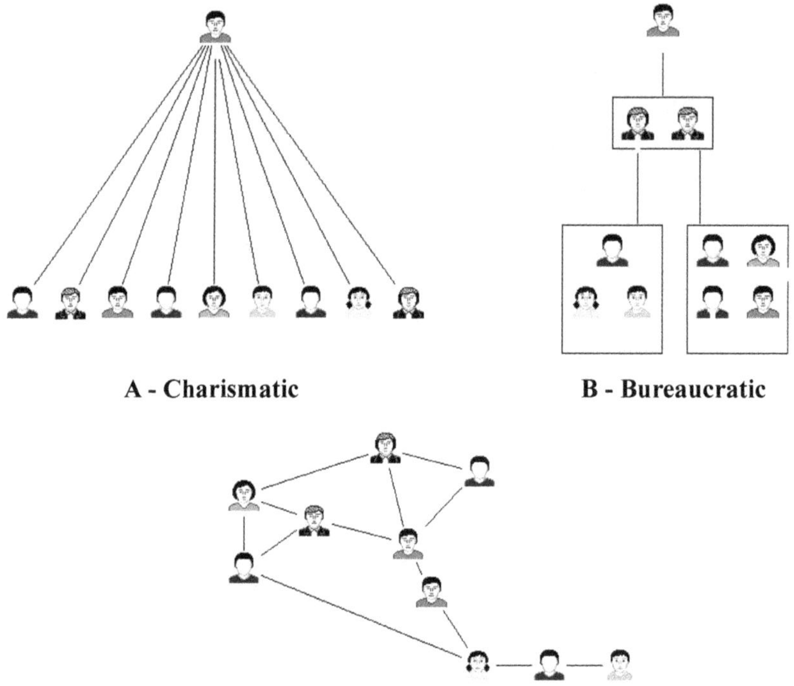

A - Charismatic

B - Bureaucratic

C - Network

Diagram 1: Types of organizational structures.

Types A and B represent the classic distinction between charismatic and bureaucratic authority (Max Weber). In the charismatic structure, the leader links directly with the mass of his or her subordinates, while bureaucracies are based on a hierarchy of echelons subordinated to a central authority. For both types of pyramidal structures, identifying the most responsible may not be too difficult, at least at the formal level (but see the requirements mentioned in the definition of most responsible, in Section 21.1. above).

Type A links are characteristic of cases of public incitement of the crime, such as Streicher (Nuremberg IMT), Akayesu (ICTR) or Brđanin (ICTY). Type B links are the basis for theories of 'organized power apparatuses' (Roxin) and the many cases about military commanders (from Jodl and Yamashita to Krstić). It is most difficult in Type C links to identify those most responsible because authority may be shared horizontally. Then, there may be mixed types; for example, the Lord's Resistance Army, which looked like A + B under Joseph

Kony's charisma and military echelon. Associations of different types are also common, like 'C+A' networks of local militias, or 'B+B' tactical groupings of conventional military units.

Beyond the formal (*de jure*) view of the structure, the critical question is to establish its real (*de facto*) functioning. The two diagrams below show the same organization, first according to its formal definition, and then according to the network analysis of its real functioning.[32]

Figure 1-1a

Formal Versus Informal Structure

FORMAL ORGANIZATIONAL CHART

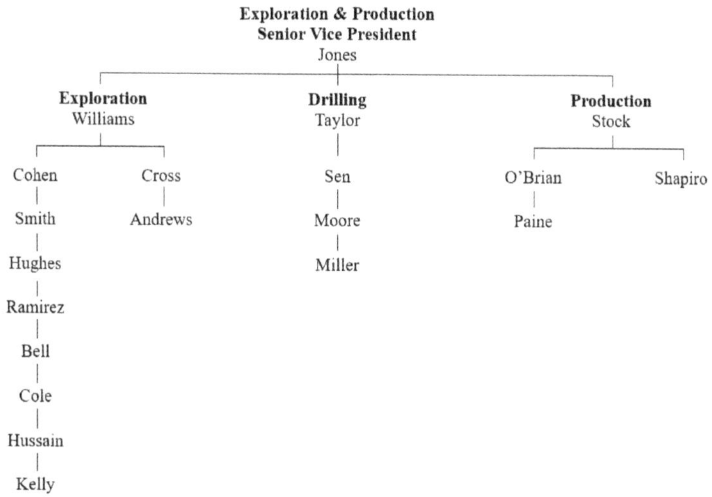

Note: This example has been substantially disguised at the request of the organization.

Source: Figures 1-1a and b from R. Cross et al., "Knowing What We Know: Supporting Knowledge Creation and Sharing in Social Networks," *Organizational Dynamics* 30, no. 20 (2001): 100–120. © 2001, reprinted with permission from Elsevier Science.

Diagram 2: Formal organizational chart.

[32] Rob Cross and Andrew Parker, "How Org Charts Lie", 6 July 2004, excerpt from their book *The Hidden Power of Social Networks: Understanding How Work Really Gets Done in Organizations*, Harvard Business School Publishing, 2004.

Figure 1-1b
Informal Structure as Revealed by Social Network Analysis

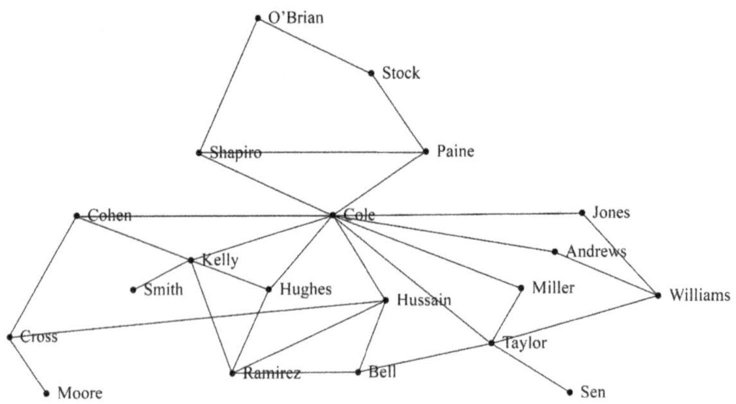

Diagram 3: Informal structure.

In this example, the most senior officer at the top of the formal structure (Jones) actually has a peripheral role in the informal structure, while the central roles are played by officers that have formally lower positions. This type of discrepancy is not rare and is the matter of much analysis and investigation when dealing with core international crimes. To shed light on the internal functioning of a structure, we may resort to the study of constitutional and other laws and regulations, to thorough interviewing of insiders (who may well contradict among themselves), analysis of archives and communication records, and various diagramming techniques and advance software (such as 'i2'). A checklist of the main elements to investigate a structure would comprise the following categories:

No.	Category	Definition
1.	Formal Status	Formal establishment and mandate of the structure.
2.	Doctrine	Ideology, group identity, guiding principles and objectives.
3.	Uniformity	Standards of organization, external signs and procedures.
4.	Authority	Ability to issue and implement plans, orders and instructions.

5.	Communications	Ability to transmit information effectively within the structure.
6.	Personnel	Number of members, and ability to manage them (fungibility).
7.	Weaponry	Weapons and ammunitions utilized or available to the structure.
8.	Finance	Economic system, including income, assets, payments and trade.
9.	Logistics	Support system for supplies, transport and infrastructures.
10.	Territory	Geographic deployment and territorial control or influence.
11.	Discipline	Including internal discipline and criminal justice).

These categories may need to be specifically analysed in reports (with proper analytical drafting and sourcing standards), chronologies, organizational charts (time-specific, duly sourced and following proper diagramming conventions), maps, *et cetera*. Such systematic analysis, based on the awareness of different types of structures and their formal-informal contradictions, should be the basis for the most objective and accurate identification of those most responsible.

21.3.4. Suspect-Driven *Versus* Offence-Driven Investigations

Suspect-driven investigations are those in which the accused is selected from the outset, and this choice determines the whole development of the investigation. Offence-driven investigations are those in which the choice of the criminal events drives the investigation, while the selection of the accused takes place at a later and better-informed stage.

Suspect-driven investigations are rather common when dealing with core international crimes. They are often preferred by the investigating authority because they are seen as faster and easier to manage. A suspect-driven strategy may be legitimate if the information available at the initial stage justifies objectively the choice. For example, a fairly compelling *prima facie* case led to a fully suspect-driven investigation for Eichmann. Nevertheless, this approach carries a risk of missing the broader picture and developing 'confirmation bias', that is, to collect and interpret evidence selectively to confirm a premise, towards incrimination of the chosen suspect. Confirmation bias is certainly a very common problem in criminal investigations that may affect the quality of the findings, and that judges may consider detrimental to the fairness of the process.

Experience shows that the best techniques to control the risks of suspect-driven investigations may be: (a) to develop parallel lines of investigation or analysis on the offence and on the suspect, avoiding that the perception of the offence is conditioned by the information about the suspect; (b) to focus on the organizational structures as such, considering simultaneously the role of multiple suspects; (c) to develop alternative hypotheses and counter-arguments, using techniques such as the Analysis of Competing Hypotheses, red teams or 'devil's advocate', aiming at the 'inference to the best explanation' after having considered different causal hypotheses; (d) to conduct systematic Source Evaluation with standard criteria for the reliability of the sources and the credibility of their information; and (e) to subject the findings to internal critical review by an independent panel of officers that have not been involved in the investigation and should not suffer from confirmation bias.

21.4. Conclusions

Based on the lessons learned and best practices from international tribunals, the use of the criteria of gravity and highest responsibility for selection of prioritization of cases would be best guaranteed by the following principles:

a. Determine the substantive offences that are regarded as gravest (such as possibly killing, rape and torture) and develop the selection process mainly around them;
b. Define clear parameters of gravity, including quantitative and qualitative aspects (number of victims, manner, specific intent, *et cetera*) and considering sentencing criteria;
c. Adopt an explicit hypothesis of the case as the outline for selection and investigation;
d. Adopt a clear definition of 'most responsible', focusing on the primary causal actors and presuming that they are the same as senior leaders only under certain factual circumstances;
e. Beware of the existence of multiple types of power structures, discrepancies between their formal definition and real functioning, and variations over time and space;
f. Utilize systematically analytical techniques, including crime-pattern databases, statistics, standard indicators check-lists, mapping, chronologies, network analysis, *et cetera*, to determine both gravity and highest responsibility;
g. Beware of the risk of confirmation bias in suspect-driven investigations and take measures to control it.

Appendix 1: DRC Killings, Spread July 2002–September 2006

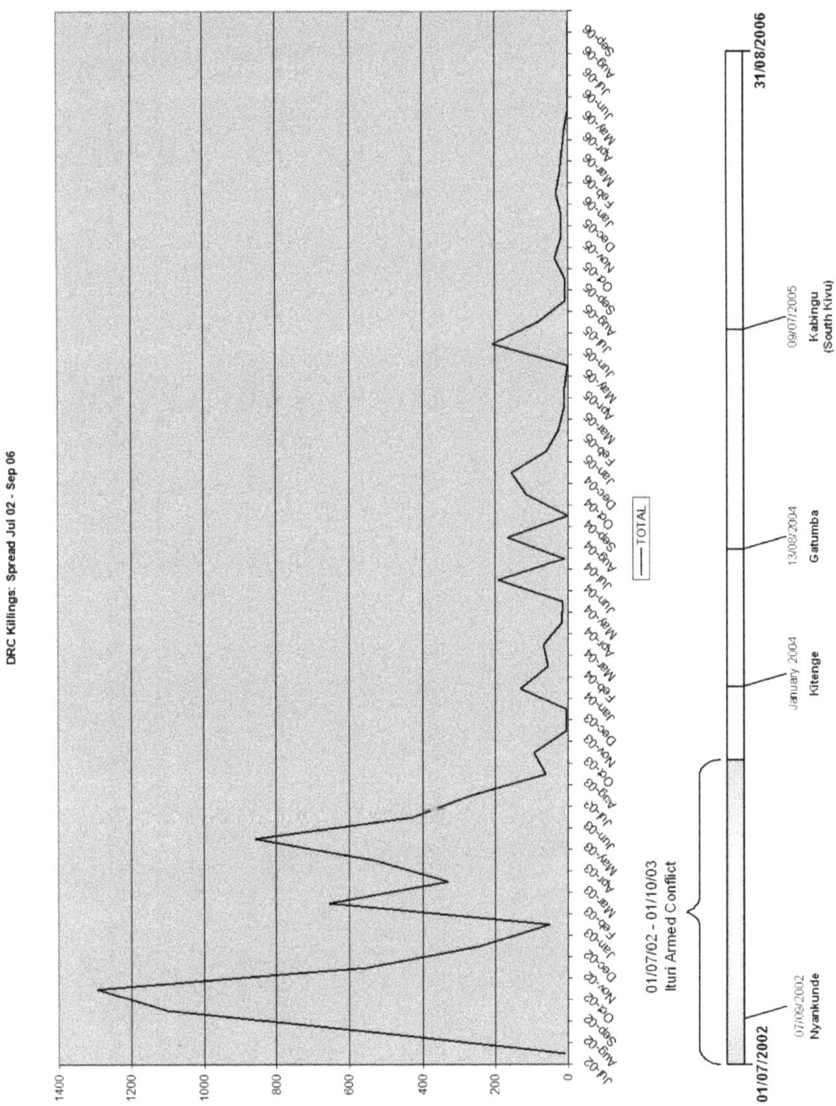

Graph 5: DRC killings (July 2002–September 2006).

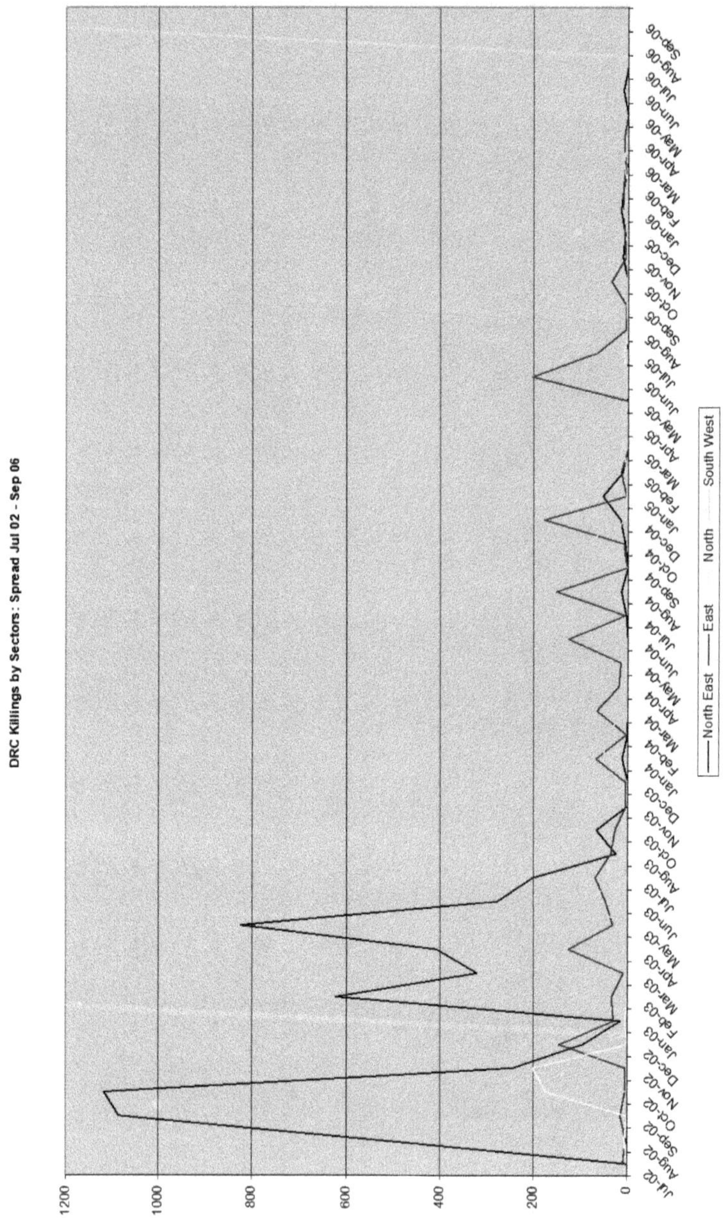

Graph 6: DRC killings by sectors (July 2002–September 2006).

22

Functions of the Gravity Threshold Before the ICC: Releasing the Prosecutor From the Gravity Constraint

Megumi Ochi*

22.1. Introduction

Is it the duty of the Prosecutor of the International Criminal Court ('ICC' or 'Court') to prosecute crimes of sufficient gravity within the jurisdiction of the Court if national criminal justice systems do not? This question is important. The answer can have a dramatic effect on the size of the Court, its impact, its respect for different traditions, its budget, and its planning.[1] The first ICC Prosecutor implicitly acknowledged this ambiguity when he asked States Parties on the question: "[m]ust the ICC Prosecutor initiate an investigation in all situations that appear to fall within the jurisdiction of the Court? Or, should the Prosecutor select amongst them the most grave and urgent situations within the limits of his resources?".[2] The question was left without an answer. But the Prosecutor explained that the main factor for the selection of his first case was 'gravity'.[3] This created a trend. The Prosecutor is understood to carry the burden of proof with regard to gravity in the selection of cases or situations. The function of the concept of gravity on the actions of the Office of the Prosecutor ('OTP') seemed 'regulatory'. A new constraint emerged, requiring the OTP to initiate investigations if, and only if, there is sufficient gravity, or to at least explain the gravity

* **Megumi Ochi** is Associate Professor at the Graduate School of International Relations, Ritsumeikan University, Kyoto. At the time of writing, she was a post-doctoral research fellow of the Japan Society for the Promotion of Science at Kyoto University. She completed her Ph.D. in Law at Osaka University and an LL.M. at Leiden University. She interned at Pre-Trial Chamber II of the International Criminal Court from April to September 2012. This chapter is based on her master's thesis. Chapter 6 (Rod Rastan) above discusses later ICC practice on 'gravity'.

1 ICC-OTP, "Statement by Luis Moreno-Ocampo, Prosecutor of the International Criminal Court: Informal Meeting of Legal Advisors of Ministries of Foreign Affairs", 24 October 2005 ('Statement at Informal Meeting of Legal Advisors of Ministries of Foreign Affairs') (https://www.legal-tools.org/doc/7bb578/).

2 *Ibid.*

3 *Ibid.*

of the selected and prioritized cases and situations. This understanding of gravity helped to legitimize one of the Court's most important decisions. At the same time, the apparent inconsistency and paradox contributed to a doubt regarding the Prosecutor's impartiality.[4] Civil society does not always agree with the Prosecutor's decisions. It questions 'why does this case display more gravity than the others?' Considerable attention has been paid to suggesting or establishing an adequate gravity threshold for the sake of credibility and transparency.

This chapter discusses whether our understanding of gravity requires reassessment. The gravity constraint entails several of disadvantages. First, the function of the gravity threshold differed between the OTP and Chambers (especially, the Pre-Trial Chamber ('PTC')). The selection process by Chambers is a 'screening-out' process. Meanwhile, the Prosecutor's selection is a 'picking-out' process. The gravity threshold functions as a 'sieve' before Chambers. It functions only as one of the elements that guide the case or situation selection before the OTP (Section 22.2. of this chapter). The gravity constraint on the OTP has four main demerits: disturbing the maximization of deterrent effect, broadening the impunity gap, blocking the Court from considering the interests of justice, and offending the victims' feelings (Section 22.3.). This chapter criticizes the concept of gravity as regulatory for the OTP, and suggests that diversification of the conception of gravity strengthens this argument (Section 22.4.).

22.2. Different Function Before the Office of the Prosecutor and Chambers

22.2.1. The Gravity Threshold Stipulated in the Statute and the OTP Regulations

The word 'gravity' can be found in some provisions of the ICC Statute. 'Gravity' seems to reflect the purpose and scope of the Court to prosecute and punish the most serious crimes that concern the entire international community. In particular, the so-called 'gravity threshold' appears as an indicator included in Article 17(1)(d) of the ICC Statute. It provides that the Court shall determine a case inadmissible when it does not have sufficient gravity to justify further action by the Court.[5]

The adopted Article 17(1)(d) of the ICC Statute was contained in Article 35(c) in the 1994 draft of the ICC Statute prepared by the International Law

[4] Margaret M. deGuzman, "Gravity and the Legitimacy of the International Criminal Court", in *Fordham International Law Journal*, 2009, vol. 32, no. 5, p. 1435.

[5] Rome Statute of the International Criminal Court, 17 July 1998, Article 17(1)(d) ('ICC Statute') (http://www.legal-tools.org/doc/7b9af9/).

Commission ('ILC').[6] The draft provision read as follows: "The Court may [...] decide [...] that a case is inadmissible on the ground that the crime in question [...] (c) is not of such gravity to justify further action by the Court". The language that is used in the Article 17(1)(d) first appeared in the commentary to the draft. In it, the ILC noted that the "grounds for holding a case inadmissible are that the crime in question [...] is not of sufficient gravity to justify further action by the Court".[7] This language had found its way into the current ICC Statute.[8] It was already widely agreed during the preliminary informal consultations that one ground for inadmissibility would be insufficiency of gravity. This idea was included in an early version of the Co-ordinator's text. It remained throughout the negotiations.[9] According to the ILC, the Court should have discretion to decline jurisdiction in cases that lack sufficient gravity. This ensures that the Court limits its focus to the most serious crimes. It also enables the Court to manage its case load.[10] If it had to address every crime that fell under its jurisdiction, including crimes of lesser gravity, the ICC would be flooded with cases and become ineffective.[11]

The negotiation history of the ICC Statute reveals little concerning the content of the gravity threshold. Nonetheless, this conversely suggests that the drafters did not envision the threshold as a very substantial limit on the exercise of the Court's jurisdiction.[12]

The gravity threshold is primarily provided as an element related to the issue of admissibility. The idea of gravity has played an important role in the selection of cases and situations. There are two stages in identifying the objects of the proceedings of the ICC. The first stage is the selection of 'situations'. This normally entails the identification of the time and place to be investigated by the Prosecutor. There are three modes of selecting situations. A Security Council

6 Report of the International Law Commission on the work of its forty-sixth session, UN Doc. A/49/10, 2 September 1994, p. 52 (https://www.legal-tools.org/doc/f73459/).

7 *Ibid.*

8 United Nations ('UN'), Report of the Preparatory Committee for the Establishment of an International Criminal Court, UN Doc. A/Conf. 183/2/Add.1, 14 April 1998, pp. 40–41 (https://www.legal-tools.org/doc/fb8414/).

9 John T. Holmes, "The Principle of Complementarity", in Roy S. Lee (ed.), *The International Criminal Court: The Making of the Rome Statute, Issues, Negotiations, Results*, Kluwer Law International, London-Boston, 1999, p. 47.

10 Susana SáCouto and Katherine A. Cleary, "The Gravity Threshold of the International Criminal Court", in *American Journal of International Law*, 2008, vol. 23, no. 5, p. 809.

11 Mohamed M. El Zeidy, "The Gravity Threshold Under the Statute of the International Criminal Court", in *Criminal Law Forum*, 2008, vol. 19, no. 1, p. 36.

12 deGuzman, 2009, pp. 1416–1425, see *supra* note 4.

referral (Article 13), a State Party referral (Article 14), and an investigation *proprio motu* (Article 15). The second stage is the selection of 'cases'. The Prosecutor conducts its investigation into a situation and chooses cases from the situation by identifying the suspect. In these two different stages, the Prosecutor makes decisions regarding the gravity of the objects of the proceedings. Article 53(1) of the ICC Statute provides that the Prosecutor shall, after evaluating the information that is available to him or her, initiate an investigation unless he or she determines that there is no reasonable basis to proceed under the ICC Statute. According to Article 53(1)(b), the Prosecutor shall consider, among other things, the admissibility of possible cases under Article 17. This eventually includes an assessment of the sufficiency of gravity. In addition, Article 53(1)(c) stipulates that the Prosecutor shall also determine whether there are substantial reasons to believe that an investigation would not serve the interests of justice. In this assessment, he or she must consider the interests of victims and the gravity of the crime.

A detailed process and criteria for the selection of situations and cases is provided in the Regulations of the OTP that entered into force on 23 April 2009 (and in later policy papers discussed in Chapter 6 above). Regulation 29 provides some clues for the assessment of gravity. Paragraph 2 stipulates that to assess the gravity of the crimes, the Prosecutor "shall consider various factors including their scale, nature, manner of commission, and impact".[13]

22.2.2. Earlier Study: Legal and Relative Gravity

At the time of writing, it has become a trend among commentators on international criminal law to argue for a dual gravity threshold. SáCouto and Cleary develop a twofold gravity approach. They state that gravity has guided the Prosecutor's selection of situations and cases warranting the attention of the ICC, and claim that it is because of the need to satisfy admissibility requirements and of policy.[14] They also explain that the OTP applies the concept of gravity at two distinct stages: the selection of situations and that of cases. They argue that a distinction can be made between a gravity threshold and the exercise of prosecutorial discretion concerning 'relative' gravity.[15] They observe that it has not always been clear when the Prosecutor refers to gravity as a requirement under the ICC Statute, or gravity as one of presumably many factors leading to the OTP's decision to prosecute certain crimes over others.[16] As the first Prosecutor

---

[13] Regulations of the Office of the Prosecutor, 23 April 2009, Regulation 29(2) (https://www.legal-tools.org/doc/a97226/).

[14] SáCouto and Cleary, p. 817, see *supra* note 10.

[15] *Ibid.*, p. 850.

[16] *Ibid.*

stated that gravity is one of the most important criteria for the selection of the OTP's situations and cases, he apparently chose to highlight the relative gravity of situations and cases as a means of determining what will be investigated and prosecuted, even after he has become satisfied that the jurisdiction and admissibility requirements of the ICC Statute have been met.[17]

Similarly, deGuzman argues that gravity has two dimensions: first, a relative (discretionary) gravity that allows the OTP to prioritize cases and situations involving discretionary decisions and, second, a theoretically static concept of a (non-discretionary) gravity threshold that requires the OTP and Chambers to reject inadmissible situations and cases that fall below this legal barrier.[18] She argues that gravity acts to legitimize the Court in two interrelated ways: the gravity threshold helps to ensure the moral legitimacy of the Court's exercise of jurisdiction, and the Prosecutor's discretionary use of relative gravity strongly affects perceptions of the Court's legitimacy.[19] She then notes the risk of using the latter means of legitimization: "a decision to prosecute only the leaders responsible for the most heinous crimes may increase the Court's legitimacy in some audiences, while others may require prosecutions of all sides of the conflict to consider the Court legitimate".[20] Her suggestion is a relatively straightforward factor-based analysis, and cases scoring at the bottom of the gravity spectrum on all factors should be excluded based on the gravity threshold.[21]

Stegmiller claims that neither the OTP nor Chambers have developed a congruent gravity approach, and they both address certain aspects of the 'gravity' prong but fail to arrive at an all-embracing interpretative approach.[22] He suggests an approach dividing the notion of gravity into 'legal' gravity, linked to Article 17(1)(d) and Articles 53(1)(b) and (2)(b), and 'relative' gravity, which amounts to the assessment under Articles 53(1)(c) and (2)(c).[23] According to him, legal gravity constitutes a low barrier, primarily requiring a quantitative check, and relative gravity addresses situation (and case) selection *vis-à-vis*

17 *Ibid.*

18 deGuzman, 2009, p. 1405, see *supra* note 4.

19 *Ibid.*, p. 1404.

20 *Ibid.*

21 *Ibid.*

22 Ignaz Stegmiller, "Interpretative Gravity under the Rome Statute", in Carsten Stahn and Mohamed M. El Zeidy (eds.), *The International Criminal Court and Complementarity: From Theory to Practice*, Cambridge University Press, 2011, p. 603.

23 *Ibid.*

other situations (or cases), for which qualitative factors should increasingly be taken into account.[24]

22.2.3. The Dual Function of Gravity: Element and Sieve

As mentioned earlier, the conceptions and roles of the gravity threshold have different understandings before the OTP and Chambers. In addition, the practice of the OTP and Chambers has clarified that gravity also functions differently depending on whether the OTP or a chamber is concerned.

The selection process by the chamber is to 'screen out' the situations or cases of sufficient gravity. The concept of gravity functions as a 'sieve'. In contrast, the selection process of the OTP is to 'pick out' the situations or cases. Gravity functions just as one of the elements. Fundamentally, whereas the selection of the chamber is exclusion, the selection of the OTP is a choice. Selection by a chamber is negative selection, and that by the OTP is positive selection. The process of choosing between similar candidates cannot be regulated in a manner of law. There is no legal requirement to prosecute cases in order of gravity. The 'sieve' is determined according to the interpretation of gravity in the ICC Statute. However, there was, at the time of writing, no clear legal guidance for the treatment of gravity as an 'element' for picking out situations and cases.

A situation is a complex of information that contains potential cases composed of multilateral links between persons and crimes. In the selection of situations, the Prosecutor picks out a complex of information that contains potential cases and puts the complex on the chamber's 'sieve' in order to verify whether it is grave enough to stay in the sieve. A case is one of those links picked by the Prosecutor out of the complex. After this picking-out process, the chamber conducts their screening-out process again in the case of a *proprio motu* investigation, or for the first time in the case of referrals.

22.2.3.1. The Gravity Threshold Before the Office of the Prosecutor

The concept of gravity functions as an element in case or situation selection before the OTP in the following three manners: policy papers, requests for the authorization of an investigation, and decisions of inaction.

The OTP has repeatedly used the concept of gravity in its policy papers, as discussed in Chapter 6 above. For example, the OTP's "Policy Paper on Preliminary Examination" was completed in 2013. The paper declared that, "[a]t the preliminary examination stage, in line with the approach regarding complementarity outlined above, the Office assesses the gravity of each potential case that

[24] *Ibid.*, p. 636.

would likely arise from an investigation of the situation".[25] In the "Policy Paper on Case Selection and Prioritisation" of 2016, the OTP clearly stated that "[g]ravity is the predominant case selection criteria adopted by the Office and is embedded also into considerations of both the degree of responsibility of alleged perpetrators and charging".[26] In the part addressing the approach to case selection, it is repeated that the "Office will select cases for investigation and prosecution in light of the gravity of the crimes".[27]

The Prosecutor has made use of the concept of gravity when requesting investigation authorization from the PTCs. For example, the Prosecutor requested authorization from PTC II in 2009 to investigate the situation in Kenya. When PTC II sought more information concerning the alleged crimes, speculation emerged that there were concerns regarding gravity.[28] The Prosecutor's submission followed Regulation 29 of the OTP Regulations. It introduced information involving the scale of the violence, the widespread and systematic characteristics of the attack, the brutal modes of commission of the crimes and sexual violence of great impact, and the selectivity of victims based on their ethnicity.[29] In the request for authorization to initiate an investigation regarding the situation in Côte d'Ivoire submitted in 2011, the Prosecutor stated that he had examined the gravity of the potential cases based on the preliminary list of persons or groups that appeared to bear the greatest responsibility for the most serious crimes.[30] The Prosecutor emphasized their high-ranking political or command positions and their alleged role in the violence.[31]

The Prosecutor has also relied on the concept of gravity in his or her decisions of inaction. Although the first Prosecutor recognized since the beginning of his work in 2005 that gravity is the most important criteria for the selection

[25] ICC-OTP, "Policy Paper on Preliminary Examination", November 2013, para. 59 (https://www.legal-tools.org/doc/acb906/).

[26] ICC-OTP, "Policy Paper on Case Selection and Prioritisation", 15 September 2016, para. 6 (https://www.legal-tools.org/doc/182205/).

[27] *Ibid.*, para. 34.

[28] ICC Press Release, "ICC Judges Request Clarification and Additional Information with Regard to the Situation in Kenya", 19 February 2010 (https://www.legal-tools.org/doc/a01740/).

[29] ICC, *Situation in the Republic of Kenya*, Pre-Trial Chamber II, Request for authorisation of an investigation pursuant to Article 15, 26 November 2009, ICC-01/09-3, paras. 56–59 (https://www.legal-tools.org/doc/c63dcc/).

[30] ICC, *Situation in the Republic of Côte d'Ivoire*, Pre-Trial Chamber III, Request for authorisation of an investigation pursuant to article 15, 23 June 2011, ICC-02/11-3, para. 56 (https://www.legal-tools.org/doc/1b1939/).

[31] *Ibid.*, para. 57.

of cases,[32] the early ICC decisions did not address the merits of gravity.[33] The issue of gravity suddenly appeared to be a controversial topic when the Prosecutor used this concept to justify his decision not to initiate an investigation concerning the situation in Iraq in 2006. The complaints that were filed with the Prosecutor regarding that situation concerned the behaviour of the British troops in Iraq since the 2003 invasion.[34] The Prosecutor clearly explained that in assessing gravity "a key consideration is the number of victims of particularly serious crimes, such as wilful killing or rape".[35] The number of potential victims of the crimes in the Iraq situation was of a different scale than the number of victims in the other situations that the Prosecutor was investigating. The Prosecutor concluded that the Iraq situation did not appear to meet the required threshold of the ICC Statute.[36] This practice was evaluated to be as close as the Prosecutor had come to providing criteria for the selection of situations.[37]

In 2014, responding to the referral by the Comoros, the second Prosecutor submitted a report that explained her decision not to initiate an investigation into the Situation on Registered Vessels of Comoros, Greece and Cambodia because of the insufficiency of gravity.[38] The humanitarian aid flotilla bound for the Gaza Strip was carrying over 500 civilian passengers when 10 were killed by Israeli Defence Forces ('IDF') and approximately 50–55 were injured. The number of passengers who suffered outrages upon their personal dignity was unclear. The Prosecutor concluded that the potential case(s) that would likely arise from the investigation into the situation would be inadmissible pursuant to Article 17(1)(d) of the Statute. The Prosecutor determined that "considering the scale, impact and manner of the alleged crimes, the Prosecutor is of the view that the

---

32 Statement at Informal Meeting of Legal Advisors of Ministries of Foreign Affairs, p. 6, see *supra* note 1.

33 See, for example, ICC, *Situation in Uganda*, Pre-Trial Chamber II, Decision on the prosecutor's application for the warrants of arrest under Article 58, 8 July 2005, ICC-02/04-01/05-1, para. 2 (https://www.legal-tools.org/doc/9870dd/).

34 ICC-OTP, "Response to Communications Received Concerning Iraq", 9 February 2006 (https://www.legal-tools.org/doc/5b8996/).

35 *Ibid.*, p. 9.

36 *Ibid.* However, because these other three situations were referred by States Parties or the Security Council, which means that the Prosecutor did not have the same discretion not to investigate, the extent to which this comparison explains his decision is unclear. William A. Schabas, "Prosecutorial Discretion v. Judicial Activism at the International Criminal Court", in *Journal of International Criminal Justice*, 2008, vol. 6, no. 4, pp. 740–741.

37 William A. Schabas, "Victor's Justice: Selecting "Situations" at the International Criminal Court", in *Journal of Marshall Law Review*, 2010, vol. 43, no. 3, p. 544.

38 ICC-OTP, "Situation on Registered Vessels of Comoros, Greece and Cambodia: Article 53(1) Report", 6 November 2014 (https://www.legal-tools.org/doc/43e636/).

flotilla incident does not fall within the intended and envisioned scope of the Court's mandate".[39]

22.2.3.2. The Gravity Threshold Before ICC Chambers

Unlike the OTP, ICC Chambers are not supposed to exercise their discretion for case or situation selection. Chambers, especially the PTCs, are entitled to conduct a judicial review of cases or situations selected by the Prosecutor. The process involves three distinct procedures: admissibility assessment of a case, authorization of investigation, and review of decisions of inaction.

Article 19 of the ICC Statute provides that the Court may, on its own motion or responding to applications that have been submitted, determine the admissibility of a case in accordance with Article 17. For example, a chamber was given the first occasion to interpret the gravity threshold in 2006. In the decision on the Prosecutor's application for two arrest warrants for Lubanga and Ntaganda, PTC I interpreted the gravity threshold. It established three clear standards: (i) whether the conduct was systematic or large-scale with social alarm, (ii) whether the suspect is one of the most senior leaders of the situation, and (iii) whether the suspect is the most responsible.[40] Having assessed the gravity of these two cases, PTC I concluded that the gravity was sufficient in the *Lubanga* case but not in the *Ntaganda* case. Responding to the appeal, the Appeals Chamber ('AC') delivered a judgement that reversed PTC I's decision on the inadmissibility of the case of Ntaganda, stating that PTC I erred in law in its interpretation of 'sufficient gravity' under Article 17(1)(d). The AC found that there was no legal basis for the requirement of large-scale or systematic conduct that caused social alarm.[41] Further, the AC held that the imposition of rigid standards that were primarily based on top seniority may result in achieving neither retribution nor prevention.[42]

---

[39] *Ibid.*, para. 142. On the contrary, one commentator suggested that based on a comprehensive analysis of the situation, there is a reasonable basis to believe that all criteria are satisfied and encouraged the Prosecutor to open a formal investigation into the situation. Russel Buchan, "The Mavi Marmara Incident and the International Criminal Court", in *Criminal Law Forum*, 2014, vol. 25, nos. 3–4, p. 496.

[40] ICC, *Prosecutor v. Lubanga*, Pre-Trial Chamber I, Decision on the Prosecutor's Application for a warrant of arrest, Article 58, 24 February 2006, ICC-01/04-01/06-8-US-Corr, para. 63 (https://www.legal-tools.org/doc/af6679/). The original decision including the statements regarding Ntaganda was unsealed by the Decision ICC-01/04-520, which was incorporated in the record of the case of *Prosecutor v. Ntaganda* as ICC-01/04-02/06-20-Anx2, 10 February 2006 (https://www.legal-tools.org/doc/d68b07/).

[41] *Ibid.*, para. 73.

[42] *Ibid.*, para. 74.

In 2010, PTC I was given another chance to provide criteria to determine sufficient gravity in the decision that confirmed the charges against Abu Garda. The Regulations of the OTP had already entered into force and provided the four factors that the Prosecutor shall consider assessing the gravity of crimes. PTC I agreed with the Prosecutor that, in assessing the gravity of a case, the issues regarding the nature, manner and impact of the alleged attacks are critical.[43] In addition, by referencing the opinion of Williams and Schabas, PTC I determined that the gravity of a given case should be assessed not only from a quantitative perspective. It stated that the qualitative dimension of the crime should also be considered.[44] Furthermore, the Chamber found that certain factors listed in Rule 145(1)(c) of the Rules of Procedure and Evidence ('RPE')[45] could serve as useful guidelines for the evaluation of the gravity threshold that is required by Article 17(1)(d) of the Statute. These factors included "the harm caused to victims and their families, the nature of the unlawful behaviour and the means employed to execute the crime".[46]

In cases of investigation *proprio motu*, the PTC assesses the Prosecutor's request to authorize the initiation of an investigation according to Article 15(3). In the decision on the Kenya situation issued in 2010, PTC II established the criteria to authorize an investigation.[47] It stated that "admissibility at the situation phase should be assessed against certain criteria defining a 'potential case'". Those criteria may include: (i) the groups of persons involved who are likely to be the focus of an investigation for the purpose of shaping the future case(s), and (ii) the crimes within the jurisdiction of the Court allegedly committed during the incidents that are likely to be the focus of an investigation for the purpose of shaping the future case(s).[48] Regarding the first element of a potential case, PTC II considered "that it involves a generic assessment of whether such groups of persons that are likely to form the object of investigation capture those who

[43] ICC, *Prosecutor v. Abu Garda*, Pre-Trial Chamber I, Decision on the Confirmation of Charges, 8 February 2010, ICC-02/05-02/09-243-Red, para. 31 (https://www.legal-tools.org/doc/cb3614/).

[44] *Ibid.*

[45] ICC RPE, 9 September 2002, Rule 145(1)(c) (https://www.legal-tools.org/doc/l3a64k/).

[46] *Prosecutor v. Abu Garda*, 8 February 2010, para. 32, see *supra* note 43.

[47] ICC, *Situation in the Republic of Kenya*, Pre-Trial Chamber II, Decision Pursuant to Article 15 of the Rome Statute on the Authorization of an Investigation into the Situation in the Republic of Kenya, 31 March 2010, ICC-01/09-19 (https://www.legal-tools.org/doc/338a6f/).

[48] *Ibid.*, para. 50.

may bear the greatest responsibility for the alleged crimes committed".[49] Concerning the second element, PTC II stated that "the gravity of the crimes will be assessed in the context of their *modus operandi*".[50]

Furthermore, responding to the request by the Prosecutor for the authorization of an investigation into the situation of Côte d'Ivoire, PTC III used the parameters from the Kenya PTC decision concerning the assessment of gravity.[51] PTC III considered the scale of the crime and especially the rank and role of the individuals who were likely to be the focus of any future investigation, particularly the former President.[52]

Finally, according to Article 53(3), the PTC may, at the request of the Security Council or the State that makes a referral, review a decision of the Prosecutor not to proceed. It can then request the Prosecutor to reconsider the decision. Against the Prosecutor's decision not to initiate its investigation in the Gaza situation, in 2015, PTC I took the view that the Prosecutor had erred. First, PTC I recalled that, in the decisions on the situations of Kenya and Côte d'Ivoire, there were two different elements to establish. These elements were (i) whether such groups of persons who are likely to form the object of investigation capture those who may bear the greatest responsibility for the alleged crimes committed, and (ii) the assessment of gravity from both a 'quantitative' and a 'qualitative' viewpoint and the use of factors such as the nature, scale and manner of commission of the alleged crimes, as well as their impact on victims, as indicators of the gravity of a given case.[53] PTC I especially noted that, concerning the first element, the Prosecutor did not provide, in its evaluation of the gravity of the potential case(s), an analysis of the factor of the potential accused's level of responsibility.[54]

This practice means that the chambers have the power to re-assess the evaluation of gravity made by the Prosecutor and ask the Prosecutor to review its determination.

---

49 *Ibid.*, para. 60.

50 *Ibid.*, para. 61.

51 ICC, *Situation in the Republic of Côte d'Ivoire*, Pre-Trial Chamber III, Decision Pursuant to Article 15 of the Rome Statute on the Authorisation of an Investigation into the Situation in the Republic of Côte d'Ivoire, 3 October 2011, ICC-02/11-14, paras. 201–204 (https://www.legal-tools.org/doc/7a6c19/).

52 *Ibid.*, para. 205.

53 ICC, *Situation on the Registered Vessels of the Union of the Comoros, the Hellenic Republic and the Kingdom of Cambodia*, Pre-Trial Chamber I, Decision on the request of the Union of the Comoros to review the Prosecutor's decision not to initiate an investigation, 16 July 2015, ICC-01/13-34, para. 21 (https://www.legal-tools.org/doc/2f876c/).

54 *Ibid.*, paras. 22–23.

22.3. Releasing the Prosecutor From the Gravity Constraint

As shown above, the concept of gravity works in three phases before the OTP (policy papers, requests for the authorization of investigation, and decisions of inaction). It works in three phases before Chambers (admissibility-assessment of a case, authorization of investigation, and review of decisions of inaction). The three phases before Chambers require legal assessments to screen out inappropriate cases or situations. However,, the three phases before the OTP require policy assessments to pick out potential cases and situations. As assessed below, the latter is not mandatory. I argue that the non-mandatory nature of the selection process does benefit the OTP, whereas the gravity constraint has burdened the OTP unnecessarily.

22.3.1. The OTP's Duty to Investigate, Prosecute or Explain Its Action?

One has to admit that there is no such provision obliging the ICC Prosecutor to initiate prosecution or investigation in a specific circumstance. The chamber is obliged not to proceed if it does not find sufficient gravity. The OTP, in contrast, is not obliged in that way.

It is not a violation of the ICC Statute that the Prosecutor does not bring a case of sufficient gravity. With regard to *proprio motu* investigations, the OTP "*shall* review the information analysed during preliminary examination and evaluation and shall collect the necessary information and evidence in order to identify the most serious crimes committed within the situation", according to Regulation 33 of the Regulations of the OTP.[55] However, the discretion to initiate *proprio motu* investigation is clear from the wording of Article 15: "[t]he Prosecutor may initiate investigations *proprio motu* on the basis of information on crimes within the jurisdiction of the Court". Paragraph 3 provides that, if the Prosecutor concludes that there is a reasonable basis to proceed with an investigation, the Prosecutor "shall submit to the Pre-Trial Chamber a request for authorisation of an investigation, together with any supporting material collected". Similarly, the wording 'shall' in Article 53(1) makes it obligatory to initiate an investigation unless the Prosecutor determines that there is no reasonable basis to proceed under the Statute. However, the OTP has to initiate only if the OTP decides at the first stage that there is 'reasonable basis'. The structure of this provision is that 'you shall decide when you decide to decide', which provides nothing but discretionary power. It means that it is still in the hands of the OTP whether to touch the issue. Thus, the Prosecutor has complete discretion in selecting among admissible cases.[56]

---

[55] Regulations of the OTP, Regulation 33 (emphasis added), see *supra* note 13.

[56] deGuzman, 2009, p. 1415, see *supra* note 4.

The OTP can bring a case of insufficient gravity. According to Article 53(1)(b), the OTP "shall consider whether: (b) The case is or would be admissible under Article 17"; however, even when it lacks a confident explanation, the OTP is free to proceed. Even if a chamber later concluded that the case brought by the Prosecutor was inadmissible, it would not mean that the Prosecutor violated the Statute. Article 17 of the Statute provides that the Court shall determine that a case is inadmissible when the case is not of sufficient gravity. However, it does not mean that the Prosecutor shall not bring a case that is to be found, eventually, to be of insufficient gravity by the chamber. It is the chamber that assesses the gravity and not the OTP.

It is true that, if the OTP brings a case that is eventually found to be of insufficient gravity and the PTC dismisses it, the Court wasted its time and resources. Therefore, it is a matter only of judicial economy and not of compliance with the law. This flexibility is fully understandable, given the limited information and evidence that the OTP would possess before the initiation of an investigation or prosecution. Pursuant to Article 15(1) of the ICC Statute, the Prosecutor can investigate "on the basis of information in crimes within the jurisdiction of the Court", which is a very low threshold. The Prosecutor can receive such 'information' by watching the news.[57] It has been found that the evidence only needs to establish a reasonable conclusion that the person committed a crime within the jurisdiction of the Court. It is not required that this is the only reasonable conclusion that can be drawn from the evidence.[58] Therefore, even one non-governmental organization report can be a 'reasonable ground'. When acting in such a circumstance, it is obvious that the Prosecutor needs to be selective. Gravity itself cannot be the only decisive factor.

In addition, the Prosecutor is not obliged to explain its inaction. At the time of writing, one of the major criticisms against the ICC Prosecutor is that he is largely unconstrained and unaccountable.[59] Another criticism is that the lack of clearly defined goals and priorities poses a serious challenge to the ICC's legitimacy.[60] Apparently, the behaviour and statements of the first Prosecutor gave

---

[57] John. R.W.D. Jones, "The Office of the Prosecutor", in Antonio Cassese, Paola Gaeta and John R.W.D. Jones (eds.), *The Rome Statute of the International Criminal Court: A Commentary*, Oxford University Press, 2002, p. 270.

[58] ICC, *Prosecutor v. Al Bashir*, Appeals Chamber, Judgment on the appeal of the Prosecutor against the "Decision on the Prosecution's Application for a Warrant of Arrest against Omar Hassan Ahmad Al Bashir", 3 February 2010, ICC-02/05-01/09-73, paras. 33, 39 (https://www.legal-tools.org/doc/9ada8e/).

[59] See, for example, Diane F. Orentlicher, "Judging Global Justice: Assessing the International Criminal Court", in *Wisconsin International Law Journal*, 2003, vol. 21, no. 3, p. 511.

[60] Margaret M. deGuzman, "Choosing to Prosecute: Expressive Selection at the International Criminal Court", in *Michigan Journal of International Law*, 2012, vol. 33, no. 2, p. 267.

such an impression. However, according to the law, does the Prosecutor have to provide legal explanations of his or her decisions of inaction?

At the beginning of the investigation, Articles 18(1) and 15(3) of the ICC Statute provide the obligation of the OTP to inform the related parties when it initiates a *proprio motu* investigation. In contrast, in the case of a decision not to take action, Article 15(6) provides: "If, after the preliminary examination [...], the Prosecutor concludes that the information provided does not constitute a reasonable basis for an investigation, he or she shall inform those who provided the information". However, no provisions can be found in the Statute obliging the OTP to provide the reasons of inaction except in the case provided in Article 53(2)(c). The Prosecutor can even take necessary measures to ensure the confidentiality of information according to Article 54(3)(f) . In making its activities public, the OTP shall be guided, *inter alia*, by considerations for the safety, well-being and privacy of those who provided the information or others who are at risk on account of such information, in accordance with Rule 49, sub-rule 1 of the RPE. The first Prosecutor mentioned in a policy document dealing with the matter that he would "use this [discretionary] power [of the Prosecutor] with responsibility and firmness, ensuring strict compliance with the Statute".[61] However, because there is no provision saying that the OTP has to disclose all the reasons for inaction, including budgetary issues or possibility of arrest, the OTP should be excused from the accusations that do not have legal grounds.

Furthermore, the attempts or efforts of the OTP to explain or disclose the decision-making process revealed its inconsistency, which is more problematic. For example, when the OTP made a statement explaining that Lubanga was charged as the first suspect because he was facing 'imminent release' from prison in the DRC, it invoked a discussion of whether the selection of the *Lubanga* case was based on gravity or his possible imminent release.[62] Moreover, while the Prosecutor declared that the decision not to proceed in the situation in Iraq was because only 12 people were killed,[63] it furthered the proceedings in the *Banda and Jerbo* case despite the fact that the actual number of killed victims was 12 in this case as well.[64] Thus, the effort to ensure transparency

[61] ICC-OTP, Annex to the "Paper on some policy issues before the Office of the Prosecutor": Referrals and Communications, 5 September 2003, p. 4 (https://www.legal-tools.org/doc/5df43d/).

[62] El Zeidy, 2008, p. 41, see *supra* note 11.

[63] "Response to Communications Received Concerning Iraq", 9 February 2006, p. 9, see *supra* note 34.

[64] ICC, *Prosecutor v. Banda and Jerbo*, Corrigendum of the "Decision on the Confirmation of Charges", Pre-Trial Chamber I, 7 March 2011, ICC-02/05-03/09-121-Corr-Red, para. 2 (https://www.legal-tools.org/doc/5ac9eb/).

ended up, to some extent, creating the belief that the Prosecutor arbitrarily selected cases without consistency.

Some commentators noted that 'discretionary' does not mean 'unfettered'. They claim that the Prosecutor should indicate if he or she declines further proceedings on the basis of legal or policy considerations.[65] However, at least as long as there is no statutory or regulatory limitation as to the gravity, the ICC Prosecutor should be released from the 'gravity constraint' which was invented through an excessively pragmatic interpretation of the ICC Statute and the relevant rules and regulations.

22.3.2. Demerits of the Gravity Constraint

It has been claimed that it may be considered legitimate to pursue factor-practical reasons, such as the likelihood of apprehending a suspect or the availability of evidence, or strategic considerations, such as a desire to shed light on the 'complete landscape' of events that occurred within a particular situation.[66] In particular, among the advantages of the flexible assessment by an ICC Prosecutor released from the gravity constraint, this chapter discusses the issues of the maximization of the deterrence effect, the impunity gap, the interests of justice and peace, and the victim's feelings. Relying on the gravity constraint as a means to regulate the OTP's activities may negatively impact these factors.

22.3.2.1. Maximizing the Deterrence Effect

The prevention of serious crimes is one of the major purposes of the ICC.[67] As a global universal criminal justice body, the Court should have a deterrent effect covering the crimes that fall within its jurisdiction. Many observers believe or want to believe that breaking the culture of impunity, holding even just one perpetrator accountable, would have a powerful symbolic effect and dissuade those who might commit future gross violations of human rights.[68] The OTP has also recognized the importance of deterrence, adopting it as the "third principle" guiding its prosecutorial strategy.[69]

A weakening of deterrence caused by the gravity constraint was recognized in the discourse on the *Lubanga* case. In the decision on the arrest warrant, the PTC stated:

---

65 Stegmiller, 2011, p. 637, see *supra* note 22.

66 Luc Côté, "Reflections on the Exercise of Prosecutorial Discretion in International Criminal Law", in *Journal of International Criminal Justice*, 2005, vol. 3, no. 1, p. 168.

67 ICC Statute, Preamble, para. 5, see *supra* note 5.

68 Chandra Lekha Sriram and Stephen Brown, "Kenya in the Shadow of the ICC: Complementarity, Gravity and Impact", in *International Criminal Law Review*, 2012, vol. 12, no. 2, p. 240.

69 ICC-OTP, "Report on Prosecutorial Strategy", 14 September 2006, pp. 5–6 (https://www.legal-tools.org/doc/6e3bf4/).

> the analysis of the additional gravity threshold provided for in article 17 (1) (d) of the Statute against the backdrop of the preamble of the Statute leads to the conclusion that such an additional gravity threshold is a key tool provided by the drafters to maximise the Court's deterrent effect. As a result, the Chamber must conclude that any retributory effect of the activities of the Court must be subordinate to the higher purpose of prevention.[70]

Then, the Court considered that:

> the additional gravity threshold provided for in Article 17(1)(d) of the Statute is intended to ensure that the Court initiates cases only against the most senior leaders suspected of being the most responsible for the crimes within the jurisdiction of the Court allegedly committed in any given situation under investigation.[71]

The PTC adopted a test for the assessment of whether a person is the most responsible to the commission of the crime, explaining that:

> [...] the fact that those persons who, in addition to being at the top of the State entities, organizations or armed groups allegedly responsible for the systematic or large-scale commission of crimes within the jurisdiction of the Court, play a major role by acts or omissions in the commission of such crimes are the ones who can most effectively prevent or stop the commission of those crimes.[72]

The PTC concluded that only concentrating on this type of individual can maximize the deterrent effects of the ICC, because other senior leaders in similar circumstances will know that only by doing what they can to prevent the crimes can they be sure that they will not be prosecuted by the Court.[73]

However, the AC found that the test developed by the PTC is incorrect. It claimed that this may cause the opposite effect. It stated:

> [the argument] that the deterrent effect is highest if all other categories of perpetrators *cannot* be brought before the Court is difficult to understand. It seems more logical to assume that the deterrent effect of the Court is highest if no category of perpetrators is *per se* excluded from potentially being brought before the Court.
>
> 74. The imposition of rigid standards primarily based on top seniority may result in neither retribution nor prevention being achieved. Also, the capacity of individuals to prevent crimes in the

[70] ICC, *Prosecutor v. Lubanga*, Pre-Trial Chamber I, Decision on the Prosecutor's Application for a warrant of arrest, Article 58, 10 February 2006, ICC-01/04-01/06-8-Corr, para. 48 (https://www.legal-tools.org/doc/af6679/).

[71] *Ibid.*, para. 50.

[72] *Ibid.*, para. 53.

[73] *Ibid.*, para. 54.

> field should not be implicitly or inadvertently assimilated to the preventive role of the Court more generally.[74]

It further explained its concern that the criteria considered by the PTC (such as the national or regional scope of activities of a group or organization, the exclusively military character of a group, the capacity to negotiate an agreement, the absence of an official position, and the capacity to change or prevent a policy) could let the Court ignore the highly variable constitutions and operations of different organizations.[75] It could also encourage any future perpetrators to avoid criminal responsibility before the ICC by ensuring that they are not a visible part of the high-level decision-making process.[76] Moreover, individuals who are not at the very top of an organization may still carry considerable influence and commit, or generate the widespread commission of, very serious crimes.[77]

The OTP welcomed the AC's findings, stating that:

> [it] has dismissed the setting of an overly restrictive legal bar to the interpretation of gravity that would hamper the deterrent role of the Court. It has been also observed that the role of persons or groups may vary considerably depending on the circumstances of the case and therefore should not be exclusively assessed or predetermined on excessively formulistic grounds.[78]

Ball suggests several factors upon which the deterrent effect is an empirical variable: (i) the social structure and value system under consideration, (ii) the particular population in question, (iii) the type of law being upheld, (iv) the form and magnitude of the prescribed penalty, (v) the certainty of apprehension and punishment, and (vi) the individual knowledge of the law as well as the prescribed punishment, and his definition of the situation relative to these factors.[79] Briefly analysing the international criminal law system through these factors, it is clear that most of these factors are weak. Because the ICC potentially addresses the whole world, an integral approach towards the diversity of value-perspectives is required, which is far from easy. Since there are still several countries that have the death penalty, the ICC's possible punishments can be

---

[74] ICC, *Situation in the Democratic Republic of the Congo*, Appeals Chamber, 13 July 2006, ICC-01/04-169, paras. 73–74 (emphasis in the original) (https://www.legal-tools.org/doc/8c20eb/).

[75] *Ibid.*, para. 77.

[76] *Ibid.*

[77] *Ibid.*

[78] ICC-OTP, "Draft Policy Paper on Preliminary Examinations", 4 October 2010, para. 69 (https://www.legal-tools.org/doc/bd172c/).

[79] John C. Ball, "The Deterrence Concept in Criminology and Law", in *Journal of Criminal Law, Criminology, and Police Science*, 1955, vol. 46, no. 3, p. 348.

regarded as less severe, such that the deterrent effect is decreased in this sense.[80] With regard to knowledge, even though it is remarkable that even the armed groups in the deep jungle in Rwanda and the DRC are aware of international humanitarian law[81] and the International Committee of the Red Cross continues its hard work educating the parties of armed conflicts,[82] it is still difficult to ensure common public knowledge of what is to be punished before the ICC. Not only the difficulties in widespread education, but also the complexity and ambiguity of the definition of the crimes under the jurisdiction of the ICC, make such an achievement difficult.

Gravity and the ICC Prosecutor's discretion are related to Ball's fifth factor. Criminological research conducted over several decades and in various nations generally concludes that enhancing the certainty of a punishment produces a stronger deterrent effect than increasing the severity of the punishment.[83] An eighteenth-century philosopher, Beccaria, was among the first to reveal the correlation between the imposed punishment of crimes and compliant behaviour of society.[84] According to classic deterrence theory, which is based on rational theory, a potential perpetrator will commit a crime if and only if his expected utility from doing so, taking into account his gain and the chance of him being caught and sanctioned, exceeds his utility if he does not commit the act.[85] Heller argues that the OTP cannot affect the utility that a perpetrator expects from the commission of a serious international crime, but its prosecutorial strategy can, and

80 The most severe punishment is life imprisonment at the ICC. ICC Statute, Article 77, see *supra* note 5.

81 ICC, *Prosecutor v. Mbarushimana*, Pre-Trial Chamber I, Decision on the confirmation of charges, 16 December 2011, ICC-01/04-01/10-465-Red, Dissenting opinion of Judge Sanji Mmasenono Monageng, para. 14 (https://www.legal-tools.org/doc/63028f/).

82 International Committee of the Red Cross, "Building Respect for the Law", 1 May 2011 (available on its web site).

83 Valerie Wright, "Deterrence in Criminal Justice: Evaluating Certainty vs. Severity of Punishment", The Sentencing Project, Washington, D.C., 2010, p. 4.

84 He described the factors of a decision to commit a crime as: being a human having a free will, rational way of thinking and ability to prospect outcome of actions, and to decide based on the simplest view of man which is primarily that pleasure is preferable over pain. Cesare Beccaria, *On Crimes and Punishment, and Other Writings*, Cambridge University Press, 1995 (originally published in Italian in 1764).

85 A. Mitchell Polinsky and Steven Shavell, "The Economic Theory of Public Enforcement of Law", in *National Bureau of Economic Research Working Paper Series*, 1999, no. 6993, p. 4; Becker hypothesized that criminals are rational calculators and that, therefore, they make their decisions about compliance with criminal law on the basis of a comparison of the expected costs and benefits of criminal and legal activity. Gary S. Becker, "Crime and Punishment: An Economic Approach", in *Journal of Political Economy*, 1968, vol. 76, no. 2, pp. 169–217.

does, affect the likelihood that a perpetrator will be apprehended and prosecuted if he or she does commit the crime.[86]

It has been found that both criminals and non-criminals tend to avoid offenses for which detection and prosecution are likely, preferring other safer endeavours.[87] It seems likely that the potential criminal contemplates both the prescribed penalty and the risk of apprehension.[88] Deterrence theory suggests that an increase in the perceived likelihood of punishment should decrease the commission of international crimes.[89] Therefore, maximizing the possibility of criminal prosecution is the key for effective deterrence.

PTC I's decision in the *Lubanga* case was the polar opposite. The decisions in the situation in Kenya and Côte d'Ivoire made a similar mistake. The implicit exclusion of certain types of people causes the neutralization of a deterrent effect. Furthermore, as long as neither the chamber nor the OTP are sure about where the lower gravity threshold is set, the discussion should be left open for the sake of deterrence. It is important to let the potential perpetrator think that it is still possible that the crime will be considered to be of sufficient gravity, rather than assume that what he or she is going to commit will not be considered sufficiently grave to be prosecuted before the ICC. From these concerns, the gravity standard should be applied flexibly at times, when, for example, pursuing lower-ranking officials could deter other similarly situated officials from committing ICC Statute crimes, with an immediate impact for victims on the ground.[90]

In the case of the ICC, its fundamental circumstances make the deterrence effect weak. It has already been noted that international courts have the disadvantage of being located at a considerable distance from the places and persons concerned, which can reduce the effect of sanctions.[91] Threats of punishment

---

86 Kevin Jon Heller, "A Sentence-Based Theory of Complementarity", in *Harvard International Law Journal*, 2012, vol. 53, no. 1, p. 240.

87 See, for example, Daniel S. Nagin and Raymond Paternoster, "The Preventive Effects of the Perceived Risk of Arrest: Testing an Expanded Conception of Deterrence", in *Criminology*, 1991, vol. 29, no. 4, pp. 561–587.

88 Ball, p. 351, see *supra* note 79.

89 William W. Burke-White, "Proactive Complementarity: The International Criminal Court and National Courts in the Rome System of International Justice", in *Harvard International Law Journal*, 2008, vol. 49, no. 1, p. 74.

90 Human Rights Watch ('HRW'), "Unfinished Business: Closing Gaps in the Selection of ICC Cases", 15 September 2011 (available on its web site); HRW, "Selection of Situations and Cases for Trial before the International Criminal Court", 2006, pp. 7–15.

91 Anne-Marie La Rosa and Carolin Wuerzner, "Armed Groups, Sanctions and the Implementation of International Humanitarian Law", in *International Review of the Red Cross*, 2008, vol. 90, no. 870, p. 337.

are already limited. They may do little to achieve immediate deterrence once mass violence has erupted.[92]

22.3.2.2. Precondition to Respond to the Impunity Gap

Smith notes that there is no doubt that focusing only on the 'most senior leaders' will, in most cases, leave a large number of potential accused untouched by the process of the ICC.[93] The question is who to prosecute and how to address the alleged perpetrators who will not stand trial before the ICC.[94] This phenomenon is called the 'impunity gap'.[95] For the crimes that are grave, but not grave enough, in the absence of a State willing and able to prosecute, the perpetrators enjoy immunity in the gap between the limited ICC action and an unable or unwilling State. Those bearing the greatest responsibility for crimes are among the most difficult for national authorities to pursue.[96] In addition, in some cases, it is theoretically and practically possible that national authorities prefer to focus their limited resources on the most responsible persons. They may request the ICC to address the rest to complete the transitional justice process.

The ICC, therefore, should not exclude potential cases by setting a clear gravity threshold. Considering the first reason for the drafters to include the gravity threshold in the Statute, the cases that the ICC can deal with depend on its budget and resources. The size of the budget is affected by various factors: the number and generosity of the donors, the global economic situation, and the budget allocated to other issues. If inaction is caused by a shortage of resources at a given moment, it does not mean that the OTP will not take action in the future.

However, it must be admitted that the concept of 'impunity' tends to be marginalized. Because the concept of gravity was first inserted to avoid the Court's overload, it is inevitable that its interpretation will change with the economical limitations of the Court. It may appear pessimistic, but the ICC will never 'complete' the prosecution of all the perpetrators of serious crimes of international concern. While there is a real danger that a failure by the Prosecutor to take cognizance of State interests may marginalize the ICC. It may provide

---

92 Payam Akhavan, "Beyond Impunity: Can International Criminal Justice Prevent Future Atrocities?", in *American Journal of International Law*, 2001, vol. 95, no. 1, p. 10.

93 Stephen E. Smith, "Inventing the Laws of Gravity: The ICC's Initial Lubanga Decision and its Regressive Consequences", in *International Criminal Law Review*, 2008, vol. 8, no. 1–2, p. 340.

94 Jan Wouters, Sten Verhoeven and Bruno Demeyere, "The International Criminal Court's Office of the Prosecutor: Navigating Between Independence and Accountability?", in *International Criminal Law Review*, 2008, vol. 8, no. 1–2, p. 291.

95 *Ibid.*

96 HRW, 15 September 2011, p. 4, no. 1, see *supra* note 90.

ammunition to those opposed to the Court, this is a situation where the Prosecutor walks a tightrope, balancing political imperatives on the one hand and legal obligations on the other.[97] The ICC is unlike other international courts or tribunals in that it is not limited by geographic or time constraints, making a 'completion strategy' (as that of the ICTY discussed in several chapters above) unnecessary.[98]

22.3.2.3. Interests of Justice and Peace and Security Concerns

Letting the Prosecutor take the decision whether to initiate an investigation freely, regardless of the gravity of the case, enables the Prosecutor to take appropriate action in ongoing or post-conflict situations where serious crimes are most likely to occur. In contrast, if the Prosecutor has to take and explain his or her decision based only on the gravity of a case, it will create serious tensions concerning not only the ICC, but also the involved region and other parties.

Among the central conflicts confronting the ICC, there is the tension between the legal goal of enforcing the rule of law to end impunity and the political requirements of negotiating an end to armed conflicts.[99] To respond to situations that require a sensitive and political consideration, some commentators discuss the utility of Articles 53(1)(c) and (2)(c). According to these provisions, if the Prosecutor is satisfied that there is a reasonable basis to believe that the case is within the jurisdiction of the Court and is or would be admissible under Article 17 of the Statute, he or she should determine whether, taking into account the gravity of the crime and the interests of the victims, there are nonetheless substantial reasons to believe that an investigation would not serve the interests of justice.

The phrase 'interests of justice' is not defined in the ICC Statute. Some commentators have interpreted it as a form of creative ambiguity that could encompass alternative justice mechanisms, such as truth and reconciliation committees.[100] Others have argued that it was intended to grant the Prosecutor broad

[97] Ray Murphy, "Gravity Issues and the International Criminal Court", in *Criminal Law Forum*, 2006, vol. 17, no. 3–4, p. 312.

[98] *Ibid.*, p. 311.

[99] Kenneth A. Rodman, "Is Peace in the Interests of Justice? The Case for Broad Prosecutorial Discretion at the International Criminal Court", in *Leiden Journal of International Law*, 2009, vol. 22, no. 1, p. 100.

[100] See John Dugard, "Possible Conflicts of Justice with Truth Commissions", in Cassese, Gaeta and Jones (eds.), 2002, p. 702, see *supra* note 57; Matthew R. Brubacher, "Prosecutorial Discretion within the International Criminal Court", in *Journal of International Criminal Justice*, 2004, vol. 2, no. 1, p. 81; Richard J. Goldstone and Nicole Fritz, "'In the Interests of Justice' and Independent Referral: The ICC Prosecutor's Unprecedented Powers", in *Leiden Journal of International Law*, 2000, vol. 13, no. 3, p. 655.

political discretion to "arbitrate between the imperatives of justice and the imperatives of peace".[101]

The OTP issued the "Policy Paper on the Interests of Justice" in 2007 to set out the OTP's understanding of the concept.[102] It ascertained that Articles 53(1)(c) and (2)(c) create an obligation to consider various factors. The interests of justice tests need be considered only where positive determinations have been made on both jurisdiction and admissibility.[103] The ICC Statute does not define the concept of interests of justice. Thorough reviews of the preparatory works of the treaty also offer no significant elucidation.[104] And Chambers had not taken, by the time of writing, an explicit position on any of the transitional justice mechanisms.[105] Furthermore, the OTP confirmed the difference between the concepts of the interests of justice and the interests of peace, and that the latter falls within the mandate of institutions other than the OTP.[106] It stated that,

> [i]n situations where the ICC is involved, comprehensive solutions addressing humanitarian, security, political, development and justice elements will be necessary. The Office will seek to work constructively with and respect the mandates of those engaged in other areas but will pursue its own judicial mandate independently.[107]

In the same vein, the UN Secretary-General has called for mediators to understand that the ICC will proceed in accordance with the law as an independent judicial body.[108]

Despite these efforts not to involve the ICC in the dynamics of international politics, it has been recognized that the Court's lack of consideration can frustrate sensitive peace processes, and that due response is required. The need for clarity on the concept of interests of justice before the ICC was first raised in the situation of northern Uganda, where community leaders argued that the ICC's continued investigation could have the potential to jeopardize peace talks. The Prosecutor had suggested that he could suspend the investigation, invoking

---

101 See the statement from Bourdon in Côté, 2005, p. 178, see *supra* note 66.

102 ICC-OTP, "Policy Paper on the Interests of Justice", September 2007, p. 1 (https://www.legal-tools.org/doc/bb02e5/).

103 *Ibid.*, p. 2.

104 *Ibid.*

105 Wouters, Verhoeven and Demeyere, 2008, p. 292, see *supra* note 94.

106 "Policy Paper on the Interests of Justice", September 2007, p. 1, see *supra* note 102.

107 *Ibid.*, p. 5.

108 UN Security Council, Report of the Secretary-General on enhancing mediation and its support activities, UN Doc. S/2009/189, 8 April 2009, para. 37 (https://www.legal-tools.org/doc/560fc5/).

the concept of interests of justice.[109] It was reported that the first Prosecutor had once concluded that it had both the power and the duty to suspend investigations pursuant to Article 53 in any situation where he determined that the investigation might interfere with political negotiations between warring factions to end an armed conflict.[110] When negotiations resumed in the South Sudanese capital of Juba in 2006, the Prosecutor was asked to withdraw the arrest warrants, which were seen as an obstacle to their completion. This was the view that persisted, even after the Juba process collapsed in 2008 when Kony refused to sign the peace accords.[111]

One cannot deny the influence of the OTP's action on the stabilization of the conflict, and the ICC Prosecutor's action appeared to have a huge impact on the peace process. In light of the experience in Uganda in the spring of 2006, forcing the Prosecutor to take a position in a politically sensitive area without clear legal guidelines may prove to be a fundamental flaw in the ICC Statute.[112] International criminal law can build on the capability and willingness of political actors to wield international coercion or intervention, but it cannot help settling a conflict without them.[113]

As mentioned above, the Prosecutor is not obliged to explain the reason of inaction unless the reason is solely related to the interests of justice. If the Prosecutor was to hold back from politically sensitive proceedings, he or she would be more likely to rely on his or her inherent discretion, meaning that the Prosecutor does not need to invoke Article 53 to hold back from a potentially destabilizing case. Rather, he or she could delay criminal proceedings and avoid public statements, at most discreetly collecting information until the political situation changed.[114] The principal cost of such an approach is its lack of transparency.[115] This could create a suspicion that the Court protects powerful actors.[116]

---

[109] HRW, "The Meaning of the "Interests of Justice" in Article 53 of the Rome Statute", 1 June 2005 (available on its web site).

[110] Amnesty International, "Open Letter to the Chief Prosecutor of the International Criminal Court: Comments on the Concept of the Interests of Justice", 17 June 2005, p. 1 ('Open Letter to the Chief Prosecutor of the International Criminal Court') (https://www.legal-tools.org/doc/ff88f7/).

[111] See Erin K. Baines, "The Haunting of Alice: Local Approaches to Justice and Reconciliation in Northern Uganda", in *International Journal of Transitional Justice*, 2007, vol. 1, no. 1, p. 103.

[112] Wouters, Verhoeven and Demeyere, 2008, p. 292, see *supra* note 94.

[113] Rodman, p. 108, see *supra* note 99.

[114] *Ibid.*, p. 123.

[115] *Ibid.*

[116] See, for example, Stephanie Wolters, "Selective Prosecutions Could Undermine Justice for Congo", 7 March 2007 (available on the Institute for War and Peace Reporting's web site).

However, Human Rights Watch made a similar proposal when it conceded that the Prosecutor has limited discretion in terms of the timing of a potentially destabilizing prosecution, but should not publicly announce what he or she is doing because it could compromise the integrity of the Court.[117]

A confidential prosecution strategy is important. No provision in the Statute or the RPE establishes a definitive time-period for the completion of a preliminary examination. This was a deliberate legislative decision in Rome. It ensured that the analysis is adjusted to the specific features of each particular situation including, *inter alia*, the availability of information, the nature and scale of the crimes, and the existence of national responses concerning the alleged crimes.[118] On the other hand, Amnesty International was strongly opposed to the idea of waiting until the right time, referring to the maxim "justice delayed is justice denied".[119] However, it is also true that the total and permanent denial of justice is worse than delayed justice. To avoid the situation of total denial of justice because of the lack of co-operation by relevant parties, it is necessary to conduct sufficient preparation, including the right scheduling.

22.3.2.4. Victims' Feelings

Victims often seek exposure and acknowledgement of the truth of the events involving the violations they suffered.[120] In addition, in a 2008 study by Frank Haldemann, it is argued that a criminal court can contribute significantly to justice through broader 'recognition' not only by making a victim a beneficiary of reparation and a witness to assist in finding truth, but also by letting them participate directly in the criminal proceedings.

The concept of 'justice as recognition' was developed by Haldemann. It is,

> the kind of justice that is involved in giving due recognition to the pain and humiliation experienced by victims of collective violence. Recognition here is essentially individual-centred. Unlike restorative approaches to justice, which emphasise the restoration of communal bonds, recognition focuses primarily on the individual's sense of injustice and threatened self-respect, drawing a clear line

[117] HRW, 1 June 2005, pp. 21–22, see *supra* note 109.

[118] ICC, *Situation in the Central African Republic*, Pre-Trial Chamber III, Prosecution's Report Pursuant to Pre-Trial Chamber III's 30 November 2006 Decision Requesting Information on the Status of the Preliminary Examination of the Situation in the Central African Republic, 15 December 2006, ICC-01/05-7, para. 10 (https://www.legal-tools.org/doc/1dd66a/).

[119] Open Letter to the Chief Prosecutor of the International Criminal Court, p. 1 see *supra* note 110.

[120] Dinah Shelton, *Remedies in International Human Rights Law*, Second Edition, Oxford University Press, 2006, p. 276.

between such matters of justice and other moral concerns (including democracy, peace, or reconciliation).[121]

Recognition in this context appears on different levels. Transitional politics of recognition must reach beyond distributive systems of goods in a society, in order to investigate the full dimension of injustice and the sense of victimization it aroused.[122] Shklar pays attention to the fact that evil-doing, especially torture or rape, not only causes the victim physical suffering, but also betokens a profound lack of concern – a kind of 'symbolic devaluation' that is not reducible to the absence of goods.[123] These points deserve more attention as a framework to offer silent support to the feelings of victims, that they were not 'forgotten'.[124]

Declaring a case or situation as 'not grave enough' in this sense will harm the victims' feelings significantly. Each crime is among the gravest incidents of a victim's life, and no victim deserves 'relative assessment' with other victims. It is important to be aware that all the core crimes within the jurisdiction of the ICC are the most serious of crimes. At least official statements should avoid declaring that any of them are of insufficient gravity.

22.4. Conclusion: Diversification of the Conception of Gravity

This chapter has argued that the understanding of regulatory gravity may require reassessment. The function of the concept of gravity differs between the OTP and Chambers and the gravity constraint has a number of demerits.

Opponents of an independent Prosecutor insist on the danger of a politically unaccountable actor and of politicized trials. In that, the Prosecutor would be inappropriately targeting nationals of a State for political reasons.[125] Certainly, a Prosecutor that is accountable to no political body at all could have negative consequences for the protection of international peace and security and for the Court itself. Furthermore, if a Prosecutor was ever to wage a personal vendetta against individuals of a particular country, it would seriously undermine the credibility and legitimacy of the Court.[126] The proposed understanding of the function of the concept of gravity permits a flexible approach on the part of the ICC Prosecutor. However, appropriate safeguards should be provided,

---

[121] Frank Haldemann, "Another Kind of Justice: Transitional Justice as Recognition", in *Cornell International Law Journal*, 2008, vol. 41, no. 3, p. 678.

[122] *Ibid.*, p. 679.

[123] Judith N. Shklar, *The Faces of Injustice*, Yale University Press, 1990, p. 49.

[124] See, for example, Janine Natalya Clark, "Transitional Justice as Recognition: An Analysis of the Women's Court in Sarajevo", in *International Journal of Transitional Justice*, 2016, vol. 10, no. 1, pp. 67–87.

[125] Wouters, Verhoeven and Demeyere, 2008, p. 279, see *supra* note 94.

[126] *Ibid.*

such as strengthened judicial review or the creation of an inquest of the Prosecution.

The above-mentioned trend of diversification of the conception of gravity strengthens my argument. In the "Policy Paper on Case Selection and Prioritisation" of 15 September 2016, the ICC-OTP clearly stated that it pays particular attention to crimes that have been traditionally under-prosecuted. It also tells that it will pay particular attention to attacks against cultural, religious, historical and other protected objects as well as against humanitarian and peace-keeping personnel.[127] Then, the document mentions that the OTP "will aim to highlight the gravity of these crimes, thereby helping to end impunity for, and contributing to the prevention of, such crimes".[128] This use of gravity is inconsistent with earlier practice. It emphasizes the relative gravity between different types of core crimes. This was never intended by the drafters. It is true that the international community is becoming aware of the diversification of values. They may change between regions, cultures, genders or individuals, and between different generations. The statement in the 2016 policy paper reflects such a new understanding of the relativity of values protected by the core crimes. This shows the necessity of releasing the Prosecutor from the gravity constraint, which is already an unrealistic way of controlling the activities of the ICC Prosecutor.

[127] "Policy Paper on Case Selection and Prioritisation", 15 September 2016, para. 46, see *supra* note 26.

[128] *Ibid.*

23

Making Justice Meaningful for Victims

Richard J. Dicker[*]

23.1. Identifying and Explaining Criteria to Affected Communities

In order for justice for the worst crimes to have an impact in post-conflict societies, its processes must be transparent and understood by those most affected by the crimes being tried. The prosecutor's selection of cases is particularly important to that end, as it offers victims their first 'benchmark' to assess how the criminal justice system can be used to address their suffering. The seminar of the Forum for International Criminal and Humanitarian Law on 26 September 2008 focused on the merits of establishing criteria for case selection and for prioritization of cases to be processed in the criminal justice system.

The benefits of adopting and implementing such criteria in post-conflict societies where widespread war crimes, crimes against humanity, and, in some situations, genocide have been committed are numerous. Developing a policy can help maintain a sense of internal coherence in the work of the prosecution and can assist in the better management of what may be limited available resources. Establishing a clear policy for prosecutions can help insulate prosecutors from pressure from outside groups to pursue cases that fall outside of the prosecutor's mandate to try the most serious crimes. It can also help protect prosecutors from allegations of bias, particularly in ethnically-polarized communities, that could otherwise undermine their credibility and effectiveness. Increased transparency about how cases are selected and prioritized can also promote predictability in the process and can contribute to managing expectations of what can be achieved through the criminal justice process.

However, the criteria underlying the policy for case selection and prioritization are really only as successful as the extent to which they are understood by the victims, the communities affected by the crimes, and the general public.

[*] **Richard J. Dicker** is a Senior Legal Adviser for advocacy at Human Rights Watch's ('HRW') and a Lecturer in Law at Columbia University. At the time of writing, he was the founding Director of HRW's International Justice Program since its beginning in 2001. This chapter has not been substantively updated since the Second Edition. He graduated from New York University Law School and has an LL.M. from Columbia University. Starting in 1995, he directed HRW's multi-year campaign to establish the ICC, subsequently representing HRW in the ICC negotiations as one of the most influential actors. He has been one of the leaders of the international criminal justice movement since the 1990s.

Communicating non-confidential elements of the criteria to affected communities and the general public is, therefore, absolutely essential. Even the most objective of criteria can be interpreted differently by different groups of victims, thus highlighting why it is necessary to explain key elements through a vigorous outreach and communications strategy to help avoid or counteract misunderstandings that may emerge.[1] This is particularly important for international tribunals that conduct proceedings hundreds, and sometimes thousands, of miles from where the crimes have taken place. But it is not limited to international tribunals.

In Bosnia and Herzegovina, for example, there was a widespread perception among members of each of the three main ethnic communities that their community suffered the most during the war, and consequently an expectation that the crimes against their community would be prioritized for prosecution. This state of affairs highlighted the need for a strong outreach and communications programme to manage expectations and to counteract attempts by extreme nationalist politicians and others seeking to manipulate or undermine the responsible courts' work for their own ends.[2] Indeed, many non-governmental organizations and victims' groups interviewed by the HRW stressed that it was difficult to obtain information regarding trials before the cantonal courts in the Federation and the district courts in *Republika Srpska* for crimes under international law and that this lack of information fed rumours and speculation.[3] Based on our research, we believe that more efforts were needed to educate victims and the general public in Bosnia and Herzegovina through widespread dissemination of accurate information, in accessible forms, about the work of the War Crimes Chamber and the cantonal and district courts in the country.

---

1 Establishing and explaining to the public the criteria used in the selection of country situations for investigation can further protect judicial authorities from broader allegations of bias. For instance, the ICC's focus on Africa in its early years led to criticism that the continent was the Court's main 'target', with the prosecution strategy being intentionally geographically-based. Underlying this criticism was the perception that the ICC was a biased court designed to try African perpetrators because they were believed to be politically and economically 'weak, despite the fact that three of the four country situations under ICC investigation at the time of writing were voluntarily referred and a fourth was referred by the United Nations Security Council. For a more detailed discussion of this debate, see HRW, "Courting History: The Landmark International Criminal Court's First Years", July 2008, pp. 44–45.

2 HRW, "Narrowing the Impunity Gap: Trials Before Bosnia's War Crimes Chamber", vol. 19, no. 1(D), February 2007, p. 45.

3 HRW, "Still Waiting: Bringing Justice for War Crimes, Crimes Against Humanity, and Genocide in Bosnia and Herzegovina's Cantonal and District Courts", July 2008, p. 60.

The efforts by officials of the Special Court for Sierra Leone ('SCSL') offer an inspiring example of how complex and difficult legal concepts can be explained to affected communities. The Special Court's Office of the Prosecutor, together with other court officials, made significant efforts beginning early in the court's mandate to explain to Sierra Leoneans the court's statutory mandate to pursue those "bearing the greatest responsibility" in its selection of perpetrators.[4] Undoubtedly, this was a difficult issue to tackle in the villages and towns of Sierra Leone, where many victims of crimes were still living in close proximity to those individuals that they believed had perpetrated horrific abuses against them. This was among many of the important initiatives aimed at making the court accessible and at increasing awareness of its activities among ordinary Sierra Leoneans.

23.2. Consistent Application of the Criteria Identified: Promoting Transparency in Practice

Articulating the criteria for case selection and prioritization is an important first step, but it is not sufficient for effectively inspiring public confidence in efforts aimed at ending impunity for war crimes, crimes against humanity and genocide. The criteria that have been identified and publicized must be consistently applied in practice. Inconsistencies can feed negative perceptions about the prosecution's efforts, which can damage the credibility of efforts to promote accountability overall.

The work of the ICC in the Democratic Republic of the Congo offers insight into the kind of negative perceptions that can emerge because of a perceived failure to follow established criteria for case selection. The Rome Statute identifies 'gravity' as one of the key thresholds that must be satisfied for a case to be tried before the ICC.[5] The ICC's Office of the Prosecutor ('OTP') has also indicated that 'gravity' is the guiding factor in its selection of cases.[6] In this context, the ICC-OTP's narrow charges against Thomas Lubanga and Bosco Ntaganda –relating only to child soldier recruitment – led to many damaging perceptions about the Court: Lubanga and Ntaganda were senior officials in the Union of Congolese Patriots militia in the Ituri district of north-eastern Congo, whose forces are believed to be responsible for committing a range of horrific

[4] HRW, "Bringing Justice: The Special Court for Sierra Leone – Accomplishments, Shortcomings, and Needed Support", vol. 16, no. 8(A), September 2004, p. 33.

[5] Rome Statute of the International Criminal Court, 17 July 1998, entered into force on 1 July 2002, Article 17(1) ('Rome Statute') (https://www.legal-tools.org/doc/7b9af9/).

[6] ICC-OTP, "Criteria for Selection of Situations and Cases", draft discussion paper, June 2006, pp. 5–6 (https://www.legal-tools.org/doc/sk0ratuy/).

crimes including murder, torture and rape. Charges relating to these crimes were not reflected in the indictment.

Many of those we spoke with in Ituri in 2007 expressed the opinion that these charges were not 'serious' given the extent of the atrocities committed in Ituri, and especially since all Ituri-based militias used children as soldiers.[7] These doubts have raised questions about the ICC's relevance among communities affected by Lubanga and Ntaganda's other alleged crimes and have contributed to rumours that the ICC must have pursued them for other 'political' reasons. This has led to speculation that the ICC was biased.[8] These questions illustrate that the perception of inconsistent application by the OTP of the primary criterion for case selection – gravity – threatened to undermine the overall impact of the ICC's work in eastern Congo.

Related to the problems that flow from perceptions regarding the inconsistent application of criteria is the matter of legitimacy. HRW believes that the legitimacy of criminal justice depends in large part on the actual and perceived impartiality of the judicial institution. To preserve this key principle, any criterion identified for case selection and prioritization must be applied equally to investigate all individuals or groups suspected of committing international crimes, regardless of ethnic or political affiliation. Indeed, an important factor that gives the SCSL real legitimacy is its having charged the leaders of three militias, including one that was actively on the side of the government in the course of the civil war there.

We saw the importance of emphasizing impartiality – and regularly communicating this to members of affected communities – in the context of the ICC's work in Uganda. The situation in northern Uganda was referred to the ICC by President Museveni to investigate abuses committed there by the Lord's Resistance Army, a group at war with the government.[9] However, there were also allegations that crimes falling in the jurisdiction of the ICC had been committed by members of the Ugandan armed forces (the Ugandan People's Defence Forces). The OTP made efforts to clarify that its investigation was not

[7] While the ICC's charges against Lubanga and Ntaganda raised the profile of and, therefore, awareness about crimes related to child soldiers, our research suggested that more efforts were needed to contextualize and humanize these crimes over time.

[8] At the time of our mission to Ituri in 2007, only Thomas Lubanga had been arrested. As a result, there were rumours that the real reason he had been taken into custody was that he was being held responsible for killing 'white people' (that is, United Nations peacekeepers). There were also rumours that the ICC's arrest warrants required further 'confirmation' from the Congolese government and, hence, that the Court was only going after "(President) Kabila's enemies". See HRW, June 2008, pp. 64–65, *supra* note 1.

[9] ICC, "President of Uganda refers situation concerning the Lord's Resistance Army (LRA) to the ICC", Press Release, 29 January 2004 (https://www.legal-tools.org/doc/f598bc/).

limited to alleged perpetrators from one group and stressed the impartiality of its investigation.[10] Nonetheless, representatives of civil society and community-based organizations that we interviewed in Kampala and northern Uganda in 2007 consistently criticized the ICC's failure to investigate and prosecute abuses by the Ugandan armed forces or to explain why this was not being done. Despite additional outreach efforts by the ICC to affected communities in northern Uganda overall, more could have been done to clarify and better convey the key messages about the ICC's approach to alleged crimes by Ugandan army personnel. As a result, the prosecutor's work there was perceived by many as one-sided and biased.[11]

The HRW can appreciate that the focus and substance of investigations are confidential and cannot be shared with the public. Nonetheless, there are a number of objectives, non-confidential factors that the Prosecutor's Office could better and more frequently explain to local communities to preserve the ICC's credibility. For example, the OTP could improve efforts to explain its policy regarding the gravity threshold in selecting cases, as well as its inability to investigate crimes that fall outside of the ICC's temporal jurisdiction. This would be significant, as it is believed that some of the most serious abuses allegedly implicating Ugandan armed forces were committed prior to 2002. Of course, no amount of explanation can eliminate all of the criticism of the court's work, particularly in a polarized society. But providing clear explanations would go a long way to better inform affected communities and to counteract some of the negative perceptions that, if left unaddressed, can damage the credibility of the ICC.

23.3. Conclusion

The criminal justice process in relation to the worst crimes must be understood by victims and affected communities to be meaningful and, therefore, effective. Developing criteria for the selection and prioritization of cases involving war crimes, crimes against humanity and genocide is essential. However, just as important as developing the criteria, is how the criteria are used and explained. Inconsistencies on any of these fronts will likely undermine efforts to make an impact in the struggle against impunity for the worst crimes.

[10] ICC, "Prosecutor of the International Criminal Court opens an investigation into Northern Uganda", Press Release, 29 July 2004 (https://www.legal-tools.org/doc/cfe941/).

[11] HRW, June 2008, pp. 41–42, see *supra* note 1.

24

The Danger of Selective Justice

Christopher K. Hall*

I am very honoured to have been invited to contribute to this anthology following the seminar on 26 September 2008 organized by CILRAP's Forum for International Criminal and Humanitarian Law (FICHL), which was co-sponsored by my own organization and many others. It is a particular pleasure to acknowledge the role of Morten Bergsmo, who has dedicated most of his career to the cause of international justice and took the initiative under the Ethics, Norms and Identities Programme of the Peace Research Institute Oslo (PRIO) to organize the seminar.

The purpose of the seminar, to explore creative ways, consistent with due process, for states to fulfil their obligations to investigate and prosecute crimes under international law – a task far beyond the limited capability of international criminal courts to do – addresses the most important challenge we face today in the field of international justice.

24.1. Defining the Problem

In my very brief remarks on this topic, I would like to strike a note of caution about the formulation of the issue that was addressed in the seminar, suggest a different foundation which guides the approach of Amnesty International to the problem of impunity, and propose some possible approaches that might be considered at the international and national levels to encourage states effectively to investigate and prosecute the enormous number of unresolved crimes under international law, not only in Bosnia and Herzegovina, but also throughout the

* The late **Christopher K. Hall** was a Senior Legal Adviser at the International Justice Project, International Secretariat of Amnesty International in London. He graduated from Columbia College in New York City (1972) and University of Chicago Law School (1978). Formerly, he was Associate at Fried, Frank, Harris, Shriver and Jacobson in New York City (1978–1982) (extensive *pro bono* litigation on behalf of Haitian and Cuban refugees); Instructor (1982–1983) and Adjunct Professor (1983–1984) at the University of Miami School of Law (1982–1984); Associate at Kurzban, Kurzban and Weinger in Miami (1983–1984); Assistant Attorney General of the State of New York (1984–1990); and Legal Adviser (1990–2004) at Amnesty International. As the author has sadly passed away, this chapter has not been substantively updated since the Second Edition.

world, and to provide reparations to victims. In doing so, I will note some of the activities that my organization has been undertaking to address this issue.

First of all, let me clarify that Amnesty International enthusiastically supports this initiative and welcomes the many insights in the paper on which the seminar was largely based.[1] However, as I will explain in a moment, our organization believes that the problem should be formulated in a somewhat different manner. The programme for the seminar took as its starting point with regard to Bosnia and Herzegovina the "thousands of open case files involving allegations of core international crimes in the various prosecutors' offices at the state and entity levels of the country". I leave aside the omission from the concept of core crimes under international law (genocide, crimes against humanity and war crimes) of other crimes under international law, such as cases of torture, extrajudicial execution and enforced disappearance, since in the situations considered most of these crimes would also amount to one or more of the core crimes.[2]

Instead, our primary concern is the limitation of the definition of the problem to "open case files". The number of such files is a matter of considerable political controversy, but one recent report suggests that there are approximately 16,000 suspects named in such files in Bosnia and Herzegovina.[3] One is struck immediately by the vast disparity in numbers between the various prosecutors' offices that can have no bearing on the degree of criminality in each area within their jurisdiction. It is clear that the number of persons responsible for crimes under international law in Bosnia and Herzegovina is considerably higher than indicated by the open case files.

24.2. The Perspective of Kant

What should be done? Let me start by citing a somewhat surprising authority for an organization that has committed itself for the past three decades to the complete abolition of the death penalty – Immanuel Kant's *The Right of Punishing*, a defence of capital punishment in his *Science of Right*, published in

---

1 The paper was published as Morten Bergsmo, Kjetil Helvig, Ilia Utmelidze and Gorana Žagovec, *The Backlog of Core International Crimes Case Files in Bosnia and Herzegovina*, Second Edition, Torkel Opsahl Academic EPublisher, Oslo, 2010 (https://www.toaep.org/ps-pdf/3-bergsmo-helvig-utmelidze-zagovec-second).

2 In addition, these remarks do not address the question of the crime of aggression.

3 According to a reliable report, the War Crimes Processing Strategy, written by the President of Court of Bosnia and Herzegovina, Judge Medđida Kreso, noted that a total of 2,098 war crimes involving 16,152 persons were reported to various prosecutor's offices in Bosnia and Herzegovina. The largest number of reports, 1,037, was filed with prosecutor's offices in the Federation of BiH. The Bosnian Prosecutor's Office had received 608 reports, and the *Republika Srpska* 418. Another 35 reports involving 714 individuals were forwarded to the Prosecutor's Office in the District of Brčko. It is not clear whether some individuals were reported to more than one prosecutor's office.

1790 as part of the *Metaphysics of Morals*. If one can put aside for a moment the particular punishment that he defended, his insight more than two centuries ago into the concept of criminal justice has much to commend itself to us today with regard to crimes under international law. In that essay, he argued that criminal law was a categorical imperative and expressly rejected utilitarian justifications for punishment as a deterrent:

> Juridical punishment can never be administered merely as a means for promoting another good either with regard to the criminal himself or to civil society, but must in all cases be imposed only because the individual on whom it is inflicted has committed a crime.[4]

Kant argued that justice was a fundamental value in itself: "For if justice and righteousness perish, human life would no longer have any value in the world".[5] To illustrate his view he gave the following famous example:

> Even if a civil society resolved to dissolve itself with the consent of all its members – as might be supposed in the case of a people inhabiting an island resolving to separate and scatter themselves throughout the whole world – the last murderer lying in the prison ought to be executed before the resolution was carried out. This ought to be done in order that every one may realize the desert of his deeds, and that blood-guiltiness may not remain upon the people; for otherwise they might all be regarded as participators in the murder as a public violation of justice.[6]

It is very difficult for us today to consider this example – or, indeed, some of Kant's other writings on justice advocating particularly harsh penalties – as having anything to teach us. It comes as a shock that so soon after his near contemporary, Cesare Beccaria, had eloquently attacked in *On Crimes and Punishments* (1764) the harsh penalties imposed in Italy and elsewhere in Europe, that Kant advocated such cruelty. However, Kant's great insight was that each criminal should be brought to justice and that whenever any criminal escaped justice – at least for a grave crime – society to that extent failed to fulfil its responsibilities.

24.3. The Implications Today for International Justice of Kant's Views

What then does Kant have to teach us with regard to international justice today? If criminal justice is a categorical imperative and if society is implicated in the guilt of those who have committed genocide, crimes against humanity, war

[4] Immanuel Kant, *The Science of Right*, in *Metaphysics of Morals*, 1790 (translated by William Hastie).

[5] *Ibid.*

[6] *Ibid.*

crimes, torture, extrajudicial executions and enforced disappearances, if it has the power to investigate and prosecute them, but fails to do so, then society must ensure that they are brought to justice. When such crimes are committed, then the society concerned is not simply an island or even a state. These are crimes committed against the entire international community and it is the entire international community that must undertake every possible effort to ensure that no criminal is left free to live out his or her life in complete impunity.

24.4. Is This Approach 'Realistic'?

The immediate response of those who espouse what they would call realism usually is that this approach is wholly 'unrealistic'. Realists in this field, however, do not have a very good track record. Realists predicted that the International Criminal Tribunal for the former Yugoslavia would have failed and that it would have tried no cases as no state in or outside the Balkans would have arrested and surrendered accused persons. Fifteen years later, it had indicted a total of 161 persons, proceedings were completed against 116 persons and 45 were undergoing pre-trial, trial or appellate proceedings (only two of whom remained at large at the time of writing).

When the United Nations ('UN') General Assembly referred the International Law Commission's Draft Statute for an International Criminal Court to an *Ad Hoc* Committee in December 1994, one government official told William Pace, who was to establish the Coalition for an International Criminal Court two months later, "[d]on't worry, Bill, you won't see this Court in your lifetime. Your children won't see it in their lifetime and I doubt that your grandchildren will see it either". Less than four years later, 120 states in Rome adopted the Statute for the International Criminal Court.[7] Less than four years after that, the Statute entered into force and at the time of writing 108 states have ratified it, the Court has issued 12 arrest warrants, and its first trial is to start in January 2009. Perhaps one would not be far wrong to say that the only realists are the idealists, since, in the long run, they are usually right.

24.5. What Resources Are Required to Bring All Those Responsible to Justice?

This is a question that the seminar on 26 September 2008 sought to address. Where should one begin? There is some merit in the advice of the King of Hearts to the White Rabbit who asked the same question. He replied, "[b]egin at the beginning, and go on till you come to the end: then stop". The beginning is mapping, in close consultation with civil society, the total number of crimes

[7] Rome Statute of the International Criminal Court, 17 July 1998 (https://www.legal-tools.org/doc/7b9af9/).

committed and the total number of suspects, then categorizing the types of crimes committed according to the difficulties that are likely to be encountered in investigating them. In some cases, there will be no bodies; in others, no witnesses. Some cases will be massively documented; others will have only a single eye-witness. Some will involve complex hierarchies of command; others will be the next-door neighbour now living in the victim's house. As this mapping exercise progresses, then estimates can begin to be made of the resources that would be required to prove each case, if it were to go to trial and then be appealed.

In the light of these considerations, there can be no rigid criteria for prioritizing – and I emphasize prioritizing, not selecting – cases for investigation. There will always need to be some room for judgement in applying any criteria to determine which crimes should be investigated first. For example, if a rigid application of a particular set of criteria were to lead to a disproportionate number of crimes committed against members of a particular ethnic or religious group to be given a low priority or to certain crimes, such as crimes of sexual violence against women, to be ignored, then those criteria need to be applied differently, modified or abandoned.

That said, the following would seem to be a far from exhaustive list of appropriate criteria or, perhaps, more accurately, factors to consider, in determining priorities of crimes for investigation:

- age and health of the victim and his or her family (investigations should be completed with sufficient time to complete any prosecution in their lifetimes);
- age and health of the suspect, when known (investigations should be completed with sufficient time to complete any prosecution in the suspect's lifetime);
- degree of access to evidence (material and witness testimony) in the forum's jurisdiction and to other evidence through mutual legal assistance;
- security of victims and witnesses during the investigation; and
- scale of the crime (number of victims).

Now, of course, for a wide variety of reasons, in all legal systems, not all crimes result in trials of suspects. Therefore, the next stage will be to estimate the percentage of crimes that will probably never be solved or will be unlikely to be solved in the near future, but which should be given eventually to a cold cases team. After that, consideration can be given to a wide variety of innovative techniques to conduct criminal proceedings in a way that will minimize the resources needed to complete them in a manner consistent with due process. Finally, a long-term action plan should be developed in a transparent manner in close consultation with civil society to investigate and, where there is sufficient admissible evidence, prosecute all suspects over several years. In prioritizing which of those cases should be prosecuted first, then the same criteria suggested for prioritizing investigations could be taken into account.

24.6. Innovative Techniques to Reduce the Resources Needed to Complete Proceedings

I am certainly not an expert in the administration of criminal justice systems. I simply wish to note here a range of measures that could be used to conduct criminal proceedings with the least resources in the fastest possible way which is still fully consistent with due process. None of what I suggest is entirely novel – all have been used before in international or national courts somewhere, but some of the steps will be new for some legal systems.

Some of the proposed techniques include:

- *Plea bargaining.* This is the most promising method for reducing the resources needed to a manageable level. In some jurisdictions, such as the United States of America, 90 per cent or more of all serious criminal cases are resolved by plea bargaining.[8] One form of plea bargaining should be avoided when crimes under international law are involved. Such crimes are so grave that the prosecutor should not offer, and the court should not grant, complete immunity from prosecution in return for co-operating in the investigation and prosecution of other such crimes, but, instead, the reward for such co-operation should be mitigation of punishment. Such co-operation is considered as a legitimate factor to be taken in deciding whether to mitigate punishment for genocide, crimes against humanity and war crimes in Rule 145(2)(a)(ii) of the Rules of Procedure and Evidence of the International Criminal Court[9] and in Article 7(2)(a) of the International Convention for the Protection of All Persons from Enforced Disappearance.[10] Of course, appropriate safeguards need to be in place, perhaps similar to

[8] In *Santobello v. New York*, Judgment, 15 November 1971, 404 US 260 (1971) (https://www.legal-tools.org/doc/kb1yi8pa/), the United States Supreme Court explained that plea bargaining was not only constitutional, but "an essential component of the administration of justice".

[9] Rule 145(2)(a)(ii) provides that "the Court shall take into account, as appropriate: (a) Mitigating circumstances such as: […] (ii) The convicted person's conduct after the act, including […] any cooperation with the Court", Rules of Procedure and Evidence, 9 September 2002 (https://www.legal-tools.org/doc/8bcf6f/).

[10] Article 7(2)(a), see *supra* note 7, provides:

> Each State Party may establish:
>
> (a) Mitigating circumstances, in particular for persons who, having been implicated in the commission of an enforced disappearance, effectively contribute to bringing the disappeared person forward alive or make it possible to clarify cases of enforced disappearance or to identify the perpetrators of an enforced disappearance.

the safeguards used in practice in the International Criminal Tribunals for the former Yugoslavia and for Rwanda or spelled out in Article 65 (Proceedings on an admission of guilt) with regard to an analogous procedure.

- *Precedent.* This is a useful approach used particularly in common law countries to avoid duplication of resources by preventing the re-litigating of exactly the same legal issues time and again once the highest court has decided the issue, subject to exceptions in the interests of justice, for example, demonstrating that the factual situation in the subsequent case was sufficiently different to require a different legal conclusion. Issues where precedent could avoid needless duplication of judicial resources include the existence of an armed conflict in the particular geographic area concerned and the nature of the armed conflict (international or non-international).
- *Judicial notice.* This is another useful tool to avoid wasting valuable court time in proving such matters as who was the official in a particular post on a certain date.
- *Use of video conferencing facilities.* This tool, subject to appropriate safeguards could increase the evidence-gathering capability of the legal system in civil and criminal proceedings by permitting victims and witnesses to participate from secure locations abroad and avoid the cost of transporting them to the seat of the court, with all the delays and security concerns entailed.
- *Joint trials.* If the court exercises effective control of the proceedings to avoid delays and to protect the right of each accused be presumed innocent, then joint trials can speed up proceedings.
- *Effective court management.* There is an increasing wealth of talent and expertise at the international level in administering the investigation and prosecution of crimes under international law, much of which can be used to develop equally effective administration of criminal proceedings at the national level. In particular, there is a long list of very sensible and sometimes innovative techniques for reducing the length of criminal proceedings based largely on the experience of the International Criminal Tribunals for the former Yugoslavia and Rwanda that was proposed by a number of experts for consideration by the Prosecutor of the International Criminal Court.[11] They are far too many to reproduce here and not all of them are relevant to national criminal proceedings, but they are well worth study.

[11] International Criminal Court, Office of the Prosecutor, "Measures available to the International Criminal Court to reduce the length of proceedings", Informal expert paper, 2003 (https://www.legal-tools.org/doc/7eba03/).

- *Extradition and mutual legal assistance agreements with other states.* Of course, it would be most effective if all states were to agree to draft, adopt and ratify new multilateral legal assistance treaties providing for extradition of persons suspected of crimes under international law, as Amnesty International has repeatedly recommended. However, pending the adoption of such new treaties, states should make the adoption of bilateral treaties governing such crimes a priority, strategically focusing on states where suspects are likely to be found. The failure of states, such as East Timor (Timor Leste) and Sierra Leone, to do so has severely limited their ability to investigate and prosecute crimes under international law.

24.7. Political Will

The absence of political will has been one of the main reasons that states have not played a more effective role in the investigation and prosecution of crimes under international law. Even if all the tools for justice are present – such as an experienced and well-trained police, prosecutors, judges, defence lawyers and representatives of victims and effective legislation – the absence of political will can defeat attempts to investigate and prosecute crimes under international law effectively and expeditiously. The adoption of the steps above can help to make it easier for political officials to give the necessary resources and support to investigations and prosecutions by making it clear that the costs of fulfilling the categorical imperative are not astronomical. However, other steps may also be needed in many countries to be taken to remove political control of prosecutions and extraditions, leaving these matters to professionals.

24.8. A Note About Amnesty International's Role

Finally, let me note a few of the things that Amnesty International has done to strength national efforts to investigate and prosecute crimes under international law. First, it campaigned since the adoption of the Rome Statute in July 1998 to persuade states not only to ratify that treaty, but also to enact effective implementing legislation defining crimes under international law as crimes under national law and incorporating principles of criminal responsibility and defences in national law in a manner consistent with the strictest standards of international law.

Second, it built links to police and prosecutors to encourage them to treat these crimes with the same degree of seriousness as other grave crimes, such as money laundering, drug trafficking, cybercrime, terrorism and trafficking in persons, and made extensive recommendations to that effect at meetings of Interpol and the European Network of Contact Points.

Third, the organization pressed states to implement rule of law programmes modelled on the UN rule of law programme for UN agencies to implement.

Fourth, Amnesty International published, having started in October 2008 (in connection with the tenth anniversary of the arrest of President Augusto Pinochet in London), a *No safe haven* series, at the time of writing comprising of 192 papers, on universal jurisdiction in each UN member state indicating what is possible and what is not, and making detailed recommendations for reform of law and practice.

Fifth, it called for states to adopt new multilateral international extradition and mutual legal assistance treaties.[12]

24.9. Conclusion

We look forward to working with the organizers of the 2008 seminar to develop and implement these ideas to ensure that the best part of Kant's vision of justice can finally become a reality.

[12] Amnesty International, Statement to Interpol in Lyon, 16 June 2005; Statement to European Union, 20 November 2006; Statement to Interpol in Ottawa, June 2007.

25

Remarks on the Characteristics of Effective Criteria for the Prioritization of Core International Crimes Cases

Mirsad Tokača*

The establishment of efficient criteria for the selection of core international crimes cases represents one of the fundamental tasks before the Bosnian-Herzegovinian society. There are several reasons why it is so. Firstly, at the moment of adoption of the Strategy for the processing of war crimes cases in Bosnia and Herzegovina ('the Strategy'), it would be very hard to imagine its efficient implementation if, at the same time, the selection criteria and prioritization criteria ('the criteria') are not ready. Secondly, prior to the very adoption of the Strategy and criteria, a number of speculations emerged about the number of war crimes cases in Bosnia and Herzegovina, varying from 10,000 to 16,000, causing widespread confusion. As the estimation was not based on detailed analysis, it caused mixed impressions. On the one hand, the impression was created that it has not been possible to deal with the high number of cases, that capacity-building for their processing has not been successful, leading to the conclusion that it would have been better to give up the entire criminal justice project and search for some other mechanisms (truth commissions or similar) to solve the issue. On the other hand, the impression is that the intention has been to blur the whole issue and prolong it indefinitely, by using the vast number of cases as a justification.

Unfortunately, only a minority seems to have argued that it is first necessary to do an in-depth analysis of the global problem of the backlog of cases, a mapping of crimes, and only after that – based on the full picture of the number

* **Mirsad Tokača** is the Founder and Director of the Research and Documentation Center in Sarajevo, since its establishment in 2004. Prior to that, he served for more than a decade as General Secretary of the State Commission for Gathering Facts on War Crimes. He has been an expert witness before the International Criminal Tribunal for the former Yugoslavia ('ICTY') and a member of the scholars' initiative of Purdue University (United States) dealing with the problem of the dissolution of the former Yugoslavia. As an independent member of the Bosnia and Herzegovina delegation, he attended the sessions of the United Nations Human Rights Commission in Geneva in 1996 and 1997. This chapter has not been substantively updated since the Second Edition.

of case files – to create and implement criteria for selection and prioritization of cases; and, on that basis, to build the long-term strategy and organization of resources necessary for efficient prosecution.

This approach has been supported by those who consider criteria as a principal operative instrument for the implementation of the Strategy for war crimes prosecution in Bosnia and Herzegovina. The approach, which I personally support, starts from the viewpoint that criteria should help the long-term directing of the inquiry of the prosecutor's office, as they can focus a well-planned use of the limited resources of the prosecution. If successfully prosecuted, such war crimes cases will produce significant societal consequences, primarily for the victims of the crimes, but also for society more widely. Criteria for case selection directly influence the prioritization of the prosecution.

Although these two dimensions interrelate, my understanding is that the focus of this volume is on operative criteria for the rational selection of cases of interest to the prosecutor's office – only in the second phase should the question of prioritization be addressed, in my view.

25.1. Prosecution or Court Independence v. Public Interest

One of the dilemmas which we have witnessed in Bosnia and Herzegovina is whether the wider (expert and even public) debate about criteria can affect the independence of prosecutors. As this proposition has been brought up in different forms, my opinion is that it should be responded to.

Broad dialogue about such criteria, at the time of their creation, can in no way jeopardize the independence of prosecution services. There are two separate processes: establishment *and* application of criteria. During the criteria-defining phase, differences of opinion should be expressed in search of the best solutions. In the implementation phase, it is the sole responsibility of the criminal justice system to apply the criteria to cases. Its independence and impartiality should not be brought into question.

Efficient selection and prioritization criteria are not only in the interest of the prosecution. They appear as the convergence of prosecution and victims' interests, providing for a joint effort to renew the rule of law, to eradicate the culture of impunity and to affirm the impartiality of the prosecutor, not through his or her inaccessibility, but through a measure of acceptable social co-operation in which all profit.

Is there perhaps a fear of an inaccessible – in some jurisdictions, for years – institution to open itself to full exposure to the public interest? Many are not aware that this kind of public consultation does not necessarily signify the undermining of institutional autonomy and independence. Or perhaps the fear –

cloaked in a veil of independence – is an attempt to hide inefficiency in the work of the prosecution service in question.

It is really hard to see how the development of transparent and efficient criteria can endanger the independence or impartiality of the prosecutor. *Au contraire*, it seems that such an approach can protect the prosecutors against unwanted external influence and pressures, with political, ethnic, religious or some other prefix. Such pressures are brought to bear on prosecution services exactly because of insufficiently transparent criteria – and a weak attitude of prosecutors towards political pressure.

I think that debates about this problem would show that their purpose is not to exercise pressure or impose any concept or solution on the prosecution, but rather reflect an effort to involve interested parties, either professional or societal, in one common pursuit of the system that would strengthen the efficiency of both the courts and prosecutors and their role in society.

There need not be any fear of confrontation among the parties to the process. It will certainly be difficult to influence the discretionary powers of the prosecutors and their authority over the practical application of criteria. Clear limits of propriety exist in this regard, but that is the subject of another discussion. However, in a new system – or one which has been radically reformed – one cannot hide behind arguments of independence and impartiality, as those standards do not mean denial of access to information on the results and work of the courts and the prosecutor's office to the public.

It is clear that with criteria we do not address many other preconditions to effective criminal justice for atrocities, including external circumstances such as the harmonization of laws, finances, organization, human resources and equipment. But good selection and prioritization criteria can assist. As criteria are not outside or above the existing criminal justice system, external circumstances can influence the efficient application of criteria.

As a matter of fact, we must be aware of and keep in mind the experience of the ICTY and the problems it faced, which criteria in no way could influence. Even under the assumption that we were able to create ideal criteria, we would not be able to raise the level of efficacy of the prosecutors and courts in the prosecution of war crimes cases.

25.2. Gravity, Scale, Nature of Crimes, Interests of Victims

There are a number of questions that should be precisely defined by criteria. The key criteria should be focused on several things: firstly, the gravity, scale and nature of the crime. Without these three dimensions it is simply impossible to build efficient and objective criteria. As regards Bosnia and Herzegovina, it is clear, primarily based on the experience of the work of the ICTY, that there are areas in which the crimes were concentrated. These crimes were part of systematic and planned military activities, executed in specific time-ranges. In that sense, the criteria must be supported by a precise demographic- and area conflict-analysis.

Secondly, it is important that criteria treat the nature of crimes in an appropriate way, insofar as the same importance – and, together with that, priority – cannot be given to individual killings and mass executions, or destruction and plunder of property *versus* the destruction of cultural and historical inheritance, or war crimes *versus* acts of genocide.

Finally, criteria must take into consideration the significant effect that war crimes prosecutions have on the whole community, that is, to which extent we fulfil the expectations and needs of the largest number of victims. It is very important in the context of Bosnia and Herzegovina that the criteria do not accommodate any kind of ethno-religious balancing – they should be strictly focused on the crime and its characteristics. This is especially important since the courts and prosecutors are under constant and persistent pressure of ethnic representation in the process. The so-called 'balanced ethnic approach' advocated by some brings into question whether the legal institutions are indeed there to implement legal norms.

26

Post-Conflict Criminal Justice: Practical and Policy Considerations

Vladimir Tochilovsky[*]

In post-conflict situations, where national resources are exhausted and the judicial system is significantly weakened or even ruined, national institutions frequently have to deal with a flood of cases from the conflict. In Bosnia and Herzegovina, for instance, several thousand core international crimes case-files were opened.[1]

There are some quasi-judicial measures to reduce the burden on the post-conflict criminal justice system. In some cultures, they apply traditional 'summary' justice (such as the *gacaca* courts in Rwanda). It was reported that the *gacaca* courts were intended to clear a backlog of thousands of genocide-related cases in Rwanda.[2] It would probably take several hundred years to resolve these cases through the regular judicial process.

Truth and reconciliation commissions with the authority to grant amnesty for low- and mid-level perpetrators is another way of dealing with the flood of complaints and cases. In the former Yugoslavia, however, attempts to set-up such commissions have been unsuccessful so far.

Thousands were involved in the conflict, including those who contributed to unlawful acts by being a part of the military, police or similar institutions (such as soldiers, camp guards and policemen) and who do not have blood on their hands. This category of low- and mid-level suspects may be considered for amnesty.

* **Vladimir Tochilovsky** is a former Trial Attorney at the International Criminal Tribunal for the former Yugoslavia ('ICTY'), which he joined in 1994. He has more than thirty years of experience in the field of criminal justice. He has authored numerous publications on international criminal justice and criminal procedure. He holds a Ph.D. from Kiev National University. He participated in the early stages of the development of the International Criminal Court ('ICC'), as an official representative of the ICTY to the Preparatory Committee.

1 Human Rights Watch, "Bosnia and Herzegovina: Local Courts Face Obstacles in War Crimes Trials", 10 July 2008.

2 See, for instance, "Perspectives on Progress and Reconciliation", *KSG Citizen*, 12 February 2001; Prevent Genocide International, "News Monitor for March 1–15, 2005", May 2005; Global Policy Forum, "Rwanda to Resurrect Traditional Justice System", 17 June 2002.

There exist some factors that reduce the scope of work in domestic investigations in states on whose territory core international crimes have occurred. Unlike international tribunals, domestic prosecutors do not need to gather information to develop their knowledge and understanding of the political, military and security structures of the parties to the conflicts. Likewise, unlike international counterparts, local prosecutors do not need to acquire knowledge of the historical and political background to the conflict. Nor is there a need to build knowledge on the area of the conflict. Much less, if any, translation and interpretation are required.

However, given the scope of investigations of war-related crimes, national prosecutors and investigators cannot investigate and prosecute every crime and every perpetrator within reasonable time. If there is no amnesty and no quasi-judicial mechanisms available to reduce the burden on the system, the prosecution has to prioritize cases. Indeed, there should be public awareness of the prosecution policy in this regard. It was emphasized that "a clear pronunciation of the prosecution policy, given in the abstract, could prevent the public from harbouring unrealistic expectations and also avoid any appearance of political bias in particular cases".[3] In particular, such transparency may prevent possible allegations of selective prosecution based on ethnicity or nationality of the perpetrators. If the criteria cannot be made public, then there may be something wrong with the criteria.

One may question the applicability of the selection criteria used in international tribunals to national jurisdictions. It makes sense to set up selection criteria in international jurisdictions. The international and internationalized tribunals or the ICC cannot, and are not supposed to, prosecute each and every perpetrator. Furthermore, pursuant to Article 17(1)(a) of the ICC Statute, the Court shall determine that a case is inadmissible where "the case is being investigated or prosecuted by a State which has jurisdiction over it, unless the State is unwilling or unable genuinely to carry out the investigation or prosecution".[4] Accordingly, only selected cases are prosecuted in those jurisdictions. It is different with national jurisdictions. There is a public expectation that, while the international tribunals concentrate mostly on the high-level perpetrators, the national institutions will prosecute all other cases generated by the conflict. However, if states are to prosecute each case in this category, then it makes no sense to set

---

3 ICC-Office of the Prosecutor, "Informal expert paper: Measures available to the International Criminal Court to reduce the length of proceedings", 2003, para. 18 (https://www.legal-tools.org/doc/7eba03/).

4 Rome Statute of the International Criminal Court, 17 July 2024, Article 17(1)(a) (https://www.legal-tools.org/doc/7b9af9/).

criteria for the selection of cases. What is necessary is to rank the cases for investigation.

Where international tribunals are involved, the national jurisdictions investigate mostly, if not only, the cases against low- and mid-level perpetrators. Most of the top-level perpetrators are to be indicted and prosecuted at the international level. Accordingly, there are not many options with regard to ranking the cases on the basis of the level of the perpetrators.

Apparently, those who contributed to the unlawful acts by being a part of the institutions (such as camp guards, soldiers and policemen) and do not have blood on their hands, shall be given the lowest priority.

The plea agreement institute may be one of the options for this category of accused to reduce the burden on resources. Moreover, this mechanism may turn a lower-level perpetrator into a valuable witness. However, the public does not easily accept plea agreements in war-related cases, especially in civil law jurisdictions.

The setting of priorities concerns primarily the gravity of the crimes rather than the position of the suspect. The highest priority should be set for the cases with the most serious crimes. In other words, it is not the actor who is at issue, but the crimes themselves. A case should be given priority because of the person's links to serious crimes. In this regard, the prosecution must identify the suspect's role and extent of direct participation in the alleged incidents, and the authority and control exercised by the suspect.

The status of evidence is another factor for ranking cases for investigation. In particular, one looks at the availability of witnesses and other evidence, as well as any work already done in relation to the case, especially by the international tribunals.

The possibility of arrest of the suspect is another aspect to consider in this regard. The cases where the suspect is in custody shall also be given priority. The European Court of Human Rights ('ECHR') has emphasized that the fact of detention is a factor to be considered in assessing reasonableness of the length of the proceedings when the right to be tried within a reasonable time is at issue.[5]

Another way to reduce the burden on post-conflict criminal justice is trial-oriented investigation. As the experience of the *ad hoc* tribunals shows, given the complex subject-matter of war-related cases, investigations are more efficient and productive if the prosecution theory is identified as early as possible

---

5 See ECHR, *Jabłoński v. Poland*, Judgment, 21 December 2000, Application no. 33492/96, para. 102 (https://www.legal-tools.org/doc/arlo36/); ECHR, *Abdoella v. The Netherlands*, Judgment, 25 November 1992, Application no. 12728/87, para. 24 (https://www.legal-tools.org/doc/a3lwia/).

to avoid investigation of matters that ultimately are not relevant or important at trial. From the outset, the investigators must be aware of the elements of potential offences and theory of liability. For instance, in superior responsibility cases, the identification of subordinates who committed the crimes by their category or as a group would be sufficient, if it is not possible to identify those participating in the crimes by name.[6] It may suffice to identify particular forces involved.[7] As noted by the head of the War Crimes Department in Ukraine's Prosecutor General's Office, "we understand that we may not find the [physical] perpetrator at all […]. It is much easier to identify the battery, regiment, and their immediate superiors […]. Ultimately, the number of cases will be much lower, and we will be able to identify the commanders of specific units".[8]

There is no universal and magic remedy to dealing with the flood of potential cases in territorial states affected by armed conflict. To reduce the burden, some of the post-conflict states apply such means as summary justice and amnesty. If such means are not available, then the cases should be ranked for the investigation. The priority should concern mostly the availability and status of evidence and the possibility of arrest of the suspect. Besides, trial-oriented investigations may also contribute to reducing the burden on the judicial system.

---

6 ICTY, *Prosecutor v. Blaškić*, Appeals Chamber, Judgement, 29 July 2004, Case No. IT-95-14-A, para. 217 (https://www.legal-tools.org/doc/88d8e6/); ICTY, *Prosecutor v. Meakić et al.*, Trial Chamber, Decision on Duško Knežević's Preliminary Motion on the Form of the Indictment, 4 April 2003, Case No. IT-02-65-PT, para. 35 (https://www.legal-tools.org/doc/1cbc12/).

7 ICTY, *Prosecutor v. Milutinović et al.*, Trial Chamber III, Decision on Defence Motions Alleging Defects in the Form of the Proposed Amended Joinder Indictment, 22 March 2006, Case No. IT-05-87-PT, para. 10 (https://www.legal-tools.org/doc/4af8e8/).

8 Yuriy Belousov, head of the War Crimes Department in Ukraine's Prosecutor General's Office, "Новий міністр оборони Росії у фокусі уваги МКС", *Ukrinform*, 3 July 2024.

Annex: Case Mapping, Selection and Prioritization of Conflict and Atrocity-Related Crimes: CMN Guidelines

Emilie Hunter and Ilia Utmelidze*

1. Introduction

Contemporary armed conflicts are characterized by an overwhelming range and scale of illegal conduct, often carried out against vulnerable or marginalized groups. Justice efforts should address the total character of victimization, including the geographic area of victimization and the affected communities, as well as the responsible organizations and individuals. However, it is rarely possible to provide criminal justice for all violations. Justice institutions are often limited in the number of cases that can be processed at any one time: without an objective and transparent strategy, cases will be pursued on an *ad hoc* basis without a clear structure – such as 'first come first served' – while many others will remain unaddressed. This type of selective approach may – inadvertently or purposely – be discriminatory, partial or unfair and could result in *de facto* impunity for certain offences, perpetrator groups or victimized groups.

Case mapping, selection and prioritization aim to address these challenges by enabling the totality of victimization in any conflict to be addressed in an impartial and socially sensitive way. They seek to balance the quest to end impunity for the perpetrators of mass atrocity with the constraints of justice and accountability mechanisms, ensuring a more efficient and transparent administration of justice. This does not necessarily mean the de-selection of cases, nor the closing of all but a handful of cases, but rather establishes an objective and

* Dr. **Emilie Hunter** is the Deputy Director of CILRAP's department Case Matrix Network ('CILRAP-CMN'). She holds a Ph.D. from the European University Institute in Florence. **Ilia Utmelidze** is the Director of CILRAP-CMN. He has worked extensively on capacity-development in a number of criminal jurisdictions around the world. These Guidelines – first released in June 2018 (https://www.legal-tools.org/doc/fd5f42/, open access version with visual illustrations), updated for this Third Edition – were prepared by Emilie Hunter and Ilia Utmelidze (with research assistance by Andreja Jerončič and Marialejandra Moreno Mantilla), building on earlier CILRAP work on case mapping, selection and prioritisation criteria (in particular Morten Bergsmo, Kjetil Helvig, Ilia Utmelidze and Gorana Žagovec, *The Backlog of Core International Crimes Cases in Bosnia and Herzegovina*, Second Edition, TOAEP, Oslo, 2010, pp. 81-127 (https://www.toaep.org/ps-pdf/3-bergsmo-helvig-utmelidze-zagovec-second), which in 2010–2011 was further developed and significantly expanded, now appearing as Chapter 5 above).

transparent process for the allocation and phasing of cases within and across appropriate justice mechanisms.

Criminal prosecution should prioritize cases involving offences committed in the areas and communities most affected by violence. Equally, organizations or institutions most responsible for the commission of offences should face criminal justice to a greater extent than, or ahead of, organizations and institutions of lesser significance. Other cases or incidents may be allocated to other accountability mechanisms, depending on the post-conflict needs of the country and its legal framework.

These Guidelines set out the approach recommended by the CMN department, which is based on our experience in different post-conflict settings as well as empirical observation and theoretical research. They outline:

- key general principles that help to guide case mapping, selection and prioritization;
- the scope and process for mapping backlogs of open case-files as well as broader incidents;
- considerations on the adoption of a policy to guide any case mapping, selection and prioritization process;
- model criteria for the selection and prioritization of cases; and
- CMN services in case mapping, selection and prioritization.

CMN has developed a complete case mapping, selection and prioritization methodology, which supports national actors in the adoption of an objective and transparent policy to address these questions. This includes the comprehensive mapping and analysis of the totality of victimization (including the backlog of all open case-files); the adoption of objective criteria for selection and prioritization and their inclusion in a broader strategic policy that establishes the rationale for case mapping, selection and prioritization and the allocation to different justice procedures (including abbreviated criminal proceedings); the application, review and monitoring of criteria for selection and prioritization; outreach; and assessment of the necessary material and infrastructural resources. CILRAP-CMN case mapping, selection and prioritization methodology has informed the practice of several institutions, including in Bosnia and Herzegovina and the Democratic Republic of the Congo, and the International Criminal Court ('ICC'). Further information is available on request.

2. General Principles of Case Selection and Prioritization

2.1. Current Selection or Prioritization Practices Should Be Scrutinized

Conflict-related cases are often addressed selectively, taking cases forward as 'first come first served', on the ready availability of evidence or as a result of political or public pressure. Delays almost always occur leading to a greater backlog and increased pressure on criminal justice services. Existing selection and prioritization practices should be reviewed to identify the realities of conflict-related adjudication, including practices which may involve inadvertent or purposeful bias, undue delays, limitations on the fulfilment of fair trial practices, as well as victim and witness protection and support.

2.2. Mapping of Open Case-Files Should Be Carried Out to Determine the Totality of Victimization

An inventory of existing open case-files should be undertaken and should form the basis of a comprehensive review of the factual circumstances of the conflict to understand the extent of victimization caused and the available legal framework(s) for accountability. This process will inform the choice of specific indicators of the selection and prioritization criteria and will ensure that the cases that are selected and prioritized remain representative of the overall victimization. In many circumstances it may be optimal or necessary to extend the mapping exercise to include incidents registered with other bodies – such as national human rights institutions or ombudsmen, commissions or inquiries – and beyond.

2.3. Case Selection and Prioritization Should Be Consistent but Flexible

Case selection should be *consistent but flexible*, taking into account newly acquired or developed evidence – or any other new information – that may render a case more or less of a priority. Exceptions can be made for justifiable tactical reasons to pursue cases where the alleged perpetrator holds greater liability. The decision to prosecute a specific case is a balancing exercise, requiring an assessment of the interests of the victims, the accused and the community as a whole. The legitimacy of the use of criteria and the cases selected must also be considered to ensure that certain types of crimes, perpetrator groups or victims are not prioritized disproportionately or, conversely, ignored or over-looked. These Guidelines provide a framework from which the interests of the victims, the accused and the community as a whole can be assessed and balanced.

2.4. A Selection and Prioritization Policy Should Be Adopted

The selection and prioritization policy should provide a roadmap for the pursuit of justice by addressing the specific needs and realities of the conflict, as well as the legal system and its resources. It should respond to the backlog of cases and violations, fair trial considerations, issues of legality and resource or capacity considerations, and include formal and objective criteria that will guide the selection or prioritization process.

2.5. Outreach to Affected Communities Should Be Conducted

Affected communities and society at large often view justice mechanisms with suspicion or even hostility. This can be exacerbated by the absence of transparent and objective information on the character of the conflict in general and their experience of the conflict and the judicial response to it, in particular. By following a clear and objective mapping, selection and prioritization policy it is possible to engage with concerns – of the scope of arbitrariness or of accusations of impunity, bias or targeting – and provide a transparent standard by which prosecutors' decisions can be evaluated. Accordingly, there are credible justifications for publicizing case selection and prioritization practices, in order to demonstrate the legitimacy of the priorities and the objective factors that inspire them.

3. Mapping Open Case-Files and the Extent of Victimization

Case mapping, selection and prioritization work on the principle that justice efforts – particularly criminal prosecutions – should be representative of the overall victimization of a conflict, including the offences, perpetrators and victims. This requires the mapping of the violations committed, which will include accurate and reliable data on the criminal conduct, the perpetrators and the victims. Existing backlogs of open case-files and complaints from the criminal justice system will need to be mapped in order to manage the process of selection and prioritization, and to ensure that the most senior level and most involved perpetrators are identified and charges against them well managed. Broader *incident mapping* of victimization may also be necessary, particularly where the registration of formal complaints has been severely impeded or compromised or where the scale and character of complaints is heavily disputed.

3.1. Backlogs of Existing Open Case-Files

Most territorial jurisdictions experience a backlog of cases or complaints of violations committed as part of a conflict or atrocity. All existing open case-files or complaints from the criminal justice system that may amount to core international crimes, violations of international humanitarian law or serious human rights violations – including new cases – should be mapped in order to create a quantifiable inventory of existing cases.

3.2. Incident Mapping

In many situations it may be necessary to expand the mapping exercise to include incidents or violations that have been registered with other bodies, including police stations, national human rights institutions or ombudsmen offices, commissions of inquiries, healthcare facilities, morgues, as well as international and non-governmental organizations and other credible sources. This may be necessary to ensure that the totality of victimization is understood, including an accurate portrayal of the scale of victimization and criminality.

3.3. Inventory of Open Case-Files, Complaints and Incidents

Mapping allows disaggregation and cross-referencing between sources to determine accurate and reliable data on the victimization caused by the criminal acts. This process should be supported by an inventory that enables accurate and reliable recording of data on criminal facts, alleged perpetrators and victims. Inventories such as the Investigation Documentation System (I-Doc) should be used to complete effective mapping and identify the totality of criminal behaviour.

This can be done through analytical functions, including:

- *catalogues of victims, suspects, incidents:* develop accurate lists searchable by geography, time, violation types, and other relevant factors including ethnicity, status, gender and source of complaint;
- *involved institutions:* reconstruct chains of command and establish links to suspects;
- *fact-finding:* link persons (victims, witnesses and suspects), institutions, material damages, incidents and context with each other before assigning criminal classifications;
- *case (re)construction:* register and (re)assign incidents to different justice procedures within the justice system including criminal cases, human rights cases and alternative procedures (for example, truth commissions, abbreviated criminal proceedings); and
- *real-time monitoring:* identify bottlenecks, delays, bias that may reduce the fairness of equality of the administration of justice, as well as monitor the progression and outcomes of all cases and complaints.

The inventory of cases and incidents provides the factual information that will inform and support the adoption of a selection and prioritization policy, and will form the basis for decisions on the allocation of cases for prioritized criminal prosecution as well as other justice options.

4. Adoption of a Policy on Selection and Prioritization

The adoption of a policy is encouraged to ensure objective, consistent and achievable selection and prioritization of cases. The policy should provide a roadmap for the pursuit of justice, by responding to the specific needs and realities of the conflict, as well as the legal system and its resources.

4.1. Analyse the Inventory of Open Case-Files

Analysis of the victimization should take place using the inventory of open case-files, complaints and incidents to determine the scale and character of the conflict or atrocity. This should include disaggregation and cross-checks of all data to verify the true extent of victimization and the alleged perpetrator groups, as well as the geographic breakdown. These are important factors in determining the potential jurisdiction of cases as well as potential conflicts of jurisdiction.

4.2. Identify Resource Gaps and Needs of the Justice System

The capability of the justice system should be assessed to understand how many cases it can realistically and fairly process within a specific time period: very few justice systems will have the capacity to prosecute all violations without unreasonable delay. It will also be necessary to understand the allocation of cases according to applicable jurisdictional requirements and procedures. This should be followed by diagnosis of the resources necessary to deliver justice, including the skills, equipment and infrastructure, along with financial assessment to ensure adequate budgetary planning.

4.3. Consultation and Monitoring

These Guidelines recommend a consultative process with relevant groups during the adoption of the policy and its prioritization criteria. This could include the various levels of jurisdictions that will be responsible for conflict- and atrocity-related cases, alongside co-operation with national and international stakeholders in building national capacity and knowledge. Equally, monitoring of the application of the policy and its criteria should also be planned for, including a response system to address ineffective, biased or zealous application.

4.4. Clarity, Precision and Equal Application

The policy should be formulated in clear, non-political and confidence-generating terms in order to be easily and consistently applied. The equal application of any selection and prioritization is essential to ensure the legitimacy of prosecutors' actions with the public and in particular the victims.

4.5. Adoption of Criteria to Minimize Arbitrariness

Fixed prioritization criteria should be adopted that consider the crimes committed, as well as the surrounding circumstances. Such criteria may reduce the scope for arbitrariness, protect prosecutors from accusations of initiating politically-motivated prosecutions, and provide a clear framework to evaluate and monitor cases.

4.6. Publication and Dissemination of the Policy

These Guidelines recommend the development of an outreach programme as part of the policy. This should include publication and dissemination of the policy in general and the selection and prioritization criteria in particular. Outreach should be directed towards the victims, affected communities and general public, all of whom have an interest in knowing how justice is done. This can help to minimize mistrust and accusations of arbitrariness, bias or selectivity, as well as to reduce misinformation and importantly, to build and strengthen trust in justice institutions.

5. Model Criteria for Selection or Prioritization

The adoption of objective criteria for selection or prioritization is an essential safeguard to ensure that the cases taken forward are reflective of the *total* victimization and that they are not discriminatory or unfair, or provide *de facto* impunity for certain offences, perpetrator groups or victimized groups. These Guidelines propose three criteria groups.

5.1. Gravity: Facts and Context of the Criminal Acts

This group of indicators examines the behaviour that may form the basis of criminal prosecution, through assessment of (i) the seriousness of the alleged offence, combined with (ii) the seriousness of the responsibility of the alleged perpetrator. The indicators help to properly establish the facts and context of the criminal acts in question and to assess their gravity in a fair and objective manner. The indicators include *quantitative and qualitative* factors that together support the determination of the gravity of the alleged offence(s), while some indicators are also significant in determining specific classifications of crimes or liabilities. Within these Guidelines, reference is made to the crimes and liabilities of the ICC Statute, but this should be adapted to the applicable law of the jurisdiction that is considering the adoption of case selection and prioritization criteria.

- *Qualitative indicators:* measurable data that demonstrate the facts of the criminal behaviour such as their scale, as well as the extent and patterns of the criminal behaviour;

- *Quantitative indicators:* data that helps to determine the motivations, reasons and patterns of criminal behaviour, which may also be reflected in findings of aggravating or mitigating circumstances.

5.1.1. Seriousness of the Offence

The indicators listed here help investigators to properly establish the facts and context surrounding the criminal acts in question and to assess the gravity of the crimes in a fair and objective manner. They include quantitative aspects that measure the scale and extent of the criminal behaviour under examination, as well as qualitative factors that may later be reflected in findings of aggravating or mitigating circumstances.

5.1.1.1. Number of Victims

This includes the compilation of data that establishes the number of direct and indirect victims. Gathering this data can be a challenging task, requiring the use of complex methodologies: in the aftermath of conflict or atrocity, data should be collected through counting reported victims or estimating their number based on samples and extrapolations.

5.1.1.2. Nature of Acts, and Duration and Repetition of the Offence

The nature of the acts refers to the specific factual elements of each offence – such as killing, torture, rape or other sexual or gender-based crimes, or crimes committed against or affecting children or other vulnerable groups. Reference should be made to the legal requirements of applicable crimes.

In many jurisdictions, an interest-based ranking of the seriousness of crimes may be employed, which will consider the interest that the offence protects, for example, the protected interest of life may be considered greater than that of property. This would elevate the seriousness of the crime of killing over plunder or looting and may lead to thematic prosecutions of specific offences: in such instances, the criminal sanctions for each offence, as well as the interests of the victims, should be taken into account. National policies on sanctions and sentencing are themselves a subjective reflection of the gravity of crimes. In many jurisdictions, sanctions for sexual and gender-based violence crimes may be lower than offences of comparable gravity: this should be taken into consideration to ensure that the former are not underrated due to the application of lower sanctions.

The duration and repetition of the offence are directly linked with the nature of the offence and the consequence(s) of the offence(s). The reoccurrence or repetition of a crime helps to determine its scale and may also indicate that the crime forms part of a plan or organized policy, which forms part of the legal requirements of the definition of crimes against humanity.

5.1.1.3. Area and Scale of Destruction, and Location of the Crime

These indicators allow investigators to assess the geographical area affected by the specific offences or acts, while also evaluating their broader and long-term impact, beyond the immediate victims or damage. Evaluating the geographic spread of crimes helps to determine their gravity and facilitates the selection of the most relevant cases to be prioritized.

5.1.1.4. Group Identity of the Victim(s) and Perpetrator(s)

Identification of the group identities of both the victim(s) and perpetrator(s) helps to determine the common features that may establish patterns of criminality. This includes nationality, as well as ethnicity, tribe or other relevant group belongings. The ability to establish the existence of such patterns may help to determine whether the crimes committed were systematic, resulted from a plan or organized policy (components of the definition of crimes against humanity) or were committed with discriminatory motives.

5.1.1.5. *Modus Operandi* of the Criminal Offence

This indicator encompasses a qualitative examination of the manner of commission of the alleged crimes, including:

- the means employed to execute the crime;
- the extent to which the crimes were systematic or a product of a plan or organized policy, or otherwise resulted from the abuse of power or official capacity;
- crimes committed with a flagrant disregard for the law; and
- the existence of elements of particular cruelty, including the vulnerability of the victims.

5.1.1.6. Discriminative Motives

The commission of core international crimes on the basis of discriminatory motives is a cross-cutting indicator: it facilitates understanding of other indicators – including group belonging, nature of acts, *modus operandi* of the criminal conduct, and consequences of crimes – and it also lends an element of particular gravity to the offences committed. For offences resulting in genocide or persecution as a crime against humanity, the existence of discriminative motives on the basis of belonging or group identity is important in establishing the following specific legal requirements:

- *Genocide:* (group belonging) the victims belonged to a particular national, ethnical, racial or religious group; and (*mens rea* of group belonging) the perpetrator intended to destroy, in whole or in part, that national ethnical, racial or religious group;

- *Crime against humanity of persecution:* any identifiable group or collectivity on political, racial, national, ethnic, cultural, religious, gender or other grounds that are universally recognized as impermissible under international law (ICC Statute, Article 7(1)(h)).

5.1.1.7. Defencelessness of the Victims

The defencelessness or vulnerabilities of the victims should be assessed: non-combatants and the civilian population, especially women and children, are afforded special protection under international humanitarian law, while refugees, internally displaced persons, migrants, indigenous persons, LGBTQI, human rights defenders as well as land defenders, are also frequently adversely affected by conflict and atrocity.

5.1.1.8. Consequence(s) of the Offence(s)

The effects of the crimes on the victim(s) and the community are inherently linked to the gravity of the criminal acts, where it results in permanent or lasting consequences. This is also referred to as the *impact of the crimes* and may include assessment of the increased vulnerability of victims, the social, economic and environmental damage inflicted on the affected communities, the illegal exploitation of natural resources, or the illegal dispossession of land. It is advisable that assessment considers the conditions before the offences occurred in order to have a baseline against which the short-, mid- and long-term effects can be measured.

5.1.2. Seriousness of the Responsibility of the Alleged Perpetrator

This group of indicators examine the position the suspect held in the leadership hierarchy and their involvement in the commission of crimes, as well as the degree of personal culpability for crimes committed by leaders or their subordinates. It considers that the higher the position of the alleged perpetrator and level of involvement in the commission of a core international crime, the greater the level of their criminal responsibility. However, the indicators also take into account the lower-level perpetrators who have committed particularly egregious offences.

This approach is consistent with the practice and strategies of international criminal tribunals in identifying the greater level of criminal responsibility amongst the breadth of perpetrators in any conflict or atrocity. However, each jurisdiction working on the formulation of criteria must choose what best serves its needs. The formulation chosen should provide adequate guidance to those who will work with it, be sufficiently clear to the public, and lend itself well to serve the interest of equal treatment of all cases.

5.1.2.1. Position in Hierarchy; Status as Political, Military, Paramilitary, Guerrilla or Civilian Leader; and Leadership at Municipal, Regional or National Level

These indicators examine the criminal responsibility of the leadership of any party to the conflict or atrocity for the commission of core international crimes and cover individuals with *de jure* or *de facto* positions of leadership in the military, police, political or judicial chain of authority, as well as paramilitaries, guerrillas and other armed groups. They apply to current as well as to past members of the leadership.

5.1.2.2. Group Identity of the Perpetrator

This indicator is used to identify the specific belonging of the actors taking part in the conflict or atrocity and aims to ensure that the prosecutorial strategy addresses the criminal behaviour of all actors involved in the commission of atrocities. It uses the perpetrator data from seriousness of the offence or group identity of the victim(s) and perpetrator(s).

5.1.2.3. Notoriousness or Responsibility for Particularly Heinous Acts

This indicator ensures that individuals who are accused of having committed particularly egregious crimes are included in assessments of 'those most responsible'. It targets individuals who have allegedly committed particularly heinous crimes and have reached a certain level of notoriety that contributes to the victimization and terrorization of the local population. It is frequently used to refer to lower-ranking perpetrators, as well as to direct perpetrators who acted with particular cruelty. Indicators from the seriousness of the offence should demonstrate the severity of the crimes, particularly the nature of the acts, *modus operandi*, defencelessness of victims, and consequence(s) of the offence(s).

5.1.2.4. Participation in Policy or Strategy Decisions; Personal Culpability for Specific Atrocities; and Extent of Direct Participation in the Alleged Incidents

These indicators seek to cover potential modes of criminal responsibility of an alleged perpetrator, whether that person commits a crime as an individual, jointly with another person or through another person. Arguably, the higher the rank of the suspect and the more directly this person is responsible for the crimes in question, the higher their level of responsibility.

5.1.2.5. Authority and Control Exercised by the Suspects; and the Suspects' Alleged Notice and Knowledge of Acts by Subordinates

These indicators seek to verify the relationship that senior leaders had with their subordinates, as well as the measures taken to have knowledge of the actions of their subordinates. They are closely linked with the concept of command or superior responsibility, or related omission liabilities. This is important in determining the responsibility of the alleged perpetrator as it establishes the seniority of suspects as well as their involvement. While the indicators of this criterion do not emphasize any one mode of liability, it is quite probable that some liabilities will become dominant, due to the scale of crimes and the typical roles of senior leaders. However, the purpose of such indicators is to ensure that the determinations of who bears the greatest responsibility is pursued on the basis of objective factors.

5.2. Objective Representativity: Case Representative of the Overall Victimization

These criteria ensure that the prioritized cases are representative of the overall criminality, taking into account the areas and communities affected by the violence and the organizations or institutions most responsible for the commission of such offences, the interests of victims and society, and the fair trial considerations that may be triggered by the prioritized case. Its purpose is to maximize the impact of prosecutorial work and minimize perceptions of unfairness and injustice that inevitably arise from the process of case selection and prioritization. By the end of the justice process for conflict, post-conflict or mass violence, the accumulated portfolio should reflect – or be representative of – the *overall victimization* caused by the criminal activity.

5.2.1. Representative of the Overall Victimization

The cases that are prioritized should be representative of the total criminality or victimization it has caused: the areas, communities and victim groups most affected by the crimes will be the subject of more cases that those in less affected communities. Equally, organizations or structures that caused the most serious crimes should have more of its responsible members – or more of the crimes caused by them – prosecuted than other such organizations or structures. The reasoning behind this criterion is underpinned by concerns for the interests of victims, as well as the ability of the criminal justice for the core international crimes in question to contribute to reconciliation and deterrence. The balancing, which the approach entails, is also intended to solve the problems that may arise due to the prioritization of the cases. It balances the interests of victims and society as a whole with the reality of limited resources and the limited capacity of the criminal justice system in question.

A representative prosecution requires comprehensive knowledge and understanding of the criminality of a given situation. It presupposes a mapping of the offences committed, which will include accurate and reliable data on the criminal offences, the alleged perpetrators and the victims. This must include broader contextual analysis of the political environment, conflict and geography, the motivations of the parties involved, and the structure and affiliations of local and regional authorities.

5.2.2. Interests of Victims and Society as a Whole

Contemporary criminal justice for atrocity has increasingly focused on being a means through which victims receive justice for their suffering: the design and implementation of any prioritization practice should include consideration of their physical and psychological well-being, dignity and privacy. Prosecution services can achieve this by working with civil society organizations and victim organizations, conducting consultations in light of the planned prioritization practices, as well as publicizing the objectives of the prioritization and any broader policy. Moreover, in interactions with victims, victim groups and civil society in general, investigation and prosecution teams should be sensitized and skilled to understand:

- local perceptions of justice, including traditional and institutional means;
- taboos surrounding conflict-related crimes, particularly sexual violence;
- social (and economic) consequences of the transmission of evidence by victims, particularly of sexual violence crimes;
- overall security situation surrounding victims and victim groups;
- 'Do no harm' and informed consent;
- possible negative impact on victims and victim groups as a result of interaction with investigative authorities; and
- adoption of measures to minimize risk, harm and damages that may be inflicted upon victims through their participation in justice processes.

5.2.3. Fair Trial and Due Process Considerations

These considerations are relevant to the public role of the criminal justice system as both a guarantor of law and order, and protector of the security and safety of the people. Applicable fair trial protections and associated protections to victims and witnesses should also be reviewed in light of case selection and prioritization and the adoption of its underpinning criteria, to ensure the adequacy of the legal framework and resource allocation and to identify any areas requiring reform, additional resources or monitoring.

5.3. Policy and Practical Considerations

Most justice systems are unavoidably constrained by practical and policy considerations when deciding whether to proceed with a case. In post-conflict and transitional situations, these constraints are likely to be amplified, and justice institutions will likely operate with an impaired infrastructure in environments with high levels of criminality, particularly in the most affected areas. It is therefore advisable to define and formalize such constraints – as part of the commitment towards greater transparency in the criminal justice process – while also ensuring that investigative and prosecutorial resources are not duplicated, that evidence is complete, admissible and reaches the required standard of proof, and that the case falls within the overall strategic direction without destabilizing other cases.

5.3.1. Available Investigative Resources

The availability of investigative resources is a decisive factor in the conduct of investigations and prosecutions. It aims to prevent the needless duplication of investigative and prosecutorial resources, as well as to encourage judicial efficacy and rational resource management.

5.3.2. Evidence or Witness Availability; Potential Rollover Witness or Likelihood of Linkage Evidence

These indicators support the objective assessment of credibility and reliability of both material evidence and witnesses in a specific case before a decision is made to prosecute a particular suspect. Measures should be taken to anticipate problems that may arise in the course of their investigation and should consider whether evidence is admissible, substantial, reliable and sufficient to establish the relevant standard of proof.

Assessment of sexual and gender-based crimes presents additional challenges for evidence and witness availability, which may need to be addressed, including availability of forensic or documentary evidence; potential standard of proof for sexual violence offences, especially concerning circumstantial evidence; social stigma and factors that deter reporting crimes and/or appearing as witnesses; intimidation and fear of retaliation; and traumatization of the judicial process and testifying.

5.3.3. Completeness of Evidence

The completeness of the evidence of criminal activity is linked to its value to prosecutorial services in aiming to prove the charged crime. This indicator is essential because the provability of charges is decisive for a prosecutor when deciding to proceed with a case.

5.3.4. Availability of Exculpatory Information and Evidence

Effort should be made to identify the existence and availability of exculpatory evidence that may indicate the provability or otherwise of achieving a conviction in the particular case. The strong presence of such evidence may suggest that a prosecution of a specific case could fail to result in a sentence and should consequently be avoided.

5.3.5. Arrest Potential

The arrest potential of a suspect is very important in a conflict or post-conflict context, and in many instances may pose a severe challenge to the national authorities, due to a number of factors that may include:

- location of perpetrators in remote, difficult-to-access areas;
- ability of victims to identify their attacker with certainty;
- interference to shield alleged perpetrators from judicial proceedings; or
- refusal to surrender accused persons or their transfer to new units.

5.3.6. Available Charging Theories; and Liability Theory and Legal Framework of Each Potential Suspect

Consideration of the charging and liability theories during investigation is fundamental in assessing the likelihood of conviction. It can also serve to double check that the prosecution would be representative of the total criminality and to encourage prosecutorial services to cover a wide range of perpetrators and types of criminal behaviour.

5.3.7. Potential Legal Impediments to Prosecution; and Potential Defences

Obstacles to the pursuit of justice, including potential legal impediments such as personal immunities and amnesties, should be considered along with potential defences such as superior orders, self-defence or diminished responsibilities, and reviewed in order that prioritized cases can proceed on a sound basis.

5.3.8. Overall Strategic Direction

These indicators seek to maximize the effects of the overall work of the prosecution, including efficient deployment of its resources.

5.3.9. Impact of New Investigation on Ongoing Investigations and on Making Existing Indictments Trial Ready; and Estimated Time to Complete the Investigation

This cluster of indicators addresses the temporal dimensions of the case, its status and impact on other cases under the rubric of 'readiness to proceed'. These factors serve to reduce delays in completing all connected investigations and ensure that cases are not put at risk.

5.3.10. Chain of Command Escalation Potential: Can the Case Take the Investigation Higher in Chains of Command?

This indicator aims to review the suspect(s) of a case in light of their political, military, police or civilian chain of command, to discern the level of involvement of commanders or senior level persons and the possibility that they could be found criminally responsible. It reinforces the objective that prosecutions address those most responsible.

5.3.11. Extent that the Case Fits into a Larger Pattern-Type of Ongoing or Future Investigations and Prosecutions

This final indicator seeks to maximize the impact of the prosecutorial workload by establishing links between ongoing and future investigations and prosecutions.

6. CMN Services in Case Mapping, Selection and Prioritization

6.1. Database: Investigation Documentation System (I-Doc)

I-Doc supports the above-described process of case selection and prioritization through mapping, application of criteria, real-time monitoring, and identification of bottlenecks or backlogs of open case-files. Earlier prototypes have been deployed in Bosnia and Herzegovina (the Database of Open Case-Files or DOCF) and the Democratic Republic of the Congo.

I-Doc allows institutions to:

- organize open case-files of core international crimes and serious human rights violations;
- obtain an overview of a totality of victimization as a pre-condition to objective selection and prioritization process;
- map and analyse open cases according to, *inter alia*, geography, time, legal classification of offences and liabilities, vulnerable groups, alleged perpetrators and their institutional belonging;
- diagnose bottlenecks or backlogs of cases during each stage of investigation and adjudication;
- increase accuracy, information-flow and transparency in processing existing open case-files; and
- apply criteria for case selection and prioritization.

6.2. Advisory Services: Technical Assistance, Diagnostics and Evaluation

CILRAP-CMN advisory services are designed and delivered according to the mandate, legal framework and material and infrastructural resources of each institution, and can include training, consultation, evaluation, review of:

- methodologies and principles for case mapping, selection and prioritization;
- backlogs and transfers of open case-files;
- selection and prioritization strategies;
- mapping or inventory systems; and
- customization, installation, training and support in the use of I-Doc to map, select and prioritize cases.

6.3. Publications

- Morten Bergsmo, Kjetil Helvig, Ilia Utmelidze and Gorana Žagovec (eds.), *The Backlog of Core International Crimes Case Files in Bosnia and Herzegovina*, Second Edition, TOAEP, Oslo, 2010 (https://www.toaep.org/ps-pdf/3-bergsmo-helvig-utmelidze-zagovec-second).
- Morten Bergsmo (ed.), *Criteria for Prioritizing and Selecting Core International Crimes Cases*, Second Edition, TOAEP, Oslo, 2010 (https://www.toaep.org/ps-pdf/4-bergsmo-second);
- Ilia Utmelidze, "The Time and Resources Required by Criminal Justice for Atrocities and *de facto* Capacity to Process Large Backlogs of Core International Crimes Cases: The Limits of Prosecutorial Discretion and Independence", in *ibid*., p. 189 (https://www.legal-tools.org/doc/d885e1/); and the revised Third Edition chapter, *id.*, "Requisite Resources and Capacity to Process Backlogs of Core International Crimes Cases", Chapter 4 of this book.
- Morten Bergsmo (ed.), *Abbreviated Criminal Procedures for Core International Crimes*, TOAEP, Brussels, 2017 (https://www.toaep.org/ps-pdf/9-bergsmo);
- Morten Bergsmo (ed.), *Thematic Prosecution of International Sex Crimes*, Second Edition), Torkel Opsahl Academic EPublisher ('TOAEP'), Brussels, 2018 (https://www.toaep.org/ps-pdf/13-bergsmo-second);
- CILRAP-CMN, "Prioritising International Sex Crimes Cases in the Democratic Republic of the Congo: Supporting the National Justice System in the Investigation and Prosecution of Core International Crimes With a Sexual Element", CILRAP, 2015 (https://www.legal-tools.org/doc/2ee277/).

<table>
<tr><td colspan="4">The adoption of objective criteria for selection and prioritization is an essential safeguard to ensure that the cases taken forward are reflective of the total victimization and that they are not discriminatory or unfair, or provide de facto impunity for certain offences, perpetrator groups or victimized groups.</td></tr>
<tr><th colspan="2">Gravity</th><th>Objective representativity</th><th>Policy and practical considerations</th></tr>
<tr><td>Seriousness of the offence</td><td>Number of victims;
Nature of acts;
Duration and repetition of the offence;
Area and scale of destruction;
Location of the crime;
Group identity of the victim(s) and perpetrator(s);
Modus operandi of the criminal offence;
Discriminative motives;
Defencelessness of the victims;
Consequence(s) of the offence(s).</td><td rowspan="2">Representative of overall victimization (presupposes mapping of the offences);
Interests of victims and the society as a whole;
Fair trial and due process considerations.</td><td rowspan="2">Available investigative resources;
Evidence or witness availability;
Potential rollover witness or likelihood of linkage evidence;
Completeness of evidence;
Availability of exculpatory information and evidence;
Arrest potential;
Available charging theories;
Potential legal impediments to prosecution;
Potential defences;
Liability theory and legal framework of each potential suspect;
Overall strategic direction;
Impact on ongoing investigations and on making existing indictments trial ready;
Estimated time to complete the investigation;
Chain of command escalation potential;
Extent that the case fits into a larger pattern-type of ongoing or future investigations and prosecutions.</td></tr>
<tr><td>Seriousness of the responsibility of the alleged perpetrator</td><td>Position in hierarchy;
Status as political, military, paramilitary, guerrilla or civilian leader;
Leadership at municipal, regional or national level;
Group identity of the perpetrator;
Notoriousness: responsibility for particularly heinous acts;
Participation in policy or strategy decisions;
Personal culpability for specific atrocities;
Extent of direct participation in the alleged incidents;
Authority and control exercised by the suspects;
The suspect's alleged notice and knowledge of acts by subordinates.</td></tr>
</table>

Table 1: Model Criteria for Selection and Prioritization.

INDEX

D

E

F

N

O

P

Q

R

S

T

U

TOAEP TEAM

VOLUMES IN THE *PUBLICATION SERIES*

Morten Bergsmo, Mads Harlem and Nobuo Hayashi (editors):
Importing Core International Crimes into National Law
Torkel Opsahl Academic EPublisher
Oslo, 2010
FICHL Publication Series No. 1 (Second Edition, 2010)
ISBN: 978-82-93081-00-5

Nobuo Hayashi (editor):
National Military Manuals on the Law of Armed Conflict
Torkel Opsahl Academic EPublisher
Brussels, 2023
Publication Series No. 2 (Third Edition, 2023)
ISBN print: 978-82-8348-226-3
ISBN e-book: 978-82-8348-225-6

林 伸生（主编）:
国家武装冲突法军事手册研究
Torkel Opsahl Academic EPublisher
Brussels, 2023
Publication Series No. 2 (Chinese Edition, 2023)
ISBN print: 978-82-8348-119-8
ISBN e book: 978-82-8348-120-4

Morten Bergsmo, Kjetil Helvig, Ilia Utmelidze and Gorana Žagovec:
The Backlog of Core International Crimes Case Files in Bosnia and Herzegovina
Torkel Opsahl Academic EPublisher
Oslo, 2010
FICHL Publication Series No. 3 (Second Edition, 2010)
ISBN: 978-82-93081-04-3

Morten Bergsmo (editor):
Criteria for Prioritizing and Selecting Core International Crimes Cases
Torkel Opsahl Academic EPublisher
Brussels, 2024
Publication Series No. 4 (Third Edition, 2024)
ISBN print: 978-82-8348-238-6
ISBN e-book: 978-82-8348-239-3

Morten Bergsmo and Pablo Kalmanovitz (editors):
Law in Peace Negotiations
Torkel Opsahl Academic EPublisher
Oslo, 2010
FICHL Publication Series No. 5 (Second Edition, 2010)
ISBN: 978-82-93081-08-1

Morten Bergsmo, César Rodríguez Garavito, Pablo Kalmanovitz and María Paula Saffon (editors):
Distributive Justice in Transitions
Torkel Opsahl Academic EPublisher
Oslo, 2010
FICHL Publication Series No. 6 (2010)
ISBN: 978-82-93081-12-8

Morten Bergsmo, César Rodriguez-Garavito, Pablo Kalmanovitz and María Paula Saffon (editors):
Justicia Distributiva en Sociedades en Transición
Torkel Opsahl Academic EPublisher
Oslo, 2012
FICHL Publication Series No. 6 (2012)
ISBN: 978-82-93081-10-4

Morten Bergsmo (editor):
Complementarity and the Exercise of Universal Jurisdiction for Core International Crimes
Torkel Opsahl Academic EPublisher
Oslo, 2010
FICHL Publication Series No. 7 (2010)
ISBN: 978-82-93081-14-2

Morten Bergsmo (editor):
Active Complementarity: Legal Information Transfer
Torkel Opsahl Academic EPublisher
Oslo, 2011
FICHL Publication Series No. 8 (2011)
ISBN print: 978-82-93081-56-2
ISBN e-book: 978-82-93081-55-5

Morten Bergsmo (editor):
Abbreviated Criminal Procedures for Core International Crimes
Torkel Opsahl Academic EPublisher
Brussels, 2017
FICHL Publication Series No. 9 (2017)
ISBN print: 978-82-93081-20-3
ISBN e-book: 978-82-8348-104-4

Sam Muller, Stavros Zouridis, Morly Frishman and Laura Kistemaker (editors):
The Law of the Future and the Future of Law
Torkel Opsahl Academic EPublisher
Oslo, 2010
FICHL Publication Series No. 11 (2011)
ISBN: 978-82-93081-27-2

Morten Bergsmo, Alf Butenschøn Skre and Elisabeth J. Wood (editors):
Understanding and Proving International Sex Crimes
Torkel Opsahl Academic EPublisher
Beijing, 2012
FICHL Publication Series No. 12 (2012)
ISBN: 978-82-93081-29-6

Morten Bergsmo (editor):
Thematic Prosecution of International Sex Crimes
Torkel Opsahl Academic EPublisher
Brussels, 2018
Publication Series No. 13 (Second Edition, 2018)
ISBN print: 978-82-8348-025-2
ISBN e-book: 978-82-8348-024-5

Terje Einarsen:
The Concept of Universal Crimes in International Law
Torkel Opsahl Academic EPublisher
Oslo, 2012
FICHL Publication Series No. 14 (2012)
ISBN: 978-82-93081-33-3

تِرج آینارسن:
مفهوم جرایم‌جهانیدر حقوق‌بین‌الملل
Torkel Opsahl Academic EPublisher
Brussels, 2023
Publication Series No. 14 (Persian Edition, 2023)
ISBN print: 978-82-8348-202-7
ISBN e-book: 978-82-8348-203-4

莫滕·伯格斯默 凌岩(主编):
国家主权与国际刑法
Torkel Opsahl Academic EPublisher
Beijing, 2012
FICHL Publication Series No. 15 (2012)
ISBN: 978-82-93081-58-6

Morten Bergsmo and Ling Yan (editors):
State Sovereignty and International Criminal Law
Torkel Opsahl Academic EPublisher
Beijing, 2012
FICHL Publication Series No. 15 (2012)
ISBN: 978-82-93081-35-7

Morten Bergsmo, Cheah Wui Ling and Antonio Angotti (editors):
Old Evidence and Core International Crimes
Torkel Opsahl Academic EPublisher
Brussels, 2024
Publication Series No. 16 (Second Edition, 2024)
ISBN print: 978-82-8348-228-7
ISBN e-book: 978-82-8348-229-4

Yi Ping:
戦争と平和の間——発足期日本国際法学における「正しい戦争」の観念とその帰結
Torkel Opsahl Academic EPublisher
Beijing, 2013
FICHL Publication Series No. 17 (2013)
ISBN: 978-82-93081-66-1

Morten Bergsmo and Song Tianying (editors):
On the Proposed Crimes Against Humanity Convention
Torkel Opsahl Academic EPublisher
Brussels, 2014
FICHL Publication Series No. 18 (2014)
ISBN: 978-82-93081-96-8

Morten Bergsmo and Carsten Stahn (editors):
Quality Control in Fact-Finding
Torkel Opsahl Academic EPublisher
Brussels, 2020
Publication Series No. 19 (Second Edition, 2020)
ISBN print: 978-82-8348-135-8
ISBN e-book: 978-82-8348-136-5

Morten Bergsmo, Cheah Wui Ling and Yi Ping (editors):
Historical Origins of International Criminal Law: Volume 1
Torkel Opsahl Academic EPublisher
Brussels, 2014
FICHL Publication Series No. 20 (2014)
ISBN: 978-82-93081-11-1

Morten Bergsmo, Cheah Wui Ling and Yi Ping (editors):
Historical Origins of International Criminal Law: Volume 2
Torkel Opsahl Academic EPublisher
Brussels, 2014
FICHL Publication Series No. 21 (2014)
ISBN: 978-82-93081-13-5

Morten Bergsmo, Cheah Wui Ling, Song Tianying and Yi Ping (editors):
Historical Origins of International Criminal Law: Volume 3
Torkel Opsahl Academic EPublisher
Brussels, 2015
FICHL Publication Series No. 22 (2015)
ISBN print: 978-82-8348-015-3
ISBN e-book: 978-82-8348-014-6

Morten Bergsmo, Cheah Wui Ling, Song Tianying and Yi Ping (editors):
Historical Origins of International Criminal Law: Volume 4
Torkel Opsahl Academic EPublisher
Brussels, 2015
FICHL Publication Series No. 23 (2015)
ISBN print: 978-82-8348-017-7
ISBN e-book: 978-82-8348-016-0

Morten Bergsmo, Klaus Rackwitz and Song Tianying (editors):
Historical Origins of International Criminal Law: Volume 5
Torkel Opsahl Academic EPublisher
Brussels, 2017
FICHL Publication Series No. 24 (2017)
ISBN print: 978-82-8348-106-8
ISBN e-book: 978-82-8348-107-5

Morten Bergsmo and Song Tianying (editors):
Military Self-Interest in Accountability for Core International Crimes
Torkel Opsahl Academic EPublisher
Brussels, 2015
FICHL Publication Series No. 25 (2015)
ISBN print: 978-82-93081-61-6
ISBN e-book: 978-82-93081-81-4

Wolfgang Kaleck:
Double Standards: International Criminal Law and the West
Torkel Opsahl Academic EPublisher
Brussels, 2015
FICHL Publication Series No. 26 (2015)
ISBN print: 978-82-93081-67-8
ISBN e-book: 978-82-93081-83-8

Liu Daqun and Zhang Binxin (editors):
Historical War Crimes Trials in Asia
Torkel Opsahl Academic EPublisher
Brussels, 2016
FICHL Publication Series No. 27 (2015)
ISBN print: 978-82-8348-055-9
ISBN e-book: 978-82-8348-056-6

Morten Bergsmo, Mark Klamberg, Kjersti Lohne and Christopher B. Mahony (editors):
Power in International Criminal Justice
Torkel Opsahl Academic EPublisher
Brussels, 2020
Publication Series No. 28 (2020)
ISBN print: 978-82-8348-113-6
ISBN e-book: 978-82-8348-114-3

Stian Nordengen Christensen:
*Counterfactual History and Bosnia-Herzegovin*a
Torkel Opsahl Academic EPublisher
Brussels, 2018
Publication Series No. 30 (2018)
ISBN print: 978-82-8348-102-0
ISBN e-book: 978-82-8348-103-7

Stian Nordengen Christensen:
Possibilities and Impossibilities in a Contradictory Global Order
Torkel Opsahl Academic EPublisher
Brussels, 2018
Publication Series No. 31 (2018)
ISBN print: 978-82-8348-104-4
ISBN e-book: 978-82-8348-105-1

Morten Bergsmo and Carsten Stahn (editors):
Quality Control in Preliminary Examination: Volume 1
Torkel Opsahl Academic EPublisher
Brussels, 2018
Publication Series No. 32 (2018)
ISBN print: 978-82-8348-123-5
ISBN e-book: 978-82-8348-124-2

Morten Bergsmo and Carsten Stahn (editors):
Quality Control in Preliminary Examination: Volume 2
Torkel Opsahl Academic EPublisher
Brussels, 2018
Publication Series No. 33 (2018)
ISBN print: 978-82-8348-111-2
ISBN e-book: 978-82-8348-112-9

Morten Bergsmo and Emiliano J. Buis (editors):
Philosophical Foundations of International Criminal Law: Correlating Thinkers
Torkel Opsahl Academic EPublisher
Brussels, 2018
Publication Series No. 34 (2018)
ISBN print: 978-82-8348-117-4
ISBN e-book: 978-82-8348-118-1

Morten Bergsmo and Emiliano J. Buis (editors):
Philosophical Foundations of International Criminal Law: Foundational Concepts
Torkel Opsahl Academic EPublisher
Brussels, 2019
Publication Series No. 35 (2019)
ISBN print: 978-82-8348-119-8
ISBN e-book: 978-82-8348-120-4

Morten Bergsmo, Emiliano J. Buis and Song Tianying (editors):
Philosophical Foundations of International Criminal Law: Legally-Protected Interests
Torkel Opsahl Academic EPublisher
Brussels, 2022
Publication Series No. 36 (2022)
ISBN print: 978-82-8348-121-1
ISBN e-book: 978-82-8348-122-8

Terje Einarsen and Joseph Rikhof:
A Theory of Punishable Participation in Universal Crimes
Torkel Opsahl Academic EPublisher
Brussels, 2018
Publication Series No. 37 (2018)
ISBN print: 978-82-8348-127-3
ISBN e-book: 978-82-8348-128-0

Xabier Agirre Aranburu, Morten Bergsmo, Simon De Smet and Carsten Stahn (editors):
Quality Control in Criminal Investigation
Torkel Opsahl Academic EPublisher
Brussels, 2020
Publication Series No. 38 (2020)
ISBN print: 978-82-8348-129-7
ISBN e-book: 978-82-8348-130-3

Morten Bergsmo, Wolfgang Kaleck and Kyaw Yin Hlaing (editors):
Colonial Wrongs and Access to International Law
Torkel Opsahl Academic EPublisher
Brussels, 2020
Publication Series No. 40 (2020)
ISBN print: 978-82-8348-133-4
ISBN e-book: 978-82-8348-134-1

Morten Bergsmo and Kishan Manocha (editors):
Religion, Hateful Expression and Violence
Torkel Opsahl Academic EPublisher
Brussels, 2023
Publication Series No. 41 (2023)
ISBN print: 978-82-8348-141-9
ISBN e-book: 978-82-8348-142-6

Gavin E. Oxburgh, Trond Myklebust, Mark Fallon and Maria Hartwig (editors):
Interviewing and Interrogation: A Review of Research and Practice Since World War II
Torkel Opsahl Academic EPublisher
Brussels, 2023
Publication Series No. 42 (2023)
ISBN print: 978-82-8348-200-3
ISBN e-book: 978-82-8348-201-0

Mark Klamberg, Jonas Nilsson and Antonio Angotti (editors):
Commentary on the Law of the International Criminal Court: The Statute Volume 1
Torkel Opsahl Academic EPublisher
Brussels, 2023
Publication Series No. 43 (Second Edition, 2023)
ISBN print: 978-82-8348-204-1
ISBN e-book: 978-82-8348-205-8

Mark Klamberg, Jonas Nilsson and Antonio Angotti (editors):
Commentary on the Law of the International Criminal Court: The Statute Volume 2
Torkel Opsahl Academic EPublisher
Brussels, 2023
Publication Series No. 44 (Second Edition, 2023)
ISBN print: 978-82-8348-206-5
ISBN e-book: 978-82-8348-207-2

Mark Klamberg, Jonas Nilsson and Antonio Angotti (editors):
Commentary on the Law of the International Criminal Court: The Rules of Procedure and Evidence
Torkel Opsahl Academic EPublisher
Brussels, 2023
Publication Series No. 45 (2023)
ISBN print: 978-82-8348-208-9
ISBN e-book: 978-82-8348-209-6

All volumes are freely available online at http://www.toaep.org/ps/. For printed copies, see http://www.toaep.org/about/distribution/. For reviews of earlier books in this Series in academic journals and yearbooks, see http://www.toaep.org/reviews/.

www.ingramcontent.com/pod-product-compliance
Lightning Source LLC
Chambersburg PA
CBHW050227271224
19514CB00016B/378/J

9 788283 482386